Thomas Heilmann (Ed.)

Manual of International Marketing

Thomas Heilmann (Ed.)

Manual of
International Marketing

Bibliographic information published by Die Deutsche Bibliothek
Die Deutsche Bibliothek lists this publication in the Deutsche Nationalbibliografie; detailed bibliographic data is available in the Internet at <http://dnb.ddb.de>.

Originally published in German with the title:
Thomas Heilmann (Hrsg.): Praxishandbuch Internationales Marketing
© Betriebswirtschaftlicher Verlag Dr. Th. Gabler/GWV Fachverlage GmbH, Wiesbaden 2006

First edition 2006

All rights reserved
© Betriebswirtschaftlicher Verlag Dr. Th. Gabler/GWV Fachverlage GmbH, Wiesbaden 2006
Gabler is a company of Springer Science+Business Media.
www.gabler.de

Project design and knowledge development by the Executive Science Project
www.execscience.org – contact@execscience.org

Editor: Thomas Heilmann, CEO Scholz & Friends Group

Editorial Director: Johannes Bhakdi, Chairman Executive Science Project

Editorial Manager & Director of Executive Relations: Kathrin Zarthe, Executive Science Project

This work is subject to copyright. All rights are reserved, whether the whole or part of the material is concerned, specifically the rights of translation, reprinting, reuse of illustrations, recitation, broadcasting, reproduction on microfilm or in any other way, and storage in data banks.

The use of general desciptive names, registered names, trademarks, etc. in this publication does not imply, even in the absence of a specific statement, that such names are exempt from the relevant protective laws and regulations and therefore free for general use.

Cover design: Nefas, Martin Hospach
Visualization of models: bottled fish GbR
Typeset and design: Appel Grafik Berlin GmbH
Printing and binding: Wilhelm & Adam, Heusenstamm
Printed on acid-free paper
Printed in Germany

ISBN-10 3-8349-0039-7
ISBN-13 978-3-8349-0039-5

Table of Contents

Foreword — 9

Introduction to International Marketing — 11
Thomas Heilmann – Scholz & Friends

Global Marketing

Global Brand Identity — 23
Niclas Friese-Greene – Siemens Communications

Global Brand Management — 39
Karen D. Halpert – MasterCard Europe

Global Customer Interaction — 53
Christa Wilhelm – Microsoft

International Product Launch — 77
Gabriele Gundel, Stefan Gundelach – Nintendo Germany

Global versus Local Marketing — 91
Frank Hermann – Electronic Arts

Intercultural Marketing — 101
J. Johan Jervøe – McDonald's Germany

International Brand Portfolio Management — 119
Peter Amon – Unilever Bestfoods

Marketing Management

Brand Alignment — 139
Dietmar Turocha – BSH Bosch and Siemens Hausgeräte GmbH

B2B Marketing — 153
Adriana Nuneva – Heidelberger Druckmaschinen

Modular Marketing Management — 169
Dr. Ralf E. Strauß – SAP AG

Retail Brand Strategy — 185
Prof. Dr. Roland Mattmüller, Dr. Ralph Tunder – European Business School

Strategic Marketing Management — 197
Barbara Schädler – Fujitsu Siemens Computers

Tailor-Made Marketing (B2B) — 213
Christina Rüter – Schwarzkopf Professional Haircare

Marketing Organization Efficiency — 227
Annegret Reinhardt-Lehmann, Nicole Ebner – Fraport AG

Brand Management

Brand Architecture — 245
Wolfgang Orians – Freudenberg

Brand Building — 257
Ivo Hoevel, Karin Kaiser – O_2 Germany

Regional Brand Expansion (Financial Services) — 271
Michaela Luhmann – DWS Investments

Branding — 285
Angela Nelissen – Unilever

Brand Value Management — 297
Dr. Wulff-Axel Schmidt, Dr. Kay Oelschlägel – Luther Rechtsanwaltsgesellschaft mbH
In Association with Ernst & Young

Corporate Brand Identity — 311
Christian Schubert, Hans Kiefer – BASF AG & Prof. Dr. Franz-Rudolf Esch, Dr. Simone Roth

Long-term Brand Migration — 325
Stefan Swinka, Peter Wolf – Tchibo AG

Brand Desirability — 345
Dr. Ulf Santjer – PUMA AG

Umbrella Brand Strategy — 361
Alexander Schwade – Akzo Nobel Deco GmbH

Regional Brand Expansion (Retail) — 379
Guido Renggli, Philip Martin – Media Markt Switzerland

Corporate Brand Building — 393
Peter Caspar Hamel, Karoline Güller – Degussa AG

Marketing Communications

Detection Marketing — 411
Dr. Burkhard Henn – eBay Germany

Image Campaign — 421
Dirk Miller – Siemens AG

Marketing Communications Controlling — 431
Jens-Thomas Pietralla, Andreas X. Müller – Siemens Mobile

Marketing Innovations — 447
Jörg Dohmen, Dr. Wolfgang Armbrecht – BMW Group

Online Advertising — 467
Markus Hinz – AutoScout24 and ScoutMedia24

Viral Marketing — 485
Michael Rüthnick, Robert Moffett – Masterfoods Inc.

Customer Relations

Community Marketing — 505
Timo Schneckenburger – O_2 Germany

Customer Service — 521
Rainer Bürkle – The Ritz-Carlton Hotel Company

Customer Retention System — 533
Harald W. Eisenächer, Sascia Hilverkus – Deutsche Lufthansa AG

Interactive Marketing — 551
Thorsten Schapmann – Imperial Tobacco Group

Innovation Management — 565
Petra Meyer – Merck Consumer Healthcare, Gabriele Neuschaefer – morgenland

Integrated Customer Retention — 575
Martin Kanis, Kathrin Henze – O_2 Germany

visit → **www.marketingmanual.org**

latest editions – latest knowledge – latest Executive Science!

Foreword

Dear Reader,

Many thanks for deciding to purchase the "Manual of International Marketing". This work, covering the basic principles of marketing, offers you invaluable and pertinent knowledge from leading marketing decision-makers, working for international companies, in a clearly structured form that is ideal for practical use.

The idea to develop a manual based on key words at decision-maker level is the result of a survey of the book market. Before we started work on the present publication, there was no product on the international book market that provided practice-oriented knowledge in a systematic manner and in a way that enabled this knowledge to be efficiently used. In the search for an appropriate publication, we came across either highly specialized knowledge on a case-by-case basis, which was of little relevance for decision-makers, or very abstract models from the academic world that were consequently of scant practical value.

Based on my experience as a guest professor at the Berlin University of the Arts and as Chairman of the Board of the international communication network Scholz & Friends, I therefore decided to develop a more suitable offering for decision-makers in international marketing and for those who are interested in the topic from an academic point of view. Consequently, I sought a content-related approach with which relevant practical knowledge could be understood theoretically and conveyed in a practical manner.

The approach I have adopted is based on the notion of "Executive Science" (developed at the Eberhard Karl University in Tübingen and at the Humboldt University in Berlin), a concept that draws on two simple ideas:

- Not only does theoretical insight have to be correct, it also has to be relevant. Consequently, the only effective test for theoretical knowledge is the practical use and measurement of the impact achieved by a theoretical concept.
- Here, theoretical knowledge incorporates all kinds of logical contexts and models – even if these are just semi-conscious concepts in the mind of their creator.

The result of this is that arguably the most valuable carriers of theoretical knowledge are "executives" in the sense of high-ranking functionaries. For the knowledge of these people does not only have to be correct, it also has to be relevant. The central problem now lies in eliciting theoretical knowledge. Although this knowledge is often used in practice, its originators are not completely aware of it in its entirety as explicit theoretical knowledge.

In the "Manual of International Marketing" we have attempted to solve this problem through three activities:

- Every author was asked to put his knowledge into a clear theoretical format.
- At the same time, the Editorial Office led by Johannes Bhakdi (Editorial Director) and Kathrin Zarthe (Editorial Manager) that was explicitly set up for this project provided comprehensive support in the explication of knowledge and the development of the articles.
- In some articles, the theoretical models have also been converted into systematic visual models, enabling implicit knowledge for decision-makers to be explained in a more precise way.

We have thus managed to create a factor model for each key word in the manual that justifies the claim of a theoretical and, at least in part, precise visual model.

In line with this approach, all the chapters in the manual adhere to the same formal structure.

The 37 key words define the 37 chapters of the manual. In doing so, each key word was developed in cooperation with the respective author so that, overall, the key words reflect the topics and problem areas which at the time of the survey – in 2005 – affected decision-makers in international marketing. (For better orientation, we divided all the chapters into the five areas of Global Marketing, Marketing Management, Brand Management, Marketing Communications and Customer Relations).

For each key word, the author provides a theoretical model, which is followed by the more operational description of process and implementation of the key word.

The framework of each chapter is formed at the start by an "Executive Summary" and at the end by "Key Insights" and "Practical Guidelines" that contain the most important fundamental knowledge and helpful tips and instructions for the implementation of the key word.

To make the introduction to the topic easier for the reader, we also wrote an overview chapter at the beginning of the manual in the sense of an "Introduction to International Marketing," which sums up the most important meta-knowledge and trends from the articles of the authors.

In view of the prototypical methodical approach and the limited scope of each article – none of the articles is longer than 20 pages – it soon becomes clear that, despite all the methodical precision, each topic can only be addressed in a basic way that is definitely not exhaustive. The complexity and challenges of international marketing are so great that I would prefer to call the models at hand initial steps rather than finished solutions for the very reason that marketing as a discipline is still at the beginning of its research compared to other fields that are the subject of scientific research. We hope, therefore, that in a few years time this book will be considered a fundamental work and will encourage a range of updates.

The innovative approach that we have pursued in this work – the specific crystallization of decision-maker knowledge into theoretical models and systematic implementation processes – can also be seen as an exciting experiment. If we have indeed managed to crystallize the knowledge of leading decision-makers that is crucial to success, and provided you, the reader, with this knowledge, we will have opened up a new approach of targeted crystallization and the systematic transfer of genuinely decisive units of knowledge.

On the following 600 pages, you will be able to decide for yourself whether this experiment has been successful or not. I wish you much pleasure and maximum added value in your reading!

Thomas Heilmann
Editor

Thomas Heilmann – Scholz & Friends

Introduction to International Marketing

International marketing is a topic and problem field of management that is growing significantly in importance thanks, primarily, to the current overall macro-economic situation. It is also moving more and more into the focus of investors and top-level decision-makers. To understand this topic from a strategic point of view, we should at least briefly recall the economic boundary conditions for companies today.

New boundary conditions of a digitalized world

Arguably, the most fundamental trend that represents one of the main causes of further developments can be described by the principle of digitalization. Digital communication has led to the dissolution of temporal and spatial boundaries between market participants.

This in turn has resulted in an overall acceleration of business processes. Internal and external company transactions can be made directly and without any delays; global virtual marketplaces are being developed; markets overall are becoming quicker and more transparent.

In addition to acceleration, another consequence of digitalization has been the expansion of the catchment area of all market participants. The dissolution of spatial boundaries is leading to a situation in which players, who have been hitherto separated, can trade with one another or compete against each other. I would like to assign the key word "globalization" to this effect, a development that is resulting in an increase in efficiency in the most comprehensive economic sense.

This globalization of markets and interactions is having a sustained impact at both the immediate operational level and from a strategic and mid-term perspective. The immediate effects are reflected in the competition for prices, product ideas, and the attention of consumers worldwide, making faster and more precise actions essential for survival. However, the mid-term strategic result is even more important. The flexibility of capital and knowledge means that whole industrial sectors can be re-localized regionally, and that second movers can copy business ideas more quickly. The outcome can be referred to as the "comprehensive commoditization" of products of all kinds. Even new products face the threat of interchangeability, as knowledge and human capital have become more flexible and production capacities can be copied quickly.

This effect of a digitalized and globalized economy is arguably the most momentous for traditional and proud industry sectors of the West. Today, products that were previously seen as secure fortresses and the result of decades of research, development, and design work, are becoming more and more frequently interchangeable goods, that are easily duplicated.

The problem associated with this is aggravated by another trend: the classical marketing functions are faced by a media reality that makes it appear almost impossible to reach customers effectively via classical routes. The communicative overflow makes every advertising campaign a bitter fight for the scarce product "attention." At the end of this, the situation, in which there are a few rare winners and many losers, is becoming more and more common.

Ultimately, the increase in global productivity and macro-economic output, along with its associated higher level of need fulfillment, is leading to an continuously strongly differentiating structure of customer requirements. Above all, the rapid change in customer requirements presents many traditional suppliers with serious problems. The solution to these can require an extensive realignment of the companies.

Constant market alignment as the basis for corporate success

Even if many of the new boundary conditions, as described above, create the impression that the world is tougher and more difficult for companies and their managers, and trigger corresponding protective instincts, the overall development should be seen and evaluated at a distance and from a strategic perspective. This unearths considerably more opportunities than risks: the possibilities of globalized markets with maximized levels of efficiency, and the existence of practically unlimited product development and product capacities, present opportunities of value creation that would have been unthinkable a few decades ago.

So, under what conditions, other than the boundary conditions mentioned above, can companies generate advantages for themselves, their products, and their brands?

One strategic implication that I believe is crucial does indeed refer to the role and function of marketing.

For in a world where products and entire production lines are interchangeable and can be copied, where product ideas and know-how are more flexible than ever, the opportunities of value creation and the safeguarding of the corporate added value are to be found less and less frequently on the production side and more and more often in the place that a company occupies in the minds of the consumers.

In comparison to all other management functions, marketing is acquiring pivotal importance in the strategy of international companies as a market-aligning and brand-forming function. Whereas actual production know-how can be copied increasingly quickly, brands and brand worlds represent more long-term and more secure assets in the overall portfolio of a company. A similar aspect applies to the entire marketing and sales organization that is less flexible and more regionally established than production capacities.

An interesting trend is emerging: brands are becoming the internal and external focus of the company because they are the central asset, which is difficult to copy. Marketing organization and structure form the actual value creation focus in a growing number of companies because production and know-how can be purchased flexibly in a globalized world of commoditization. The key to long-term corporate success is the safeguarding of access to consumers and the satisfaction of needs.

To be able to implement this development successfully, many companies need to change their way of thinking. Product-driven management must give way to so-called "customer-centric management." The company must see itself as a comprehensive value-creation structure with the sole objective of satisfying customer needs. Consequently, it must possess and manage analysis and delivery systems from and to the market as the most important part of its infrastructure.

Indeed, some developments can be observed that confirm this thesis of strategic change in corporate structures. Marketing is being increasingly elevated to a function at board level. At the same time, the topics and focus in many marketing departments are changing: classical tasks such as communication and sales are supplemented in favor of new strategic aspects such as customer retention strategies, brand management, and stronger competence in product development.

The most interesting question here is this: looking at the management level, what fields and drivers can be identified that divide the previously-mentioned strategic developments into operationally effective fields of activity?

Working with authors on the "Manual of International Marketing" gave us the opportunity to examine this crucial question. On the basis of the articles in this book, we were able to crystallize a number of areas of activity.

It should be taken into account here that every research approach is confronted by a host of unanswered questions, contradictions, and topics that have only been rudimentarily developed from a research point of view. The complexity of the field and the unclear number of impact variables represent a particular challenge. I believe, therefore, that this overview and the chapters in this book can provide an impulse for advancing the progress of knowledge.

Fields of activity in international marketing

1. Internationalization of the marketing functions

The first and probably most obvious field of activity in international marketing, in the context of the developments described above, is the strong internationalization of the various marketing functions. From consumer research through product development to communication and brand building in general, globally active companies are faced with the growing challenge of coordinating marketing at an international level and implementing the corresponding operational divisions.

Here, there are also considerable opportunities for the quality and efficiency of marketing activities: campaigns and research results can be called up via global marketing platforms, thus saving valuable time and resources. Know-how can be exchanged in the same way between regions and countries. And successful product developments in one region can be made available to all other regions, more or less simultaneously.

To be able to make use of this opportunity, however, a few prerequisites in marketing management are necessary, and these are described in the corresponding chapters of the manual:

- The introduction of a global marketing platform is necessary. This platform will create the technical and organizational basis for international exchange. The chapters "Global Customer Interaction" (Christa Wilhelm) and "Intercultural Marketing" (J. Johan Jervøe) provide relevant know-how on this.

- The efficiencies provided by global marketing must be balanced by management systems that safeguard the relevance of these marketing activities and ensure that materials and concepts that may have to be adopted, can actually be used at regional level, and that a potential lack of local relevance (and, thus, fall in sales) can be avoided. The safeguarding of regional and cultural relevance is vital. Fundamental insights into this are provided by the chapters "Global vs. Local Marketing" (Frank Hermann), "Global Brand Management" (Karen Halpert) and "Intercultural Marketing" (J. Johan Jervøe).

- In general, the decision has to be taken on how central or decentralized brands and products are to be managed internationally. Above all, the definition of a system with clearly transparent rules of organization is decisive for success here. Insights into the division of local and global competences are provided by the chapters "Regional Brand Expansion (Retail)" (Martin Renggli, Philip Martin), "International Brand Portfolio Management" (Peter Amon, section on management styles) and "Global Brand Management" (Karen Halpert).

- The international expansion of brands necessitates the exact analysis of brand, brand architecture and target markets. Relevant know-how is supplied in the chapters "Regional Brand Expansion (Financial Services)" (Michaela Luhmann) and "Regional Brand Expansion (Retail)" (Martin Renggli, Philip Martin)

In addition to these specific dimensions of success, it is also a fact in international marketing that all existing challenges of local marketing appear in multiplied strength. Slower and less transparent feedback from the regions means that it is more difficult to draw conclusions for the respective international marketing activities. The same rules apply in local marketing, but infringements against these are punished more comprehensively and in a more perceptible way. Organizations that want to internationalize marketing successfully have to – in addition to the specific requirements mentioned above – do their classical marketing homework particularly well and professionally. A good example of how local core functions of marketing can be internationalized is shown in the chapter "International Product Launch" (Stefan Gundelach, Gabriele Gundel).

2. Redesign of marketing as a management function

As a consequence of the new boundary conditions that companies face – above all, the commoditization of large product areas and ever-changing consumer requirements – marketing continues to grow in significance as a core area of strategic company management. This leads to two major effects that can be seen in many articles in the manual:

- Marketing has moved up as a management function and is also frequently being institutionally anchored at board level. This is reflected, on the one hand, in newly created functions such as the CMO (Chief Marketing Officer), and on the other hand, in a comprehensive description of the tasks of the highest marketing function in companies. This includes, above all, a fundamental significance of brand management in the sense of a trend-setting function for the entire company, but also the responsibility for areas such as Market Research, Product Development, and Sales that were mostly separate before. Of course, this development does not apply to all companies, yet a higher-level trend can be discerned.

- Probably as a result of the increase in support for the marketing function, its structure is also changing in the sense of the divisional definitions it embraces. A particularly interesting observation within the articles in the manual was the reevaluation of the 4Ps of marketing: Product, Price, Promotion, and Place, in the sense that most articles now only speak of 3 Ps, namely Product, Promotion, and Place. This development can be explained by the new significance of product development and positioning. Whereas the price determination strategy was previously an essential and stand-alone component in the marketing mix, because the entire repositioning of the new introduction of products represented rather the exception to the rule, in times of constant product innovation and reaction to changed market conditions, the focus shifts to a holistic view of the product and brand positioning (product) in which price only plays a matter-of-course role as a classified element. Today, it is all about which segment a product is positioned in – the price is a logical variable that can only be changed to a limited extent within the product positioning.

This example shows how priorities are also reflected in the daily naming and definition of divisions.

In addition to the reorganization of existing tasks and fields of activity in marketing, the development of new fields can be observed in the marketing function. Terms such as "Brand Alignment" – the alignment of production logics and communication activities to the brand (Dietmar Turocha), "International Portfolio Management" as a strategy for maximizing the profitability of multi-brand companies (Peter Amon), and "Strategic Marketing Management" (Barbara Schaedler), show that marketing today has acquired a more comprehensive importance for company management.

Arguably, the most important field continues to be brand management as a meta-function of marketing management. Furthermore, the brand emerges as a lighthouse in a sea of complex options – both externally for the consumer and also more and more frequently internally for product developers and the strategic alignment of the company overall. The articles "Long-term Brand Migration" (Peter Wolf, Stefan Swinka), "Global Brand Identity" (Niclas Friese-Greene), "Umbrella Brand Strategy (Alexander Schwade), "Brand Architecture" (Wolfgang Orians), "Brand Building" (Ivo Hoevel, Karin Kaiser), "Brand Desirability" (Ulf Santjer) and "Corporate Brand Building" (Peter Caspar Hamel, Karoline Güller) are very informative on this point.

Overall, our observations show that marketing has become more holistic. The cause appears to lie in the new significance of marketing as a strategic management function that aligns the company to the market. The result: traditional structures and categories of marketing that resulted, above all, from its function as sales promotion are being replaced by new strategies and aspects that are making marketing into a market-aligning function in companies.

Incidentally, a further result of this development is what we can call "professionalization" of marketing management. Marketing management is increasingly taking fundamental management and organizational aspects into consideration, as described in the articles "Marketing Communications Controlling" (Jens-Thomas Pietralla, Andreas Müller) and "Modular Marketing Management" (Ralf Strauß) or "Marketing Organization Efficiency" (Annegret Reinhardt-Lehmann, Nicole Ebner).

3. Customer loyalty and relevance as a global value driver

In the course of increased competition and margin pressure on the efficiency of marketing activities, the phrase "Customer Lifetime Values" has contributed, above all, to making the topic of customer loyalty one of the most important trends in international marketing.

For globally active companies in particular, this presents a specific challenge in a field such as this that is dependent on precise local activities. Different cultural ideas, regionally different brand traditions and differences in consumer attitudes make activities to increase international customer loyalty the touchstone for the competence of a company in international brand management and customer care.

Above all, the strong professionalization of this relatively recent topic is visible in the articles. In "Customer Retention System" (Harald Eisenacher, Sascia Hilverkus), the Lufthansa Miles & More system is explained as a prominent example of global customer retention systems. However, particularly in the case of a frequent flyer program, many of the intercultural problems only occur in a mild form because the clientele is a global target group. It is, therefore, not surprising that, with regard to the technical side, an impressive specification of the customer retention was achieved at this point. However, many hitherto unanswered questions are raised here particularly for companies with more heterogeneous international target groups.

A further interesting aspect is supplied by the article "Global Customer Interaction" (Christa Wilhelm), in which the problem of targeting customer interaction is described for Microsoft as a company with different product divisions and strongly globalized activities. A possible concept for solving the problem is also shown.

Another highly auspicious approach can be found in the article "Tailor-Made Marketing," which shows a B2B approach and describes in a particularly explicit manner the adaptation of the service portfolio and the development of added values in line with customer requirements in an international context.

Articles such as "Community Marketing," "Viral Marketing," "Brand Desirability," "Integrated Customer Retention" and "Customer Service" depict further interesting and very promising approaches of how companies can adopt retention and service measures for international target groups in order to further enhance the overall value of their customer portfolio.

4. Innovation and organizational learning

To be able to manage brands and products successfully in global markets that are changing at an ever more rapid pace, companies must examine their offerings to a greater extent than up to now, with regard to their relevance for the different consumer groups, and must make appropriate adaptations. Innovation in the sense of constant further development of product and brand worlds thus becomes one of the most important factors for success.

To be able to use this factor for success, a multitude of variables must be successfully managed and brought together. This begins with market research and insight generation, continues via flexible adaptation and implementation processes in research and development and ends in tasks such as the concept of rapid prototyping that is known from the automotive industry. Overall, it can be observed that the field of activity of innovation management is being established as an independent field of international marketing in more and more companies ("Innovation Management"- Gabriele Neuschaefer, Petra Meyer).

Here, innovation does not only mean the innovation of products, but also a higher-level attitude and objective. The constant innovation of offerings, and also communication measures, organizational structures, and brand designs, is becoming one of the most important requirements for short- and long-term corporate success.

The article "Marketing Innovation" (Jörg Dohmen, Wolfgang Armbrecht) shows a system that helps to identify innovation potential and implement this primarily for the communicative activities of companies.

Furthermore, the creation of new technical possibilities opens up strategic innovation fields for marketing. In doing so, the new forms of communication are more tangible through increased empirical values and the further development of management models, permitting marketing fields that were hitherto only vague, to become clearer and more systematically tangible – this is shown particularly convincingly in the articles "Online Advertising" (Markus Hinz), "Detection Marketing" (Burkhard Henn) and "Viral Marketing" (Michael Rüthnick, Robert Moffett).

Perhaps the most important framework condition for successful innovation management here is the development of a corporate culture that integrates constant learning as an obvious process in its organizational DNA. The objective of a learning organization is gaining fresh significance and new priority on the management agenda ("Global Customer Interaction"; Christa Wilhelm) at a time when innovation is becoming an important lifeline in companies.

Overall, it can be established that the global innovativeness of companies is one of the economically decisive requirements in international marketing, but is also one of the most elusive. The articles included in the manual can make an initial contribution to systematic reconditioning – and, I hope, provide an impulse for further examination of this extremely promising lever of international corporate development.

5. Race to catch up in B2B marketing

Finally, I would like to refer to an interesting observation from my work that concerns the development of international marketing in an area that was not previously focused upon to a great extent: business-to-business marketing (hereinafter referred to as B2B marketing).

Marketing between companies, i.e., in the widest sense in the investment goods sector, was perceived for a long time as a poor relation in practice and research. The reason for this is clear: investment decisions by companies can generally be understood in a more rational way and thus – viewed on the surface – as less relevant to marketing.

However, the articles in the manual originating from classical B2B companies such as BASF, Degussa, Heidelberger Druckmaschinen or Freudenberg open up a new perspective on this field. Particularly in the B2B sector, a race to catch up with regard to the professionalism and significance of marketing seems to be taking place. This applies at least to part of the market. There is also a development in the opposite direction that I will come back to at the end of this point.

Primarily strategic topics such as "Corporate Brand Building" (Peter Caspar Hamel, Karoline Güller), "Corporate Brand Identity" (Christian Schubert, Hans Kiefer et al.) or overall systems of marketing ("B2B Marketing" – Adriana Nuneva) are gaining in significance for manufacturers of investment goods.

We can only briefly go into the reasons for the strong increase in the importance and professionalization of marketing in this field at this point. However, the explanation does seem rather obvious that all the framework conditions in a globalized and digitalized market environment are leading to B2B companies being faced by a greater number of target groups, potential customers, and competitors. The relationship with the customer that was once so settled and based on many years of trust and exclusivity in the actual production competence is being replaced by more relaxed relationships that are subject to greater pressure from competitors. Larger, more anonymous target groups of decision-makers need to be reached; furthermore, these are having to make their investment decisions faster and on the basis of less information and specialist knowledge. The result is the emergence of success components that have already applied in the mass market for a long time:

- The brand as a confidence-building variable that can have an all-important effect on the purchasing decision, particularly with faster decision processes and an unclear basis for information.
- Optimized communication as a catalyst and orientation system for the customer now faced by a complex range of services and products in this sector, too.

In brief: the B2B sector is changing in many areas to a kind of mass market, and is adapting the instruments of professional mass marketing.

Interestingly, in addition to this race to catch up by B2B companies, in which the flow of knowledge runs primarily from the consumer goods' manufacturers to the B2B companies, an increase in knowledge in the opposite direction can also be observed. Particularly in the B2B sector, other factors of marketing have being playing a major role for a long time and these are only now acquiring strategic importance in other sectors. At the very forefront are dealings with key accounts, in other words, particularly important customers. Taking care of the customers that generate the most sales is a truism that is crucial for survival in many B2B companies, and that has led to a corresponding professionalism in this discipline (see "B2B Marketing" – Adriana Nuneva). Today, in times of increased profitability pressure, this competence is also important for other sectors, as the articles "Customer Retention System" (Harald Eisenächer, Sascia Hilverkus) and "Integrated Customer Retention" (Martin Kanis, Kathrin Henze) show.

In this respect, an alternating learning relationship between the various sectors can be observed that is subject to a central paradigm: the importance of marketing is growing in many areas, and the pressure to make all marketing disciplines more professional suggests that the mutual exchange of knowledge between industries should be strongly encouraged.

However, as already mentioned, a development in the opposite direction in the B2B sector can be discerned with this trend: many companies see their opportunity rather more in a symbiotic relationship with one major customer. They adapt themselves to this customer with activities that are rather alien to marketing. This includes the networking of infrastructure as well as the development of tailor-made production and service competences that cannot be copied in the short term, the reduction of vertical integration and outsourcing activities to the skills that are important to the customer and thus maximum flexibility with regard to this customer.

These two major trends – B2B goes over to mass marketing vs. symbiotic relationships with a core customer – primarily affect B2B companies with an unclear positioning. These companies need to decide which route corresponds to their own core business. The pressure on the central positioning area is growing in favor of the two more extreme poles.

Open topics

In our work as an international communication agency, we come across further contentious topics of marketing management that we have not been able to cover yet due to the limited scope of this work. In conclusion, I would at least like to refer to three other fields of activity in international marketing that, in my opinion, are growing in importance:

A International Marketing Risk Management

The issue of the communicative handling of crises in companies – whether it is communicative, product-dependent, or otherwise induced – continues to increase in importance with internationalization and digitalization. International companies are also finding themselves more quickly facing international crises that have to be dealt with on an international level. Above all, the organizational complexity this entails, and the variety of consumer cultures that have to be taken into account, make global risk management in marketing a new important field that requires substantial know-how, and also the right tools if it is to be dealt with successfully in corporate practice.

Open research issues in this field consist primarily of how an image crisis spreads internationally, and which cultural factors are to be taken into consideration if this crisis is to be managed in a communicative way.

Another fundamental area is also the analysis of the development of marketing-induced crises and the explication of the most important risk factors in international and intercultural marketing.

B International Advertising Management

Global campaigns require the global management of highly complex advertising activities. Here, too, issues are raised over and over again that have not been satisfactorily dealt with, such as the cultural effect dependencies of communication, and issues concerning possible tools and management mechanisms, and concepts for the selection and management of local and global vendors.

However, from our day-to-day work as an international advertising agency, we know that this area especially often has great potential for development, both on the agency and the client side, which should be reflected in future primarily in more sophisticated communication, management and reporting systems. Scholz & Friends has found a system response for this that is new in our sectors (we call it "Partner System"). We consider it more appropriate to position this in our company portrait rather than in this work.

C Internal Marketing

The internationalization of companies is also leading to new communicative challenges. From lobbying for new strategies and concepts, to the conveyance of fundamental value systems such as brand image and corporate identity, the following applies: the internal communication of rational and emotional content is becoming a central organizational skill for company management itself and also for the management of change processes.

Above all, in global groups that are increasingly growing as the result of acquisitions and other non-organic development activities, internal marketing, in terms of conveying central concepts and visions, is becoming a decisive factor for success.

The factors that determine the success of internal marketing are in part the same as the success factors for external marketing: target groups need to be convinced of concepts and content through clear messages and corresponding media activities, and taken to the purchasing or adaptation decision. In part, however, new aspects are emerging that are given by the specific organizational framework of a company: channels and feedback systems differ, and a hierarchical system with multipliers, which on the one hand have a higher obligation to implement the content, but on the other hand first need to be convinced themselves of their relevance, brings a new aspect of communication into play.

The growing importance of change and communication processes in global companies suggests that this research field should also be put on the shortlist of important issues.

The Editor

Thomas Heilmann, CEO

Thomas Heilmann is CEO of Scholz & Friends AG, one of Europe's leading marketing service agencies.

During his career he worked at the Munich branch of the management consultancy firm McKinsey and Lufthansa's marketing department in New York before joining the Scholz & Friends Group. Heilmann is a visiting professor at the Berlin University of the Arts and editor of several publications.

Global Marketing

→ www.marketingmanual.org/global

Niclas Friese-Greene – Siemens Communications

Global Brand Identity

Leveraging inherent strengths of a brand through a positioning that combines global attractiveness with local relevance to ultimately drive market impact and business success

▶ Executive Summary

"A brand identity expresses who we are, what we stand for, and what we aspire to become!"
- A strong brand should have a rich, clear brand identity – a set of associations that a brand seeks to create or maintain among all primary and secondary target groups.
- In contrast to a brand image (the brand's current associations), a brand identity is aspirational and may imply that the image needs to be changed or augmented.
- For the formulation of a successful and differentiating global brand identity it is mandatory to develop a thorough strategic foundation that builds on an analysis of all market forces and a clear understanding of relevant market dynamics across all markets worldwide.
- All strategic brand work should be validated against the different stakeholders of a brand, both internally and externally, to ensure highest relevance and success of the chosen positioning.
- As one of the most important elements of brand and marketing communication, the creative direction and CI needs to fully reflect the core values and brand identity elements.
- Adapting the global brand strategy with regard to the local peculiarities is the core prerequisite to implement the brand consistently across regions while still accounting for the specific situation and demands in different markets.
- A brand strategy has to be brought to life, both internally and externally, through a focused and comprehensive roll-out plan.
- Ultimately, the full success potential of a brand identity can only be leveraged through the consequent implementation of brand driven processes across all relevant internal functions and departments, beyond brand management and marketing communication.

▶ Theoretical Model of a Global Brand Identity

Background

A global brand identity defines what a brand stands for in a compelling way. The brand identity is used to provide the overarching strategic direction, to rally decision-making around bringing the brand to life in any kind of marketing communication and to directly guide and shape management actions. It is reflected in the visual identity and represents the core and fundamental thoughts that you want to bring into the mind and heart of people, may it be customers, consumers, employees, or anyone else that has a relationship to the brand at any place in the world. Creating and managing a successful global brand identity demands a deeply founded and comprehensive understanding of all relevant local markets while still maintaining a global view to define an overarching set of brand values. In order to leverage the full potential of a brand on a regional level, it is important to define specific adaptations of the brand identity that account for the peculiarities of the different markets. This task requires a direct and open interaction with the marketing headquarters and local marketing organizations, both to leverage their market expertise and drive their buy-in for the brand identity. The following article will first describe the different aspects of a strong global brand identity and then illustrate the ideal process to develop and implement a differentiating brand strategy within the organization. We have undertaken this brand work at Siemens Mobile Devices over the past two years and I believe this article will help to showcase the significant positive impact and success potential of this approach.

1. Definition and core principle

A brand is the face, personality, and promise of a company to internal and external audiences. It symbolizes the culture, values, and goals and also reflects the business strategy of a company. It derives from elements such as our history and identity – and from experiences with people, products, and partners.

The global brand identity provides a structure for communicating the core elements of a brand, including who you are, what you do, and who you aspire to become. In its nucleus it is comprised of the brand essence and core identity elements that reflect the strategy and values of the organization.

The brand identity is not meant to be communicated explicitly in the form of claims or phrases. It represents the core foundation for all internal and external brand communication. It is translated into a unique visual identity and the strategic direction for all relevant business processes, like product development or brand alliances.

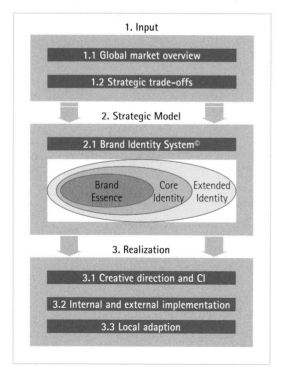

Fig. 1: Global Brand Identity Model

The chart above shows an overview of the core elements of a Global Brand Identity Model. These will be described in further detail in the following sections of this article.

2. Factors of global brand identity

2.1 Input

2.1.1 Global market overview
Any successful and differentiating global brand identity has to be built on a solid and complete understanding of the current market situation. Aiming to create a globally appealing brand positioning, this view should never be restricted to the core markets of a brand or driven by a pure "revenue based" approach but rather enclose all relevant regional markets the brand actively targets or plans to target in future.

It is important to incorporate strategic input from different departments and regional teams within the global organization, especially concerning the core objective of developing a globally relevant and successful brand identity. At the very early stage of any strategic brand initiative, this ensures the necessary breadth of the market overview and also lays the basis for an efficient and fast local implementation of the brand strategy.

One major element of the market overview is the awareness for any current and future industry dynamics that define the overarching frame of the business. This regards the interplay and relationship between market forces on the one hand (e.g., manufacturer and retailer), but it is also highly relevant to identify relevant market trends that can reshape the whole industry.

A second aspect of the market overview is a thorough comprehension of the demand landscape, the different customer (B2B view e.g., mobile service operators, retailers) and consumer (B2C view, end-users) groups targeted by the brand's offering.

In order to describe this demand landscape it is very important to understand the purchase and loyalty drivers in the market, for business customers on the one hand and end-consumers on the other hand. All market assessment that is conducted in this context has to explicitly regard the different regional markets and the specifics that drive and explain individual customer and consumer behavior. This enables a company to identify global commonalities as well as regional differences within the demand landscape. Building on this knowledge, it is possible to create a brand identity that answers the purpose of a globally appealing and at the same time locally adaptable brand identity. Aiming to create such a differentiating brand positioning necessitates a deep understanding of what drives and what potentially prevents success in the industry. Overall, the demand landscape view answers the core question: "What do I have to stand for, what do I have to deliver to the market to be successful?" This is strongly linked to the business strategy of a company, which makes it very obvious why the brand strategy has to be fully aligned with the business strategy in order to address the market challenges.

A third and very important aspect of the market overview is the assessment of the supply landscape, which includes the complete competitive set as one major element and the company (e.g., Siemens Mobile Devices) as the second element. Basically, the supply landscape shows targets that provide answers to two questions:
- "How strong are my competitors in fulfilling the needs and expectations of the customers and consumers and how much differentiating potential does this leave for my brand in the market?"

- "How well prepared is my company to deliver on the core market demands and how credible would it be for my brand to position around those specific benefits?"

Combining the three elements of industry dynamics, demand landscape, and supply landscape allows a company to identify attractive positioning white-spots that are not fully covered by competition and are also credibly addressable by the brand. A powerful tool to drive such a comprehensive global market overview is the Strategic Brand Analysis (SBA) that will be presented in part II of this article. The Strategic Brand Analysis approach was developed by Vivaldi Partners, a global marketing and brand strategy consultancy that worked in close collaboration with the marketing team of Siemens Mobile Devices on the development and implementation of the new brand identity.

2.1.2 Strategic trade-offs

Based on the global market overview and the identification of strategic white-spots that would provide the attractive starting point for brand identity and positioning it is important for a company to decide on a focused strategic path for its future business. Many brands do not encounter problems in defining what they want to stand for in the marketplace but rather in defining what they do not want to stand for. A brand should never try to be "everything to everyone," just to avoid leaving any potential market segment behind. By choosing a too broad an approach in its positioning, a brand will lack clear focus and profile, thus making it hard for people to really understand the core messages the brand wants to communicate. Diluting a brand positioning by avoiding strategic trade-offs is a major reason for brand failures in the long run. Especially with regard to the increasing information and marketing overload in the market, a simple, dedicated, and concise brand identity is the way to future success and a strong brand-consumer relationship.

2.2 Strategic model

2.2.1 Brand Identity System

After having seen many different philosophies and strategic approaches for the development of a global brand strategy, I feel that the Brand Identity System from Vivaldi Partners is the most credible and applicable model for Siemens Mobile Devices. The Brand Identity System is a proprietary strategic model of Vivaldi Partners that defines a set of brand values and associations that a company aspires to create or maintain. It is the foundation for communicating the brand benefits to all internal and external stakeholders. Driven by a global market view and clear strategic trade-offs, the formulation of a Brand Identity System turns the results of a Strategic Brand Analysis into strong brand values and a distinctive positioning.

The Brand Identity System includes the following core elements:

- Articulation of the brand identities, including:
  - Brand essence: a single thought capturing the soul of the brand.
  - Core identity: fundamental elements of a brand that define what the brand stands for and aspires to be.
  - Extended identity: dimensions that add texture and completeness to the brand by formulating values according to the four perspectives Brand as Product, Brand as Organization, Brand as Person, and Brand as Symbol.

- Formulation of brand positioning statement: a declared defensible space for the brand in the competitive landscape. The positioning statement defines how a company wants its customers, consumers, and employees

to perceive, feel, and behave towards its brand. It is the foundation for communicating who the brand is and will help align how the brand is lived, perceived, and broadcasted. It communicates along the three founding elements of every strong and differentiating positioning statement.
- Frame of reference: the competitive space of a brand.
- Brand promise: the value proposition or benefit delivered by the brand to its target audience.
- Reason why: the unique advantage or differentiating factor of a brand.

- Definition of target-group specific value propositions for different constituencies (consumers, business customers, employees, etc.), including functional, emotional, and self-expressive benefits. Those value propositions also form the basis for the formulation of the brand-consumer relationship.

2.3 Realization

Any strong and distinctive brand strategy can only leverage its full potential when it is successfully implemented and activated across the whole organization and throughout all relevant functions. The creative direction and CI as a visual expression of the brand identity and positioning is a core and powerful tool to "bring the brand to life." In addition to this, a successful internal and external activation of the brand strategy demands a well designed global roll-out plan and also a consistent establishment of brand driven business processes within the company. Finally, as a decisive success factor for any global brand identity, the local adaptation and implementation of the brand strategy in the different regions completes an optimized brand and marketing approach.

2.3.1 Creative direction and CI

The creative direction and overall CI is one of the most important aspects of brand and marketing communication, especially for consumer driven markets such as mobile phones. Building on the core strategic aspects of the brand's positioning, the creative direction is the outside face of the brand towards all target groups. When the brand strategy defines "what the brand wants to stand for," then the CI is the one most important medium to define "how the brand wants to appeal to its audience." In order to carry the brand identity through all communication vehicles and across all consumer touch-points, its is necessary to have a complete set of creative guidelines in place that guide and determine all marketing communication (TV spots, print ads, POS, events, packaging, shop design, etc.)

2.3.2 Internal and external implementation

There are two critical phases that determine the success of a brand strategy. One is the launch phase of a new brand identity, internally and externally, and the second is ongoing brand governance.

During the first phase of the launch and roll-out of a brand identity, all relevant internal stakeholders across the different departments have to be informed about the new strategic direction the company wants to take with the brand. This should also showcase the extensive strategic work that was done in identifying the most attractive and relevant positioning themes in the market. In order to create buy-in and excitement among the work force, both the rational and emotional aspects of the brand strategy have to be brought together to form a compellingly convincing message that can be carried on throughout the organization. The launch should build on all existing vehicles of internal communication and, besides that leverage, some strong roll-out tools like a brand book or a "brand day" to bring the soul of the brand identity to life.

Subsequent to this internal launch, the brand has to be activated against all external stakeholders; most importantly of course the customers and consumers. As mentioned before, a differentiating creative direction represents a powerful way to communicate a change within the brand approach and create awareness and interest among the primary and secondary target groups. It is important to get the buy-in from the CEO and the top management team at this stage to have them act as ambassadors for the new brand strategy within the organization. Dedicated PR activities also play an important role for the external brand launch as they allow communication of the strategic background of the brand. Thus, this helps to create relevance for the brand beyond the often very emotional marketing driven messages of mass advertisement.

While the brand roll-out is undoubtedly a highly significant phase laying the foundation for the success of a brand identity and positioning in the market, it is often even more relevant and decisive to ensure a consistent incorporation of the new strategic brand direction into all major internal processes. This enables a company to live up to the brand promises made towards the target audiences and covers a broad variety of functions and processes like the product development ("design to brand"), marketing governance, KPI measurement and management, just to name a few.

2.3.3 Local adaptation

"Play global – win local." This simple phrase states one of the major challenges for any global brand identity. On the one hand, the brand identity has to be consistent and recognizable across the world to benefit from positive spill-over effects in marketing and create one look and feel for the brand. But on the other hand, it is also important to account for potential local peculiarities by adapting the global brand positioning and identifying elements with regard to regional requirements. The decision on the regions and countries that should be provided with a dedicated adaptation has to be taken on a case-by-case basis in consideration of available resources and overall timing requirements.

Building on the strategic work that informs the global market overview as well as an individual analysis of market specifics in a certain region, the local adaptation has to follow a clear and comprehensible framework. This defines the areas of potential adjustment and also distinguishes elements that have to stay the same across all regions. For example, the brand essence as the nucleus of a brand identity should ideally remain unchanged and consistent across all markets.

The regional adaptation of the global brand identity should always be developed in close collaboration and agreement with the local marketing departments. This bears a range of benefits for the corporate headquarters. First of all, the regional organizations have the best insights into the market and have access to a broad expertise regarding the peculiarities of the market forces, both from a demand and supply landscape view. Secondly, the regional marketing team represent powerful brand ambassadors who carry the spirit and soul of a brand identity into the local organization. Based on their buy-in and excitement, they support the headquarters in bringing the new brand to life in a relevant and engaging way.

CASE   Siemens mobile (MD)

In 2000, Siemens Mobile Devices had an image of the "grey planet," driven by aspects like cold, distant, and purely rational. In order to emotionalize its brand, Siemens decided to take a bold and very different approach for its marketing communication, called "be inspired." It was a very lifestyle driven communication that focused on emotional and self-expressive benefits, leaving the technology-based communication behind that was predominant in the market at that time.

In the beginning "be inspired" was simply a claim for one of the product campaigns in that year. But based on initial positive internal response it soon raised to become the new brand direction. However, "be inspired" was not the result of a deeply founded brand assessment and therefore it was not really a new "strategy" but rather a communication approach (for an example ad, please see Fig. 2 below). By that time the mobile phone market was increasingly driven by service providers and the competition between manufacturers became fiercer than ever with new players entering the market. Against this backdrop, Siemens mobile had risen from being a peripheral player with 3.6% market share in 1998 to become the 4th player in global mobile communications in 2002 with 8.3% market share.

The Siemens mobile brand helped this success; in particular, the "be inspired" campaign contributed to a consistent look and feel, and increased brand awareness. However, by late 2002 the markets had changed significantly. Almost every competitor was following a similar, very emotional communication approach. Relevant and motivating product superiority combined with distinct and consistent brand communication were becoming critically important again as consumers were faced with more and more choice and seemingly never-ending lifestyle advertising.

By the end of 2002 the "be inspired" approach had lost most of its differentiating power. In addition to this, research showed that people in general had some difficulty in linking for the idea of "inspiration" with the mobile category and "inspiration" driven attributes turned out to be not really competitive advantages of Siemens mobile. The overall insight was that "inspiration" was too abstract and philosophical; therefore it was difficult to connect it with clear product and consumer benefits.

At that time, I decided that it was time to take the brand to the next level and create a new brand identity that successfully addressed the market challenges while providing the basis for a distinctive market communication.

Fig. 2: Example of "be inspired" ad for C55

Global Brand Identity

	1	2	3	4	5a	5b	6	7
	Global Strategic Brand Analysis	Positioning hypotheses	Elaboration of initial Brand Identity System	Development of new CI	Design and preparation of global market research	Global validation & refinement of brand identity and CI	Internal and external activation	Development and implementation of local adaptations
Goals	Understanding of market and trends; Identify purchase and loyalty drivers; SWOT Analysis	Create the strategic foundation; Ensure market relevance	Create a brand identity; Develop the basis for future marketing measures	Perfect visual translation of the brand identity; Basis for implementation of the new CI		Test the resonance of the new direction; Clear implications for the final brand identity	Activation of the new brand strategy; Integrate brand strategy into core business functions; Finalize the Brand Identity System	Regional adaptations of the brand identity and CI; Internal buy-in in the regions
Actions	Review current business and brand; Compile information on market; Analyze existing market research; Interviews with internal departments; Additional desk research	Positioning hypotheses; Discussion with relevant internal departments; Finalize most attractive hypotheses	Compile potential brand identity elements; Condense initial ideas and define the brand essence; Formulate additional elements of the Brand Identity System	Develop a creative brief; Select 2–3 creative concepts; Present concepts to relevant internal stakeholders; Create visual stimuli for the global validation		Research design; Fieldwork; Analyze survey results and refine brand positioning/CI	Overview of all current communication vehicles; Develop roll-out plan; Additional roll-out tools to increase impact of the launch phase; Develop main messages and messaging architecture; Implement new brand strategy into other departments	Discuss the global brand strategy with regions; Potential areas of adaptation; Develop and activate dedicated regional adaptations

Fig. 3: Process steps for the development of a Global Brand Identity

▶ Process & Execution

1 ▶ 2 ▶ 3 ▶ 4 ▶ 5 ▶ 6 ▶ 7

Phase 1: Strategic Brand Analysis (SBA)

The objective of the first project phase is to gain a comprehensive global market overview as the foundation for the identification of attractive positioning opportunities for the brand in the competitive environment. The tool that can be applied here is the Strategic Brand Analysis (SBA). It allows a detailed assessment of all relevant market forces (customer, consumer, and competitor), the company, and current market dynamics/industry trends by leveraging both internal and external expertise.

CASE The marketing team of Siemens Mobile Devices worked on the strategic market assessment and the following formulation of the global brand identity in close collaboration with the Munich office of Vivaldi Partners, a global brand, marketing, and business strategy consultancy (headquartered in New York). During the course of the two year project, Vivaldi Partners supported the marketing team at Siemens Mobile Devices throughout the development and implementation of the new global brand identity.

Key Inputs: Based on data gathering and research there are four multiple key inputs that drove the analysis of consumers, customers, competitors, and Siemens Mobile Devices. In this phase, it was crucial to access and analyze strategic information from different departments and regions and incorporate direct input through personal interviews with internal representatives across the organization. In addition to this, market studies and expert interviews were used to create a deep understanding of the market dynamics and decisive future trends.

Analysis: This phase included an assessment of the situation and potential trends in the industry as well as customer and consumer dynamics. In addition to this, we analyzed the competitive positioning along with their respective communication activities and finally Siemens Mobile Devices as a business and brand. This was specifically evaluated in the context of the Siemens AG, one of the most successful and long-standing technology companies in the world.

Implications: The overall objective of the Strategic Brand Analysis was to identify distinctive brand opportunities to which the competitive advantage of Siemens Mobile Devices could deliver compelling value propositions. The brand challenges and opportunities were derived from the thorough assessment of the demand and supply landscape in the global market. As the core outcome of the SBA, these strategic insights represented the foundation for the development of overall positioning hypotheses.

The SBA showed that the market was facing a lack of differentiation between the different mobile phone manufacturers on the one hand and also the mobile service operators on the other. All market forces were attempting to appeal to the consumer's values, belief systems, and needs, e.g., freedom, individualism, friendship, and self-fulfillment through a very lifestyle-driven brand positioning and communications approach. But more and more consumers were looking for something different. In a market with an increasing abundance of choices, both in mobile phones and possible tariffs, people felt confused and insecure about their purchase decision.

The big opportunity for us in this situation was to move away from the mass of brands in the market by focusing on brand characteristics related to the mobile phone itself so as to appear authentic and act as the credible authority in a complex market environment.

Phase 2: Positioning hypotheses

CASE During this project step, I had many heated discussions with Vivaldi Partners and internally with the members of the project team in order to find the most attractive direction for our brand. After the finalization of the core hypotheses, they were translated into specific brand identity elements as the central element of the Brand Identity System (see Phase 3).

Based on the results of the SBA, the next step is to formulate a set of dedicated positioning hypotheses that form the foundation for the development of the brand identity along with a sustainable and successful future brand positioning. These hypotheses have to be broad enough to allow for a rich interpretation while they already have to carry some clear strategic trade-offs to focus the initial brand positioning around strong core values.

The "breakthrough solution" for Siemens mobile was reflected in the one idea of „celebrating the product as the hero." Moving the brand away from the lifestyle-driven clutter in the market and positioning around real consumer values and benefits that the Siemens mobile phones provide was the bold move. By building on the ability of Siemens Mobile Devices to develop and produce great products, the new brand direction was also much closer to the heritage of the corporate Siemens brand.

The challenge for Siemens Mobile Devices was now to leverage the history of Siemens as a technological leader for almost 160 years while still fostering the emotional side of their brand. The new brand approach is very much about being true to the heritage of Siemens. Ultimately, this also helped to strongly engage everyone who has contact to the brand internally and make them proud of what the company has achieved over the past years.

The message that this brand positioning gives to the people at Siemens and to the outside worlds is very bold and easy: "No other company has the equivalent combination of expertise in packaging high quality, continuous improvement, design leadership, and enduring and balanced relationships with its stakeholders. To its customers Siemens mobile is a strong and reliable business partner, enabling them to offer a broad set of attractive mobile devices. And it is by being more relevant in consumers' everyday lives and by addressing their challenges that Siemens Mobile Devices will gain leadership in the marketplace." This commitment formed the basis for the formulation of the Brand Identity System for Siemens Mobile Devices.

Phase 3: Elaboration of initial Brand Identity System

The brand identity is a powerful tool to guide all internal and external marketing and brand initiatives around a common focus. It is not meant to be communicated externally through any marketing communication vehicle.

Starting from the identified positioning hypotheses, a preliminary idea for the brand identity is derived and communicated internally to all relevant representatives. Based on their feedback and with regard to the overall strategic direction that is selected for the brand, the marketing team develops the initial Brand Identity System. This encompassed the brand essence, core, and extended brand identity elements and also a positioning statement and dedicated value propositions for the different stakeholders of the brand.

CASE   The new brand essence became "Ingenuity." This powerful idea captures the spirit that is unique to the brand. Ingenuity describes the ability to invent things or solve problems in clever new ways. It is more than pure innovation simply for innovation's sake. Ingenuity is about making technological expertise relevant to consumers by turning it into products that deliver relevant benefits.

The brand essence is complemented by three distinctive core identity elements: real, coherent, and timeless. The aspect of "real" carries the idea of "the product as the hero"; it positions the brand around values such as authentic, genuine, and unpretentious. The second aspect of "coherent" has strong links to the product experience by driving the brand promise around values like clear, logical, and uncomplicated. Finally, the "timeless" identity element positions the brand actively against the battle of many competitors to deliver the latest and trendy, but quickly outdated gadgets in their phones. Siemens mobile phones offer classy and elegant design – showing the confidence not to follow every technology fad in the market.

The brand essence and core identity is completed by the extended identity elements of "brand as person" (open-minded, honest, and optimistic), "brand as organization" (focus and consistency, commitment, and expertise in engineering) and "brand as product" (classy design, superior quality, and essential functionalities). The positioning statement and value propositions (functional, emotional, self-expressive) for customers, consumers, and employees were also formulated at this stage of the process and further refined based on internal discussions among the project team.

As an element of the verbal translation of the brand identity, a new claim was developed to accompany the future marketing communication of the brand. With regard to the results of the global validation survey (see also step 5), the final claim for Siemens Mobile Devices was "designed for life." It communicates the timeless and iconic character of the brand while combining the excellent quality and reliability of Siemens mobile phones and the overall design strength of the company.

Phase 4: Development of new CI

Following the formulation of the Brand Identity System, the fundamental strategic direction of the brand has to be translated into a catholic creative framework that defines the visual basis for all future brand and marketing communication.

During this process step, the task is the formulation of a variety of creative approaches that have to be built on a thorough understanding of the brand strategy as well as of course the design equity of a brand. With regard to the fact that the development of the creative brand direction is usually outsourced to a CI agency, it is important that the creative briefing for the agency is developed in close collaboration with the project team that developed the Brand Identity System.

CASE   After several pitches we selected MetaDesign, a leading CI agency with headquarters in Berlin for the development of the visual stimuli that delivered on the core aspects of the new brand identity. MetaDesign developed three alternatives for the new creative direction that were tested in the course of the global validation survey (see also Phase 5). The research design and preparation was conducted in parallel to the development of the CI options. This enabled Siemens Mobile Devices to incorporate all necessary testing material, both strategic and creative, while ensuring a fast and efficient validation and refinement phase.

The research results proved that the "iconic" design framework received by far the strongest acceptance among the global audience. This design approach strongly reflects the new positioning anchor around the aspects of high quality engineering and distinct design while delivering on the need for simple but appealing communication, beyond the undifferentiated market clutter. The picture below shows an example of a current print ad for the S65, the premium business phone launched in mid 2004.

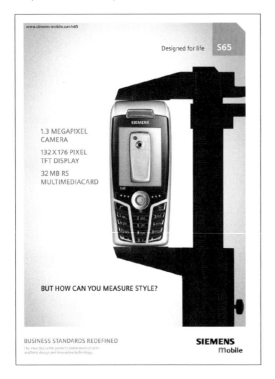

Fig. 4: Current print ad for the S65

Phase 5: Global validation and refinement of brand identity and CI

The overall objective of this process step is to conduct global research among all relevant target groups to validate and refine the proposed strategic direction for the brand along with the new creative direction. Addressing customers, consumers, and employees in different regional markets enables the company to gain valuable insights for a finalization of the brand identity in a global view. In addition to this it also provides the basis for the potential adaptation of brand strategy and CI for specific regional markets.

On the strategic side, the findings from this phase also help to add more texture and relevance to the description of the different brand identity elements and support the formulation of dedicated brand messages for the different stakeholders. Regarding the creative direction, the research results provided a core input for the elaboration of a complete set of creative guidelines for all marketing communication channels and related aspects (e.g., advertising, fairs, packaging). The global research ideally encompasses both qualitative and quantitative research, with the former being conducted first. Qualitative research helps to assess the constructs behind the brand identity in great detail and in addition to this it also represents the more vivid and rich possibility to analyze the response of key stakeholders on the proposed creative directions. Defining the research design of the quantitative survey based on the insights from qualitative interviews allows testing specific and clearly focused questions among a sufficiently large sample which is statistically relevant.

CASE   We conducted more than 2,500 interviews in 12 countries among customers, consumers, and employees in the course of the global validation survey. In order to leverage current market research work within the company, the global validation was tied directly into current research structures and approaches. This ensured comparability with existing and future data. Our validation survey was conducted in close collaboration with GfK, a global market research agency that is also the long-term partner regarding advertising tracking. Following the validation research, a core set of brand items was incorporated into the advertising tracking to allow consistent measurement and management of the new core brand values.

Phase 6: Internal and external activation

6.1 Operational roll-out

After the finalization of the new global brand strategy and its creative interpretation through a unique brand CI, the next process step is the preparation of an internal and external roll-out. In this phase, it is highly important to assess the existing internal communication channels and vehicles to develop a dedicated roll-out plan.

The next challenge is to translate the strategic foundation of the brand strategy and the core brand values into compelling brand messages that are tailored to the different internal stakeholders. For example, the marketing departments in the headquarters and the regional organizations have to be supported with a detailed briefing on all aspects of the new brand identity, whereas the sales department should only receive specifically adapted core messages about the new brand direction. The objective should always be to create awareness and engagement for the brand identity by illustrating the potential of the brand strategy and its positive impact on the business performance of the whole company.

CASE   Besides the existing internal communication vehicles, we introduced new roll-out tools such as a brand book as well as conducting several brand launch events around the globe to excite the people across the organization. We also organized a Media Summit in Berlin where we invited all leading creative and media agencies as well as all key marketing personnel within Siemens Mobile Devices. The objective was to introduce the new global brand identity and CI among the different stakeholders who would work directly with the brand in future. In addition to this, the external roll-out was prepared and coordinated by my marketing team across all communication channels.

6.2 Brand-driven business processes

The future market success of a brand identity and positioning is strongly dependent on the ability of an organization to deliver on the brand promises it conveys to its target audiences. One of the most important aspects in this regard is the product development process. Successful brands, for example in the automotive sector, have a comprehensive system in place to ensure that all product development efforts are checked against the brand fit of the individual product.

CASE We started this integrative approach in early 2004. Other core aspects besides the product development are, for example, the marketing management process or brand partnerships and sponsoring activities.

Phase 7: Development and implementation of local adaptations

Any global branding approach has to keep a solid balance between the objective to achieve one core brand positioning and one "look and feel" across all markets while still accounting for fundamental regional specifics that demand an adaptation of the global brand identity and CI. With regard to the necessary involvement of resources and the need for a fast and efficient activation of the new brand direction, there are again clear strategic trade-offs to be made when answering the question of which region will get a dedicated interpretation of the brand identity and creative direction. As the regional marketing teams are a core target group during the internal roll-out meetings, the feedback from their side provides valuable initial input in taking this strategic decision. Other aspects that drive the selection of relevant regions are of course also turnover and future potential of the market.

The development of a dedicated regional adaptation of a new brand identity represents an important starting point for all future regional brand management. This ideally occurs in an open and highly responsive interplay between the corporate headquarters and the local marketing teams. With the headquarters providing basic strategic directions and guidelines, and the local organizations taking over the responsibility for the operational work, this ensures the highest efficiency and consistency throughout the process. Hence, the marketing team develops a framework for the local adaptation that describes the potential areas of change while also defining limits of potential refinement. Close interaction between the headquarters and the regions enables a company to build on the unchallenged expertise of the regional team in the relevant markets while creating strong buy-in among those employees who will be the main brand ambassadors in the regions in the long run.

CASE We found that the one region with the most urgent need for adaptation was China (with regard to maturity of the mobile phone segment, consumer behavior, cultural environment, and market position of Siemens Mobile Devices). Therefore, the marketing team at headquarters developed an overall approach and framework for the regional adaptation in close collaboration with the local marketing team and Vivaldi Partners regarding the strategic aspects. In parallel, MetaDesign also worked on the development of dedicated creative guidelines for the Chinese market. Based on in-depth secondary research and additional primary research in different cities, a set of adaptation hypotheses was developed. These represented the core input for the following refinement of the Brand Identity System within the given strategic framework. As one aspect of the adaptation, the global claim "designed for life" was changed into "design enriches life" to account for the cultural specifics in China. As an overall outcome of this approach, the adapted brand identity was very positively received across the Chinese organization and now represents a core input of all brand and marketing related initiatives.

▶ Key Insights

- The brand strategy has to be directly linked to business strategy.
- Building a successful global brand identity is a task that demands the effort and consistent contribution of the different departments within the organization and across all regions.
- A brand identity needs to be aspirational and achieve strategic trade-offs.
- Leveraging existing brand equity (e.g., heritage) can strongly impact a positive internal and external acceptance.
- Just following category trends in brand positioning is often likely to under-leverage a company's inherent strengths.
- A brand's identity and positioning need to comprehend three interrelated factors to become relevant and enduringly successful:
  - Consumer relevance
  - Competitive distinction
  - Core capabilities of a company.
- Periodic renewal of a brand is critical for success in fast-changing markets.

▶ Practical Guidelines

- Leverage existing material – across the organization and across the globe.
- Get the key stakeholders involved – always build a brand strategy on an open and "inviting" process.
- Account for regional peculiarities while creating the global picture for a brand.
- Incorporate the brand into all communication channels to ensure consistent involvement of the organization – not just for the roll-out phase.
- Testing a new strategic and creative direction on a global base should tie into existing research and potentially be integrated into future market research. Use it as the starting point for ongoing tracking of the brand performance.
- Translate the brand strategy into easy and understandable guidelines to ensure that the people find it easy to understand the new brand direction and its impact on their daily work.
- Institutionalise brand champions throughout the organization, especially on a global view, who act as ambassadors, both internally and externally.

The Author

Niclas Friese-Greene

Vice President Marketing Communication Mobile Phones (Siemens Communications Mobile Devices) and Vice President Brand Management (Siemens Communications Group). Niclas Friese-Greene joined Siemens mobile in October 2002 and is responsible for driving Siemens mobile's transformation into a major international consumer brand. He also oversees tactical marketing execution across a diverse multi-dimensional product offering that includes category leaders and emerging markets. Niclas joined Siemens Mobile following his role as Vice President Marketing and Sales for a new media subsidiary of Grundig AG and has over 13 years of brand marketing management expertise acquired at high profile consumer electronics brands such as Loewe, Grundig, and Nintendo. A native Englishman, Niclas holds a CIM (Chartered Institute of Marketing) Diploma, and a BA (Dual Honors) in International Marketing from Greenwich University, London.

Literature Recommendations

D. A. Aaker and E. Joachimsthaler, "Brand Leadership," 2000
D. A. Aaker and E. Joachimsthaler, "The Lure of Global Branding," in: Harvard Business Review, Nov–Dec/1999
N. Friese-Greene, "Neupositionierung als Teamaufgabe," in: Absatzwirtschaft, 12/2004

Karen D. Halpert – MasterCard Europe

Global Brand Management

Global brand success through global strategy, local relevance, and an internationally aligned corporate structure

▶ Executive Summary

- ☐ The management of global brand and product portfolios faces the task of achieving the greatest possible global success through optimal utilization of different local markets.

This success presumes

- a precise understanding of the company's own global brand and product world,
- the effective analysis of local markets and consumers through definition of collective global research criteria,
- a global market strategy and the corresponding clear prioritization of the markets according to growth potential, local brand strength and strategic corporate targets,
- development of an internationally aligned corporate culture through the selection, training, and structural support of the employees on a global and local level,
- successful local realization of the global brand strategy through experienced employees and suitable infrastructures in local markets,
- support of global brand strategy through the decision-makers on global and local levels.

- ☐ The provision and safeguarding of these factors is the cornerstone of successful global brand management and thus the growth of international companies.

▶ Theoretical Model of Global Brand Management

1. Definition and core principle

Over the last 30 years, the term "global brand management" has increasingly become a synonym for other, less popular management tendencies:

- Marketing colonialism, whereby the centrally developed concepts are used as a one-size-fits-all concept for all markets.
- Cost-cutting through centralization and reduction of local personnel, and downsizing of infrastructure.

These tendencies neglect one aspect that is the top factor for success in a global competitive environment: growth. Today, a brand can only be successful if a company effectively exploits local market potential whilst simultaneously increasing global management efficiency. For global brand management this means: "glocal" is key. Without neglecting global efficiencies, local markets must be understood and managed in terms of their special characteristics in relation to competition and resources. Primarily, this stipulates a global brand strategy in which the company's own portfolio is precisely defined and understood, and in which a clear prioritization of the markets occurs. The following model describes how these factors are to be understood and applied in detail.

2. Factors of global brand management

2.1 Definition of the company's own brand range

Precise understanding of your own range of products and brands, together with the definition of brand architecture and the service and value system behind it, are prerequisites for successful global brand management. This sounds trite, but in many cases it is not. Brands and products usually develop from a local history on the home market. They encompass the perceptions that have grown in the heads of local consumers and local management. A brand that is well known in one market, where it has developed over a period of years and has a corresponding image, could be perceived as an unknown or quite differently positioned brand in another market. This means: real understanding of their own brand in local markets presents global or regional management with a task that can only be accomplished within the local markets with the involvement of local consumers and experts. The aim is to find a precise definition of globally applicable brand and product logic that is conclusive and, wherever possible, self-explanatory. Necessary information on the definition of global and local brand logic is, correspondingly, always on a global or local level:

- Brand status: analysis of strengths and weaknesses (SWOT).
- Brand portfolio: all brands and their products within the associated categories from which the elasticity of the brand is determined (to what extent is the brand elastic across various categories and product lines without weakening its profile and its brand values?).
- Competition: international and local rivals based on the perception of the consumers.
- Prerequisite: knowledge regarding the buying decision process of the consumer.

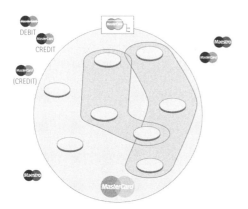 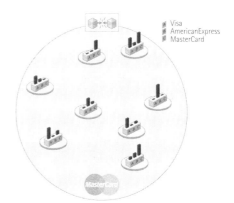

Fig. 1a: Testing of the product and brand portfolio in the various countries provides an overview of the actual local brand and/or product strategies that exist

Fig. 1b: The investigation of the competitive environment (strength of the competition) in the various countries provides information on how difficult the expansion is in the relevant market

CASE   MasterCard

The challenge for the definition of the brand portfolio at MasterCard was the existence of the different brands Maestro, Cirrus, and MasterCard. All these brands stand for payment services for the end-consumer, and for the simplification of personal payments. This leads to potential confusion for the consumer.

The solution: First of all, we differentiate between "pay now" (debit cards) and "pay later" (credit cards) products. At the core, Maestro is the brand for debit cards, and MasterCard is the brand for credit cards. The Cirrus brand stands for a system for obtaining cash from automated cash machines and, thus, plays a less important role in brand management. Due to various market introduction histories and framework conditions, there are, however, also markets where the MasterCard brand covers both areas.

Therefore, the following questions must be clarified for the development of the global brand strategy:

- Should the MasterCard brand on a global level only cover credit cards, or should it represent credit cards and debit cards?
- Can it perhaps stand for an even broader portfolio of payment solutions? What could it include?
- Should there be a brand with sub-brands – e.g., MasterCard pay now, MasterCard pay later, MasterCard prepaid, MasterCard paypass, etc.) – or should there be one brand that identifies the product types, e.g., MasterCard credit, MasterCard debit, MasterCard prepaid, etc. or two brands: Maestro for debit cards and MasterCard for credit cards?

The decision should be based on an analysis of the relevant brand recognition and brand image in each market, on brand elasticity and, above all, on the risks and the upside potential of possible changes. A particularly critical factor is always the cost of implementing a new branding strategy.

2.2 Analysis of the international markets

The international analysis of the local markets forms the most important prerequisite for a well-founded strategic development. The analysis should primarily consider the psychological criteria in the minds of the consumers, in order to discover indicators for the positioning of the brand. The intention is to achieve a deep insight into the attitudes of the consumers, the buying decision process, demand structures, and the resulting brand/product fit.

The great challenge in this kind of global investigation of consumer needs is developing a globally comparable collection design as a basis: only if all variables are set equally across all local markets, an international comparison can be undertaken.

In addition, such a study should offer results that facilitate the decision on which marketing measures to adopt. The most important step is the identification of the international "common denominator" as a basis – i.e., the psychological and socio-demographic research dimensions, that allow sensible statements to be made, in all local markets, on the attitude and the socio-demographic profile of the existing and potential consumers, and thereby, on the future marketing strategy.

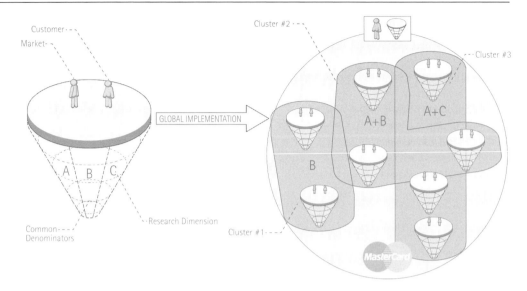

Fig. 2: During global research design, it should be ensured that the research dimensions to be investigated are the dimensions that can be compared globally: the "common denominators." The common denominators are investigated in all markets and divided in accordance with the results into regional clusters, in which similar consumer perception exists

CASE Mouthwash

In order to illustrate this principle, we can look at the "oral hygiene" sector: following a comprehensive investigation of the various markets, it became clear that the attitudes of the consumers in international markets could be split primarily into two fundamental dimensions:

- The social function of oral hygiene: fresh breath is important for social acceptance – particularly with the opposite sex – and this is the decisive factor in buying decisions.
- The medical health function of oral hygiene: fresh breath is a consequence of healthy bacterial flora in the mouth and, thus, is an indicator of healthy teeth.

Market research also showed that these attitude dimensions were directly associated with the development of the relevant markets in the oral hygiene sector. Consumers in markets that show high levels of development in the oral hygiene sector expect, above all, health benefits from their oral hygiene products, whereas markets with a lower level of development place more emphasis on socially-related benefits. The background lies in the varying levels of knowledge amongst consumers. As soon as they become aware that bad breath is substantially the result of poor oral hygiene, their preference shifts from purely cosmetic products to hygiene-oriented products. This realization makes it possible for the company to develop a globally standardized brand, and to form "clusters" of markets in accordance with the development of their oral hygiene standards. By "clusters" we mean regionally independent collections of markets, depending on the extent to which the consumer perceptions are in similar dimensions or not. Depending on development levels, relevantly adjusted product ranges were then presented, which met the current requirements of the market.

2.3 Analysis and development of the "global corporation"

2.3.1 Global corporate organization

In order to be able to implement global brand strategies in the local markets, your company must possess relevant implementation competence for the various markets. An understanding of its own local offices, resources, and competencies constitutes an important part of the analysis. With this implementation competence, it is not just a question of organizational infrastructures, but also of the development of a "global corporation": a company whose employees think globally and have intercultural understanding, whose structures and processes support international interaction, and which embodies local and global excellence as a total organism. In short: it is about much more than just the operational implementation of a strategy – the creation and nurturing of a corporate culture in line with the international management activities is required. The following dimensions are important aspects in this respect:

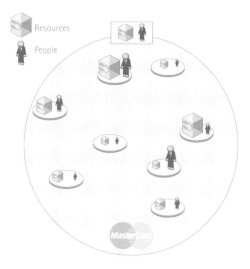

Fig. 3: A global analysis of company resources and management competence (people) creates an evaluation basis for the capability of serving a certain local market

- Corporate structure: are the corporate structures in accordance with the requirements of a global strategy?
  - processes,
  - reporting lines,
  - central positions of power, both local and global.
- Employees: are the right employees included in the teams, and are they supported by relevant training and education in relation to intercultural appreciation?
- Infrastructures and service-providers: is there a global vendor strategy, i.e., a global, coordinated network of service providers that helps to structure the international activities?
- Local characteristics: is there sufficient knowledge of local characteristics such as statutory regulations or religious restrictions?
- Global decisions: do the guidelines and strategies from global or regional headquarters influence the characteristics of the local markets?
- Growth: are the necessary processes and systems in place to support growth in local markets? A company must constantly test whether its structures and processes are still fulfilling the changing requirements of customers and markets. If they are not, then they become a hindrance.

All these questions show how important the concept of "glocalization" is. Local brand and/or customer relevance is the decisive prerequisite for every type of global business success – the central task of global brand management is to safeguard it and to utilize global synergies at the same time.

CASE MasterCard Europe

MasterCard is a company that operates in 210 countries. As the U.S. is the home market and also the market with the highest turnover, the control and the majority of innovation development take place there. At the same time the company knows that each market has its own laws and history and, therefore, uses corresponding local sales and marketing groups in order to stay close to the business. The local offices are manned by experts from the local markets. The global topic of security is a decisive factor for success in the credit card business, which is also heavily influenced by local statutory regulations. For this reason, MasterCard has a network of security experts who work closely together on a local and global level. In contrast to this, product development is mainly carried out on a regional level in order to keep the local costs low and, at the same time, retain a critical closeness to the market that would no longer exist on a global level. In order to constantly ensure and improve the efficiency of the organization, the following questions are asked at MasterCard at regular intervals:

- Do the strategies and innovations at global and regional locations take local market conditions sufficiently into consideration?
- Are the employees trained in intercultural capabilities? (Only in this way can they understand and utilize the similarities and differences in local markets).
- Does the company have the necessary system and processes in order to effectively support growth?
- If functions are centralized – how do we ensure that local requirements are taken into account?

All these questions help the company to effectively realize the principle of "glocalization." This can be understood as a bottom-up approach, in which all global activities are based on a foundation of local understanding, and maximum local market relevance is therefore guaranteed.

2.3.2 Corporate willingness

In the end, the implementation success of a global brand strategy depends on the willingness of the management at global, regional and local levels. Only if all decision-makers on all three levels support the strategy, can it possibly be successful. The associated buy-in process should definitely start at top management level: the global level decision-makers must be convinced of the global brand strategy. A prerequisite for this is a clearly structured strategy, which is clearly defined in terms of profit and growth targets. As an effective global brand strategy follows a holistic approach (and is not just oriented to marketing communication), it should also be clearly recognizable how

- the corporate philosophy,
- the selection and the training of employees,
- the cooperation of global, regional, and local levels,
- the communication systems,
- incentive programs,

and further aspects resulting from the specific internal conditions within the company interrelate. Perhaps the most important aspect: each global activity takes place in a highly dynamic global environment. Preparation against market fluctuations, along with the flexibility of the strategy and management, should therefore be clearly communicated as an inherent concept.

2.4 Prioritization of markets

Besides brand definition and global market and consumer analysis, the prioritization of possible local markets is of great importance. In this process, it is important to know that the definition of a "local market" is not always in accordance with geographical, national borders, but that it can (and should!) be defined independently of this according to consumer perceptions and company structures. The strategic prioritization makes the effective allocation of resources and management possible in markets with the highest potential for the company. Here, the main focus is on the ranking of the existing and potential local markets with regard to their turnover and development potential. An analysis of the global markets in accordance with the following aspects is a prerequisite:

- Global corporate goals: market share, turnover, profit.
- Size of the market and its growth potential, degree of saturation of market and brand.
- Competitive situation of the brand in the relevant market: no. 1, no. 2, no. x?
- Dimensions: turnover, media power, distribution, etc.
- Costs of (further) market development.

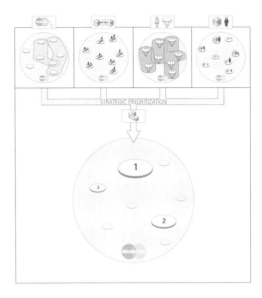

Fig. 4: Based on the analysis dimensions, a prioritization of the markets can be carried out. It serves as a strategic measure for the allocation of resources and management

Depending on the specific strategic situation of your company, other aspects can also become important. At the core, the strategic decision on where the key markets for your brand are located forms the focus – whether this is early entry into growth markets, presence in the lead market for your category, or the market with the most promising short-term revenue growth, depends on the specific corporate aims.

CASE Sport shoes

A well-known American sporting goods manufacturer wanted to expand its international business. The company had a strong sport shoe brand on the home market, which stood for high performance, and was aimed at keen all-round sportspeople and semi-professionals. The brand had sufficient cash reserves to add new markets. The target continent was Europe. The markets were analyzed according to the following criteria:

- Attitude of the consumer towards sport.
- Usage behavior.
- Sales channels and infrastructure.
- Competitive environment and, derived from this, the necessary effort involved in becoming a key player in the relevant market.

- Price structures, in order to test profit potential.
- Production and logistics capacities, in order to guarantee short delivery times.

Based on this first analysis, the following estimation of the European market resulted:

- The European market could be split into two types of market: into highly developed markets where the perception of sport shoes exists as technologically based goods, and into markets with a low level of development where sport shoes continued to be seen primarily as practical shoes.
- In the highly developed markets, a suitable consumer structure for the company's products was already in place: these markets had a highly developed sports culture with regard to participants and audiences in the most important market segments.
- Existing product lines were suitable for the markets and could be transferred without a problem.
- The analysis also revealed profitable innovation potential in three further sports that were not sufficiently relevant in the U.S. home market.
- The price structure and, thus, the profit potential were relatively high.
- A very strong competitor was already active in the markets. Its brand did, however, show some weak points that the U.S. company was able to use to its advantage.
- The U.S. brand also already had a fairly high level of awareness and a good image in these markets.
- The less developed markets, on the other hand, did offer higher growth potential, but this was on a lower level and under the provision that the brand was itself able to become the growth driver for the market as a whole.

For these reasons, the company decided to invest primarily in the more developed markets. In doing this, the company relied heavily on its American origins, which had a positive perception in the sports sector, and which displayed a clear differentiation criterion to the main competitor. At the same time, the brand was positioned as young and cool and, thus, effectively tackled the competitor, that had a somewhat older image.

2.5 Realization of the global brand strategy

Strategy is the "necessary" condition, whereas its successful implementation is the "adequate" condition. When prioritizing the markets, it is possible to identify the important strategic similarities or differences between them – analyzing the success factors for the local implementation is, however, a further condition that a globally active company must consider. These success factors are not based on strategic aspects such as sociodemographic analyses or turnover forecasts, but rather of problem areas

- local traditions,
- language and humor,
- local trends and fashions,
- and cultural nuances (color, expressions, story lines).

If this is not taken into account, then the best strategy may not be successful. The target must be as follows: the local management uses global know-how and resources (e.g., through integration of campaigns, designs, or product innovations), and from these resources and know-how, develops a concept that still gives the consumer the feeling that the product/the campaign was developed just for them!

CASE   MasterCard Europe

MasterCard Europe received input from the various markets that a mutual opportunity existed with the customers: A "brand spot" was needed in order to communicate to the customer how and where the MasterCard could be put to everyday use. In order to develop a pan-European concept for the brand spot, the local markets defined which individual shopping situations should be communicated.

In actual fact, it was shown that the markets had differing priorities and, thus, wished to communicate different situations. MasterCard Europe decided, after comprehensive consideration, to film two different spots that were kept fairly neutral on a cultural level, and could be adjusted to local requirements in various dimensions. Locally, this concept proved to be successful (the consumer relevance materialized) and, at the same time, substantially less expensive than the production of spots for each key market.

This case shows what "glocal" means: a global concept, oriented primarily to cost savings, would have provided the markets with only one, perhaps not even culturally neutral, spot (e.g., in order to save adaptation costs). A totally local concept would have cost several times as much. In the "glocal" concept, the best compromise was found from local relevance and global and/or regional synergy.

▶ Process & Implementation

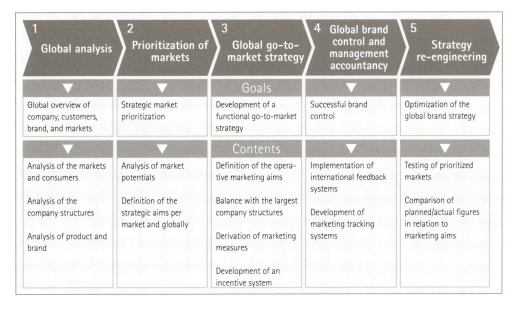

Fig. 5: Global brand management process

Global Brand Management

Phase 1: Global analysis

1.1 Analysis of the markets and consumers
Analyze the following for each region where your company is active:

- The size of the market.
- Market growth (based on population development, trends, econometrics).
- Consumer insights: cultural characteristics, needs in the category, problems, brand status with consumers.

In the overall planning of the analyses, take into account the perspectives that will later result in concrete, usable results for the operational planning of measures. As the analysis of the markets requires both internal and external resources, the return on investment should be clearly calculated beforehand.

1.2 Analysis of the corporate structures
Analyze the following for each country where your company is active:

- The central persons (who are the key persons for global brand management? What expertise exists?), resources (which budget, instruments, departments are available?), and the company size (revenues, profitability, overall trend).
- The structure and composition of the management team, attitudes and motivation of the employees in relation to international cooperation.

The aim of this analysis should be to obtain a clear insight into the framework conditions within all the markets. This is a necessary prerequisite for the implementation of the global brand strategy in the markets.

1.3 Analysis of the products and brands
Analyze the following for each region where your company is active:

- Your company portfolio on the market.
- The brand portfolio and its status.
- The competitive environment (note that products in other categories may also represent competition for your products in the mind of the consumer – depending on consumer perception, the definition of competition can differ greatly on a regional level).

This should result in an exact overview of the international product structure of your company and the central competition on a regional level, from which the global key competitors can also be derived.

Phase 2: Prioritization of the markets

2.1 Analysis of market potential
The analysis of market potential has the aim of identifying the markets with the highest short-term potential (harvest), on the one hand, and identifying those markets with the highest growth and future potential (invest)

for your company, on the other. This should produce two shortlists (harvest and invest) that show the top priority markets.

2.2 Definition of strategic aims per market and globally

The question of which markets are particularly important from a strategic point of view can only be answered precisely with knowledge of the relevant company strategy. Strategic growth markets can be identified for each product strategy and global situation. These can be both emerging and mature markets, depending on the concrete brand strategy. Depending on this, the market potentials identified in Phase 2.1 can also be compared with the strategically most important markets. The markets that are both on a shortlist and on the list of the strategically important markets are your top priority markets.

Phase 3: Global go-to-market strategy

Starting with the global marketing strategy, which is mainly based on the prioritized markets, you should derive the operational marketing targets as a next step. This involves setting quantitative business targets (turnover and sales targets, market shares, etc.) and qualitative targets that, for instance, relate to brand development (changes to image dimensions, etc.). Especially in markets where the potential exists in the future, qualitative strategic targets should be formulated. Depending on the corporate structures, as outlined in Phase 1.2, the operative marketing measures must then be derived. The traditional marketing areas should be covered:

- Brand control and measurement.
- Communication and promotion.
- Product and pricing strategy.
- Sales and distribution.
- Customer loyalty.

The concrete measures for the achievement of the marketing targets always depend on the existing local resources within the company, and also on the market and competitive environment. Here, at the latest, a more intense involvement of local experts is necessary in your company. The global synergies should certainly be made usable in the development of local marketing measures:

- Create and optimize a global marketing portal in which all local offices can search for and upload pools, spots, tools, and know-how.
- Promote a culture of international exchange, in which local offices constantly check the activities of culturally or structurally similar markets, and are willing to learn from one another.
- If in doubt, ensure that local relevance is given precedence over global synergies. In the end, the consumer in the local market always decides whether your product or brand will be successful!

A decisive factor for success in the entire Phase 3 is the support of all global and regional decision-makers. If in doubt, develop an internal incentive system that creates motivation for all those involved to communicate with one another and create the maximum glocal strength for your brand(s)!

Phase 4: Global brand control and management accounting

Successful brand control presumes the use of a globally functioning feedback system. In principle, this kind of feedback system has a simple task: creating a transparent information flow and effective tracking systems based on this. This, in turn, presumes a corresponding IT infrastructure and motivation systems for the local offices to make their data available accordingly. The development of an effective tracking system presumes that the central tasks and strategies are used intelligently in local activities and programs. For this purpose, process checkpoints that enable a follow-up of procedures in local markets, and which contain both content results and the corresponding budgets and timings, should be set up for all important processes. A more technical feedback and tracking system such as this should also be expanded to include communications instruments and institutionalized processes, in which the local, regional, and global levels communicate regularly on developments and interesting results. With this method, there is a risk of over-bureaucratization of the system. Ensure that the necessary technical, organizational, and process-related structures are put in place, but that superfluous reporting procedures are avoided, at the same time. The tracking system must be very easy to use and easily integrated into the current processes.

Phase 5: Strategy reengineering

Global Brand Management must remain a system that is capable of reaction; that can react as quickly as possible to changes in the local markets, the global competition situation, or the strategic forecasts. For this purpose, the whole strategy and the derived measures must be inspected regularly for relevance – in all dimensions previously named in the process:

- Are the markets developing as expected?
- Are the measures having the planned effect?
- Are the marketing targets being achieved? If not, why not?
- Have the strategic targets of the company changed? Are changes in global brand strategy necessary?
- Are new local or global resources available that should be utilized? Have resources been removed?
- Is the balance right between local and global? Is the development of the global marketing plan locally relevant?

As important as constant tracking and the improvement of structures are, it is also important to keep the system stable as soon as it is working – the constant changing of structures on an international level is very complicated and often entails more risk than opportunity for brand and company.

Key Insights

- Marketing is a "social science": success is based on a constant process of research and knowledge development. The figures are only as good as the interpretation. **Gut feelings are a part of this.**
- As a result of constantly changing global markets, long-term flexibility of international marketing must be incorporated as an integral part of the company's processes. **Keep moving!**
- Only those who do not hide behind research results and figures, but rather, who absorb themselves personally and subjectively in the "real" consumer world, will be able to successfully carry out brand management. **Go out and open your eyes!**
- People are at the center of marketing – and they can neither be pinned down nor retained. **People are unpredictable.**
- It is precisely for this reason that highly talented employees are of fundamental importance in global brand management. Only people can sense and understand people. **Employees with good instincts are decisive to success.**
- The complexity of global brand management makes it impossible to cover all management facets in depth. **Less is more – set priorities.**
- Only make changes if the market really demands it. **Changes for their own sake endanger the brand and the company.**

Practical Guidelines

- Develop a precise understanding of your own glocal brand and product world.
- Identify the "common denominators" as a basis for your brand, and align your global market research activities with them.
- Get an exact overview of the current condition of your company (people, structures) in all important markets.
- Develop a clear ranking of the markets based on this overview, and set corresponding priorities in your global brand strategy.
- Realize global brand strategy in the local markets by selecting the right employees, creating incentives for international cooperation and promoting the development of local infrastructure in accordance with the prioritization of the markets.
- Ensure the support of top management on global, regional, and local levels.
- Ensure that decisions, once made, are followed consistently. Don't keep changing your team members – strategies need time to become effective, especially on a global level.
- Don't forget: in the end, the success of global brand management can only be measured against the development of your brand's sales.

The Author

Karen D. Halpert

Karen D. Halpert is a brand management expert with broad experience in the development, positioning, and introduction of international brands. At present, she is Vice-President, Head of Marketing, Central Europe at MasterCard Europe. Before joining MasterCard Europe, she worked as Global Marketing Director at Goldpfeil AG, and as Brand Communications Director at Nike Germany, where she developed the first national communications program for the brand. Before her career in industry, Karen Halpert held several senior positions in various advertising agencies such as Saatchi & Saatchi GmbH (Frankfurt) and J. Walter Thompson Company (Frankfurt, New York).

Literature Recommendations

P. Underhill, "Why We Buy," New York 2000
R. J. Kriegel, L. Patler, "If it ain't broke, break it!," New York 1991
D. C. Thomas, K. Inkson, "Cultural Intelligence," San Francisco 2004
P. Kotler, various marketing titles
A. Ries, J. Trout, various titles on positioning

Christa Wilhelm – Microsoft

Global Customer Interaction

A brand-driven management system aimed at specifically targeting the customer's wishes within marketing, sales and service functions

▶ Executive Summary

- For an international brand leader with a broad product and service portfolio, there exists a large amount of information that has to be communicated to customers and partners. This set up often results in partners and customers being approached in an uncoordinated manner by different corporate areas – marketing, sales, partners, services.
- The sheer number of different messages can be a source of irritation to the customer. He is not interested in taking the time and effort to filter out any relevant information from the overabundance of messages. Uncoordinated interaction with customers and partners thus damages both the brand and the 1:1 relationship.
- The aim of the Global Customer Interaction approach is to optimize all interactions with the customer. Communication between all the corporate divisions on the one hand, and customers and partners on the other, is controlled and coordinated systematically. The right message is delivered to the right target group, at the right time, and via the correct medium.
- Moreover, Global Customer Interaction utilizes a uniform database in order to process customer wishes across all corporate areas and functions.
- The effect: strong and loyal connection of the target groups to the company, and a positive corporate brand recognition resulting from consistency and precise satisfaction of customer wishes.
- Several conditions must be met in order to successfully manage Global Customer Interaction:
  - An international Customer Interaction Strategy must be adopted, which defines business, marketing and operational objectives, and provides a framework for the process.
  - Top management must be committed, and a (small) global team with clout should be nominated. The global team should be composed of employees who have a special interest in relationship marketing.
  - The service provider landscape is consolidated, and the most important suppliers (agencies, etc.) should be manageable on a global basis (think global, act local).
  - A Global Marketing Platform, in which data warehousing functions permit division-specific customer data to be accumulated, should be implemented. This platform supports world-wide interaction processes from all corporate divisions, and facilitates central control.
  - A learning cycle revolves. Regular customer surveys take place as part of an institutionalized process. Lessons are learned from the results, and are implemented in all customer-related corporate functions.
  - A long-term, modular and step-by-step project plan is in place to implement the whole system.

This article highlights the key properties and success factors, and outlines a process for implementing Global Customer Interaction.

Theoretical Model of Global Customer Interaction

1. Definition and core principle

Globally active companies today are confronted with developments that lead to high levels of complexity in a variety of dimensions:

- Markets and target groups are becoming more heterogeneous.
- At times, extremely varied market segments need to be serviced worldwide.
- Corporate brands embrace a growing number of highly differentiated product segments. The portfolio is very heterogeneous.
- Globally active customers (key accounts) do not always have clear structures and contact points for the corporate divisions of the provider brand.

This whole constellation of elements results in inconsistency in dialogue and interaction with customers when viewed globally. The various product groups or departments of your company run the risk of contacting the same customer independently and conveying different messages about your corporate brand that are uncoordinated in terms of both timing and substance. If lack of coordination in structures also applies to the customer's side, then you have perfect chaos. The consequence: negative awareness of your corporate brand.

Microsoft encountered this problem relatively early on. Due to the great number of very different products (Windows, Office, Server, MSN, Xbox, etc.), overlapping target groups were sometimes approached by different corporate divisions. Just a few years ago, such instances of communication with customers and partners were still isolated from each other.

The approach to a solution that I describe in this article relies on the development of a central interaction system – Global Customer Interaction (also termed "GCI" below). The basis of Global Customer Interaction is that the dialogue and interaction of all units in a company and their corresponding service providers is controlled via a common platform. Furthermore, the customer should be in a position to help control which communication channel is used to inform him on which subject. This permits a relationship profitable for all parties to be established with customers and partners. In order to achieve this, Microsoft decided to ensure that meaningful dialogue is pursued with customers and partners and managed via all communication channels. Marketing, sales, service and infrastructure aspects are optimally coordinated in this process.

In addition to the technical components of a worldwide data warehouse (2.4 – Global Marketing Platform), this approach encompasses internal organizational aspects (2.1 – Global Interaction Strategy and 2.2 – Global Team), external aspects (2.3 – Global Vendor Strategy), as well as a company's fundamental mindset of constant growth in terms of customer orientation (2.5 – Learning Cycle). I will explore these factors in greater detail in the next section.

2. Factors

2.1 Customer Interaction Strategy

The basis for successful implementation of Global Customer Interaction is an appropriate worldwide strategy. The strategy must facilitate clear goal orientation and allow the derivation of operational milestones. The logic of a Customer Interaction Strategy is simple to explain – it is founded on the guidelines

- of business planning:
  - Planning for existing business fields (per business field: win – win customers, drive – drive sales, grow – secure growth)
  - Identification of future business fields – which are likely to grow with particular force? Which are important strategically? Which new business fields can be penetrated?
  - Quantified business goals

- of the resulting marketing planning:
  - Which target groups exist in which business fields?
  - Which target groups should be more intensively approached in the future?
  - Budgets, existing structures (customer data, CRM)
  - Actors within the company (departments, key individuals) on an international and local basis

- of the resulting communication planning:
  - What are the communication goals for which target groups? How should communication take place in order to achieve these goals?
  - Who are the current agency partners in the different regions in which the plan is to be implemented?

- as well as of the Global Brand Strategy:
  - Definition of the brand core
  - Corporate brand strategy (e.g., relationship of the Microsoft brand to the individual products; definition of core vision and core message that rises above all topics and is always of benefit to the customer. For example, the Microsoft core vision: "Any device, any time"; and for example the Microsoft core message: "Your potential, our drive.")

The Global Customer Interaction Strategy can be developed based on the chain "business planning – marketing planning – communication planning" and the paramount Global Brand Strategy. This should, in particular,

- bring together global target groups in meaningful clusters,
- define the central corporate divisions that enter into dialogue with these target groups,
- define the vendors (agencies) for all areas in all countries,
- develop system logic and architecture in the dimensions described below (Phase 2.2 through 2.5).

2.2 Global team

In order to successfully develop and, above all, implement Global Customer Interaction, you need a strong team at the international level. The team must assume responsibility for the success of the project and must be equipped by management with the appropriate level of decision-making and implementing authority.

This team should

- be established for the long term (implementation can last up to five years in a company the size of Microsoft),
- be situated at the global level,
- be small, but dedicated (at Microsoft, a team of five people started up – today several small teams are responsible for daily operations),
- be recruited from marketing units: team members must bring with them broad marketing know-how and a specific background in relationship marketing (CRM). They must possess a passion for customer and partner satisfaction,
- be composed of employees who already have an overview of the individual business fields (bird's eye view), but are still sufficiently involved in operational processes to be able to assess the effects of the project.

In the case of Microsoft, the team consisted primarily of division managers or business development managers who were personally supported in this venture by a member of the executive team. In addition to professional qualifications, intercultural group dynamics needed to be taken into consideration, precisely in the case of international projects:

Task	Capability	Appropriate cultural group
Define scope	Ask numerous questions, closely examine what works and what doesn't.	Asia/Australia
Planning	Attention to detail. Take everything into consideration. Have a plan.	North Central Europe
Team work	Southern Europeans like to work in teams – "socializing" is the key word.	Southern Europe
Organization	Colleagues from the US/Canada are very pragmatic with respect to organization. Which meetings, how often, setting the agenda, taking minutes.	USA
Communication	Colleagues from the US/Canada understand not only how to set up a communications structure, but how to implement it in a disciplined fashion.	USA
Implementation	UK and Australia are very pragmatic. Rapid implementation is in the forefront – energy not dissipated in details.	UK/Australia
Debrief	This again needs the discipline of the US/Canada. Determine the process, exchange high points/low points and learning.	USA

Fig. 1: Depending on the task and the capabilities required, the employees' cultural background can be an advantage or a disadvantage

- An international project is always characterized by its intercultural aspects; this constitutes both its appeal and its risks.
- Important in this process is to take into account the strengths of individual nations. Depending on the nation involved, the emphasis may be on comprehensive planning, perfect organization, specific implementation, or teamwork (see Fig. 1). In addition, any number of organizational problems may arise (from customs to implementation).
- Learning that can take place this way determines the success or failure of international projects!
- Centrally transmitted core messages in conjunction with national cultural adaptation and specific implementation in the respective local languages are key success factors in international projects.

The team's task consists, above all, in

- developing an overall strategy,
- defining the next "building blocks" in system construction (modular project planning),
- coordinating the project, including communication and incentives with respect to the business divisions involved in all markets.

It is key to the success of the project as a whole that the Customer Interaction System is built up in manageable units. An overall project of unmanageable size subdues, unsettles, and demotivates staff and is often destined to fail. Moreover, the project must have the unconditional support of one or more individuals on the uppermost management level who are able to communicate a clear project vision internally and to "kick-start" the project (empowerment).

CASE Microsoft

The project at Microsoft developed historically by stimulating marketing employees in various countries. The vision of a central system that managed customer contacts and communication was promulgated at the uppermost level, while several branches (Germany, Australia, ...) demonstrated its realization at the local level.

Today, the individual project components are a permanent fixture in the annual Microsoft Strategy Memo, in which worldwide executive management documents its view of the past and formulates its outlook for the future. The memo is based on discussions and conversations among all executives worldwide, as well as on ideas and opinions that have been encouraged to flow from all divisions. In this manner, the range of impulses and developments are interconnected and points of emphasis for the coming fiscal year established. Initiatives for the Global Marketing Platform are presented, as are necessary measures for enhancing customer satisfaction. Projects are adapted or, if necessary, reformulated, depending on the annual memo.

2.3 Global Vendor System

Consolidating marketing vendors into a manageable number and integrating them into system logic is an essential success factor of the Customer Interaction System. For it is the vendor, after all, who executes the communication of your corporate brand.

The task consists of constructing a marketing vendor network at the global or regional level that is incorporated to the extent possible in coordination and internal processes. As a result, you will be able to achieve the following important goals:

- All global communication activities occur via one or a manageable number of vendors or regional vendor groupings.
- The operational side of communication becomes transparent, manageable, and subject to rational budgeting.
- Vendor structures act as additional organizing entities – if only one agency is used by all corporate entities, it ultimately has an overview of your activities and can intervene strategically if necessary. If, for instance, Unit A and Unit B develop conflicting messages or plan unfortunate overlaps in customer approaches without coordinating with each other, then an agency that is being used jointly can provide appropriate feedback and suggest corrective measures.

A prerequisite is that the relevant vendor network exists worldwide. The agency partner must be in a position to provide the appropriate know-how or centrally controllable partner agencies in the respective local markets. Additional criteria in selecting agencies are:

- Industry experience.
- High degree of global presence.
- Good price/performance ratio for retainer management.

In order to work together successfully, it is necessary to clearly establish the expectations of the agency partner as well as the precise processes of cooperation:

- Scalability requirements of the vendor team (manpower, areas of responsibility, specialty knowledge).
- Exchange within the vendor network (learning curve, allocation within the network, who can best accomplish which task).
- Reporting and information flows.
- Cooperation processes standardized to the extent possible.

In order to convey a better idea of the manner in which a Global Vendor System can be managed, a brief example follows. Optimization of efficiency and effectiveness is the central focus:

- According to previous logic, each branch could allocate its marketing budget for orders to any local vendor, provided it satisfied certain basic conditions. The advantages: high degree of flexibility, short run-up times. Disadvantages: no planning certainty, discounts could not be planned, implementation not uniform.
- In the new Global Vendor System, a specific order volume is negotiated with global or regional vendors, which is managed via a central retainer. Depending on the level of the retainer used at the end of the year, a discount is applied for the following year.
- Moreover, global and regional vendors are bound to adhere to quality standards and reporting requirements.
- Implementation of the contractually agreed provisions and retainer management is in the hands of the respective local office: Think globally. Act locally.
- Global offices of the customer and the agency partners are available as escalation points in this system.

This approach allows a global structure to be created in which information flows are clearly definable, and quality management has a fixed framework. Specific work on contents (customer benefits, value propositions, offerings) is, as ever, the responsibility of the local office – to enhance customer relevance!

In order to implement a vendor consolidation successfully, pilot opportunities should be identified first. This can occur on a regional basis (individual markets, small or large countries, regions) or according to communication discipline. At Microsoft, initially a mixture was decided on – consolidation was introduced as a first step for traditional advertising under the label "global advertising," and, in turn, step-by-step in the individual regions. In this manner, we could first gather experience, convert this into learning events, and then apply this to further implementation.

2.4 Global Marketing Platform

A central IT platform that controls the coordination, manageability, and transparency of all communication and interaction processes forms the core of Global Customer Interaction. An important factor: data protection is taken very seriously worldwide, in order to assure the customer's privacy. The goal is to create a 360 degree view of the customer on the customer's behalf. By collecting all essential aspects per customer from all regions and corporate divisions, we make sure that we do not overwhelm the customer with information and we assure that the demands that the customer makes of us are accurately converted into action. This is the only way in which a targeted and coordinated approach and a uniform corporate brand image are possible.

Prerequisites for building up a Global Marketing Platform are:

- central collection of all customer data in a global data warehouse,
- development of suitable applications (service elements) for access to the central data warehouse that are adapted to the requirements of the respective vendor, department and their task portfolio,
- integrating the system in the corporate processes of both the vendor and in-house departments, compelling all processes to be dealt with by the system,
- guaranteeing data security and data protection for the customers and partners.

2.4.1 Global data warehouse

A technical prerequisite for the Global Marketing Platform is that all databases in which customer data is included must be combined into a global data warehouse. In organizations that grow organically, every department and corporate division acquires its own databases of their customers over time. A total 360 degree overview of the customer is, however, impossible until the databases are linked to each other. A data warehouse is nothing but a meta database with the customer as its central organizing factor. Every customer entry is allocated data from all the subordinated databases.

This allows one to query the most varied data on a customer (sales, interaction with the service, product requests, contact history, etc.). In order to build a proper warehouse for your company, the following questions need to be answered:

Input – Which channels transmit information to my company? Where and how is this information stored?
Output – Who acts from the company's side/who uses the data? For which purpose is the data used?
Security – Are data protection guidelines followed, or are adjustments necessary?

Interaction with globally operating business customers and their networks harbors additional challenges. If the individual offices of your company communicate with the respective local offices of the customer, then more or less individual solutions are devised according to the customer's local requirements. This is not a problem per se, but may cause complications; for example, if a global audit is conducted on the part of your customer and centralization efforts ensue, the products and solutions developed by your local office are compared to each other. If inconsistency on a global level is discovered, this casts a negative light on your global image. This is a key reason for globalizing your marketing platforms. Further consolidation of your internal information flows in a global data warehouse facilitates international coordination of customer interactions and guarantees interaction with global customers that is consistent worldwide.

2.4.2 Applications

While creating a data warehouse forms the basis for the Global Marketing Platform, appropriate applications or user interfaces make the relevant data useful to employees and partners. The goal of appropriate applications is to ensure convenient access for those responsible to precisely that data that they may need in their corporate division and for their tasks (needs-oriented design).

CASE Microsoft

An example from the communication planning division at Microsoft shows what this can mean. In this division, appropriate applications are developed for the preparation of relevant information from the data warehouse for the entire communication process – analysis, planning, pre-execution, execution, and post-execution. During each phase, a tool is made available that enables precise activity planning based on the corresponding information.

2.4.3 Taking root

Probably the most interesting question from the top management perspective is: how do I get my company to actually use a Global Marketing Platform developed at such a great cost? As it is only when all participants conscientiously use the system that the requisite information base representing the key to success is actually created. The answer is simple – by ensuring that both within the company and among the partners there are no other options. The Global Marketing Platform must be established as a strategic organizational instrument – it is far more than an optional tool. It serves as a reporting system via which all metrics and evaluations can occur. If it's not in the system, it doesn't exist. This method of taking root organizationally compels all participants to be fully involved with the system. The Global Marketing Platform becomes the eye of the needle through which all marketing information must pass. Clear vision and determination on a global level by top management is a prerequisite for this design approach, as for the whole GCI concept.

2.4.4 Effects of the Global Marketing Platform

Once the platform has been established, it can be used to control the dialogue with the customer. One example is contact strategies in which only a certain number of contacts per customer are allowed in a given time interval. So, if product division A wishes to send a direct mailing to interested customer decision-makers, only those contacts from the target group are automatically included in the mailing list, whose contact values permit such a mailing at time X. Moreover, all internal activities can be tracked, inter-regional comparisons drawn, customer responses measured and, depending on the tasks set, further analyses conducted. The result: a level of transparency

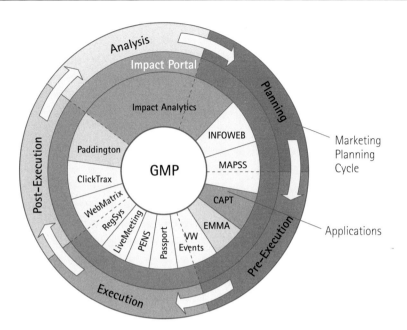

Fig. 2: At Microsoft, a series of applications throughout the Marketing Planning Cycle allow access to data from the Global Marketing Platform

and control over the interaction between corporate divisions and customers that is not possible with traditional methods and that, above all, is in the interest of the customer.

CASE Change management at Microsoft

Probably the biggest hurdle in implementing a Global Marketing Platform is the internal reasoning: why should my employees around the world abandon the usual processes to deal with a completely new system, especially if this system generates a level of transparency that many will find intuitively unpleasant?

Great value must be placed on supervising the process when implementing such a system. Only if the introduction of the system is accompanied by a well-conceived change and communication strategy that conveys a convincing core argument will the project be successful in the long term. The core argument may differ from one company to the next, in fact, even from one branch to the next. At Microsoft in Germany, we decided to build our core argument around the theme of data privacy. For Microsoft as a global player in the German market, it is precisely the security of customer data that plays a central role. Breakdowns in this area would have a significant negative impact on the company. Once adherence to data protection and data security guidelines became the responsibility of a small team and their significance was clearly understood throughout the company, the need for a central database was no longer questioned. This allowed the centralization of all customer data to begin. Whatever the clincher is in any specific case is not important – there simply has to be a plausible and forceful argument for introducing the Global Marketing Platform.

2.5 Learning Cycle

Possibly the most important effect of a GCI is the worldwide improvement in customer relationships and the resulting increase in customer satisfaction. In order to achieve this, it is not enough to communicate consistently with the customer. It is even more important to pursue a dialogue with the customer and offer opportunities for interaction. This interaction should primarily have the goal of constantly improving products and services by responding to outstanding customer needs.

The Global Marketing Platform offers the required basis for this. Using the customer information gleaned and made accessible on a global basis, semi-annual or annual (customer satisfaction and loyalty) surveys are conducted on the various product categories. The results of these surveys are then implemented as specific measures in the Learning Cycle:

- The results are evaluated and strategic recommendations are provided and forwarded to the development, sales, service, and marketing departments.
- Process reengineering in the respective corporate divisions (e.g., in marketing) or product development takes place.
- The new results are implemented.
- The "Learning Cycle" closes.

In this manner, problem areas are identified in a semi-annual or annual rhythm, service and marketing optimized and improvements measured systematically. In this case too, the prerequisite is top management support and the will to view the company as a learning organization. Only if all departments are convinced of the need for constant optimization and the teams responsible for the Learning Cycle actively communicate the logic and the objectives of the system, can true performance improvements be achieved.

CASE   Microsoft customer survey

Once a year at Microsoft, a global survey of customers and partners takes place. Items in four strategic areas are dealt with:

- brand awareness and image
- customer perception
- loyalty
- customer behavior.

Evaluation of the results is reviewed differently according to target group and thus offers specific approaches for change. Based on what is learned, measures are devised, training initiated, and optimization approaches that have been developed are implemented in the relevant corporate divisions and their departments.

Communication Index

	Image/Customer perception	Customer retention Loyalty	Customer behavior
Brand awareness/Image	Value proposition Painpoints	CSAT	CSAT
Image (sympathy, trust)	Value of investment Value of money	Engagement	Contact
Product image (image items)	Customer care/corporate culture	Repurchase	Interest
	Microsoft helps "Realizing potential"	Share of wallet	Order

Ascertainment of Influencing Factors

B: Measuring categories according to product/target group

Products		
Technical support		
Competitive pricing		
Sales of marketing material		
Licensing programs		

Fig. 3: Determining influential factors using the communication dashboard

① Problems at the local level

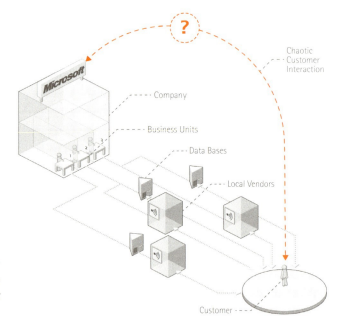

Fig. 4: Problems at the local level
Different departments that utilize vendors and data on customers in an uncoordinated fashion result in chaotic interaction with the customer

② Detail: Problems due to uncoordinated data management

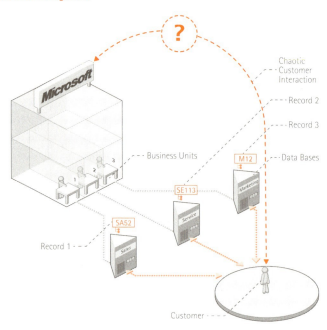

Fig. 5: Uncoordinated data management
A key reason for chaotic customer interaction is uncoordinated data adivisions (e.g., Sales, Service, Marketing) all have their own databases in which every customer entry has a different coding and other allocated information

③ **Solution approach 1: Marketing platform**

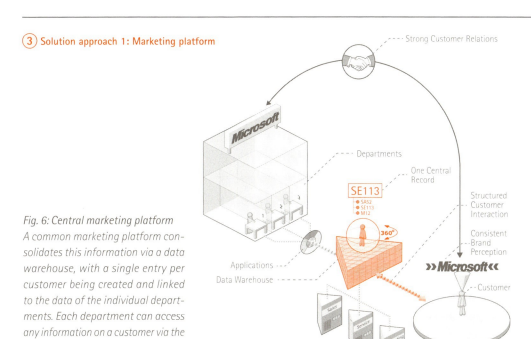

Fig. 6: Central marketing platform
A common marketing platform consolidates this information via a data warehouse, with a single entry per customer being created and linked to the data of the individual departments. Each department can access any information on a customer via the appropriate application - a 360-degree view of the customer is created

④ **Solution approach 2: Central vendor**

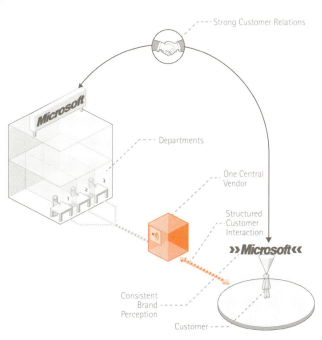

Fig. 7: Central vendor
In addition to a common marketing platform, the use of one vendor for all divisions is a further essential organizing factor: the central vendor organizes the activities of all departments and helps to engage in orderly interaction with the customer

⑤ Problems at a global level

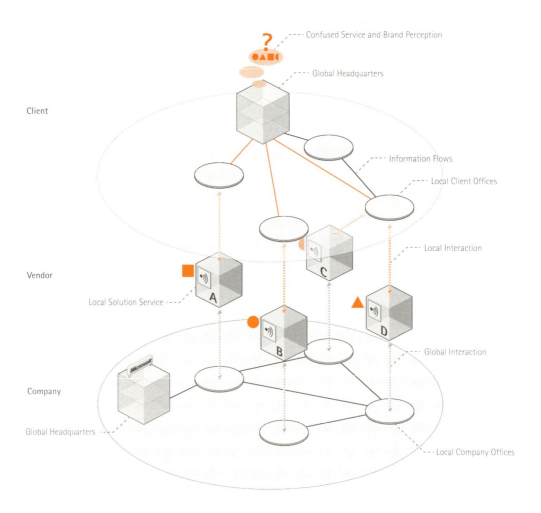

Fig. 8: Problems at the global level
At the global level, inadequate data coordination and a lack of vendor strategy can result in further problems. So, it is precisely globally active customers who experience inconsistent interactions of individual local offices in a particularly negative way

(6) **Global solution approach 1: Global Vendor System**

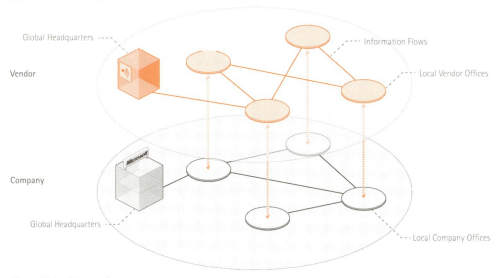

Fig. 9: Global Vendor System
Use of a global vendor ensures that all activities of a company worldwide can be further controlled and filtered. Moreover, it affords Global Headquarters an overview of budgets and activities

(7) **Global vendor – task distribution**

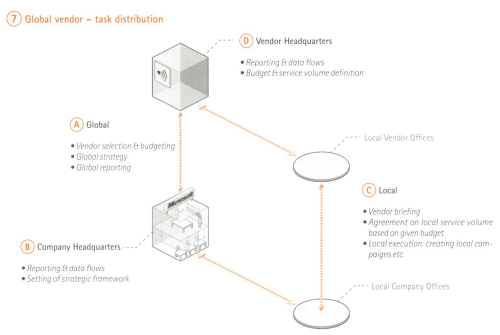

Fig. 10: Global vendor – task distribution and data flows

Global Customer Interaction   67

⑧ Global solution approach 2: Global Marketing Platform

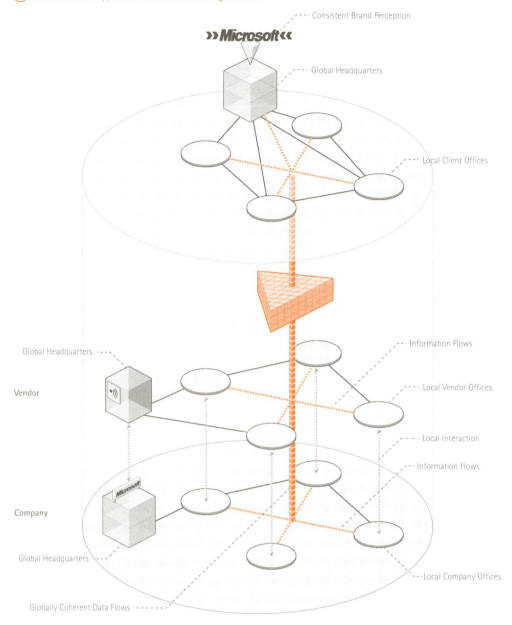

Fig. 11: Global Marketing Platform
A Global Marketing Platform ensures that activities of local offices and vendors are transparent worldwide and organizes them. The result: a clear and uniform perception among international customers

⑨ Local Learning Cycle

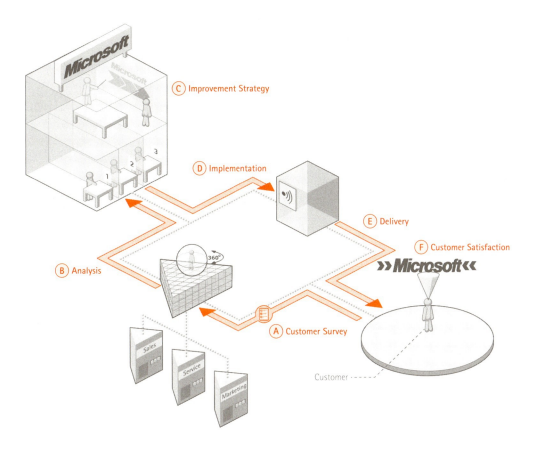

Fig. 12a: Local learning cycle
Based on customer surveys, customer needs can be systematically observed, analyzed, converted to optimization strategies, implemented and delivered. In this manner, the entire delivery of a company can be optimized in a six-month cycle, for instance

⑩ Global Learning Cycle

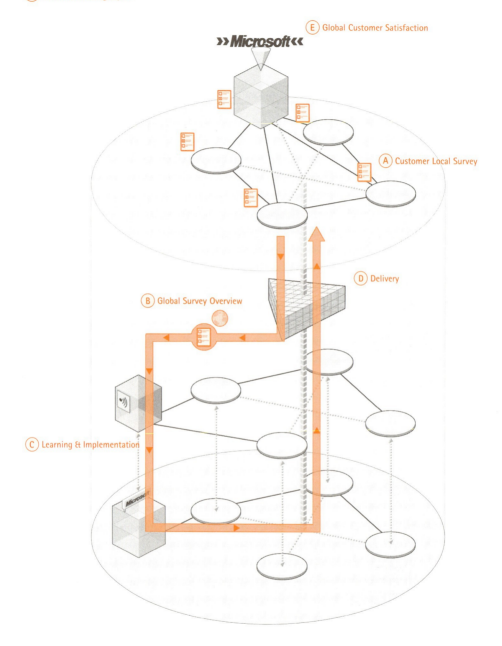

Fig. 12b: Global learning cycle
On a global level, the introduction of a Learning Cycle creates the potential for supra-regional learning processes, allowing information to be exchanged and implemented at the supra-regional level

Process & Implementation

Phase 1: Definition of goals and auditing

1.1 Top management support and strategic planning
The basis for successful implementation must be established at the beginning of the process:
- Secure top management support for the project. Top management must be fully behind the project and make an example of the measures taken.
- Derive the goals for GCI from the brand strategy, business, marketing, and communications plans.
- Define the long-term plan – what should be achieved and by when? Less is more. Divide the whole into realistic partial goals.
- Estimate expense (in terms of costs, time, and human resources) and introduce transparent project financial control.

For all plans, take into account that you should never plan the entire project, but proceed with building blocks. The precise definition occurs in Phase 3.

1.2 Global auditing
As soon as a clear strategic line and top management support is assured, an audit of the following areas should take place:
- corporate divisions concerned
- functions concerned in these divisions
- regions concerned
- international status of vendors/supplier divisions; benchmarking with comparable companies.

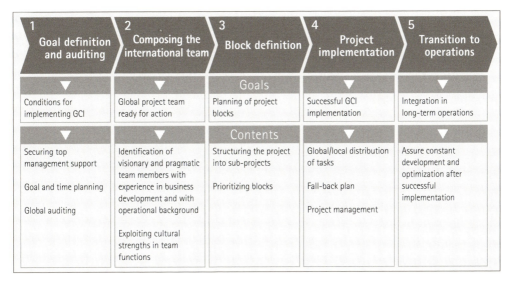

1. Goal definition and auditing	2. Composing the international team	3. Block definition	4. Project implementation	5. Transition to operations
▼	▼	Goals	▼	▼
Conditions for implementing GCI	Global project team ready for action	Planning of project blocks	Successful GCI implementation	Integration in long-term operations
▼	▼	Contents	▼	▼
Securing top management support Goal and time planning Global auditing	Identification of visionary and pragmatic team members with experience in business development and with operational background Exploiting cultural strengths in team functions	Structuring the project into sub-projects Prioritizing blocks	Global/local distribution of tasks Fall-back plan Project management	Assure constant development and optimization after successful implementation

Fig. 13: Gobal Customer Interaction process

Phase 2: Composing the international team

Consider how to identify team members for the global team. Concentrate on finding innovative employees with global interests, who, on the one hand, strive for a total overview and yet, on the other hand, have enough operational know-how to design GCI. Take into account cultural differences when composing the team too, and try to combine people with different cultural backgrounds. Intercultural teams allow team members to take responsibility for functions that fit them and their culture. A short, experience-based view of the team functions and cultural groups is shown in Fig. 1.

Phase 3: Block definition

3.1 Breaking down the project into building blocks

If you start by planning the project as a whole, and present team members exclusively with the overall goal, you are doomed to failure. Introduction of GCI is a multi-year process and a variety of external development and learning instances can change the course of the entire process over the long term. The most important prerequisite for success in implementation is employee motivation, and you can best ensure such motivation if you define manageable sub-projects – building blocks – with clear, achievable, and quantifiable interim goals. Begin by viewing the entire project as modular and breaking it down into building blocks. Consider which portions will produce the greatest benefits most rapidly and the interdependencies of the different system components.

3.2 Prioritizing the building blocks

Next prioritize the building blocks with respect to their significance for the entire project and the benefits they may bring to your company as individual components (find the 'low-hanging fruit'). This may mean specifically:
- Reduce your vendor system at the start to those vendors that have the greatest impact and the largest budgets (e.g., advertising).
- Concentrate initially on the largest and most important markets.
- Identify the applications and areas of the Global Marketing Platform that provide the greatest leverage.
- Build your data warehouse first for the corporate divisions/functions that most urgently need a 360 degree perspective of the customer.

Phase 4: Project implementation

4.1 Global/local task distribution

The right task distribution between the global and local levels is important in implementing the building blocks. This implies that:
- vendor selection and budgeting,
- application development, as well as
- data warehousing

are tasks at the global level;

- briefing of vendors and negotiation of specific services,
- integrating applications in the corporate processes,
- input on information required from the data warehouse for application development

are taken over by the local offices.

4.2 Fall-back planning
Planning of fall-back scenarios is an important safeguarding function during implementation. The significance of the change process in implementing a GCI is great, so breakdowns can have major consequences. Simple and effective fall-back planning consists of being able to return to traditional processes as quickly as possible in the event of breakdowns. Structures and processes adapted during the ongoing implementation process must, therefore, have been mapped in advance, and responsible individuals designated for emergency cases, in order to facilitate a rapid return to established structures. Fall-back planning should address potential weak spots in the new system, which should be identified in advance to the extent possible. There must, for instance, be an emergency plan when the data warehouse is introduced, one which keeps the old access paths to customer data open and which does not gear all the processes completely to the new platform in an initial test phase until a reliable "running system" has been established.

4.3 Project management
The key to implementation success, besides those aspects mentioned above, lies in professional project management. There should therefore be (at least) one experienced member in the global team, who is engaged exclusively in coordination, definition of milestones and fall-back plans.

Phase 5: Transition to operations
When all the building blocks have been finalized and GCI is in operation, the system must continue to be updated and optimized. The process of transitioning from the completion of the change project itself to your company's daily operations is not always automatic, but rather conceals additional pitfalls. The goal is to have GCI take root for the long term in your company's organizational DNA and thereby secure a value-creating, self-optimizing interaction with the customer on a worldwide basis.

▶ Key Insights

- **GCI can only be implemented in small steps**
  Dividing the total venture into clear and manageable projects (building blocks) is a prerequisite for ongoing motivation. It allows continuous implementation of lessons from the Learning Cycle and thereby ensures complete success.
- **GCI needs top management support**
  The strategic importance of GCI requires that top management wholeheartedly supports the project in its entirety and actively participates in communications in this respect. It is only if top management buys into the system that a change of this magnitude can actually take hold.

- **GCI = Global Vendor System + Global Marketing Platform**
  GCI is primarily composed of two core elements – a Global Vendor System and a Global Marketing Platform. Consolidating the vendor landscape in a Global Vendor System allows marketing activities to be channeled and utilizes global partners as a management instrument. A Global Marketing Platform is a prerequisite to the coordination and manageability of customer interaction worldwide.
- **GCI requires a learning organization**
  In order to integrate knowledge gained from customer interaction successfully into further processing, a learning organization is necessary. If learning is not a fixed component in a company, such attributes can be stimulated by creating fixed structures with clear check points and processes.
- **GCI needs global teams**
  International composition of a team has two positive effects:
  - project work is more effective, since different cultures can apply their specific capabilities, and
  - the regional effectiveness of strategies can be tested at an early stage.
- **GCI creates a strategic competitive advantage and needs a strong lobby**
  Implementing GCI affects the entire orientation of a company and creates a strategic competitive advantage at the global level – it is precisely for this reason that it requires a strong lobby within the organization.
- **GCI means: optimize customer dialogue. Maximize the brand relationship worldwide**
  GCI's core philosophy is to enter into an ongoing, learning dialogue with the customer, allowing him to guide this dialogue himself and thus maximize his relationship with the brand globally.

▶ Practical Guidelines

- **Celebrate your successes – large and small!**
  Think about identifying low-hanging fruit and reward small successes with big celebrations. This motivates people and keeps them going, particularly with projects that last several years.
- **Top management should be in the forefront with convincing examples.**
  It is not enough for top management to assure you of support and express this support in memos. It is only when top management actively lives the new processes and does not accept exceptions that you will be successful in implementing new systems such as the Global Marketing Platform or the Global Vendor Strategy.
- **Pick up people where they are stuck!**
  Define a core argument – everyone has an Achilles heel. Once you have identified this and turned it into your project's core argument, you've won! You will be able to guarantee the solution of a problem and no one can say no to that.
- **Create transparency!**
  It is often precisely the big projects that lack transparency for the rest of the company. What are the team members doing all day? Why are they considered so important? Why are they praised so much for their successes? Ensure that what happens is transparent to the rest of the company. And always emphasize the benefit to the individual – the core argument, well, you can take it from here ...

- **Always keep an ace up your sleeve!**
  It is especially in large projects that bring about major changes that things may go wrong! Actively manage risks. Prepare a fall-back plan and pull an ace out of your sleeve in emergency cases.
- **Transfer responsibility to the project team!**
  Define the framework within which the project team has decision-making authority. Only a team that has been given true responsibility is going to assume responsibility.

The Author

Christa Wilhelm

Christa Wilhelm (39) has been Chief of Marketing Communication at Microsoft Deutschland GmbH since April of 2004. Wilhelm started at Microsoft Deutschland in 1998 as project leader for the CRM (Customer Relationship Management) solution Siebel. Subsequently, she assumed responsibility in a variety of positions in the Marketing division. After finalizing her business studies in Vienna, which included an emphasis on marketing and languages and two sojourns abroad in Italy and England, Wilhelm started her marketing career as a management consultant with the Österreichische Industriellenvereinigung (Austrian Industrial Association). From 1994 to 1998, she was employed as a business economist in the Austrian company UpDate AG, a medium-sized company specializing in CRM solutions. Her functions there included two years as Sales Manager. Her last function there was heading up the division of Professional Services in Germany. Wilhelm was born in January of 1966 in the Salzkammergut in Upper Austria.

Gabriele Gundel, Stefan Gundelach – Nintendo Germany

International Product Launch

European umbrella campaign and country-specific communication as illustrated by the introduction of the Nintendo DS in Germany

▶ Executive Summary

An international product launch embraces four phases and comprises a host of complex elements:

Development phase
- Well-founded market research.
- Precise determination of the target group and the brand personality.
- Development of a key message as the core message of the campaign.
- Definition of the street day.
- Alignment of the regional communication activities with the international umbrella campaign.

Implementation phase
- Selection of the communication activities and channels.
- Alignment of the content of all activities.
- Sophisticated timing for the concertation of all activities.
- Flexibility in reacting to the unexpected.

Post-launch phase
- Sustainment of functioning activities for the firm establishment of the product.
- Deployment of additional activities for a broad market penetration.

Analysis phase
- Detailed analysis of the efficiency of the campaign.
- Preparation and planning of future activities and subsequent campaigns.

▶ Theoretical Model of the International Product Launch

1. Definition and core principle

Europe has always stood for unity in diversity. This factor must be taken into account by every company that intends to bring a new product onto the market Europe-wide. Its success is fundamentally dependent on whether it manages to combine an international umbrella campaign with regional communication activities that consider country-specific and cultural characteristics. The right timing of these activities is a second deciding success factor for an international product launch. Only in the interplay of supra-regional and regional activities, that are well concerted with regard to timing, can it be possible to constantly increase the buyer's interest in the product. The aim must be to generate product hype, an increasing wave of attention, interest, tense expectation, and enthusiasm in several success phases of activity, and for this to reach its peak exactly on the street day, i.e., the market launch.

For all this, well-founded market research is the first requirement, in which there should be an initial focus on the exact definition and analysis of the target groups. From this results the determination of the international and national project timing, as well as the exact communication and sales targets in the individual markets. Only when these objectives are clearly defined can a creative umbrella campaign be developed that is tailored to the language, wishes, and expectations of the target groups, and that turns the product into a brand, into a striking personality with an unmistakable face that potential buyers find appealing and trustworthy.

2. Factors

A product launch is based on a number of strategic activities that need to be tailored to the conditions of the market and to the positioning of the product. In doing so, a few core factors have to be taken into account, and these ultimately play a part in deciding whether a campaign is a success or a failure.

2.1 Market research

The central importance of market research lies in determining the real market conditions – mostly with the help of statistical methods. Consumer habits and specific interests, for example, can thus be determined, and target groups can be defined in detail.

CASE   In Japan and America, the launch of the Nintendo DS was extremely successful. In order to repeat this success in Europe, those responsible at Nintendo of Europe initially evaluated the market research results and experiences from the product launches in the two countries. They then also started their own market research at European and national level.

2.2 Key message

From the positioning of a product and the analysis of its specific qualities, (at least) one key message can be derived. This core message plays an important role in the communication. To a certain extent, it is the main argument for the purchase and, at best, distinguishes the product as being unique.

CASE   In the case of Nintendo, the results of the market research showed that the communication for the Nintendo DS should concentrate on four core points: on the two screens, on the touch screen, on the innovative technical features of the appliance, and on the new game experiences that it would facilitate.

The innovativeness of the Nintendo DS, therefore, presented opportunities and challenges in equal measure: the opportunity to tempt potential buyers with innovative technical features, and the challenge of first having to make the meaning and the attraction of these features easy to understand. Every campaign, no matter what kind of campaign it was, had to vividly present to the consumers – in every country and in every target group – the totally new possibilities of the portable video game. It was to become clear: the Nintendo DS is a revolutionary appliance that opens up hitherto unknown game worlds and game experiences for its user.

2.3 Combination of umbrella campaign and regional activities

In the case of international campaigns, it is important to take regional preferences and differences in mentality into consideration and, at the same time, to coordinate the individual communication activities and instruments with one another in such a way that they do not contradict each other. The umbrella campaign and its regional offshoots must present themselves as coming from the same source. In this way, they can enhance the credibility of the core messages reciprocally.

CASE   The key messages for the Nintendo DS were kept absolutely standardized across Europe. PR, classical advertising, promotions, events, online and guerilla actions had to march to the same tune and in the same direction.

2.4 Timing

The selected date for the launch, the street day, can be one of the deciding factors for the success or failure of a product. Seasonal fluctuations, public holidays, or great events in world politics sometimes have considerable effects on consumer behavior, both in the general and specific sense.

CASE   The Nintendo DS appeared in the U.S.A in the week before Thanksgiving 2004. It was the first world premiere of a Nintendo hardware product outside of Japan, where it was launched on the market a few weeks later, just before Christmas. In both countries, the appliance proved to be a resounding success right from the start. And the aim was to repeat this success a short while later in Europe. For the European countries, 11, March 2005 was planned as the first day of sales – in time for the Easter business.

2.5 Flexibility

A further, highly important factor for the success of a broadly applied campaign is flexibility. Precise and detailed planning is a must, but it must not prevent the company from reacting quickly and appropriately to unforeseen events. Flexibility also means checking the company's own activities and instruments, at all times, for their functionality and, where necessary, modifying these. For this, it is absolutely necessary to integrate so-called feedback loops into the campaign as early warning signals.

CASE   In the case of the Nintendo DS, the aim was to keep an eye on a rival product that had been announced. The launch date for this product was unclear for a long time, and was then ultimately postponed. That is why it was possible for the Nintendo DS campaign to operate in a much broader field than originally expected.

Process & Implementation

Phase 1: Development of the international campaign

1.1 Analysis of the market and competitor situation

A successful product launch starts well before the first day of sales. The systematic collection, preparation, analysis, and evaluation of data about the European markets, and about the possibilities for influencing them, unearthed valuable information that was to enable the development of a successful campaign – hence, only those who have a complete knowledge of their market – its structure and its current situation – as well as of the competition, will find the right strategy and make the right decisions. However, in addition to professional, high-quality market research, good common sense is also of essential importance for the right communication strategy: the market research data must not distort the view of the creative, human moment of a campaign.

Firstly, however, all phases of the market research process need to be carefully planned, thought through, and ideally guided by a company-internal market analysis and research management team.

CASE In the case of Nintendo DS, the market research process went through five phases:
1. Formulation of the questions and the research objectives.
2. Design of the research plan.
3. Analysis.
4. Analysis of the data and interpretation of the results.
5. Creation and presentation of the market research report.

Nintendo initiated several of these market research studies before developing the European umbrella campaign. In each study, active video players and casual gamers between the ages of 10 and 35 were surveyed in England, Germany, France, Italy, Spain, and Holland. The so-called active gamers frequently use video games in their freetime, but not exclusively. On the one side, they differ from casual gamers, who only occasionally occupy themselves with video or computer games, and on the other side, from hardcore gamers, for whom playing represents a fundamental part of their life.

The surveys were to find out which features of the Nintendo DS are most appealing. What is more important for the consumers in the next generation of handhelds? The playing experiences that they make possible, or their multimedia ability? What is the general awareness regarding the Nintendo DS like? What can be said about the readiness to purchase, price expectations, the image of the appliance, and the current key trends? The studies were able to answer all these questions – broken down according to age and preferences. Even after the start of the campaign, market research was still done to indicate possible changes in the attitude of the target groups.

It was already demonstrated in the first survey that the most striking innovations to the Nintendo DS impressed the trial persons most: the fact that the appliance had two screens, and games could be controlled via one of them (the touch screen) by mere touch.

1. Development of the international campaign	2. Local implementation	3. Post-launch campaign	4. Results analysis and evaluation
Goals			
Realistic assessment of the market	Strong presence of the brand before, during, and after the launch	Firm establishment of the product on the market	Factual substantiation of the campaign efficiency
Precise definition of the target group(s) and the brand personality	Reaching the target group emotionally	Enduring presence of the product in advertising, PR, and at POS	Experience gain for the benefit of future activities
Definition of the core message for the campaign	Consistency of the advertising message despite different instruments and channels	Broad as possible market penetration	Mid- and long-term efficiency increase
	Constant increase in hype until launch	Where necessary, expansion of the market	
	Independence of the campaign		
Contents			
Detailed market analysis	Selection and use of varied, original, and emotionalizing media activities and integration of regional factors	Maintaining functioning communication channels	Detailed efficiency analysis: comparison of the campaign objectives with the actual results
Interpretation of the results and inclusion in the campaign strategy		Use of new measures	
Development of an unmistakable brand personality	Coordination of content of all communication activities	Where necessary, use of cross-promotional activities for synergy effects	Preparation and planning of future activities and subsequent campaigns
	Meticulous timing of the instruments	Flexible planning and implementation of the further procedure taking into account the results up to that point	
	Specific integration of secondary target groups such as media representatives and trade		

Fig. 1: International product launch process

1.2 The definition of the target group

The right assessment of the target group is of crucial importance for any campaign. Careful target group research is necessary for defining and assessing the target group.

CASE With regard to the potential buyer groups, the market data collected in Germany provided the same results as in the other European countries. Detailed enquiries, for example, about the integrated chat function of the Nintendo DS provided information on the potential for e.g., extending the target group for the appliance. Picto Chat, as the integrated chat function in the appliance is called, particularly fascinated the girls and the casual gamers, some of whom were not active game players.

The secondary target group includes journalists from TV, radio, and online media, as well as from general, specialist and trade press. With retail, the campaign should focus above all on the top purchasers and on the sales personnel at the POS. For all of them, it should deliver clear and strong arguments in favor of the Nintendo DS. To implement these objectives, Nintendo cooperated with various creative agencies.

1.3 Brand value and brand personality

When a new product is launched on the market, it does not yet have any brand personality. The brand personality first has to be created. The more innovative the article is, the more complex and diverse the effort becomes to define its value and brand personality in the eyes of the public.

CASE   In the case of the Nintendo DS, the creative agencies, together with Nintendo Germany, were to develop a brand personality that ideally linked the two sides of the desired brand image together: on the one hand, the Nintendo DS was to be regarded as a revolutionary appliance to clarify the immense innovative thrust in the video games market. On the other hand, the campaign should be able to make fun of itself and act in a humorous way. In addition, it should be easy to understand (as it would address active and hardcore gamers) and should also help expand the target group.

1.4 The core message of the campaign

In addition to a large presence among the target group, it is crucial for every campaign to emphasize the uniqueness of the product. Even if the USP is sometimes composed of different factors, it is recommended to emphasize just one single, particularly strong and vivid aspect.

CASE   With Nintendo, the decision was made to emphasize the touch screen of the DS. This technical innovation was to contribute to creating an unmistakable brand character. In doing so, the benefit of the touch screen for the enjoyment of the game was to be presented in such an easy-to-understand way that it would make sense for anybody.

The aim was to convey to the consumers the core message that they can influence the virtual worlds of the Nintendo DS games quite easily at the touch of their finger. Reduced to a simple and easy-to-understand sentence, the message of the campaign was: "You've got the power and can change the world." The claim that was to be disseminated during the teaser and launch campaign, across print advertisements and TV spots, shortened all this once more to the slick but effective invitation: "Touch me!"

Phase 2: Local implementation

2.1 Task definition

Every market is subject to its own laws. These can differ regionally to such an extent that one and the same product can be advertised with the same activities in one country and be a huge success, and in another country, be an utter flop. That is why it is important to find the right communication activities for a country, activities that are specially tailored to that country.

Fig. 2: German teaser and launch advertisements

CASE The German Nintendo DS campaign was to be based on comprehensive communication activities from media, PR, online, events, promotions, and POS, which were all to be professionally tuned to one another. In addition, very target-group specific marketing and communication activities such as guerilla campaigns were to convince the target groups of the strengths of the Nintendo DS. As envisaged in the umbrella campaign, a bold and surprising approach that differed from the usual one, was explicitly requested. In short, the integrated communication concept was to provide consumers, opinion brokers, and dealers with the same messages about the Nintendo DS – but via different channels and with a form of address that was specific to the respective target group.

2.2 Definition of objectives and means of the campaign

A campaign as an advertising campaign over a limited period of time can pursue very different objectives. The activities that are used to reach these objectives are also very varied. To achieve results that are as efficient as possible, and to minimize wasted coverage, the means of the campaign must be very precisely tailored to its objectives.

CASE Right from the start, the general objective of the Nintendo campaign was: until the first day of sales, the DS was to be a constant topic of discussion amongst the target groups: in the specialist media and in retail, as well as in school playgrounds and on the video game scene. To achieve this, the appliance had to be present in many places before, during, and after the launch, as the aim was to take one thing into consideration: due to its many innovative features, the Nintendo DS was a product that needed explaining in the pre-launch phase: people who decide to buy a new video game system want to know beforehand exactly what specific benefit the technical features will give them with regard to game enjoyment. Another strategic objective, therefore, had to be to bring as many people as possible into contact with the Nintendo DS even before the sales started, to make it literally "easy to grasp."

For this, creative and emotional activities were required that could be just as innovative as the product itself. That is why more funds than usual were made available for POS material and interactive displays – for example, for large pre-launch events or POS campaigns in retail – but also for guerilla activities. In addition to this, PR work and classical advertising, such as television, Internet, and SMS, were to repeatedly spread the key messages about the Nintendo DS. Their focus at all times was to be the most noticeable product features of the appliance, i.e., the aspects "touch" and "dual."

2.3 Timing and tuning of the instruments

Like the instruments of an orchestra, the communication instruments of a launch campaign also have to be tuned to one another. Only if the timing of their use, their content, and their tonality is right, can they enhance one another, convey clear messages, and arouse expectation that reaches its peak at exactly the desired moment.

CASE

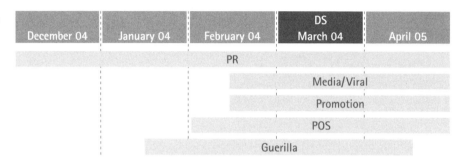

Fig. 3: The German Nintendo DS campaign was designed for five months, from December 2004, through the street day on 11, March 2005, up until the first weeks after the product launch

2.3.1 The PR activities

A good PR activity is capable of touching its target group emotionally. However, most people are very experienced in the reception of any kind of advertising, and are correspondingly "hard-nosed" about it. It is, therefore, very difficult – but just as important – to constantly seek new ways of impressing, fascinating, moving, hence emotionalizing, with PR activities.

CASE   The intensive PR activities for the Nintendo DS started as early as the beginning of December. The aim was to generate a constantly increasing hype about the forthcoming launch of the handheld console. For this, a specific form of address for the respective individual target groups was developed, as well as specific, creative communication activities that were to impress retailers, journalists, and video players in equal measure. As with every other campaign, the work of a professional press office formed the basis for everything else. This included the creation of press texts and specials for the trade press, the provision of further press material and the agreement of media cooperations, e.g., of competitions. To set itself apart from other product launches, this foundation work was supplemented by a number of unusual activities.

This is how, for example, very special, creative press material was created: lifestyle photos and artwork, such as manga-style pictures, which were much better received than normal press photos by the anime and hip-hop magazines with a particular affinity to the target groups.

Fig. 4: German Nintendo DS press photos

As an additional incentive for the media partners, "modding variants" of the Nintendo DS were used with the individual competitions. These were individually designed appliances that would not be available in that form in the shops. A special cooperation was made with the fashion show Bread & Butter in Berlin at the end of January 2005. This is where Nintendo DS was presented as a cool lifestyle product.

In its communication with the media, Nintendo attached particular importance to sampling actions, in order to convey a "tangible" idea of the new console to the journalists as well. As early as December 2004, an editorial journey began in a "touch mobile," a specially designed caravan in which editors could test the first Nintendo DS games themselves. The tour was directed primarily at public media, e. g., lifestyle magazines that usually plan their reporting several months in advance and, therefore, needed to be informed as early as possible.

From December 2004 onwards, the curiosity and attention of the trade press was stimulated by sending "touch parcels." In addition, they contained a number of funny gimmicks to feel and touch. At this point in time, the press office subsequently sent out more than 200 copies of the Nintendo DS to selected journalists.

The Europe-wide press conference on the launch of the Nintendo DS at the end of January was a first highlight of the PR campaign. For the occasion, journalists from Germany and all over Europe were specially flown into Paris, where they received a first impression of the innovative quality and the great variety of the software that would be available to the Nintendo DS players from the street day onwards.

Nintendo tried out a new path of communication in February with a school newspaper competition. The editorial teams of school newspapers from all over Germany could take part in the competition. The best of them – just like their colleagues from the big public media – received one of the sought-after advance copies of the Nintendo DS for review purposes. The activity was suitable for addressing the primary target group directly. It was also particularly credible because it was done via peers.

In the weeks directly before the product launch, the "Nintendo DS Touch Tour" accompanied and supported the press activities. This was a costly promotional activity in six German cities; it ended in a big party on the street day (see below).

2.3.2 Media activities

The mass media print, radio, TV, and online are the most important channels for the majority of advertising forms. With skillful placement of the advertising content, the number of target group contacts is particularly high with these media forms. They are indispensable for any large campaign. However, significant results can also be achieved through other channels, as these sometimes permit very personal contact.

CASE   The Nintendo DS media planning aimed for direct access to consumers with an affinity for video games. At the same time, the retail sector had to be taken into account as a target group. In as broad a media mix as possible, all relevant advertising media were to be taken into account for the launch phase (Spring 2005). The objective: through a multi-level campaign – from the teaser via the launch to the post-launch phase – every potential buyer of the Nintendo DS was to be informed about the new product as early and as thoroughly as possible.

A central element of the media activities was the costly, classical TV campaign that focused attention on the Nintendo DS from 15, February 2005 onwards. In the teaser phase, a whole series of crazy, cool spots under the slogan "Du hast die Macht!" ("You've got the power!") aroused curiosity for the market launch on 11, March. In the actual launch phase, slightly longer spots of the same kind highlighted the key features of the Nintendo DS. The TV campaign had the entire core target group in focus, and was positioned in all broadcasting environments relevant to them, such as for example, on MTV, Giga TV, Pro 7, RTL, RTL II, and SAT 1. The TV was flanked by a print campaign. This included advertisements in the specialist trade press, as well as consumer advertisements. Online advertising is also essential for products like the Nintendo DS. The presence on the Internet pages of MTV and Giga was combined with the TV advertising on both television channels.

2.3.3 Promotions

Generally speaking, promotions are advertising activities that bring the potential consumer into direct contact with a promoter or include him or her in an event. They are particularly suited for addressing consumers and, at the same time, incorporating retail and regional media. An event promotion is only successful when it manages to be used in a way that is relevant for the media. If there is no interest from the media and/or no communication of the key messages via the media, then it is questionable whether the usually very high investment in its design and implementation is at all worthwhile.

CASE   The strongest argument for the Nintendo DS – something those responsible for the campaign were convinced about – is the Nintendo DS itself. For this reason, too, it was of crucial importance to offer as many people as possible the opportunity to pick up the new console and test it before its market launch.

The construction of the Nintendo DS Wallride in Flachau-Winkel in Austria was mixture of guerilla and classic PR activity. The snowboard ramp with the highly visible Nintendo DS branding is the highest of its kind in Europe. For its inauguration at the beginning of March, some of the biggest snowboard aces in Europe came for a night photo shoot.

Fig. 5: The Nintendo DS Wallride in Flachau-Winkel (Austria)

The highlight of the campaign in Germany was the large-scale "Nintendo DS Touch Tour" that undertook a tour through six German conurbations from 19, February 2005 until the street day. Shopping centers with high numbers of visitors were transformed into so-called "Nintendo DS arenas." In these gaming zones, that were designed in the optics of the advertising campaign, several thousand video game fans were able to test the new appliance at attractive demo displays, and take part in exciting contests against each another. The best from each city were invited to Hamburg, where the finale of the tour took place on the evening before the first day of sales.

Fig. 6: The Nintendo DS Touch Tour and the Nintendo DS launch event in the D-Club

2.3.4 Trade marketing

A good POS presence can only be expected if it has active and huge support from the trade. This can be achieved, for example, through high-quality deco material, attractive giveaways, and promotions. An attractive design of sales areas and shop windows increases the attention, curiosity, and the interest for a new product.

CASE Precisely through such activities, Nintendo involved the retail sector in all phases of the campaign. All elements strictly adhered to the optics of the advertising campaign with the striking Nintendo DS logo and the claim "Touch me!". In the pre-launch and launch phases, Nintendo sent out e.g., professional decorators to some 500 outlets to support retail. An attention-grabbing demo display was one of the eye-catchers.

During the launch phase, Nintendo increased its commitment to the retail sector once more: at selected retailers, specially trained promoters were present at POS for more than four weeks from market launch. They attempted to inspire potential buyers with the new handheld in advance through product demonstrations. At the same time, they trained the retail partners of Nintendo intensively on the subject of the Nintendo DS.

Phase 3: Post-launch campaign

Immediately after the market launch of a product, the aim must be to maintain the established hype as long and as intensively as possible. Depending on the respective product, the activities to attain this objective sometimes differ greatly from the activities in earlier phases of the campaign.

CASE

Strategy

Nintendo Germany developed – based on the activities up to that point at European and national level – a post-launch campaign that embraced both PR and media activities. One of its targets was to address girls and casual gamers more, in order to expand the target groups. If the communication up until then had been concentrated on the innovative hardware, it had to achieve an about-turn to the software in the first weeks of sale. In this phase, it was decisive to make clear that a comprehensive range of different games was available for the new console right from the start. At the same time, the communication for the software was to repeatedly emphasize the new features of the hardware. Consequently, of the games proprietary to Nintendo, the focus was to be primarily on those on which the innovative feature of the appliance could be particularly well demonstrated.

Activities

In the area of classical advertising, the duration of the TV spots, that had been very well received during the pre-launch and launch phases, was first extended until mid-April. This was supplemented by online activities, e.g., banner advertising or pop-ups on lifestyle portals or other Internet pages relevant to young people. Furthermore, cooperation was agreed with portals such as T-Online, Yahoo, and GMX that facilitated an integration of the advertising in the editorial sectors. With regard to PR, the issue was finding additional response to the software innovations using means that went beyond the day-to-day press activities. Nintendo, therefore, developed a special campaign under the slogan "Summer – Fun – Nintendo DS," the aim of which was to ensure that the product remained a topic of conversation amongst the target groups and that the media interest in the product was maintained.

Phase 4: Results analysis and evaluation

In the final phase of every marketing campaign, a detailed results analysis, evaluation and response analysis are done. Questions do not just focus on the pure sales figures of a product, but also on whether the self-set targets of the campaign, with regard to the target group and key messages, have been reached, and whether the instruments used for this have served their purpose. In this way, communication instruments can be constantly refined further, and target groups and their expectations defined and addressed more precisely. Sepp Herberger's wise old football saying still applies here – in slightly modified form: "After the campaign is before the campaign." Therefore, these concluding analyses serve primarily to prepare and plan future activities and subsequent campaigns.

CASE As the Nintendo DS campaign was designed to run until the end of 2005, the corresponding analyses are not yet available at the time of going to print. Nevertheless, three months after the market launch of the new handheld, both the success of the European umbrella campaign and that of its national offshoots can be ascertained using a few data and facts:

Numbers of units sold:
- 500,000 copies on the European market in the first two weeks (77% of the amount supplied to shops).
- Added to this, a multitude of games sold; 250,000 copies of the title "Super Mario 64 DS" were sold in the Easter business across Europe.
- At the beginning of June, more than one million appliances had been sold.

Media response:
- Coverage of the Nintendo DS PR campaign: just under 430 million readers of public and trade press, as well as of special interest media, radio listeners, and television viewers, in addition to the visitors of corresponding Internet pages in the pre-launch phase up until 11, March.
- By 1, July 2004, the contact figures had risen to approximately 530 million.

Strategic objectives:
The market for portable systems should grow overall, and not at the cost of the existing series of Game Boy products. In the summer of 2005, it became clear that this target would also be fulfilled. In Germany, shops even recorded additional business growth with the Game Boy after the Nintendo DS had appeared. This was a first indication that the consumers had understood an important message of the campaign: the Nintendo DS is an independent product.

Conclusion:
The first results from the German and overall European market show that the country-specific activities and the umbrella campaign are optimally intertwined and have enhanced each other's impact. In a short space of time, the Nintendo DS has established itself in all the important markets in Europe.

▶ Key Insights

- The goal of a launch campaign is the constant increase of product hype until the street day.
- With an international product launch, all activities have to be tailored to the regional characteristics and, at the same time, match the umbrella campaign.
- A successful launch campaign necessitates a profound knowledge of the market and of the target group.
- Secondary target groups such as media and trade representatives are important elements for a convincing product presence.
- An advertising message works best when it is clearly formulated and originally and emotionally charged. It should stand for the USP of the product.
- The orchestration and the timing of the advertising activities and channels play a fundamental role in the success of the campaign.

▶ Practical Guidelines

- ☐ Get to know your target group, do intensive market research!
- ☐ Opt for a coherent and easy-to-understand key message for the core message of the campaign.
- ☐ Select the most favorable date for the street day of your product.
- ☐ React in a flexible manner to unforeseen events during the campaign, and integrate all your experiences in the further course of the campaign.
- ☐ Rely on creative and emotional advertising activities that set themselves apart from the monotony of high-gloss pictures.
- ☐ Bundle the power of your advertising message by using different channels that are coordinated with one another.
- ☐ "After the campaign is before the campaign." Evaluate your work carefully and learn from it for the future.

The Authors

Gabriele Gundel

Gabriele Gundel was born on 27, July 1969 in Hamburg. In 1996, she completed her degree in Business Administration, majoring in marketing, at Fulda Polytechnic. From September 1996 to July 2000 she worked at Konami of Europe GmbH as a marketing assistant, European Marketing Coordinator and, finally, as Marketing Manager. Since August 2000, she has been Head of Marketing for Nintendo Germany at Nintendo of Europe GmbH.

Stefan Gundelach

Stefan Gundelach was born on 14, January 1973 in Schweinfurt. He studied at Würzburg University and University College London, where he successfully completed his M.A. degree. From 2000 to 2004, he worked as a Senior PR Consultant at Euro RSCG ABC in Frankfurt. His last position there was as deputy site manager for the Frankfurt office. There he was responsible for advising customers such as Vodafone Germany, MGM, Samsung Electronics and Nintendo. Since August 2004, he has been PR manager and press spokesman for Nintendo Germany at Nintendo of Europe GmbH.

Frank Hermann – Electronic Arts

Global versus Local Marketing
The right balance between an internationally standardized brand presence and optimum local market development

▶ Executive Summary

By nature, international marketing requires the coordination of cross-border communication. Borders are not only set by countries and regions, but also by cultural differences, market structures, and various other influences that may not always correspond to national frontiers. This article will highlight some key factors and processes that can help to achieve a better understanding and management of international marketing decisions. It will focus in particular on the area of tension between local and global strategies for problem solving.

- There is no "golden rule" that states whether a global or local marketing approach should be adopted. Each decision has to be made individually, based on a predefined set of parameters relevant to the objective.
- A global communication approach offers greater advantages for brand-focused companies if it is directed at a globally homogenous target audience.
- A local approach seems more appropriate when companies want to extend their market share beyond globally homogenous consumer segments.
- The variables in the decision process "global or local approach" are derived from the respective management focus, cost effects, and brand consistency.
- The decision-making process should also be made on the basis of a set of parameters defined by the respective company. Any changes to this set of parameters must be supported by top management.
- Even globally active brand companies with a unified communication policy should have strong marketing and sales organizations in their key markets that constantly monitor the relevance of the communication.
- Communication in the Fast Moving Consumer Goods (FMCG) sector should have a globally consistent core idea, but by all means offer the option of local adaptation, i.e., be adjustable to different cultures.

▶ Theoretical Model of Global versus Local Marketing

1. Definition

Brand management decisions with global consequences incorporate a host of factors, such as the global and regional economic situation, the geo-strategic position of the markets, price formation and distribution, and corporate identity. However, discussing all these factors in detail would far exceed the scope of this article. The focus below will therefore be on the strategic elements of product and marketing communication. Furthermore, the article needs to be limited to the FCMG sector as different findings and conclusions are possible in other industries.

So what are the challenges in deciding whether a global or local communication approach should be adopted? Let us have a look at the overall development: in an ever-shrinking world in which consumers travel extensively and frequently use the same media, it is difficult to see an argument for advertising and promoting global brands in entirely different ways in different countries. Firstly, this could confuse the consumer because the same brand looks different in different places. Secondly, this would fail to capitalize on the economies of scale that should be one of the central benefits of having a global brand.

But what is the best way to proceed? How can a global brand successfully and effectively create a consistent image of itself in different places? A frequent mistake is to automatically run the same advertising and communication everywhere. Unfortunately there are many brand companies that adopt precisely this approach. Typically, the internally strongest country develops an advertising presence that every other country has to adopt, and only the language and the pack shot are allowed to be adapted to local requirements. Yet this is precisely the situation where the rule "advertising does not translate" applies. The words do, but they are only a part of the ad or press release or any other form of media used. It is the culture that matters and that is crucial for success or failure.

2. Factors: global versus local marketing

2.1 Global consistency of product and communication
Even if the core values of a brand need to be consistent at global level to serve global markets, an American advertisement in perfect German still sounds like an American speaking German. It lacks the richness and emotional resonance that only a country's own culture can convey to the target groups in that country. Ideally a company therefore draws up a globally relevant communication idea that will reflect the product's advantages to the consumer and also leave space for local implementation of this idea.

The global alignment of consumption cultures indicates that products and communication need to be consistent at global level. Internationally active firms with a strong focus on marketing may even create global trends by expanding into national markets and providing consumers there with a new and global consumption experience. This has been successfully demonstrated by companies within the food and beverage industry such as Starbuck's and Red Bull, companies which – to a certain extent – have even managed to change national consumption habits. If companies really are to expand beyond national markets, they therefore require global vision and strategy.

2.2 Understanding of local markets
But why are local markets relevant at all? First, depending on their size and structure, they will certainly add to the revenue of any company expanding into them. Even countries of smaller size or with comparably lower per capita income can still be very profitable to globally active companies. The degree of profitability depends on the management objectives of each firm and also on the available infrastructure and the processes in the local markets.

2.3 Local consumer segments
However, achieving profitability in a local market also depends on the special characteristics of that market. An important factor here is the consumer segments that vary from country to country.

CASE   In the case of Electronic Arts, for example, the segments of gaming people in Germany are divided into the so-called "core gamers" (see Fig. 1), who play at least ten hours a week and spend at least 200 euros per year on video and computer games, and the "casual gamers."

Core gamer PC/Console → 39% market relevance
23% of all gamers

Console gurus → 28% market relevance
10% of all gamers

Fig. 1: Electronic Arts core gamer segments in Germany in 2004

These segments constitute two-thirds of overall revenue although they represent just one-third of the gaming population. Comparative research showed that a "console guru" segment, i.e., gamers who predominantly played games on consoles could be found in most countries, yet the preference for the PC as a gaming platform is a specific aspect for Germany that is not found in any other major country of the Western hemisphere. Ignoring this segment and their specific needs from a product and communication perspective could have resulted in at least two-thirds of the potential market for computer and video games in Germany being ignored.

2.4 Local culture

In addition to consumer segments, different cultures also have a significant influence on market performance. Cultural sensitivities may stem from religion, language, or other factors. This can result, for example, in product names that may have a less favorable meaning in another culture depending on the region. Accordingly, values and virtues also vary in different social environments.

CASE   In the case of video games the level of violence within a game is a decisive factor for the acceptance of this game and its potential market performance. Germany and the Scandinavian countries, for example, have very strict regulations on violence in games whereas within the Anglo-American cultures violence – including in video games – is more accepted. This may lead to management launching a game on the market in the U.K. and the U.S. that is banned in Germany because of its violent content.

2.5 Local media landscape

Another important factor in opting for globally consistent or local marketing is the media landscape of the markets. Here, too, a comparison between the U.K. and Germany is intended to help in understanding this factor. For example, in the U.K. the communication culture focuses more on TV and the tabloids, with London being the clear media capital. The opposite is true for Germany, where communication is print-oriented with the highest number of newspapers and magazines published worldwide. Moreover, Germany has no clear media capital like London. Instead, it has at least five different media centers. Be it product PR or media planning, knowing and taking these special local characteristics into account is essential for any marketing organization.

To understand the opportunities and challenges of global versus local marketing better, a look at the theoretical opportunities of product and communication policies (Fig. 2) may be helpful.

Globally standardized product and communication	Globally standardized product, local communication
Advantages: · High cost efficiency with regard to product development and advertising · Basic organizational infrastructure needed in foreign markets · High brand consistency and awareness can be achieved (in theory) **Disadvantages:** · Less knowledge of local markets may lead to "trial and error" situations with marketing activities · Ignored local consumer needs generate a risk of losing market share · Smaller scale of feedback from territories not favorable for further development of product and communication · Only works in globally homogenous markets	**Advantages:** · High cost efficiency with regard to product development · Local infrastructure enables feedback on product and communication for optimized development · Localized communication adaptable to culture of local market · High brand consistency and awareness can be achieved **Disadvantages:** · Higher SGA budgets for maintaining local marketing organization
Local product, global communication	**Local product and communication**
Advantages: · No clear advantages recognizable **Disadvantages:** · High costs for product development · Global communication not able to reflect special characteristics of local products	**Advantages:** · High relevance for local markets · Optimal communication flow from local consumer needs to product development and communication **Disadvantages:** · Extremely high costs for product development and communication · No global brand presence and awareness achievable, may lead to customer confusion

Fig. 2: Global versus local marketing opportunities in the FMCG industry

Within this context, "local" has to be understood as a clearly distinct alternative to the basic product or basic communication, wherever this may be necessary. Obviously the preferred route in the majority of cases should be to offer a globally standardized product that is accompanied by optimized local communication. A company can thus best reach local consumers and offer them a range of services – in addition to an attractive product – through a local marketing organization with its own decision competence within the guidelines of a globally consistent brand appearance.

However, this route requires a management culture that enables the necessary freedom for local organization and allows for consumer feedback from local territories. The establishment of processes between headquarters and local offices that support the consistent presence of brand and products are fundamentally important here. These processes thus permit the attainment of the company's economic targets.

▸ Process & Implementation

The following process shall reflect on how Electronic Arts as a global market leader in the interactive entertainment industry has established routines to optimally communicate within different markets while still offering globally identical products.

Phase 1: Evaluation

Before starting the first conceptual stage of product development and communication all relevant factors for achieving the set objectives must be analyzed and linked to one another. Naturally, such an analysis will start with existing market research data highlighting parameters such as:

- Current market size
- Main products of competitors

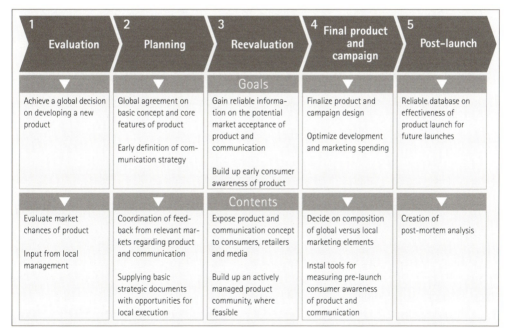

Fig. 3: Global versus Local Marketing process

- Feedback on consumer interests
- Overall economic situation
- Consumer groups
- Post-mortem analysis of previous products, if available.

Based on this information, a first draft of the product's main content and benefits as well as cost and timing implications will be developed. If this draft concept is approved by top management, it is ideally shared, even at this early stage, with territory management and marketing executives. Based on the local buy-in as well as an initial rough estimate of the market success, the company starts to set up a development team.

Phase 2: Basic planning of product and communication

Early feedback from at least the most relevant regional markets including forecasts of initial sales figures leads to the decision on whether the product content will be globally identical, offer some local variation or extra content, or if the product will not even be launched in particular markets. The decisive criterion is the forecasted market performance of the product based on relevant local market data that is as in-depth as possible. Most firms take this step very seriously as launching a product in a local market against better knowledge will not only harm the product's success but cause a lot of unfavorable developments for the respective company, such as bad product reviews and negative publicity or even losses due to returned products. Thus the product should contain all features identified as relevant by the most important markets, as long as they conform to the basic concept of the product. But within the given scope of product features the opportunities for the integration of additional local content has to be balanced against the danger of missing global timelines. The focus is thus mostly on a regionally adapted communication policy.

Nevertheless, the product needs to offer precisely these opportunities during its development to ensure that it will be a long-term success on its home market and globally. A major factor for this success is to not only gain early clarity on the product features but also exchange basic communication ideas and coordinate them in an effective manner. The basic elements of the communication, for example, the advertising idea or the launch communication strategy, should therefore be centrally coordinated and supplied to the local offices as the basis of their local communication strategy.

Phase 3: Reevaluation

Once the basic features of product and communication have been agreed upon, they need to be tested further in the markets to "fine tune" the content. There is a large number of ways to do this, the most frequently used being:

- Focus group testing of both product and communication ideas.
- Early demonstrations of the product to media and retailers at trade shows.
- Media invitations to product previews.
- Consumer surveys.

Another measure that has become increasingly important in the recent past is community management, i.e., a firm systematically taking care of its customers with shared interests in the same product. Normally, the basis for this is a web-based communication approach that continuously supplies relevant information for these customers on selected sites and also provides them with a platform for constant exchange with the company and among themselves hosted by a webmaster. In its wider sense, community management may even comprise incentives or events that are exclusive to community members. The benefit for the company is an extremely loyal and well-informed base of customers that supplies high-quality feedback at all stages of product and communication development.

Balancing the flow of feedback and the progress of product development is of course a complicated matter. Opportunities to integrate feedback diminish the closer the product comes to its launch. Still, this is often anticipated by companies that consequently integrate appropriate "development windows" into the cycle. None of these measures are limited to just the phase of reevaluating the product and communication policy. Instead they all start here and usually last until the market launch of the product.

Phase 4: Final product and campaign

When the basic set of product and communication values has been defined, a final decision is made on the degree of localization, i.e., which elements of product, such as:

- packaging
- design
- local content, where possible (e.g., local statements in video games)

as well as which elements of communication will be transferred into the local context. However, this decision should be based on reliable consumer feedback with regard to product and advertising to reach an optimum effect in the respective local market, without questioning the core benefits of the product and the supporting communication campaign. Obviously a fully global as well as a fully local approach defines the poles of opportunities with most launch campaigns being of a hybrid nature, balancing global core elements with local added value elements.

Other important decision parameters with the global versus local approach are of a financial nature, i.e., local managers have to prove that a more localized approach creates more profit than globally standardized products and communication. A possible indicator of such an improved profit may be the "3 to 1 spending rule" which demands that any extra cost for local content must pay off with a profit of at least 3 times the profit compared to the existing global approach. In any case this flexibility depends on the global management culture of the company. In general, however, companies that are able to localize products and communication in their key markets seem to fare better than those that rely on a globally homogenous approach.

Once the decision is made, all elements of communication need to be aligned to the strategy, and these usually include:

- advertising
- public relations

- customer relationship management (CRM)
- promotions
- retail activities and communication
- internal communication.

These form a communication master plan, which defines the content as well as the timing and the budget assigned to the product launch.

To ascertain the effectiveness of communication even before the launch, the definition of a set of parameters that measure the awareness of target audiences towards the product is recommended. Important parameters both quantitatively and qualitatively may be the scope of media coverage achieved, pre-launch ratings from consumers and retailers, pre-order figures and website statistics. Data from previous launches may help to evaluate the success potential of the new product. It may also indicate if the chosen communication approach is on course and, if not, alternatives may emerge from the observations.

Phase 5: Post-launch

Irrespective of whether the chosen strategy has been successful or not, a post-launch analysis is a very important source of information. This analysis should include all basic elements of the communication used, the sales forecast and actual data as well as available feedback from retailers, media, and consumers. Where available, ratings regarding the product as well as comparisons with competitor products must also be integrated into the analysis. This document will be vital when deciding the launch of product sequels, as it contains all relevant data and reflects the strategic process from product conception to launch in the local market, including the decision for a global or local approach.

CASE   German launch of "The Sims 2" by Electronic Arts in 2004

In the case of "The Sims 2" there was a substantial amount of information material on the predecessor PC game "The Sims," giving various details of the market size and consumer needs. Consequently, the German management team of EA was happy to put its faith in the idea of a sequel from the earliest phase onwards. During the process of developing "The Sims 2" a great deal of local consumer feedback was incorporated into the new product. It emerged, for example, that Germany had the largest Sims community outside North America. Furthermore, EA Germany constantly invited key authorities from communities, the media, and retailers to enable them to participate in development and to be in direct contact with the studio team responsible for developing the game.

To give the product content an even more local flavor, EA Germany negotiated with German pop star Jeanette Biedermann for a cross-promotional integration with Jeanette being integrated into the game and vice versa Jeanette producing a song and video reflecting her involvement in the Sims world. This enabled the German team of EA to also develop a national campaign approach by using the international advertising creatively and adding some locally related activities to it. The consumer feedback was overwhelmingly positive and both Jeanette and EA Germany won several awards for "The Sims 2" launch campaign. In addition, the German version of "The Sims 2" sold 60 percent of the volume of the whole of North America in the same period, making it the most successful launch of a PC game in Germany ever.

Fig. 4 & 5: The official logo of EA Germany's cooperation with pop star Jeanette (left). Jeanette's song "Run with me" reached No. 3 in the German pop charts (right)

▶ Key Insights

- The potential for locally adapted products, and communication is first and foremost a matter of corporate culture. Flexible companies usually fare better in international competition.
- A firm's size and product range are further key parameters when deciding on implementing a local management infrastructure.
- Establishing balanced global and local communication requires an established internal organization that communicates well.
- Even in a more globalized world many local markets preserve their special characteristics and these may be decisive for a product's success.
- Consumer segments and their breakdown by markets are vital in deciding on a more global or local approach.
- Only very few products are suitable for standardized marketing across the globe.
- Decision-making with regard to the degree of local content in the product and communication requires an intensive analysis of local data.

▶ Practical Guidelines

- All activities in the design of product and communication campaigns must be oriented at all times to consumer research that represents the local market.

- Integrating consumers into communities offers companies a source of invaluable and highly up-to-date consumer feedback.
- Global or local management decisions require a detailed set of fixed communication processes within a company.
- Good contacts between headquarters and local offices avoid miscommunication and enable a constant up-to-date flow of relevant consumer data.
- Creative communication, especially the advertising idea, must include opportunities for local implementation.
- Right from the start of the product design process, local relevant feedback must be integrated into development.
- The measurement and tracking of product and brand recognition helps to evaluate the efficiency of the overall concept and provides information as to whether the approach needs to be made more global or more local.

The Author

Frank Hermann

Frank Hermann, 41, Marketing Director Central Region heads the German marketing team of Electronic Arts (EA) and coordinates marketing for neighboring countries to the south and east of Germany. After completing his studies in German Literature and History with a Master's degree at the University of Cologne he began his professional career as a PR consultant at ABC Eurocom and later moved to KohtesKlewes. During this time he worked for national and international clients in both product and corporate communications. In 2000 he assumed the position of Head of Public Relations at EA Germany. Since Fall 2002, Frank Hermann has been the Marketing Director Central Region at EA.

My special thanks to Roger Clayton whose great experience and support have made a major contribution to the concept and content of this article.

Literature Recommendations

I. Dole, R. Lowe, "International Marketing Strategy," 3rd edition, Thomson, 2001
W. Keegan, "Global Marketing Management," 7th edition, 2001
D. E. Schultz, P. J. Kitchen, "Communicating Globally: An Integrated Marketing Approach," McGraw Hill, NTC, 2000

J. Johan Jervøe – McDonald's Germany

Intercultural Marketing
Building global brands by generating local consumer relevance

▶ Executive Summary

- Globalized markets enable and require the internationalization of strong brands.
- It is only possible to extend the brand into new markets and cultures by creating the maximum possible relevance for consumers in the local market.
- Consumer relevance is therefore the key variable in international marketing. Each market and the corresponding culture must be regarded as a unique psychological environment with its own specific product-related consumer requirements; these determine the success of a brand.
- Consumer relevance can only be systematically achieved by:
  - identifying the key cultural consumer insights,
  - establishing a skilled and highly trained management team,
  - making use of local marketing experts at operational level with the necessary cultural awareness.
- Regular international discussion amongst regional management teams of new consumer insights, campaigns, and methods helps to accelerate learning and create global synergy. This exchange of ideas should take place within a global and structured talent management process.
- The development and use of a Global Marketing Platform enables marketing resources to be shared, and guarantees rapid access to innovative ideas, insights, campaigns, and strategies for all regions.
- By strategically leveraging these tools it is possible to build a strong global brand, and to fully exploit market opportunities in all regions through cultural consumer relevance.

▶ Theoretical Model of Intercultural Marketing

1. Definition and core principle

For global companies and brands, penetration of new markets and the exploitation of regional growth potential offer the greatest opportunities for business growth. However, each and every country, and each and every region, has its own cultural values. These determine consumer needs, sometimes leading to significant differences in the perception of brands and products.

Since business success and growth are primarily based on consumer relevance, intercultural marketing has a key strategic role to play in the globalization of brands and products. The goal is to make brands and products relevant within the target market culture without eroding their global brand identity. To gain cultural relevance, it is necessary to generate cultural consumer insights, to deploy effective management teams, to develop strategies and activities geared to the local cultural environment, and to exploit global opportunities for synergy. The following model highlights the key factors.

2. Key factors

2.1 Understanding the local culture

All regions have their own psychological rules that have evolved over the course of hundreds if not thousands of years. These have a profound influence on the (purchasing) behavior of each region's population. Understanding these rules is one of the keys to regional business success. Cultural awareness is, however, not just about understanding fundamental cultural items. It is primarily a matter of hands-on knowledge of consumer perceptions and preferences with regard to categories and brands. Effective consumer insight research is therefore the all-important foundation of intercultural marketing. The more comprehensive and psychologically relevant those insights are, the better the basis for developing regional marketing strategies. What is needed are insights into the perceptions and needs of consumers, creating a platform for positioning and developing products. Insights must be new in character, fundamental in nature, and must strike a chord. Five elements need to be considered:

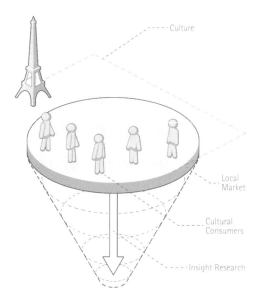

Fig. 1: Insight research is the basis for penetrating deep into the cultural perceptions of consumers

Identify needs
- Gain an understanding of the specific needs of the people in your region. This rarely means conscious or directly expressed wishes. It is more meaningful to gain insight into unconscious experiences and perceptions.
- The central question is: to what degree does your product satisfy these needs? What do you have to do/change to make your brand or product (more) relevant?

Define the competitive environment
- Find out who your competitors are IN THE MINDS of consumers. Identify your competitive environment in terms of consumer perception.

Provide a solution to a problem
- Identify the category-specific problem within your region. To what extent does your product solve this problem?

Spot emerging trends
- Trends influence the future structure of the market you serve. It is therefore vital to identify key trends before your competitors do. You need to be quicker or better than your rivals.

Develop a feel for language and humor
- You need to gain a thorough understanding of the appropriate language in your region. This includes common sayings and expressions, popular, modern folklore, and subtle word associations and connotations. You need to acquire a feeling for local humor, and for its impact. Every single word within a particular language engenders

a wide variety of associations that are specific to the local culture. You need to find exactly the right words to generate exactly the right image in the minds of your consumers.

To gain consumer insights of this kind, psychological skills need to be combined with a thorough understanding of local market conditions. It is only possible to identify relevant insights when you are fully aware of the competitive environment, market trends, and consumers' subjective perceptions.

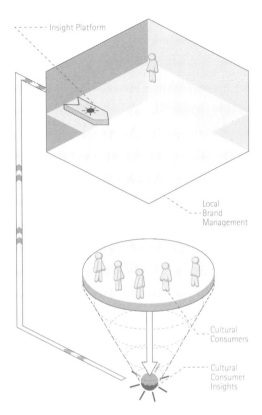

Fig. 2: Insight research leads to the generation of cultural consumer insights that serve as a strategic basis for marketing

CASE The McDonald's rice-burger

In many parts of Asia, McDonald's faced the challenge of gaining greater relevance within the scope of consumers' daily eating habits. For much of the Asian population, for example, rice is a central element of any meal. However, McDonald's products were primarily meat-based burgers.

Insight
For the vast majority of the Asian population, a proper meal always includes rice.

Need
Develop a rice-based meal, alongside products such as the Big Mac, that corresponds to the McDonald's DNA (Selbstähnlichkeit).

Competitive environment
There is an established culture of casual, convenience dining in Asia, i.e., street food. This is ideal for McDonald's.

Solution to the problem

Following market research studies, McDonald's developed a rice-based "bon," which could be used as a replacement for the conventional sesame-seed bon – the concept of the rice burger was born.

This maintained the McDonald's DNA (Selbstähnlichkeit) (the classic burger architecture remained intact), and fulfilled the cultural needs of large sections of the Asian population. Moreover, the rice-burger idea dovetails neatly with an important concept in the Asian region: namely the desire to combine a modern outlook with respect for traditional roots. For the informal eating-out category this meant twinning traditional Asian eating habits with more recent western concepts (family restaurants) and brand identities. Against this background, McDonald's also developed new Asian-inspired side orders, e.g., clam chowder.

To fulfill local needs in terms of language and humor, the entire campaign was developed locally, but taking into account McDonald's-typical features: the McDonald's focus on "food, folks and fun," is the main theme of the TV campaign. This was designed in line with the overall McDonald's DNA (Selbstähnlichkeit). My Asian colleagues deserve all the recognition for this innovative food approach.

Fig. 3: Rice-burger with corresponding value meal

2.2 Recruitment and training of the management team

Although cultural consumer insights are the vital theoretical basis for marketing success, the choice of local management is the critical factor at operational level. When dealing with markets with very diverse cultures, it is essential to develop and implement local marketing strategies by means of a management team that has marketing intuition, intelligence, ability, and, above all, a shared motivation to achieve success. In fiercely contested and culturally demanding regional markets, the staffing philosophy must be: find the best, work with the best, forget the rest.

The local team must be selected extremely carefully, and systematically trained in the marketing processes of your company. It is important that the entire team, from members of the field sales organization to executive decision-makers, is fully committed to achieving success in the marketplace. The team must ask itself: "What can we do to make it work?" and not "Why isn't it going to work?" When assembling a team, all employees should be judged on two criteria using a scale of 1 to 10:

Personal fit

How well does someone fit into a particular project, a particular team, and how well do they get on with the others within the team?

Professional fit

Does the potential employee have the experience, abilities and skills needed for the task in hand?

Each employee must score at least seven points for each criterion to qualify as a potential candidate. One of the greatest sources of failure for brands at local level is a willingness to compromise on these two criteria – for example, as a result of appointing staff for tactical reasons, i.e., because they are simply "available" or because they have been released from other tasks for this particular project – irrespective of personal or professional fit. Should it become apparent that a member of the team simply does not have the skills or personality needed, there is only one solution: let them go. For more information on selecting and motivating team members, I very much recommend the book Hot Groups, described at the end of this article.

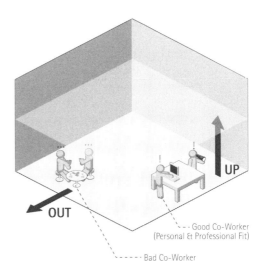

Fig. 4: The recruitment of the most capable employees for local management is vital

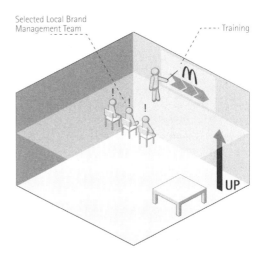

Fig. 5: Local management should be trained in international processes to prevent time-consuming and frequently expensive learning-on-the-job

CASE   McDonald's Hamburger University

McDonald's has a dedicated staff training organization: the McDonald's Hamburger University. This has facilities at all key locations, and provides a wide range of skills-development opportunities:

- All management-related disciplines.
- Both hard (professional) and soft skills (personal development, inter-personal skills).
- Training for all staff – from restaurant crew to top management.

Professors are not just external professors, but also in-house staff recruited from the appropriate departments. This additional role as an instructor contributes to their further development within the talent management process.

2.3 Creating consumer relevance

Once a skilled local management team and the corresponding cultural consumer insights have been established, the basis for the hands-on development of operational marketing activities is in place. The following components need to be combined:

2.3.1 Product development and marketing strategy

Based on cultural consumer insights, existing products are repositioned or new products developed. The aim is to:
- Take account of specific attributes of the local culture.
- The core competencies of the company.
- Global branding requirements.

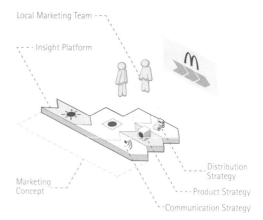

The marketing strategy needs to be tailored on the basis of consumer insights, in particular with regard to the four Ps, particularly promotion, POS/POP (point of sale/point of purchase) and packaging. Of central importance is the development of core brand/product positioning within the region, and the alignment of all marketing activities with this positioning. It is also important that the rationale behind the strategy can be clearly communicated to global management, and can be logically derived from the combination of cultural consumer insights at local level and the global brand framework.

Fig. 6: Leveraging consumer insights, the local marketing team develops concepts and strategies for product, place, and promotion

2.3.3 Implementation

The implementation of marketing strategy in a foreign market requires excellent understanding of the cultural perceptions and sensitivities of local consumers. Even the best possible strategy is doomed to failure if cultural details are ignored or neglected within the scope of operational implementation of communications and product design – in other words, in comparison to the home market environment, operational implementation is an

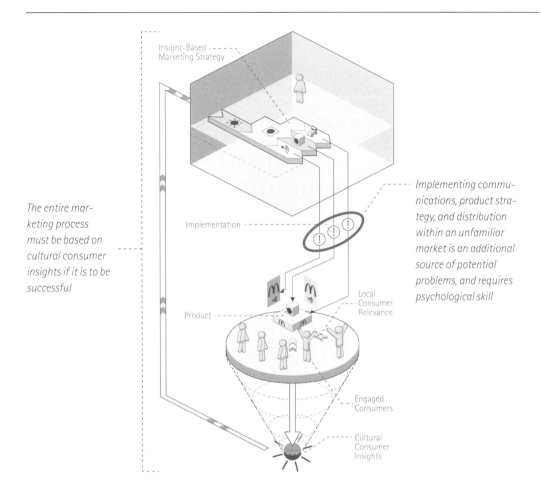

The entire marketing process must be based on cultural consumer insights if it is to be successful

Implementing communications, product strategy, and distribution within an unfamiliar market is an additional source of potential problems, and requires psychological skill

Fig. 7: Insight-based marketing process for the generation of local consumer relevance

additional source of potential problems. For example, communications can only address consumer needs, wishes, and problems if expressed using the consumer's day-to-day language. Language usage, references to current folklore, and all other elements within the scope of advertising, at the POS/POP, on packaging and other media, need to correspond 100 percent to the nuances of the local culture, and their impact on the consumer must be precisely and carefully studied. It is not enough to employ a professional translator – attention must be paid to the linguistic nuances inextricably linked to the current zeitgeist, to current language, and general social trends. The list of faux pas committed in this area is unfortunately far longer than the list of successful transfers. Neglecting cultural, in particular linguistic nuances, can lead directly to the failure of a product. As a result, great attention needs to be given to implementation. Work closely with, and listen to the advice of your local advertising agency. Market success is simply not possible without local relevance.

Consideration must also be given to components that directly impact upon language, such as humor and the art of storytelling. Again, it is essential to involve local marketing experts to verify such elements before a campaign goes on air or before a product is launched. In addition to these predominantly linguistic issues, the character of the product itself should be verified in terms of cultural preferences such as taste, color, and style – and humor.

2.3.4 Evaluation and feedback systems

The impact of marketing activities must be monitored and measured, and the findings forwarded to headquarters. In particular, two key criteria need to be considered:
- Are the business goals (in monetary terms: sales, market share etc; in qualitative terms: awareness, likeability, etc.) being achieved?
- Is consumer relevance being generated?

Consumer relevance can be measured by means of two variables:
- A. Purchase intent
- B. Re-purchase intent.

Two issues need to be considered:
- A and B are of equal importance with regard to the further development of the product.
- Both variables need to be studied with regard to a concrete product or service – in other words, you should specifically test individual aspects of the offering (e.g., different sizes of packaging for a chocolate bar: single bar, pack of three, etc.) and not just the general attitude to the product (attitude towards the product brand).

2.3.5 Summary

The right combination of consumer research, product development and marketing strategy, implementation and evaluation, leads to a brand being accepted within a given culture, and being perceived as a relevant offering within the market. The result is high consumer relevance, and, consequently, the profitable exploitation of a regional market.

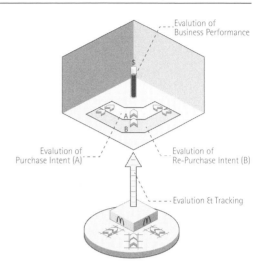

Fig. 8: Marketing activities need to be evaluated and tracked continuously to ensure they are creating consumer relevance

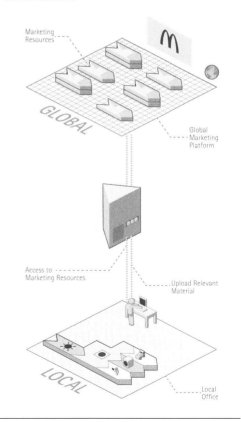

Fig. 9: Global Marketing Platform for the exchange of campaigns and other resources

Manual of International Marketing

2.4 Global synergy
Good ideas and resources from one local campaign can often be deployed elsewhere. Two tools are available to achieve global synergy of this kind:

2.4.1 Global Marketing Platform
Regional and global pools give all marketing teams anytime access to the latest campaign developments, research findings, and strategic tools. This requires a corresponding IT infrastructure in the form of the Global Marketing Platform. This comprises a global database fed with the corresponding data on campaigns, products, consumer insights, etc., from all regions.

CASE McDonald's intranet

Both companies and agencies have access to several central intranets (McDonald's, internal for all management areas, and specifically for marketing, with multiple intranets (agencies and other companies; e.g., Omnicom, DDB)). Each employee has a personal user profile with defined access privileges. If an employee in the U.K. discovers a particularly interesting chicken burger in LA, and tells a colleague, both can immediately view a selection of the latest burgers with all key information by means of Menu Management/Global Regions/U.S.A/New Products/Product Architecture.

As a result, all marketeers can access information on all product developments and campaigns, often leading to significant savings – not merely by adopting existing marketing concepts, but in terms of the development of new products. Rapid access to innovations and campaigns around the globe is a very powerful and cost-effective driver of ideas.

2.4.2 Ongoing marketing reviews

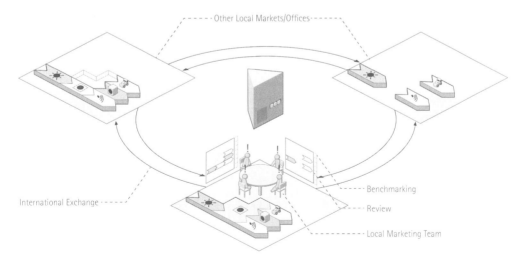

Fig. 10: Reviews at international level promote close collaboration and global synergy

In addition to the global marketing platform, local marketing teams should hold regular reviews of product innovations, insights, and campaigns at international level. Institutionalized exchange generates greater understanding and more ideas, and enables the best to be gathered and shared with the aim of achieving the greatest possible synergy.

However, the overriding criterion for deciding which idea is suitable for which market remains local consumer relevance. The required cultural expertise in terms of consumer insights and the structures of the specific markets only exists at local level.

CASE   McDonald's reviews

In Germany, McDonald's and the agency hold regular joint reviews of new ideas or existing campaigns, comparing them with internal (other regions) and external (leaders in other industries) benchmarks. This review and benchmarking process has clear benefits: for instance, imagine you were to take a look at all TV commercials aired in the last 18 months in sequence, and would compare them with those from another industry leader. It would soon become apparent whether there is a common thread throughout all your company's communications (a consistent brand identity or not). If YOU end up confused, what do you think the impact on your customers is?

If you are responsible for multiple regions or countries, then you should ensure that your local marketing teams meet regularly every six to 12 months to identify creative input, constructive criticism, weaknesses, and potential improvements. It is important to engender a spirit of "let's be better at being better," and not one of finger-pointing.

Hazards
The greatest enemy of global synergy is not-invented-here syndrome: often, successful concepts in one market are not implemented in another simply because they were conceived by "someone else." This can occur at local, regional, and global level, and emanate from individual employees or entire departments. Regional campaigns are often dismissed as too provincial and small-minded by the global office. And within local offices, there is a danger of jumping to the conclusion that proposals and campaigns of a global nature are irrelevant to the regional market. The best antidote is to create clearly defined incentives for mutual exchange, and to introduce a global marketing platform and marketing reviews, combined with a performance-driven culture of international exchange and learning – led from the top.

In conclusion, really good employees understand their own capabilities, and do not have a problem with adopting concepts and campaigns developed by others in their own markets. There are no frontiers when it comes to really good ideas.

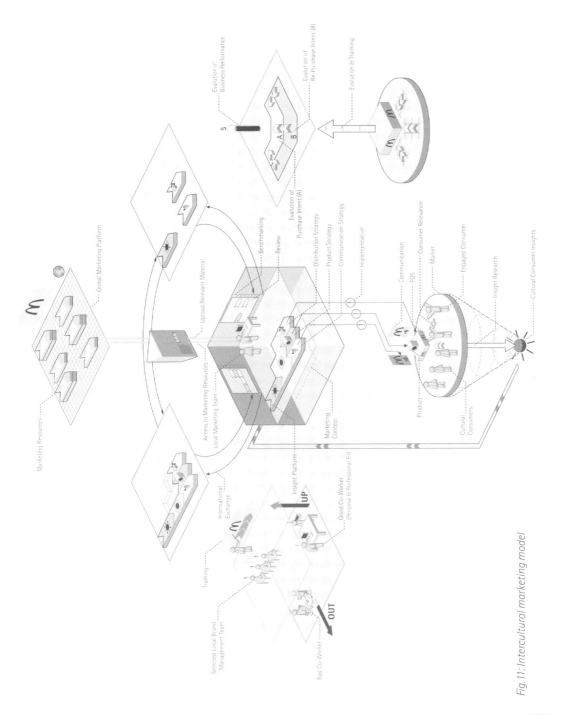

Fig. 11: Intercultural marketing model

▶ Process & Implementation

1 ▶ 2 ▶ 3 ▶ 4 ▶ 5 ▶ 6 ▶ 7

Phase 1: Consumer insight research

The first phase of the insight research process is of vital importance to all subsequent phases as it determines the insight of the culture and region relevant to the purchasing decision.

1.1 Definition of business goals and checks on existing data

To perform focused insight research, it is necessary to precisely define business goals. Moreover, it is essential to collate all existing insights into the local market and consumer perceptions at local and global level. By checking the availability and accuracy of internal insights it is often possible to save a considerable amount of money.

1.2 Selection of insight specialists

Successful insight research is highly dependent on the selection of the right specialists. These can be either experienced employees or external professionals. A successful insight researcher combines psychological skills

1 Consumer insight research	2 Definition of consumer relevance	3 Strategy development	4 Check on suitability of international marketing resources	5 Development of marketing mix	6 Roll-out and execution	7 Evaluation of consumer relevance and market impact
Goals ▼	▼	▼	▼	▼	▼	▼
Cultural consumer insights	Develop key cultural leverage points for product/brand	Marketing strategy	Synergy through existing global resources	Executable marketing mix	Successful roll-out	Verify consumer relevance
Content ▼	▼	▼	▼	▼	▼	▼
Definition of business goals and checks on of existing data	Springboarding and concept development	Definition of global/general requirements	Check on what is available in global pool	Product optimization	Successful cooperation with regional vendors	Measure roll-out performance
Selection of insight specialists	Concept evaluation	Agreement of marketing plan	Decision on exact procedure	360 degree campaign planning	Set up experienced regional team of experts	Measure consumer relevance
Perform insight research				Design of tracking and evaluation system	Holistic, integrated approach	Analyze weaknesses and strategic re-engineering

Fig. 12: Process of intercultural marketing

and in-depth knowledge of the culture with marketing and methodological expertise – and the creative ability to transform insight into marketing innovation.

1.3 Cultural consumer insight research

Genuine insight research is about identifying highly subjective perceptions. It is therefore dependent on the skills and personal strengths of the insight researcher. The insight researcher and his team enter into the personal world of the target group, conduct in-depth one-on-one interviews, workshops, etc., in order to break out of the sterile conditions of the research laboratory and to gain relevant insights into the target group and purchasing decisions. Often, the consumers are themselves not aware of their decision-making processes, and instead the researcher must unearth unconscious needs that can be translated into product and marketing activities. However, many market research studies lead to findings that are not necessarily clearly defined, relevant consumer insights – because as the saying goes, "research is not going to tell you what to do."

Faced by a large number of findings, the key task is to pinpoint the one essential insight that weaves a common thread through all studies and consumer statements. This requires internal and external expertise, and interpreting skills. Clearly, differing culturally-determined responses to questions, particularly within the context of international marketing studies, need to be taken into account. For example, there is some evidence to suggest that respondents in Asia tend to be exceptionally positive in their judgements of new products compared to respondents in other geographics.

Phase 2: Definition of consumer relevance

Phase 2 of the process is about boiling down findings to the essential insights for product and brand strategy, and using them as the basis for developing corresponding concepts.

2.1 Springboarding and concept development

The first step is to create concept platforms on the basis of the insights gained as the foundation for consumer-relevant innovations/variations or fine-tuning of brand positioning. Generally, this work is contracted out to external specialists (e.g., the Insight Institute), who develop concrete concept platforms in conjunction with insight specialists and the local marketing team within workshops.

2.2 Concept evaluation

Once a critical mass of concepts with apparent relevance has been obtained, prototypes (products, positioning, campaigns) can be developed and tested with the direct involvement of consumers. This serves to pinpoint the most suitable lever for generating consumer relevance in the target market.

Phase 3: Strategy development

When clarity has been achieved with regard to the lever for generating consumer relevance in the target market, the next step is to develop a marketing strategy.

3.1 Definition of global requirements

The strategic goal, for example enhancing brand image or maximizing revenues and earnings, depends upon the requirements laid down by global management. These requirements also determine marketing activities.

3.2 Agreement of strategic marketing with headquarters

Then the work of strategic marketing planning can commence. This includes issues such as a precise definition of the target group and of the business objectives: how many units are to be sold, with what profit margin, how much market share do we want, what market penetration, what purchasing frequency? These strategic goals are then used to develop marketing activities by means of a conventional marketing planning process, complete with time lines (what products are to be sold? Do existing products need to be changed or evolved? What type of communications are to be deployed? What are the design requirements for the point of sale and packaging? What sales organization structures need to be established? Do we need time schedules and evaluation plans? etc.) Once the marketing plan is in place, the budget, and strategic methods and plans, need to be agreed with headquarters.

Phase 4: Check on the suitability of international marketing resources

Once the consumer and his behavior have been described in Phases 1 and 2, and strategic goals have been verified in Phase 3, the next two phases concentrate on choosing between adopting campaigns developed at global level, or in other countries, or developing local campaigns from scratch. From personal experience, the author can confirm that Phases 4 and 5 are frequently neglected. However, this often results in the transfer and implementation of inappropriate or less-than-ideal campaigns.

4.1 Check on what is available in the global pool

First of all, a decision needs to be made on whether campaigns or other resources at international level are suitable for local campaigns, and whether these should be adopted and adapted in order to save costs.

4.2 Decision on exact procedure

Three basic scenarios are possible at the end of Phase 4:

Scenario 1
A campaign developed elsewhere is available, and corresponds to local cultural insights. In this case, the campaign should be used, but adapted to local conditions.

Scenario 2
A campaign developed elsewhere is available but does not correspond fully to local cultural insights. In this case, a decision needs to be taken on whether it is worth investing in the development of an entirely new campaign. Where costs are an issue, the existing campaign should be used, but re-engineered to a greater degree.

Scenario 3
The existing campaigns run contrary to local cultural insights. In this case, it is essential to develop a local campaign. An existing campaign that conflicts with local culture would be counterproductive and damaging to the

brand image, with a negative impact on product sales. If a decision has already been taken to deploy an existing campaign, this needs to be subjected to a cultural check, with a local cultural expert verifying the story line, design, and language. If it becomes apparent that there are still slight conflicts with the local culture in terms of details, these must be eradicated during Phase 5.

Phase 5: Development of marketing mix

Building on the marketing strategy, Phase 5 entails developing a concrete marketing mix, encompassing the four Ps: product, place, price, and promotion. In the ideal instance, the global concept is compatible with the local culture, and must simply be translated and fine-tuned. For example, a storyboard developed for a TV commercial in the U.S. may be suitable for China, but needs to be re-shot with local actors and in a local setting. Packaging will also need to be localized in terms of language and legal disclaimers, etc. Generally, localization should also take account of cultural preferences in terms of style, colors, and taste. However, a campaign which includes certain elements alien to the regional culture can have a considerable positive impact if this corresponds to a new trend, or starts one itself. Decisions on this type of optimization need to be taken by the local marketing experts. But campaigns should, of course, never fly in the face of local cultural insights. After an initial high-level cultural check, the concepts should be fleshed out, and subject to a pre-test with the target group to gauge the impact on consumers. Care should be given to the development and testing of language and humor, as these are highly dependent upon subtle nuances of the regional culture, and can have a huge influence on purchasing behavior. If a campaign developed at global level is to be employed, it is important that the developers of the global campaign and the managers responsible at local operational level work hand in hand. This is important for localization work, but also helps professionals responsible for global campaigns to gain greater understanding of regional markets and cultures. Any time lines should take account of the competitive situation, and possible action by rival players to ensure your company is able to respond in an appropriate and timely manner. Wherever possible, your company should be a proactive trendsetter and not a reactive trend follower.

Phase 6: Roll-out and execution

Campaign launch needs to be monitored at operational level by local decision-makers. Central control of operational marketing activities by global or regional executives would be too rigid, slow, and inflexible due to a lack of local knowledge and contacts. Local control of campaign execution, by contrast, enables rapid response to unforeseen opportunities and problems. As a result, it is possible to hold local events, find local sponsors, and make tactical use of unforeseen circumstances in a much simpler, faster, and more effective way. Moreover, a locally controlled campaign enables better exploitation of below-the-line communications.

Phase 7: Evaluation of consumer relevance and market impact

It is important to continuously track and evaluate marketing activities to ensure their efficiency and effectiveness. In addition to "hard" performance indicators, such as market share, number of units sold, and purchasing frequency, "soft" parameters are also of importance to establish the impact of marketing with regard to product relevance for the consumer, and to obtain information that could be used to fine-tune marketing. These include top-of-mind awareness, the popularity of a product and the brand, and advertising acceptance. Consumer relevance can be measured, as described above, by means of purchase intent and re-purchase intent, and a number of other criteria. Concrete information on competitor behavior is of key importance to employee motivation, and particularly to franchisees, i.e., if rival players modify their offering, prices, or advertising in response to activities executed by your own company. Competitor monitoring and evaluation are again best performed by local experts, as they are best able to judge the regional market structure and competitors.

▸ Key Insights

- Successful intercultural marketing is the result of a combination of components, focusing on local consumer relevance.
- Precise and relevant cultural consumer insights lay the foundations for in-depth, product-related, and category-related understanding of a given culture.
- An able local management team, trained in the international processes of your company, is vital to the intelligent translation of insights into innovations, strategies, and concrete activities. The culturally sensitive implementation and verification of strategies, with the involvement of local experts, drives forward strategy and innovation. Ongoing international exchange, including the deployment of elements from the marketing mix developed in other regions, creates synergy and cost savings.
- In this way, local management can combine the strengths of a global brand and its existing resources with maximum consumer relevance in their own region through their own cultural awareness.
- Worldwide implementation and ongoing optimization of these strategic components enables maximum exploitation of market opportunities in various regions, and the building of a brand that is both strong on a global level and relevant on regional level.

▸ Practical Guidelines

- Be strict when it comes to recruiting employees: find the best, work with the best, forget the rest.
- Your intercultural marketing activities should revolve around one key task: generating consumer relevance.
- Be relevant.
- Within each market, pinpoint the all-important number one consumer insight.
- Within each market, identify the key consumer need that will earn you money – ideally, a need not currently satisfied by any product on the market.
- Pay attention to both profitability and feasibility: there are needs with great relevance but which, on account of existing market potential (the number of consumers) or development costs, will never be profitable.
- For each market and each product, you need to ask the following question: how can we solve the problem/satisfy the consumer's need (better than before/better than our competitors)?

- Identify a test market with the conditions that underpin reliable forecasts on the success of innovations and campaigns. Austria, for example, is an ideal and highly compact test market for all of German-speaking Europe.
- The following applies to all product and brand launches: take a decision and stick to it. Even the best idea is useless if it is not put into practice.

The Author

J. Johan Jervøe

J. Johan Jervøe, a Dane, joined McDonald's in 1996. Previously, he was Milka brand manager at Kraft Jacobs Suchard in Austria, and a consultant at Roland Berger & Partner in Vienna. At McDonald's, he has held a number of regional positions within the Central Europe Region. In April, 2000, he was named Director of Worldwide Sports Marketing at McDonald's headquarters in Oakbrook, Chicago. Since July, 2002, J. Johan Jervøe has been Vice-President of Marketing at McDonald's Germany, and a member of the McDonald's Germany Board. Johan served four times as Professor at McDonald's Hamburger University.

Literature Recommendations

J. Lipman-Blumen, H. J. Leavitt, "Hot Groups: Seeding Them, Feeding Them, and Using Them to Ignite Your Organization," Oxford 1999

Peter Amon – Unilever Bestfoods

International Brand Portfolio Management
Successful brand portfolio management as the basis for corporate success

▶ Executive Summary

- Successful brand portfolio management is the basis for corporate success.
- It aims to concentrate management resources on the most profitable and top-selling brands, and to strictly couple the selection of brands with opportunities for growth in the relevant markets.
- This is how a brand focus portfolio is created – a brand portfolio that is optimized with regard to its opportunities for growth and its profitability.
- The creation of a brand focus portfolio requires a global brand audit for the entire existing brand portfolio, which covers the dimensions of strategic role, scale, and balance, as well as the strategic allocation of each brand to one of the quadrants ("Divest," "Milk," "Invest" or "Question Mark") in the brand matrix.
- When the brand focus portfolio has been developed, the success of the portfolio, and the ability of a multi-brand company to maneuver, depend primarily on the successful management style of its key local and global brands.
- In doing so, every brand may be assigned to one of the management styles "Global Brand Management," "Multinational Brand" or "Local Brand Management."
- In Global Brand Management, the following applies:

  • Global Brand Management does not exclude taking into account local characteristics.
  • There is no optimal point between global and local brand management. Instead there is always an optimal point in relation to the respective situation, that is also dependent on the organizational form and portfolio.
  • Even for brands with a strong local heritage, it makes sense to bundle parts of the strategic brand management, in order to ensure synergies and a harmonized presence in all countries.
  • An international corporation can be very successful with local brands, too.
  • A balanced mix of global brands and local jewels, as well as management styles that are adapted to fit the respective situation, are the basis for the success of brand portfolio management.

Benefits

- Balanced portfolio of strong global and local brands which optimally satisfies the requirements of consumers
- Cost savings and economies-of-scale effects.
- Avoidance of cannibalisation effects.
- Increase in the maneuverability of complex multi-brand companies and their brand portfolios through structured management styles.
- Greater profitability and competitiveness of the entire company.

Theoretical Model of International Brand Portfolio Management

1. Definition and core principle

Today, multi-brand companies are facing special challenges in many ways.

- More global markets require multinational management and the regional expansion of existing brands.
- Greater pressure from competitors increases the pressure to operate at a profit for individual brands as well as for the entire portfolio.
- Shorter innovation cycles necessitate a more specific innovation management that is compatible with the brand for each individual brand.
- Growing media volumes increase minimum expenditure in brand communication (minimum investment levels).

Overall, this scenario leads to a significantly higher pressure on profitability and management intensity of each individual brand within a brand portfolio. The answer to this challenge can only be: concentration of resources on the most important brands, i.e., those with the most promising chances for growth and those that are most profitable, and creation of maximum synergies between brands in relation to their coverage of relevant market segments and strategic importance. The task of current and future portfolio management lies in these strategic objectives and the optimization of operational management efficiency for each brand. The following factor model shows instruments and mechanisms for successfully completing this task.

2. Factors

2.1 Corporate vision

A rule of thumb with multi-brand companies is that a small number of brands account for by far the largest share of turnover and profit. At the same time, all brands require similar management resources, indirectly increasing the efficiency of the core brands. Consequently, the actual portfolio of a multi-brand company should comprise of a small number of decisive brands. The strategic objective of international brand portfolio management should therefore be the concentration of the company on its core brands. In the following, I would like to call the focused brand portfolio created in this way "brand focus portfolio."

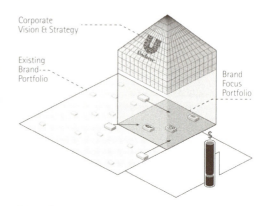

Fig. 1: Corporate vision and strategy serve as a strategic model in the identification of core brands and the resulting focusing of the brand portfolio (brand focus portfolio)

To be able to define the brand focus portfolio, a precise brand audit is needed that incorporates various perspectives, and which evaluates each brand accordingly. The starting point and the basis of the brand audit is the corporate vision and strategy. Particularly for multi-brand companies, the following applies here: the corporate vision creates a bracket in which the competences, brands, and strategies are applied. Without a credible corporate vision, the strategic decision benchmark, which helps in the selection or enhancement of a brand portfolio, is missing. The result: the company loses itself in too many different competence areas and favors short-term profitability of individual brands over long-term synergy effects. In this respect, the development of a strong corporate vision that provides direction plays a pivotal role in brand portfolio management.

CASE   Unilever Vitality Vision

Unilever has made it its objective to improve quality of life. "We meet the requirements for nourishment, hygiene and body care with brands that help people to feel good, look good and get more out of life." Consumers use products from Unilever more than 150 million times a day in 151 countries around the world. The Vitality Vision is a strong bracket for aligning all current and future activities with one common goal.

2.2 Brand auditing and decision tree
Based on the corporate vision, a three-stage decision tree is available for examining the existing portfolio in relation to its key brands.

2.2.1 Strategic role

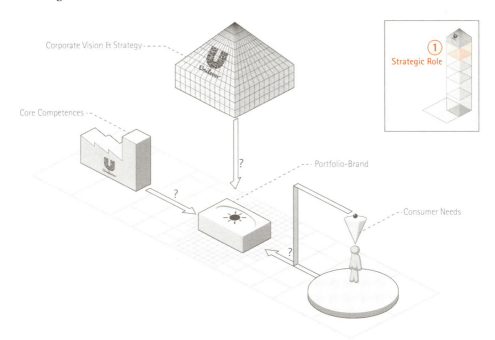

Fig. 2: The first dimension in the development of the brand focus portfolio is the establishment of the strategic role of each brand in the portfolio – the aspects of corporate vision and strategy, existing production competences (core competences), and the status of consumer requirements (consumer needs) play a role here

Here, the focal point is which strategic growth role a brand has in an increasingly global portfolio. At the first stage, the core competences of the company are analyzed, and the brands are measured by how closely they relate to these core competences. The more strong brands there are that relate to any one of a company's core competences, the higher their synergy potential is in relation to, for example, production and Research and Development. This may also affect different product categories: a particular core competence in fats can be strategically important in both the body-care sector and for margarine brands. In this respect, the analysis of the strategic role requires not only comprehensive knowledge of the market-related aspects of a brand, but also the technical and commercial production background of this brand, as well as the knowledge base available in the company. Moreover, the use of common core competences does not guarantee that a brand will remain in the portfolio. It is more important to ask if the brand fits in well with the corporate vision of the company. That is why brands that are suitable with regard to their required core competences, and are well positioned on the market, may also be approved for sale. Particularly because of their market strength, these products generally demand a good price and, thus, serve the further development of the entire company.

2.2.2 Scale

At the second stage, an analysis is performed as to how much media volume is necessary for the brand to be sufficiently heard in the markets. The central variable here is the so-called minimum investment level (MIL) as it is referred to below. MIL must be defined for every category and for every market. It can be determined e.g., through an analysis of media expenditure for the entire market over the last two years. Using these figures, the MIL can be calculated and with this it is possible to define which monetary minimum investment is necessary to communicate the company's own brand sufficiently. Whether the media volume derived from the MIL can be achieved by a brand, is defined in most cases by the market position and/or by turnover and profitability of the brand. Only in exceptional cases can strategic corporate budgets be used above the turnover generated by the brand to further the expansion of the brand.

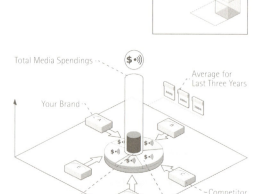

Fig. 3: The second dimension of brand evaluation is the determination of the media scale that every brand has in its market. For this, the media spending of all competitors (competitors/brands B-E) over the last three years is added up and the required minimum spending volume (minimum investment level [MIL]), which the brand has to reach, derived

2.2.3 Balance

A fundamental objective of a brand portfolio is to adopt as many profitable positions as possible in the market within its core categories without cannabalizing its own brands in the process. That is why it needs to be checked, firstly, to determine whether each brand has a clearly defined place for itself in the market and, secondly, that it is not competing with another company-internal brand. If two brands are too close to one another, cannibalization effects are the result. A portfolio is balanced when a balanced positioning of the brands within the crucial image dimensions and price segments of a category has been created. Here, an entry into lower price segments can make sense, in order to ensure that they are not ceded to cheap trade brands. This also applies to renowned brands.

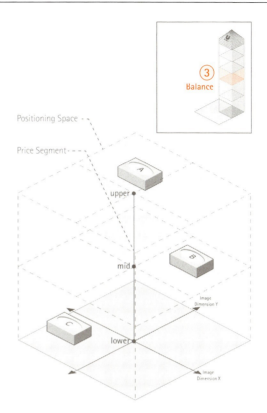

Fig. 4: The third dimension for brand evaluation is the analysis of the brand's positioning that distinguishes it from other brands in the portfolio – for example, this can be through the localization to two image dimensions and one price dimension

CASE   Multi-brand management in the margarine market

If several brands are managed in the same product category, we talk about a multi-brand strategy. This is characterized by the fact that consumers can select between different brands of the same company instead of having to choose between the company's brand and the brand of a competitor. A prime example is the market development by Unilever in the margarine market. Rama, for instance, is positioned as a family margarine, whereas Becel addresses the health-conscious consumers.

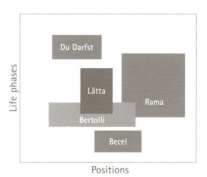

Fig. 5: Positioning space of some Unilever brands

International Brand Portfolio Management   123

2.2.4 Operational instructions for using the decision tree

Despite systematic recording, brand evaluation necessitates a high degree of knowledge about the market and comprehensive consumer insights. Assigning this task to third parties is therefore difficult. It makes most sense to work with international experts in cross-functional marketing teams. The members of these teams should always have a high seniority. Prerequisite for a successful creation and evaluation of the brand focus portfolio is a high degree of openness with which the evaluation is conducted. Established ideas about brands, and subjective attitudes, must not be allowed to influence the analysis and transfer into the matrices. Only in this way can weak points be detected and improvements be initiated. The process is ideally managed from head office, or the management transferred to a management consultancy. The aim is to establish, where possible, a fitting and harmonized scheme of criteria for all countries, markets, and brands. This should be done in close coordination with some key markets to ensure that the company does not suffer from "ivory tower syndrome". At the second stage, it is then the task of individual countries to record the data. At the third stage, the data is consolidated and evaluated at headquarters.

2.3 Derivation of the brand focus portfolio

2.3.1 Allocation of the brands to the four-field matrix

On the basis of the three-stage decision tree (strategic role, scale, and balance), any brand of a global brand portfolio can be positioned in a four-field matrix that defines the future strategic line for the respective brand.

The logic of the four-field matrix emanates from the following consideration: on the two axes, the growth rate (and thus the economic potential) of the market concerned is marked on one side and, on the other side, the relative position of the examined brand to the competition. The following four quadrants then result:

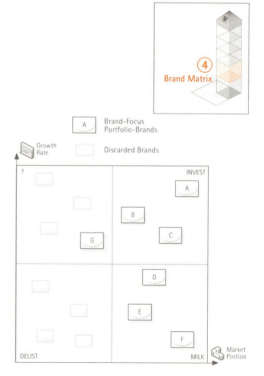

Fig. 6: On the basis of the three dimensions of analysis, the brands of the portfolio can be allocated to the four quadrants of the four-field matrix, enabling the decision to be made on whether the company should discard the brand (Delist), invest in it further (Invest), capitalize existing brand potential (Milk) or subject the brand to closer examination (Question mark)

1. Divest: If the brand is in a market with few opportunities for growth, and also has a poor competitive position, it should be divested. This decision needs to be considered well because brands are ultimately the lifeblood of a brand company. However, if a brand does not fit in with the corporate vision of a company, or if it uses up too many resources, another company may be a better home for the brand. With divesting, the motto is: sale before closure. A sale of the brand to another company gives the brand dignity, safeguards jobs, and also prevents possible negative PR for the company that sells the brand.

2. Milk: If a brand demonstrates a strong position in a market, but has few opportunities for growth, its resources need to be used so that a large cash flow continues to be generated. The brand is continued, although under tougher conditions in relation to expenditure for product development and marketing. The objective is the maximizing of profitability, not the strategic further development of the brand.

3. Invest: With a strong market position in a clearly growing market, the company should invest in a brand to secure the strategically important position and maximize future turnover. The motto here is: strategic investments can be more important than short-term profitability. The degree of investment should be done in a classical manner according to growth forecasts and the qualitative evaluation of the brand potential (trend and consumer strategy).

4. Question mark: Brands that are located in this quadrant are slightly more difficult to evaluate. This quadrant concerns brands that are relatively weak compared to the competition, although they are in markets with strong growth. The question of whether brands of this type should be taken out of the portfolio or given particularly strong support to achieve a better position in the market depends on their strategic importance to the company (see "Strategic Role"). In any case, the following applies: if a company opts for a question mark brand, this decision will automatically lead to a decision in favor of strong investment. In today's climate, a weak position in dynamic markets automatically leads to negative profitability.

CASE Mondamin – successful development of a question mark brand

Fig. 7: Mondamin shaker bottle and Sial d'Or

When the Mondamin brand decided to diversify away from its traditional sector (that of the classical binding agent for sauces) into the sector of sweet dishes, this market was clearly dominated by Dr. Oetker. The only chance was, therefore, in the introduction of unique innovations to win the consumers over to Mondamin. A very good example is the introduction of the Mondamin shaker bottle for pancakes. With this new product, the company managed to acquire several million consumers on the German market in just one year. The market share of the brand was significantly improved. This introduction was the most successful product introduction in 2004 across all food categories in Germany, and was awarded the Sial d'Or.

The allocation of the portfolio brands to the four quadrants can be done at both international and national level. It is perfectly possible for a brand to be in the "Invest" quadrant at local level, and in the "Divest" quadrant in a particular region.

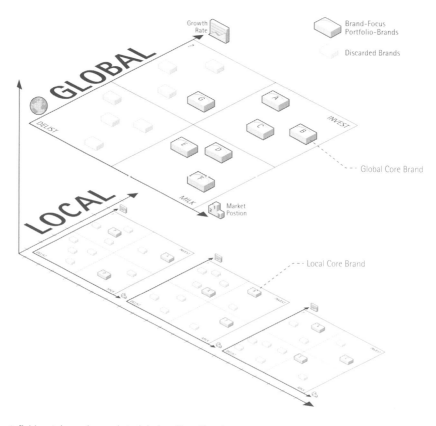

Fig. 8: The 4-field matrix can be used at global and local level

2.3.2 Derivation of the brand focus portfolio

The brand focus portfolio is based on the allocation of the brands to a local and global 4-field matrix. Brands that are located in the quadrants "Milk" and "Invest," or that are to be promoted further in the "Question mark" quadrant for strategic reasons, remain in the portfolio. All other brands should be removed from the portfolio. Overall, two fundamental types of brands can be distinguished in the brand focus portfolio: the global core brands are represented in different countries under the same name and share the same common vision, even if they are positioned differently. The local core brands have a strong local heritage and achieve high rates of growth. However, they are not marketed under the same name and are not represented in all countries.

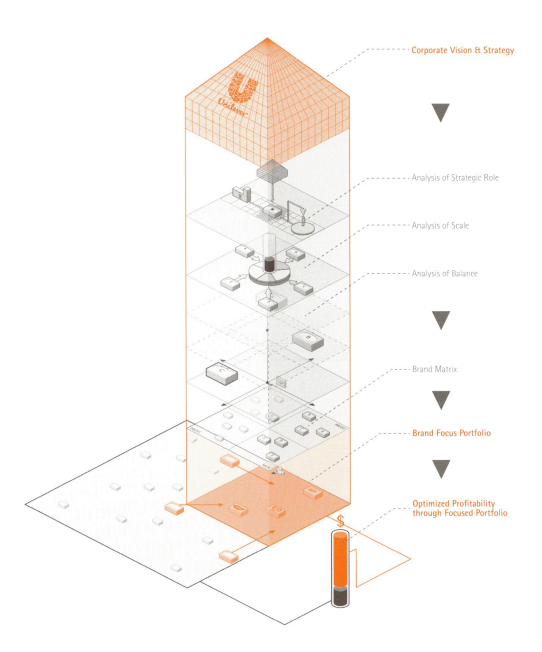

Fig. 9: Model of international brand portfolio management

2.4 International brand management

2.4.1 Management styles
Once the right brand portfolio strategy has been developed, the operational management of the selected brands is crucial for overall success. In the management of global, multinational, and local brands, you often encounter a classic area of conflict, that has a significant effect on work at an international level: the need for local consumer and market know-how, as well as excellence in execution, versus the efficiency effects of global brand management. From experience, operational management tends to oscillate between the two poles over time.

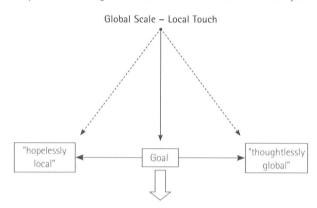

Fig. 10: Area of conflict between "hopelessly local" and "thoughtlessly global"

It is important that this area of conflict adheres to a natural system of logic. In principle, it cannot be solved: local relevance must always be linked to global efficiency. Above all, it is important to give priority to longer-term stability in the structure, rather than constant reorganization activities, if the performance of a brand is not ideal at any one time. The deficits lie frequently in the execution and not in the structure.

All in all, the brands of the portfolio should be assigned to one of three possible management styles to permit a clear management structure in the brand portfolio:

A – Global Brand Management

With global brand management, a central department makes all the strategic decisions that concern brand management. Communication, product development, and research strategy are developed at the headquarters. The tasks of local brand management are reduced to a minimum here and primarily cover the areas of trend and consumer reports, tracking of current business trends, and local adaptation of the globally developed elements of the marketing mix.

However, the balance between local and cultural competences and the global specifications is also important with this first management style. Particularly in the areas of communication and nomenclature, local and cultural characteristics must be taken closely into account to avoid any loss of market share.

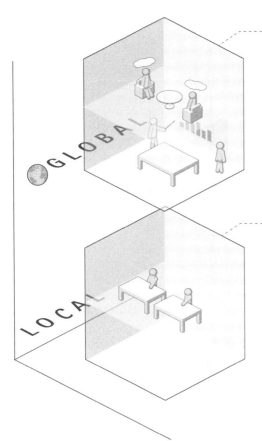

Tasks of the global brand team

- International brand strategy
- Basic marketing activities (above-the-line communication, brand presence)
- Branding
- Product development

Tasks of the local brand team

- Details and special forms of communication that demand an exact knowledge of regional infrastructures (below-the-line communication)
- Linguistic adaptations and cultural check
- Input on trends in the regional market, in particular those concerning competitors, trading partners, and consumer perceptions

Fig. 11: Global brand management: task allocation between global and local teams

Global brand management lends itself if:

- Consumer trends for a brand are globally similar.
- The consumer insights for the corresponding category adhere to the same principles all over the world, and only nuances are subject to cultural characteristics.

CASE Bertolli

Bertolli has now been introduced into more than 40 countries, and is managed very successfully with the global brand management approach. It uses the same advertising campaign in all countries, focusing on vitality into old age. Not even the language has to be adapted to the respective country. Due to the pleasant sound of the Italian language, the campaign works with subtitles:

Fig. 12: Bertolli TV spot used internationally

B – Multinational brand management

With multinational brand management, the strategic management of the brand is in the hands of the global management team. However, within a stipulated corridor (brand vision), various strategic directions can be taken in different regions. The local management teams have the freedom to react to cultural characteristics of the markets and target groups in all dimensions of the marketing mix. Depending on requirements, the development of products and campaigns can be done locally.

An important aspect in multinational management is that the global vision is identical in all countries and that only the operational interpretation is adapted to regional conditions. Otherwise, a company risks losing control over the core profile of the brand – the brand is no longer manageable on a global basis.

Multinational brand management lends itself if:

- (Fundamentally) different consumer trends for a brand are available in different regions.
- The consumer insights for the corresponding category adhere to different principles worldwide, and cultural characteristics have a strong influence on the brand.
- Strong regional marketing teams exist to whom the strategic management competence can be transferred.

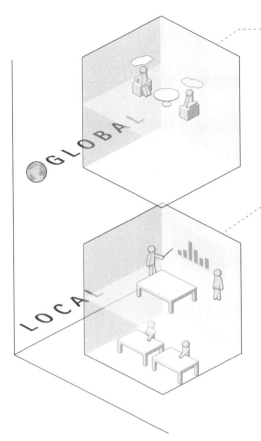

Tasks of the global brand team

- Development of the strategic corridor (brand vision)
- Development of management specifications and business objectives
- if necessary, branding specifications
- if necessary, above-the-line concepts

Tasks of the local brand team

- Development of the regional/local brand strategy
- Development and implementation in all basic areas of the marketing mix (above-the-line communication, brand presence)
- Product development
- Details and special forms of communication that demand an exact knowledge of regional infrastructures (below-the-line communication)
- Input on trends in the regional market, in particular regarding competitors, trading partners, and consumer perceptions

Fig. 13: Multinational brand management: task allocation between global and local teams

CASE Knorr

Fig. 14: Knorr packet soup and tetra pack

International Brand Portfolio Management

Knorr is one of Unilever's largest and most geographically widespread brands. Interestingly, Knorr has managed to become perceived as a national brand over the course of many years. For example, many Swiss consumers think that Knorr is a Swiss brand although the brand originates from Germany. This national identity has often given Knorr a sound basis for growth, enabling it to establish itself against global as well as local competitors. Particularly in the fields of seasoning and refining of dishes, local characteristics are very strongly defined, and the brand that best meets these taste preferences wins the favor of the consumers. For example, packet soups are the dominant form on offer in the German market, whereas in France the market is characterized by soups in tetra packs. Attempts to establish the respective other segment in the market have not been particularly successful.

C – Local brand management

With local brand management, the sole overall responsibility for brand management lies in the hands of the local team. Consequently, this style of management should only be used in the case of local jewels, i.e., important brands that only exist in one country. From a global perspective, locally managed brands primarily play a role in

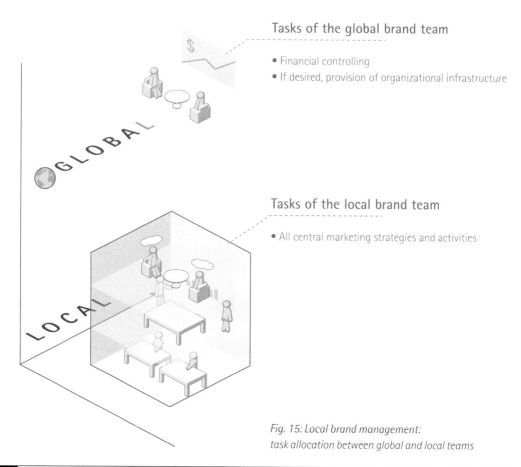

Tasks of the global brand team

- Financial controlling
- If desired, provision of organizational infrastructure

Tasks of the local brand team

- All central marketing strategies and activities

Fig. 15: Local brand management: task allocation between global and local teams

reporting (turnover, market share) in portfolio management, as well as taking the brand into consideration in the regional balance with global brands of the same company that may exist. It is often the case that local jewels have an extremely strong position and dominate global brands in their market.

▶ Process & Implementation

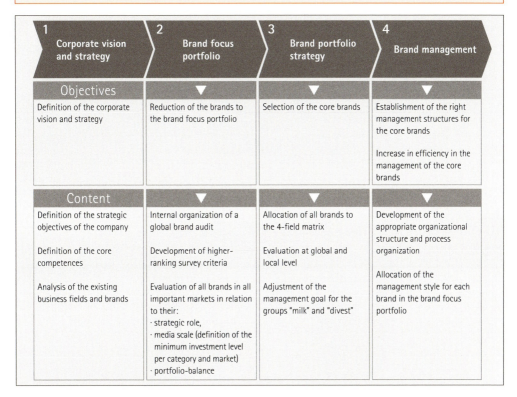

Fig. 16: International brand portfolio management process

Phase 1: Corporate vision and strategy

- It is best to combine top-down and bottom-up approaches. Be clear in your own mind where the lead head office for the process is located, and ensure that it initiates and supports the process.
- Try to find the BHAGs, i.e., the "big, hairy, and audacious goals": a vision and a strategy without ambitious objectives are pointless.
- A profound understanding of core competences is not easy to acquire, yet it is decisive for all diversifications and M&A considerations. In this respect, the process is essential for successful portfolio management. It forms the factual basis for your management decisions!

Phase 2: Brand focus portfolio

- All activities must be based on detailed knowledge of consumer insight in the relevant markets and countries.
- Do not aspire to 100% perfection; doing 80 percent properly over a short period of time is better.
- Use cross-functional and international teams with a high level of seniority, and do not delegate downwards.
- The prerequisite for successful creation and evaluation of the brand focus portfolio is a substantial degree of openness when carrying out the evaluation.

Phase 3: Brand portfolio strategy

- A meticulous classification of the brands is necessary to adapt the strategic direction.
- The right balance between global and local markets is essential for success.
- With divesting, the motto is: sale before closure.

Phase 4: Brand management

- People make brands. The selection of suitable people with responsibility for the brand is therefore crucial to success. This is more important than any organizational form!
- Taking local features into account on a daily basis is also an important success factor in the marketing mix for global brands.

▶ Key Insights

- ☐ The concentration of the portfolio on key brands (can be global or local brands) is therefore the fundamental prerequisite for the successful management of a multi-brand company.
- ☐ The development of a brand focus portfolio necessitates that a brand audit be conducted worldwide. In this audit, all brands in every important market are analyzed for their strategic role, their media strength, and balance in the portfolio. The 4-field matrix serves as a strategic platform, helping to distinguish key brands from unimportant brands.
- ☐ The operational management of the individual brands should be assigned to three basic management styles.
- ☐ Brand portfolio management is a top-level priority.
- ☐ Brand portfolio management is the basis for corporate success and must therefore be dealt with in a sensitive manner.
- ☐ Successful brand portfolio management is characterized by the following factors: classification and, thus, prioritization of brands, derivation of management styles, and consistent implementation.

The Author

Peter Amon

After completing his degree in business administration, Peter Amon joined Unilever in 1991 as a management trainee. His career at Unilever then developed further with various marketing and staff positions in Germany and abroad, including in the Foods Executive in Rotterdam. In 1998, he moved to Kraft Foods where he held various positions in marketing and general management, including Marketing Director, Kraft Foods Germany. He then became Director Strategy Cheese, Meals, and Enhancers Division, responsible for North America, and finally Director of Commercialization in Europe. Since June 2004, Peter Amon has been the Managing Director of Marketing Unilever Bestfoods Germany with responsibility for the brands Knorr, Lipton, Pfanni, Mondamin, BiFi, and Dextro.

Marketing Management

→ www.marketingmanual.org/management

Dietmar Turocha – BSH Bosch and Siemens Hausgeräte GmbH

Brand Alignment
Fulfilling the brand promise with professional processes and methods

▶ Executive Summary

- The most important element in global competition is the brand: one of the company's most valuable assets and a central symbol of trust and orientation for consumers.
- Successful brands with superior product ranges and services have a relevant use to the consumer, a definite competitive advantage and a clear, homogeneous brand image.
- Methods and instruments of brand alignment should ensure that all brand services, which are recognizable in the market, work collectively in the sense of the brand promise.
- Conversion of the strategic targets in the measures of the marketing mix as a whole and implementation of the brand credo in the sense of "to walk the talk" must be guaranteed.
- When used correctly, the range of instruments for brand alignment help to develop the brands internationally in the light of the intended brand image. They also help to set and take advantage of trends, and to develop fields of competence, thus making brands bigger and stronger.
- To facilitate the congruence of words and deeds, of strategy and measures, organization and processes within the company (through to the consumer level) must be directed towards fulfillment of the brand promise. This can be achieved through mutual understanding of the brand, management tools, and the motivation and commitment of the top management and employees.
- All international functions and especially sales relatet units of companies that have direct contact to customers via their own sales organizations, e.g. airlines, gas station networks, and fast-food francises, have a clear duty to communicate a uniform coporate identity.
- In globally operating multi-brand companies that generally bring their brand performance onto the market via commercial outlets, that themselves are brands with their own profiling goals, the demands on brand alignment increase.
- In these multi-market groups, one aim is to achieve necessary synergies and cost efficiencies via platform concepts in the sectors of technology, production, and administration. On the other hand, the brands must also be differentiated from one another, and strengthened individually, in order to achieve higher market utilization. It is precisely in this area between industrial platform concepts and necessary brand differentiation that the use of professional brand alignment instruments is of great importance.

In the following, control instruments and professional methods of brand alignment are outlined on the basis of a theoretical model, and the challenges in the process of development and implementation are described.

Theoretical Model of Brand Alignment

1. Definition and core principles

1.1 The brand alignment model between company, brand, and customer

Against the triangular framework of brand, company, and customer, brand alignment methods aim for purposeful control of all the performance dimensions, within the whole value creation chain of a company, that are relevant for the strengthening of the brand. In order to achieve effective brand alignment, brand management controls all the relevant company functions that are necessary to create the total brand performance via a defined brand promise in the sense of the brand culture. This is valid for defined product dimensions and the corresponding emotional experience dimensions. In order to create an understandable, competitive and attractive brand range, it is necessary to produce a consistent image via product and service performance, sales presentation, sales promotion, advertising and price positioning.

Fig. 1: Theoretical model

As employees are behind the corporate functions of product development, design, sales, sales promotions, advertising, pricing, and customer service, it is necessary to determine the brand promise clearly and unambiguously, and to disseminate this throughout the company, across all performance and departmental areas. The requirements that are derived from this must be communicated internally to all employees, unequivocally and with relevance to their specific tasks. Only then is there a chance that an integrative brand experience, across all relevant performance criteria, is forged amongst the customers, thus, motivating them to buy.

For effective and efficient brand management, it is particularly important to measure recognition amongst customers for all the decisive performance criteria, and in relation to competitor brands, by using suitable market research methods. This recognition should also be compared with the target values, and individual performance areas should be improved within the brand management cycle.

1.2 Expanded model: company, brand portfolio, trade, and customer

In the following model, typical multi-brand companies are covered, which, in the management of their brand portfolios, are always positioned in the area of conflict between the use of internal company synergies and differentiated brand use.

Those companies are also included that do not sell their brand products and brand performance to the end customer via their company's own organizational unit, but rather via independent trade channels and companies, who are always in competition with one another. Very many large branded product companies have this characteristic. And both criteria are valid e.g., for a household appliances company such as BSH Bosch and Siemens Hausgeräte GmbH.

Fig. 2: Expanded model

2. Factors of Brand Alignment

2.1 Platform concepts

It is no secret that corporate groups with a strong market position must secure their competitiveness via cost-based synergy potential. Within the framework of the brand portfolio, cost efficiency is achieved via platform concepts in development and production, as well as through the use of internal company synergies in the company's administrative divisions. On the other hand, a brand portfolio opens the doors to expanded sales opportunities and greater market utilization through differentiated use of the brand for various target groups. These target groups, with their various requirements, will not, of course, be excited by platform concepts of almost identical brand ranges, but must be shown brand personalities that have decisive differences in their uses and the experience that they provide. Thus, through the methods of brand alignment, brand management also finds itself in the areas of conflict between necessary cost synergy through base platform concepts, and consciously-formed brand profiling in performance criteria that are important and visible to the consumer. There is a rule of thumb: cost efficiency and platform concepts are possible in areas that the consumer cannot experience directly, and additional investment, or rather, reinvestments from the platform synergy, are necessary for demonstrative performance factors that our customers perceive consciously, and which are highly valued in their buying motivation.

2.2 Trading activities

In contrast to brand providers with their own outlets or franchisees with exclusive sale of a brand to the end consumer, e.g., in the case of fast food chains and gas station networks, the majority of goods are sold via many forms of retail organization. In the household appliances sector, for example, products can be sold through single specialist retailers, large specialist retailers, kitchen studios, large furniture retailers, department stores, and mail-order businesses. Some of these retail channels have their own brands, and are in direct or indirect competition with one another, which is expressed through various distribution channel concepts and, to a significant extent, through price factors. As most household appliances are sold through consulted service channels, a multitude of retail-oriented activities must be performed for the household appliance brands in relation to the brand alignment e.g., sales promotion concepts, brand sales brochures, point of sale measures, training concepts for retail sales.

2.3 Marketing mix – overlapping concepts

The necessity of strengthening and differentiating brands through brand alignment relates to the entire marketing mix. In the broader sense, detailed control instruments, that enable effective and efficient brand control, are presented by using the example of the product and communication areas, that are particularly important in the performance mix and difficult to process in the company. For the sake of completeness, however, all the components of the marketing mix, which must be considered in the brand alignment, are outlined below:

- Product: the product is the brand's figurehead. It not only includes experienceable utility but, primarily, the design and packaging, as these elements are the first things to be communicated to the interested parties. Taking into account the increasing product and performance homogeneity in many sectors means that the design factors will become increasingly important in the buying decision.
- Price: a sustainable and constant price position of the brand is decisive for long-term success. Brands with large product ranges are defined through their price position. The planned position is usually placed in a scale of six levels from 1a to 3b. As an effective resale price fixing only exists in very few sectors, e.g., printed products and cigarettes, price maintenance is a particularly important alignment task in the other sectors, as very strong price volatility leads to uncertainty amongst the consumers in relation to the actual value of the brand. However, in most cases, the brand must be defined within a certain price range, as retail channels with differing cost structures vary their offer within a certain scope, and clearance sales also have to be taken into account in the price perception. A non-binding price recommendation can support the planned range for branded products, but this requires flanking measures for price alignment.
- Communication: the most important communication element is, and will remain, the brand name itself: as a word symbol or as a word/image symbol. A strong word/image symbol in connection with a strong brand promise, expressed by a claim, is the basis for the communication mix as a whole. These elements also form the anchor for all further, broadly-diversified activities: advertising campaigns sales promotions measures, public relations, brochures, internet presence, trade fairs, etc. The number of opportunities makes it clear that brand alignment has a particularly important coordinating task here. The temptation to follow the latest creative variations and fashions is great. Brand management, in the sense of brand alignment, does, however, require consistency and continuity, in order to produce a sustainable brand profile. All communication activities are oriented to the market, and aim to create a predisposition and motivation to buy the brand. The company-internal effect of highly-effective advertising measures should also not be underestimated. Claims and advertising campaigns help to form identity among all employees, especially in the functions close to the market, and to create pride in their own company and in the brand itself.
- Sales and distribution: brand alignment measures are particularly important in the departments of sales, logistics, pre- and after-sales service, that are closest to the customer, as this is where the brand is communicated via people that often have a more lasting impression than all other communications measures. It is particularly important to follow the aim of "walking the talk," and to bind all relevant functions and employees to the company and the brand codex via training measures, workshops, and auditing. Only in this way can sales functions in the retail sector be persuaded and won over on an emotional level in the context of the represented brand.

2.4 Control instruments

The belief that brand alignment is the sole responsibility of the marketing and sales functions that are in direct contact with the customers does not suffice for the widespread task of brand alignment. It is important for all employees and external partners that work on the strengthening and differentiation of brands, such as advertising agencies and design consultants, to share a mutual image of these brands, and to have knowledge of their characteristic values, properties, and targets. Besides the content requirements, the main challenge is mainly to develop a suitable, internal, integrated set of instruments for brand alignment.

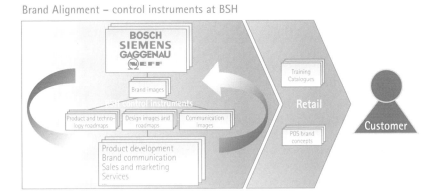

Fig. 3: Control instruments

These control instruments must succeed in illustrating relevant content for the employees and partners in a clear manner, and in a language that they are able to understand. After all, the set of instruments should serve as orientation for both the work of the communications expert and the product developer. Only if there is clarity within the company on the target profile of the brands, is it possible to communicate an understandable, strong, and uniform brand image, externally towards the market.

Brand guidelines

The brand guidelines form the foundation of determining brand territory, making the main competencies of the brand understandable on rational and emotional levels. The guidelines describe and visualize the self-image and the characteristic properties of the brand, document the aims and the basic promise associated with them, and develop a clear vision of the brand values. The contents of the brand guidelines, that describe the strategic framework for action on the brand presence, must now be made concrete in important facets of marketing. As a consequence of this, the brand guidelines instrument is expanded through the addition of further suitable control instruments, that act in accordance with the specific requirements of the main marketing mix components. An important role in this process is played by both the product range and the communications. For this reason, some product and communications oriented control instruments will be described below in detail.

Product-oriented control instruments: product- and design-roadmaps, fingerprints

From the brand guidelines, all relevant fields of the product profiling are described using the fingerprints instrument. These detailed planned fingerprint profiles give product developers medium to long-term orientation for the further development of products for the specific brand. Thus, the general development and innovation efforts of design teams encounter a catalogue of requirements from the brand targets, and, therefore, a scheme for collective selection and for decisions concerning product use and differentiation characteristics.

The design guidelines and design-roadmaps have the task of describing the design requirements for the brand in more detail, in relation to the brand guidelines, and of securing them in the long-term. Design-roadmaps represent the planning framework for larger, investment-related creative intervention, which, in synchronization with product-roadmaps (i.e., the production-oriented series planning), forms the basis for the brand launch and re-launch planning.

Communication-oriented control instrument

The decisive control instrument for the communication presence of the brand is summarized in the communication guidelines. This instrument translates the brand values, as defined in the brand guidelines, into a semantic, design-related, and visual brand world, and forms the basis for the creation and inspection of all the advertising and communication materials.

The main communication idea also forms the basis for the action mix of sales and distribution marketing, sales promotion and for sales catalogues, training content, etc. As corporate functions with direct customer contact are involved in the realization of measures, it is particularly important to communicate the brand idea in a very delineated manner. After all, the behavior of the employees who work closely with sales and service is often more important for the formation of the brand image with the customer than mass communication measures are. It is, however, not sufficient to establish the range of brand alignment instruments. Moreover, the contents of the control instruments must be tested regularly through continued, systematic market research and performance measurement. Only through planned/actual discrepancy analyses is it possible to correct measures in a purposeful manner, and to effectively control the marketing mix. Brand alignment without market research is like hiking without a compass.

2.5 Integration of international aspects

It is almost self-explanatory that the brand must be aligned to an international standard in its core competences and important communicative statements. This requirement has two important consequences: the concerns and points of view of regions with strong market potential and high turnover must be included in the preparations for brand management. Secondly, it must be defined clearly which formal and content-related constants of brand management are aligned to central guidelines, and which measures in the marketing mix can be varied regionally in an interpretation corridor, in order to optimize brand activities in relation to regional target groups and different competitive environments in the countries.

Successful, internationally-active brand companies direct their brand guidelines towards international validity from the beginning while, however, including important international trends into the brand management. This means that the set of brand alignment tools as a whole must integrate and assess important regional aspects into the brand management process. The international markets in Europe, America, and Asia display similar demand tendencies in nearly all brand and product categories, all of which follow similar mega-trends within a certain brandwidth.

The possibilities and effects of international communication networks also create the prerequisites for a more effective and efficient brand management, aligned to an internationally valid and uniform brand image. The decisive factor in the inter-regional validation of brand guidelines, product performance, and emotional values, in addition to the essential creative base elements of brand-CI, is a foundation of the total guideline design on an international fact-based analysis, e.g., internationally designed target group cluster analysis, brand image investigations in the competition environment, and trend analyses in relation to the brand performance being offered.

On the other hand, it is important to differentiate between the immovable basic dimensions of the brand guidelines and the necessary regional adjustments via regional marketing planning. This need for adjustment can occur in all areas of the marketing mix, but must also be analytically founded. This is true for product and range adjustments, equipment, communications, and media mix, etc. It is not, however, true for brand-CI, basic design, and basic experience values of the brand. Brand design in the dialogue between central brand management and regional marketing is a broad field. In relation to effectiveness and efficiency, it can generally be said: as much of a uniform brand platform as possible and as little regional adjustment as necessary. And both should, preferably, be based on international analyses and decisions by international working groups.

▶ Process & Implementation

Along the process chain, the strategic and executable working steps for successful brand alignment can be split into three areas:
- The analytical and strategic groundwork to establish a brand image and/or differentiated images for the brand portfolio, as well as the development and adoption of the brand alignment control instruments for the key elements of the marketing mix.

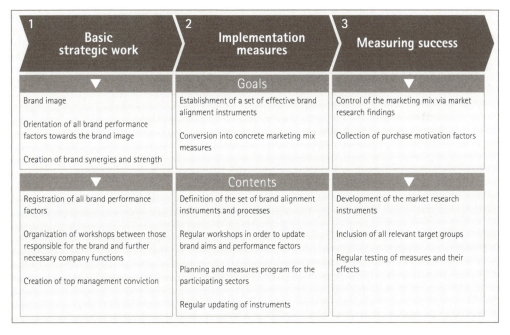

Fig. 4: Brand alignment process

- The development of concrete implementation measures with a direct market effect, that (and this is of vital importance for the long-term success of all measures) only create a comprehensive and strong brand image when flanked by brand alignment.
- Measurement of success, and auditing of the most important brand performance characteristics, as perceived on the market, in order to derive new control impulses for optimization steps.

CASE The procedure of successful brand alignment can be demonstrated and processed quite well by using the example of household appliances, as household appliance groups generally have a brand portfolio that must be divided and aligned to target groups. Furthermore, the sales and distribution to the final customer is carried out via mediators, who are primarily in service sales and not in self-service. The retail level, therefore, plays a more decisive role in the household appliances sector than it does in the FMCG sector, as it also has to take on a consultancy role in addition to the presentation.

Phase 1: Basic strategic work

The set of brand alignment instruments apply at the important interfaces for the development of brand performance, and, consequently, have two main directions: firstly, all relevant function areas in relation to the development of the product range, and, secondly, all functions surrounding the sector of brand communication and sales-related functions. The primary credo of the brand is created through the development of brand images that describe the brand comprehensively in accordance with the product-oriented and emotional competence profile.

Therefore, brand alignment is internal corporate "interface work": the very early inclusion of relevant employees from all departments is decisive for success, both on the sales side, and on the technology and development side. The same is true for the international functions that come into question. Early workshops, before the projects begin, are essential for success. Insufficient inclusion of necessary departmental functions will cost much more time in explanations and corrections later on in the process.

The following measures represent a suitable set of instruments to ensure the success of the strategic ground work:

1.1 Brand images

As the brand image determines the fundamental, strategic alignment of the brand and all other instruments therefore relate to the image, brand images must be developed and demonstrated in a highly professional manner. The brand image characterizes the planned situation of the brand in the market-relevant competence dimensions and, thus, also provides information on the intended superiority profile in relation to competition. It is, therefore, not only recommended, but rather absolutely necessary to develop a brand image based on facts. The basis, therefore, is systematically collected knowledge on the status quo: where does the brand stand today in the competitive environment in relation to its most important attributes? What are the decisive buying factors on the market? This knowledge can either be achieved through internal or external auditing, and through market research. Furthermore, it is necessary to collect systematic ideas on which competence factors will determine the market in the future. The aim is to achieve a future-oriented brand image with medium to long-term prospects.

Quality

Performance
Durability
Value

Experience
Innovation
Use superiority

Technical competence

Quality of life

Together
Balance
Sympathy

Principle loyalty
Reliability
Trust

Responsibility

Fig. 5: Brand image

In comparison to the classical positioning statement (which is a word depiction), the brand image includes the word and image depiction, in order to make the brand position even easier to understand, consciously and emotionally. A good brand image is effective because of its convincing range of areas of expertise and attributes. Anyone who places superlatives in all fields will not achieve anything. A good image is ambitious, but not utopian. Utopian concepts land in a draw, and not on a desk. One more comment is important: a brand image can and must be produced on a working level. However, the unequivocal commitment of top management is necessary for the company-internal realization.

1.2 Detailed instruments in company division processes

In the planning and work process of the main areas product creation and communication, detailed control instruments are adopted, which are tailored to differing work content and working methods. In terms of structure and content, a development engineer requires different information and briefing specifications than a creative director who wishes to develop an advertising campaign.

1.2.1 Communication platform between product and brand: design-roadmaps and fingerprints

Common instruments for medium-term product planning are technology- and product-roadmaps, that facilitate the planning of new products, product ranges, and decisive product changes. These roadmaps are produced in various degrees of detail for the various working levels and involved functional areas. Based on a similar pattern, design-roadmaps are now being developed that document important design plans and necessary design steps from the brand perspective: facelifts, new advertising and service concepts, additional design equipment such as light design, material variations, etc.

One important aim, particularly in the household appliance sector, is to achieve brand alignment between the various product categories of chillers, heaters, dishwashers, washing machines, etc. Design-roadmaps are the connecting element for the product roadmaps in the product sectors. After all, the consumer buys a kitchen as a complete unit, including oven, extractor hood, microwave, dishwasher, etc, and expects from the brand that everything fits together, and that the brand displays a design signature.

For this reason, intensive planning discussions between product planning, construction, and development, on the one side, and the design and marketing functions, on the other side, are decisive. In these workshops, all ideas and concepts are discussed and harmonized until an agreed plan, that sets a clear time horizon for the synchronized product and design events, can be documented, thus, ensuring brand alignment.

As already described, the household appliance sector is mainly characterized by companies that work in several product categories (such as chillers, heaters, and dishwashers), and which must manage several brands from within these product categories. To this extent, products and brands form a matrix within these companies, in which brand alignment has to be effectuated in relation to product use profiles. If, for example, a brand arrives with the argument "extremely quiet," then the consumer expects that this will not only be true of the dishwasher, but also of the washing machine. Therefore, it is advantageous if the principle development within one product category (that, after all, secures the general and long-term competitiveness within the category) is flanked by a product use briefing from the brand's perspective. This briefing of the use factors is represented by the fingerprints instrument.

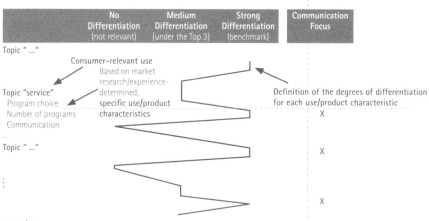

Fig. 6: Fingerprints

Fingerprints represent a catalogue of use criteria, that consciously does not communicate via technological factors or features, but rather, via consumer-relevant use. The fingerprint illuminates the product from brand benefit perspective, and sets the priorities of the brand profiling. The point is to set the focus, and not to define all performance dimensions to the same extent with the claim of superiority. Credible brand profiles are only created by purposeful selection of suitable performance criteria that match the total statement of the brand image, and for which it is, therefore, worth postulating the competitive superiority from the product. Brand portfolio control based on the division of labor can only be created within the company through differentiated weighting and, thus, different brand performance profiles.

1.2.2 Agreement platform between communication and the brand: communication guidelines, briefings, etc.

In most companies, the advertising departments are accustomed to controlling advertising campaigns and sales promotions through suitable instruments (such as standardized briefings, communication guidelines, etc.), as external advertising agencies and communications specialists are usually allocated the task of developing creative realization measures.

The main focal points for brand alignment in this sector lie less in the further professionalization of the processes, than in the effort to achieve continuity and consistency of all measures within the extensive communication mix, and in uniform statements, recognizable signals, and sustainable management of brand topics. The brand claim, advertising story, brand CI, design style, and the creative mechanism of the advertising campaign only result in a sustainable effect, and only lead to brand profiling in the intended sense, if they are holistically orchestrated, and communicated as a consistent message over an extended period of time.

Phase 2: Implementation measures

Important for the implementation of brand alignment is that the topic is not regarded as a "private function" of the marketing department. In order to achieve this, it is necessary to already include all areas concerned in the development and definition of the brand alignment instruments, in order to ensure the routine suitability and the transfer of planned target formulation into the workflow of the sectors. Like all planning tools, the brand alignment instruments also require regular discussion on planning, with a record of the current situation, agreement on targets, and a discussion of measures. In this regard, brand management should not just be organized with the various company divisions through individual workshops for the creation and concretization of the individual brand alignment instruments (such as roadmaps, fingerprints, brand event, and sales round planning). More importantly, it should take the form of inter-departmental brand alignment decision workshops. This is the only way to ensure that the implementation plans in the company sectors intertwine with one another, and that a strong, uniform collective action package is later created around the brand on the market.

It is strongly recommended that the planning instruments of the brand alignment are integrated in the relevant business planning calendar of the company. Hereby, it is necessary that the execution and conception of the brand alignment strategy and planned measures are also incorporated into the company's annual business planning process.

This both strengthens the acceptance of the brand planning requirements for brand management and makes it clear within the company that brand alignment planning is not an "exercise in relaxation," but rather, that it follows economic aims of increasing brand value, that can be measured by using brand performance figures (as described in the next chapter).

Phase 3: Measuring success

Professional control via the set of brand alignment instruments presumes fact-based knowledge via reception and acceptance of all the important performance factors in the market. The market effect needs to be tested at the consumer level at regular intervals. On one hand, the purpose is to test performance characteristics such as active and passive recognition, motivation to buy within the relevant set, etc. and, on the other hand, the allocated brand competences and the quality image of the brand. These tests are usually carried out at intervals of one to three years in accordance with market dynamics, in order to evaluate the development of the brand over time. The brand image tests usually need to be carried out at the consumer level. In sectors such as the household appliance industry, in which the retail outlet performs additional important functions besides presentation (such as consultancy and service, etc.), retailer satisfaction surveys are considered to be important, as the retailer is in direct contact with the consumer and, thus, has specific knowledge of consumer behavior and consumer attitudes. Also, as the satisfaction of the trade partner has a direct influence on sales motivation across the entire performance mix of the brand, his personal attitudes to product quality, design, value for money, service reliability, etc. are decisive for the competitiveness of the brand "on the shop floor." In order to let the brand alignment system function synergetically, it is important that the terms and semantic content of the brand image, design image, communication guideline briefing, and fingerprints are formulated to such a use-oriented and consumer-oriented extent, that they can be represented in empirical market research as mirror images on a retailer and consumer level. In this way, findings from market research and auditing can easily be converted into control impulses in the sense of brand alignment.

▶ Key Insights

- Today's consumer is confronted with a confusing number of brands, of which he can only record a limited number. At the same time, the growth and increased fractionalization of the media landscape is responsible for an increasingly confusing range of advertising messages. This makes brand alignment an urgent necessity, in order to merge all the facets and performance factors of a brand into a uniformly strong brand image.
- Growing internal corporate complexity in organization and processes, particularly in multi-brand companies, requires the establishment of a set of professional instruments, in order to achieve the targets of brand alignment.
- These detailed control instruments must extend across all the brand's relevant performance ranges, and be interwoven with one another via a brand image.
- Each functioning control instrument of the brand alignment applies at the interface between brand management and the relevant performance sector (e.g., product development or communication), and creates a tailor made communication platform between the brand and the functional area.
- Technology and production platform concepts do not contradict brand alignment if cost efficiencies are sensibly balanced with necessary investments for the differentiation and profiling of the individual brands within a brand portfolio.
- Brand alignment means integrity, and is an integrated starting point for all questions of brand management.
- Both the effectiveness and efficiency of the brand work and, most importantly, the relevance of the brand strengthening topics, must be tested with customers and consumers through systematic market research.
- International demand trends and the global networking of communication are advantageous for effective and efficient brand management, based on the principle: as much uniformity as possible and as few regional discrepancies as necessary.

▶ Practical Guidelines

- ☐ Analytical and strategic ground work to define the status quo, and determining the target corridor for the brand work, is essential for the creation of a professional, fact-based set of instruments for brand control.
- ☐ All responsible employees from the relevant performance sectors must be involved in the work process at an early stage.
- ☐ The contents of the control instruments are intended for various target groups inside and outside of the company, and, in order to be clear and accepted, must be presented in a language that is understandable for the relevant target group.
- ☐ Brand concepts with defined, product-oriented and emotional competence fields, in addition to brand CI, have internationally valid guideline characters. This presumes an interregional, analytical foundation and establishment of the guidelines in an international team.
- ☐ A clear commitment from top management is necessary for realization within the company.
- ☐ Successful brand alignment can only be achieved through content continuity and consistency in all facets of marketing.
- ☐ A clear brand profile always means concentration on certain performance dimensions and, thus, also doing without others.
- ☐ The contents of the control instruments and the success of their use must be tested regularly through systematic market research and performance tests.

The Author

Dietmar Turocha

Dietmar Turocha, Divisional Manager for brand management at BSH Bosch und Siemens Hausgeräte GmbH, is responsible for corporate marketing: brand portfolio management, market research, brand communication, and brand design. Career-steps: industrial sales representative, university student (economics and politics), sales and marketing positions at Colgate-Palmolive, Beiersdorf, and Reemtsma cigarette factories.

Literature Recommendations
A. Meyer, H. Davidson, "Offensives Marketing," Freiburg 2001
K. Lane Keller, "Strategic Brand Management," New Jersey 1998

Adriana Nuneva – Heidelberger Druckmaschinen

B2B Marketing
The convergence of B2B marketing with the success factors from the B2C sector

▶ Executive Summary

Above all, B2B marketing differs from B2C marketing in that the demand comes not from end-consumers, but from organizations such as industrial companies. The personal interaction between supplier and customers is a decisive factor for success. Today, manufacturers of industrial goods are confronted with a situation that is comparable to B2C marketing.

- Due to the diversity and similarity of the products, purchasing decisions in the industrial goods sector are also shaped to an increasing extent by complexity and uncertainty for the customers.
- In this situation, brands, brand policy, and brand management have a growing importance in B2B marketing. Accordingly, through brand building, suppliers of industrial goods are also making use of the tried and tested methods of B2C marketing to communicate quality information and trust in the products offered.
- The form of market development for manufacturers of industrial goods is becoming a decisive feature of differentiation over competitors. The issue is to establish, maintain and support a successful relationship with customers in the long-term. This understanding is reflected in the model for holistic market development in B2B marketing.
- Here the dimensions of the model embrace:
  1. the sales approach that is specific to the segment and derived from a careful customer segmentation
  2. the focusing of the communication on exactly defined content, as well as
  3. the specific use of those communication instruments that realize the necessary degree of proximity ("relationship magnitude") to the customer.

▶ Theoretical Model of B2B Marketing

1. Basics of B2B marketing

As a result of sectoral framework conditions, manufacturers of industrial goods are seeing some special characteristics that fundamentally differentiate industrial goods marketing, i.e., business-to-business marketing (B2B marketing), from consumer goods marketing, i.e., business-to-consumer marketing (B2C marketing). To distinguish B2B marketing from B2C marketing, the issue of the target group is of primary relevance: is the company's offering directed at an individual person as the end user, or does the customer take the form of an organization? Correspondingly, the so-called organizational procurement behavior forms a pivotal starting point in industrial goods marketing for numerous marketing-related decisions. It is defined by the following characteristics:

- Derived character of demand
  The demand of an organization is not original, but derivative. In other words, it is the result of the requirements of an organization's customers. Accordingly, it should be noted that the customers of the demand have a corresponding influence on the latter's procurement behavior. That is why the suppliers should always create preferences among the customers of their own customers (as, for example, Intel has succeeded with "Intel inside").
- Multi-personality and multi-organizationality
  Multi-personality refers to the fact that purchasing decisions in industrial goods marketing are not usually made individually. Instead, several members of an organization are involved in the purchasing decision process in the form of a "buying center." Usually, this is mirrored by a "selling center" on the supplier's side. In this case, in addition to the actual customer company, other organizations, such as banks or management consultancies, are usually involved. This is when we speak of multi-organizationality of the procurement.
- Long-term nature of the business relationship
  Particularly in industrial goods marketing, the successful management of the business relationships represents one of the central success factors over a long period of time.

Personal interaction between supplier and customer organizations.

- Based on the long-term nature of the business relationship, personal selling is of paramount importance in B2B marketing. Correspondingly, systematic customer management is another success factor.
- High level of individualization ("customized goods").

Despite all the differences between B2B and B2C marketing, manufacturers of industrial goods see themselves confronted with a situation today that, to all intents and purposes, is comparable to that of B2C marketing in some areas.

- Growing buyer power is leading to a situation in which manufacturers of industrial goods are also having to implement specific and costly marketing activities to successfully market their products.
- Due to the number and growing similarity of the products, purchasing decisions in the industrial goods sector are also being shaped, to an increasing extent, by complexity and uncertainty for the customers.

As a result of these developments, brand communication is playing an increasingly important role in B2B marketing.

1.2 Core model of B2B marketing

With market development in the B2B sector, the issue is primarily to establish, maintain, and support a successful relationship with the customers in the long-term. Successful market development is characterized by the fact that, while taking into account cost aspects, it influences the purchasing decisions of the customers in the interest of the company. To better understand the requirements of comprehensive market development, a model was developed that establishes the corresponding procedure with the help of theoretical concepts and knowledge.

Basically, a model for market development must cover the following three dimensions:

- Definition of the target group.
- Definition of the content to be communicated.
- Definition of the suitable channel for interaction with the target group.

Based on these dimensions, the questions on the requirements of an effective market development are:

- How can the various target groups be segmented?
- At what time should which content be communicated?
- Which channels and/or instruments realize the necessary degree of proximity ("relationship magnitude") to the customer?

In developing a model for market development, it is therefore a critical objective to depict these issues in their entirety. As the interdependencies also need to be considered during such an integrated market development, a complex decision problem arises. To solve this problem, it was depicted with the help of a three-dimensional space (see Fig. 1). The defining characteristics of the three dimensions of the model are based both on recognized concepts of market research and marketing theory for segmentation and customer retention, as well as on knowledge taken from behavioral sciences regarding effective and efficient sales approaches.

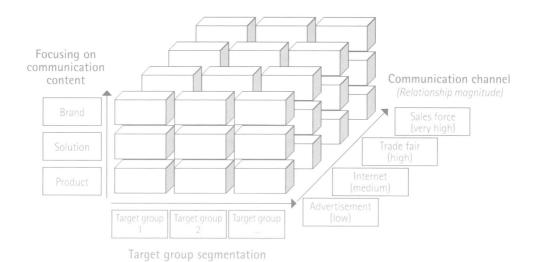

Fig. 1: Model for integrated market development

An essential prerequisite for the adoption of holistic market development is the availability of a customer database with globally standardized terminology, processes and data fields. Furthermore, the customer data must be up-to-date and permanently maintained.

2. Factors of B2B marketing

2.1 Target group segmentation
Target-oriented market development necessitates identifying target groups that behave in a homogeneous way. In the second step, those customer segments should be identified that have the most relevance for a profit-oriented market development. The necessary segmentation for this should take place in B2B marketing on four levels.

On the first and higher-ranking level, the question must first be answered as to whether a direct customer group is the subject here, i.e., the customers of products, or an indirect group in the area of the technological, social, ecological or economic environment.

The direct customer groups are segmented in a second step according to the following criteria:

- Kind and/or type of customer: what kind of company (type of company) does the customer have?
- Customer life cycle phase: in what phase of the customer lifecycle is the customer? Is the customer simply interested in our products, or already want to buy them or even a repeat buyer?
- Business cycle phase: in what phase of the business lifecycle is the customer? In the start-up phase or is it a company that is already established on the market?
- Cultural group: what cultural group is the customer from? Here, it should be noted that in B2B marketing there are broad areas where an applicability of the culture-free thesis can be assumed. However, experience shows that, in direct dealings with the customer, their cultural affinity must be taken into consideration.

After this, the issue of the respective interaction partner on the customer side is relevant on a further (third) level: who is the respective counterpart to the seller in the buying center? These can be, for example, heads of production, financial director, or the owner.

The fourth and last phase of segmentation deals finally with the profitability of the customer: is the customer an A, B or C customer? How much turnover does the customer represent and/or how profitable is he/she for the company?

2.2 Communication of content

Communication activities can also be differentiated as to whether they are directed more at products, complex solutions that can embrace, for example, product-service bundles, or at the image of the company. Whereas product communication in the classical sense deals with an advantage argumentation of benefit and performance, the issue with the communication of solutions is primarily about addressing customer requirements in an integrated way, and through a combination of products and services that is specific to the target groups. Brand communication ultimately opts predominantly for values and emotions with the objective of having a positive influence on the attitude of the customer towards the company and its services. The various types of communication content have different psychological effects on the addressees in the individual phases of the purchasing cycle, and these can be decisive to the purchase in due course. Psychological effects of the communication policy in industrial goods marketing are, for example, attention, recognition, attitude, conciseness, competence, appeal, or trust. Particularly because organizational procurement behavior in industrial goods marketing is so complex, and typically involves several people from different functions with different requirements and expectations (see above), it is important with regard to the content focusing of communication to make both products and solutions, and the corporate brand the subject of communication activities. For instance, the company management on the customer side needs to be convinced just as much as the controller or skilled worker. Furthermore, it needs to be taken into account and ensured that the indirect target groups are reached in addition to the direct ones. These, too, react correspondingly to different stimuli.

2.3 Significance of the "relationship magnitude" of a communication channel

Communication instruments of B2B communication have different customer retention effects, and differ with regard to their interactivity. In B2B marketing, "relationship-oriented" communication activities, such as company tours, road shows, or visits by the sales force, that lead to a social integration of the customer into the sphere of influence of the company, are particularly effective. Adverts or brochures, on the other hand, only have a low potential for customer retention, but are important for generating particular psychological effects. Instead of the classic communication channels, such as daily newspapers, posters, radio or television, in industrial goods marketing, communication channels that permit a specific sales approach to the specialist public are being used more. In addition to adverts in the trade press and specialized product catalogues, industrial goods companies also woo their customers with costly public relations measures. For example, trade journalists are informed specifically about company news, advertorials are initiated, and specialist events with high-ranking speakers from the company are arranged, in addition to lobbying activities being organized. All of these activities aim to position the respective company as a competent partner and problem-solver amongst its target groups. For some years, many companies have been using multi-level dialogue marketing programs very successfully by incorporating interactive media, including call center support, into their sales approach. Through the Internet, many new interactive possibilities have been created, such as product configurators with direct ordering options or personal access portals for important customers of the company. Expensive international customer magazines also belong to the repertoire of marketing communication. Many manufacturers of industrial goods also operate their own training and conference centers for enhancing and improving the communication about their products that require explanation.

Customer retention activities form an important element of communication. These include special events such as customer trips, events, etc., and also customer clubs and the specific cooperation with selected customers in the development of new products and during the test phases.

With investment goods marketing in particular, the participation of companies in trade fairs has a long tradition and an outstanding position in the marketing mix. In addition to very cost-intensive personal selling, these are among the most important instruments of market development in B2B marketing. In times when communication activities are being intensified, competition density is growing, and interest in classic communication measures is falling, a situation of stimulus flooding and information overload can be ascertained. In this environment, the trade fair offers a very good platform for direct and personal communication with individual consulting and support, and a high degree of interaction between the company and visitors. This personal communication with existing or potential customers is important for industrial goods companies. Through the complexity of the products, a bilateral and dialogue-oriented communication can lead to an understanding of the product more quickly and in a more sustained manner than, for example, communication via classical media. For this reason, the trade fair budget of many industrial goods companies has the biggest share of the communication budget with 37 percent. Trade fairs can be carried out by a trade fair organizer on a trade fair site or by a company itself as an in-house fair. From the company's point of view, in-house trade fairs have the advantage that the investment goes into setting up the company's own infrastructure and the customers can be looked after and managed in a more targeted manner.

▶ Process & Implementation

On the next page, the implementation of the individual process phases is shown by using the example of Heidelberg.

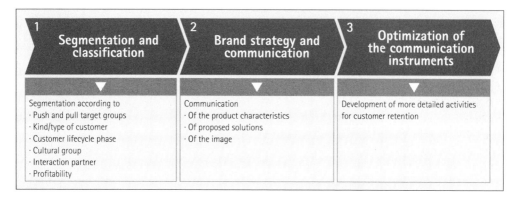

Fig. 2: Process phases of realization

Phase 1: Segmentation and classification

1.1 Segmentation according to push and pull target groups

For Heidelberg, the segmentation on the first level, that is the differentiation between direct and indirect target groups, is of great importance (see Fig. 3). Here, printing companies represent the direct target groups. The indirect target groups that Heidelberg also woos are primarily the "print media decision-makers", i.e., the graphic artists, designers, and production personnel in advertising agencies that can convince their customers of the quality of Heidelberg products and services, as well as members of the print media community (persons with marketing responsibility and clients of print media campaigns). Direct target groups are developed with push activities; indirect target groups with pull activities.

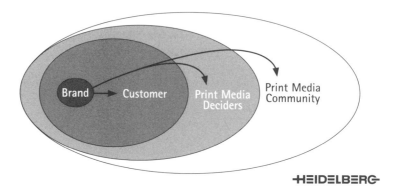

Fig. 3: Direct and indirect target groups of Heidelberg

1.2 Segmentation according to the parameters of customer type, customer lifecycle phase, business cycle phase, and culture group

For a targeted sales approach, Heidelberg segments its direct customers in relation to the kind and type of their business model, the company size (number of employees, shift operation, sales, etc.), as well as the respective end product creation (for example, packaging print and further processing; segmentation of the second level). These target groups embrace the following customer segments:

- Commercial Printer
- Industrial Printer
- Packaging Printer
- Label Printer
- Post-Press Specialists
- Inplants and Authorities
- Pre-press Services
- Direct Mail Printer
- Digital Printer
- Quick Printer
- Web Printer
- Newspaper Printer
- Other Speciality Printers

The focus in the market development varies from country to country; in most cases, it is on the six first mentioned segments. Within a customer segment, the respective lifecycle of the customers is identified from the Heidelberg perspective (see Fig. 4).

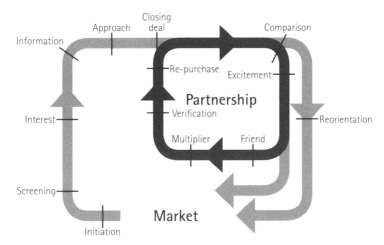

Fig. 4: Customer lifecycle phase

Heidelberg's goal, above all, is to position itself as a partner of the printing companies and enter into a long-term relationship with them. Within the framework of the initial contact, the information about Heidelberg and its services should take the customer to a point of interest stimulation and the desire for more specific information. If the customer can be persuaded by Heidelberg's offering, a contract agreement should result. Between the initiation of the contact and the conclusion of the contract, several months or even years can pass, and a multitude of decision-makers and influential people are typically involved in the purchasing process. After the purchase, the customer needs confirmation of making the right decision with the purchase decision and that Heidelberg's products and services fulfill his/her preferences better than the other suppliers. If this succeeds, the customer will very probably become a multiplier, in other words, will encourage other potential customers to buy the product. For a more precise determination of the information requirements, a further characterization of the customer with regard to his/her business cycle phase, by a member of the sales force from Heidelberg, is necessary. If the customer is in the company set-up phase, the sales force member will choose a very different approach than for a company that has already been established in the marketplace. The personal relations between sales employees and customers are, however, different in their intensity and duration, depending on the respective cultural group. Furthermore, Heidelberg also analyzes the cultural features of the respective customer on this segmentation level.

1.3 Segmentation according to the respective interaction partner on the customer's side at the buying center

The segmentation and characterization of the actual contact persons on the customer's side are conducted by the sales force member and/or key account manager. Using these criteria, the contact persons and sales teams are determined on the side of Heidelberg. The question of who the respective counterparts on the customer's side are is of crucial importance. Particularly here, it will show whether an individualized sales approach is successful – the interaction with different functions on the customer's side (boards of international companies, purchasing organizations, owner, partner of the owner, technical head, controllers, printers, etc.) also has to be designed and arranged differently.

1.4 Classification of the customers

To arrive at a decision regarding the effort for customer development, attractive customers have to be differentiated from less attractive customers, and current and potential customers have to be classified according to their contribution to the company's success. Correspondingly, an efficient allocation of sales and marketing resources – aligned to the parameter "customer value" – has to be ensured.

The decisive parameters in the definition of the customer value are:
- Customer potential (current and future customer value)
- Customer profitability ("input/output" relation)
- Customer penetration ("share of wallet", i.e., what share of the expenditure of a customer is for Heidelberg products?).

At Heidelberg, customer classification implies a decision about the communication channel, the contact frequency and the intensity of the customer development. Furthermore, customer segmentation and classification, in relation to mailings, allow for an individual, situation-relevant addressing of the customer. This in turn results in higher response quotas, higher conclusion rates, and lower campaign costs. Finally, customer segmentation and classification allow for a more efficient handling of customers in relation to their requirements and their expected investments. Moreover, they facilitate the exploitation of cross, and up-selling potential.

The support of these activities via IT tools is of crucial importance. Based on a global, totally heterogeneous system environment, Heidelberg has introduced harmonized standards for data fields, terminology, and processes that have permitted a centralization of both ERP and CRM data into one business warehouse solution. The business warehouse then serves as the central analysis tool.

Summing up, in Phase 1 Heidelberg split the entire market up into homogeneous sub-markets, evaluated the customers of the sub-markets with regard to lifecycle, business cycle, and cultural group, defined the various interaction partners and finally classified the customers according to ABC criteria, so as to be able to develop the market in a specific and targeted manner.

Phase 2: Brand strategy and communication

In principle, it should be noted that, with industrial goods (in contrast to consumer goods), the trust in the brand does not usually relate to the product itself, but rather to the supplier: supplier-related aspects, such as credibility, partnership, and competence, play a special role here. This trust in the supplier is exceptionally prominent in the Heidelberg brand. Furthermore, Heidelberg benefits from being associated around the world with traditional German qualities. Studies that were conducted between 1999 and 2004 prove that a core element in the differentiation of Heidelberg from its competitors lies in the strong value of the Heidelberg brand – and less in individual products. That is why the first task was to develop a brand strategy that bridges the gap between the traditional brand values, i.e., the "inheritance" of the Heidelberg brand (qualitatively high-class engineering) and the conveyance of "new" brand values such as, for example, the high competence in printing-related IT solutions for integrating the entire printing process.

A great challenge was presented by the heterogeneous brand presence due to rapid internal and external growth. This growth was accompanied by non-standardized product designs and means of communication. Figure 5 shows the heterogeneity of the market presence that prevailed until 1999.

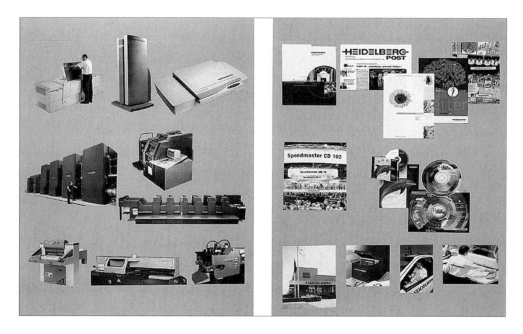

Fig. 5: Heterogeneous brand presence

As a result of these insights, a standardized brand strategy with a strong umbrella brand was developed, and in further steps, three supporting and supplementary "sub-identities" were created. An expression of the umbrella brand strategy is not just the Heidelberg logo, which can be found on all products and services of the company Heidelberg, but also a globally standardized corporate identity concept (corporate design, corporate behavior, and corporate communications), as well as a harmonized product nomenclature. Diversity has become a unity that ensures the recognition of the brand Heidelberg, and makes it considerably easier for customers to orientate themselves in the product portfolio.

HEIDELBERG

Fig. 6: Standardized Heidelberg logo

The clear and geometric language of form and the strong impression given by the Heidelberg design provide an additional contribution to realizing the abstract umbrella brand promise of "highest quality, innovation, fascination and precision". All machines manufactured by Heidelberg are created in a harmonized design and have been given numerous "Red Dot Design" awards (see Fig. 7).

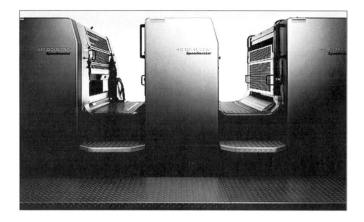

Fig. 7: Reduced stylistic featuring in product design

The customers have a high emotional attachment to the brand, are proud to work with Heidelberg technology and also want to use this for their own presentation. To support and promote this, the logo "technology by Heidelberg" (see Fig. 8) was created and used in two ways. On the one hand, the logo was presented to our customers so that they could differentiate themselves from their competitors and show the printed matter procurement personnel that their company works with Heidelberg products. The customer is provided with a marketing package, containing everything to do with the logo, as a starting aid.

On the other hand, the logo is used on all applications, such as print samples, to show everything that is possible by using Heidelberg technology. The push and pull effects complement each another and together lead to increased demand.

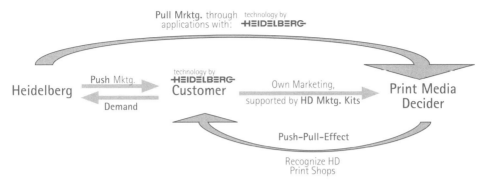

Fig. 8: Customer and application logo: "technology by Heidelberg"

Communication architecture

Heidelberg's communication architecture consists of three elements: product, solution, and brand-related communication, and includes a different weighting of the direct and indirect target groups.

For efficient communication at product level, the company concentrates on the purchase-relevant characteristics, particularly on the use of the product, which can be either technical or commercial. The solution-related communication is based on Heidelberg being the only turnkey provider able to support the entire chain of printing processes with their own hardware/software/brainware portfolio. This unique selling point is transported via corresponding communication that brings the problem-solving and application competence of Heidelberg to the fore. Pivotal arguments are the continuity and compatibility of the solutions, as well as "total cost of ownership" arguments.

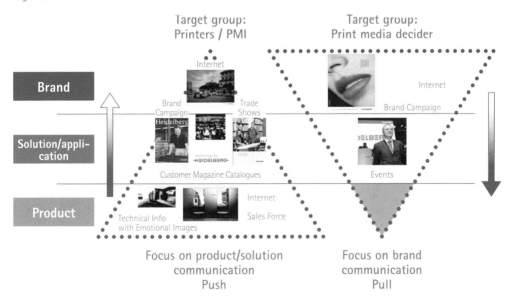

Fig. 9: Communication architecture

Above all, brand-related communication intends to influence the values and attitudes of the customer towards the company in a positive manner. The customers perceive Heidelberg as the only "real" brand in the print media industry. This goes along with the fact that the customers of Heidelberg allow themselves to be touched in a more emotional way by Heidelberg than by any other competitor. Heidelberg promotes this with specific image campaigns. A current and very successful example of this is the "Passion for Print" campaign, with which the emotions of the direct and indirect target groups of Heidelberg are addressed. To take into account the different requirements of various countries, three different motif sections were developed. Figure 10 shows the motif section cut to the North American market.

Fig. 10: The brand campaign "Passion for Print"

Phase 3: Optimization of the communication instruments

In line with the customer lifecycle (see Fig. 11), the communication activities of Heidelberg are primarily aligned to establishing a close relationship with the customer. In this respect, Heidelberg has developed a number of very specific, target-oriented communication instruments, for example, by setting up various worldwide customer clubs for which special certification is required. An example is the selected concept customers with whom Heidelberg works intensively in the development and test phases of product innovations.

In addition to the use of fully integrated campaigns (PR, advertisement, mail, call, micro-site, a global customer magazine, customer visit), Heidelberg not only has a globally standardized web-based customer portal and an online shop, it also conducts professionally organized company visits, so-called customer tours, during which potential buyers get to know the company Heidelberg and its portfolio of products very closely, and are able to test these. The central element here is professionally conducted product demonstrations in the show rooms (print media centers), in which the solutions from Heidelberg are set up specific to the target groups and in full working order. The presented solutions in the respective show rooms are globally selected in such a way that the countries are able to support each other, and not every country has to keep every solution in reserve for demonstration purposes. These demonstrations are the most important sales and marketing instrument for keeping the brand promise of Heidelberg. For customers who want to test the machines on site and in depth, this often represents the deciding impetus to purchase. In Fig. 12, the different elements of a customer tour are listed, that are compiled individually for the respective customers.

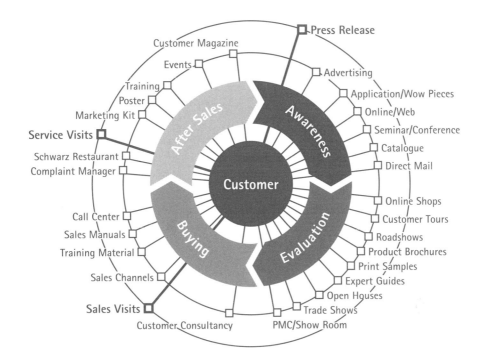

Fig. 11: Use of the communication instruments aligned to the customer lifecycle

A Customer Tour Consists of a Combination of Several Elements

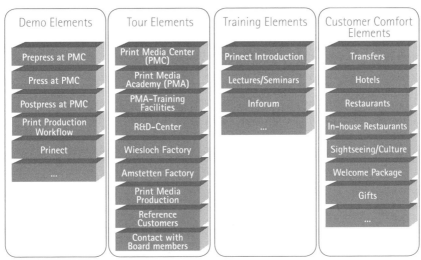

Fig. 12: Elements of the customer tour

However, not only the technical elements contribute to keeping the brand promise. The entire customer care division does, as well. On site at Heidelberg, for instance, in addition to a lounge, there is a high-quality restaurant on the 12th floor of the Print Media Academy (see Fig. 13). A visit to the restaurant makes a decisive contribution to shaping the overall emotional experience. With regard to the topic of customers and service orientation, Heidelberg regularly conducts benchmarking comparisons with the global market leader in matters of customer orientation, the Ritz-Carlton. Furthermore, Heidelberg offers a comprehensive and financially successful merchandising program. The products can either be ordered online or bought in our own shops.

Within the framework of road shows, Heidelberg also goes to the customers. Here, the latest developments at Heidelberg with regard to hard-, soft- and brainware are explained on location and the capabilities of Heidelberg proven.

Heidelberg is also comprehensively represented in the central trade fairs of the printing industry. For instance in the DRUPA, which takes place every four years in Düsseldorf, the PRINT in Chicago, the China Print in Peking, the IPEX in Birmingham, and the IGAS in Tokyo. For every DRUPA, Heidelberg develops a comprehensive marketing concept three years in advance, which is used over and over again in subsequent years after the DRUPA at the other print media trade fairs, in accordance with the philosophy "create once, use many times". This guarantees an efficient use of the marketing resources deployed. The preparation, implementation, and follow-up of the trade fairs are underpinned with comprehensive project planning processes and past values, so that the efficiency of the respective trade fair presences can be assessed at any time. This measurement of efficiency is important, as the costs incurred for a trade fair presence often reach millions. For this reason, Heidelberg has significantly reduced its participation in trade fairs over the last few years, and now only opts for important focus trade fairs in the different regions, and invests more in in-house trade fairs and, thus, in its own infrastructure, i.e., in its own show rooms (print media center).

Fig. 13: Schwarz – the restaurant

In addition to the direct costs for trade fair set-up, the indirect trade fair costs are also substantial. In the run-up to all trade fairs, all sales employees worldwide are, thus, prepared for their task by using, for example, specially developed web-based learning programs and presence training.

Furthermore, Heidelberg has been training customers for some years in its own training centers around the world – the print media academies in Heidelberg, Atlanta, Kabul, Cairo, Kuala Lumpur, Moscow, Mexico City, Sao Paulo, Shenzhen, Sydney and Tokyo – to guarantee that the customers get the maximum benefit from Heidelberg's products. However, not only product-related training courses are offered here. Training is also given that covers all aspects of printing operation, i.e., also on administrative, financial, or personnel topics, for instance. The print media academies also offer a global platform for seminars and conferences of the entire communications industry.

Heidelberg supports various specialized printing institutions (for example, the University for Printing and Media in Stuttgart, Germany) and engineering faculties of selected technical universities by setting up printing machines for testing purposes and providing teaching materials. In this way, Heidelberg ensures that future specialist workers in the printing industry, who will approach Heidelberg again in the future as customers or users, are already familiarized with Heidelberg's products and methods of operation in their training phase.

The most important instrument of relationship-oriented communication is the sales force, which supports current and potential customers in 250 sales and service companies in 170 countries around the world – economic activity, and especially purchasing decisions in the investment goods sector, do not take place between isolated players, but rather, are constituted in the frameworks of continuous systems of social relationships and institutional structures.

To use the synergies between the individual activities, and to ensure a consistent presence amongst the target groups, Heidelberg opts for a rigorous integration of the communication activities. Integration means, amongst other things, a formal and widely harmonized communication design, the geographical coordination of the communication policy across 170 countries, consistency of content, and the timely planning, implementation and assessment of the activities. For this, an international team was set up that agrees on issues worldwide in regular telephone conferences and meetings.

Finally, it should be noted that the strategy of long-term intensive relationship management – which can also be referred to as the strategy of social integration – is increasingly at the forefront of Heidelberg's marketing work.

▶ Key Insights

- Holistic market development in B2B.
- Establishment of a clear brand architecture for improved customer orientation.
- Segmentation of the target market and analysis of the target groups.
- Adjustment of the portfolio.
- Analysis of all the company's "customer touch points" and planning measures accordingly.
- The permanent monitoring of the business models of the customers.
- Corresponding organizational anchoring of marketing.

▶ Practical Guidelines

- ☐ Create a simple corporate design and implement it rigorously.
- ☐ Concentrate your activities on the most important target markets.
- ☐ Position yourself as the mouthpiece of the customers and form the bridge from sales to development.
- ☐ Observe alternative technologies and their impact on the business models of the customers.
- ☐ Take into account the cultural and social aspects of other countries.
- ☐ Never underestimate the personal attachment of the customer to the sales person and to the company, even with investment goods.
- ☐ Make your results transparent and communicate alot internally.
- ☐ Build up a global network to recognize country-specific requirements and take these into account.
- ☐ Ensure that you have the backing of the CEO and be persistent.

The Author

Adriana Nuneva

Adriana Nuneva studied Business Administration in Mannheim, and has been Senior Vice-President Global Marketing at Heidelberger Druckmaschinen AG since 2000. She is also head of the global network of the company's own further training academies for customers and employees, and the worldwide network of customer demonstration centers. Before she joined Heidelberg, she worked as a strategic marketing consultant for various companies in Germany and abroad.

Literature Recommendations

K. Backhaus, "Handbuch Industriegütermarketing: Strategien, Instrumente, Anwendungen," Wiesbaden 2004
I. Doole, R. Lowe, "International Marketing Strategy," London 1994
M. Granovetter, "Economic Action and Social Structure: The Problem of Embeddedness," American Journal of Sociology, Vol. 91, No. 3, 1985
C. Homburg, H. Krohmer, "Marketingmanagement, Strategie – Instrumente – Umsetzung – Unternehmensführung," Wiesbaden 2003
H. Meffert, "Ziele und Nutzen der Messebeteiligung von ausstellenden Unternehmen und Besuchern," in: G. Kirchgeorg, W. M. Dornscheidt, W. Giese, N. Stoeck (eds.), Handbuch Messemanagement, Wiesbaden 2003
R. Ziegler, "Psychologische Aspekte des Interaktionsansatzes im Investitionsgütermarketing," in: Kliche, M.; Baaken, T.; Pörner, R. (eds.): Investitionsgütermarketing, Wiesbaden 1990.

Dr. Ralf E. Strauß – SAP AG

Modular Marketing Management
Building block approach for the realignment of the marketing function

▶ Executive Summary

- Growing market saturation and internationalization, in combination with evermore demanding customers, are leading to an increase in competition. The focus is on the improvement of customer satisfaction and on the establishment of a long-term, comprehensive customer orientation and loyalty.
- Against this backdrop, the marketing function needs to be transformed gradually: the orientation to a more strongly individualized marketing approach implies the accurate, mass depiction of all possible customer requirements in the marketing planning, and also in the subsequent implementation.
- The aim is to address the more demanding, more extensively informed customers about the variety of communication channels, and to satisfy their requirements.
- In a market environment that is undergoing such changes, marketing management finds itself increasingly confronted with the challenge of increasing marketing efficiency against sinking marketing budgets, reducing costs, and sustaining marketing successes.
- On the basis of interviews with international marketing managers, and case studies, this article presents a building block concept with which managers can identify weak points in marketing and address these specifically. The systematic integration of the various building blocks forms a stable foundation for successful marketing management.

▶ Building Blocks of Strategic Marketing Management

1. Challenges and proposed solutions in strategic marketing management

If the marketing models are analyzed in detail, it becomes clear that these have changed considerably over the course of time. Into the sixties, entrepreneurial marketing activities followed the mass marketing model, that was replaced in the seventies by a target-group oriented approach in the form of direct marketing. After database marketing concepts, with their strong focus on databases and analysis systems, an approach to comprehensive customer management has been discussed and implemented since the beginning of the nineties. Facilitated by modern information technologies, this approach is referred to as "Customer Relationship Management" (CRM). Whereas in traditionally defined marketing, the tendency was towards short-term oriented sales generation, market share, and the unidirectional information of the customer, in the relationship-oriented approach, the focus is on the establishment of long-term business relationships, the knowledge of individual customers, as well as the (abundant) interaction with individual customers (Strauß/Schoder, 2001). The reason for the increasing focus on the customer lies in the knowledge that, in the majority of cases, dissatisfied customers are irretrievably lost and can also leave negative signals on the respective sales market. The retention of satisfied customers, on the other hand, necessitates considerably lower costs than new customer acquisition and opens up cross-selling potential.

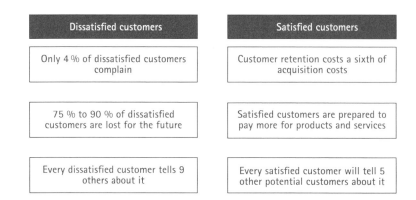

Fig. 1: Comparison of the effects of satisfied and dissatisfied customers (Tiwana, 2001)

Project examples, as well as numerous empirical studies, show that the reasons are complex for inadequate efficiency and target group precision within the scope of existing marketing activities. In addition to wrong forecasts within the scope of the marketing analysis, even companies with international marketing organizations and high volumes of investment cite conceptual and strategic challenges. For example, the discussion arises as to whether certain campaigns could be target-oriented, often with regard to the tactics that are to be conducted, such as mailings or events (Fig. 2). After a decision on a particular tactic has been reached, the strategy, target group, or even the content that is to be communicated, are determined. Answers to fundamental strategic questions – for example, with regard to the communication objective – are often overlaid by tactical discussions. Inadequate customer data systems make a target-group specific approach additionally difficult, and display a customer profiling (attribution) that is defined strongly by company-internal perspectives. With the increasingly international orientation of the marketing organization, experience shows that these types of effect mechanisms intensify. The challenge in marketing management lies, therefore, in overcoming a procedure that is rather more tactically defined, in favor of a thoroughly methodical and strategically secured approach that is specific to the target group.

In the following, means and ways are shown (in the building block concept) in which companies can address the most important challenges in the marketing function in a systematic and target-oriented manner – within the framework of a strategically orientated and conceptually based market communication. Nevertheless, the modular structure of the building blocks should not disguise the fact that marketing is primarily an integration task that needs to be actively shaped and managed. The emphasis here is intentionally on "marketing management": this is intended to underline that the success-oriented implementation and use of all potentials necessitates an active and decision-oriented design with the support of all affiliated functional areas. Case studies and interviews with marketing managers in the German-speaking and Anglo-American regions show that at least five specific and tangible activities lend themselves to operationalization and practice-relevant implementation (Fig. 3):

Marketing planning			Execution (e.g.)			Analysis
1 Marketing strategy and planning	**2** Detailed planning of campaign	**3** Campaign coordination	**4** Data management and target group segmentation	**5** Mailing management	**6** Event	**7** Review and analysis
Understanding of target groups	Use of target groups used so far	Insufficient possibilites in the CRM system	Owner for permanent maintenance of data not defined clearly	Flooding of mails (spamming)	Presentations insufficient	Despite dependency, no comprehensive KPIs beyond marketing and sales
"Binder on the shelf" syndrome	Technical: target group = selection result	Too broad a target group definition (focus on quantity)	No suitable data basis (quality, quantity, topicality)	Insufficient usage of new media	Orientation of different target groups in the variety of topics	No systematic reporting and feedback loop
Understanding of detailed brand requirements	Unclear campaign objective	Overlapping with other campaigns	Ad-hoc-selection based on existing data	Different look and feel	Content preparation unsatisfactory for target group	
Focus unclear: lead generation, awareness, etc.	Mass instead of class (figures instead of composition)	Late planning	No up-to-date attributes/profiling of customers	Future risk of "opt out"	Love of detail vs. mass marketing	
Starting point tactics, not target group	Content from an internal perspective, content not interesting/ differentiated enough for target group	Without a concept as purely tactical for sales	No responsibility for permanent attribute maintenance		No harmonized formats	
No systematic and consistent communication architecture	Unsuitable tactics		No transparency with regard to possible used selection criteria			
	Depiction appropriate to the target groups					
	One-level campaigns					

Fig. 2: Illustration showing examples of challenges along the market value creation chain

Marketing strategy and planning	Data quality	Analysis and KPIs	Campaign execution	Organization
Planning process	Attribute definition	Campaign scorecard	Mailing and event guidelines	Specialist career @marketing
Sales and marketing strategy	Fundamental adjustment	Marketing dashboard	Campaign pre-testing	Team structures
Planning template	Maintenance process	Campaign objective definition	Target group inventory	Campaign coaches
Infocube (collision matrix)	Review mechanism	Marketing balanced scorecard	Presentation rehearsal	Project management
Brand strategy	IT Systems and tools	Contact lead mgmt. process	Agency management	
		Lead calculator		

Fig. 3: Building block concept for marketing transformation

- In the area of marketing planning, the focus is on the planning process, including the marketing strategy, the harmonization with sales planning, as well as the detailing of planned campaigns, through to how frequently the target group is approached with different and possibly conflicting content.
- Data quality embraces areas of action such as the fundamental data adjustment and the integration of all existing customer data systems, as well as the establishment of loops for data maintenance, and the control mechanisms to ensure that data-related processes are adhered to once they have been established.
- Necessary prerequisite for the monitoring of campaign objectives (analysis and KPIs) is the establishment of a contact lead management process that spans sales and marketing. This also permits the depiction of all customer interaction in the IT system, as described below.
- Within the framework of campaign execution, complex methods for ensuring the quality of the implementation, and also the consistency of the market presence, are conceivable, such as communication guidelines or the definition of particular communication formats.
- The implementation is to be ensured by accompanying measures in the area of organization, such as through the development of highly team-oriented structures. An essential element is systematic and continuous project management.

The building blocks shown here overlap in many places. Their full potential is often opened up by their combination with other building blocks. For example, the clear identification of customers and associated user profiles within the framework of customer data management forms the (necessary) basis for a subsequent individualization within the framework of marketing planning. The building block concept thus deliberately depicts heterogeneous categories as being equal, and foregoes taking overlaps and interactions between the individual problem areas and building blocks into account. Here, within the framework of a transformation process, it is important to observe all building blocks as a whole, where possible, and within the framework of an integrated perspective, to holistically reflect on all marketing activities beyond national boundaries. Practical examples in various European countries, for example, show that often up to 40 different building blocks have to be taken into account within the framework of such a transformation approach.

2. Factors of strategic marketing management

2.1 Marketing strategy and planning

The basis of marketing strategy is the analysis of the existing, as well as the future market environment, and the appraisal of the company's own core competences and resources. In the first stage, the focus is on the external market, competition, and customer analysis. In addition to the analysis of existing market structures, it should also be examined which customer segments, and with which requirements profile and sales potential, come into question for which offerings. Here, both classical market research procedures, as well as "share of the wallet" analyses, are used in the framework of the market potential analysis. The competition analysis ultimately focuses on the business models, the positioning, as well as the offerings of competing market participants. The attractiveness and the average profitability of a market segment can be described by factors such as competition intensity between companies, barriers to entry, the existence of substitution products, supplier and customer clout, as well as the availability of complementary products. In the most favorable case, the various analyses already show potential market niches and positioning options in the respective industry segment.

In addition to the classic, mostly quantitative analysis procedures through direct surveys, qualitative survey designs such as morphology and semiometry are lending themselves increasingly. Whereas in semiometry both today's and the desired market positioning from a customer point of view are elicited using more than 200 attributions, in the scope of morphology, the attempt is made to ascertain the real motives of a customer. The focus here is on the issue of the actual motives within the framework of deeply psychological interviews – beyond socially desired answers.

For the determination of target and actual positioning of a brand and the subsequent brand strategy, rational and emotional brand levels are analyzed, for instance, in the framework of SWOT workshops to assist the rational brand evaluation, of the brand value creation chain (brand funnel), or of the emotional brand level (via a semiometric approach). Through the discussion of various positioning spaces, a target positioning can be developed that manifests itself in a guiding principle for the brand. This reflects the desired positioning, and serves as a shift mechanism for the transition to the target positioning, through consistent alignment of the entire brand communication. Building on this, a campaign architecture is developed, within which every campaign has its own idea. All campaign ideas are developed under the guiding principle of the brand, and must contribute to and work for the overall guiding principle of the brand. Every campaign thus receives a specific and also an overall brand task. Together with the marketing and communication strategy, detailed campaign formats can be subsequently defined. A missing or insufficiently operationalized brand strategy leads to inconsistent market communication, and reduces the evaluation of individual campaign elements to the personal intuition of the decision-makers. The operationalization of the brand strategy ideally ends in binding communication guidelines that help to secure the alignment of all marketing activities in conformity with the brand.

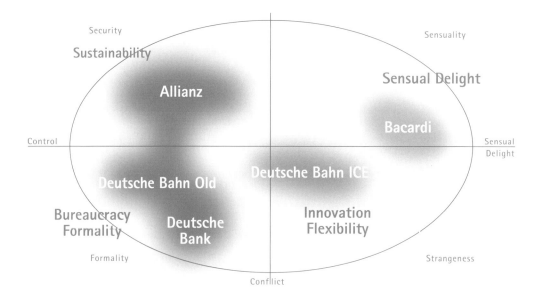

Fig. 4: Example of an illustration of brand perceptions in the framework of semiometry

In addition to the market analysis, a comparison needs to be carried out, among other things, between existing sales, the profit margins or even the sales structures. In the majority of cases, tangible business potential can already be identified or described further on this basis. The exact determination of this business potential opens up the possibility of discussing positioning options in a detailed way, including the respective target group segments that are to be addressed, sales channel strategies, organizational implications, as well as potential strategic partnerships (Strauß/Schoder, 2001).

The process for developing the marketing strategy, and also that of the subsequent planning, is thus based on complex multi-layered content. Differentiated analyses of market potential, typologies, roles in the decision process, and preferred communication channels are also included in the overall company strategy as the basis and prerequisite of the marketing strategy. In individual cases, the coordinated and target-group specific market approach is ensured by a planning workshop for discussion of the marketing plans across all industry and topical areas. Joint workshops lend themselves to the synchronization between sales and marketing planning, within which the detailed bottom-up sales planning is developed, and specific sub-target groups and their respective preferences are discussed. The actual marketing planning is conducted in an extensive "planning workbook," within which all fundamental parameters based on strategy, focus topics, specifications on the preferences of different target groups, through to the planning of all tactical activities, are covered. The inclusion of all campaigns, divided according to industry segments, functions of the contact persons, and topics, permits a differentiated analysis of how often target groups, in which segments and functions, and with which content, are to be addressed over a particular period of time. In practice, the use of a "collision matrix" (Fig. 6) has proven its worth. Within the framework of the campaign coordination, this permits a simplified overview of all planned campaigns, and enables improvement potential (contact strategies) to be elicited early on ex-ante in the approach frequency of individual

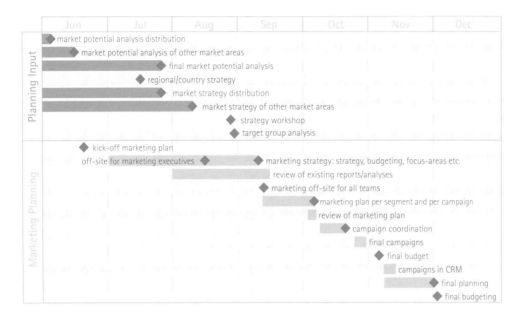

Fig. 5: Example of the procedure in the framework of the marketing planning

target groups. The focus on marketing and campaign planning is on the development and subsequent monitoring of operationalized target specifications and performance indicators (such as an "increase in the brand perception by x percent" or the "y leads in a particular target group for a particular solution offering").

2.2 Data Quality

Case studies and projects show that, in the majority of cases, a systematic survey and maintenance of individual customer data in many companies fails for the same reasons (Strauß/Schoder, 2001).

- Lack of data collection: often, customer data is systematically collected neither passively (for instance, tracking of the customers on the web site), nor actively (direct survey).
- Lack of data aggregation: different sources of information across various functional corporate areas are seldom merged (for instance, technical hotline, ordering service, online behavior).
- Lack of profiling: insufficiently differentiated attributes prevent the profiling of customers according to requirements and/or segments.

At the heart of customer data management lies the merging of the customer data inventories, spread across several corporate divisions, applications, and systems, into one standardized data resource that is accessible across the company. In addition to customer master data (such as the address) and socio-demographic features, action data (for example, marketing activities of the company), reaction and transaction data about the effects of these activities, as well as any eventual potential data, are aggregated here. In addition to the company-internal data sources, customer data can be enriched with external information from address publishing houses, list brokers and market research institutes, behavioral patterns, as well as product preferences. On the basis of these data resources, forecasts can be conducted on the status within the customer life cycle, or aggregated customer values, for instance.

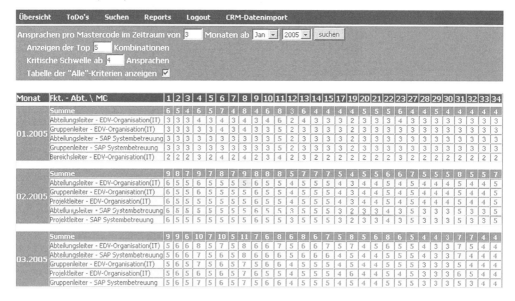

Fig. 6: "Collision matrix" in the framework of campaign planning

In this context, a systematic database management is faced with two essential challenges. Firstly, due to relocations, name changes and the like, every data resource finds itself in a permanent state of updating, that affects 20 percent and more of a data resource within a year. This gives rise to the necessity for constantly ensuring that the data is up to date. Secondly, the duplications that occur in the customer data resources, such as the supplementation with third party addresses and more detailed qualification criteria, necessitate continuous comparison procedures to clean up the addresses. Practical experience shows that, without standard classification facilitated by the same entity (key identifier), the comparison of customer data belonging to different data owners causes considerable problems in the use of automatic matching procedures. In this case, the automatic allocation quotas can sink to just a few percent of the stored data. Accordingly, applications for data cleansing are provided such as:

- Flexibility: possibility to specify tolerance limits of the calibration procedures (degree of focus) for the similarity check.
- Phonetic validation: validation not only of faulty letters, but also of addresses that sound similar, with free parametrization per data field.
- Validation across several data resources: several different data stocks can be synchronized among themselves, whereby different priorities should be given per data field (such as data stock A is leading in the address, data stock B is leading in the name, etc.).
- Fuzzy logic procedure: automatic consideration of different criteria in the classification, dependent on the level of consistency. After an initial verification, additional evaluation criteria are gradually and automatically supplemented within the synchronization, so that the system can adjust itself with an increasing number of cycles, and adapt to the requirements of the data stock currently being verified.

Permanent changes to stock and transaction data, the necessary adjustment of the procedures for data synchronization, as well as the conducting of an advertising performance check, necessitate the establishment of an independent database marketing process. Once the data has been extracted and analyzed, the results of the marketing activities are to be retained permanently in the database, so that all customer experiences can be taken into account for further data analysis and for the activities that build on this analysis (Fig. 7). The attributing of the customer data must fulfill two opposing requirements here: on the one hand, the attributes should be able to depict the true customer requirements as selectively as possible. On the other hand, however, to ensure a pragmatic use, they should be limited in number and, for their maintenance, should be equally understandable across various corporate function areas. A necessary prerequisite is the establishment of a clear "data authority."

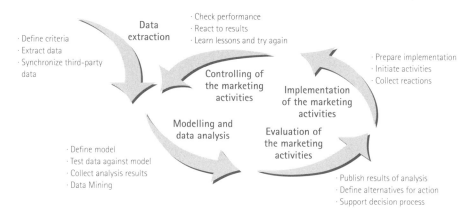

Fig. 7: Database marketing loop

2.3 Analysis and KPIs

Increasingly, marketing managers are faced with the problem of having to accurately prove the value of each activity. Through clearly defined key performance indicators (KPIs), the success can be verified and evaluated. The Balanced Scorecard (BSC) has established itself as a multi-dimensional control and analysis instrument that works with a manageable number of measurable key figures. In doing so, for example, financial performance measurement systems (such as the number of generated leads) can be supplemented by a customer, process, or development perspective. Cause-effect chains between the different perspectives permit the analysis of causal connections (Fig. 8). Deviations from the target can trigger tactical adaptation measures, or contribute to the continuation and/or revision of the adopted marketing planning.

In practice, a campaign scorecard has proven itself to be a specific version of the Balanced Scorecard. This is where all relevant KPIs, such as the number of contacts, leads, and opportunities, are recorded per campaign, up until the figure in the respective contract. Concentrating on a manageable number of KPIs can be supported by a so-called marketing dashboard. In an analogous manner to the dashboard of a car, it shows all the key figures of a BSC that are permanently updated. The necessary requirement for the monitoring of the KPIs is a continuous contact lead management process across all cooperating functional areas. The overall process ensures that, on the one hand, the workflow for processing customer inquiries unfolds without breaks in media and processes. At the same time, the syntactical and semantic standardization of the key figures used is ensured. The objectives of individual areas can be determined within the framework of the marketing planning, for example, through a

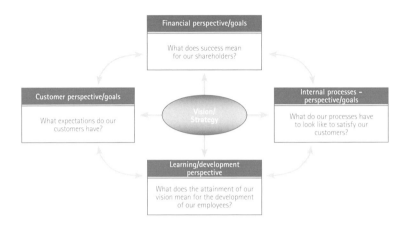

Fig. 8: Perspectives of the Balanced Scorecard

lead calculation for the whole year, that subsequently cam be broken down into individual campaigns. Ideally, the objectives of a respective campaign are already defined in advance with the assistance of "conversion rates" and sales figures (for example, "generate 2000 contacts by 20 leads and 4 contracts"). Analogous procedures lend themselves to non-lead oriented campaign objectives (such as the increase in the level of recognition, etc.).

2.4 Campaign execution

The classical advertising campaign has long been supplemented by events and sponsoring, by Internet campaigns and one-to-one marketing – and this differentiation creates a new marketing problem: ensuring the uniformity of communication is becoming increasingly difficult. Accordingly, the necessity of clear and binding guidelines is growing. These can embrace the entire market communication or have a reduced focus, such as mailing and event guidelines. To control the transfer from guidelines that maintain identity, to campaigns that attract great attention, advertising media can be subjected to pre-testing before it goes live. By having new campaigns assessed by a representation group of test users, under laboratory conditions, breaks in the brand perception are identified – and can be prevented by revision of the advertising media and/or the entire customer sales approach.

In the area of events, there are outstanding examples of how the quality of live communication can already be considerably enhanced by simple presentation rehearsals. In this case, all speakers are asked to give their respective presentations beforehand, in front of a selected (company-internal) audience, and to include their feedback in the presentation and/or the presentation style. Where necessary, the speakers are to be offered media trainers.

Over and over again, the planning of individual campaigns is problematic, as it is conducted for target group segments of sizes that do not really exist. For example, campaigns are designed for the target group of "human resource managers" with a circulation of 2,000 contact persons, whereas in the course of the data selection in the company-internal data resources, only 100 contact persons in the target segment are encountered. The insufficient qualification of existing data resources leads to a delay in execution as additional data qualification measures or even the revision of the campaign concept are necessary. In this case, the use of a target group inventory can prove itself to be worthwhile. Through a target group inventory, the currently available data resources can be analyzed early on in a simple search inquiry with regard to the criteria sought, and then allows either the concept of the campaign to be revised and/or the additionally required qualification measures to be taken into account in the scheduling.

In order to execute an optimally harmonized campaign for every target group in international marketing, agency management is becoming a key activity for marketing departments. Whereas only larger agency networks can offer the infrastructure required for an international campaign, a highly specialized local agency can deliver better results with special tasks, particular media or target groups. The advantage of internationality, and the broader experience spectrum of agency networks, is often contradicted by less flexibility, less target group orientation and the use of standard tools. Experience shows that agency commissions are suitable for gaining transparency about the quality and services, for verifying conditions, and for redefining and/or recompiling the agency pool, where necessary.

2.5 Organization
The following emerge as the most important requirements and design principles of the marketing organization:

- Flexibility: the safeguarding of a sufficient organizational flexibility for adaptation and speed in reaction to high market and competition dynamics. With regard to employees, this mostly means making working time, work content or qualifications more flexible.
- Culture: the substitution of formal organizational structures with distinctive team-oriented organizational cultures, both internally (intra-marketing, internal partners such as Sales), as well as externally (for example, service providers and agencies).
- Innovation speed: as preparation for prompt reaction to changing market conditions and, associated with this, a rapid revision of existing campaigns or services offered.
- Teamwork: ability to cooperate with changing tasks in different roles (Neck/Manz, 1994).
- Integration of functions: horizontal and vertical integration of functions for integrated task processing, for example, by taking over tasks not only in the planning, but also in the execution of campaigns.
- Learning organization: establishment of a learning organization as the permanent continuation of individual know-how, the sustained provision of the competences acquired in the entire organization, as well as the permanent adaptation of the "organizational knowledge" to changing environmental and competitive structures (Daft/Huber, 1987; Strauß, 1996). This can be supported, for example, through team structures, multi-layered marketing training, topic coordinators or also campaign coaches.
- Self-organization: a high degree of self-organization amongst employees and the organizational structure, with great freedom of disposition; associated with this is the formation of a "trust organization" through delegation of responsibility, where possible, to operational levels (Hackman, 1986).

The successful implementation of these design principles requires a high degree of own responsibility from all members of the organization along the value creation processes, and is always accompanied by a high level of organizational decentralization. Linked to this is the prompt formation of teams and interaction across hierarchical levels and functional areas, and the necessity for a culture that permits errors (Schein, 1994).

With regard to the competences available in the company, new areas of competence emerge:

- Competences in innovation management ensure the implementation of the differentiation strategy that the

company is striving for in relation to its competitors. At the heart of innovation management lies the establishment of a standardized process for the systematic development and integration of product and process innovations, for example, innovative customer sales approaches.
- At the same time, the professional selection and monitoring of high-quality content, external service providers and partners requires know-how in alliance management. Alliance management is the permanent analysis of the market with regard to attractive partners (for example, for co-marketing), the development of possible partnership concepts, as well as the permanent maintenance of acquired alliance partners.

In contrast to this, hierarchical forms of coordination often necessitate the overloading of higher-level instances and formal official channels, that hampers the possibilities for coordination of the value creation processes and/or makes them time-consuming. Furthermore, too much third-party organization prevents the perception of requirements on the part of employees with regard to autonomy at work, self-responsibility, and self-realization. The formal framework is provided by defined paths for realizing a specialist or management career, including competence and function profiles that are aligned to the requirements of a marketing department.

To be able to agree very complex, cross-functional and/or international campaigns, that are difficult to agree upon, companies often shape the role of a campaign coach or manager in their marketing organizations. In the role similar to that of a project manager, he or she is to ensure that all the areas involved carry out their tasks, which have been defined beforehand, on time and in accordance with a project plan. The basis for this is often formed by a temporary project organization without direct hierarchical authority of the project manager. This results in:

- the implementation and operationalization of the strategy being ensured across different campaigns and countries,
- the process requirements that occur between these campaigns being optimally aligned with one another in terms of time and content,
- a high degree of transparency about the status of all projects,
- risks and tasks being consolidated and actively managed across different projects,
- the optimal deployment of employees in accordance with their competences being ensured within the framework of all campaign projects,
- a continuous and consistent market sales approach being ensured (Strauß, Schoder, 2001).

▶ Process & Implementation

Practical examples in European and American companies show that the implementation of the building block concept for strategic marketing, as outlined here, ideally also follows a classic project approach. After the detailed analysis of existing weak points in strategy and concept, the building blocks concept needs to be adapted and/or supplemented accordingly. The development of the individual building blocks and fields of activity should be done within the framework of workshops with all divisions that need to be involved in the framework of the marketing value creation chain. After the building blocks concept has been adopted, individual topic areas should be handed over to the responsible specialist divisions for implementation. The early involvement of all functional areas affected ensures that both the proposal solutions developed and the subsequent implementation are carried out in the necessary detailed depth of content, and at the same time, that those affected are involved from the start in the necessary change process.

Reference examples, both in the German-speaking and Anglo-American region, demonstrate that projects like these are normally done in three stages:

- 1st Phase: after a short analysis and concept phase of around eight weeks,
- 2nd Phase: approximately one year is needed for the second phase. For this, a permanent program management is necessary, that is ideally carried out by an external consultant. He or she monitors the implementation in accordance with the project plan set up at the beginning, and ensures that the concepts are not softened in day-to-day business once they have been set up.
- In a 3rd phase, the change processes need to be further monitored for at least another year by use of review weeks and checklists.

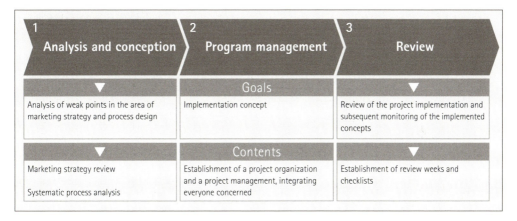

Fig. 9: Marketing management process

▶ Practical Guidelines

- Use the building block concept as a checklist to localize problem areas in the marketing of your company.
- Do not get lost in reflections about the two-way interrelationships between the individual marketing elements; in the majority of cases, starting with individual building blocks is more promising.
- Align the marketing strategy and the marketing planning as early as possible with the market analysis, sales planning, and brand strategy.
- Understand and conduct the improvement of data quality as a continuous process.
- Use the possibilities of the analysis and KPIs systematically to analyze your marketing success and document it as best practice.
- Select the respective optimally suitable agency for the campaign execution – sometimes one with a lot of resources and operating on a global level, sometimes highly specialized and regionally established. Communication guidelines help with a strict implementation.
- Organize your marketing consistently as a learning department that strengthens teamwork and is tolerant of errors.

The Author

Dr. Ralf E. Strauß

Dr. Ralf E. Strauß is Head of Marketing at SAP in Germany and EMEA Central. After earning his degree in Business Administration at Passau University, he completed his doctorate in telematics at Freiburg im Breisgau University. He is a specialist author of more than 50 publications, projects and project management in the area of telecommunications, new media, one-to-one marketing, e-business, Customer Relationship Management, and networked company structures. Dr. Ralf E. Strauß has several years' professional experience in consulting, focusing on the telecommunications and media sector, as well as on e-business. He is also the author of three of the largest and most representative surveys in Germany and Europe on the topic of e business. His book "e-Reality - Auf der Suche nach Spitzenleistungen im e-Business" was published by the FAZ-Verlag in October 2001.

Literature Recommendations

D. A. Aaker, E. Joachimsthaler, "Brand Leadership," New York 2000
S. L. Brown, K. M. Engelhardt, "Competing on the Edge," Boston 1998
R. L. Daft, G. P. Huber, "How Organizations Learn: A Communication Framework," in: Ditomaso, N.; Bacharach, S. (eds.): Research in the Sociology of Organizations, Vol. 5, 1987, pp. 1–36
J. R. Hackman, "The Psychology of Self-Management in Organizations," in: Pallak, M. S.; Perloff, R. O. (eds.): Psychology and Work: Productivity, Change, Emplyoment, Washington 1986, pp. 89–139
A. Kieser, "Fremdorganisation, Selbstorganisation und evolutionäres Management," in: Zeitschrift für die betriebswirtschaftliche Forschung, 1994, No. 3, pp. 199–228
P. Kotler, F. Bliemel, "Marketing-Management: Analyse, Planung und Verwirklichung," 10th edition, Stuttgart 2001
M. Krafft, "Der Kunde im Fokus: Kundennähe, Kundenzufriedenheit, Kundenbindung - und Kundenwert?," in: Die Betriebswirtschaft, 59. Jg., No. 4, 1999, pp. 511–530
C. P. Neck, C. C. Manz, "From Groupthink to Teamthink: Toward the Creation of Constructive Thought Patterns in Self-Managing Work Teams," in: Human Relations, Vol. 47, No. 8, 1994, pp. 929–952
W. Pepels, "Darstellung und Bedeutung des Kundenlebenszeitwerts im Business-to-Business Marketing," in: Helmke, S.; Dangelmaier, W. (eds.): Effektives Customer Relationship Management, Wiesbaden 2001a, pp. 49–84
D. Peppers, M. Rogers, "The one to one future," New York 1993
F. T. Piller, "Mass Customization," 2nd edition, Wiesbaden 2001
R. T. Rust, V. A. Zeithaml, K. N. Lemon, "Driving Customer Equity", New York 2000
E. Schein, "Innovative Cultures and Organizations," in: Allen, T. J.; Scott Morton, M. S. (eds.): Information Technology and the Corporation of the 1990s, New York 1994, pp. 125–146
P. Schnäbele, "Mass Customized Marketing," Wiesbaden 1997
P. B. Seybold, "The Customer Revolution," New York 2001
R. E. Strauß, "Determinanten und Dynamik des Organizational Learning," Wiesbaden 1996
R. E. Strauß, D. Schoder, "eReality. Das e-business-Bausteinkonzept. Strategien und Erfolgsfaktoren für das e-business-Management," Frankfurt am Main 2002

R. E. Strauß, D. Schoder, T. Hummel, The Learning Laboratory – Supporting Learning Organizations with Agent Systems, 1996 IEEE Annual International Engineering Management Conference: "Managing Virtual Enterprises: A Convergence of Communications, Computing and Energy Technologies," Vancouver, August 18–20, 1996, Kanada, January 1996, pp. 611–615

A. Tiwana, "The Essential Guide to Knowledge Management," Upper Saddle River 2001

Prof. Dr. Roland Mattmüller, Dr. Ralph Tunder – European Business School (Oestrich-Winkel, Germany)

Retail Brand Strategy
How retail brands can ensure competitive advantages of trading concerns

▶ Executive Summary

- Many retailers are interchangeable in the eyes of the customers.
- One of the most important success factors to free from interchangeability is to give one's own products or shops a clear image, or in other words: a brand.
- The basic structure of a brand is, in a first step, the positioning of the products as
  - generics,
  - classic private label,
  - premium brand.
- Then the requirements for the product have to be set
  - price-oriented,
  - premium-oriented.

This article will analyze which possibilities proceed from the individual product alone, in order to develop a brand.

▶ Theoretical Model of Retail Brand Strategy

1. Definition

A retail brand strategy can be seen as a "make-or-buy-decision": it can be based on a private label strategy, where three alternatives are conceivable (Mattmüller/Tunder, 2004, pp. 226 f.):

- Product brand,
- Category brand,
- Assortment brand.

Or, it can capitalize on certain activities with manufacturer brands. In this case the retailers take some measures, that serve the reputation of the brand and therefore contribute to their own identity. Two alternatives are conceivable:

- Price leadership,
- Exclusive leadership.

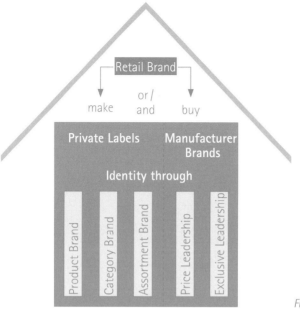

Fig. 1: The house of retail brand

2. Factors of retail brand strategy

2.1 Factors of a private label strategy

2.1.1 Product brand
The product brand corresponds to the classic branded goods concept. The brand is only allocated to a certain product, in which case various differentiating features of the product, like different flavors, and/or package sizes are also included. The discounter Aldi can be named as a typical example of brand management orientated to product brands, which with the brand "Tandil" (heavy-duty detergent) probably stocks one of the most prominent representatives of product brands (Lauer, 2001, p. 18). The advantages of the product brand are that the degrees of freedom and hence also the design possibilities are very great, so that concentrated positioning for a specific target group is definitely possible. The boundaries between the distributor's brand and the manufacturer's brand are therefore hardly noticed. However, in order to achieve an independent brand identity with the product brand, a high level of capital expenditure or a very long period is necessary as in the case of Aldi. One drawback of this strategy is the fact that the development of independence begins with the success of the product brand. As a result herefrom the transfer effect from the product brand to the trading concern decreases. "This effect can only be avoided if the trading concern succeeds in becoming the main image factor itself, as in the case of Aldi." (Bruhn, 2001, p. 33).

2.1.2 Category brand
In the case of the category brand, products covering analogous needs are offered under one and the same brand name. For example, the trading concern Rewe (Germany) groups together its food under the brand "Salto" and its cosmetics under the brand "Today." With this strategy, trading concerns specifically try to achieve synergy effects,

hoping that the greater facing of a brand suggests competence and strength. This hope is cherished as long as the trading concern can, as far as possible, unite the category brand with a benefit philosophy. If the brand gets lost in a greater extension of the category, there is a danger of brand erosion.

2.1.3 Assortment brand
In the case of the assortment brand, the area of application of the brand is spread even wider by being transferred to other products too, that are not in any direct group relationship. However, this greater scope results in an increasing reduction in the level of aspiration of a brand, which is why such a strategy is used more for brands that are positioned in the lower range from the outset. "Ja!" (Rewe) and "A & P" by Tengelmann (Germany) can be mentioned as examples of these brands. The central advantage of this brand strategy is to distribute the cost of keeping the brands over as many products as possible. This can be seen against the disadvantage that the heterogeneity among the products automatically increases. The brand management is then faced with the difficulties of conveying to the customer a problem-solving competence for the brand. It is therefore not surprising that the assortment brand is sold less on the basis of performance and more on the basis of price.

2.2 Factors of a manufacturer brand based strategy

2.2.1 Price leadership
The retailer offers the manufacturers' brands at a low price e.g., by advertising inducements or as part of the concept of "low pricing every day." With this aggressive price strategy the retailer tries to establish an identity as a price leader. The building of the retail brand thus takes place at the expense of the manufacturer's brand. Therefore one speaks of opportunist behavior on the part of the retailers. In this case, the trade uses both the reputation of the manufacturer's brand in general and the price premium associated with the brand in particular as instruments for establishing a specific price competence in relation to its customers. The trade succeeds in doing this particularly when falling back on manufacturer brands that have a high purchase frequency as well as a relatively large amount of room for maneuver from a price-policy, quasi-monopolistic point of view (Bauer/Huber 1997, p. 13; Henning-Bodewig/Kur 1988, pp. 51 f.). In specific terms, the trade deliberately foregoes the enforcement of the price premium of a manufacturer's brand via offers referred to as bait in order to create the impression of being a retailer who is, on the whole, low-priced.

In order to bring about this effect mechanism throughout the specific price competence of the trade, the price premium of a manufacturer brand must fulfill two criteria. On the one hand, it must be recognisable for the customer as well, via the stating of a recommended retail price by the manufacturer and, on the other, this price recommendation must also be accepted by the customer in that he would also be willing to pay the price recommended by the manufacturer. It is with this willingness to pay that price competence comes into play with the trade signaling to its customers a certain "readiness to make sacrifices" with a selling price below the manufacturer's recommended retail price and, at the same time, feigning an apparent saving effect for them. The message "strong brand at a favorable price" communicated by the trade therefore acts as a substitute for the dealer's price-worthiness.

2.2.2 Exclusive leadership
This strategy is the opposite of price leadership. The retailers profit from their selected position as authorized distributors. The high image of the manufacturer brand is intended to give the retailer's identity a boost. Consequently the behavior of the retailer conforms to the ideas of the manufacturers.

The trade makes a specific investment in the management of the manufacturer's brand with its conforming behavior by investing in attractive furniture and fixtures, shop fitting concepts or in the qualification of the staff for example. However, it must be mentioned that these specific investments usually do not relate only to a manufacturer's brand and if in fact they do, are then not based on voluntary choice, but are tantamount to an obligation of the trade within the scope of a distributional restraint system implemented by the manufacturer.

▶ Process & Execution

Purely to consider the process the private label strategy will also be dealt with in this article. The manufacturer based strategy will not be explained, as this would go beyond this article's scope. Crucial elements of this manufacturer-based strategy are still to be dealt with from the manufacturer's perspective. Here, we restrict this article to the trading concern's perspective.

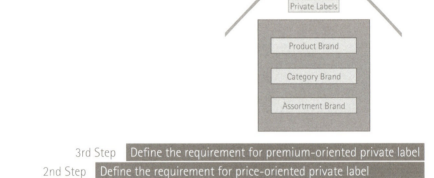

Fig. 2: The three steps to build a retail brand with private labels

Phase 1: Define the positioning of the private label

Brands or products that are positioned worldwide hold possibilities, but also dangers. If a brand or product is introduced to more than one country and its market, it is crucial to know about the differences between the markets. That means knowing about the competition in every market, which is not necessarily the same even if the competitors are identical, but also knowing about general international marketing problems, such as language, national preferences and habits, or distribution issues. Factors that can vary are for example: the purchasing power, the economic situation, the existent retail structure, particularly the discount scene and the general price level. It can be observed that price sensitivity differs explicitly between Germany and Switzerland, that is a result of the above-mentioned factors.

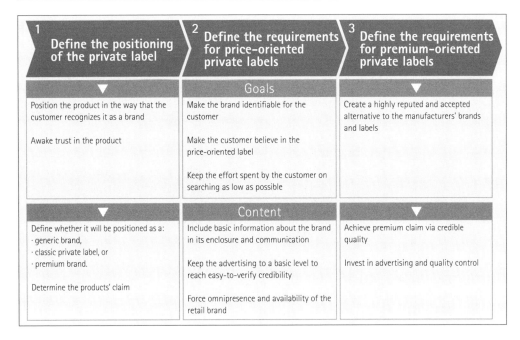

Fig. 3: Process of retail brand strategy

Penetrating means a more difficult coordination and expenditure due to the greater and more complex target group. Furthermore, the manufacturer needs to decide on the basic strategy: international differentiation or standardization. Is the product exactly the same in all countries or are national preferences or habits respected and is the product therefore adapted? Is the product branded identically or are individual brands introduced to facilitate the product's launch? Nationally and internationally, there are three possibilities to position a private label:

1.1 Generics
Generics show the lowest aspiration level with what are referred to as basic products. Their quality merely meets minimum requirements, which is why they range in the price entry level. Originally the retail trade used generics in the early 1970s, in order to defend themselves against the discounters' own brand policy. Meanwhile, however, they serve the purpose of assortment supplement, by rounding off the assortment at the bottom end. Examples of generics in Germany are "Ja" by Rewe or "A & P" by Tengelmann.

1.2 Classic private label
The classic retail brand, such as "Salto" by Rewe or "McNeal" by Peek & Cloppenburg, satisfies the differentiated mass demand. It ranges with regard to quality and price structure in the average level of all comparable products of manufacturers and other trading concerns. In its appearance it is often orientated to the established manufacturer brands, which is why it is also referred to as an imitation brand. Originally, the retail trade intended to set a counterpoint to the manufacturer's brand with the classic private label by having it participate in the market success of the manufacturer brand using aggressive prices. In the course of time the classic brand has become liberated. It is perceived by the customer as the clever alternative in comparison to the manufacturer brand (key word: smart shopper).

1.3 Premium brand

The premium brand ranges at a high price level and also justifies this with the highest demands made on quality, which is why it need not be afraid of being compared with the manufacturer's premium brand. In an accordingly vague way the customer perceives the premium brand as a retail brand as well. The boundaries between the manufacturer brand and the retail brand become fluid with the premium brand at the latest. Examples of premium brands are "Füllhorn" from Rewe or Karstadt's attempt to establish the former manufacturer brand "Dual" as its own brand at the premium level.

Phase 2: Define the requirements for price-oriented private labels

In addition to the international problems mentioned above, the international requirements for price-oriented private labels have to be respected. The nationally different expectations about prices have to be figured out in detail.

2.1 Branding by price-fixing

Branding lies in the nature of the brand. The product is raised out of its anonymity with it, and in that way experiences an external individuality for the customer (Dörtelmann, 1997, p. 77). The primary task of branding is accordingly that the customer distinguishes the retail brand from the manufacturers' brands when purchasing for the first time, and can also find it again in the case of intended repeat purchases. However, this requires that the customer can deduce the particular trading concern from the retail brand. At the same, time the way the branding is done has to set signals with whose help the consumer can carry out a classification of the brand. That means in the case of the price-oriented retail brand that the branding must not be expensive, but should on the contrary emphasize the reasonable prices by means of plainness and simplicity. The price-oriented retail brand sets itself apart from all other products particularly by the simple type and manner of the branding, which in the extreme case goes as far as the emphasized "Non-branding" in the sense of "No Names."

2.2 Price-informative advertising

Without doubt advertising has often had to struggle with credibility problems on the customer's part, since after all, the customer knows the commercially motivated background of the advertising. In particular, the advertising messages that cannot be checked by the customer are mistrusted by him or her as a matter of principle (Kaas, 1990a, p. 50). In contrast, the customer can check price-informative advertising with relatively few problems as regards credibility. Here it is less necessary to convince the customer of certain messages than to supply the relevant and objective price information (Irmscher, 1997, p. 217). With this conveying of information the advertising for price-oriented retail brands simplifies the customer's information process (Mattmüller/Tunder, 2002, pp. 348 f.).

2.3 Shop-specific ubiquity

Basically two demands are made on the retail brand with shop-specific ubiquity. Firstly the omnipresence and availability of the retail brand are meant to ensure that the amount of time and effort spent by the customer on searching and looking for information is kept as low as possible. The price advantage that a price-oriented retail brand promises must not be negated by an extensive search and/or procurement effort. Secondly – and that goes hand-in-hand with the branding – the customer should also be able to allocate the retail brand to the corresponding trading concern, in order to permit a purposeful visit to the point of purchase. In this case not only the cognitive transfer between the retail brand and the point of purchase is of importance, but also the constant availability of the products at the point-of-sale. An "out-of-stock" situation, i.e., the temporary empty placing of price-oriented retail brands would again counteract the price advantage.

Phase 3: Define the requirements for premium-oriented private labels

The customer's willingness to substitute premium-oriented private labels for manufacturer's brands can vary greatly among different nations. This can depend upon the prestige awareness of a culture. The higher a people regards reputation as a crucial factor of society, the more manufacturers' brands are purchased. This has to be respected.

With the premium-orientation the trading concern tries to position its own brand in the upper price and quality segment and thus create an alternative to the leading manufacturers' brands. Since, however, the original product competence still rests with the manufacturer, retail brands can only provide originality to a limited extent. The retail brand thus always appears as a "brand follower," whether actually justified or not. Even if this were not the case, the retail brand is always at least preceded by such a latent reputation. For this reason the premium-oriented retail brand always has difficulty in being defined via sociological or emotional benefit statements. Its premium claim is achieved rather via its credibility with regard to the quality characteristics communicated. The brand thus has a substitution function for credibility (Tunder, 2000, pp. 171 f.). In this connection the customer draws confidence from the expenditure in the setting-up, and the management in the premium-oriented appearance of the retail brand, in the fact that the promised quality characteristics are actually right – even if they refer to characteristics that themselves cannot be checked even after purchase (confidence characteristics).

Accordingly, the premium brand has to meet certain requirements in order to achieve a confidence-promoting effect. These requirements can be understood as being what are known as "exogenous costly signals," i.e., for a trading concern it would, from an economic point of view, not be advisable to feign the meeting of these requirements. The reason for this is to be found in the nature of the "exogenous costly signals," since the cost of achieving this signal effect correlates positively with actual (objective) quality of the product (Spence, 1976, p. 592). Three requirements for the premium-oriented retail brand can be deduced from this:

- High price (together with a high reputation),
- Investments in advertising,
- Investments in quality control.

Even if these three requirements initially incur the same costs regardless of the actual product quality, for the customer they suggest credibility. This is due to the fact that the economic efficiency of these requirements is aligned to the relevant brand being purchased several times and not once. The customer thus possesses a kind of sanctioning power over the promise of quality of the brand. Should he or she have been deceived, there would be no repeat purchase and no refinancing of the requirements for the brand. As a result of this sanctioning power, the potential revenue that a trading concern achieves once with a "dishonest" retail brand remains below the present value of future revenues of an "honest" brand (Klein/Leffer, 1981, p. 624). Seen against this background, the above-mentioned requirements are illuminated more closely.

3.1 High price standard with a high reputation

The inference from a high price of an equally high quality is possible only to a certain degree, for two reasons: firstly the customer can hardly understand the connection between the cash value of the future revenue with the "honest" brand and the profit with a "dishonest" brand. Secondly there are no specific investments associated with the price, which the trading concern has to write off as "sunk costs," if the customer feels deceived (Mattmüller/Tunder, 2002, p. 351).

Under these circumstances, the confidence-building effect of a high price does not act in isolation but together with a "credible transaction environment" (Irmscher, 1997, p. 177), which is in turn manifested in the reputation of the trading concern. The reputation serves the customer in that case finally "as a mirror image of the brand's credibility" (Tunder, 2000, p. 167). In this context the customer understands the reputation as a kind of "hostage in the customer's power whose life is jeopardized again with every purchase" (Kaas, 1990b, p. 545). For this reason the reputation also kindles the expectation in the customer that the trading concern will exercise the necessary care in order not to run the risk of a discrepancy between the price and the actual quality of the products and/or the retail brand (Spremann, 1988, pp. 619 f.).

3.2 Investment in advertising

As already stated, the credibility of advertising is frequently doubted. Since in particular advertising statements regarding certain quality characteristics are based on experience and/or confidence characteristics, no credibility is radiated from them, even initially. It is with corresponding distrust that the customer encounters those advertising claims that raise a brand to a premium level. Nevertheless the customer can draw conclusions from the appropriate investments in advertising to the effect that the retail brand can be trusted. That is to say, the specific advertising investments do not pay off for a trading concern as a rule if they only motivate a one-time purchase. Their amortization requires several repeat purchases. Seen against this background the amount of advertising expenditure has a confidence-building signal effect on the customer. From it the customer gains the impression that the trading concern is only willing to carry out specific advertising investments because it is convinced that it will satisfy the customer and can thus induce him or her to purchase it repeatedly.

3.3 Investment in quality control

Besides the price and the advertising expense the investments in quality control behind a retail brand serve as a further signal to win the customer's trust. In the case of these investments, a relationship applies which is analogous to the one applying to the advertising expenditure. Decisive here are not so much the statements made on quality control, but rather that certain expenditure is incurred or efforts are made to maintain the quality and that these are also conveyed to the customer. These expenses thus also correspond to "exogenous costly signals."

Finally, summing up, it can be stated that the premium-oriented retail brand does not in fact necessarily experience an added value and thus entitlement to a premium from the customer with regard to the sociological or emotional benefit, but as a result of the meeting of certain requirements as regards its credibility that can also satisfy high demands made on the quality. Basically, the reputation of the trading concern and that of the retail brand determine the credibility of the promises of quality. However, this conclusion leads to a paradox, as the reputation of the retail brand depends on credibility, which in turn is actually supposed to be developed by the brand. In the final analysis the premium brand strategy only functions in the case of a retail brand if the company sets the highest quality aspirations for itself and its own brands. Quality control serves also as self-protection in this case in order not to allow any "initial suspicion" of a fall-off in quality to arise as compared with a manufacturer's brand.

3.4 Summarising assessment of opportunities and risks

The building and the management of retail brands require extensive and permanent investments in the brand alongside long-term planning. The decision in favor of a retail brand is consequently associated with a number of opportunities and risks that must be taken into account in advance.

Besides a purely economic consideration, further opportunities and risks in the way retail brands take effect and function must be assessed. In this case attention must be drawn in particular to the possibility of gaining the consumers' trust in the retail brand. This line of argument points to one of the main advantages of strong retail brands – the loyalty potential. As in the above statements concerning the individual forms in which retail brands appear, the loyalty of the customers achieved within the scope of positive image transfers can also be utilized for new business models and sales lines.

In any case, marked loyalty to the retail brand serves the set-up of positions that are easy to defend against competitors. In addition, the trading concern can therefore set up a counterweight to strong manufacturer brands to a certain (restricted) extent. In the clearest case the customer again purchases from a certain trading concern although he or she does not (any longer) find a manufacturer's brand, that was originally looked for by him/her (the strength of the retail brand beats the manufacturer brand). The result is that the retail brand leads to growth in the power of the trading concern as compared with its product suppliers.

In the same way that the positive image transfer can be stated as an opportunity, the danger of negative transfer effects are also highly visible. A poor quality perception of individual articles or of other elements of the business model can have direct negative effects on the business model as a whole. In this case the consumers tend to transfer negative experiences with one product not only to the respective manufacturer but rather also to the whole assortment and hence to the retail brand. "The consumer will in fact still feel a specific individual case to be an exception, but a few such exceptions can, however, cause lasting damage to the image of a retail brand" (Roeb, 2001, p. 297). As a prerequisite for a permanently successful retail brand it must once again be emphasized that the perception of quality by the consumers with regard to all of the articles offered should be harmonized with the particular brand philosophy of the trading concern and/or of the retail brand. This requires pronounced quality management on the part of the trading concern in the assortment area.

The food discounter ALDI demonstrates in a striking way how the strategy of price leadership can be successfully combined with the concept of the retail brand. On the basis of a streamlined assortment of merely 600 to 700 articles, ALDI succeeds in permanently positioning itself in the market as the supplier with the lowest prices. The prerequisite for this is the achievement of a unique cost/benefit ratio by a systematic uniform positioning in the dimensions of price and quality. The assortment predominantly consists of the company's own brands and is supplemented by manufacturers' brands only in individual areas. In order to meet the requirement for a uniform price level ALDI always offers the majority of the products at least at prices that are exactly as low as the lowest comparable offer in the market. With regard to quality, ALDI also makes use of the institution "Stiftung Warentest" (Goods Testing Foundation) in Germany, in order to have the quality level of selected ALDI articles objectively and provably checked. The objective of ALDI here is to reach or even surpass the quality level of the most important brand article of the product category in each case. As this objective is applied to the whole core assortment, this leads to a uniform quality perception on the part of the consumers (Roeb, 2001, p. 304). On the basis of this brand philosophy ALDI succeeds in sustainability promoting the consumers' confidence in its retail brand (Ahlert/Kenning/Schneider, 2000, p. 135).

ALDI therefore combines the different variants of the brand-strategy tactics in particular of individual brands and company brands, whereby the perception of the latter on the part of the consumer clearly predominates ("I buy the champagne from ALDI!"). As a result, and due to its decades of high market presence, ALDI in Germany achieves a profile recognition of 96 percent. Through the combination of high profile recognition and sustainable confidence-building on the basis of a unique cost/benefit ratio ALDI has succeeded in successfully positioning itself as a retail brand in food retailing.

▶ Key Insights

- The consumers' trust in the retail brand as a substitute for the manufacturer's brands must be gained.
- The loyalty potential towards a retailer's brand must be fully tapped.
- Poor quality perception of the retailer's brand products can have direct negative effects. Consumers tend to transfer negative experiences with one product to the respective manufacturer and to the retail brand.

▶ Practical Guidelines

- The building and management of retail brands require extensive and permanent investments in the brand and long-term planning.
- In a first step, the product's positioning (generics/classic private label/premium brand) is defined. Accordingly, the requirements for the product are set (price-oriented/premium-oriented).
- The product's claim and quality must be harmonized with the particular brand philosophy of the trading concern and/or of the retail brand.
- The internationally different requirements must be found out and respected, according to varying market structures and distribution channels.

The Authors

Prof. Dr. Roland Mattmüller

Univ.-Prof. Dr. Roland Mattmüller is Head of the Chair for Strategic Marketing at the EUROPEAN BUSINESS SCHOOL, International University Schloß Reichartshausen. His major fields of research are in Strategic Marketing, Retail and Services Marketing. Besides various activities in the field of international education and further education, he is a lecturer and consultant for enterprises at home and abroad. He is also speaker of the board of the IMMF: Institut für Marketing-Management und Forschung (Institute for Marketing Management and Research), Professor for Marketing at the Sino-German college at the Tongji University in Shanghai as well as a member of various juries and committees.

Dr. Ralph Tunder

Dr. Ralph Tunder is a Junior Professor at the Department for Market-oriented Management at the EUROPEAN BUSINESS SCHOOL, International University Schloß Reichartshausen. His major fields of research are in Strategic Marketing, Trade Marketing, and Branding. Besides various activities in the field of education and further education, he is a lecturer and consultant for enterprises at home and abroad. Before joining the EUROPEAN BUSINESS SCHOOL he did an apprenticeship as an Advertising Merchant with Grey in Düsseldorf.

Literature Recommendations

D. Ahlert, P. Kenning, D. Schneider, "Markenmanagement im Handel. Von der Handelsmarkenführung zum integrierten Markenmanagement in Distributionsnetzen. Strategien, Konzepte, Praxisbeispiele," Wiesbaden 2000

H. H. Bauer, F. Huber, "Der Wert der Marke," Arbeitspapier Nr. 120 des Instituts für Marketing der Universität Mannheim, Mannheim 1997

M. Bruhn, "Bedeutung der Handelsmarke im Markenwettbewerb. Eine Einführung," in: Bruhn, M. (ed.): Handelsmarken. Zukunftsperspektiven der Handelsmarkenpolitik, 3rd revised ed., Stuttgart 2001

T. Dörtelmann, "Marke und Markenführung. Eine institutionentheoretische Analyse," Bochum 1997

F. Henning-Bodewig, A. Kur, "Marke und Verbraucher – Funktionen der Marke in der Marktwirtschaft," Weinheim 1988

M. Irmscher, "Markenwertmanagement. Aufbau und Erhalt von Markenwissen und -vertrauen im Wettbewerb. Eine informationsökonomische Analyse," Frankfurt am Main 1997

K. P. Kaas, "Langfristige Werbewirkung und Brand Equity," in: Werbeforschung und Praxis, No. 3, pp. 48-52, 1990

K. P. Kaas, "Marketing als Bewältigung von Informations- und Unsicherheitsproblemen im Markt," in: DBW – Die Betriebswirtschaft, Vol. 50, No. 4, pp. 539-548, 1990

B. Klein, K. B. Leffler, "The Role of Market Forces in Assuring Contractual Performances," in: Journal of Political Economy, Vol. 89, No. 4, pp. 615-641, 1981

A. Lauer, "Vertriebsschienenprofilierung durch Handelsmarken," Wiesbaden 2001

R. Mattmüller, R. Tunder, "Zur Bedeutung von Marken und Markenwert für Anbieter und Nachfrager," in: Hommel, U./Knecht, T.C. (eds.): Wertorientiertes Start-Up-Management, München, pp. 335-354, 2002

R. Mattmüller, R. Tunder, "Strategisches Handelsmarketing," München 2004

T. Roeb, "Von der Handelsmarke zur Händlermarke. Die Retailbrands als Markenstrategie für den Einzelhandel," in: Bruhn, M. (ed.): Handelsmarken. Zukunftsperspektiven der Handelsmarkenpolitik, 3rd revised ed., Stuttgart 2001

M. A. Spence, "Informational Aspects of Market Structure. An Introduction," in: Quarterly Journal of Economics, Vol. 90, pp. 591-597, 1976

K. Spremann, "Reputation, Garantie und Information," in: ZfB – Zeitschrift für Betriebswirtschaft, Vol. 58., No. 5/6, pp. 613-629, 1988

R. Tunder, "Der Transaktionswert der Hersteller-Handel-Beziehung. Hintergründe, Konzeptualisierung und Implikationen auf Basis der Neuen Institutionenökonomik," Wiesbaden 2000

Barbara Schädler – Fujitsu Siemens Computers

Strategic Marketing Management
Marketing as a long-term management tool

▶ Executive Summary

- Marketing expenditures have become a treasure trove for a number of top financial executives these past few years. When business growth slows, many CFO's perceive this area as the easiest opportunity of lowering costs rapidly and in the long-term.
- Tougher competition and greater cost pressures make it ever more important for a company to align its products strategically to the market and target customer needs.
- Particularly in the case of stagnating markets, providers must leave the well-trodden paths that focus on products and techniques and, rather than dropping prices in order to attract buyers, develop strategies that focus on customers.
- The key component in a customer-oriented product array is the implementation of integrated, strategic and operational marketing at the executive level.
- It is only when knowledge of the wishes, wants, and needs of customers penetrates into the uppermost decision-making levels, and from there in turn, into the organization as a whole, that a company is likely to experience long-term success.

▶ Theoretical Model of Marketing Management

1. Definition and core principle

Strategic marketing management at the executive level allows a company to achieve a marketing impact that is both quantifiable and of high quality. It is only when the marketing function is viewed as being equivalent in importance to production, sales, and finance that it can fully exploit its strategic competence, thereby contributing significantly to the company's long-term success. In contrast to operational marketing activities, that are frequently aimed primarily at original and creative execution, strategic marketing management must guarantee that the customer remains the central focus of business activities – at all times and regardless of the company's position in the market.

In order to secure good long-term results, products, strategies, processes, and marketing activities must be aligned to the customer's needs. Indeed, successful companies are able to anticipate their customer's wishes so far in advance that their range of offerings continue to correspond to market requirements for another two to three years.

Four problem areas
What happens in a company in which marketing is decentralized and operates at a lower level? Four problem areas can be identified.

Fig. 1: Strategic marketing model at the executive level

Problem 1: Marketing as marcom

Marketing is often equated with marketing communication and advertising – an inadequate interpretation. Such an oversimplification of the function has several disadvantages:

- Marketing (= "advertising") is only thought of at the very end – when a product has already been developed and produced. Then the creative crew is supposed to think up campaigns in order to "flog the stuff."
- If marketing is confused with advertising, the risk arises that a product manager who has received no central guidelines will operate freely according to his own ideas. For a group with a variety of product divisions and numerous products, the results can be disastrous – customers are confronted with a welter of advertising activities, resulting in a dilution of the company's positioning.
- Last but not least, with such an oversimplified understanding of marketing, its pivotal function between development, production, and sales cannot be fulfilled. A significant portion of the company's value creation chain is missing.

Problem 2: Internal resistance

Marketing must create a need for the company's products amongst customers – in other words, it must generate demand. But before specialists are in a position to do this, there are frequently in-house hurdles to be surmounted, particularly the following three:

- To date, many (managing) employees have given little thought to the topic of marketing. The "old school" colleagues in many cases grew up in a sellers' market and cannot fully relate to the transformation to a buyers' market.
- In many companies, cost-reduction is currently paramount. The rule is to manufacture as cheaply as possible and to lower costs, and when in doubt, preferably in marketing.
- Marketing has a difficult time vis-à-vis financial control, partially because its impact is not measured, in the case of many companies (although this is clearly possible), as compared to a production site that has a quantifiable output and for which profit share and contribution can be measured in a precise manner on a regular basis.

Problem 3: Decentralized marketing
Marketing that is not closely linked to corporate management

- cannot plan strategically and for the long-term,
- is dependent on decisions by colleagues/supervisors that may not correspond to the market,
- is limited to conducting short-term campaigns to advertise products already produced,
- struggles for internal recognition and for the chance to set a course for the future with its valuable knowledge,
- is not included in management decisions,
- is perceived as a cost factor that supposedly does not produce measurable results,
- expends double and triple the amount of funds necessary for marketing activities, because individual product divisions/branches do not coordinate with each other,
- cannot establish an image that spans all products, because in certain circumstances, each individual responsible for marketing is in pursuit of his/her own objectives,
- cannot create a (global) recognition factor,
- dilutes the company's public image,
- cannot weigh in with its market knowledge in corporate decisions early enough,
- cannot contribute to product development,
- cannot influence strategic corporate development,
- is reduced to one of the various marketing functions – a service function for sales.

Problem 4: Potential areas of conflict in introducing centralized marketing
At first glance, however, a centralized structure harbors risks, too. Because local sales or marketing staff want to

- address their regional target groups individually,
- create and time their campaigns themselves,
- have their own budgets,
- prevent supervisory entities from intervening in their areas.

1.3 Core tasks of a centralized marketing function
Centralized marketing on the other hand wants to

- guarantee a uniform brand image,
- implement cost-effective and efficient campaigns,
- network service providers,
- achieve integrated communication via all channels,
- enhance cost efficiencies for the organization as a whole,
- generate as much demand as possible with clearly planned resources,
- perform integrated marketing success measurement.

2. Factors

2.1 Marketing as an entrepreneurial philosophy
Whether a one-man operation, a mid-sized company or a global player – whoever wants to establish themselves long-term in the market and secure sustainable profits, must not view marketing simply as an operational function.

Marketing is an entrepreneurial type of thinking. It is, of course, not enough to simply want to be customer-oriented. This customer orientation must also be implemented and become a consistent way of life. This will only succeed, however, if the uppermost management level thinks in marketing terms. It's fine if the CEO can participate with the required understanding and know-how. As the top decision-maker, however, he must give consideration to a number of divisions. So it is important, in the interests of a common goal, that a marketing professional has a voice at the Executive Board level.

It is not enough to merely equip the sales function with supposedly powerful sales arguments and send them off to the customer. Whether the company is selling

- a customer benefit
- or a gadget that only makes product development happy,

is not decided during the sales discussion, but much earlier. Starting with product development, through manufacture, to service, the customers and the market must be the central focus of all efforts. This is the only way a product or service will emerge that stimulates enthusiasm and motivates buyers.

Topic: Companies need a market-oriented function – and this can only be provided by integrating marketing into senior management!

Marketing must see itself as the unit in the company that assists all corporate divisions in market orientation. Marketing can, however, only fulfill this important task, if it is lodged high up in the hierarchy. Marketing must be a strategic management responsibility, just as is the case with the Finance and Production divisions.

2.2 Marketing as a market-oriented corporate function

According to a study conducted by the market research company Market Lab, 79.4 percent of German start-ups do not reflect on their (potential) customers, whom they urgently need in order to succeed in the market after the establishment phase has been completed and the production phase begun. The "Happy Engineering" phenomenon is rife. Many new companies – and not infrequently larger groups – develop new products without sparing a thought as to whether these new developments are needed or even wanted on the market.

Companies that place their marketing function at the strategic management level can easily avoid these development failures. For if a function with in-depth knowledge of the current market and future trends participates in the decision-making process, then dubious products from the customer's perspective are (as a rule) identified earlier and costly development failures avoided as a result.

2.3 Healthy conflicts

It is not marketing's task to promote every product, but rather to generate demand for the various product lines and the company as a whole. Of course, such a definition always leads to "healthy conflicts" between marketing and sales. In case of doubt, most sales staff always want a short-term sales promotion from marketing.

It is not enough for marketing from a strategic perspective to concentrate on short-term demand generation; rather, an understanding of how customer needs develop in the medium and long-term must exist. Marketing should, therefore, always keep a slightly longer period – up to approximately three years – in view. It is the task of marketing to bring the customer perspective into the company – not the individual customer perspective of the sales manager, but the representative customer perspective that is, in part, determined by market research.

2.4 Influence on processes, products and strategies
Situating marketing at the executive level ensures that strategies key to corporate success become reality, too. In particular for large companies with a large number of products and branches, this implies

- that the marketing chief must manage employees outside of his department in other marketing functions via reporting lines or at least functionally,
- that his/her competencies must impact vertically through the hierarchical levels, as well as horizontally over all product groups and customer segments,
- that every marketing area to be found throughout a group cooperates closely with headquarters,
- that the marketing organization in countries has to be structurally linked to the central marketing department with clear interfaces.

This allows for more intelligent savings opportunities than a crude cutting of the advertising and promotion budgets.

2.5 Customer focus
Marketing from a strategic perspective not only envisions today and today's customers, but the markets of tomorrow as well. The Marketing Director can set a course in-house to ensure that market orientation functions in various aspects:

- in the case of market analysis,
- in the case of marketing planning,
- in the case of project management and the implementation of planned activities,
- in measuring marketing impact,
- in the pivotal function between product development, sales and service.

Marketing is the interpreter that allows the world of technicians to communicate with the world of sales. It translates the wishes of the respective colleagues, who often do not speak the same language and helps

- determine,
- better address,
- and satisfy

the customers' needs. But what are the customers' needs? Companies must focus on the following:

- What problems does the customer wish to solve?
- Which benefits does he wish to buy?
- What demands does he have in this connection?
- What situation is he in?
- How can you help him?
- What solution will he be comfortable with?

Most companies make the mistake of answering these questions themselves. Not infrequently, they miss the point and their creation flops.

2.6 The task: marketing must bring the representative customer perspective to the company

An essential marketing task is to determine

- what the customers want,
- and how they are most easily accessible with respect to product benefits.

Every branch and every product division does not need to conduct such studies themselves. It would be a waste of resources to generate a multiplicity of market studies and customer analyses.

A central marketing function can work much more efficiently since it can

- exploit synergy,
- draw conclusions from a networked analysis,
- contribute integrated expert knowledge
- consistently think from a market perspective, in other words, place the customers' wishes in the center of corporate management.

CASE Digression: even legendary entrepreneurs such as Henry Ford have continued to manufacture for a disappearing market

Because markets and customers change, companies must regularly review their strategies and adapt them to new conditions. If this is neglected, setbacks, such as that experienced by Henry Ford, are risked. He sold his legendary "Model T" fifteen million times over and earned huge profits due to assembly line manufacture, that cut costs, and his concentration on the one model only (black, simple, and affordable). However while his competitors started to offer cars with extras, Ford held tightly to his limited selection. Since he had given the market what it wanted, he simply assumed that the market continued to want the same thing: a simple, inexpensive car with a uniform appearance. His ignorance was punished by dramatic losses.

"Most companies can barely resist the appeal of drastically reduced unit costs with rising production. The profit outlook is breath-taking. All efforts are geared towards optimizing production. The consequence is that marketing is neglected," criticized Harvard Professor Ted Levitt as early as 1960 in his famous article "Marketing Myopia" in the Harvard Business Review. He accused companies of being short-sighted with respect to marketing: the most important responsibility of a company was to satisfy customer needs and not to produce goods willy-nilly.

In the IT field as well, suppliers in the early years followed the (in this regard bad) example of Henry Ford: higher unit numbers, lower prices. But what had happened to the customer?

2.7 Develop customer benefits

"Hardware manufacturers" and traditional IT service providers have been used to thinking in bits and bytes and not in their customers' dimensions," warn Stephan Kloess and Manuel J. Kreutz of the consultancy Nexum Strategy in Zurich. For an IT sales person's discussion partner, however, the speed or capacity of a computer is less important than the question of how the solution offered assists him in his day-to-day business. The goal, therefore, is to provide the customer with solutions, not blank products. For customers

- do not buy a drill, but a neat hole in the wall,
- do not buy software for their computers, but greater working ease, time savings, or simply entertainment.

Or as Harley Davidson puts it: "We sell an attitude towards life – the motorcycle is thrown in for free." Marketing must also support the company in defending the price credibility argument. Although thrift may be appealing, most customers are indeed prepared to pay more for good quality and service and, as always, for the provider's image.

3. Conclusion: marketing as a leadership function

Central integrated marketing thus plays an indispensable role: strategically, it ensures that all marketing functions cooperate efficiently and are pulling together, so that the company can operate successfully in the market. In addition, it assumes a pivotal function among different corporate divisions – by better and more competitively satisfying customer demands.

▶ Process & Implementation

The Fujitsu Siemens Computers Case

Strategic marketing management is a leadership and management responsibility that should generally be situated at a company's Executive Board level, regardless of size and industry. Operational implementation, however, depends on the particular corporate environment, which is why we are demonstrating the process based on the specific example of Fujitsu Siemens Computers, that completely reorganized its marketing function between 2002 and 2005.

1. The position of marketing at Fujitsu Siemens Computers prior to reorganization – problem areas

Today marketing at Fujitsu Siemens Computers is a cross-functional executive function that helps to align the company strategically to customer requirements. This was not always the case. Prior to the restructuring, marketing departments and functions were located in a number of corporate areas.

- There were dedicated marketing departments, such as marketing communication or partner and alliance management.
- A department for corporate communication existed, and product marketing colleagues occupied positions in individual product divisions.

- Other marketing colleagues in turn were located in the sales companies.
- Moreover, due to a lack of central support, there were marketing functions in many corporate divisions, that provided the absolute minimum of marketing support in varying degrees of quality.
- There was barely any communication between all these units of marketing responsibility, much less coordination or common goals. The term "marketing plan" was unknown and marketing measurement not even contemplated.

1.1 Reasons for the problem situation

This non-strategic and non-functional distribution of competencies was rooted in the company's recent past. Fujitsu Siemens Computers, created in 1999 from the merger between the hardware divisions of Fujitsu Ltd. Europe and Siemens AG, was a joint venture in which many structures were still being established. Responsible managers, therefore, who needed marketing support, simply found a few marketing people themselves and placed them in their divisions. It was for this reason, for instance, that the service division was responsible for the company's web site for a long time – of course, not networked with other functions, however.

1.2 Consequences of decentralization

In the long-term this situation was found to be unsatisfactory, not just by the Executive Board, but by the marketing managers themselves. The consequences of the decentralized structure were:

- Internal turf battles were fostered.
- Business concentration was thus prevented.
- Conflicts regularly had to be escalated to the Sales Manager or even CEO level.
- Budgeting was rudimentary and when it occurred, it was only on an individual basis rather than spanning all departments.
- Funds were not used according to objectives or in a quantifiable or strategic fashion.
- Or at the end of the year it was noted that the marketing budgets as a whole had been significantly exceeded, simply because each division was somewhat over budget.

1.3 Missing functions

Functions that were absent:

- a marketing strategy geared towards the corporate strategy and business plans,
- common directions spanning all departments,
- integrated rather than individual budgets,
- measurement of marketing success,
- financial marketing control,
- systematic lead generation and closed loop processes,
- adequate sales support,
- clear authorities regarding instructions.

The only marketing functions represented company-wide were the communication divisions of corporate communication and marketing communication.

2. Goals of the reorganization

The goal of the wholesale restructuring was to establish integrated and coordinated marketing according to the following specifications:

- the marketing organization was to be organized anew – with transparent roles, competencies, and interfaces,
- efficiency and quantifiability of the function was to be increased,
- marketing expenditures to be lowered,
- end-to-end marketing processes to be generated,
- focus to be aimed at customer needs,
- brand to be strengthened.

3. Four preliminary considerations

3.1 Consideration no. 1: synergies can be consistently exploited only with a central infrastructure

Fujitsu Siemens Computers decided to dispense with a purely product-line oriented marketing function during the first reorganization discussions. Only a true integration guarantees access to joint resources. After all, a large company is only justified when it actually utilizes the synergistic effects offered. Otherwise it may as well be transformed into a holding with four or five legally autonomous companies. In a marketing organization geared strictly towards product lines, however, each division would have to have its own corporate communication, events management, market research, etc. Such an organization would be inefficient to an extraordinary degree. Moreover, with an integrated, functionally designed marketing organization, services can be provided from headquarters that can be used, not only by the individual product divisions, but also by the various country branches.

3.2 Consideration no. 2: one-to-many approach from the beginning

An intensive one-to-many approach in marketing comprised part of the considerations from the start. This approach not only increases efficiency, but reinforces the company's overall strategic alignment. It is important to offer an integrated appearance to customers – not just with the brand, a uniform corporate design and corporate identity, but with all announcements, products, and programs.

3.3 Consideration no. 3: promote cooperation amongst marketing functions

The history of the various marketing functions found throughout the company prior to the reorganization, was a particular challenge. Most department chiefs had created teams that were responsible, for instance, for event organization or campaign management for their own divisions. These overlapping activity fields had to disappear in the new integrated marketing organization. They represented an enormous source of inefficiency and moreover, as a rule, quality problems. In addition, the various marketing divisions were to work together at the point of go-to-market and demand generation, providing their respective know-how.

3.4 Consideration no. 4: link central integration and regional know-how

In integrating and coordinating Fujitsu Siemens Computers' marketing function, the point was not to disable the sales marketing functions or to merge them with central marketing. As always, cultural, legal, and economic differences play a huge role, especially in Europe. So the aim was always to link integration and the utilization of regional customer and market expertise.

4. The position of marketing in the company as a whole – new orientation in three steps

- Even before the substantive, as well as organizational, new orientation, there was an Executive Vice President for Sales, Marketing, and Customer Services. But during the first two years, this individual had to put a strong emphasis on sales processes and sales structures, with an immediate positive impact on profits. The new marketing orientation was to take place in the second step.
- In July of 2002, a working group of marketing managers recommended to the Executive Board that a Chief of Marketing function should be introduced. On October 1st, 2002, this function was created and I assumed its responsibilities. As Chief of Marketing, I reported to Bernd Bischoff, then Head of Sales, Marketing, and Customer Services for just two years.
- When Bernd Bischoff rose to President and CEO of the German-Japanese joint venture in the summer of 2004, he aimed his focus primarily on the company's continued strategic development in parallel with its operational excellence. As of July 1st 2004, marketing became an executive function and I was appointed Vice President Corporate Marketing.

Fig. 2: Corporate organisation

5. The process

The new orientation of the marketing organization was implemented in three phases:

Phase 1: Marketing planning and marketing structure

1.1 An overview of the new marketing infrastructure

In the new structure, there is no marketing division that does not report functionally or, in some cases, directly to the VP Corporate Marketing. The following report to the VP Corporate Marketing functionally or directly:

Fig. 3: Marketing organization process

- Marketing operations: marketing planning, market assessment and research, marketing infrastructure, and process development.
- Marketing alliances and partners: with software partners and system integrators such as SAP, Intel, Microsoft, Oracle, Siemens Business Services, Accenture, and numerous medium-sized and smaller partners.
- Corporate communications: traditional PR and press affairs, internal communication, Intranet, analyst communication.

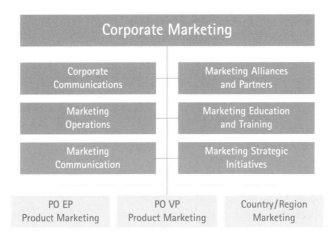

Fig. 4: Corporate marketing organization

Strategic Marketing Management 207

- Marketing communication: brand management, advertising, on-line marketing, events, publishing.
- Marketing education and training: pre-sales, sales and post-sales services for employees and 30000 reseller partners. Since Fujitsu Siemens Computers sells exclusively via these partners in the small and medium enterprise market, these training sessions are a significant component of our cooperation with partners.
- Marketing strategic initiatives: a staff position for special strategic tasks.

The following are functionally linked via a matrix organization with the Vice President Corporate Marketing and the central marketing function:

- Sales marketing, situated in 25 sales companies. The marketing organization in those countries was structured in such a fashion that clear interfaces to the central marketing organization now exist.
- Product marketing that belongs to the two Product Operations.
- Marketing financial control, which relates to the function of Chief Financial Officer.

1.2 Marketing planning: analysis instruments for increased customer orientation

Fujitsu Siemens Computers constantly gives consideration to customer benefits and to providing solutions and products in this regard. Above and beyond its coordination and integration function, the Marketing Operations division bears the responsibility of continuously developing the marketing back-end. This involves measuring achievement of marketing goals or defining and implementing the closed-loop marketing processes for the company as a whole. No information should be lost, business opportunities should be grasped at the right moment. Here, too, the customers are the central focus of considerations, since without integrated processes and information, the topics that interest them individually cannot be specifically addressed.

The RAD matrix (Retention Acquisition Development) is central to the new strategic and analytical orientation. This is a customer database analysis with which marketing control and sales management refines the major customer segment. It offers answers to the following questions:

- Which customers are currently in the acquisition phase?
- Does every sales company have sufficient focus on this segment to grow?
- Which products are sales selling, and at what profit margins, to customers who have long been the company's partners?
- Do up-selling and cross-selling opportunities exist?

When used consistently and continuously, this instrument helps to align the marketing structure better to the customer needs, and to manage sales strategically.

Phase 2: Project management

Implementation of sound process management: marketing operations as the core of the new organization

Fujitsu Siemens Computers created an entirely new department for process definition and implementation, integrated marketing planning, and project management for plan execution two years ago – Marketing Operations.

This department is at the core of the new organization. Market assessment and market research – in other words, those employees who provide the company with market intelligence and, thus, essential knowledge about the customers and their wishes – form part of this structure.

The program office, the central coordination team in the marketing operations department, is responsible for marketing planning. Marketing plans specific to customer segments and product lines are prepared here – plans that supply marketing basis support.

Actual demand and lead generation occurs via the marketing topic plans, also newly implemented. These GTMs are oriented towards specific customer wishes above and beyond the hardware. In concise terms – it is not the box that makes the difference, but the fact that Fujitsu Siemens Computers thinks about its customers and offers them solutions for specific problems.

Fujitsu Siemens Computers divides its customers into

- Large companies (large enterprise segment – the major sales generator),
- Mid-sized companies (small and medium enterprise segment), and
- Private customers (consumer segment).

All these areas of the company are incorporated in the preparation of the go-to-market plans. The sales marketing departments, with headquarters support, roll out these programs in all sales regions in Europe, the Middle East, and Africa, in which Fujitsu Siemens Computers is present. The marketing topic plans, together with the corporate marketing plan of all marketing areas, provides the company with the direction and the common approach for the fiscal year. They are the core of integrated and coordinated marketing.

Phase 3: Efficiency measurement

Efficiency measurement in the end-to-end process

Measurement of the marketing impact on the business is indispensable in an end-to-end marketing process. In the marketing departments themselves, the concern often arises that such efficiency measures will primarily be used to make life difficult for employees working there, since they now have to prove the success of their work. Fujitsu Siemens Computers' approach is different – marketing measurement is attributed a high value, because the marketing impact on the business cannot in fact be proven without such measurement. And if this impact is not proven, then marketing will always be the first place a company looks to for cost savings. In other words, this is not about control. It is only by means of efficiency measurement that a return on investment for marketing can be determined. This much is certain: it is only a marketing measurement system set up for the relevant marketing organization and the specific company that can succeed in convincing CEO's that marketing cannot be perceived as a cost center, but rather as the company's investment in its customers, the market, and its own future.

▶ Key Insights

- ☐ Marketing is a company's market alignment function, and thus an indispensable key to success.
- ☐ Marketing should be an executive function, also because "healthy conflicts" must be generated between product development, sales and marketing in order to achieve the best results. This is in part why we talk about strategic marketing management at the executive level.
- ☐ Marketing must bring the representative market and customer perspective to the company, so that all the company's processes, products and strategies can be directed towards customer needs.
- ☐ Marketing shouldn't focus itself on only a single product line, but must reflect the entirety of a company, both organizationally and substantively. Only the totality of products determines the specific value of a company and its differentiation potential.
- ☐ Marketing must be orientated towards the medium- and long-term for sustained success (what are the most important products to be offered in the future?) and should not restrict itself to short-term sales support.
- ☐ It is not marketing's task to sell individual products, but rather to stimulate general demand, not just for current sales periods, but for future sales periods as well.
- ☐ Marketing's task in an IT company is to translate technology into customer benefits from the product development to the product marketing stage.
- ☐ Last but not least: Marketing must deliver measurable results. The aim is to increase business, not busyness.

▶ Practical Guidelines

- ☐ Make clear the importance of marketing as strategic success factor within your company.
- ☐ Clarify that marketing is not a cost center, but an innovation center and key investment. Locate the marketing function at the top management level.
- ☐ Change the company's structures so that strategies and ideas can flow from top to bottom, and vice versa, rapidly and without bureaucracy.
- ☐ Strictly align your corporate strategy to customer needs. Only those who align their business activities to the customer will achieve long-term market success.
- ☐ Integrate all employees in the marketing concept and illustrate to everyone what customer alignment can signify for him or her individually on the job.
- ☐ Measure the success of your marketing strategies and activities. This is the only way in which you will obtain the internal support and recognition (from colleagues in other departments) that you need for your work.

The Author

Barbara Schädler

Barbara Schädler has been with Fujitsu Siemens Computers since 2000. Previously she was head of Corporate Communications at the energy provider RWE Energie, and from 1994 to 1998, Press Chief for the German Ministry of Finance and Ministerial Spokesperson. Barbara has been head of the Marketing & Communications division at Fujitsu Siemens Computers since October 2002. She has been a member of the Executive Council since July of 2004. Since October 2005 she is Chief Marketing Officer at Fujitsu Siemens Computers.

Christina Rüter – Schwarzkopf Professional Haircare

Tailor-Made Marketing (B2B)

The marketing evolution from a product focus to a holistic business focus creating real added value for the customer.

▶ Executive Summary

"Profit in business comes from repeat customers, customers that boast about your project or service, and that bring friends with them."

W. Edwards Deming

- Competitiveness today requires a stronger customer focus and a more holistic perspective in our offers. A "technical" product focus is no longer sufficient enough to satisfy the existing customer, win new customers, and/or create a long-term customer relationship with higher barriers to changing a supplier.
- The highest level of service to our customers comes always with a tailor-made solution. In order to be able to offer Tailor-Made Marketing, a standardized marketing concept has to be developed that offers enough flexibility and room for adaptation to create marketing measures satisfying the individual customer's need.
- The case study outlined in this article explains the creation of an international business solution program that enables the sales and key account division to drive the customer's business with individual and target oriented marketing measures. These measures will create real added value to the customer's business and a win-win-situation for both companies.
- This change of business towards a holistic service requires a change not only in the mindset of the employees but also in the appropriate structure, resources, and people within the company.
- Results of Tailor-Made Marketing:

  - Increasing customer satisfaction.
  - Strong winning reasons for prospect customers to join.
  - Stronger binding factors for existing customers.
  - Higher prices and profits due to unique and tailor-made offers.
  - Job enrichment within sales organisation.
  - An internal emotional "pride" factor.

▶ Theoretical Model of Tailor-Made Marketing

1. Definition and core principle

Tailor-Made Marketing involves the transformation from a classical product focused marketing to a value added marketing, offering holistic business solutions rather than single products to the customer.

Stage 1: The focus on a core product offer

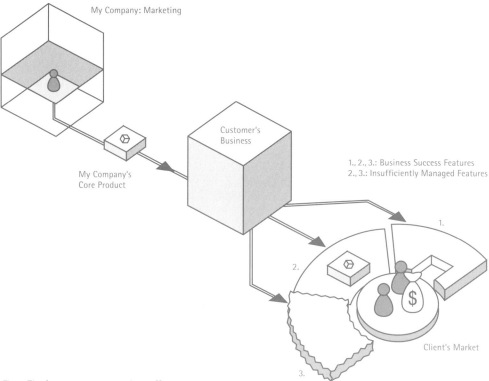

Fig. 1: The focus on a core product offer

Originally a company's focus was dedicated to a specific product offer reflecting the company's core competence. The marketing activities were strongly absorbed by the ongoing effort to maximize and update the product benefits and build the product awareness and success in the market. The marketing teams were in danger of being driven by single product features rather than taking into consideration how and what the customer might need in a wider and holistic business sense and perspective. The Stage 1 model illustrates that the core product is therefore only relevant in one of the three business success factors in capturing the customer. That means that the company's offer only solves one single business answer and other business success factors are not satisfied within the company's portfolio.

Market background and development

In a B2B environment there is often a very trustful and close relationship between the company and their customer. As it is not a mass market approach, individual business offers and personal relationships play a major role in binding the customer and developing the business into a reciprocal win-win approach. In order to compete successfully and to increase the customer base further, the company has to offer more than the "single" core product. The customer is looking for holistic business solutions. This market demand is visually reflected in Stage 2 of the marketing model.

Stage 2: The holistic business solution approach

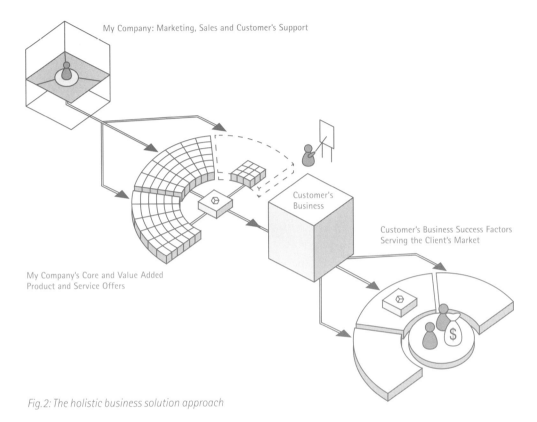

Fig. 2: The holistic business solution approach

A crucial internal understanding has to take place within the company's internal structure. In order to be able to develop holistic business solutions, the marketing knowledge has to be merged with sales experience, and client support knowledge. This creates a strong knowledge pool detailing the customer's business and their demands. The more these three departments bring their competencies together, the higher is the success rate in developing new value added products and/or service offers. The core product should be complemented by other products and service offers reflecting the business success factors of the customer.

The overall targets behind these new offers should be to:

- enlarge the company's portfolio with customer-driven offers,
- maximise the business success of the customer,
- enhance the mutual business relationship,
- bind the customer closer to the company,
- increase the company's turnover and profit,
- reduce internal fluctuation.

2. Factors of Tailor-Made Marketing

2.1 The company's departments and competencies
Marketing: The expertise about the product features and benefits is essential. New product ideas and product improvements should be developed on the basis of market research. Product launches and re-launches are the final outcome of the marketing efforts.

Sales: The expertise about the customer and their business demands. Through their daily contacts the sales team observes the customer's business habits and understands what kind of activities may be required to further bind the customer to the company and extend the company's portfolio. The sales force knowledge contains a detailed information pool about the customers. These "business" driven sales people require a sophisticated business consultation profile.

Customer support: The expertise and knowledge of the customer's business success factors. The customer support team knows exactly how to run and drive the existing customer's business operations. Its members' background could be derived from the customer's business itself. Because of its solid understanding of the customer's business, the customer support team is often able to develop new product and service offers, creating at the same time a business link to the company's core product.

2.2 The company's core product and extended product and service offers
Core product offer: This is the originally manufactured product that is the base of the company's portfolio. A detailed core product knowledge lies within the company and often has a long history of manufacturing underlining the company's reputation and image.

Extended product offers: these are the new product offers that are developed around the core product, enhancing the product usage and binding the customer closer to the company. Targets for these extended products should be to answer to a concrete business issue for the customer or make the application and usage of the core product easier, more economical, quicker, more beautiful and fun.

Extended service offers: these are the new service offers that are developed on the basis of an understanding of the customer's success factors. The company's targets for these services are to increase the customer's business success and find new ways to bind the customer, emotionally but at the same time financially.

2.3 The customer's business success factors
- Success factor 1: the technique, the original "handcraft" or core that is offered and sold to the clients of the customer's business. In our case this is the handcraft of cutting and coloring hair within the hairdressing industry.
- Success factor 2: the business knowledge of the customer translates into the rational side of the business. The knowledge of the customer is often the financial driver of their business.
- Success factor 3: the service knowledge of the customer, including ideas and approaches on how to win and bind clients to the business through service quality and offers.

All success factors are enhanced by a solid base of clients' data showing clients' demographic details, purchasing behavior, retention rates, satisfaction rates, and overall behavior and demand trends.

CASE The hairdressing industry

Company background
Schwarzkopf Professional is the hairdressing division of Henkel's cosmetic business sector and is a truly global business with its main markets in Japan, U.K., Spain, Germany, France, Oceania, and Russia.

Fig. 3: Website of Schwarzkopf Professional

Customer background
The hairdresser is looking for one main partner or supplier for the technical products offering color and form. In the retail segments of care and styling products, the hairdressers offer in most cases multi-brands from different suppliers. All these products represent the core products of Schwarzkopf Professional with a long history and expertise of research, development, and production.

Market need and company development
In order to create a stronger bind between the hairdresser and Schwarzkopf and gain a competitive advantage, there existed an obvious need to enhance the company's portfolio into a more holistic and business-driven direction. This development needed not only top management support but had also to be found in the right people with the right skills in the appropriate positions. A new department was developed in the area of customer support, named Professional Partner Service. Here the team's background was based around a solid understanding of the hairdressing operations. Often, working experience in hairdressing salons supported this understanding. As the hairdressing business is a very emotional industry with strong "intuitive" success factors the emotional skills are crucial for a successful team. The new team developed ideas and approaches on how to improve Schwarzkopf's portfolio into a stronger hairdressing-driven direction and offer new tools and services that were truly dedicated to the hairdresser's operation and business success. On the one hand, these are emotional service factors and image driven aspects reflecting the hairdressing spirit, on the other hand, practical and operational tools that were developed for making the hairdressing life easier, more professional, and effective. The challenge for Schwarzkopf was to bring the Marketing experts together with the Professional Partner experts in order to develop products, services, and tools that are connected to the core products (of color, form, care and styling) and at the same time create new business opportunities for future turnover and profit.

Within the fusion process of the Marketing and the Professional Partner Teams a third area of competence was obviously required for developing the international structure. This was the "rational" business area that was another field for potential new offers. Here the experience and knowledge of sales people was needed, combined with conceptual skills about how to develop new business tools and approaches. This is referred to as the area of "Business Sales." The closer Marketing, Professional Partner Services, and Business Sales join their expertise, their creativity, and hairdressing understanding, the greater the possibility to develop new and real added value products, services, tools, and approaches for the customer. These new offers have a great potential to demonstrate to the customer that Schwarzkopf truly understands the hairdressing business and is able to provide the customer with the right solution for their hairdressing business needs. This means much more than a "classical" offer of color, form, care, or styling products, it is business solutions for any relevant hairdressing need.

CASE In order to illustrate an example of the newly developed business tools, the following case will explain the creation of an international Business Solution Program.

Market background, segmentation, and needs

The hairdressing market is divided into different customer segments. There are many criteria to define these market segments. Here are a few example criteria:

Quantitative segmentation
- Annual turnover of the salon group and per salon.
- Number of salons.
- Number of employees per salon.
- Relative price level (in comparison with the local price index) of salon services.

Qualitative segmentation
- Image and design quality.
- Creative reputation.
- Technical skill level of employees.
- Professional business and marketing concepts.

According to the different market segments, different key customer groups are defined. These groups require different support levels from Schwarzkopf and, as well, the company's differentiating business growth potential.

For example a bigger-sized salon group with 50 salons in the middle price segments with a lower image and design quality, lower creative reputation, and low professional level of business and marketing concepts translates into a high growth potential for the business through active client oriented measures. Therefore there is high interest in acquiring professional support in these fields from the industry partner.

The kind of support measures needed for a customer are very individual and therefore there is no standardized tailor-made support plan.

Tailor-made support measures are, however, expensive to develop and execute, and the customer is usually not willing to pay too high a price for these measures.

Objective of the Business Support Program
The target was a standardized approach that offered enough flexibility to adapt the business measures to the individual business requirement. The Business Support Program would be a "tool box" from which standardized trade marketing measures were offered to the customer with room for modification according to the needs of the individual salon.

▶ Process & Execution

"A vision without action is a daydream, an action without vision is a nightmare."

Phase 1: Understand your customer's business and need

- Use your customers and also any existing in-house experts to completely understand the relevant business questions your customer faces. Consider all relevant areas beyond your products' offer to fully develop a holistic picture of all the core success factors necessary for your customer's business.
- Approaches: interview and hold focus groups with customers and in-house experts who have a deep understanding of the customers' business and needs (e.g., Sales, Customer Support, and Marketing).
- Data research: analyze your customer business patterns based on market studies. Cluster your customers in segments accordingly and discover what kind of business support they receive from where, as this might indicate service gaps with a potential for future tools.
- Use existing ideas and approaches that have already been developed in local markets and check their success rate.

CASE In the past Schwarzkopf offered different support measures, such as marketing activities, for different customer groups. However, these measures were time bound and always dedicated to one specific target (e.g., increase the color share of the salon). As the customers' business situation varies from salon to salon and over time as well, these "standard" activities were not flexible enough to satisfy the customer or to realize the highest business potential of the salon at the time. The development of the Business Solution Program needed a clear understanding of the most relevant business opportunities that the salons would have. Therefore the Schwarzkopf team of Trade Marketing & Sales started to analyze all the different but crucial salon opportunities. Internal workshops with brainstorming sessions started the process, and also interviews with selected customers gained additional insights. After a good month of work, a selection of the most important business opportunities was developed.

Examples of business opportunities for salons:

- Gain new clients.
- Gain client's loyalty.

- Increase client bill through retail sales.
- Increase color business.
- Increase team motivation.
- Create salon awareness.

Phase 2: Business concept and business plan

- Create a comprehensive concept for the business tool in order to be able to sell it internally. An agency might support this process with the visualization of the idea.
- Analyze the value that the support tool will generate for your customer. On the basis of this estimation a financial calculation should be possible to define the income.
- The costs of the tools need a rough technical concept, including cost and timing proposals. These financials are then the base for the business plan.

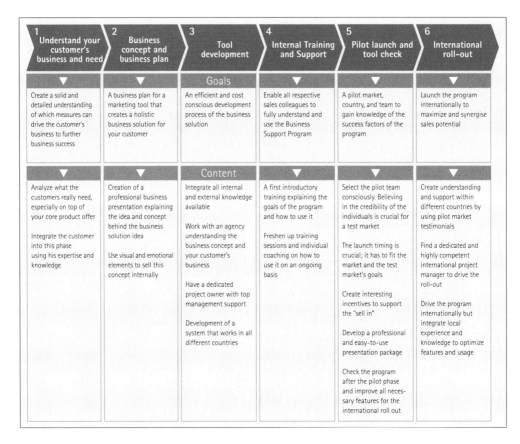

Fig. 4: Tailor-made marketing process

CASE   The first generation of the Business Support Program was developed not internationally but on a local level. Therefore the concept, as well as the technical side, was focused around the requirements of the specific country. This had the advantage of a quick and pragmatic technical solution, however, one not suitable for international usage. As the success of this tool was not yet proven, it seemed obvious to test and utilize the tool in one country first. The concept was driven by the local Key Account Team, where the customer need for tailor-made solutions was very strong. A local agency developed proposals for the technical concept as well as the look and feel of this program. These proposals were discussed particulary in terms of easy usage and practicability. The entire Key Account Team was heavily involved in the discussion and decision process as they would be the key users for the program. The more the key users felt comfortable and involved in the program's development, the greater the acceptance was which was experienced later during the launch phase.

Phase 3: Tool development

- According to the business concept the requirements of the tool have to be specified and defined. These requirements have to be checked with the user's profile and skills.
- The content should be defined by internal experience and external benchmarks. The internal experience should be gained at an international level, as local knowledge and ideas enrich the content development process. Evaluate as well the competition's offer (if there is one) and analyze other branches to see if there are content ideas available.
- Find the right agency and partner for the tool development. They have to fully understand the business concept, as well your customer's requirements and the relevant market environment.
- A local agency in the pilot country could have the advantage of local knowledge and efficient working procedures.
- Find internally an appropriate project manager who is dedicated to drive this project to success. As well, a "mentor" on a high management level helps to support the project against any internal obstacles, especially if this project explores a new business area for the company where there might be barriers internally.
- If there is a technical system involved, the technical requirements for thc international system should be discussed at an early stage with the respective IT departments – both in the pilot country and on an international level.

CASE   The first generation of tool development in the pilot country took nearly six months to initiate. The target was to have a very comprehensive program with many activities to be as flexible as possible and was also to utilize any successful promotional ideas or concepts from the past. Here the trade marketing expert was the driver of the project while the technical concept was provided by the agency. This local approach of the program was centered on software, including the use of a CD Rom that combined PDF files. This solution was pragmatic for the first launch, but was however, not suitable for the international roll-out. Therefore the second generation international system later included a completely new technical concept and was programmed as an interactive website, which was downloadable on to a CD Rom. The advantage of the first and second generation tools was clearly an educational opportunity to learn from experiences in the pilot country. We were able to improve all weak elements of the first generation while drawing on all the strong elements that were proven in the pilot country. The international roll-out in other countries was also supported by the local experience of the pilot country.

Other countries' teams quickly believed in the program and understood the impact that this tool could create for their country's success. The disadvantage of the local pilot phase was that we had to build the program more or less completely anew which translated into additional budget and time resources costs.

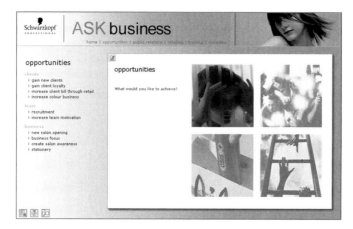

Fig. 5: The Business Solution Program: introduction page

Phase 4: Internal training and support

- If you explore a new business area for your company be aware that you have to intensively train all the internal users in the use of the new business tool. This is crucial for successful acceptance and its usage in front of the customer.
- Internal training is especially of importance for sales people, but will cost time and money. This has to be clear to all involved departments, including top management. It is of importance because if the users don't feel 100 percent comfortable with the new business tool, they will not use it in an effective and winning manner in front of the customer.
- If your business tool is somehow connected to your business IT, the technical implementation has to be 100 percent perfect. Any technical faults will endanger the whole tool not to work effectively. This might cause the users not to use the tool.

CASE   How much training is appropriate for a new business tool? In the pilot country introductory training included some role playing activities based on how to use the new tool with a customer. However, some of the users did not feel as comfortable with the program as was necessary to present the tool in a professional manner to the customer. The training needs depended very much on the individual skill profile of the user. Some needed more technical, IT, and usage training; others required more content training. Individual coaching sessions, after the introductory training, helped to support learning on an individual level. Training should be delivered as a permanent support action to the team. The introductory sessions initiate the training and fulfill the requirement to explain the overall tool and its basic functionalities. The ongoing training and coaching should then answer all the questions that will come with the use of the program by the customer. It is important to clarify the responsibility of the training and appoint someone who has the right skills and at the same time enough impact and the appropriate competence, to instruct all users to become program experts.

Phase 5: Pilot launch and tool check

- Find a test market within your organization to launch the tools in order to gain experience and feedback for all countries. The test market should fulfill some criteria:

  - a dedicated team that believes in the tool and its benefits, and also has the resources to develop and launch the project,
  - a market environment that is ready for this new tool and approach,
  - a strong position of the pilot country as internal credibility is vital to the international roll-out process later.

- The closer the international department and the pilot country work together, the better the chance that the pilot tool will be used without too many modifications at the international level. Make sure that the project manager in the pilot country feels closely connected to the international department that is responsible for the project.
- Timing is crucial for a new business tool. Find the right launch month when there is enough time for the sales force to explain the tool and therefore have enough focus and support behind it.
- Support the launch with incentives for the sales force. For some of the more traditional sales people there might be a barrier to "sell" and present a service – not a product – beyond the core product offer. An incentive can help to motivate them to present the system.
- Offer presentation support for the first launch phase using dedicated people from internal departments such as Trade Marketing or Customer Service. This prevents the sales people feeling "left alone" with the new tool.
- The price and costs of the tools need to be 100% clear to all internal users of the program. Make sure that the basic training includes how to sell the price of the new service to the customer.

CASE The launch phase took longer than expected. Although the launch timing was good and there was enough focus behind the program, the sales team and the customers as well had to get used to this completely new offer from Schwarzkopf. Time and support was needed at an individual level to make the main advantages of the program clearer to the customer and to allow for the development of enough trust and belief in the new system. The support was important from the head of sales and national management who backed the program and actively asked for feedback and launch results. This created an internal awareness of the importance of this tool as an essential aspect of the company's focus and as a "normal" part of the product portfolio. Success stories of individual customers about how the program was utilized helped to create the belief and success drive within the internal departments. We also used individual success stories to create other customers' belief in the program. This gave strong credibility and helped the roll-out in the first launch phase. Customers' testimonials should be used in the presentations to other customers. The outcomes of the individual measures of the program have to be monitored and analyzed. If there are weak measures in the program they should be eliminated as soon as possible. The strong ones have to be celebrated and shared with internal users and customers. Feedback and results are crucial for the successful launch of a tool that was not part of the company's core product range before.

Tailor made elements of this activity are an individual Salon Logo, a percentage off price, and copy elements. The modification can be done directly on the laptop of the Schwarzkopf user; the program

Fig. 6: This is one example of a Trade Marketing Measure from the Business Solution Program. Business Opportunity: Gain new clients

generates the final stage of this creative artwork activity and is sent directly to the printing house. This ensures an effective and very fast production time.

Phase 6: International roll-out

- Use the experience and success stories from the pilot country for the international launch of the tool to other countries. Invite the key drivers of the pilot country to international presentations and meetings to celebrate their success with the international audience. This gives a high pride factor to the "heroes" of the pilot country and creates strong credibility for the tool.
- Use customer testimonials from the pilot country and later different countries to underline the benefits of the tools.
- The international system has to fulfill other requirements than a local system. This makes the process more complex. Make sure that the international project manager understands the local and international requirements for the system in order to be able to develop it in the right direction. Again, the teamwork between the pilot country and the international department is crucial to eliminate local weaknesses and allow for the development of a future-oriented international system.

CASE   As the first and local generation of the Business Solution Program did not offer enough flexibility in terms of language adaptations, international accessibility, and update opportunities, we had to build a completely new technical system for the program. This took another six months with a new agency using better and more advanced technology.

The international generation offers advanced functionalities and is much more economical for all the other countries than the first local generation. The synergies of the international approach were obvious and the countries are able to launch their local version, based on the international system, with an economical budget and high quality.

The content and the look and feel of the program as well are driven and controlled by the international department. It is important to understand that the international program is an open and flexible system, that can be improved and further developed, based on the local experience of the countries. The exchange of these experiences is crucial for the information flow and the development potential of the program.

▶ Key Insights

- The deep knowledge of your customer's business is the starting point for successful Tailor-Made Marketing.
- The belief and the development of added value tools on top of your "classical" product offer is a strategic decision that needs to be promoted and endorsed by the top management.
- The development of these new offers creates an impact on all levels of the company – possibly even through new departments, new human resource profiles, and new training approaches for employees.
- Time to market is crucial for these tools. If a pilot country develops the tool, allow the international department to join the development process in order to avoid local solutions and to build international approaches from the very beginning.
- There must be a clear and profitable business plan behind the new tools.
- Always develop the tool from an international perspective, this saves time and budget expenses for the international roll-out later.

▶ Practical Guidelines

- Have a strong believer and mentor in the top management for these new approaches and tools – this will generate credibility and support on all levels of the company!
- Do not outsource the development of these added value tools – it is crucial business knowledge that you generate and create within your organization!
- Be sure that the whole company understands the new direction and strategy behind these added value tools!
- Involve your customers with the development and the sales process, they know the requirements and they can contribute great testimonials!
- Find both international and local/national project managers dedicated to the tool in order to have a strong engine behind the project while maximizing local knowledge with international features and aspects.

The Author

Christina Rüter

After studying economics, the author worked for 11 years for Unilever and Schwarzkopf & Henkel in various management functions and regions in International Marketing and Sales. She is responsible for international business support for Key Accounts within International Strategic Sales.

Literature Recommendations

S. C. Lundin, H. Paul, J. Christensen, "Fish! Ein ungewöhnliches Motivationsbuch," München 2003
R. A. Buckingham, "Customer Once, Client Forever: 12 Tools for Building Lifetime Business Relationships," 2001

Annegret Reinhardt-Lehmann, Nicole Ebner – Fraport AG

Marketing Organization Efficiency
Management competence and organizational culture as levers for improving marketing efficiency

▶ Executive Summary

- The cost efficiency of goods and services defines the level of a company's competitiveness.
- Specific cost and revenue patterns are recorded and modified with the aid of various analysis and measurement procedures. Marketing efficiency is mostly mentioned in this context in order to assess the financial impact of marketing decisions, and to be able to use budgets more efficiently.
- The organizational shift of controlling into corporate divisions such as marketing and corporate communications – areas that, up until now, have been defined more by a qualitative understanding of performance measurement – shows the growing influence of results orientation on market orientation.
- Measurement procedures and instruments can only make a contribution to recording efficiency. Management tasks such as the formulation of objectives, the implementation of strategies, the creation of organizational structures, the development of ideas, the communication of knowledge, and strategic decision-making still remain the principal levers for improving efficiency and effectiveness.
- This is of particular relevance for marketing, because it is connected to other corporate divisions via a large number of interfaces.

▶ Theoretical Model of Marketing Efficiency

1. Definition

The terms efficiency and effectiveness are often not differentiated from one another. The following definition helps to clarify the difference:

- Marketing effectiveness describes an objective or result. "Effectiveness is doing the right things."
- Marketing efficiency refers to the process of implementation. "Efficiency is doing the things right."

This gives rise to a close interdependence. After all, doing the right thing properly is a substantive prerequisite for successful marketing. Often, however, the mutual dependence ends in the conflict between the two principles. An activity that can increase the efficiency of goods and services, such as the economization of a process step in customer care, does not necessarily increase its effectiveness at the same time. Often, it actually reduces it. In this thoroughly problematical interrelationship, marketing controlling provides instruments and methods that permit continuous feedback between the original plan, its actual development, and the ultimately effective result. On this basis, adaptation activities are made or deviations anticipated.

Fig. 1: Influencing factors on marketing efficiency (source: Fraport AG)

2. Factors

2.1 Importance of marketing

Marketing can acquire different importance in an organization. In American companies, market orientation is very pronounced, which is why marketing is usually an important strategic function here. Most European companies give greater weighting to results orientation. Here, the management has a special focus on strategic controlling. In addition to this influence of economic culture on the corporate philosophy, the respective industrial sector, in which the company operates with its services, particularly with regard to the sector-specific competitive intensity, has an influence on the significance of marketing. It is, not infrequently, the case that marketing is confronted with pejorative prejudices in the division of responsibilities within the company.

- Marketing is a philosophy. What counts is selling in the hard, everyday world of sales.
- Marketing is a "cash burner." You don't earn money by looking after your image; other people are always responsible for the actual result.
- Marketing sits in the ivory tower and follows any trend it likes.
- Marketing managers are aloof theorists with no operational know-how. They spread anglicisms, create colorful pictures, and know nothing about the business.

In view of this conflict potential, activities for increasing the efficiency of marketing should initially concentrate on breaking down prejudices like these, even if the spreading of stereotypical ideas is part of everyday corporate life. Proof of the effectiveness of activities that have been carried out, and their contribution to value creation in a company, are particularly suited for refuting clichés that have a negative effect on the marketing function.

2.2 Organization

Depending on the importance of marketing, marketing tasks are perceived as peripheral activities by other departments, are assigned to Sales, or are organizationally anchored as an independent department next to Sales. In some companies, Sales is, in turn, assigned to Marketing. Only in this case we can speak of integrated marketing that places its emphasis on the strategic and conceptual level, and adopts corresponding directive functions. Hybrid forms of centralized and decentralized marketing and sales organizations are by all means prevalent, mainly in large companies and corporate groups. Arising problems which can have a negative influence on the level of efficiency achieved, are:

- lack of decision competencies.
- different priorities.
- coordination effort and process intensity.
- unclear responsibilities, internal competition and redundancy.
- self-orientation instead of customer orientation.

The transformation of organizations does not allow any long-term, optimal structures. To limit, where possible, the listed frictional losses in marketing to a minimum, considerations regarding the organizational structure should primarily take into account the customer interface along the business processes of the company or group, along with its brand strategy. The following applies in the case of an umbrella brand strategy: The more contact points one and the same customer has with the various products or services of a company, the more the marketing and sales organization should be integrated or coordinated. An appropriate example is given by the organizational dynamics of Deutsche Telekom AG, that satisfied this necessity by reintegrating independent subsidiaries to the parent company. In contrast, a small number of overlaps at the customer interface, or a single brand strategy, require a lower level of integration. Here, the proximity to other departments is often more important.

The organizational structure can, therefore, make a decisive contribution to clearly defined responsibilities and decision competences. However, efficient processes between interacting departments, parent companies and subsidiaries or teams can only then be realized if roles, tasks, and interfaces are defined so clearly that at least theoretical requirements for the division of work have been created. Particular attention is to be paid to semantics. They are often the vehicle to formally record self-interests "without these being noticed."

2.3 Communication

Despite regulations with regard to organizational structure, self-interests, non-transparency, and other barriers to the transfer of knowledge can hinder efficient cooperation. This can occur between companies and departments, as well as within departments. The result of this is an on-going deficit in circulating information, or an out-of-hand communication culture of meetings and group sessions, every participant has a voice in. Here, the potential for increasing efficiency lies in meaningfully structured communication, as well as in the use of instruments that bring transparency to processes and the tasks of individual employees or divisions. These include:

- immediate formal communication possibilities, such as meetings.
- formal communication and information options transmitted via media.
- informal communication options.

The removal of barriers is best encouraged through the direct cooperation of all players. Meetings that take place within the framework of this cooperation must always follow a specific objective and a fixed agenda, so that they do not become a time trap. Only employees who can make a specific contribution or are directly affected in their field of work should take part.

There are many technical auxiliary instruments for the formally transmitted exchange of information. They extend from joint drives through SAP applications, to Internet-based portals or databases. However, communication cannot be reduced to this level, for technology alone cannot ensure either the exchange of information or the finding of objectives. Only continual usage by all participants turns it into an efficient tool. The prerequisite for this is a common understanding and similar priorities. The introduction of CRM technologies without a preceding strategy process, for example, does in no way solve the classic question of whom the customer or contact belongs to.

A further important type of communication is informal communication. It promotes the formation of networks that can speed up decision processes enormously, and is of particular relevance especially in the context of international cooperation. Furthermore, unofficial information is also passed on through it. While planning and implementing activities, the undocumented knowledge about company processes, and the comprehension of situations are very important sources.

2.4 Competence and leadership

Power ambitions and corresponding conflicts that can be found on all levels of the organization also lead to frictional losses. The interest of those involved consists of influencing matters in such a way that they can be used for individual benefit or for individual profiling. In their interaction, specialists and executives are confronted with many behavioral strategies, that serve to enforce the own will of individual players by using all the possibilities that present themselves and, thus, to slow down or completely prevent decision processes. Assuming that specialist competence is available, this hurdle to efficiency places high demands on the social, personal and, in the framework of international cooperation, intercultural competence of the marketing management, that interacts with other divisions, companies or teams.

There is no patent remedy for handling power struggles and conflicts successfully. Neutrality, results orientation, objectivity and the ability to recognize the interests of other players, and to analyze these with emotional distance, are vital. In the majority of cases, addressing conflicts openly also helps. Marketing managers find this neutrality and ability for abstraction very difficult, particularly when they are dealing intensively with a task or a project and have corresponding responsibility. Instead of driving the process on reflexively, there is a risk of resignation. The desire for recognition is supposedly thwarted by its opposite. This emotional problem needs to be overcome.

If conflict situations are particularly muddled, escalation can help. So that this leads to an efficient solution, the authority above must be prepared to intervene, make decisions, delegate tasks to the right department, and network the players. Working on cross-divisional or cross-company tasks, this can only succeed if marketing is accepted at board level, and if those responsible are also in agreement about the fundamental orientation. If this culture is not lived, the inefficient motto "loyalty before agreement" usually applies.

2.5 Marketing process

A systematized marketing process is also an indispensable prerequisite for marketing efficiency. If marketing only enjoys a low level of attention, the tasks are often limited to operative marketing or ad-hoc activities that primarily serve as direct support to the board or individual divisional heads. These often include ad-hoc activities and goodwill measures that barely have sustainable impact. Marketing activities do not develop their full impact until they have been checked for their effectiveness, and have been planned and implemented coherently with regard to both time and content. Without a systematic process, activities to increase efficiency also end in cost reduction activities that are planned in the short-term, and that have a negative impact on the effectiveness and performance of marketing.

The marketing process is an element of a market-oriented corporate management and, in most companies, is not distinguished from the tasks of corporate or business field development. "Analysis of the internal and external environment," "strategic corporate planning," "strategic marketing planning," "operative marketing planning," "implementation," as well as "control and feedback," are named as typical stages in the process. The dilemma of interpretation is shown in the example of marketing planning. "Determination of strategic business development objectives," "evolution of market development strategies," etc., are seen as top management, but not as marketing tasks. The comprehension problem lies in the fact that marketing is not recognized as a cross-sectional function, and is reduced to department level. Irrespective of which department initiates and controls the process and the company-wide implementation of the individual steps, process thinking and process management make the fundamental contribution to marketing efficiency.

2.5.1 Marketing planning
In the marketing planning phase, corporate, financial, and marketing objectives are first harmonized with one another. Together with the portfolio of a company, as well as information and key figures from the market, they form the normative planning framework. Focusing results from this higher-level target specification, that forms the basis for finding the strategy, planning activities, and allocating the budget. Only when these are linked with one another efficiency and effectiveness in marketing can be increased.

2.5.2 Implementation and performance measurement
Focusing makes an essential contribution to efficient actions and effectiveness. However, it only serves as a lever if adherence to outdated customs can be overcome, if innovations have a chance, if conflicts of distribution are prevented, and if all decision-makers support the overall corporate alignment. For this, these must be closely involved in the planning process. This is the only way to ensure that strategy objectives receive tactical counterparts, activities are implemented in a mandatory manner, necessary resources are made available, and that procurement synergies are used.

Poor implementation makes any planning process obsolete. It also has a negative impact on the implementation of performance measurements, as these do not only supply the basis for adaptations to goals, but also reveal weak points in results and processes. Reasons for why marketing performance is not measured are mostly:

- the controls are perceived as intervention or punishment,
- marketing managers are already occupied with the next task,
- setting up a suitable measurement procedure takes too long,
- there is basically no management interest in key marketing figures,
- existing instruments are not used further after reorganizations.

2.6 Marketing controlling
Controlling and marketing have different planning horizons, that can be illustrated, for example, in how they use budgets. Marketing views marketing expenditure as an investment in the future and in the establishment of long-term values. Controlling understands it as positions without quantifiable benefit that can potentially be deleted

in the short-term. However, both disciplines are essential functions for market-oriented corporate management. Furthermore, marketing without performance measurement is not capable of depicting its contribution to value creation. Controlling is therefore one of its most important support functions.

Interdisciplinary conflicts are founded in mutual prejudices and in the apparently incompatible methods of the two approaches. Implementing special marketing controlling processes has an efficiency-enhancing impact when it

- supplies marketing management with information about customers, competitors, market partners, and the brand,
- provides a management system that permits an overview of the marketing instruments, depicts the implementation of activities in a transparent way and, thus, facilitates coordination,
- controls the marketing performance by conducting checks on both results and procedures. Performance measurements should be coupled closely to the provision of information, so as to generate a benefit for the marketing manager.

The requirements of marketing controlling, therefore, exceed the performance measurement of the marketing process and include analyses of the organization, management, competence, coordination, and communication. And this is also true for companies and groups that operate at international level.

Marketing controlling has a multitude of different analytical methods at its disposal. The evaluation of a campaign's results of course necessitates the use of other instruments besides the analysis of the marketing efficiency or the marketing performance. The conducting of a marketing audit is a suitable measure for uncovering weak points in the

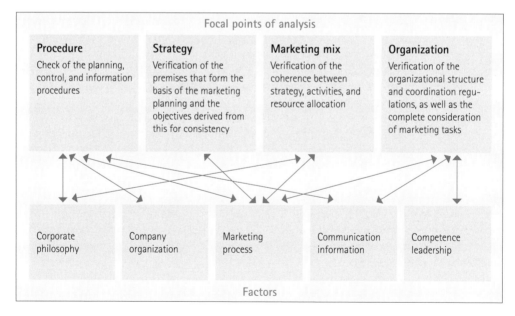

Fig. 2: Depiction of examples of interdependencies between focal points of analysis and efficiency factors (source: Fraport AG)

marketing efficiency. The objective of such an audit is the verification of the premises and conditions that are seen as being particularly influential with regard to the activity procedures and results of marketing. This means

- verification of existing procedures,
- verification of the strategy,
- verification of the marketing mix,
- verification of the organization.

The quality and importance of existing procedures, strategies, etc. is influenced to a large extent by the factors that determine efficient and effective action.

Marketing audits should be carried out at regular intervals. When the auditing takes place for the first time, and is accompanied by a change process at the same time, it is then wise to initiate a project. However, if auditing is already an established instrument, the task can be performed in existing organizational structures within the framework of correspondingly defined processes.

The process approach outlined below concentrates on a project-oriented procedure for conducting a marketing audit.

▶ Process & Implementation

The individual process steps of a marketing audit, with subsequent correction of weak points, can be structured in five higher-level phases.

1 ▷ 2 ▷ 3 ▷ 4 ▷ 5

Phase 1: Planning of a marketing audit

A reflexive corporate culture is the prerequisite for internal organizational projects being conducted within the framework of critical feedback and adaptations. If this requirement is not fulfilled, the auditing should be accompanied by an external consultant acting by order of the company management. To avoid any gaps in implementation and losses in knowledge once the project has been concluded, it is best for the consultant to work in tandem with an internal project manager. Here, the classical division of responsibilities consists of the consultant contributing methodological knowledge and analytical competence, whereas the internal project manager supplies organizational and sector-specific knowledge with a strong relation to its application. Abstract specialist knowledge and applied process know-how must nevertheless be available on both sides to align the project planning individually to the requirements of the organization, and to implement an efficiently designed and effectively positioned project.

The project planning is the decisive strategic and conceptual thinking process that precedes the actual conducting of the audit. Basically, it is to be closely agreed with the client, as it is a critical success factor in the subsequent course of the project and the project results.

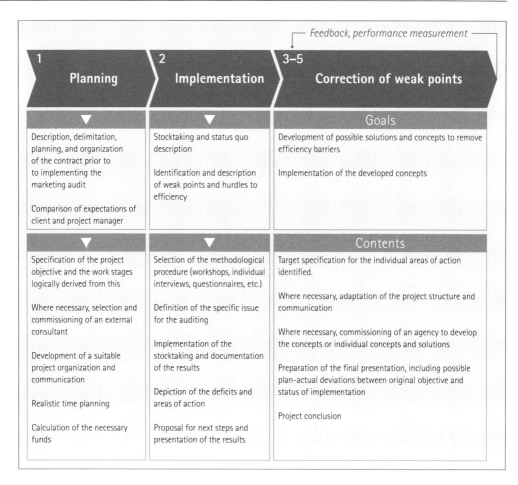

Fig. 3: Marketing efficiency process

How the project is ultimately organized depends on whether the subsequent implementation of the results necessitates a change in thinking or action of the players. If a high proportion of convincing throughout the organization has to be performed, a project organization is recommended that takes into account the multipliers that will have a later influence on the proper implementation of the solutions developed. Typical divisional interfaces in an efficiency-enhancing project within marketing result:

- between marketing divisions (e.g., market research, product management, marketing communication, etc.),
- to Corporate Communication (press, public relations, internal communication, investor relations, etc.),
- to Production and to Sales,
- to Procurement and Controlling,
- to Corporate Development and company management,
- to other companies that belong to the group.

Project structure and communication are important levers for maintaining the course of the project. They specify roles, tasks, and the routes to preparing and finding decisions.

Important project roles within the scope of a marketing audit start with the actual client. The client issues the contract for the audit and approves the results. As a marketing audit is of high strategic relevance, the client should be a member of the Executive Board or the Board of Directors. In addition, the project organization should consider setting up a steering committee. This committee is responsible for the cross-divisional decision-making that has been prepared by the project manager and those involved in the project as a preliminary step to the approval of the results by the client. The project manager guides and accounts for the overall project. It is not sufficient that he has well-founded knowledge of project management. He also needs additional specialist knowledge, so that communication barriers and gaps in comprehension can be avoided. To create a high level of identification with the project, the others involved in the project should be actively integrated and have individual responsibility for results. This contributes to acceptance with projects across divisions and sites, and makes a decisive contribution to the success of the implementation.

In the different project phases, the structures of the project organization and, thus, also the communication patterns can change. However, the decision-making is always guided via the project communication, which needs to be taken into account with adaptations.

Phase 2: Conducting a marketing audit

From a methodological perspective, a variety of procedural approaches are available. Interviews and questionnaires are particularly suitable. An extract of specific issues that can be the subject of an auditing is listed here.

Examples of procedural issues are:

- Is there a planning and control process in marketing? Has this been defined in a methodical way and with regard to time?
- Are strategic and quantitative planning coupled with one another?
- Is the procedure to define and control the size of the marketing budget derived from objectives?
- Are innovative ideas being assessed, and are profit analyses and savings potential being considered?
- Are decision-makers sufficiently involved in the planning and control?
- Is there a routine to adapt the plan during the year in a coordinated manner, in which the annual values are projected onto quarterly and monthly values?
- Are market trends with regard to customers, products, areas, competitors, interest groups, etc. being taken sufficiently into account?
- Is the planning and control process formalized and standardized in such a way that it proceeds easily?

Examples of strategic questions are:

- Is the fundamental mandate of the company expressed clearly?
- Are there formulated assumptions, scenarios, or forecasts as the basis for this fundamental mandate?

- Have all macro-economic and influencing factors that concern the direct working environment been taken into account?
- Are the corporate objectives and the target figures for marketing defined in such a way that marketing planning and performance measurement can be oriented to this?

Examples of marketing mix questions are:

- Are the marketing objectives linked to strategies and activities?
- Are strategic instruments (analyses, measurement procedures) for finding, planning, and focusing of the marketing strategies being used?
- Do the marketing strategies correspond to the personal, material, and temporal resources that are available long-term?
- Are sales channels, advertising, public relations, etc., effective?
- Are the activities harmonized to one another with regard to content, time, and form?

Examples of organizational questions are:

- Are the areas of marketing responsibility structured in a resonable manner? Have all functional areas been taken into account, and are they equipped appropriately?
- Are there interfaces between the functional areas or other departments?
- Do those with marketing responsibility have sufficient authority and responsibility?
- Is there an attachment of the marketing objectives to responsible employees, and are there appropriate incentive systems, particularly in Sales?
- Has marketing controlling been taken into account as an institutionalized department in the marketing organization?
- Do instruments exist (e.g. Intranet platform or forms) that contribute to the coordinated and harmonized planning and control?

Phase 3 to 5: Removal of weak points and performance measurement

A continuation of the project after the actual auditing ensures that the action fields identified in the stocktaking can be brought to an appropriate solution. The objectives of the project must now be specified on the basis of the results available from the analysis of weak points, and transferred to a target concept, the implementation of which contributes to correcting the existing deficits. However, weak points can also be corrected by solutions that already exist. Indeed, concepts are often already available in organizations – they are, however, unknown to the majority of the players, as they are only conveyed and used in a manner specific to the department. A cross-divisional use of such local solutions saves time and is easy to realize. Across sites, it should be checked beforehand whether existing concepts will meet with acceptance in other markets or if cultural differences necessitate other solutions.

During the implementation of the conceptual specifications, the individual tasks are transferred into the line organization, whereby the implementation process is monitored and supported, where necessary, and the on-going exchange of information between the players is ensured through the project. This usually occurs without more detailed external support. The project ultimately concludes by comparing targets with results.

CASE Marketing communication audit at Fraport AG

The methodical procedure, in addition to some results of an audit, are briefly outlined below by using a practical example that focused on an analysis of the communicative activities, information, and communication processes, as well as on possible savings in material costs.

Initial position and objective
The initial position of the project was as follows:

- The number of communication instruments is growing.
- The diversity of media is continually increasing, addressees are suffering from information overload, target groups are hard-fought.
- Cost pressure on companies is growing, the communicative differentiation in competition is becoming more difficult, a harmonized brand image is becoming a "survival strategy."

This gave rise to the following objectives:

- Creation of a harmonized internal and external presentation through the coordinated use of media. This means the optimization of the internal and external media landscape through coordination of the communication activities with regard to content, time and form.
- Optimization of the process organization for the creation and implementation of communication activities. This means the structuring of processes within the organization, starting with the generation of information, through to the selection of the right medium and the coordination of priorities, to the production and distribution.
- Identification and realization of savings potential. This means recording of redundancies, the identification of interfaces, and the creation of synergies.

Results of the survey and identified areas of action
The auditing showed that there were redundancies in the media mix with regard to content. For instance, the same content was communicated to the same target group in different publications. Moreover, it was also shown that information was either not always received by the recipient in a target-oriented manner, or it had been prepared in a way that was non-specific to the target groups. Furthermore, it was demonstrated that a common understanding, with regard to the communication objectives, was missing, and this resulted in different priorities and a variety of messages.

The allocation of division-specific roles and responsibilities was not clear enough. In part, competition situations between the departments arose. Cross-divisional and networked thinking was weakly defined, action based on divided labor was either totally non-existent or defined by high synchronization effort due to the insufficient definition of coordination- and clearing-centers, as well as standardized editorial processes. In the procurement of external services, there was obvious savings potential.

Necessary fields of action emerged as follows:

- focusing of strategic communication goals,
- reduction of the diversity of media,
- canalization of the content and the target group approach,
- creation of clear roles and responsibilities along the communication processes,
- standardization of editorial, production and distribution processes,
- as well as the realization of synergy potential and a consolidation of external service providers.

Efficiency-enhancing activities through savings and innovations

Through the auditing, all weak points in the communication were identified. Not just inefficiencies were uncovered, but also deficiencies that could have an impact on the effectiveness of communication, such as an inadequate organizational provision for crisis communication. In all, the project made it possible to realize material costs savings amounting to a six-figure sum. Classical levers that contributed to it were a bundling of requirements and a reduction in the purchase costs, standardization of layout templates and formats, relocation of print media to electronic channels, reduction of circulation numbers and adjustment of distribution lists, reduction or consolidation of media and applications such as picture databases, etc. Furthermore, the activities initiated and implemented through this project have contributed to increasing the quality of the communication itself, and to enhancing the efficiency of the procedures connected with its planning and implementation. Extracts from a few solutions are shown below:

Strategy solutions

Communication is not an end in itself. It takes place in order to achieve company and marketing objectives. Communication objectives and focal areas were, therefore, derived consistently from these, and are contributing to the positioning of the company. For the measurement of performance, regular image- and brand recognition-analyses are suitable.

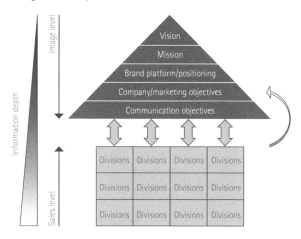

Fig. 4: Coherency principle (source: Fraport AG)

Media mix solutions

The media mix was revised in two respects: firstly with regard to the mix of the adopted communication tools, and secondly with regard to the number of publications. This resulted in, for instance, a

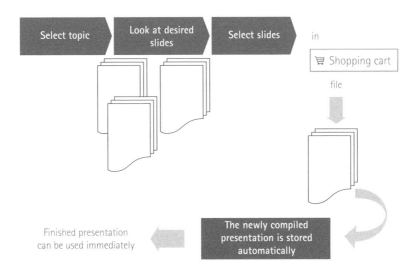

Fig. 5: How the presentation kit works (source: Fraport AG)

reduction of printed media in internal communications, that were, however, replaced by events, etc. The previously-mentioned savings potentials could primarily be realized through these optimizations and their associated production and procurement processes. However, innovative ideas were also adopted, such as the development of a presentation kit that follows the procurement principle on the Internet. As a result of this development alone, savings of around EUR 180,000 a year are being realized.

PowerPoint presentations are used for all types of communication events. The creation of the documents needs time, research, and coordination. The presentation kit developed now provides all the important slides on strategic and product-specific topics. They are maintained and updated by the responsible specialist departments. Updating is ensured by a monitoring process. Employees who are preparing a presentation can rely on the quality of the data and statements. They order the slides according to the shopping cart principle, and only need to put them in the desired order.

Procedural solutions

The marketing and communication planning process was coupled directly to the strategic and quantitative corporate planning. It starts with a marketing strategy meeting, in which tactical objectives across divisions are defined for the coming year, planned division-specific activities are presented, synergies identified, and responsibilities defined. Specific inquiries are also made about external results that have already been recognized, and that could have an influence on the company or products of the company in the following year. These are included in the planning. This ensures that resources are available and that potential crises are anticipated. To take into account changes in the boundary conditions, and to be able to make adaptations, the strategy meeting is repeated during the year.

The consolidation of the budget planning and the recording of all activities are done subsequently via the controlling. All marketing activities and communication means recorded there are ultimately included in an intranet-based platform that depicts the planned activities on a calendar with all additional information. This creates transparency and avoids task redundancy. The Intranet platform also incorporates all other supporting information and applications that were developed and implemented within the scope of the project. They significantly contribute towards less re-production, time saving, and the use of standards.

Procedural-organizational solutions
For the media categories of print, electronic media, and events such as trade fairs, sample processes and a role-rights concept were created, to be used across the divisions. This was also done for the communication in the case of a crisis.

▶ Key Insights

- From a strategic point of view, marketing effectiveness and efficiency are continuing to grow in importance. This is connected to the demand for a reduction in marketing costs, while, at the same time, the performance is to be increased.
- Qualitative management tasks are the decisive levers for increasing efficiency and effectiveness.
- Marketing controlling has to provide methods and instruments that clearly show the correlations of effect between management actions and quantifiable results. This also applies in the international context and is of particular importance for groups that operate on a global level.
- To increase the importance of marketing within a company or group, it has to be in a position to depict its performance contribution to value creation.

▶ Practical Guidelines

- Organizational solution options for marketing should be based on the customer process and the brand strategy.
- Roles, tasks, and interfaces between marketing and sales departments, as well as subsidiaries, must be clarified. Different terminology should not allow any room for interpretation.
- Sustainable communication structures need to be created between companies of the group, departments and teams. Technical solutions alone are not sufficient.
- Assuming that well-founded specialist knowledge is available, strategic competences, such as specialist knowledge of process management, should be taken into account when filling marketing positions.
- The budget distribution should be coupled to objectives, strategies, and specific activities.
- Important decision-makers should be directly involved in the planning process to ensure successful implementation.
- To demonstrate marketing performance, efficiency, and effectiveness of marketing activities, the specific function of marketing controlling should be created.

The Authors

Annegret Reinhardt-Lehmann

Annegret Reinhardt-Lehmann was appointed Senior Vice President of Marketing in 1997. She is in charge of Marketing, Strategy, Boards and Committees. Mrs. Reinhardt-Lehmann holds a bachelors and a masters degree in American studies and French and Spain cultural studies. She studied at the University of Frankfurt am Main, Germany; Jamestown, ND, U.S.A.; Salamanca, Spain. She spent the major part of her professional carrier working in management positions for Fraport in Marketing, Communication and International Projects. She was in charge of developing Fraport's international investment activities and setting up the investment division. Mrs. Reinhardt-Lehmann is a member of the Supervisory Board of Saarbrücken Airport. She is married and has one daughter.

Nicole Ebner

Nicole Ebner started her career in 1998 in the marketing department. As a senior executive manager she subsequently took over the management of the divisions Electronic Media, Integrated Communication, as well as Marketing Strategy and Sales Support. Her management tasks are currently concentrated on strategic fields such as the marketing planning and international regional-market coordination of Fraport AG. Furthermore, she is responsible for the company's brand management across the group. Nicole Ebner studied Romance Languages, German, and Political Science at the universities of Mexico City (Mexico), Cordoba (Argentina), and Frankfurt am Main, where she completed her M.A. degree. She is married with a son and daughter.

Literature Recommendations

R. Köhler, "Marketing-Controlling. Konzepte und Methoden," in: Reinecke, S., Tomczak, T., Dittrich, S. (eds.): Marketingcontrolling. Fachbuch für Marketing, St. Gallen 1998
P. Kotler, F. Bliemel, "Marketing-Management. Analyse, Planung und Verwirklichung," Stuttgart 2001
H. Meffert, "Marketing. Grundlagen marktorientierter Unternehmensführung. Konzepte – Instrumente – Praxisbeispiele," 9th edition, Wiesbaden 2000
J. Meurer, P. Ott, S. Reinecke, D. Fuchs, "Marketing Efficiency: Budgetierung," in: Absatzwirtschaft, special issue 2004
S. Reinecke, "Marketingcontrolling. Eine neue Perspektive. Sicherstellen der Rationalität marktorientierter Unternehmensführung als Herausforderung," St. Gallen 2000
Roland Berger Strategy Consultants, "Marketing Efficiency," 2002
P. Schütz, "Die tausend Tode der Effizienz," in: Absatzwirtschaft, special issue 2002

Brand Management

→ www.marketingmanual.org/brand

Wolfgang Orians – Freudenberg

Brand Architecture (B2B)
Key factors for the development and maintenance of brand architecture

▶ Executive Summary

- The importance of brands will increase further – even in the B2B sector.
- Therefore, brand management will also become a factor for the success of your company.
- Brand management requires a brand strategy and brand architecture.
- Brand strategy and architecture reflect the company strategy.
  Brand architecture can be structured in five phases:
  1. Evaluation and systematization
  2. Research
  3. Positioning
  4. Development of theoretical brand architecture
  5. Realization as permanent process.
- Brand architecture is the systematic reflection of the company to its stakeholders.
- Development of brand architecture is a permanent process that visualizes the development of the company.

▶ Theoretical Model of Brand Architecture

1. Definition

1.1 The importance of the brand is increasing
The idea that it is worth investing in brands is nothing new. In the consumer goods industry, brands are created and maintained with large budgets. According to estimates by the Interbrand agency, Coca-Cola, the best known brand in the world, has a value of 70 billion dollars, which is more than the market capitalization of the company.

The question of accounting measures for brand values is also being discussed more and more. When a company is acquired, the brand values must be determined individually and valued in accordance with the respective accounting principles, e.g. US-GAAP (US-American accounting standard), IFRS (International Financial Reporting Standards) or HGB (the German statutory accounting standard). The capitalization of self-developed (original) brands is not allowed under German GAAP (HGB), US-GAAP or IFRS. This might result in a distorted picture of the actual company situation, and the company value, as displayed in the accounts, can be set too low.

In accordance with US-GAAP, group accounts must include the breakdown of total goodwill into separately identifiable intangible assets and, thus, the value of brands is to be determined individually and shown in the accounts. For foreign companies listed on the U.S. stock exchange, this regulation is valid as of January 1st, 2003.

In light of the globalization of financial markets, a unification of various methods of rendering accounts is to be expected and, therefore, a renewed discussion of brand values can be presumed.

The proportion of the brand value in the company value as a whole differs according to sector: an investigation by PricewaterhouseCoopers showed that this value is 62 percent for perishable consumer goods, 53 percent for non-perishable consumer goods, 43 percent for services, and 18 percent for industrial goods. With this average value of 56 percent, it is clear that there is a large, previously untapped potential in brand development, especially for industrial goods. The constantly increasing relevance of brands has the following origins:

- Products and services are becoming increasingly similar, technical advances continue to be short-lived in the globalized information society. Thus, it is becoming more important to develop and apply other differentiation factors. In the industrial goods sector, the advancing standardization and norm introduction efforts are an additional factor. According to a study by McKinsey, the number of European standards has risen by 60 percent between 1997 and 2001 to a total of 12,967.
- A trend exists, especially in the industrial goods sector, to connect not only products, but also complex performance bundles. So, the item being sold is not just a seal, but rather the solution to a seal problem that can extend way beyond that one product.
- Constantly increasing pricing pressures make it necessary to offer the customer added value beyond the purely functional product, in order to justify a price premium.

Given this background, brands have three particular functions:

- Improving information efficiency. This relates to the brand property of concentrating as much information as possible about the product and manufacturer, in order to act as a "concentrated brief message" on the important capacities of the provider of investment goods.
- Risk reduction. "Nobody ever got fired for buying an IBM" is already a familiar phrase. It expresses the following: if you, as a purchaser, decide to go for the offer at the lowest price and something goes wrong, then your job is at risk. If you decide to buy IBM you are not only buying a product, but also the reputation and quality promise of IBM. If something goes wrong anyway, nobody will blame you because you bought the best product on the market.
- Brands can also serve an idealistic use. In the consumer goods sector, they offer the consumer the opportunity for self-realization and displaying their values. For industrial goods, this use is somewhat more complicated. The additional use is made up from the external effect on various groups with different requirements.

1.2 Professional brand management increases profitability

While the importance of brands in the B2C sector is undisputed, the discussion in research and practice with regard to brand relevance in the Business to Business sector has increased over the past years. In a questionnaire sent to 769 companies, McKinsey found that brands also have a clear influence on the buying decision process in the B2B sector. This influence does, however, vary in different product markets.

Professor Dr. Christian Homburg from Mannheim University carried out a branding excellence study, in which he questioned 360 companies. He came to the conclusion that the importance of brands in the B2B sector will increase.

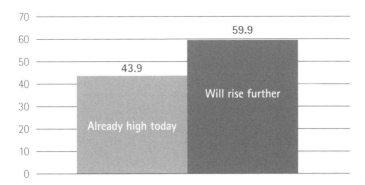

Fig. 1: The importance of brands (as a % of those asked). Source: Branding Excellence Study by the institute for brand-related company management at Mannheim University for approximately 360 companies from the B2B sector.

According to the Branding Excellence Study, a connection can also be found between turnover revenue and brand management. Professor Homburg found that the companies in which the degree of brand management was high also had substantially higher turnover revenue (degree of brand management low: turnover revenue = 6.2% – degree of brand management high: turnover revenue = 9.4%).

2. Factors for brand architecture

2.1 Systematization of the brand portfolio

The creation of the brand portfolio is only the consequence of a planned process with a strict direction in a minority of cases. Particularly in the investment goods sector, companies often grow through mergers and acquisitions. If there is no brand strategy in such cases, the company that is purchased and/or its brands often continue to be placed in the market with the old branding. If this takes place in an uncontrolled manner and without a strategic background, synergy effects will be lost, at the least. In the worst case scenario, the original brand is even damaged. A further cause for the uncontrolled growth of brands and pseudo-brands is the multitude of products and the continuing diversification. In principle we can say that not every product name is a brand, even if it is a registered trademark. Not every product must be a brand.

Besides these objective factors, there are also psychological reasons within the company to continue creating new brands. A brand not only allows delineation in the market, but also within the company organization. A brand needs its own image, brand management, a budget. It makes it possible to defend against demands that are made: "In my market, the situation is totally different," "My customers have very specific needs," etc. Thus, having the responsibility for a brand also results in limitable power. Developing the potential for power is appealing to the individual and he will defend the potential for power that he has already achieved with all his strength. The systematization of an organically grown brand portfolio will, therefore, always meet strong internal resistance that cannot be broken with rational arguments alone. Rather, it is necessary to make the affected individuals into participants by involving them in the process.

Determination of brand architecture is the key decision for the brand management within a company. Design of brand architecture includes deciding which brands should be used on each of the company levels, their positioning and their specific roles. Brand architecture is oriented to the company organization without transferring the organizational diagram to the brand level. Thus, a company organization as a management company – business field – strategic business unit on the brand side (corporate brand) – faces the company brand and product brand on the other side.

Brand architecture has the task of structuring the often historically and organically created composition of the brand portfolio, so that it can be controlled. It determines the brands to be used on the individual company levels, the positioning thereof and the relationship of the brands to one another. In the first step, it is necessary to define the brand types. Only a few companies, for example Sony, work with a brand that is valid for both the company and the products. At first glance, there appear to be two categories: the product brand and the corporate brand. While the product brand bundles the characteristics of the product and, therefore, makes the buying decision easier for the customer or gives him the prospect of participation in a "brand world," the corporate brand is generally more rational in that it symbolizes the values of a company, that can thus increase the value of the company. The relationship between the corporate brand and the product brand can vary greatly. It is, for example, only of secondary value to the very strong washing powder brand Persil that this product is manufactured by Henkel. If, however, a regionally known washing powder, such as Spee, is introduced into other markets, it is helpful to point out that this is also a quality product made by Henkel.

2.2 Definition of brand types

In principle, observance of the effect of the brands on the relevant target groups is well suited to differentiating between corporate brand and product brand. A study by the mcminstitute in St. Gallen offers the following framework: the product brand is of great importance to the customer, and the corporate brand is of great importance to the financial community, because the customers are primarily interested in the product characteristics, while investors are more interested in how solid the company behind the product is. Corresponding allocations can be made for all other demand groups. For the employees, both a strong product brand ("I am proud to produce, sell, etc. the product xy") and the corporate brand are of importance ("I work at the company z, which is successful, creates jobs, pays good wages, etc.").

Target group	Product brand	Corporate brand
Customers	+++++	++
Employees	+++	+++
Suppliers	+++	+++
Press	+++	+++
Community/authorities	++	++++
Universities	++	++++
Local environment	+	++++
Financial community	+	+++++

Fig. 2: Target group orientation of brand types. Source: mcminstitute study, Corporate Branding Study. S. Einwiller, 2001

With companies that are active in various business sectors, or with groups that are made up of various companies, the introduction of a further category, termed Company Brand, is useful.

- Product Brand – bundles product characteristics,
- Company Brand – positioning in the relevant market,
- Corporate Brand – bundles common values and creates added value.

In the example of the automobile group Volkswagen, this differentiation would be as follows:

- Corporate Brand: Volkswagen,
- Company Brand: Skoda,
- Product Brand: Octavia.

2.3 Brand strategy

The brand architecture now has the task of describing the relationship of the various brands to one another. In order to do this, it is necessary to decide on a brand strategy and/or to use existing corporate strategy on a relevant brand strategy. In literature, the two pure forms of "branded house" or "house of brands" are differentiated. In the case of a "branded house" the corporate brand dominates on all levels (Siemens, Bosch, Sony), in the "house of brands" the corporate brand is in the background (Unilever). In corporate reality, these pure forms do not, however, often exist. Thus, for example, product and service brands can be presented as dominant, but still be supported by a corporate or company brand (endorsed brand). Based on the differentiation between corporate brand, company brand and product brand, we have defined the following brand strategy as the basis of brand architecture:

Fig. 3: Possible brand strategies

The choice of fundamental strategy made by a company depends on various, individual factors. None of the above-named models are superior to another by definition; rather, it is a case of finding the right one. The assessments in the following chart are based on a company with decentralized organization, that possesses a broad portfolio, and is managed by a holding company. The assessment was carried out from the point of view of the management company, and from the point of view of the (independent) business groups, as the interests of the various units within the group are not uniform.

2.3.1 Taking international aspects into account

In principle, brand architecture is a strategic instrument that also has a multi-level character in an internationally structured company. However, the architecture forms relationships between brands that previously existed independently of one another. In order to guarantee acceptance of the brand architecture in all regions, specifically national characteristics must be taken into account. Thus, for example, the color white is a symbol for grief in Asian countries, and a white frame can be interpreted in the same way as a black border. In the case of words as brands, the differing meaning of words in different languages must be taken into account. The story of the Italian car manufacturer who found it hard to sell its small car in Finland, because the (Italian) name of the car meant "idiot" in Finnish, is

	Option A Company/ Product brand strategy	Option B Mixed brand strategy	Option 2 Corporate brand strategy
Assessment from the point of view of the management company	This option increases the work for the brand management as a whole, the brand of the parent company is substantially weakened and, thus, the visible unity of the company group is also diluted	This option both strengthens the parent company brand and leaves sufficient scope for the individual business groups to acquire a strong image in their markets with their own brands	This option allows higher savings potential to be realized, the parent company brand is strengthened and a uniform identity is promoted. On the other hand, it requires strong centralized measures and makes a suitable brand image more difficult
Assessment from the point of view of the business groups	Although this option gives the business groups the largest possible scope for design, it also removes the opportunities for forming a strong image via the parent company brand	The business companies can achieve a strong image in their specific market environment while simultaneously using the existing potential of the parent company brand	With this option, the companies are more or less structured in the same way, and no longer have the opportunity of forming a strong image in the market environment via their own brands

Fig. 4: Decision for a fundamental strategy

legendary, as is the Japanese manufacturer who brought a car onto the Spanish speaking market with a name that was a gutter term for masturbation. In the same way, abbreviations must be handled with care. In the U.S.A, an abbreviation including an F with a dash can be interpreted as a short form of the socially unacceptable word "fuck."

There are also less obvious problems and situations that result from the inherent hierarchy in the architecture. Hierarchy is interpreted in a completely different way in Asia than in America or Europe. In order to rule out, where possible, conflicts that could endanger the acceptance of the brand architecture, representatives from the most important international markets should be involved in the creation process.

2.4 Brand matrix

The fundamental prerequisite for the success of brand architecture is that it is sufficiently clear and simple. It must offer an understandable follow-up for existing brands and make a fast (also understandable) allocation possible for future brands within the framework of the company strategy. An auxiliary instrument here could be a brand matrix. In this case, too, it is not possible to present an ideal solution. The following matrix is therefore only an example, and each company must develop its own matrix.

In our case, the matrix has two axes and four fields. The horizontal axis shows the participation quota, the vertical axis the positioning of the brand in the company strategy. The proximity to the corporate brand is shown by the positioning within the four fields, illustrated by visual characteristics. Thus, for example, a brand that is allocated in the lower, left quadrant would have an independent image, with its own brand management, without or with only a weak tie to the corporate brand. Brands that form the core business of the company and that are majority owned by the group can be found in the upper right quadrant.

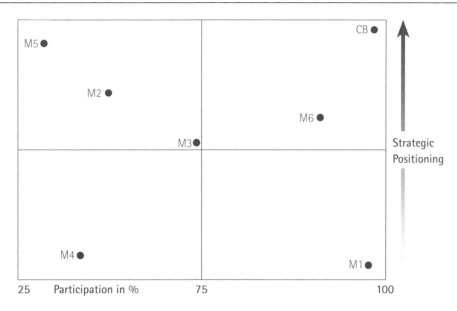

Fig. 5: Example of a brand matrix

This example deals with a corporate brand (CB) and six sub-brands. The brand M1 is 100% owned by the company, but the product is not included in the core business and does not, therefore, contribute to the brand core of the CB, and may not include references to the corporate brand besides the legally obligatory information. The same is true for M4, which is 40% owned by the company but is managed outside the core business. M2 is 50% owned and M5 only 25%, but both brands are part of the core business and should, therefore, have clear references to the corporate brand. M3 is 75% owned, but there are plans to sell this brand in the next few years. Thus, the connection to the corporate brand should be gradually reduced. M6 is 80% owned, but there are plans to take it over completely. It represents a strategic development business field. A strong connection to the corporate brand is desirable here. The connection to the corporate brand is formed via the logo or constituent parts of the logo, the corporate color or the font, or via the endorser.

Logo (complete)	Only CB
Logo part	can ⟶ May not be used
Endorser (clear/hidden)	Must be used
Color (corporate color)	can ⟶ May not be used
Corporate font (Futura)	Must be used
Design element	Can be used
Positioning of logo	Must be used
Image style	Can be used
Wording	Can be used

Fig. 6: Similarities through mutual design elements and language

The similarity of the various brands that belong to the company is created by using mutual design elements and a mutual language. There are clear guidelines for brand management, that are decided on centrally for the mutual design elements. It is even possible that a ban on the use of corporate brand design elements may be announced for companies in the lower quadrants.

▸ Process & Implementation

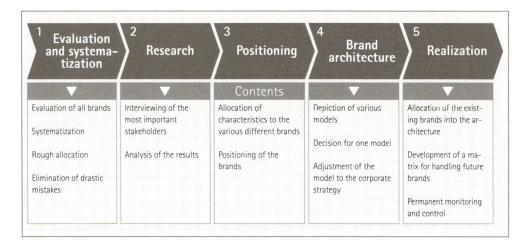

Fig. 7: Phases of brand architecture

The development of a brand architecture can be split into five phases:
1. Evaluation and systematization
2. Research
3. Positioning
4. Structure of the theoretical brand architecture
5. Realization as a permanent process.
Several years must be planned as a suitable period for the process as a whole.

Phase 1: Evaluation and systematization

Ideally, the company will have a central department that manages all the brands, monitors the extension of registrations, and follows up cases of brand piracy and misuse. Particularly in international and decentralized companies, it is, however, often several different offices carrying out brand administration. Also, corporate brands are not always registered or, in the case of commonly used names, cannot be registered. As brands can be registered in various market categories and countries, this kind of evaluation often results in several thousand brands. In principle, the motto "less is more" is applicable, as a successful brand requires management and investors. It should also be remembered that not every product name is a brand or needs to be one. The name "1 D 495 a" can be very helpful for internal purposes and a certain customer segment, as each number and letter provides a reference to a certain performance characteristic of the product. This kind of name is, however, certainly not a brand and, therefore, has no place in a brand portfolio. Usually, a systematization of the brand portfolio into business sectors, product groups, etc. already reveals substantial potential for the reduction of brand numbers. For reasons already mentioned above, this will not, however, be possible without substantial resistance from within the organization.

Phase 2: Research

Brand architecture structure requires a strong foundation of data, that must be collected through the analysis of existing documents and brand images, and interviews with the most important stakeholders. Important questions are as follows:

- What is the degree of awareness of the individual brands?
- Which brand core do the target groups allow the brand/brand core to have?
- How important is the corporate brand for the company or product brands?
- Are the internal and external points of view the same?

This data, collected both internally and externally, forms the basis for the decision of which basic strategy/architecture should be used.

Phase 3: Positioning

In the next step, the existing brands must be systematically allocated to a brand group. In the case of the corporate brand, this is usually still possible without problems, but at the company brand level, there are often boundary problems in relation to product brands. The above brand typing guidelines and the mcminstitute grid of target groups can help in making decisions.

Phase 4: Structuring the theoretical brand architecture

When the individual brands within a company have been suitably allocated, the next step is to develop the brand architecture. At first, possible models for brand architecture must be shown. The company strategy or organization will probably rule out certain models from the start. Despite this, there will be more than one model of which the advantages and disadvantages must be assessed. Once the decision for a theoretical model has been made, the model must be adjusted to suit the company strategy/reality. This means clearly defining the possible exceptions and laying them down in writing.

Phase 5: Realization of the brand architecture

In a final step, the existing brands are allocated within the architecture. A matrix can be helpful here, especially in order to categorize newly added brands. Brand strategies and brand architectures require consistency over a long period of time, so that they can establish themselves. Thus, the observance of the requirements must be tested constantly. Where a brand architecture is first developed with an existing brand portfolio, a longer period (up to several years) should be scheduled for the realization. Once the brand architecture has been established, it must be developed further on an ongoing basis.

▶ Key Insights

- Brands are becoming increasingly important, also in the B2B sector.
- Professional brand management increases profitability.
- There are various brand types with different tasks and target groups.
- A brand architecture is necessary in order to control complex brand portfolios.
- The foundations of brand architecture are the brand strategy and the company strategy.
- A brand architecture must be understandable in all the countries and regions where the company is active.
- A brand architecture must be structured in a clear and sufficiently simple way.
- Brand management is a continuing process.

▶ Practical Guidelines

- Place the brand architecture project at the highest level.
- Plan in a "buy in process" that will take time.
- Expect enormous resistance.
- Move beyond a national perspective and make very sure to involve representatives from the most important markets.
- Plan the project in steps that will be decided consecutively, so that the entire project cannot be put at risk by one decision.
- Make it clear from the beginning that the project is designed to achieve an improvement in market processing (an increase in turnover and profit).
- Define clear structures and processes for brand management.
- Plan a lot of time for the implementation.

The Author

Wolfgang Orians

Wolfgang Orians studied social and communications sciences in Mannheim before working as a journalist. He took his first steps into public relations with the "Deutscher Bundesjugendring," the lobbying organization of youth organizations in Germany, developing a new logo, amongst other things. He held further positions as departmental head for the national press office at Ruhrgas and head of communications at the listed chemical and plastics group ROTGERS. For the past four years, Orians has managed corporate communications at the internationally active family firm and technical equipment supplier, Freudenberg. There, he has introduced corporate brand management and is in the process of developing a brand architecture.

Literature Recommendations

Ch. Homburg, M. Richter, "Branding Excellence: Wegweiser für professionelles Markenmanagement," Institut für marktorientierte Unternehmensführung Universität Mannheim, Reihe: Management Know-how, No. M 75, Mannheim 2003

H. Meffert, A. Bierwirth, & C. Burmann, "Gestaltung der Markenarchitektur als markenstrategische Basisentscheidung," in: H. Meffert, C. Burmann, M. Koers (eds.): Markenmanagement: Grundlagen der identitätsorientierten Markenführung, Mit BestPractice-Fallstudien, Wiesbaden 2002

Ivo Hoevel, Karin Kaiser – O₂ Germany

Brand Building
Building a new brand in existing competitive markets

▶ Executive Summary

- The building of a new brand requires high levels of investment, and presents great challenges for the marketing department. Brand building should, therefore, be prepared in an optimal manner and carried out in a structured process.
- A thorough analysis of the market and the market environment forms the basis for the brand and market access strategy. "Courage to differentiate" content must already be shown at this stage.
- The primary aims for a brand launch are maximum attention and fast development of brand recognition. The corresponding structuring of communication and the inclusion of as many external factors as possible (e.g., trade fairs, events, testimonials) are necessary prerequisites of this.
- Following a successful launch, existing customer loyalty must be maintained and increased. The content of the brand must be developed further in this phase and also charged further.
- The transition to "classical marketing" can then take place.

This article will explain the individual components in the building of a new brand, along with the correct arrangement of the individual components in relation to one another in a phase model. The article can thus serve as a guideline for brand building.

▶ Theoretical Model of Brand Building

1. Definition and core principle

Brand building describes the structuring of a new, previously non-existent brand. Thus, it must be differentiated clearly from a brand extension, which, in contrast to new structuring, describes the expansion of an existing brand into a new product category.

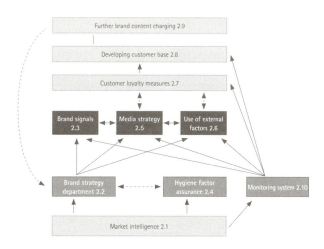

Fig. 1: Brand building

2. Factors of brand building

2.1 Market intelligence
A comprehensive analysis of the market and the market environment serves as a basis for a possible entry into the market. One of the most common analyses is e.g., Porter's Five Forces model. This determines the power of suppliers and consumers, as well as competitive pressure and the threat of potential new competitors and possible substitutes. In combination with an analysis of the general environment – split into political, economical, socio-cultural, and technological sectors – it provides a great depth of information on the market conditions. In addition, the market as a whole must be split into homogeneous partial markets (market segments) by target group segmenting. Possible criteria for the segmentation of the market are geographical, socio-demographic (e.g., gender, age, marital status, education), psychographic (e.g., lifestyle, character traits) or behavior-related (e.g., intensity of consumption, stadium of readiness to buy, choice of shop location) characteristics.

2.2 Brand strategy
Each brand requires a long-term and differentiated orientation guideline: the brand strategy. One elementary factor is the determination of the core competence of the brand, i.e., the determination of what the new brand should stand for. Further important factors that should be included in a brand strategy are the benefits (what am I offering my target groups) and the characteristics by which the brand should be recognized. All future marketing activities are derived from the brand strategy.

2.3 Brand signals
The brand signals serve the differentiation and recognition of a brand in the market environment. When building up a new brand, these brand signals must be redesigned. The following aspects are the main focus:

- Brand name,
- Color Code (specific color or color combination),
- Brand logo,
- Font type,
- Design elements (e.g. packaging or product design),
- Brand slogan,
- Communicative elements (key visual).

2.4 Hygiene factors
Each new brand must ensure the "hygiene factors" of the product or service category. "Hygiene factors" are criteria that have no differentiation potential, but which must be fulfilled in order to even come into the relevant set (readiness to buy) among the target group(s). The hygiene factors must be fulfilled in the dimensions of product quality, price positioning, and sales alignment.

2.5 Media strategy
The media strategy is determined on the basis of the media objectives and the main target groups, as well as the available budget. The media mix is an important variable in the media strategy. It determines which media are best suited to efficiently communicating an advertising message to the target groups, and how the individual media should be weighted. In order to determine the optimal media strategy, both the prerequisites and the media planning of the competition must be taken into account.

2.6 External factors
External factors are directly or indirectly influenced conditions, e.g., multipliers, opinion leaders, specialist magazines or trade fairs and events, that must be put to optimal use for the brand.

2.7 Customer loyalty measures
Retaining customers that have already been won over is one of the fundamental tasks of each brand marketeer, as the cost of acquiring a new customer is many times higher than the retention cost for an existing customer. Various tools can be used to intensify the customer's loyalty towards the new brand, based on a customer value analysis. Some "classic" retention tools are loyalty promotions and/or loyalty discounts or "one to one" communication in the form of personalized mailings. A good customer database is always the starting point for these measures.

2.8 Developing the customer base
Besides the retention of existing customers, it is, of course, also important to win new customers for the brand. One of the ways in which to achieve this is through expansion of the existing target groups. It should, however, be considered to what extent the potential in the previous main segments has been exhausted. Expanding the target groups too early can lead to the dilution and damaging of the new brand. It should, therefore, be considered in depth beforehand.

2.9 Further charging of the content of the brand
Besides a high level of market recognition, an independent brand is also a factor in successful brand management. It is important to ensure a stringent realization of the brand strategy at all contact points between the target group and the brand. Relevant content for the target groups must be associated with the brand in the long term.

2.10 Monitoring system
A monitoring system should contain both sales figures at the point of sale, and tracking within the target groups. This tracking should take place on a weekly basis in order to measure the development of brand recognition, advertising memory, and buying preferences within the target groups. In this combination, learnings can also be determined in order to achieve optimal use of materials.

2.11 International aspects
The introduction of an international brand further increases the complexity of brand building; a balance must be found between a holistic international brand strategy and positioning that is relevant in all markets. Culturally specific backgrounds must, of course, be taken into account in the introduction of the brand signals – the pronunciation of a brand name alone can become a limiting factor. If the brand is at different stages of development in the different countries, then this will also have an impact on brand perception: in a more saturated market, a newcomer can be perceived as a "young player" – with all its positive (e.g., innovative, dynamic ...) and negative (not serious, not established) facets. Uniform brand perception must be maintained, particularly given the increasing mobility and dynamics of the target groups. Despite this, the introduction of an international brand also holds substantial opportunities: on the one hand, the development of one market into another can be anticipated and, thus, it is possible to have a substantial effect on the market in the other country. Also, a small market is always a suitable "test market," from which successful further developments can be transferred to other countries.

Process & Implementation

Phase 1: Set-up

1. Discover a niche
The first step in the building of a new brand should be a comprehensive analysis of the market. The starting point is the general market situation: besides market value, it must also be determined whether the market is new, or whether it is mature or even saturated. A lot of information can be collected by "desk research" (secondary research): first points of communication should be economic associations, company information, analysis assessments and perhaps also market research institutes. If the market is still developing, then the building of a new brand can be especially easy as the new brand is being built in a new category where it may come up against (maybe only a few) non-established competitor brands. In a mature or saturated market, the launch of an additional brand must be considered very carefully. In this case, the new brand must survive against competitors that are already established on the market and are competent in the category. Despite this, a new brand can also be successful in a saturated market: for a market leader, the building of an additional brand can protect its own market position and secure it against attacks from competitors (e.g., a second brand in a lower price segment). It can, however, be stated that a brand launch is particularly rewarding in high volume and newly developing markets with only a few players.

Apart from the market situation, an analysis of the general environment is also necessary: both an analysis of the sales structures and a check on the political-legal components, which could influence the market in the near future, should be carried out (e.g., regulatory authorities, protection regulations, adaptations of controls, etc.). For existing players, a comprehensive determination of strengths and weaknesses must take place.

Following the segmentation of the market as a whole, attention must be focused on individual target group segments. In this, the orientation is either towards particularly attractive segments, or towards segments that are insufficiently supplied by the brands that are already on the market or that considered themselves to be insufficiently supplied. When characterizing the target segments, socio-demographic characterization must also be taken into account, as this simplifies communication with the priority target groups. A new brand has the opportunity of focusing and polarizing. This potential should definitely be utilized!

2. Determining brand strategy
A position for the new brand must be derived from comprehensive market, environment, and target group analysis. It must be taken into consideration that pure "follower" behavior of copying the market leaders is not sufficient. A differentiated counter-weight to the existing players must be created with the new brand. The new brand strategy must be consciously aligned against existing weaknesses in the competition, and not only towards certain market topics. Otherwise, there will be no clear reason for your target group to try your brand! This is particularly true of brands that are to be launched into a mature market.

3. Optical differentiation
You must form the counter-weight to the existing players, not just on a contents basis, but also optically. You need to have the courage to be different: implement a creative and differentiated performance. Ensure that your

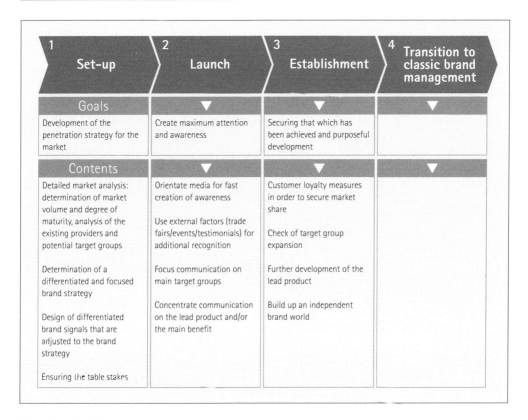

Fig. 2: Brand building process

brand strategy and/or the brand tones defined in it are also reflected in your brand elements. A concise and differentiated brand image is a "must," especially when building a new brand!

4. Fulfill core needs

Before the new brand is launched, you must ensure that all hygiene factors (basic requirements of the target groups) are fulfilled by the new product and/or the new service. Most importantly, there must not be any objective quality deficits in the product and/or the service. Especially with a new brand, the trust of the market participants must first be won – this doesn't happen if there are obvious defects.

During price positioning, attention must also be paid to the framework within which price willingness exists in the market. The price positioning must of course be adjusted to suit the brand strategy – a high quality brand cannot be sold at low prices. There are, however, certain price points in every market in whose vicinity one must move. These price points can be determined very effectively with the help of conjoint analyses, as well as with an orientation to the competition. In addition, you must consider the old marketing principle of "advertising follows sales" and ensure sufficient distribution density – after all, the target groups must have the opportunity of buying the new brand. The best differentiation strategy and the best USP can fail if the table stakes are not fulfilled.

CASE Building the O₂ brand

1. Find a niche

The story of O₂ begins seven years before the actual birth of the brand: in May 1995, VIAG Interkom was founded as a joint venture between VIAG AG, Telenor, and British Telecommunications.

The company was granted the fourth mobile telecommunication license in Germany two years later. In October 1998, VIAG Interkom began its mobile telecommunications service as the youngest network operator in Germany, and bid for and received a UMTS license in 2000. The brand of VIAG Interkom was not well established and had an unsupported brand recognition level of only 32 percent at the beginning of the new century.

In general, the mobile communications market appeared to be very attractive in the years 2001 and 2002 with double figure growth rates. The first saturation tendencies were, however, beginning to be seen in Germany with a penetration rate of almost 70 percent (December 2001). In addition, D1 (or T-Mobile), and D2 (or Vodafone) took very dominant positions within the market, with a joint market share of approximately 80 per cent.

Market segmentation resulted in five differentiated segments. Here, the "ambitious techies" and "young socials" showed themselves to be particularly attractive, as these were groups of demanding, high-consumption users who were only marginally attracted to the existing players. These two segments were to become the main target groups for the new O₂ brand – in all three markets (Germany, U.K. and Ireland).

2. Penetration strategy

Fig. 3: Appearance of the brand O₂

From the very beginning, the brand was positioned as being refreshingly different, innovative, and customer-oriented. O₂, as the chemical symbol for oxygen, stands for the openness, transparency, and ease that characterize the brand. Oxygen is essential and universal: as essential for people as the communication that O₂ is offering.

"O2 can do" is the brand promise and self-image of O₂. On the one hand, the company will make the use of mobile telecommunication easy for its customers, and will offer it at a low price. On the other hand, "can do" stands for innovative products and services to try out new possibilities via which O₂ presents itself as "refreshingly different."

The product O₂ Genion is a unique product with which customers can call from home, or any other desired address, at landline prices. This product was placed at the center of brand communication as the lead product.

3. Optical differentiation

O_2 has clearly-defined brand elements, which provide clear identification and a high level of recognition in public appearance.

Besides the main color indigo (dark blue), the memorable brand claim "can do" and the key visual (the "bubbles") ensure a strong perceived image.

Fig. 4: The O_2 "bubbles" as key visual

4. Core needs

The previous VIAG Interkom shops were used for distribution and rebranded as O_2. In May 2002, O_2 had a sufficient sales density with its 260 shops, especially in the conurbations.

Fig. 5: O_2 shop

The network coverage, a decisive buying criterion in the mobile telecommunications market, was almost complete with its own mobile communications network and an additional roaming agreement with T-Mobile.

Phase 2: Launch

1. Start with a "big bang"

The first two or three months are often considered to be decisive for the success or failure of a newcomer to the market. Therefore, the launch of a new brand must be optimally prepared and carried out with as much power as possible. The crucial objective at a brand launch is achieving rapid increase in brand recognition. Besides appearing in the classic media (TV/print/radio), the launch phase should be supported by flanking measures. When weighting in classic advertising, it should be taken into account that RV is still the medium with the broadest distribution, and it is particularly suitable for the development of fast, national awareness. Flanking "below the line" measures, that should be used, can, for example, be POS games for prizes, (multi-level) mailing activities, or promotions. Support from PR events rounds off a successful launch.

2. Use external factors

All external factors that could be used for a brand launch should be put in place. The main focus is on those factors that could attract additional attention to the new brand or that could provide proof of competence for the brand. Factors that can increase attention are e.g., trade fairs, events, sponsorship, or also testimonials, that advertise the new brand. Quality statements or tests by particular institutions or specialist publications are suitable to support brand competence. An examination needs to be carried out regarding how many of these factors can be used for the new brand. These external factors must, of course, have a certain "impact" in their core target groups, as, otherwise, their contribution will only be small.

3. Concentration and focus

As the target groups must complete a "learning curve," particularly at the beginning, the launch phase relies on a few messages. Besides the new brand image, communication should be limited to individual main benefits and the lead product. Too many messages or a frequent switch of central advertising content does more to confuse the target groups. Focus on the main target group(s) and align your media plan to them. Illustration in the media is very possible, especially where socio-demographic characteristics exist.

CASE Building the O_2 brand

1. Big bang

The cut took place in May 2002. The O_2 brand was launched in all three markets (UK, Germany, Ireland). In Germany the brand change was carried out overnight, despite all concerns.

"VIAG Interkom is now O_2." "O_2" – an English name that had to first be learned in Germany to achieve correct pronunciation.

In the first six months, with almost four fifths of the media budget, the main concentration was on the medium of TV. This served to quickly increase brand recognition, that was already above the brand recognition of VIAG Interkom five months after the launch of O_2.

2. External factors
The brand O₂ was announced at CeBIT in March 2002 – two months before the actual brand launch – with its own O₂ trade fair stand. This alone resulted in widespread press attention.

Fig. 6: Appearance of O₂ at a trade fair

The use of celebrities was decided upon as an "accelerator" for the fast increase in awareness. Franz Beckenbauer was the first to change over from the direct competition. Beckenbauer was joined by Anke Engelke, Germany's most successful comedienne, and Dieter Bohlen, the most successful music producer. With these famous advertising partners, O₂ succeeded in sending signals to various worlds (entertainment, comedy, music, and film). Today, the testimonials act as 'turbochargers' in the communication of the brand.

3. Concentration and focus
Even after the first six months of the brand launch, the concentrated media planning (focus on TV) was retained. The lead product, Genion, was the clear focus of the communication activities, thus creating a clear counter-weight for a confusing market with over 600 packages and tariff options, and making the buying decision substantially easier for the customer at the POS.

Phase 3: Establishment
1. Securing what has been achieved
Secure the customers you have already won. The basis of good customer relationship management is always a good database. You can use loyalty promotions or promotions at the POS to generate addresses.

You can then enter into a dialogue with your customers – depending on the alignment and the available funds, this can range from dialogue marketing, through to the creation of your own bonus system or even customer club.

2. Purposeful development
Expand your brand further in this phase. Try to win additional distribution points. Use the customers you have already reached: focus on community marketing and the radiating effect of your target group.

Your brand can be expanded and/or "enriched" with additional values in this stage: besides the central content that your brand stands for, allow additional and corresponding tones and benefits from the brand strategy to be communicated with the target groups from the brand strategy. A good way to make a brand into an "experience" is through sponsoring measures.

The lead product can also be developed further and optimized with further features or components. The core use must, however, remain standing. The launch of additional products within the brand is also a possibility. This must, however, be carried out in accordance with the motto "less is more," as this can otherwise cause confusion within the target groups and dilution of the brand.

3. Development control
Set targets for each phase of the brand building and check these on the basis of the monitoring system. A monitoring system in the form of a balanced scorecard or a brand cockpit can include both pure sales figures and brand awareness targets, advertising memory and buying preferences (these can be collected, for example, during weekly tracking within the target group). You have thus gained a basis for the fine adjustment of the marketing activities and can check your media spending on their efficiency and optimize it if necessary.

CASE Building the O_2 brand

1. Securing what has been achieved
The mobile telecommunications market has the special characteristic that a customer with a tariff for a contractual period ("post-paid") chooses to remain with the supplier for two years. In contrast to this, there is also the option of the "prepaid" card with which the customer can use the service up to the value of the card. In Germany, the ratio of prepaid to post-paid is approximately 1:1.

O_2 has had the highest proportion of post-paid customers, namely almost 60%, in the market since its brand launch. Despite this apparently stable customer relationship, the aim since the beginning has been to reduce the proportion of customers who switch to another supplier after the 24 month period (so-called "churners"). Various customer loyalty measures are implemented for this purpose, such as the customer magazine "can do" or a bonus system aligned to the intensity of telephone use. Furthermore, the after-sales service, particularly the hotlines, was constantly expanded and improved. The incentive to extend a contract after these 24 months was provided by attractive special offers.

The above measures have been successful: at 16 percent, O_2 has the lowest churn rate on the German mobile telecommunications market.

2. Purposeful development
In the phase after the brand launch, the facets of the brand were continued in communication and the POS presence. The clear and differentiated brand bracket was strengthened by increasing the content of "customer management"; the content of the brand idea "what can we do for you" is translated into the two main aspects "how can we help you?" and "how can we entertain you?" This method is also valid for the product portfolio.

The lead product, Genion, was further developed under the aspect "how can we help you?" Besides attractive additional options, surf@home was a revolutionary concept (e.g., the mobile option with which you can use all mobile networks for the same price). This allows O_2 Genion customers to access the Internet via UMTS, simply and at low cost – with up to six times the ISDN speed. Thus, O_2 Genion is now able to completely replace a landline connection.

The facet "how can we entertain you?" was also illustrated in the product portfolio: in March 2004, O_2 was the first mobile telecommunications supplier to start a mobile music service. Over 100,000 songs are available to customers for download via the mobile phone – on the move, legally, and at a good price. The songs can be loaded directly onto the mobile phone in mp3 quality.

For customers who like to use data services and mobile Internet, O_2 was the first supplier in Germany to introduce a flat rate for mobile phone surfing and mobile phone e-mailing. O_2 Active, the mobile portal of O_2, offers a comprehensive range of services that are already well-known from standard Internet.

Sponsoring that focuses on entertainment, ensures strong emotionalization for the brand, and enables target groups to experience the brand, rounding off the aspect "how can we entertain you?"

3. Achieving aims

The aims that were defined for the brand O_2 at its launch have been achieved in less than two years. The development of a unique brand world, with clear brand elements, was at the forefront and has been successfully realized: today's market research shows that O_2 is the most recognized and differentiated telecommunications brand in Germany. With a supported brand awareness of 98 percent, the brand O_2 is on the same level as established competitors. The slogan "can do" has now achieved the highest level of recognition on the telecommunications market and is attributed immediately to O_2. The lead product O_2 Genion is now the best know post-paid tariff amongst tariffs in Germany.

Several factors were responsible for the establishment of the new brand: efficient media planning, the consequent networking of the campaign on all levels, the focusing on the brand, and the readiness to operate with special advertising forms and surprise programs.

In the company itself, the brand promise is kept in the quality of products and services. The brand achieves internal identification and external differentiation.

Phase 4: Transition to classic brand management

After the preparation phase, the market launch and the establishment phase, the transition to classic brand management is introduced.

The central success factors are the continuity in the use of brand images and brand elements, and securing holistic brand experiences at all contact points between the target groups and your brand.

▶ Practical Guidelines

- A realistic brand assessment should take place at the very beginning – brand building requires high investments that should be seen as relative to the attractiveness of the brand (volume/maturity).
- Carry out a detailed analysis of your (future) competitors – based on their weaknesses (e.g., lack of attraction in certain target groups), an entry niche can be found into the market.
- A totally clear brand strategy with an unmistakable formulation of brand competence must be followed from the beginning – the brand must differentiate itself clearly from the competition.
- Courage to differentiate also relates to brand signals – ensure that these are unique and that they make your brand easily recognizable; brand signals do not stop at the logo and the color code!
- Secure the table stakes – the best differentiation strategy is useless if it does not fulfill its "homework" (= basic requirements).
- Allocate your media budget to the fast development of brand awareness in your target groups – this can mean a high TV share for national brand building.
- Try to use as many external factors as possible for your brand (events/trade fairs/testimonials) in the launch phase.
- Think about developing a good customer database from the beginning – relationship marketing ensures multipliers for your new brand.
- Set yourself concrete aims for each phase – not just sales targets, but also aims for brand awareness, readiness to buy, etc. Implement a tracking system (e.g., balanced scorecard) in order to monitor these aims and be able to react promptly to unwanted developments.

The Authors

Ivo Hoevel

After his studies in applied economics, Ivo Hoevel worked for T-Mobile in the area of product management. In 1998, he moved to Viag Interkom/O_2, where he has held various positions of responsibility in product marketing and marketing – most recently as the Head of Marketing for Germany. He has been the Vice President of Brand Management since 2004, and heads European brand management at O_2.

Karin Kaiser

After her studies in economics, Karin Kaiser held various positions in brand management at the publishers Egmont Ehapa Verlag. She then worked as senior brand manager at Danone, in addition to being a university lecturer and brand consultant. Since 2004, she has been the Head of Brand Strategy and International Branding at O_2.

Michaela Luhmann – DWS Investments

Regional Brand Expansion (Financial Services)

Brand core, brand perception, and brand architecture confronted with the six most important parameters of local market conditions

▶ Executive Summary

- Brand management has been a central topic of market-oriented company management for a long time; moreover, in the current times of global thinking, international brand expansion as a component of modern corporate and growth strategy is becoming more important.
- Internationalization of brand strategy means access into a new league, a higher division, the new demands and surrounding conditions of which should not be underestimated.
- Neither core competencies nor resources should be overstretched in the creation of a strong international brand structure.
- Business instinct, operational sensitivity, and a pronounced willingness to communicate are important factors for success, as well as a comprehensive and profound knowledge of all dimensions of the target market.
- Inter-cultural competence and readiness to carry out constant reflection are the characteristics of both international brand and business strategies.

CASE   DWS Investments – initial situation

- The opening of sales and distribution capacities, that had, until recently, been exclusive and internal, to fund providers outside the company, catapults the national fund management companies from a monopoly to an oligopoly situation within a very short period. The need for external competitiveness becomes necessary for survival, in which brand management becomes one of the most important criteria for success.
- An increase in displacement competition in the market, characterized by high production capacity of large, national suppliers and increased presence of international suppliers from the Anglo-American countries, intensifies the battle for the "share of wallet" amongst the customers. Further growth options are required besides market defense strategy: international expansion is one of the alternative growth strategies.
- Brand expansion of a subsidiary brand within the group (such as, for example DWS Investments as part of the Deutsche Bank Group) implies other important decision aspects: how do the involved brands react, which reciprocal transfer effects occur, and how may they change in the course of internationalization.
- DWS Investments' leading position in the market, developed and defended over many years, at 24 percent of the market of assets under management in Germany, sets a high standard for the success of a new, international business and brand strategy: this position on the domestic market must not be put at risk by the brand expansion.

Theoretical Model of Regional Brand Expansion

1. Definition

Brand expansion is defined as the expansion of an established brand strategy to new application areas, categories, or markets. The expansion of business activities can take place either horizontally or vertically within business strategy. A brand expansion can, therefore, take place as a brand extension in the sense of line extension, brand transfer to new product categories, or a multinational extension of business activities of one brand and/or a company. In this article, expansion should be understood as the geographical extension of the brand with an otherwise almost unchanged positioning of the business. The "export" of a brand into international markets, that is to be considered here based on a corporate market expansion strategy, materializes the components of a classic target system: increase of turnover or profit, strengthening of market position, and increase in company value, on the one hand, can however cause a rejuvenation or change in the image of the main brand, on the other hand.

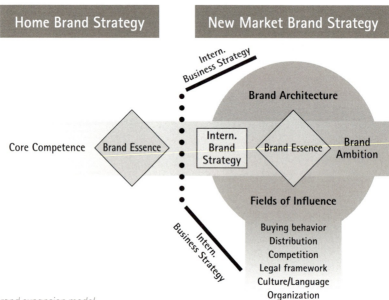

Fig.1: The brand expansion model

2. Factors for successful brand expansion

International brand expansion means, per definition, an expansion of the company model based on the successes and competencies achieved on the home market. It is precisely here, however, that one of the important risk factors lies: this business success and the proven brand strength must be exported successfully into new, international environments – without having to accept the sacrifice of competitive strength in the initial market and, thus, a reduction in profitability as a whole. The model describes the important framework conditions and success factors on this path. As the brand expansion is to be seen as part of a corporate market expansion strategy, all the factors described below are to be considered as part of the business analysis as a whole.

2.1 Brand essence and brand perception

The first step in any strategy expansion or change must be a detailed analysis of the brand. A two-stage concept is recommended, that merges practice-oriented and market research elements into an overall picture of the brand.

The definition of the core competence of the brand is recruited from the totality of all relevant performance dimensions of the company. It is determined within the framework of brand essence and reflects the assessment of the core competencies, that will ideally coincide with the actual performance capabilities of the company from the point of view of product, sales and service. This brand essence often seems to be generic, which is not surprising in the case of a market leader within a category: the category leader stands for the category, for the performance promise of not only its own products, but for the added value of the category. The question of brand perception supplements the external view of the brand and, thus, enables the identification of gaps and future communication focus when comparisons are made. The attitude "perception is reality" was adopted here: the brand perception tested in comparison to the actual performance dimensions, in order to develop a solid concept of the brand, which reveals the basic idea for the brand expansion.

CASE DWS Investments

- The brand essence of DWS also comprises brand attributes, that are closely associated with the brand essence of DB, but should also communicate further, independent ambitions: performance, innovation, service, and trust. As the market leader in the fund management market, these attributes are certainly also generic, but are equally relevant for the purchase decision process in the fund market.

- In contrast to this, the internal and external perception of the brand differed widely in the year 2000 within the dimensions of innovation. The internal perception of the permanent production of innovative fund concepts did not coincide with the external image to the same extent. This was a sign to optimize future communication content and, thus, the conscious control and penetration of singular messages.

2.2 Brand architecture

The logical structure of the brand architecture is an important prerequisite for a valid, long-term, solid brand and business expansion. Brand architecture is the term describing the systematic organization of all brands within a company or group, and has the target of allocating a specific role, level, and position to all sub-brands. The important factor for brand expansion of a company within a group is how closely the sub-brand relates to the family brand, in order to assess the brand elasticity and the importance of brand inheritance: which positive attributes does the parent brand transfer as a contribution to the internationalization of the brand, which reciprocal transfer effects, and perhaps also, which restrictions need to be taken into account and need to be overcome within the framework of target positioning and its later communicational realization. Within the framework of brand expansion, we must, therefore, check which specific market constellations of the target market to date, could possibly necessitate a change in the brand portfolio position.

CASE   DWS Investments

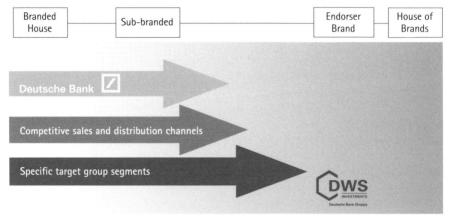

Based on David A. Aaker, E. Joachimsthaler: Brand Leadership, 2000

Fig. 2: Brand architecture of the Deutsche Bank Group with DWS Investments

- DWS Investments is defined on a brand level within the brand house of the Deutsche Bank Group, which allows the freedom and flexibility resulting from the distribution strategy, to position itself closely to Deutsche Bank.
- Simultaneously, all positive transfer effects can be activated through this categorization.
- The identification of these reciprocal transfer effects between the house brand and the sub-brand forms the basis for the new target positioning of DWS Investments and, thus, for the strategically conform and target-oriented realization of the brand strategy.

2.3 The six dimensions of influence on the target market

As part of the internationalization of a brand, the framework conditions of the target market and their reciprocal effects must be checked with regard to whether the brand promise remains relevant in the previous form, or if it needs to be adjusted in a manner that should still, however, be compatible with the brand essence. These framework conditions can be divided into direct and indirect fields of influence:

Direct fields of influence
Buying behavior and product use
Besides the corporate core competence, buying behavior and product use are the important determining factors for brand positioning and brand communication, whereby category-specific consumer needs must perhaps also be taken into account. It is also important to analyze the extent to which final consumers make their own decisions or have their buying decisions influenced by intermediaries, which is the rule in the financial services sector where advisors inform investors. Thus, an additional decision level is added, which determines the target group strategy (B2B vs. B2C or combined) and, thus, also affects brand positioning and brand communications. As both factors are also affected by the consumer and/or the intermediary as a person, the relevant determinations are also subject to cultural traditions, which must also be taken into account as part of the brand expansion.

Exact knowledge of the buying decision process and, thus, of the purchaser and the distribution mechanism in the target market, is of substantial relevance to success: the corresponding process phases should be seen as levels on which the buyer is permanently perceiving and inspecting the product (quality and communicative message) and either accepts it or refrains from the purchase. The more detailed the analysis of this buying process, and the more precise the identification of the relevant and possible countermeasures that persuade the customer to make the purchase are, the more promising the range of products and the brand communication design can be. From a classical point of view, this process begins with the fundamental relevance of the product to the user, the necessary brand recognition, along with its position and anchoring within the relevant set, brand likeability, and resultantly, purchase and repeated purchase – it should ideally end in a recommendation. Each of these stages represents a potential hurdle at which the customer can be discouraged from making the purchase. The corresponding motive situation and the possible countermeasures that can be offered, as a result of these findings, must be identified in order to be able to recognize possible brand barriers and counteract them. The level of maturity of each of the target groups must also be taken into account in this sense: how much experience does the target group have with the product category or the specific product so that it can be addressed directly at each of the named levels? Where and which measures can be put into action in the most efficient manner, and with which resources?

CASE   DWS Investments

- One of the most elementary questions that had to be answered at the beginning of a conscious structuring of the brand was: does the brand have any influence on the buying decision process of a financial investment or on the concrete purchase of an investment fund? Or are financial decisions mainly made based on performance, costs, or solely on the recommendation of the financial advisor?
- A correspondingly designed process analysis shows clearly that the quality of a financial services brand is one of the most important buying decision criteria. Thus, the brand structure and brand management have the same anchoring functions in the financial services sector as in the FMCG market.

New competitive position
The logical and clear positioning of the brand among the competition in the target market is a further key to international success. If it is successful in occupying an unoccupied, relevant, and credible position, then the brand has the famous "foot in the door." The brand then also represents a promise with news value and, thus, a competitive character.

If there is excess supply of brands on the target market with almost interchangeable products, then this task is extremely difficult: the competitiveness must be recruited most substantially from advanced performance and quality. Otherwise, an aggressive pricing strategy is the only, albeit risky, solution. Coming from a leading market position on the home market, the new competitive environment must be seen in a different light; as a market in which the business is already distributed, in which a further participant in the market is essentially superfluous. The export of the brand is, therefore, a market entry strategy, whereby the company is confronted with new requirements, both mentally and with regard to content: the leading brand on the home market is a rather unknown market participant, initially, that must work hard and possibly fight for its identity and market position at the same time, in order to achieve a profitable turnover response.

In connection with the position in the new competitive environment, the question of necessary differentiation versus sensible standardization arises repeatedly. In principle, the answer should be: as much standardization as possible, because brands travel in the age of the Internet and global technology. A truly international brand has an almost identical identity globally, and an almost identical brand promise. Differentiation can and must, on the other hand, be permissible, particularly in the distribution and the selection of communication methods. Brand management, as such, is a central process and is, therefore, standardized in principal initially. The most convincing examples for stringent brand management are very well known: Coca-Cola, Nike, Nivea, McDonald's. Their lasting and undisputed success speaks for itself.

CASE   DWS Investments

- The basis for brand expansion was a surprisingly dominant market position on the German home market, characterized by almost total sales and distribution presence, an extremely strong parent brand besides its own strong brand, and national competition that only recently existed for sales capacity.
- Market entry without any brand recognition on the target market, on the other hand, means a contrary initial situation and, thus, an initially unexpected challenge. Being a market leader with a market access strategy, therefore, initially requires a fair amount of mental strength in order to work in a new market with new, often unknown constellations.

Culture and language

Especially in markets that are geographically close to the home market, such as countries in the EU, the impression can quickly arise that the EU constitution and the free movement of money and goods will also lead to a uniform perception of brands and services. However, the culture and language of the target market are parameters that differ, despite possible geographical vicinity, and that influence or limit the positioning and/or acceptance of the brand on the target market to the same extent. Perception and meaning of quality and service, or even the success of a brand, can certainly take on different characteristics: in southern countries, success is not necessarily seen as being positive. Excruciating thoroughness, that is often regarded in a negative light in Germany, is still a convincing brand promise abroad: German Engineering. Cultural differences do not only occur with regard to consumers; they should also be anticipated within the organization. Processes and interface management are sometimes also subject to different interpretations, depending on national culture. In an inter-cultural environment, great importance must be placed on sensitivity and internal communication at the various contact points with target groups or internal organization. One thing also remains valid here: necessary differentiation yes, but sensible standardization is the key, and above all: the essence of the brand should not be damaged.

CASE   DWS Investments

- The new brand image, also realized in its logo and claim, faces the challenge of having to survive in an international market.
- The claim was translated into all relevant European languages and validated in pre-testing: surprisingly, it achieved a comparable, above-average relevance and expressiveness in all European countries.
- The advertising framework and the visuals had to be internationally strong. A balancing act: to be seen as relevant at a local level, but also to allow the roots of the German home market to show through and to communicate a part of the brand promise and/or the reason why.

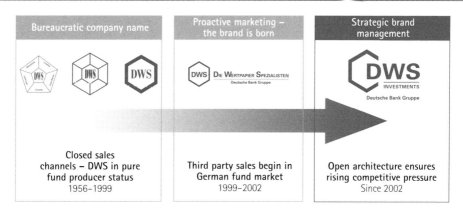

Fig. 3: From company name to strategic branding

Indirect "fields of influence"
Statutory and regulatory restrictions
Special rules on the target market can result from statutory and other regulatory conditions. They can relate to both product technology and distribution or communication. In the latter aspect, that is important for the realization of brand positioning in the target market, consumer protection regulations deserve special attention. Brand promises on the home market can be levered by this kind of local restriction, so that the proof could be questioned, on the one hand, and the unity of the proposition in various markets/countries could be undermined, on the other hand. Thus, early examination of the relevant regulations is recommended, together with any necessary feedback on findings regarding brand positioning.

Distribution
The structure of the distribution network on the target market is a further determining factor, that has a substantial influence on measures for the establishment of the brand on the target market. We must differentiate between the types of distributors on the market and both their possible interlocking structure and their price structures. The question of core competence of the brand and the company in relation to sales management, sales capacities, any established key account connections, etc. is also important here.

CASE   DWS Investments

- Because of the market potential in the funds sector, the international business strategy of DWS also included countries where no Deutsche Bank sales structure could be used for support, where fast penetration into so-called third party sales channels outside the Deutsche Bank group was necessary.
- The structure of professional, international key account management and opted pricing guidelines necessarily became the basis of business activities.

Organization
Marketing organization is not only a subsequent function of corporate and brand strategy. The correctly selected organizational form also plays a substantial role in the success of brand expansion – and can simultaneously

be seen as an indirectly influencing factor of brand expansion. What is the background of this observation? At first, organization is only a secondary element of any strategy; in the study of the implementation of brand expansion, however, the organization of brand management and marketing function itself have an important support function. This refers to both hierarchical organization and the content-related definition of the brand and marketing duties. When a brand is internationalized, focus is on the question of "central versus local." This involved distribution of tasks amongst the headquarters that had to be created, which should, of course, be established in the strongest market, probably the home market. This is where the most detailed and profound knowledge and findings regarding the core of the brand should ideally be located, that serves the purposeful and healthy control of the brand. Branding is per se a more centrally organized function than sales, which should be allocated a more local flavor.

CASE DWS Investments

- Marketing and especially strategic international brand management is considered to be a mainly central duty at DWS Invest.
- A centre of competence became necessary to secure the function of a planning- or a coordination-function, as well as for controlling strategic conformity.
- Successive special marketing disciplines were created to supply the local, more generally characterized marketing functions with professional added value.
- The continuities of communication in the new international marketing network were the factors for success – unconditional, understandable rules and framework conditions that contribute to an orderly and, thus, smoothly functioning marketing organization, that makes a contribution to sales success.

▶ Process & Implementation

The realization of an international brand strategy was only to be carried out sensibly as part of a valid international business strategy, as described briefly above. "Branding always follows strategy" is the guideline; branding is seldom a sensible company purpose in itself. The following process sequence, with a focus on brand strategy, is the result of this philosophy.

Phase 1: Core competencies

A realistic analysis of strengths and weaknesses, that includes all relevant business sectors, must be the platform for all international plans. This results in the most important concepts and starting points for the expansion. The identification of brand strengths and weaknesses is a reflection of both the internal and external perception of the brand. A classic SWOT analysis of the brand can already provide information on which components could prove to be strong and, thus, suitable for export in the brand expansion. The status quo analysis must be expanded to include a positioning plan that shows the brand ambition on the home market: what is the vision, which associations should the brand stimulate in the consumer? Should the brand fill the category – the ideal

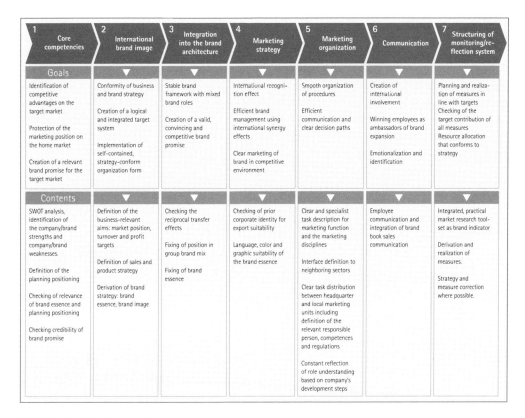

Fig. 4: Regional brand expansion process

position for the brand strategy of a market leader? Does it take the potential of the target market into account? In order to answer these questions, the above idea of "brand essence" has proved to be successful: the question of the content of the brand core, the important and unique components that make the brand unmistakable – the DNA of the brand. All answers to the above-mentioned questions must, however, always pass the test of two counter-questions: firstly is the defined aim, the ambition and/or the brand attribute relevant to the consumer and, thus, an important factor in the buying decision process? Secondly, is it a credible and, thus, achievable promise for the starting point and the legacy of the brand? Only if this question can be answered positively, i.e. if the expansion can be realized without a negative effect on the brand and the company results, is there a promise of success for the internationalization.

Phase 2: International brand image

If a competitive strength and/or a corresponding contribution can be identified in the important business sectors, then logical conversion into a satisfactory business model is the next step. What does this mean? The international business model first formulates ambitions from a market point of view, then from a financial and finally a profit-oriented perspective. All other function sectors in the company are then positioned within this target system. This is also valid, on the one hand, for the international strategy of the brand, in line with the motto "branding follows strategy." On the other hand, the brand strategy derived from the business model is a clear framework for corporate decisions: if the brand core and the brand image were defined on the basis of core competencies, and address relevant purchasing motives, the brand strategy simultaneously becomes a reflection of the business strategy. This means that brand positioning and brand promise result in clear directions, not only for communication, i.e., the language-related and visual code of the brand, but also for example selection of sales partners, price policies, product design, etc. Ideally, the brand represents the same values and promises at all contact points to the consumer, in all media, to each representative. This discovery, that is of course equally valid to the same extent for the home market, acts as a guideline and perhaps also as a correctional factor for planned initiatives or opportunities in international expansion.

Phase 3: Integration into brand architecture

The meaning of brand architecture and the important interdependencies and possible restrictions were already discussed in 2.1 and 2.2. The internationalization of this framework necessitates the examination of interrelationships and dependencies in the participating brands. The previously reciprocal transfer effects can certainly change in this process: because of the international activities of a brand, the perception of this brand can change to an image that has changed to such an extent that it also strengthens or changes the brand transfer. On the other hand, the role distribution of brands in principle is quite seldom questioned because of a brand expansion. No important changes should be made to the brand essence as a result of brand expansion. The core statement of the brand may not be changed "genetically." It should, however, be expanded to include the international components, that then enables a rejuvenated, dynamic brand image. On this understanding, the framework in and for the home market is maintained in principle.

Phase 4: Marketing strategy

The internationalization of the brand means both the expansion of activities and the inspection of the brand image elements for international suitability. Color codes, image worlds, symbols, and the identity of the statements and messages must be observed for this purpose. The target corresponds to the original aim of brand expansion: stronger recognition across borders, in order to create synergies and strengthen the brand. Discipline in the realization is elementary: both creativity and, in particular, discipline, are required in the implementation phase, together with consistent realization, which often initially also means the limitation of local design freedom in an international environment.

CASE DWS Investments

- Production of a positioned corporate design manual for the whole of Europe.
- Provision of template platforms for all printed material, ideally Internet based.
- Translation of the claim into all relevant national languages.

> 1 > 2 > 3 > 4 > **5** > 6 > 7 >

Phase 5: Marketing organization

The contribution of a satisfactory marketing organization – adapted to the target system and the resources – to success should not be underestimated. The brand comes alive with its consistent realization – and this is the only way it can support the entire target system.

In this process, functions should be defined in accordance with requirements, not in accordance with or in association with existing persons. The most important question in internationalization is: "what is central responsibility – what is local responsibility"? This is a question that may only be answered based on factual points of view – its stringency may not be subject to individual interests. Brand management is a central function. But still: project allocation, the responsibility of local resources, e.g., for certain disciplines, classic job rotation, etc. are helpful instruments in order to live out internationalization in the organization.

Another interesting finding is the fast changeability of the function contents and/or the understanding of the execution of the function of brand management. If the strategy definition is still the focus in Phase 1 of the implementation, the strategic role takes the form of control and local execution of the brand and marketing strategy. Particularly in the market introduction phase, clear local discrepancies from brand communication are not desirable. In a solidly defined and working organization, this control function should change into a value-adding instance in the short-term: in the course of further business activities, in addition to discipline, creativity and business support are in demand. The central brand and marketing management must increasingly take over the role of consultant and idea supplier. This change in the understanding of duties ideally changes in relatively short cycles and requires both very intensive reflection on the organizational development and the measures and realization qualities it provides. On the other hand, it supports the marketing organization at headquarters with regard to its own flexibility and change in self-image. This is a very interesting challenge, also from a personnel point of view.

CASE DWS Investments

- Definition of marketing function and the distribution of tasks between central and local marketing units.
- Establishing an Internet-based, so-called "marketing workbench," on which most of the communication of marketing organization runs (provision of all guidelines, templates, advertising, including detail data, campaign information and execution from all countries, best practice examples from the organization including some from other industries for know-how transfer purposes).

Phase 6: Communication

Brand book
Great importance is placed on explaining the important changes in the brand to employees and customers though illustrations and background information. In the implementation phase, employees are the first target group to be involved – moreover, they should work as multipliers and ambassadors for the expansion. Employees, especially sales employees, are the direct contact point of the brand to the customer and, thus, must be well informed about the brand attributes and ambitions. It is especially important that the brand is lived out at this point. The more new brands and, thus, new employees work with the brand, the more they must be familiarized with the history and character of the brand.

Phase 7: Creation of a target-oriented monitoring and reflection system as a revolving system

The creation of an international brand absolutely requires constant maintenance and reflection – in order to control the strategy conformity of all measures, as well as the analysis of relevance from a market and consumer point of view. A practice-oriented, i.e., a negotiable market research tool set is, therefore, of great importance. Relevant tools from an international point of view must be identified and adjusted for any existing framework. The core of the market research activities, however, is on one hand always their promptness following the reason for the research and their practice-related processing for the optimization of measures. This enables the creation of an interwoven network of indicators, that gives the international brand and the corporate aim important tips for strategy optimization or any new business sectors.

CASE   DWS Investments

- Expansion of German market – and marketing-research to include further useful tools, in order to create comparability of individual initiatives and their characteristics.
- A regular, internationally applied satisfaction analysis of all relevant sales partners became an important operational control tool.
- Other tools were put together into an indicator system that enabled the development of the brand and, thus, any prompt corrections.

▶ Key Insights

- A strong brand can travel.
- A local strategy that is based strictly on core competencies, and that is effective in a competitive environment on the home market, is certainly worth examining with a view to international expansion, in order to open up the business model and the brand to future potential. Internationality is a new league.

- International brand strategies require an exponential increase in commitment and professionalism, more system and purpose and the mental readiness to consistently question tried and tested concepts and to make new findings.
- Branding always follows strategy: a brand expansion can only be successful on the foundation of a business strategy based on core competencies; it does not serve its own purpose in the name of brand expansion.
- Internationality also means cultural discussion: and it is often elementary but also surprising how often identical buying reasons or market mechanisms can be found in the basic structures of international markets. Thus, thorough identification of the really necessary differentiation of the brand position is needed.
- Logical organization is a contribution to the achievement of the target. The organizational structure is not only the resulting function of the strategy and, thus, a troublesome obligation, but rather, in the correctly selected form and execution, an important contributing factor to the success of brand expansion.
- Brand management must be willing to develop. The international function of brand management that is created within the framework of the expansion must be prepared, as a headquarter function, to adjust its function to the life cycles of brand expansion.
- Emotionalization of the brand begins internally. Besides analytical fundamentals and disciplinary processes, the emotional charge of the brand also plays an important role in internationalization. The effect of internal brand sympathy and brand loyalty on success and the dynamics of the brand expansion can not be acknowledged clearly enough and supported by corresponding measures.

▶ Practical Guidelines

- Brand expansion requires vision, courage, and creativity – but also discipline.
- Brand and marketing are only creativity on a cure: pay attention to the greatest possible stringency in entering the target market, particularly in the implementation phase.
- It is educational to look outside your own sector. Identify industries that work with similar parameters and abstract their success factors for your sector. Only invent the wheel yourself when you are creating value by doing so.
- Strategic brand decisions are not democratic.
- A logical brand expansion that is based on core competencies may not be undermined by individual interests. You are allowed to say no!
- Enable know-how transfer in all directions.
- Establish open and constructive communication paths between the home market and the new target markets, in order to leverage value-adding and exportable specifics. This is often the way in which startling innovations are created simply, quickly, and effectively.
- In spite of all strategic consistency, international brand expansion still also means permanent change and permanent reflection on what has been achieved, findings and information.
- Above all: do not stand still.

The Author

Michaela Luhmann

After studying applied economics and writing a thesis on the marketing of fund investment management, Michaela Luhmann completed a trainee program at Deutsche Bank in Düsseldorf. After a period working on the stock market and in central fund sales, she began her career with DWS Deutsche Gesellschaft für Wertpapiersparen GmbH in 1994. There, she developed the marketing function and established brand management. Since 2002, she has developed marketing activities in both Germany and Europe, and in 2003 she took over the responsibility for marketing Deutsche Asset Management, the institutional asset management sector. Since the spring of 2005, Michaela Luhmann has been responsible for Global Brand Management at DWS Investments.

Literature Recommendations

D. A. Aaker, "Management des Markenwertes," Frankfurt/New York 1992
D. A. Aaker, E. Joachimsthaler, "Brand Leadership," New York 2000
F.-R. Esch, "Moderne Markenführung," Wiesbaden 1999
P. Kotler, F. Bliemel, "Marketing Management," Stuttgart 1995
M. Haig, "Brand failures," London 2003

Angela Nelissen – Unilever

Branding
A consistent appearance of the brand as the basis for brand success

▶ Executive Summary

"A product without clear and strong branding, is like a set of tones without a melody."
- To be competitive today, every company needs differentiated and clearly perceptible brands.
- The mission and content of these brands must define and shape the day-to-day communication with employees, customers, and suppliers – both internally and externally.
- Branding is the expression of the corporate strategy and necessitates the involvement of senior management.
- Branding activities should not be seen as a passive stamping of the brand, but rather as an active and strategic contribution to the overall brand building.
- The benefit of branding: the intensity and quality of brand perception is increasing, and a company's market position and ultimately its value are profiting from this.
- The internal and external identification potential with the company increases.
- Internal processes and decisions can be synchronized in the interest of the brand.

▶ Theoretical Model of Branding

1. Definition
By branding, we mean the coding – acoustic, visual, or multimedia-based – which creates a brand message out of a product presence. The sum of the codings should not only consistently lead through all media and contact points to a clearly recognizable brand identity, but should also coherently reflect the brand values in "bundled" form. From the classical view, this "labeling" gives a product its identity. It turns a homogeneous product into a product of its own. As early as 1939, the brand specialist Domizlaff spoke about the value of a manufacturer of branded goods being based on the familiarity of the consumer with the face of the brand product. The recognition, content-related strength, and relevance of the brand are, therefore, the objective of branding. Although these factors with successful brands are measurable to a large extent through qualitative and quantitative market research activities, their creation or development process can often not be planned in its entirety. Rather, many of the brands known to us have been defined by development over many years, a history that is only attributable in part to planned branding. The text below attempts to present the branding factors that can create strong brands when they are used properly.

Why is branding important?
"Trust creation is a fundamental goal of brand design."

- Information overflow and lack of time are factors that are crying out for fast and clear options for orientation.
- The brand bundles the functional and emotional product information together into simple imagery that is quickly recognizable.

- The brand is the basis for every price differentiation.
- The brand creates the prerequisites for effective internal management processes as it represents an orientation point for values, decisions, and processes.

2. Factors of branding

The following model intends to show which factors are of significance for a holistic branding, and how these are used in practice.

2.1 Brand essence

The prerequisite of branding is the existence or determination of the brand essence. The brand essence says, in a few words, what constitutes the brand. It is decisive for expressing the brand clearly for all those involved internally, and shows the direction for the development of all activities that support the brand. The brand essence is, so to speak, the core of the brand.

With established brands, this essence can often be found in the brand history and is connected to the original reason for the development of the brand. An updated brand essence can be developed on this basis for future work. With new brands, the brand essence is the main idea that defines the brand development. Usually, consumer research should be used when defining the brand essence of existing and new brands to verify the consumer relevance and motivation of the brand essence.

It is important for there to be agreement in the entire management team (internally and externally) on the content of the brand essence, because only then, in working together, can all activities build coherently on this brand essence and thus a strong clear image of the brand with the consumer develop. The brand essence is the lynchpin of the brand key (5 below) that brings together all decisive brand-relevant information.

2.2 Brand design

When the brand essence has been established, it has to be expressed in all brand appearances and at all contact points with the user with an appropriate coding. Identity books or brand style bibles are proven methods to anchor the semantic and semiotic design guidelines of a brand. They are an important requirement for brand signals to be used consistently. If these are used coherently in various communication channels, a holistic image of the brand is created.

How can brand design be used to create a strong brand?

2.2.1 Visual brand design
- Logo – individually designed brand flourish, defined in its form and color, often in the typography and color specific to the brand (e.g., Coca-Cola). The logo is the universal recognition symbol of the brand.
- Brand icon – unique symbol that condenses the brand idea. It works across all media and is the visual spearhead of an integrated brand program (e.g., Nike swoosh, BP shell). Symbols are of significance particularly with brands that operate on an international basis, as they overcome language barriers more easily.
- Brand figures (e.g., Meister Proper, HB man, building society fox) – these offer a high dynamic dimension beyond logo and brand icon as the figure personifies partial aspects of the brand personality and can make direct contact/direct dialogue with the target group. In addition, it offers great emotional projection space.

- Typography (e.g., Mercedes Benz, Nivea have a font that has been specially designed for their brand in their overall appearance). Of great importance in particular with product fields (e.g., automotive, telecommunication) that require a high degree of explanation.
- Layout – classic example is the VW appearance – harmonized page conception across all print media.
- Picture sequences (e.g., Dove drop, Jacobs coffee crown, Maggi's spoon). These picture sequences are typically used to emphasize special brand qualities in film form.

2.2.2 Auditory brand design
Serves in particular to emotionalize the brand message, and creates additional differentiation, especially in markets with low functional depth (e.g., alcohol).

- Sound logo: short two- to five-second sequence of sounds, can be instrumental, spoken, or sung version of the brand name or slogan.
- Brand slogan: e.g., "A Mars a day helps you work, rest, and play" pinpoints in a short form both the brand differentiation through the statement of the content, as well as brand values in the form of address and tonality. Is often supported in a musical or rhythmic way.
- Brand topic: an exclusive piece of music that defines the acoustic image of a brand (e.g., Bacardi, Beck's).
- Sound engineering: is of great importance in the automotive sector. Every passionate driver will therefore not only be able to recognize "his" brand by the sound of the engine but also even by the sound of one of the car doors shutting. These features are also being given increasing attention in the consumer goods sector, too. In this way, the exact clicking sound of a cream can closing can indeed be seen as an element of brand building.

2.2.3 Sensory brand design
- Haptic product features have a high sensual component and work very much sub-consciously. Here, too, identification and preference options for brands are generated. The surface form and the finish of cosmetics and many other products is correspondingly not only a product feature, but can also be used strategically to give the brand profile. The correct sensors are a real messenger of the brand promise because they are tangible.
- Olfactory features: the use of brand-specific scent coding is not yet extremely widespread, but is already normal in some industries. These include not only the perfumes and cosmetics industry. In the automotive sector, the issue of the interior smell (at least at the time of sales) is of just as much importance as in the up-market retail sector.

2.2.4 Semantic brand design
- Speech characteristics, tonality: the choice of brand-specific language suggests "the brand is speaking here": as with a person, language not only conveys content, it also conveys, much more, values and personality, and thus offers great identification potential. Just imagine the poster adverts of Sixt or Lucky Strike without text. Even without a voice or language characteristics, it was possible in these examples to create very tangible brands. In combination with a voice, this can be enhanced even further. (e.g., After Eight TV, Ikea, Ferrero Rocher).

The active integration of as many design features as possible in the brand formation leads to branding becoming a contribution in brand management that creates value. The name, logo, image or word brand, and the smell or sound mark, all individualize the brand performance and, thus, enhance its value.

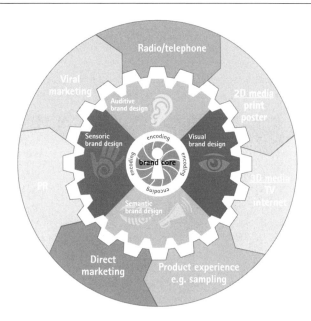

Fig. 1: Holistic brand design

CASE The examples of T-Online, the car rental company Sixt, and the cosmetics brand Dove illustrate the importance of holistic branding for various business fields.

T-Online
Telekom, as a classical supplier in the multimedia communication business, needed an extremely rapid build-up in recognition for its brand T-Online in the very dynamic Internet sector. The selection of TV as the decisive medium, due to its speed and strong coverage, was therefore clear. Here, the design of sound logo and visual logo could work together coherently. The catchy sound logo conveys digital competence, precision and speed, whereas the color combination magenta-gray represents the symbiosis of technology and modernity. The design of the logo and the Internet presence adopt this in equal measure. Sensory components of brand design are not yet relevant for the Internet – the semantic brand design is particularly important for this news- and explanation-intensive product category.

· · · · · **T** · · Online ·

Fig. 2: T-Online logo

Sixt
In the case of Sixt, the dominance of the visual factors can be recognized. As a car rental company, Sixt reaches its customers primarily at airports and railway stations where the spontaneous decision to hire a car is made. In these places, Sixt draws attention to itself through large, cheekily formulated brand messages in the striking colors of orange and gray. Since the introduction of the brand, logo, typography, and layout have been consistently used at all contact points with the customer . They create a brand continuum, from the first point of contact (by use of a large poster above the Sixt

counter), right through to stepping into the car. Auditory and sensory brand design plays practically no major role. Quite the opposite to the semantic factors; few brands have used form of address and language characteristics so clearly for the recognition value of the brand as Sixt. Singular brand or product promises are pinpointed in a brief, precise, and cheeky way, creating a clear communication of the brand promise: clever, precise, cheeky – yes, almost aggressive – but with style and humor.

Fig. 3: Sixt ad

Dove

In the case of Dove, almost all factors of brand design play a role in creating the overall brand. At the consumer's first point of contact with the brand, the logo and brand icon (the stylized dove) are of extreme significance. These two elements symbolize, through the language of color and shape, the mildness and care of the brand, and are used coherently in all visual media. The same can be found in a prominent place on all types of packaging. For a global cosmetics brand, the simple visual brand icon is of great importance for achieving rapid recognition independent of local fonts. In the hard fought cosmetic market, TV is essential for the rapid spread of product news to the target group, that mostly consists of women. Here, logo and brand icon are supplemented by a picture sequence – a flowing drop of milk that symbolizes the richness of the products. This is also to be found on the front of all types of packaging of the core range. Furthermore, the clarity and trustworthiness of the brand is communicated through a coherent simple layout (reduced gray/blue text on white background) and a no-frills typography. With regard to the auditory brand design, there is a philosophy of reduced, simple impression, but no coherent sound logo, brand topic or even brand slogan has been used, except in the respective brand introduction phases, to meet the requirements of the variety of the range. Sound engineering plays a major role at Dove in the framework of product development, but has not been used so far as a brand design feature.

Sensory brand design is decisive at the second point of contact with the consumer – at the shelf. Haptic features of the packaging influence the form language of all packagings that are oriented to organic forms. Even in the soft, smooth finish of the surfaces, Dove tries to live up to its brand promise. Scent is also of crucial importance in the cosmetics industry where products can be experienced by the senses directly on the skin. However, here a balance must always be found between optimal product scent and brand scent coding. In cooperation with scent experts and perfume houses, a scent range was defined for all products at Dove and, in addition, a typical brand scent for the core area of business.

Finally, there is the semantic brand design. A central advertising team at Dove monitors the tonality of each communication – even across many languages, and checks whether it corresponds to the brand spirit. In international business, however, it is practically impossible to turn language into a brand-building feature. In addition, the brand statement must subordinate itself in some cases to the product content. However, a clear, no-frills style ensures that the brand always remains true to itself and communicates with its target group in a familiar, unpretentious, and honest manner.

Fig. 4: Dove

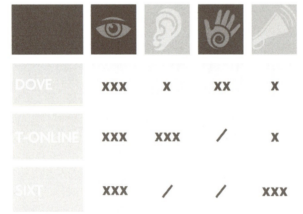

Fig. 5: Importance of the design features

▶ Process & Implementation

"The process is the process – but then you need a spark of genius."

Below, a typical procedure for the entire branding process is to be described. A complex repositioning under ideal conditions is assumed. In reality, it is seldom that you can take so much time, and not all the phases are necessary. It has been shown in international marketing practice that a period of two to three years for all phases, from the brand audit to the global introduction and/or repositioning, is utterly realistic. This applies in particular to the international context, as cross-border solutions are more sophisticated in their conception and more time-intensive in their market research. Furthermore, local adaptations of parts of the brand design and the communication solutions will be unavoidable.

When a brand process is started, this does not mean that all market activities or new introductions, regarding the brand concerned, stop. Often, such a process takes place in the background while many other brands and product activities continue.

Phase 1: Quo vadis?

The beginning of any brand discussion must be the determination of the brand identity, that is also called brand audit. What does the brand stand for today? What should or can it stand for in the future? What changes are necessary to make the new brand promise credible and interesting? Competitive environment, brand essence, brand vision, brand character, emotional and functional brand benefit, and the target group should be part of the discussion. A well-known presentation form for this information is the brand key that records the crucial data in short form. A brand book or a brand bible have also proved their worth. Although they are more complex to create, they give the brand personality more room to show itself visually.

Both the company management, agencies, and also all the departments within the company, should be involved in determining/defining the brand identity that the brand presents to the outside world (e.g., outdoor sales force). Brands are seldom created on the pinboard. Instead, in most cases they have grown and have a history. Often, information about the brand identity and the brand character can be found in the beginnings of the brand. Sometimes, however, a brand has to be totally redefined. In almost all cases, the integration of market research – both about the brand and about the competitors and the general market environment – is important. A time frame of eight months is therefore absolutely realistic and may be longer with very complex or global brands, until the current

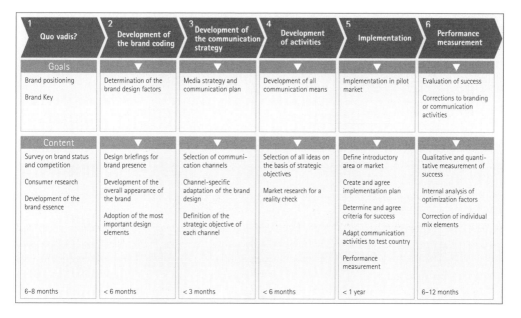

Fig. 6: Branding process

and/or desired brand identity is clearly established. Phase 1 is the basis for all subsequent steps and should not be underestimated in its importance. Only when the strategically correct prerequisites for the brand positioning are created here, can the subsequent phases lead to success.

Phase 2: Development of the brand coding

As soon as agreement has been reached about the desired brand identity, the design phase starts. How is the brand to be presented? How should its content and values be communicated to the target group in an effective and appealing manner? Multidisciplinary cooperation, under the coordination of a lead agency or an internal brand director, is the usual procedure. In doing so, there should only ever be one goal: the creation of a harmonized brand appearance that can meet the requirements of any communication medium, both internally and externally. In practice, the 2nd and 3rd phases can overlap time-wise, as every medium has special requirements for a successful brand coding.

The starting point for this phase is always the creation of one or several design briefings for the various factors of brand design. These vary from case to case, but nearly always embrace the brand logo and/or brand icon and the layout. Depending on requirements, thought should also be given in this phase to the design of subordinate design factors, and the suitable brand agencies, corporate identity agencies, and packaging agencies, up to the classical advertising agency and event agencies, should be briefed. Now is also a good moment to get the company management on board again to ensure that they are behind the project. It makes sense to organize an intermediate presentation for core areas of the company so that internal identification and support for the brand design can be created early on.

Phase 3: Development of the communication strategy

Where can my brand message meet my target group in an ideal form? Where can I achieve my communication objective most effectively? How can I make my brand message come alive for the target group? In cooperation with the media agency or the internal communication department, the brand communication plan should be devised. This will provide information about in which form the brand best communicates with its target group, in addition to revealing opportunities for new communication possibilities. It does not have to involve just the classical media such as TV, print, or poster. A communication strategy based on new media or via consumer events can also be promising. In the majority of cases, the communication plan will have a 360-degree approach that consists of a mixture of classical and modern media, in cooperation with PR, events, direct marketing activities, and possibly viral marketing, etc. The role of each medium with regard to its qualitative communication task and quantitative media performance should now be defined clearly. TV, for example, could ensure rapid establishment of brand recognition, PR strengthen the credibility of the brand, while print and direct marketing activities offer detailed information on the product range. In this phase, the importance and differentiation between the various media and the specific brand design for the core media are defined. It is essential that the brand is expressed very strongly in the core media as, for instance, can be seen in the example from Sixt in exterior advertising, Dove on TV, and T-Online on the Internet.

Phase 4: Development of activities

The role of each medium has been established. So has the desired brand coding. Now the next task is the special implementation. How can each medium reach its objective best? The specific brand message must be implemented effectively for each medium, and the interaction of all media must become a consistent and coherent overall message. A brand agency or a network of specialized agencies is often briefed on the communication tasks, taking into account the brand coding that has already been defined. However, it is also possible that individual elements of the brand coding are not completed until now, as the "inspirational" idea is created in the framework of the special media.

Once the communication ideas are all on the table, their assessment needs to be based on the strategic objective (from Phase 3). What was the strategic task of each medium? Can the idea presented achieve this? It is to be recommended that a reality check with consumers is carried out in this phase. Typically, quantitative or qualitative surveys of the target group help to hone clarity and strength of the creative idea. All in all, around six months should be planned for this phase. In the end, ideally there is still time to look at the whole communication mix from a holistic perspective to answer the following questions: Does the communication mix fit together? Is a coherent message being generated? Do all brand design features build on one another? What is missing? What is redundant?

Phase 5: Implementation

From theory to practice. Depending on the situation, a test market, a market simulation or the selection of a pioneer country can make sense in this phase before a national or international introduction is done. An implementation that is as planned as possible, but is still flexible and that satisfies national market and sales conditions, is crucial to success. That is why early cooperation with the launch partner, whether it be a sales channel or a country, is very important. This should begin as soon as possible, so that the market information and special requirements can be taken into account in the design. Often, it is just minor operational details that can lead to failure. Many good brand concepts fail because of the sub-optimal implementation. Good documentation of the implementation phase, from the setting of objectives through implementation details to individual results, is the prerequisite for using this learning phase to optimize all brand design features and communication activities before the final introduction is started.

Phase 6: Performance measurement

If a market introduction has taken place, continual monitoring of the individual activities is decisive for long-term success. It is important here to agree the decisive criteria for success beforehand, and to monitor these in the long-term. Using the same market research methods over a longer period has stood the test of time, as only in this way are results and long-term analyses comparable. Not only the company's own brand and its communication activities should be monitored, but also competitors, the market environment, and consumer behavior. All these factors have an influence on the perception of the brand design. Furthermore, they provide information about when and why the brand should adapt to new conditions, and/or about how new trends can be generated out of the brand itself. With successful major brands, it can often be established that a continuous and/or cyclical branding process is taking place behind the scenes. The resulting adaptations of the brand design ensure that the brand appears up-to-date at all times without this having to be totally "overhauled" at any time. On a smaller scale, this continual process would undoubtedly be recommended for smaller brands and even crucial for success of these in fast-lived markets.

International Aspects

If the branding process is carried out for an international brand, the following factors in particular are to be taken into consideration:

Time frame – More and more brands are being developed for several markets and/or regions. The time frame depicted in the model applies to an international branding process. If the same process were to be carried out for just one country, experience shows that a project duration of slightly less than one year can be assumed. However, the exact duration depends on the complexity of the brand design and communication tasks.

Team – A multinational project team, with experience in the different regions, will be able to manage an international branding task more easily. Furthermore, it is advisable to pay attention to the selection of a project manager with experience in similar projects and sufficient seniority to facilitate the consultation with other regions. Without the support and the active involvement of the core customers within the company, an international branding can hardly become a success. The understanding, identification, and support from all core departments of the crucial countries are decisive for success.

Complexity – The increased complexity of international branding processes must be taken into account by an extremely professional project management. As market data, consumer behavior and preferences, market research methods, competitive environment etc. are different in the markets involved, the project team should define clear criteria for the success of the project and, wherever possible, use harmonized methods. Nevertheless, some project decisions will have to be taken based on uncertainty or incomplete data. Particularly with complex requirements, not everything can and should be tested in detail. There should be a sensible balance between effort and result. That is why it is even more important that the decision competences of the project manager, as well as the exact project requirements, are clarified in advance and communicated to the deciding departments in the company.

Costs – With international processes, a multiple of the project costs with national processes can be assumed. An additional requirement of consumer information, cooperation with internationally experienced agencies, and the development of a brand design that is successful in the international context, lead, as experience shows, to significantly higher costs. However, these are compensated by the long-term advantages of a centrally managed brand that operates at international level.

▶ Key Insights

- Branding bundles the functional and emotional product information in coherent symbolism.
- The start of any branding must be the determination of the brand identity – giving direction for the internal corporate identity and external brand presence.

- Branding is part of the corporate strategy and must therefore be supported by the top management of the company.
- Branding is created through the coherent and consistent use of brand design.
- Brand design consists of four factors – visual, auditory, sensory, and semantic brand design.
- The design of all brand signals is created out of the understanding of the brand identity with the goal of communicating this in an effective and synergetic manner.

▶ Practical Guidelines

- Do not delegate branding – the coordination of all activities is in the company's hand. A neutral selection from all available options can only be made internally!
- Ensure that the entire company, as well as external agencies and partners, understand the brand and live its values.
- Learn to say no – make sacrifices to get a clear branding. Typically there are too many ideas!
- Beware of tactical and short-term changes in the brand design! They often cause long-term damage to the strength of the brand.
- Learn about good examples of branding outside your sector!
- Involve your "customers" – internally and externally – to optimize the holistic appearance of the brand.
- Give yourself and your agencies time to create or optimize the brand presence in its entirety before you communicate it to your external customers.

The Author

Angela Nelissen

After her degree in political economics and her international MBA, Angela Nelissen has been working in the national and international brand management of successful cosmetics brands in Germany and France for twelve years. Since 2001, she has been the European head of Dove skin care, and since 2005, the European head of the overall Dove brand.

Literature Recommendations

M. Neumeier, "The Brand Gap," Berkely 2005
A. and L. Ries, "The 22 immutable laws of branding," New York 2002
E. Joachimsthaler, D. A. Aaker, "Building Brands without Mass Media, Harvard Business Review on Brand Management," Boston 1999
A. Wheeler, "Designing Brand Identity," Harvard Business Review on Brand Management, New Jersey 1999

Dr. Wulff-Axel Schmidt, Dr. Kay Oelschlägel – Luther Rechtsanwaltsgesellschaft mbH In Association with Ernst & Young

Brand Value Management

Maximizing the value of a company's trademark portfolio

▶ Executive Summary

- ☐ The brand is part of a company's assets. It can be utilized to spur growth, to improve the awareness and image of both the company and its products, and to preserve the company's market position in the face of competition. It also improves revenues, enhances company and credit ratings, reduces costs, and facilitates the successful conclusion of merger and acquisition deals.
- ☐ Frequently, companies do not properly keep track of the existence of their intellectual property assets. This, in turn, often results in a failure by such companies to fully utilize their intellectual property assets in their brand's best interest. Additionally, the lack of an efficient monitoring system might also result either in the loss of intellectual property rights due to non-utilization or their non-protection.
- ☐ Consequently, companies are often unable to protect their brand to the fullest extent possible.
- ☐ In addition, limited knowledge of available intellectual property or restricted protection of a company's intellectual property assets sets limits to marketing efforts whose purpose is to increase the value of the brand.
- ☐ Brand Value Management offers a centralized instrument to handle, form and promote a brand. It organizes and administers the intellectual property rights of a company thus helping the company to find rights it may otherwise not have been aware of. Brand Value Management also improves the utilization of these rights, cuts costs, opens up new revenue streams, improves the legal protection of the rights and supports unified branding efforts.
- ☐ Brand Value Management integrates the marketing, legal, tax and financial aspects involved in maintaining a brand thereby enhancing company growth and profit margins.

▶ Theoretical Model of Brand Value Management

1. Definition

Brand Value Management is a unified approach for managing a company's trademark portfolio. It integrates the marketing, legal, tax, and financial aspects of a brand with its contributing elements in order to develop a brand strategy with an integrated financial and legal control mechanism. Its aim is to achieve (1) brand growth, (2) enhance the control and legal security of a brand and (3) ensure that the markets, financial, tax, and legal aspects of a company's trademark portfolio are utilized optimally.

2. Factors of Brand Value Management

Brand Value Management is a networking model which seeks to facilitate communication between the three core brand value contributors, i.e., the Strategic Marketing Value, Financial Value, and Legal Value Contributors,

Fig. 1: Elements of Brand Value Management

by adopting a policy which carefully guides the participants toward the necessary communication contents. The network is formed in a way in which all groups can easily communicate with each other.

In theory the information should have already been shared among the members of the different task groups and in fact such information usually is – at least partly – shared among the contributors. But frequently the information shared is shared at the wrong point of time or in insufficient forms thereby resulting in the members of these different task groups taking different and independent approaches to the handling of their tasks. Accordingly, the current approach hampers all involved parties and jeopardizes the defined goals.

In connection with the target-oriented networking, the main contributors are assigned new tasks aimed at improving their contribution to the value of the brand by either direct value driving actions or by facilitating the brand value driving tasks of the other two main contributors.

The Marketing Manager is in a unique position to administer this process and by way of the networking model gains not only additional information but also new options for his strategic development endeavors. This is especially true in international corporations or groups of companies which have to cover all subsidiaries under their main or core brands.

2.1 Strategic marketing value contributors

Strategic marketing value contributors are the marketing department, corporate communication department, and other internal and external contributors, who work with, define, develop, and communicate the brand; in other words, those who are responsible for the market creativity approach and the classical brand values. As part of the Brand Value Management, in addition to their regular tasks, they are requested to communicate both their understanding of the brand, itself, and their understanding of the relationship between the brand's core strategic marketing values and the intellectual property assets of the company to the other two main contributors. They have to define the necessity/the value of all existing intellectual property rights for their chosen brand and communicate the results of this process to the other two main contributors. They also have to assess the strategic marketing value/potential of intellectual property rights independent from the brand and any activity of the company. In addition they are requested to communicate, in advance, their branding projects to the other contributors to allow for incorporation into the studies of these contributors. The strategic marketing value targeted process will result in a more unified brand strategy, better awareness of the existing intellectual properties in the company by the creative contributors and will integrate the marketing of these brands. In short, this approach will lead to better brand management. In addition this approach gives the company's creative forces new options for the strategic development of the brand.

The market creativity approach within the Brand Value Management system can be described as follows:

Firstly, the market creativity approach requires an accurate assessment of the market, the customers, and their needs. During this phase, the core needs of the customers have to be identified. The identification of customer's needs is one of the keys for successful marketing measures. After being identified, the core needs need to be analyzed. Within the analysis it is necessary to determine, whether the customer's needs reconcile with the products offered or will be offered by the company. Based on the results of the analysis, the marketing department will be able to create a brand and arrange the brand and market strategy for the brand.

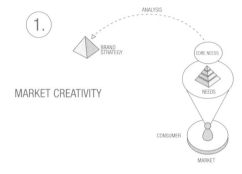

Fig. 2: Analysis of customer's needs

The next step will be to implement the brand strategy on the market. In doing so, the marketing department has to take the right and relevant measures as a basis. The measures will be dominated by the 4 Marketing P's (product, place, promotion, price). In this context, measures regarding the "product" are all aspects relating to the design of the product. Aspects around the "place" deal with problems such as the question where the products should be launched or the best means of distribution etc. "Promotion" measures relate to classical go-to-market aspects such as promotion activities during and after the inauguration phase of a brand and/or product. Finally, the market strategy has to deal with all questions relating to the determination of the "price."

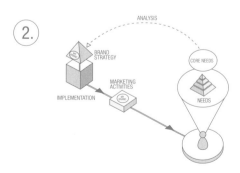

Fig. 3: Brand strategy development and implementation into the market

In addition, the marketing department also has to identify the customer's unconscious needs by analyzing their buying behavior. The identified unconscious needs have to be integrated in the market strategy of the brand. This process is not rigid, but has to be brought in line with the current consumer needs in regular intervals.

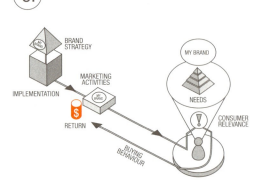

Fig. 4: The brand strategy based on customer's needs is causing a stronger customer acceptance and will generate more sales and revenues

2.2 Financial value contributors

Financial value contributors are the company's auditing and tax departments as well as external consultants in this area. They are requested to assess the financial value of the brand as a whole, as well as of all the existing

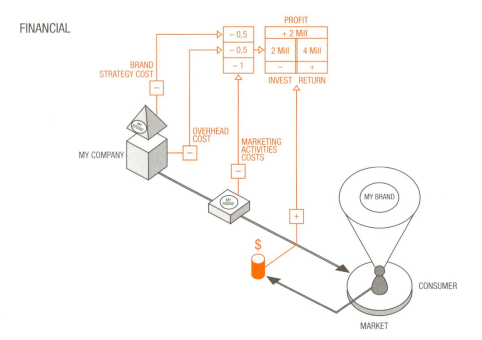

Fig. 5: A clear brand controlling leads to transparency as regards costs and effectiveness of the brand activities and results in a more precise allocation of the monetary ressources

intellectual property assets. The financial value assessment is to be based on the different strategic marketing value assessments of the strategic marketing value contributors (depending on either its general marketability or its brand-related value) and the scope of legal protection afforded by these intellectual property assets as reported by the legal value contributors. Although it is admitted that the value assessment is already an integral part of these contributors' normal operations, the introduction of an improved communication supported by way of a database will greatly facilitate their work. The financial value contributors also have to set the financial value in comparison to the costs for protection. This information is to be applied to – together with the strategic marketing value contributors – assess the market value of the intellectual property assets and to improve the asset balance. Furthermore, the information will also help these Financial Value Contributors to decide which intellectual property assets should be eliminated to reduce costs. In addition the assets are to be considered regarding their tax implications. At the end of the financial value targeted process an increase of the return on investment shall be achieved.

The tax/financial tasks within the Brand Value Management system are mainly the regular brand valuation and the financial control, i.e., the controlling of the investment costs and the returns on investment in connection with the conception and implementation of a market strategy for a brand. Brand valuation is a special subject which in particular must deal with the different methods of brand valuation. Due to its large scope the subject cannot be discussed further within this essay.

In comparison with brand valuation, aspects of financial control can be simplified as follows: in order to know, whether a brand strategy is a profitable investment, it is necessary to compare the balance of the investments on the one hand and the returns on the other hand. Investments are the brand strategy costs based on conceptional work (marketing, legal, and financial), the overhead costs (e.g., personal fix costs) and the marketing activity costs for the implementation of the brand strategy on the market. Returns are the turnovers which have been realized in connection with the brand. It is well-known that in case the returns are higher than the investments, profit has been made. The financial control has to be conducted at least every year. It is expected that in the first year and probably the year after only a small profit or no profit at all will be realized. However, profit should be realized thereafter. Otherwise the market strategy has to be reconsidered.

2.3 Legal value contributors
The group of legal value contributors is formed by the legal department, the IP department (if such exists) and external consultants (IP lawyers). They are required to compile and to maintain a complete catalogue of existing intellectual property rights and their status (ownership, licensing deals, protection scope, renewal-dates). The catalogue has to be shared with the other value contributors and especially has to be compared to the list of intellectual property assets incorporated into the branding concepts of the strategic marketing value contributors. Although most legal departments already maintain such a catalogue frequently it is not aligned with the inventory lists of the other departments. The legal value contributors also have to acknowledge and to assess the concepts of that strategic marketing contributors in order to define the necessity for the establishment of additional intellectual property protection or for the extension of protection scope and then have to realize those. The information is to be shared with the financial value contributors as well as with the strategic marketing value contributors. In a joint effort with the tax specialists the intellectual property assets are to be transferred into a tax-optimized set-up (e.g., a centralized IP holding company). The legal value targeted process eventually results in an optimized IP-portfolio as well as an improved protection for the brand. The legal approach within the Brand Value Management system can be described as follows:

To understand the legal approach, one should anticipate the optimized scenario: a company has established and implemented a brand strategy. The brand is accepted by the customers and the customers identify the company with the brand. All investments that customers make in favor of the brand are direct revenues of the owner of the brand (i.e., the company).

This scenario will change rapidly if another company uses an identical or similar brand for identical or similar goods or services. In this case, the customer will spend at least part of his investments not for the brand of the company, but for the plagiarism. As a result, the company will lose revenues.

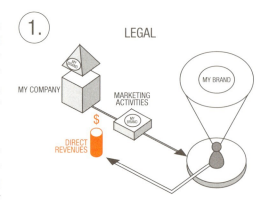

Fig. 6: Scenario of a market without identical or similar brands: all investments by customers in the company's brand are direct revenues of the brand owner

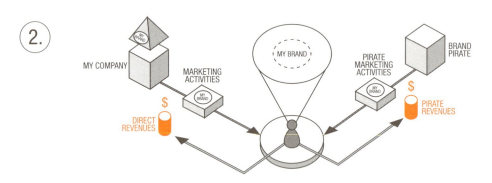

Fig. 7: Scenario with identical or similar brands: the owner of the original brand will lose revenues

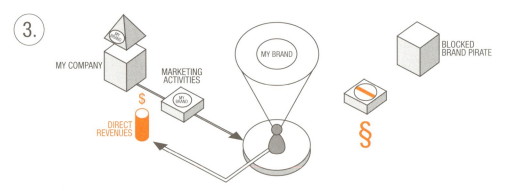

Fig. 8: A brand protection strategy hinders brand piracy – all revenues of the brand potential are revenues of the owner of the brand

At this point legal activities should commence. The brand has to be protected to prevent market confusion and loss of revenues. For example, a pirate brand user has to be stopped and undertake a cease-and-desist declaration in favor of the company in order to avoid repeated breaches and enduring loss of value. Should the pirate brand user refuse to undertake a cease-and-desist declaration, it is necessary to institute legal proceedings in order to prevent further use of the brand. Once the pirate brand using has been stopped successfully, the customer will again spend his investments in favor of the company's brand completely.

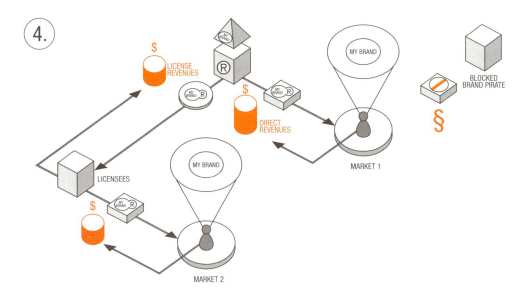

Fig. 9: License systems improve brand potential and according revenues of the owner by way of developing new markets

The protection and defence of the brand is further relevant for installing a license system and for receiving royalties. A licensee will only be willing to pay license fees, if no other party uses the brand or a similar sign without the owner's authorization. Therefore, the brand owner is obliged to protect the brand against identical or similar signs. In order to do so, he has to observe the market intensively and block every single use of a confusing brand.

2.4 Summary

Overall result of the Brand Value Management model is an ongoing, target-oriented communication, that sets up a system of checks and balances that not only assures the company of a sound protection of all necessary elements of a brand and related IP's, but also an improved Return on Investment (RoI) (due to potential cost reduction, additional revenue generated from unused IP's etc.) and extended freedom for the marketing creativity forces, as they are able to step outside the border of former restrictions and to open up new options for the strategic development of a better brand management.

▶ Process & Execution

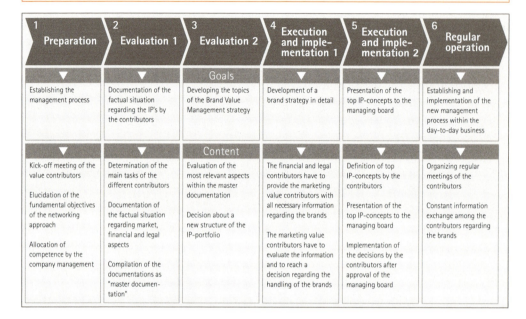

Fig. 10: Brand value management process

Phase 1: Preparation – network set-up and management adaptation

Phase 1 starts with a "kick-off" meeting of the strategic marketing value contributors, the financial value contributors and the legal value contributors organized and chaired by the marketing management. Depending on company internal structure the departments or the personnel belonging to the same "contributor class" may want to meet in an-internal kick-off event or even form a task group. Reestablishing or tweaking existing network channels will allow for concentrated information flow and assure that the marketing manager is able to gain the maximum strategic advantage for the brand.

The network set-up is followed by the elucidation of the fundamental objectives of the networking procedure. At the beginning, it is necessary to inspire confidence and to dispel potential notions that the network is meant to allow one contributor or manager to control the other involved parties. The benefit of the shared information has to be emphasized and it should be clarified that the specific information helps each contributor most if shared.

If necessary, company management must notify and confirm that the contributors respectively selected members of a "contributor class" are granted the competence that allows them to request the information necessary for the network, e.g., requests subsidies to report all necessary intellectual property assets and their content and use etc. Furthermore the competence of departments which are not contributors must be adapted so that any relevant competence is transferred to contributing departments, assuring that those receive all information necessary for the Brand Value Management regarding e.g., newly established intellectual property assets and can assure that they are entered into the system properly (in order to receive appropriate legal protection, to utilize them to the fullest extent possible, to represent them with the correct asset value in the balance sheets – if allowed – and to build a tax-optimized position).

Phase 2: Evaluation 1 – initial documentation of actual situation by the contributors

The complexity as well as the expected time and financial implications of this step vary widely depending not only on the company's size, but also on the level and quality of documentation and organization prior to the introduction of a coordinated Brand Value Management. In fact, this step may be unnecessary in respect of preparations already done by individual contributors of the "contributor class." The main tasks of the different contributors in their areas are listed below.

The strategic marketing value contributors have the following tasks:

- definition of the brand,
- comprehensive inventory list of intellectual property assets integrated into/utilized by the brand and other intellectual property assets due to the knowledge of the contributors including information for each intellectual property assets whether it is used currently or whether there are plans to use it in future,
- assessment of the intellectual property assets regarding their necessity/value for the brand and activities of the company,
- assessment of the intellectual property assets regarding their non-brand and non-company activity related strategic marketing value/potential.

The financial value contributors have the following tasks:

- assessment of the financial value of the brand and intellectual property assets as far as those intellectual properties are known to the task group,
- assessment of the tax related situation.

Finally the legal value contributors have the following tasks:

- compilation of a list of intellectual property assets based on the data of different contributors and their departments and from all other available company data,
- examination of the protection scope and status (renewal dates etc.) of the intellectual property assets.

The documentation compiled during Phase 2 should be exchanged between the contributors. If differences are detected regarding the inventory of intellectual property assets the evaluation has to be repeated regarding the information received from the other contributors. Finally the compilation and adaption of the documentations will be designated as the "master documentation" to which all contributors have access. Ideally the marketing management is again heavily involved in this step or may even guide it.

Phase 3: Evaluation 2 – developing of a Brand Value Management strategy

In this phase of evaluation a Brand Value Management strategy has to be developed by the strategic marketing value contributors. Within this development the strategic marketing value contributors have to consider legal and tax/financial aspects as outlined by the other contributors. The effort with the legal value contributors is to decide whether the IP-portfolio should be reduced or expanded and whether the administration, prosecution, and litigation proceedings of the IP's should be improved or changed. The input of the financial value contributors shall give answers to the questions whether an IP-holding should be established in order to achieve a more efficient IP-organization within the company and to reduce tax costs.

Phase 4: Execution and implementation 1 – contributor level

In this phase the different value contributors have the following tasks:

The strategic marketing value contributors have to deal with building up a strategy regarding each brand within the trade mark portfolio in detail. The main tasks are the following:

- joint decisions with the legal value contributors which brands might be used for licensing to third parties or could (and should) be surrendered,
- development of a strategy for the future of each brand of the trade mark portfolio considering potential of "new found" intellectual property assets and new options made available due to the improved information exchange process within the network,
- implementation of the updated strategy and potential concepts for brand development improvements.

The financial value contributors main tasks are the following:

- adaptation of balance sheets to incorporate the evaluated brands – as far as admissible,
- adaptation of loans to the changed credit-rating due to the improved asset-base,
- development of a tax optimized concept for the intellectual property assets and its realization in close relationship with the legal value contributors – the tax optimized holding concept can be adapted to allow for control of the intellectual property assets as instrument of a control system for subsidies etc.,
- set up of tax optimized IP holding concept.

The legal value contributors have to fulfill all tasks regarding the legal aspects, e.g.:

- adjustment of the protection scope for brands, if necessary establishment of new protection or waiver of protection – in close discussion with the marketing manager as head of the strategic marketing value contributors,
- set up of the tax optimized IP holding concept, transfer of brands,
- set up of licensing business to third parties.

Phase 5: Execution and implementation 2 – management level

Some of the plans and decisions decided upon by the contributors in Phase 4, especially regarding strategic decisions in marketing – e.g., the surrender of a trademark or an extension of business into the licensing of trade marks to third parties – have profound effects on the whole corporation. Depending on the corporate structure and possible advantages the board or other top level management members may want to or need to approve these. A marketing manager who is chairing the whole Brand Value Management may receive extended competence to handle these jointly received and prepared decisions

Phase 5 consists of e.g., presentations of proposals regarding tax optimized IP holding concepts or regarding the options for third party licensing of no longer utilized brands. Phase 5 is insofar dominated by the adaptation of the concepts and the following implementation by the contributors after approval of the managing board.

Phase 6: Regular operation with established Brand Value Management

All members of the contributors operate normally incorporating the newly received information into their regular operation in order to optimize the impact of their actions on the brand value. For example the strategic marketing value contributors may be able to expand the brand into new areas they were not aware of before, by having new instruments at their hands for the brand's strategic development. They are herewith enabled to optimize its brand management and improve the clarity of the brand message.

New relevant data/information are to be shared among the contributors through the proven channels in an ongoing process. For example the strategic marketing value contributors inform the other contributors about changes in the utilized intellectual property assets and about, new or adapted brand concepts. The legal value contributors on the other hand contact the strategic marketing value contributors in advance of the renewal of brand protection to assure that decisions cover all relevant aspects.

The marketing manager may invite the other contributors in the network to regular meetings to help sustain the network communication. During these regular meetings a constant information exchange is taking place that assures that none of the contributors create or affect trade marks which could have an effect on the strategy or require action of the other contributors without the knowledge of those. Once the management system is established the expenses time- and financial-wise for the necessary information exchange and concerted actions by the different contributors are minimal. It can also be considered to expand the established Brand Value Management to an comprehensive IP Value Management, which would establish a second network formed by the financial value contributors and the legal value contributors from the Brand Value Management network. The strategic marketing value contributors would be replaced by technology value contributors, representing the departments responsible for the technology knowledge in the company (administering patents etc.). Depending on the scope of the brand and related intellectual property assets it might be recommendable to repeat the compiling of the master documentation regarding the brand and related intellectual property assets by the different contributors regularly.

International aspects

The implementation of Brand Value Management in is not limited to national regions, but rather gains great impact in matters of international marketing activities and international trademark portfolios. As a rule, the recognition and acceptance of brands does not stop at borders and brands are targeting different markets. Consequently, in international business, a company will usually organize its IP-portfolio a lot more cost-effectively and efficiently, if it has a fully functional cross-border Brand Value Management system. On the other hand, the exchange of information will definitely be more complex in an international approach. Because of that, someone should be appointed as the person centrally in charge for the cross-border Brand Value Management system. In this respect, the obvious procedure would be to engage the marketing manager of the main country the company is headquartered.

The person in charge then should be responsible for the cross-border approach and the establishment of the Brand Value Management system in the individual countries. He or she has to set up guidelines which make sure, that the national contributors provide to him or her with the information necessary to decide about the arrangement of the trademark portfolio and, on the other hand, to implement the decisions in the participating countries.

Decisions and actions that can be made more quickly and cheaply on a regional level, should be implemented on that level. As an example, the actions of the legal value contributors can be mentioned. Strategies for registration and enforcement of property rights need to reflect the international aspects and to be centrally managed, i.e., guidelines which trademarks shall be registered in which countries and which similar trademarks shall be attacked. In contrast, the surveillance of the protected trademarks as well as their legal protection can best be accomplished locally. Therefore, it is important to have a steady flow of information to the marketing manager in charge at the company's headquarter.

▶ Key Insights

- Brand value is not limited to its strategic marketing value, meaning its potential as leverage for the company and its products on the market – brand value is a company asset that can – for acquired intellectual property rights – actually show up as asset in the balance sheet.
- Brands do cost time and money to sustain, to promote, and to protect (both from a marketing and a tax/financial as well as a legal point of view).
- If marketing, tax, and legal departments work without or with limited communication between them, time and money is wasted – e.g., by utilizing the wrong, undefendable trademarks in a brand message, wrong value assessments, non-ideal tax implications, over-dimensioned or non-sufficient protection of trademarks etc.
- Establishing a Brand Value Management in only one of the three areas does not shield the positive results as those stem from the fusing of the different information and approaches of the three areas. Therefore, the marketing manager has to bring the legal and financial resources of the company on board the strategic development process.
- Brand Value Management brings the involved parties to one table to coordinate their tasks and by doing so optimize them and the trademark portfolio, increasing the brand value and the RoI just due to the knowledge sharing.

- The set-up process of Brand Value Management allows the handling of branding and related intellectual property assets to centralize and reorder and has the potential to unearth valuable intellectual property rights no longer utilized.
- Once installed Brand Value Management results not in a major additional bureaucratic system but in a better workflow of the involved parties and improved brand management which means Brand Value Management pays for itself!

▶ Practical Guidelines

- The creation of the "master documentation" is especially important after a merger or an acquisition because the brands and related IP's at that point are not as yet integrated into the administration of the relevant departments which have to familiarize themselves with the new assets.
- If no longer utilized IP's have accumulated do not surrender them immediately, enquire about the potential of licensing them to third parties take thereby opening a new line of business for the company – even if such a license deal may take some time to place.
- The personnel charged with the data collection for the "master documentation" need to be equipped with the necessary competence – it can be surprising in how many different places brand related IP's can show up, especially if subsidiaries exist or the company is at the head of a corporate group of companies.
- Make sure to centralize the brand related IP competence and responsibility with the contributors as Brand Value Management requires that the master documentation is always kept up to date; due to his strong influence of the strategic brand development the marketing manager is a natural choice to chair this project as his team is also making the most creative use of the information provided by all contributors.
- Brand Value Management is a long-term strategy that provides best results if embedded as an integral element in the normal day-to-day-operation of the involved parties.
- Consider simplifying the legal side of the Brand Value Management by centralizing the trademarks as this also allows for better control over subsidiaries and their implementation of the main and core brands
- Once a Brand Value Management has been established, consider the option of establishing an extensive IP Value Management policy that basically transfers the concepts to the patents, technical designs etc. owned by the company – with similar positive bottom line results!

The Authors

Dr. Wulff-Axel Schmidt

Dr. Wulff-Axel Schmidt is a Partner of the Service Line Intellectual Property/ Information Technology of Luther Rechtsanwaltsgesellschaft mbH. He gives advice on all questions regarding trademark law, copyright law, competition law as well as IT law. In particular, he is a specialist on the realization of intellectual property rights strategies, for example, in the context of the acquisition, sale, and reorganization of companies. After his education as a bank clerk he studied jurisprudence in Frankfurt/Main and Berlin. Since 1995 he has worked as a lawyer. wulff-axel.schmidt@luther-lawfirm.com

Dr. Kay Oelschlägel

Dr. Kay Oelschlägel has been a lawyer at the Service Line Intellectual Property/ Information Technology of Luther Rechtsanwaltsgesellschaft mbH for almost 7 years. He is an expert in the legal fields of trademark law and passing off law, fair trading and marketing law, intellectual property and internet law as well as license law. He advises international and national clients in all of these legal areas including forensic activities. Furthermore, he has published several books and scientific articles about trademark law, passing off-law and commercial law and also gives lectures in the aforementioned law fields. Dr. Oelschlägel studied law at the University of Freiburg i. Br. in Germany and the University Aix-en-Provence in France. He has got his PHD in trademark law at the University of Freiburg i. Br. (Dr. iur). kay.oelschlaegel@luther-lawfirm.com

Literature Recommendations

U. Klein-Bölting, M. Maskus, "Markenwert als zentraler Treiber des Unternehmenswertes," Stuttgart 2003
K. Lane Keller, "Strategic Brand Management," New Jersey 2002
D. A. Aaker, "Brand Protfolio Strategy," New York 2004

Christian Schubert, Hans Kiefer – BASF AG & Prof. Dr. Franz-Rudolf Esch, Dr. Simone Roth

Corporate Brand Identity
Creating value by further developing brand identity using the brand steering wheel

▶ Executive Summary

- Corporate brands serve to increase a company's value
  - Internally: common, internationally unifying element (e.g., activities, hierarchy levels, regions, cultures) and stronger employee identification and commitment result in greater performance.
  - Externally: clear identification throughout all stakeholder groups (e.g., customers, financial community, media, politics and society); unique brand image creates preference.
- Corporate brands need to be managed and developed. They are subject to internal and external influences (e.g., portfolio changes, mergers and acquisitions, shifts in markets and business environments).
- A successful brand must be implemented in accordance with global requirements.

▶ Theoretical Model of Corporate Brand Identity

1. Definition and core principle

The brand identity is the brand definition from the point of view of the company, the so-called picture of self. It involves strategic definitions of the core characteristics of the corporate brand and takes into account the views of its various stakeholders. The brand identity expresses what the brand stands for from the internal perspective. Thus, the internal perspective in a way forms the inner nature of the brand. By contrast, the corporate brand image reflects the external perception of the corporate brand, and is formed in the minds of the target groups through repeated direct and indirect contact with the company. However, an image is not only created by steering the brand identity in a particular direction. An image is also formed when the identity of the corporate brand is not clearly established. If, for example, communication measures have not been coordinated in an identity-oriented fashion, the resulting brand image is often fragmented. The objective of the whole identity process is to attain as high a degree of correspondence as possible between the identity and the image of a corporate brand in the minds of the various target groups.

Various models are available to capture the identity of a corporate brand. Some of them have been developed from practical experience, others have a more scientific basis. Most models are convincing because they are able to capture the major characteristics of a brand. One model that is particularly helpful for developing a brand identity is the brand steering wheel created by the agency Icon Added Value. The advantage of this model is that it is based on the results of brain research that shows that knowledge is stored in two different but strongly connected parts of the brain: the left and the right hemispheres. The left hemisphere works analytic-sequentially with strong cognitive control and is therefore especially activated when processing language, arithmetic, and logic. Processing in the right hemisphere is analog-holistic with low cognitive control and is especially activated by emotions, images, or fantasy.

The brand steering wheel is divided into a left side and right side to reflect this brain split (see Fig. 1). The left part of the steering wheel contains corporate brand competence as well as benefits and reasons why. These segments correspond to the rational characteristics of a corporate brand. The right side includes the corporate brand tonalities and the corporate brand images or iconography. These two segments are mainly related to the emotional elements of the corporate brand. In order to create an integrated band identity, the four dimensions have to be considered together.

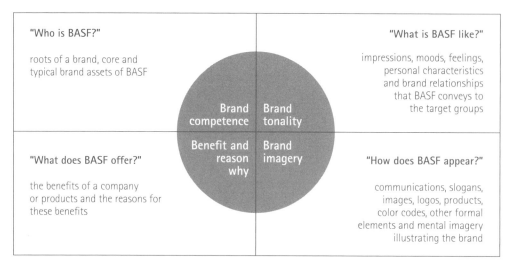

Fig. 1: Brand steering wheel of icon added value

2. Factors of corporate brand identity

2.1 Brand competence
This is related to the roots and the basic characteristics of a brand, for example, the origin or foundation of a brand. This segment also defines the role of a brand on the market and the main brand assets. The brand competence of BASF, for example, could be summarized as "The Chemical Company."

2.2 Benefits and reasons why
This segment covers the attributes, abilities, and concrete benefits for the target groups. It is necessary to distinguish between benefits and attributes. The only interest for target groups is the benefit of the product, service, or company. For example, the attribute of cost saving does not have any value for a customer, but a low price is the corresponding benefit.

2.3 Tonalities
These reflect the emotions, impressions, and feelings that are associated with the corporate brand. Tonalities can be defined as personal characteristics and relationships or experiences with the corporate brand. Relationships between the corporate brand and the target groups can be described, for example, as formal/informal and short-term/long-term. The starting point for defining tonalities for a corporate brand is the development of a specific bundle of emotions. BASF can more or less be defined as reliable, powerful, and hands on.

2.4 Imagery or iconography

The imagery or iconography of a corporate brand is formed from a variety of impressions, but primarily from mass communication and personal communication measures. The layout of sales areas, packaging, the sales force, the homepage design as well as the layout and design of all mass marketing instruments all provide impressions of a corporate brand. This brand steering wheel part includes all elements of the visual appearance of the corporate brand, such as the logo, sounds, typography, color codes, etc.

The definition of these four segments and therefore of the brand identity is a strategic task and has a long-term focus. However, in this form, it is not precise enough to be put into action. In order to change the perception of the corporate brand in the minds of the target groups, a unique and sharp brand image must be conveyed. Accordingly, it is important to concentrate on only a few attributes of the brand identity in the markets. These condensed attributes should be summarized in a positioning statement consisting of a single sentence. All marketing mix instruments can then be derived based on a precise positioning and implemented accordingly.

CASE   BASF AG

The brand steering wheel model described above can be used to develop a brand identity. The completion of the brand steering wheel is made more difficult the greater the number of business activities, targeted countries, and target groups. However, definition of a clear brand identity is not restricted to companies with a single type of product. As detailed here, even companies like BASF with more than 8,000 products can develop a consistent and clear corporate brand identity.

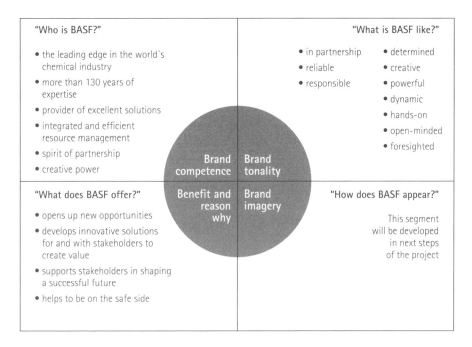

Fig. 2: Target brand steering wheel for BASF

In 2001, BASF started a project to further strengthen and sharpen its corporate brand. This was all the more challenging since BASF has 55 business units and different target groups in more than 170 countries. A detailed analysis of the brand steering wheel in 2001 showed potential areas for improvement:

- The picture and the associations concerning BASF in the external target groups included a large number of industry-specific items, such as: big, strong, good quality. Although these items did not differentiate the corporate brand, BASF "owned" high levels of likeability, trust, and loyalty in different countries and target groups, especially amongst its top customers.

- The internal target groups experienced the company quite similarly, but also here the perception was different from sector to sector. Based on the detailed analysis of the existing brand steering wheel, different options for its development were defined to derive the desired global brand image in different target groups. Figure 2 shows the target brand steering wheel for BASF.

Tools for corporate brand identity development

Brand identity development is easier for new companies than for existing companies. In general, the following tools are available to support corporate brand identity development (see Fig. 3).

Desk Research	Explorative Research	Quantitative Research
• Content analysis of communication and PR activities of the own company and of major competitors • Analysis of strategy papers • Analysis of interviews of the board of directors	• In-depth interviews • Semi-structured interviews • Focus groups • Creative workshops of employees and target group members • Trend scouting	• for example, Standardized interviews within the target group e.g., about a brand's image or a brand's positioning

Fig. 3: Tools for corporate brand identity development

If a company already exists on the market, it will have sent out signals to its target groups. A content analysis of the communication and PR activities of the company as well as of major competitors is the best tool for identifying the meaning and content of these signals. Image fragments of the corporate brand are also stored in the brains of stakeholders. Interviews with the relevant target groups should clarify the current corporate brand image. Regardless of whether the company already exists or is new, interviews and workshops can give indications of the strategy and development potential of the corporate brand. Therefore, all levels of the hierarchy should be involved – top management as well as middle management and lower hierarchical levels. This approach offers two benefits: it includes all those affected, and the involvement of top management ensures that strategic issues are taken into account.

Process & Execution

Steps for developing the corporate brand identity

The development of a corporate brand implies systematically working through a series of steps (see Figure 4).

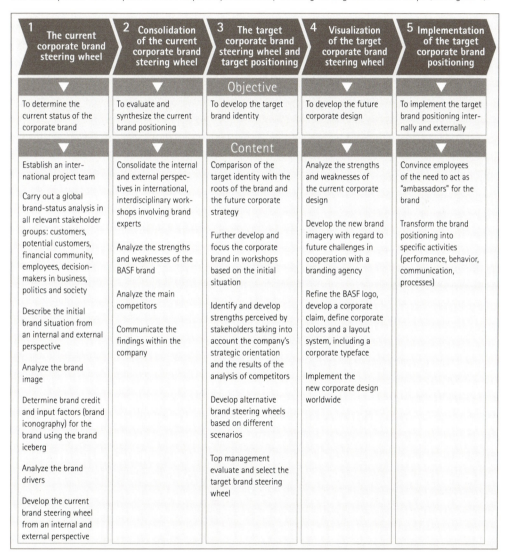

Fig. 4: Development process for a corporate brand

The extent of the development process depends on the starting point of the corporate brand: a corporate brand that already exists needs more extensive analysis than a new corporate brand. The following process shows the more extensive approach necessary for existing corporate brands like BASF. The steps can be taken considerably faster when creating a new corporate brand.

Phase 1: The current corporate brand steering wheel

The development process starts by defining the current situation of the corporate brand. This is done using the internal and external points of view of the corporate brand. The internal point of view is reflected by the company's management and employees. All levels of hierarchy can be involved in this step, but this may be extremely complex depending on the size of the company. A variety of techniques are available to assess the points of view of internal stakeholders. Conducting personal interviews is the most effective method, but this is not feasible if the company has a large workforce (BASF, for example, has approximately 81,000 employees in more than 170 countries). One pragmatic approach is to use personal interviews only at the top and middle management levels, and survey managers responsible for various business units. In the case of BASF, semi-structured face-to-face interviews were carried out with members of the BASF Board of Executive Directors and top-level managers. The results showed that although BASF's image varied from sector to sector, managers had a clear and consistent image of the company. In a next step, blue collar workers from production and employees in different functions were surveyed to reflect the current positioning. Focus groups offered a manageable way of eliciting internal perceptions in various countries and functions. At least sixteen focus group interviews were conducted in Europe, Asia, the U.S., and Brazil, involving 100 blue and white collar workers. The results showed that the picture of BASF was very similar among both employees and managers. At the end of this process, the managers' and employees' perspectives were combined to develop a single brand steering wheel from the internal point of view.

The corporate brand also has an outward effect on its environment: external stakeholders have knowledge structures and conceptions of the corporate brand in their minds. It was therefore necessary to determine the external point of view in this phase. The external perspective may be defined more or less broadly – the decision as to which external groups the corporate brand should be targeted at and, therefore, as to the most relevant target groups for the company, is a strategic one. Clearly, consumers are the most important target group for corporate brands that already exist in the end consumer's market. However, if a company like BASF sells its products predominantly to other companies, the external point of view is more general and focuses on customers. A brand like BASF also deals with a broader target group including neighbors, high potentials, the media, the financial community and politicians. In BASF's case these external stakeholders were identified as relevant target groups for determining the external point of view of the corporate brand. In total, more than 600 people in Europe, the U.S., Asia, and Brazil were questioned via computer-aided telephone interviews. The interviews were structured to analyze three important aspects:

- The mental image of BASF: open questions were used to reflect the content of all parts of the brand steering wheel.
- Brand iceberg analysis: a brand iceberg was used as a symbol of the brand value within the target groups. The iceberg model consists of related six-short term items (brand iconography), and three related long-term items (brand credit). The brand iconography was measured by brand awareness, perceived advertising pressure, memorability of advertising, vividness of brand imagery, uniqueness, and appeal of brand imagery. The brand credit was evaluated with the items brand likeability, brand confidence, and brand loyalty.

- Brand driver analysis: certain benefit claims as well as emotional statements were analyzed in two ways. Firstly in terms of their driving power. In other words, what does the item contribute to the brand credit. Secondly, in terms of BASF's performance for a specific item relative to its main competitors. For example, a high relative performance for a statement indicated that BASF "owns" this item more than a competitor and it is therefore a BASF brand asset.

After questioning, the results for the various external target groups were combined. The findings can be summarized as follows:

- The associations concerning BASF were industry-specific: big, strong, good quality.
- In different countries and target groups, BASF "owned" high levels of likeability, trust, and loyalty, especially among top customers. As a result, BASF had good credit because of its long history, the quality of its operational business, and the personal relationship with its target groups. The results also showed that there was a hidden potential for BASF to strengthen its brand image and to prevent values missing from today's brand imagery from jeopardizing tomorrow's brand credit.
- The brand driver analysis showed excellent opportunities for further developing the BASF brand.

Finally, the results were used to develop a brand steering wheel of BASF from the external perspective. It might be expected that internal and external points of view are too indistinct, and that it might not be possible to summarize these in a brand steering wheel that combines both. On the contrary, BASF's practical experience with this technique shows that it is indeed possible to define common and diverging facets of a corporate brand. The complexity of the outcome might also be surprising: managers often expect a lot of distinct and clear associations with the corporate brand, but normally they can be condensed into a small number of benefits, tonalities, iconography, and core competences.

Phase 2: Consolidation of the current corporate brand steering wheel

First of all, the outcomes of the external and the internal points of view were compared. The evaluations and consolidation of the current brand steering wheel were made by considering which associations:
- are shared by the employees, managers and external target groups,
- focus on the companies' specialties,
- make the corporate brand attractive to the stakeholders,
- are perceivably different to those of competitors, and
- have a long-term focus.

Here, a comparison between the intended brand positioning and associations stored in the target groups' minds was also interesting. It revealed gaps in the implementation phase. The comparison between the intended positioning of the corporate brand and the signals sent out to the stakeholders can also be an eye-opener and can show where work still has to be done. If there is a gap between the intended positioning, the communicated signs and the perception in the minds of internal and external stakeholders, efforts must be invested in building up a strong brand identity and then implementing it in the market. A highly important factor in this phase is the involvement of the employees themselves, especially managers. Awareness of the current corporate brand image is necessary to open up minds to change or can further reinforce loyalty to and pride in the corporate brand. This means that the evaluation and consolidation of the current brand steering wheel should not be done in only one special department within the company, in order to obtain more credible results and a greater appreciation of the difficulties involved. BASF therefore carried out various workshops with all relevant countries and divisions. The core team consisted of international marketing managers, assistants to the board of directors, and external consultants. In some phases of the discussion, the workshops also included specialists such as members of the strategic development department.

At the end of this phase the strengths and weaknesses of the corporate brand image reflected in the current brand steering wheel were established. The results were communicated within the company, creating broad awareness of the strengths and weaknesses of the corporate brand. This then formed the basis for the future development of the BASF corporate brand.

Phase 3: The target corporate brand steering wheel and target positioning

Based on these insights, the BASF corporate brand was further developed and focused. The development of the target brand steering wheel and the brand positioning required an enormous effort. In general, the following prerequisites need to be observed in developing a corporate brand identity.

- Focus: the corporate brand should provide a shorthand device or means of simplification for the core of what the company stands for. As the corporate brand is directed towards different stakeholders, both internal and external, focusing the message is essential. Only then can the corporate brand convey the core messages about the company and help to build the brand image within the target groups.
- Integration: the corporate brand needs to represent the complete product portfolio because it is strongly connected with the company's business activities. It is not so demanding to develop a brand identity for companies with a homogeneous product portfolio. An extensive product range makes it more challenging but not impossible to develop a brand identity. For example, the corporate brand BASF stands for business activities like chemicals, plastics, performance products, agricultural products, fine chemicals, crude oil, and natural gas.
- Strategy: the determination of the strong corporate brand influences the strategic orientation of the complete brand portfolio of a company and vice versa. The placement of only the corporate brand on the market (branded house) means that the content of the brand identity should be targeted at all stakeholders, whereas the placement of various single brands on the consumer market (house of brands) implies that the corporate brand can be focused more on other target groups rather than on customers.
- Emotionality: the corporate brand should represent emotional as well as rational arguments. Ultimately, unique corporate brand associations should be stored in the mind of the target groups. However, the brand should not only refer to logical arguments and promises of benefits. It should also contain emotions and tonalities. Emotions in particular can differentiate brands in saturated markets. Moreover, emotions and feelings offer companies with a wide range of products and business activities an opportunity to find matching identity components.
- Synergies: all parts of the brand identity definition should fit together. It only makes sense to create emotional and rational, verbal, and nonverbal parts of the identity that match one another. All elements of the corporate identity work together. They either create an entire picture or a fragmented and confused conglomerate. If all parts fit together and support each other, the whole is more than the sum of its parts.

- Relevance: what are the possible future needs of the target groups? A future target brand steering wheel can only be developed if expectations of the future needs of the target groups are also included.
- Distinctiveness: the objective is to create a clear and distinctive corporate brand image. This means that it is not possible to focus only on one's own company. The major competitors and their brand images should also be taken into account.

However, in developing the target brand position, its origin cannot be disregarded. The target position needs to relate to what the corporate brand currently stands for. Generally speaking, it is possible to decide between two distinctive approaches to developing the corporate brand: evolutionary or revolutionary. The evolutionary approach includes the willingness to keep the strength of the existing brand knowledge in the stakeholders' minds; the revolutionary approach means starting to work as if it were a completely new corporate brand. For the revolutionary approach, the future brand identity needs to be communicated so strongly that other stored associations are eclipsed. Evolutionary development only makes sense if it is possible to identify strengths in the current brand image in the target groups' minds.

To sum up: the target brand steering wheel balances the current brand image, the strategic orientation, and scenarios showing future needs and trends for both stakeholders as well as major competitors. In the case of BASF, the target brand position was derived with the help of internal workshops composed of experts from marketing, research, and strategic planning with support from external experts. The essential task was to integrate the corporate brand process with the refocusing of the company's strategy, called BASF 2015. At the end of this process, different strategic options of the target brand steering wheel were derived depending on the different expectations and scenarios. The decision which target brand steering wheel will be chosen is a strategic decision that can only be made by the head of the company. At BASF, the brand steering wheel and the corporate brand position were decided by the board of directors (Fig. 5).

- As the world's leader in the chemical industry, BASF opens up potential for success together with its partners.
- To this end, BASF develops and maintains partnerships that are characterized by mutual trust and respect.
- BASF helps shape the future successfully and sustainably by means of intelligent solutions.

Fig. 5: Final brand positioning statement

Phase 4: Visualization of the target corporate brand steering wheel

In the next phase, the brand position has to be transferred to the way that a company "appears." The brand imagery must reflect the other three elements of the brand steering wheel. Therefore, on the one hand the brand imagery needs to provide visual support for the presentation of the brand, and on the other hand it needs to ensure a high degree of recognition. At the same time, the new brand imagery provides momentum for internal and external change. It signals change and progress and thus acts as a impulse to motivate employees.

How was BASF's new brand imagery developed?

Initially, in stage one, BASF evaluated the existing corporate design to identify its strengths and weaknesses. This showed that further development was necessary in order to convey a consistent, brand-adequate imagery of BASF to the company's stakeholders. In a second stage, the new brand image was developed in collaboration with a brand consultancy and an agency specializing in corporate design. Various visual BASF worlds were drawn up and depicted on so-called mood boards. In a multi-stage process, these worlds yielded the design approach that, in the eyes of experts and the Board of Executive Directors, fully reflected the future brand positioning. This design approach formed the basis for the detailed elaboration of the corporate design elements. These included:

- Refining the BASF logo. The four letters "BASF" were retained. They stand for the tradition and success of the company. Two newly added squares supplement the four letters and symbolize partnership and intelligent solutions.
- Developing the corporate claim "The Chemical Company." It underscores BASF's commitment to chemistry and signals leadership.
- Introducing six corporate colors. These serve to support the brand's visualization and allow BASF to appear as a dynamic and diverse company.
- Developing a layout system – the so-called "banner system." Along with the other design elements, this ensures that BASF is presented consistently and is thus easily recognized.
- Using a uniform font. We opted for Helvetica in selected weights.

This corporate design system was successfully tested for usability in expert groups and extensive market tests across the entire spectrum of communication requirements. The complete set of the corporate design guidelines was then made available internally to BASF users as "BASF Brandweb" and externally as an Extranet option to

Fig. 6a: Communication before implementing the new BASF corporate brand identity

BASF suppliers. A key factor in the implementation of this system was to make people understand that all forms of communication must reflect the spirit of the brand and visualize BASF "The Chemical Company."

Fig. 6b: Communication after implementing the new BASF corporate brand identity

Phase 5: Implementation of the target corporate brand positioning

The internal and external implementation is often underestimated. It is a change management process by which the newly developed brand values and characteristics lead to a brand-adequate behavior by the company. This phase is too complex to be covered in detail in this article, but in order for the process to be successful, two basic requirements need to be fulfilled:

- The employees must be convinced of the brand's merits: the employees act as "ambassadors" for the corporate brand on the market. If they are not aware of or do not buy into the values of the corporate brand, no external stakeholder will believe in it.
- The brand identity should be transformed into a concrete form for different markets, functions, and divisions: the definition of the target brand identity for the corporate brand is done on a general, more abstract, level. The day-to-day experience shows that the creation of a positive attitude towards the corporate brand identity is based on a concrete derivation of implications and advantages for each function and division.

International aspects of brand management

BASF is the world's leading chemical company. The company's initial situation is very heterogeneous in its core businesses, markets, regions, and countries. This is compounded by socio-cultural differences worldwide. Development of the global BASF brand requires that the brand strategy and brand management takes account of these different initial situations. BASF therefore steered the entire development process – the analysis, development, and implementation phases – via an international, interdisciplinary project team. Individual local and stakeholder-related requirements were identified, evaluated, and taken into account during brand development. All key decision-makers were involved in the process via a global management buy-in and informed of major development steps and results at such an early stage that they were able to exert a direct influence. The biggest challenge was not finding a lowest common denominator but defining the strongest common point of reference for the BASF corporate brand. This goal was achieved using a binding global process that ensured the use of global and local expertise and thus guaranteed the commitment of international management. In this way, it was possible to develop the corporate brand systematically and implement it globally in a consistent fashion that took appropriate consideration of regional and local requirements. The global network of Brand Champions is an important success factor in ensuring implementation at the day-to-day level.

Summary: overview of the process

To sum up: the process of developing a corporate brand is based on four phases: definition of the current brand steering wheel, consolidation of the current brand steering wheel, development of the target brand steering wheel, and the implementation and monitoring of the target brand steering wheel. Each step involves three perspectives: the strategic orientation of the corporate brand, the perception of the corporate brand from the target groups' perspective (internal as well as external), and the major competitors. These three perspectives are essential for developing the corporate brand identity. The challenge in the first three steps lies in working with a general, more abstract point of view. Only this enables all categories, businesses and target groups to be taken into account when defining the corporate brand identity.

▶ Key Insights

- It is possible to develop a corporate brand for companies with a complex and diverse product portfolio in a business-to-business environment.
- Current market requirements mean that emotional elements are extremely important in the corporate brand identity definition.
- The corporate brand is perceived differently in different countries but can nevertheless be a powerful international umbrella.
- Effective corporate brand development needs the support of the company's top management.
- The conviction of employees ensures that the corporate brand acts like a lighthouse toward all target groups and the company's general environment.
- Only what stakeholders clearly perceive as unique, relevant, and integrated can create a clear corporate brand image.
- A strategy is only as good as its implementation. The complexity of the implementation process should not be underestimated.
- Corporate brand strategy drives business strategy. It acts as a guide rail for future decisions.

▶ Practical Guidelines

- ☐ Do not forget to include the current perception of the corporate brand in the development. Otherwise you may lose some roots and core assets of the brand.
- ☐ Learn from benchmarks, especially in other categories. However, do not focus too much on competitors. Copying competitors means losing one's own identity.
- ☐ Do not search for the smallest common denominator in the brand identity definition.
- ☐ Step out of the comfort zone in your company: challenge the attitudes of your employees and be aware that this requires a tremendous effort. There may be a lot of resistance, especially in companies with a long tradition.
- ☐ Use global and local expertise in the corporate brand development process, for example by establishing an international brand development team.
- ☐ Consider the corporate brand identity for each segment, business unit, and target group. The target image can be adapted for various countries.
- ☐ Do not take only external target groups into account.
- ☐ Last but not least: "Become what you are" (the Oracle of Delphi).

The Authors

Christian Schubert

Christian Schubert has been head of Corporate Communications BASF Group since November 2001. He studied management and engineering in Berlin, Germany, and Hoboken, New Jersey, U.S. Christian Schubert started his career in the German Foreign Office in Bonn in 1993, where he worked in the Economic Directorate-General. In 1996, he joined the strategic planning department of DaimlerChrysler Services AG in Berlin, where he moved on to become head of the press department in 1997.

Hans Kiefer

Hans Kiefer studied both communications and economics in Germany. Prior to joining BASF in 1985, he worked in the medical and pharmaceutical industry; initially as Communications Director and subsequently as Managing Director of a medical publishing house. During his time at BASF, Hans Kiefer has held several positions in market and corporate communications. In 2002 he was appointed as Senior Manager Corporate Brand Management.

Prof. Dr. Franz-Rudolf Esch

Professor for Business Administration and Head of Marketing, Director of the Institute for Brand and Communication Research at the Justus-Liebig-University Gießen, Germany; Founder of ESCH. The Brand Consultants, Saarlouis (Germany), Vice-President of the German Marketing Association.

Dr. Simone Roth

Former senior consultant of ESCH, the brand consultants. Since 2004, Roth has worked in international marketing at Schwarzkopf & Henkel.

Literature Recommendations

D. A. Aaker, E. Joachimsthaler, "Brand Leadership," Sydney 2002
F.-R. Esch, "Strategie und Technik der Markenführung," 3rd edition, München 2005
F.-R. Esch, "Moderne Markenführung," 4th edition, Wiesbaden 2005
F.-R. Esch, T. Tomczak, J. Kernstock, T. Langner, "Corporate Brand Management," Wiesbaden 2004
J. N. Kapferer, "Strategic Brand Management, Creating and Sustaining Brand Equity Long Term," London 1998
K. L. Keller, "Strategic Brand Management – Building, Measuring, and Managing Brand Equity," New Jersey 2003

Stefan Swinka, Peter Wolf – Tchibo AG

Long-term Brand Migration

Trust, sympathy and loyalty as the driving elements of brand credit and, thus, of long-term company growth

▶ Executive Summary

- Brand credit, comprising of trust, sympathy, and loyalty, is the foundation of long-term, stable growth.
- In order to maximize assets for a brand, it is necessary to have a brand strategy through which both internal processes and external marketing measures are controlled.
- This brand strategy must unite the factual strengths of a company with the central values of the brand and the needs of the customer, and must represent the centre of strategic company management.
- The aim is to create a consistent, 360 degree perception of the brand, both amongst the company's employees and its customers, and thus to maximize the variables trust, sympathy, and loyalty (brand credit).
- The development and realization of such a strategy presumes a strategic feedback system between the responsible brand team, the employees, and the customers, in which unsettled requirements are considered and the brand strategy is adapted correspondingly.
- A successful brand strategy leads to "Long-term Brand Migration," in which brand credit increases constantly, growth is maximized and brand values are stabilized and optimized.

Benefits

- A "learning organization," which constantly adapts its brand values and strategy to fundamental changes in the market and society.
- Maximized brand credit through stable brand values and constantly optimized brand strategy.
- Long-term, stable growth on the basis of strong brand credit.

▶ Theoretical Model of Long-term Brand Migration

1. Definition and core principle

Stable and sustainable growth is the most important foundation for the profitability of a company. However, the number of factors upon which sustainable growth depends appear at first to be confusingly high: management functions, instruments, and strategies form an immeasurable number of possibilities, many of which promise growth and sustainability.

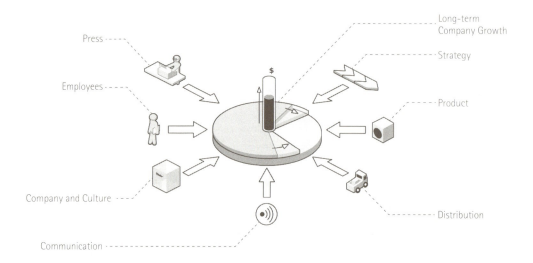

Fig. 1: Many factors influence the growth of a company. The central question is: which ones are decisive?

The model of "Long-term Migration" presumes that these factors can be pulled together into a single element: the brand. The structure of a stable and strong brand makes it possible to direct the entire company towards the requirements of the market and, thus, towards the source of all value creation, and to keep it relevant at all times. In this respect, a company strategy that concentrates on "Long-term Brand Migration" sees the brand as the strategic focus of company management and not as a special task for the marketing department.

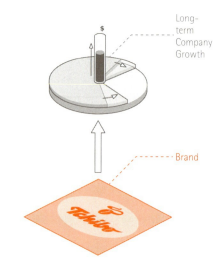

Fig. 2: The brand as the central driving force of long-term company growth

Brand credit as a basis for evaluation

In order to be able to use the brand as a strategic control instrument within the company, a concept for the evaluation of brand strength must first be developed. In our case, this is the idea of brand credit building of the variables trust, sympathy, and loyalty. These variables are always related to the values of the competition or to another reference system (market average; average for power brands etc.). These three variables of brand credit may not on any account be equated with the character of the brand (the brand values): trust, sympathy and loyalty are target values that must be aspired to by every brand, and that are the result of actual activities and the positioning of the brand. This means: the variables of brand credit are identical for all brands.

The activities and strategies surrounding the brand can be evaluated based on brand credit. In the event that brand credit increases, the probability for long-term growth also rises – the brand strategy and its realization are successful. If the brand credit decreases, then the brand strategy and its realization are failing to meet their fundamental aim: the economic strengthening of the company.

The concept of brand credit thus enables the introduction of a clear measurement figure into the labyrinth of seemingly random evaluation methods for marketing and company development; a figure that is clearly linked to the actual company target of growth. The measurability and comparability of its three dimensions turns brand credit into a variable with which the actual strength of a company on the market can be measured and evaluated, and with which the individual growth of the company correlates. The central question in the following factor model is how brand credit can be successfully increased.

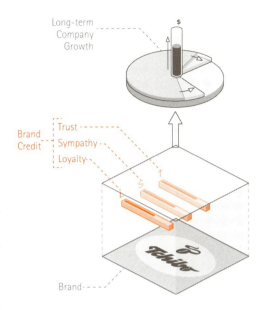

Fig. 3: The strength of a brand with regard to company growth is crystallized in the three dimensions of trust, sympathy, and loyalty – the brand credit

2. Factors of Long-term Brand Migration

2.1 Foundation: consistent brand strategy

A long-term brand strategy is the foundation of an increase in brand credit. The brand strategy is created based on the needs of the customer and the long-term capacities, abilities, and aims of the company. It is the symbiosis of the possible (company, resources, core competencies, markets) with the desirable (consumers), and forms the company vision, from which all further strategies must be derived. The brand values form the foundation of the brand strategy. The brand values constitute the core of the brand and form its DNA. They embody the innermost beliefs and convictions from which the brand promise and the central use dimensions for the customer are derived.

The relevance of the brand values for the customer must be assured by orientation of the brand strategy towards the basic needs of the target group. On one hand, this ensures that the target group turns to the brand based on an established interest, and on the other hand, it is possible to give the strategy a long-term alignment, thus ensuring a strict direction for the company as a whole. The brand strategy forms the operational foundation for the realization of the values, both internally and externally, on the basis of the brand values. Correspondingly the brand strategy has two aims:

1. Its internal aim is the formation of a corporate culture, that reflects the values and aims of the brand. The formation of a corporate culture that corresponds to the brand is of great importance in many respects, such as the long-term maximization and retention of brand credit. Employees create the values of which the brand's contribution is composed. Quality management, service, and innovation in the sense of the brand are only possible if the employees understand and live the values for which the brand stands. Employees are the spokespersons of the company and communicate directly (personally) or indirectly (through press and rumors) with those outside. Perception of the brand is only all-embracing and credible if this communication occurs in the spirit of the brand. Employees form the influencing system surrounding the further development of the brand and its values – a brand cannot be developed successfully in an atmosphere lacking in credibility.

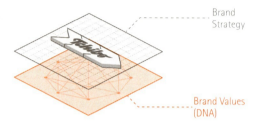

Fig. 4: The brand values form the identifying foundation of a brand and make the development of brand strategy possible

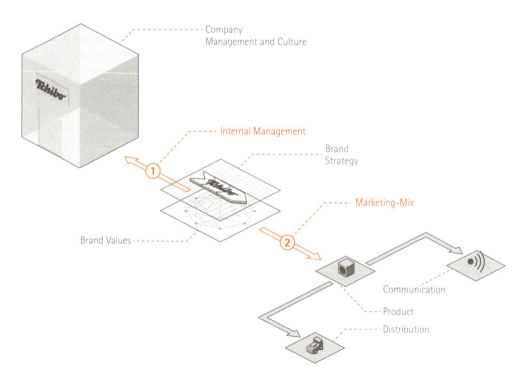

Fig. 5: The brand strategy aligns the marketing mix and the internal management of a company with the brand values

2. The brand strategy controls the marketing mix and the measures derived from it. In this, it is important to achieve the integrity of the marketing measures and their strict alignment with the marketing strategy and its core values.

2.2 360-degree perception as the target of the brand strategy

2.2.1 Alignment of corporate culture

The operational aim of brand strategy is to create a 360-degree perception of the brand and its values in the internal and external target groups. The consistency of brand perception is one of the most important factors in the creation of credibility, that in turn has an effect on the factors "trust" and "loyalty" in the brand credit. In contrast to a purely advertising or marketing-driven brand concept, the creation of real 360-degree perception not only presumes successful alignment of the externally targeted marketing mix, but also of the corporate culture. Only when perception in the market is also supported by direct or indirect communication from the employees can trust and loyalty be built up in the target groups. This assumes that both the communication of the employees in their circle of friends and acquaintances, and the perception and reporting of the press, do justice to the brand values. The two things are only possible if the brand world and its values are accepted inside the company and amongst its employees, and only if these are represented convincingly.

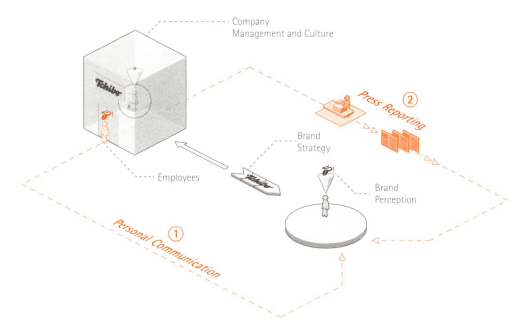

Fig. 6: 360-degree understanding of the brand values within the company requires that both personal communication through the employees and possible reporting by third parties on the market reflect the brand values

2.2.2 Alignment of the marketing mix

Besides the convincing reflection of brand strategy and values within an organization, the successful realization of the brand values and the marketing strategy in the marketing mix is the second decisive factor. The basic rules of successful marketing should be given special attention:

- The application of purposeful and well-coordinated multi-channel communication, in which individual channels are aligned with one another and to brand values.
- The application of a multi-channel sales strategy, in which the most important sales channels are identified, used and designed for the purposes of consistent brand perception. The sales channels represent an important and often underestimated component for the total impact of a brand. The consumer comes into personal and direct contact with the brand, and expects a corresponding brand experience.
- The development and delivery of a product portfolio in accordance with the brand.

When internal and external variables are aligned successfully with the brand values, this results in consistent and relevant 360-degree perception by the customers.

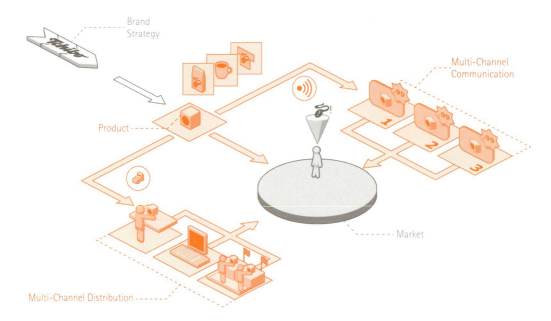

Fig. 7: The consistent multi-channel realization of the marketing strategy in distribution and communication, as well as the development of a product portfolio that is in line with the brand, is the second prerequisite for a consistent 360-degree perception of the brand by the customers.

2.3 Effects on market credit and application of the learning cycle

Thus, the brand strategy can have an effect on the consumer and his perception via the factors of corporate culture, product, distribution, and communication. It is primarily the multitude of routes and the lack of control at the end of the execution chain that make it necessary to apply the strategy as consequentially as possible to these factors, so that its content is not diluted.

If all sections of the company communicate the same brand values in this way, then the consumer must become aware in the medium-term that the brand is the carrier of a fixed and reliable set of values. He cannot withdraw from this communication as long as he is located in the market. The communication of values also continues outside the direct market activity where the PR department and employees act as ambassadors. The sustainable and consistent creation of a 360-degree perception by the customers therefore leads to the build-up of the dimensions trust, sympathy, and loyalty and, thus, to a rise in brand credit.

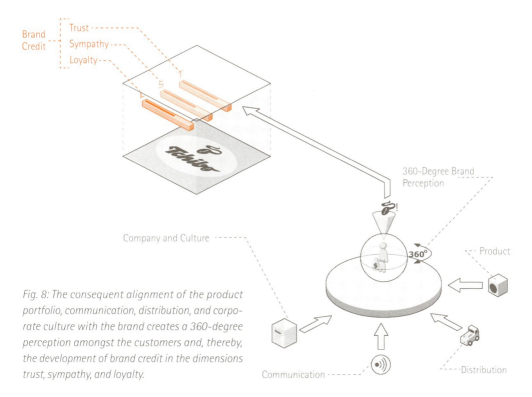

Fig. 8: The consequent alignment of the product portfolio, communication, distribution, and corporate culture with the brand creates a 360-degree perception amongst the customers and, thereby, the development of brand credit in the dimensions trust, sympathy, and loyalty.

In order to achieve a lasting relevance of the brand and its values amongst the target groups, brand values and brand strategy must be subjected to regular consideration and optimisation. The associated process is generally termed the "Learning Cycle" and can be described briefly as follows:

The measurement of brand credit makes an initial estimate possible on how the status and the performance of the brand are positioned in the market. Derived from this, optimization and solution concepts in the brand strategy or its realization need to be developed using weak-point analysis and corresponding consumer/employee research. In the event of particularly fundamental problems, it can also be useful to consider the brand values and adjust them to new social or business environments where necessary. The optimized brand strategy thus developed should then be implemented in the company, and the corresponding learning and optimization processes should be tackled. The resulting effect for the customers can be seen in turn in brand credit – the learning circle is complete.

The establishment of a learning cycle and its process-related anchoring in the company as a whole are very important for the long-term success of brand management. Only those who concentrate on the market and on customers, and who adjust their measures and strategies accordingly, will add and increase value in the long-term.

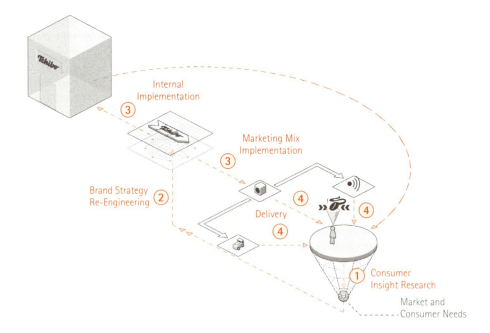

Fig. 9: The learning cycle increases brand relevance by considering current customer needs, optimizing brand strategy, and reacting to customer requirements in internal and external dimensions.

2.4 Long-term optimization of brand strategy

In order to optimize brand and brand strategy in the long-term, it is necessary to apply the named factors in a stable and balanced way. The prerequisite for this is a high level of commitment to the brand and its values within the organization – even when changes are made at board level. The safest guarantee for this kind of comprehensive, company-enmeshed brand consistency is the anchoring of the brand in the company guidelines (vision, philosophy, history) and, most importantly, the shareholders' awareness of which function and meaning the long-term stability and strength of the brand have on the company's total performance. It is worth performing at least a rough consideration of the brand strength, the planned brand strategy, and its consistency with the fundamental brand values, especially from the point of view of the investor. Turnover and growth forecasts should be checked for plausibility on this basis. A classic range of aspects must be taken into account with regard to the reengineering of a brand strategy and, especially, the adjustment of brand values to new market and business environments – namely pole stability and change. The development of a brand that is to be stable in the long-term always requires stability of its cosmos of values. At the same time, social and economic changes can also make an adjustment necessary. The solution for this apparent dilemma lies in a sensitive process of optimization of the brand values, in which the values are not simply changed, but rather, polished and given a change of perspective where necessary. The true core of a brand should always be in accordance with the basic needs of a category and, thus, should be able to remain stable for as long as the psychological foundations for the relevant product category exists.

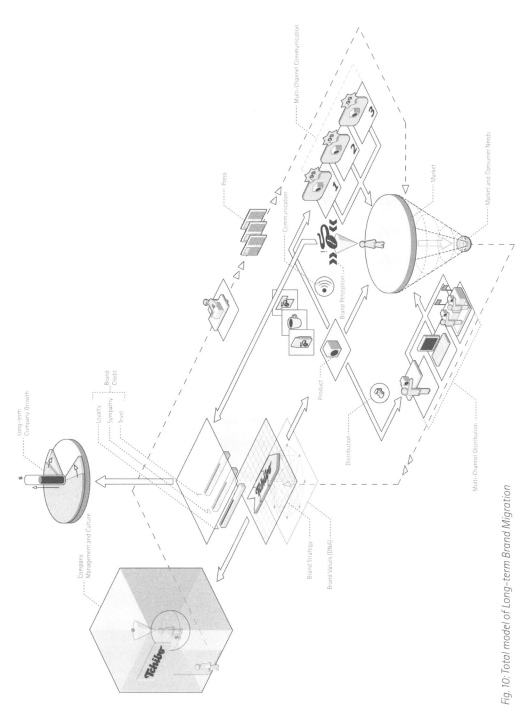

Fig. 10: Total model of Long-term Brand Migration

▶ Process & Implementation

The following process implements the concept of Long-term Brand Migration for an existing brand. The following scenario presumes an initial situation where both brand management and brand credit are sub-optimal. Correspondingly, the aim is the fundamental processing of the brand, leading to the achievement of Long-term Brand Migration.

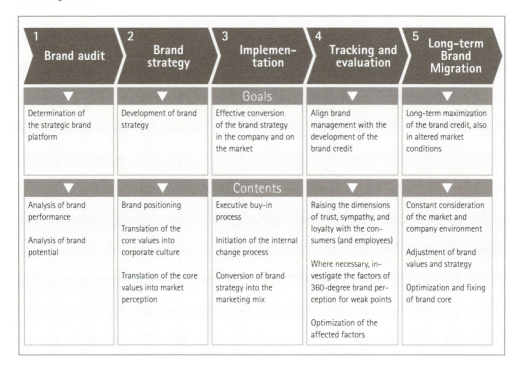

Fig. 11: Long-term Brand Migration process

Phase 1: Brand audit

1.1 Brand performance

At the beginning of the process, the performance of the brand must be assessed. The aim is to develop an analysis of strengths and weaknesses (SWOT) as a starting point for the development of the future brand strategy.

1.1.1 Analysis dimensions

The determination of brand credit should be the core of the analysis. Further dimensions can then be assessed based on these findings, whereby the concrete selection of the dimensions to be examined is dependent firstly on the existing data, and secondly on diagnostic hypotheses on the causes of the current level of brand credit.

Possible analysis dimensions could be:

The Market	**The Brand**	**Brand Perception**
· Market size	· Hard facts	· Image
· Strategic importance	· Turnover	· Awareness
· Growth potential	· Cost of brand management	· Likeability
· etc.	· Brand value	· etc.
	· etc.	

Strategic Importance of the Brand for the Company	**The Customers**	**The Competition**
· Contribution to the brand portfolio	· Definition of target group	· Competitors
· Importance for corporate culture	· Core needs of the category	· SWOT for each competitor
· etc.	· Consumer Insights	

1.1.2 Analysis result
An analysis of the brand's strengths and weaknesses (SWOT) should result from the potentials analysis. The SWOT analysis collects the results of the brand audit and, thus, produces a platform for the development of the brand strategy.

1.2 Brand potential

Case 1 – Brand in a brand portfolio
The core question: which brands can help the company to grow and which cannot? A Brand Focus Portfolio is developed based on this question, in which the brands that drive growth are identified and their strategic Key Leverage Points defined.

Case 2 – Individual brand
The core question: which facets of the brand are particularly promising and which are not? The following facets should be investigated in this regard:
- profitability and growth prospects of the brand sectors,
- position in relation to competition within the sectors and markets in which the brand is represented,
- negative und positive image dimensions of the brand for the customer,
- negative und positive image dimensions of the brand for the employees.

Possible strategic platforms are then derived from the investigated facets.

CASE   Tchibo

> 1. Tchibo is a combination of two core business fields: food and non food. These two components constitute the brand.

2. Tchibo is also a combination of a retailer and a brand item retailer.

Both components must be built up to an attractive brand, that the consumer can comprehend. For this purpose the DNA of Tchibo was first defined. The specific strengths in both the food and non food components of sales were defined. This definition process includes the entire company. This is the only way of creating an unchangeable DNA structure. The tasks: definition of the DNA

Fig. 12: Results of the brand audit

Phase 2: Brand strategy

2.1 Brand positioning
Brand positioning is carried out primarily through the determination and fixing of brand values. The brand values should embody the innermost core of the brand – its character and its central promise to the customer. Other aspects of brand positioning, such as brand vision, mission statement, benefit, reason to believe, etc., are subordinate and tend to represent operational characteristics of the core values of a brand.

2.2 Transfer of core values into the corporate culture
Besides the externally oriented measures, a further aim of the brand strategy is to develop an effective concept for the internal (employee-related) realization of the brand values. This is a comprehensive concept that anchors the brand values in the various company sectors as fundamentally as possible:

- brand values in employee communication,
- brand values in training, further education and selection of employees,
- brand values in the design of the working environment, architecture, processes, and structures.

The aim of the internal application of brand values is the creation of a credible and comprehensive perception of the brand by the employees – 360-degree perception. Only a comprehensive perception and understanding of the brand by the employees can create a corporate culture in which the brand values are lived and, thus, become an important guideline element in the value creation structures within the company.

2.3 Transfer of core values into market perception

The transfer of the core values into the perception of the market requires a classic marketing mix strategy. The most important factor in this regard is the strategic planning

- of brand communication in the various channels,
- of the development of a product range that is appropriate to the brand,
- of the distribution channels used, which lead, in combination, to a uniform perception of the brand by the consumer (360-degree perception).

Thus, it is not only the technology in these areas that must be taken into account (which distribution and communication channels are required?), but also and especially the emotional and communicational effect of sales channels (location selection, PoS, human resource etc.), product portfolios (does the range reflect the core values of the brand?), and communication (do the various channels communicate the same brand message using the same brand symbolism?).

CASE   Tchibo

Phase 2a

Every brand has several layers. For this reason, the core values of the brand must be defined exactly. The fact that these values can be understood credibly, both internally and externally, is a prerequisite. Market positioning is examined and fixed using internal audits and external market research.

The tasks: examination of DNA

- internally
- externally

Phase 2b

The finalized brand values are anchored in "company purpose and company values" following their consideration for internal brand management. They regulate the relations amongst the employees, create the necessary trust, and anchor the comprehension of the brand. Thus, every employee becomes an ambassador of the brand. In external brand management, the aim is to transfer the core dimension to the sales route and/or the sales routes in the same way as in the marketing mix.

26,000 Tchibo points of contact

Fig. 13: Brand DNA and transfer into various channels

The tasks: transfer of the brand core

- for employees
- for customers
- on the sales level
- in the marketing mix

Phase 3: Implementation

3.1 Executive buy-in-process

The successful internal implementation of Long-term Brand Migration presumes support at the executive level, as well as the absolute commitment of those responsible for the brand, along with a clear brand strategy. Further implementation – especially the alignment of the corporate culture as an important success factor for long-term brand management – can only be carried out successfully when the executive level has accepted the necessity of successful Long-term Brand Migration, and recognizes its obligation to execute the brand strategy.

The executive level is usually made up of board members and the key positions responsible for the implementation of the brand strategy. The latter must be identified for each company and case individually. A successful buy-in process is a pure people business – the interests and organizational roles of the key personnel must be known to the responsible brand manager as completely as possible, in order to be able to build up an effective communication and lobbying strategy.

3.2 Initiation of the internal change process
- Top-down process: use of an organizational snowball system, in which the superiors are obliged to realize the relevant brand aspects in their departments.
- Continuity in the exemplification of the process and the brand strategy by the superiors and the board level is of central importance.
- The successful realization of the change process absolutely requires that the brand is accepted at board level as the central focus of the company (see executive buy-in process).

3.3 Realization of the brand strategy in the marketing mix
The implementation of the brand strategy in the marketing mix mainly involves modern marketing skills that will not be explained in detail here. The guideline is: product development and delivery, brand communication, and distribution must be aligned completely with the brand values, and regarded in every way as the value-holders and representatives of the brand. Accordingly, samples of all measures in the marketing mix – from product innovation to the POS show cards and the selection of the sales channels – can be examined for consistency with the brand values.

CASE Tchibo

Internal implementation
A brand lives off its core values. They determine the behaviour of a project internally via the company purpose and the derived corporate culture. The brand begins to live in a written statement and the exemplification of this culture, and to transfer itself onto the behaviour of the employees. Only people who are convinced are able to convince others.

External implementation
Only the integrated marketing concept, including all media mix factors, from ATL communication to BTL communication, from the individual sales route to the point of sale, must communicate a uniform image to the customers.

The tasks: transformation of the core values in

- company principles
- company purpose
- media-Mix
- PoS
- outlet

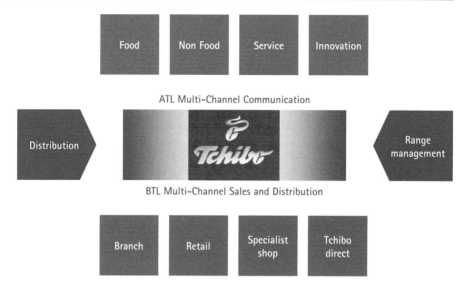

Fig. 14: Integrated external implementation of the Tchibo brand in multi-channel sales and distribution and multi-channel communications

Phase 4: Tracking and evaluation

Tracking and evaluation are central control elements of brand strategy – they give feedback on the perception of the consumer.

4.1 Brand credit as the central measurement variable

The central measurement variable here is development of brand credit – it is the only decisive factor in whether a brand strategy is successful or not. The brand credit is the only factor that correlates directly with the turnover growth of a company. The dimensions of trust, sympathy, and loyalty must be considered both in internal target groups (employees) and external target groups (customers), in order to evaluate and further develop a comprehensive brand strategy.

4.2 Analysis for weak points

A systematic analysis of weak points must be performed in the important brand management sectors, based on an examination of brand credit with employees and customers. This is carried out by means of systematic, mostly qualitative, market research in the target groups, in which ruptures of perception or negative elements of brand perception must be discovered and defined. The analysis of weak points should result in the clearest possible weak point profile in the sectors of communication, sales and distribution, product, and corporate culture.

4.3 Introduction of a learning cycle

The identified weak points form the basis for concrete optimization concepts in the corresponding sectors. The successful realization of the optimization concepts presumes an organization that is ready to learn. The following takes place in a learning cycle:

- identification of weak points,
- derivation of optimization strategies,
- implementation of optimization measures,
- evaluation of success,
- installation of incentives over the entire process for the employees.

CASE Tchibo

The examination of brand strengths at regular intervals, particularly on a qualitative level, allows the necessary feedback for correct, credible, and sustainable brand management. This includes everything from normal advertising tracking to employee questionnaires. The customer's brand image should be tested regularly: how was the brand perceived? – and these findings should then be examined with regard to the brand credit. The results are fed back and could lead to an adjustment of strategy and/or the realization mechanisms. The tasks:

External
- tracking
- competition
- chain
- logo
- degree of recognition
- advertising image
- brand image

Internal
- employee questionnaires
- value workshop

Phase 5: Long-term Brand Migration

The aim of Long-term Brand Migration is the long-term maximization of brand credit and, thus, the resultant generation of long-term and stable growth for the company. The most important instrument is the constant optimization of brand strategy and further improvement of the brand core (the core values of the brand). This improvement presumes constant tracking of brand credit and exact observation of changes in the macroscopic positioning of the markets. The art is to enable changes in brand strategy and brand core, and to simultaneously identify actual core values beyond fashion and trends, and to keep these constant. The identification of the actual core values of a brand can only take place over an extended period, in which brand strategy, the value cosmos, its changes and their effects on the target groups (measurement by brand credit) are examined in a circular process.

Long-term Brand Migration means understanding inter-relationships between changes in the brand strategy and changes in the market and company environment, and to react to these effectively without fundamentally changing the course of the brand. In the final, constant phase of the process, the point is therefore to transform the brand in a long-term process of brand management, based on a learning organization that is oriented towards the market and the needs of the customers (implementation of the learning cycle).

▶ Key Insights

- Long-term Brand Migration means leading a brand, through the alignment of internal strategies and the marketing mix, in a stable and successful manner.
- Measurement of success can only take place via long-term turnover growth and the indicator of brand credit (comprising trust, sympathy, and loyalty) on which it is based.
- The system of Long-term Brand Migration thereby allows a direct connection between internal measures, marketing mix activities, and long-term turnover growth via the indicator of brand credit.
- The important aim both internally and externally is to achieve a consistent 360-degree perception that is focused on the needs of the employees and the customers. It forms the basis for the growth of brand credit.
- The prerequisite for this is a commitment on all levels to the mutual brand and corporate vision, as well as the introduction of a learning organization that is constantly developing in the interest of the target groups.

▶ Practical Guidelines

- Fix long-term brand management as the strategic focus of company management.
- Understand the brand status in all dimensions, both internally and externally.
- Develop a long-term brand strategy that unifies the factual strengths of the company with the central values of the brand and the needs of the customers, and that represents the central focus of strategic company management.
- Implement long-term and active change management that, in order to remain transparent and controllable, should be assigned to the central points within the company based on the division of labor and modularity.
- Introduce a learning cycle into the organization: constant re-engineering of the brand based on consumer and brand research.
- Introduce a system of control and adjustment of all components by tracking the brand credit (trust, sympathy, and loyalty).

The Authors

Stephan Swinka

After joining Tchibo in March 1998 as Head of Product Management and Purchasing Non-Food, Stephan Swinka became Member of the Board at Tchibo for the Non-Food division in November 1998. Under his responsibility, the consumer product business was continually expanded, and the move into additional product segments such as insurances and credit business began, along with a cooperation in the mobile telecommunications sector with O_2. Stephan Swinka was also responsible for the internationalization of the Tchibo system business, and was head of the companies in England, Austria, and Switzerland, as well as the Internet and mail order businesses. After completing his degree in industrial engineering, he worked in a variety of marketing and sales functions for Unilever GmbH, Fielmann GmbH and Effem GmbH/Mars Inc. Stephan Swinka was also employed as a consultant for the management consultancy Gruber, Titze & Partner/Gemini Corporation in Germany and the U.S.

Peter Michael Wolf

In February 2003, Peter Wolf took over responsibility as Member of the Board for the Food Division at Tchibo GmbH. In this function, he expanded the market and competence leadership of Tchibo coffee, and led Tchibo into new growth segments with Espresso (Gusto Originale), single portion system (Cafissimo), and premium chocolate with a high cocoa content (Privatschokolade). Peter Wolf is also responsible for the Tchibo brand management worldwide (Corporate Branding), and for the Central and Eastern European region. Before his responsibilities as a Member of the Board, Peter Wolf was Managing Director at BTM Tabakspezialitäten (formerly Roth-Händle GmbH), a subsidiary of the Reemtsma Group. After completing his bank traineeship at Dresdner Bank AG, and his degree in business administration at Mannheim University, he started his professional career in product management for the Laundry and Home Care Division at Henkel KGaA in Düsseldorf. He subsequently held company management positions at the international advertising agencies J.W. Thompson and the Bates Group in Frankfurt.

Dr. Ulf Santjer – PUMA AG

Brand Desirability
Basis for the turnaround and the resurgence of established brands

Initial position
In a world of evolving media forms that can often be overwhelming, marketing is being forced to adapt to the increasingly converging requirements of more and more experienced, better informed customers and globally thinking consumers. Today, products and offerings from a whole range of areas such as sport, music, film, telecommunication, or EDP are competing against one another for the attention of the consumers. Manufacturers of brand products are therefore being forced to focus on a differentiating yet unmistakably clear brand communication to strengthen the brand and achieve brand desirability in the long-term. This includes a convincing concept for creating brand desirability that first makes the turnaround and resurgence of established brands possible.

"Brand management is not a fight between products. It is a struggle between perceptions."

Michael Brandtner

▶ Executive Summary

- Against the backdrop of stronger competition and increasing internationalization of markets, brand management is forced to react to the increasing qualitative exchangeability of products that is leading to a reduced ability for differentiation amongst consumers. To gain the perception of the consumers permanently, the implementation of a concept for brand communication, that promotes consistent investment in the increase of the brand desirability, can help.

- The necessary requirements that are fundamental for increasing brand desirability include a long-term brand strategy, creativity, an innovative brand communication, a selective distribution, as well as clear brand messages. The elements of brand desirability can be shown using a theoretical model. This refers to the fact that new contemporary norms and values, which are reflected in a particular lifestyle, have to be continually associated with the brand.

- In practice, the most important factors for creating and/or increasing brand desirability are associated closely with the entire corporate development. In the first phase, a comprehensive restructuring of all company divisions can create the basis for developing brand desirability. In the second phase, significant investment in the brand is necessary for the desired turnaround. In the third phase, the strategic objective of increasing the desirability of the brand and transforming it into profitable growth must be pursued. In the fourth step, that is orientated towards expansion, specific investments in the brand are necessary that aim to open up new sales potential. This also includes, for instance, the acquisition of second brands that supplement the existing portfolio. However, central to this and future development phases of the company that are decisive for brand desirability, is always an unmistakable and innovative brand communication.

This article offers the reader an overview of the creation and building of the desirability of a brand. People with marketing responsibility will find the fundamental elements and factors of brand desirability, in addition to the theoretical basics. They can understand, using different development phases that are presented, which instruments have to be used in the different phases of a company's development to increase the brand desirability and, thus, the brand value in a sustained manner.

▶ Theoretical Model of Brand Desirability

1. Definition

The desirability of a brand is achieved and/or enhanced through the combination of design and innovation, a clear distribution strategy, as well as brand-building concepts and marketing initiatives. Only the creation of brand desirability leads to a sustained increase in the brand value.

2. Factors of brand desirability

2.1 Long-term brand strategy

To create brand desirability, a management process is necessary that embraces the planning, coordination, and control of a host of long-term marketing activities. Elements of this strategic brand development are a specific development of the brand, the ongoing maintenance of the brand, and effective brand product marketing. The basis for a successful positioning of a brand is a strategy that ensures emotional charging on the basis of an innovative marketing mix and, thus, strengthens the desirability of the brand in the long term.

2.2 Creativity

The desirability of a brand is in constant interaction with trends and rapid changes in the market and competitive environment. To meet these challenges, creative management is necessary. The basis for this is the ability to develop unusual and innovative ideas – creativity is the key to innovation. That is why, in the development and implementation of a brand strategy, a company must be able to rely on employees who can meet these creative challenges. The prerequisite for successful creative work is the creation of a corresponding environment in the company in which creativity can develop. This includes the promotion and further development of common values that are in line with the brand personality. A corporate culture that is defined by creativity includes values such as passion, openness, self-belief, and entrepreneurship actions. Under these conditions, creativity functions as a motor of the corporate culture. A two-way dynamic process results, permitting the development of a strategy that, when implemented, leads to a sustained increase in brand desirability.

2.3 Innovative brand communication

The brand communication must support the brand strategy by giving the brand an unmistakable profile and setting a new direction on the market through innovative concepts. Marketing must take up new and exceptional topics and concepts to enhance the brand desirability through brand-building activities and innovative products. The area of public relations has a central role to play here. It has to make use of unusual and creative communication concepts to strengthen the image of the brand in the long term. For this reason, the brand communication must surprise, stimulate, and entertain over and over again. As the brand communication supplies the unexpected and ever new perspectives of the product, the desirability of the brand is permanently strengthened.

2.4 Design orientation
A fundamental contribution to the creation and strengthening of the brand desirability is made by the permanent further development of creative designs. The focus must be on the development of new products that depict, in a concise manner, the innovative aesthetics of the brand. All essential product concepts should consist of collections that are harmonized with one another, whereby the individual products are optimized in their functionality through use of innovative materials and technologies. The traditional view that functionality is at the heart of every product development is being replaced by changed consumer behavior. The consumer of today demands an innovative design combined with functionality. The purchasing decision is made increasingly via the design or the emotional perception of products. This must also be reflected in the product communication.

2.5 Selective distribution
To increase the brand desirability, a selective distribution lends itself as a market coverage strategy. Through this instrument, different products can specifically reach the respective consumer group via selected distributors. The requirement is the consistent implementation of a distribution strategy that aims to offer products only via the clearly defined sales channels. The development and use of a company-wide, web-based order management system is also one means to increase competitiveness and to support the flow of goods and information along the logistical process. The level of distribution derived from this acts as a key figure for the brand desirability and for the control of demand in retail.

2.6 Clear brand messages
Increasing competition and exchangeability of products are constantly requiring new communication activities. The efficiency of these activities must be verified repeatedly due to the information overload amongst consumers. Against this backdrop, the communication of clear brand messages is crucial. A brand must stand behind its own products, reduce the complexity, create orientation for the consumer through clear brand messages, and possess a unique personality. The starting point for this is the development of its own brand personality. This makes the company's own brand recognisable for the consumers, and it can be permanently differentiated from the competition. To increase desirability, the brand messages must reflect, above all, the positioning of the brand and the positive assessment of the brand from the consumer's point of view.

Model of brand desirability

The necessary prerequisites shown for an increase in brand desirability (factors 2.1 to 2.6) are based on a theoretical model, which assumes different brand layers that build on one another. The peak layer displays the visible brand identity with its public presence and the conveyed offerings of the products. The invisible layers of the brand personality include specific values, ideas, and characteristics that build on the origin of the brand. To achieve the objective of increasing the desirability, the existing characteristics of the brand personality must be supplemented by new elements that contribute to the increase in brand presence and the uniqueness of the brand identity. The model shows that not the past, but rather, new norms and values need to be associated with the brand, and that these need to be in harmony with the zeitgeist. This factor is fundamental to brand desirability.

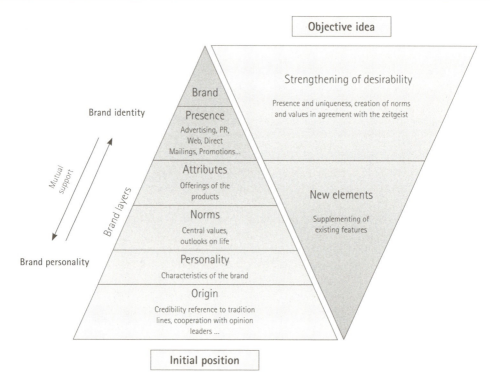

Fig. 1: Model of brand desirability

Process & Implementation

Phase 1: Turnaround of the company

If a company fails to adapt quickly and flexibly to changing market conditions, this can lead to a development that may threaten its existence. To achieve a turnaround here, a rigorous restructuring of the company is necessary, that is carried out in several steps. Firstly, it means conducting an analysis of the restructuring requirements, as well as a reorganization of company divisions and functions. Secondly, the aim must be to create a company that works efficiently and is profitable. The activities associated with the process of restructuring are orientated towards giving the company an efficient organizational structure again and, thus, safeguarding its competitiveness in the long term.

1 Turnaround of the company	2 Brand turnaround	3 Momentum	4 Company expansion
Goals			
Adaptation of the company to a changed market situation	Repositioning of the brand	Increase in the brand desirability – design, innovation, selective distribution strategy, brand forming concepts, marketing initiatives	Growth of brand and company
Reorganization of company divisions and structures	Development of brand desirability		Increase of the market share of the company's own products
	Increase in brand presence		
Profitability and competitiveness	Global alignment of the brand	Conversion of the brand desirability into profitable growth	Specific value-creating acquisitions
			Exploration of the corporate potential
		Exploration of the company potential	
Contents			
Analysis of the restructuring requirements	Investment to reposition the brand, marketing, product development, infrastructure	Promotion of the brand strategy – communication through PR concepts	Regional expansion
Development of an organizational structure – formation of core categories	Implementation of the brand strategy	Strengthening of the brand image with the aid of PR	Product expansion
			Acquisition of further brands
Creation of a contemporary corporate culture, entrepreneurial thinking, teamwork, creativity	Creation of a unique brand identity and brand personality	Conveyance of concise brand messages	Opening up of new sales potential – moving forward into new product categories, expansion of the product range
Development of a globally oriented brand strategy	Use of innovative concepts for the brand communication.	Continuation of the selective distribution strategy	Strengthening of the international orientation – shifting of the global market shares
	Uniformity, conciseness, internationality	Combination of brand personality and product design	Transfer of a lifestyle concept to new product categories
	International organization of the brand communication – strengthening of the brand image in the key markets, investment in improving product availability	Promotion of the corporate culture – values that are in line with the brand personality: passion, openness, self-belief, entrepreneurship	Support of the corporate and brand strategy – communication of the strategic activities through PR
	Optimization of functionality and design, product placement – selection of good promotion partners	Use of the virtual organizational structure – improvement of the operational efficiency, optimization of internal process procedures, effective distribution of competencies	Alignment of the brand communication with a strategic target specification – leading position of brand and company
	Development of a virtual organization structure to support the global brand strategy – decentralization, promptness, efficiency	Maintaining social and ethical standards	Communicative accompaniment of the expansion phase – innovative brand messages, selective distribution strategy, brand personality, product design
	Introduction of a selective distribution strategy		Integration of new employees
			Expansion of the virtual organizational structure and transfer of social and ethical standards

Fig. 2: Brand desirability process

CASE   PUMA – Phase 1 of the company's development (1993-1997)

Jochen Zeitz takes over as Chairman of the Board in 1993, and Phase I of the long-term company development at PUMA begins, with the objective of consistent restructuring. In this phase, PUMA concentrates on creating a lean, effective, and flexible organizational structure as the basis for future growth, and the possibility at a later date of being able to invest specifically in the brand and the creation of brand desirability. The main measures that the management introduces include, for example, the dismantling of company hierarchies, the creation of profit centers, and the closure of all remaining proprietary production facilities through consistent outsourcing. Through the formation of core categories, such as football and running, the extremely diversified product lines are streamlined to significantly reduce the overall number of individual products. The development of a corporate culture that promotes entrepreneurial thinking, teamwork and creativity is an indispensable part of this. The company concentrates for the first time in its history on a globally integrated brand strategy by developing global marketing concepts to strengthen the image of the brand in core markets. In its communication, PUMA concentrates on TV advertising, and on the marketing of a newly compiled portfolio of top sportsmen and sportswomen that fits the brand personality.

Phase 2: Brand turnaround

In the course of progressive globalization, companies are being shaped by a radical transformation. The use of new media permits trade and communication around the clock. Marketing has to adapt itself accordingly to the ever more strongly converging requirements of experienced and well-informed customers, as well as globally aligned consumer markets. A standardized, concise and internationally aligned brand communication is, therefore, decisive for business success. For the repositioning of a brand, the focus is on consistent investment in the areas of marketing, product development, and infrastructure. Through strategic alliances and cooperations, the brand presence must be extended and strengthened further. The desirability of the brand is the prerequisite for further growth.

CASE   PUMA – Phase 2 of the company's development (1998-2001)

After the successful restructuring and strengthening of profitability, PUMA decides, in the fourth quarter of 1997, to invest aggressively in the brand within the framework of its second five-year plan, whereby the funds deployed are way above the industry average. Since then, the company has continually developed its globally oriented brand strategy and its brand position further. With high investments in communication and product design, PUMA is consistently pursuing its long-term goal of becoming "one of the most desirable sportlifestyle brands in the world." By fixing the brand desirability in the mission statement of the company, its strategic importance is particularly emphasized.

1. Brand identity
In accordance with its brand identity, PUMA is the brand that successfully combines the influences from sport, lifestyle, and fashion. The great history of sporting achievements gives the brand a high

level of credibility for new and creative paths in design, technology, and communication. Concepts and products are therefore developed that cover the entire spectrum, from traditional to extreme sports. As a result of the increasingly rapid convergence of individual markets into one global marketplace, the consumer is confronted by a wealth of information. Here, a brand no longer achieves success through the quality of its products alone. Rather, behind the products, there must be a brand that reduces complexity, creates orientation for the consumer through clear brand messages, and that possesses unique personality. Only then will it stand out from the "white mountains" of its competitors. PUMA wants to be one of those special brands that tackle things differently: unmistakable and convincing. Amidst the white mountains, PUMA wants to be the "blue mountain." Although PUMA might not be the biggest mountain here – it is unmistakably one of the most desirable sportlifestyle brands.

2. Innovative brand communication

With the brand communication, PUMA concentrated on strengthening the image of the brand in the key markets, and increasing its brand visibility. Traditional sponsoring expenditure is transferred in favor of specific investments aimed at improvements in product availability. These sales promotion activities include, in particular, additional investments in the improvement of the product presence in retail, for example, through expanding in-store merchandising. Effective visual merchandising has thus facilitated a concise brand presence at the point of sale. As a smaller supplier in the concert of leading sports article companies, the right marketing mix and the rigorous networking of sales promotion, sports promotion, public relations, advertising and marketing services, in core categories such as football and running, are decisively important for PUMA. The development of a new and globally oriented portfolio of promotion partners with the top tennis player Serena Williams, the world class track athlete Wilson Kipketer, and the Cameroon national team, whose personalities match the brand perfectly, has made a decisive contribution to the creation of brand desirability.

In the area of running, at the end of the nineties, PUMA concentrated on equipping a group of almost 60 top Kenyan athletes, who were marketed globally. The dominance of the Kenyan athletes in middle and long-distance running made PUMA into one of the main players in the international world of running. For example, in 1999 alone, on the distances between 800m and 10,000m, 50 percent of the races at the Golden League meetings were won by PUMA athletes.

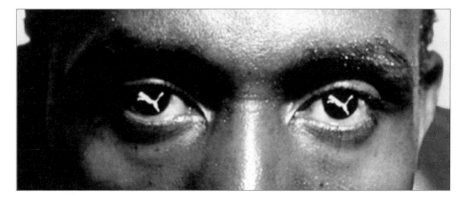

Fig. 3: The cat of prey firmly in his sights: Linford Christie with the PUMA contact lenses

3. Products

Functionality and the design of products are of outstanding importance. The development work is done primarily in Herzogenaurauch, Boston, and Taiwan. This permits the optimal use of the existing resources and competencies of the individual teams. The product portfolio has been decisively strengthened by external know-how on cooperations. PUMA adopted a pioneering role for the industry when it entered a cooperation with the fashion label Jil Sander in 1998 and, thus, expressed the fusion of sport and fashion within the framework of an innovative shoe collection. This partnership has opened up the possibility for PUMA to develop fashionable designs and, thus, provide the brand with access to new target groups. Since then, the cooperation with Jil Sander has been continued with new collections of ladies' and men's shoes. The shoe models combine authenticity and sports performance with an unmistakable fashionable flair. With the aid of targeted product placement in the print and TV area, the company has thus set a course and increased its brand presence considerably. Through the strategic alliance between PUMA and its shareholder Monarchy/Regency, one of the leading companies in the Hollywood entertainment industry in the areas of film, television, and music, product placement is further promoted. PUMA products regularly appear in Regency productions and actors, too, wear them increasingly in their free time. With the aid of Regency, PUMA is building up a unique portfolio of international promotion partners. The equipment contract with the American tennis player Serena Williams is the first of its kind. Serena Williams has not only worn PUMA products, she has also committed herself to participating in film, music, and TV projects of Regency. The company has thus strengthened the combination of sport and lifestyle, and promoted its brand desirability further.

4. Virtual structure

For the support of its global brand strategy, PUMA has developed a virtual organization structure that differs significantly from a conventional, centralized set-up. Associated with this is the challenge to design communication and processes more quickly and more effectively. For this reason, PUMA is building up its global company based on several cornerstones: a virtual company structure, strategic planning, and the employees of the company. The virtual company headquarters consists of decentralized competence centers located in Germany, the U.S.A., and Hong Kong. These competence centers are divided into the seven company functions of product, (goods) logistics, brand, growth, structure, company value, and culture. Each functional unit contains further sub-functions that all follow the higher-level global orientation. The individual functions are strategically located where specialization and management know-how are optimally available and can be used. Marketing was therefore moved to the U.S.A. as part of the functional unit "brand," so that new trends could be picked up more quickly.

In contrast, distribution as part of the goods logistics is managed from Germany, where PUMA laid the foundations for the virtual company. Within the matrix structure, PUMA achieves a geographical focus through its subsidiaries, of which Germany, the U.S.A., Hong Kong, Austria, and Australia act as regional hubs to manage distributors, licensees, and subsidiaries in the respective regions. Germany serves Western Europe, the U.S.A. the American continent, Austria serves the regions of Eastern Europe, Africa and the Middle East, Hong Kong the Asian region, and Australia the Pacific region. With this, PUMA can react dynamically to regional and local characteristics and optimally integrate the specifications of the individual markets into the company's strategies. In order to be as close to the market and consumers as possible and thus provide the company with competitive advantages, PUMA has developed a strategic planning model. Strategic planning is used, among other things, to define, plan, and implement strategies for growth and profitability of companies and brands, as well as to optimize company processes through the exploitation of all technical options that support and promote the virtual structure of the company in the best possible way.

The employees make the most important contribution to the success of the company. PUMA has therefore developed a corporate culture in Phase 2 of company development, in which work is fun, creativity can be fostered, and processes serve only as a means to an end – there is no place for traditional bureaucracy.

Phase 3: Momentum

The central objective of the company strategy must be to increase the desirability of the brand further and convert it into profitable growth. This objective is pushed by the interaction of different elements such as design and innovation, a selective distribution strategy, and brand-building concepts.

CASE PUMA – Phase 3 of the company's development (2002-2005)

With the aid of a clear and concise brand communication, the brand strategy is supported that includes a successful combination of different influences from the world of sport, lifestyle, and fashion. The challenge here is the communication of the innovative concept "sportlifestyle." Sportlifestyle is the challenge of a new market which realizes that consumers are demanding sporty products and styles that they can wear not only in the fitness studio or on the pitch, but also in their free time. The brand communication accommodates this modern interpretation of the term sport by thematically recharging the sportlifestyle concept over and over again and, thus, strengthening the brand further within the target groups. Sport today is active lifestyle, divided according to the multi-layer consumer groups. This is also reflected in the communication. On the one hand, this means the rigorous orientation of all PR instruments and activities towards the sports-enthusiastic athletes in the categories of football, running and motor sports, through to the extreme categories of sport. On the other hand, however, it is also fitness and wellness, in addition to the business traveler who is active en route, or the fashion-conscious consumer who is seeking luxury with a sporting slant. PUMA is concentrating on enhancing the brand value in a sustained manner by forcing the concise brand message and, thus, giving PUMA an unmistakable voice in the segment of sportlifestyle. The results are more than convincing. According to a 2004 study by the market research company Interbrand, PUMA is among the top 14 most influential brands worldwide.

1. Brand communication

1.1 Football
Football belongs to the core segments of PUMA. The equipment and marketing is concentrated on national teams (e.g., Italy, Czech Republic, Cameroon, Paraguay), club teams (e.g., Lazio Roma, AS Monaco) and individual players (e.g., Freddie Ljungberg/Arsenal, Samuel Eto'o FC Barcelona). Here,

Figs. 4 and 5: Samuel Eto'o and his untamable lions from Cameroon with the revolutionary one-piece kit from PUMA.

PUMA can draw on high product competence and brand recognition that has developed in the course of more than 55 years of company history. Sport, lifestyle, and fashionable flair are embodied above all by the Italian national team. The expression of this partnership with the Italian football association is that not only the kit, but also an own fashion collection by the well-known designer Neil Barrett was designed. The aim is to create an unique brand message and thereby set new accents in the market.

1.2 Running

In addition to football, running also belongs to the core categories at PUMA. Through specific merchandising, effective advertising, and innovative products, PUMA wants to inspire its customers and break new ground in running. Running products are convincing through high-quality, functional materials, and innovative designs. In the international arena, the successful cooperation with the Jamaican track and field athletics team is being continued. With this cooperation, PUMA uses the option of being able to advertise using one of the leading sporting nations in the world. In doing so, not only the image as one of the globally leading running brands is strengthened – the fun, the joy of life and the enthusiasm of the Jamaicans, who represent an active lifestyle, is also conveyed. In addition, the company is accompanying a development program for young sportsmen and sportswomen, that is intended to push the Jamaican role as pioneers in track and field athletics. With sports articles and financial means, not only sport at universities is being supported, but also the training of young potentials and the junior competitive program.

1.3 Motorsports

In 2005, PUMA expanded its commitment in the area of motorsports and now has five Formula 1 teams in its portfolio with the racing teams Scuderia Ferrari, BMW Williams, Mild Seven Renault, Sauber Petronas, and Minardi. Not only the new partnership with the World Rally Championship (WRC), but also the continued cooperation with Porsche, and the involvement with the German Touring Cars Championships (DTM), round off the spectrum and ensure an impressive presence in the world of motorsports. Through these partnerships, the company gains the unique possibility to equip drivers and teams with shoes, accessories, and apparel that reflect the typical requirements and challenges of motorsports. In 2005, a further cooperation was agreed with Ferrari's top driver and the sevenfold world champion in the Formula 1 driver ratings, Michael Schumacher; in the 2005 season he wore the racing shoe "Future Cat": Products such as the Future Cat, that combine form with function, embody the fashion and style of motorsports, even away from the racing track. The first racing shoes from PUMA were worn in the Seventies and early Eighties by drivers and teams. Since 1998, PUMA has re-entered the motorsports arena and has put together an extensive sponsoring portfolio.

Fig. 6: PUMA motorsports racing shoe "Future Cat"

2. Sales

PUMA is rigorously continuing its selective distribution strategy, and checks its implementation constantly in order to strengthen the desirability of the brand. Products are initially introduced onto the market via selected, limited sales channels. If there is appropriate acceptance on the part of the customers and consumers, the decision is then made to what extent and in which form these products will be marketed. The consistent development of the retail business makes it possible to deepen customer retention further, and to present product innovations in a way that is appropriate to the brand. The PUMA stores are "shop windows for the brand," and offer the possibility to test new products and collections, to strengthen customer loyalty further, and to rigorously align the collection offering with consumer demand.

3. Products

Through the connection of the PUMA brand personality with a high design claim, PUMA has achieved a unique positioning as a desirable sportlifestyle brand within the sports industry. Sport still has pivotal importance. Today, however, it is defined in a much more modern way. That is why the design of the products plays a crucial role. Through the combination of influences from the world of sport, lifestyle, and fashion, the consumers are offered both functionality and technology, and the design leadership in the sportlifestyle market segment is thereby underlined. The combination of innovative, design-oriented products with a consistent product lifecycle management strengthens the desirability

Figs. 7 and 8: PUMA campaign "Hello" and advert Easy Rider Evo

of the brand. Product management is, therefore, working continually with Sales to develop new concepts and to ensure their distribution. New individual and innovative products are to supplement the existing product portfolio or set modern accents. This is a sign of the continuous and consistent rejuvenation of the product range. The current collections embrace a variety of styles and product lines, and are supported by innovative marketing activities.

4. Employees

For years, PUMA has been growing, and the company has the exceptional commitment of its employees to thank for its success. Around the world, more than 4000 employees are employed. PUMA is striving to develop the company and its culture further by promoting common values that are in line with the brand personality. These common values can be summed up in four words: fascination, openness, self-belief, and entrepreneurship.

Passion: The business of PUMA is deeply rooted in the world of sport and inseparable from the unforgettable sporting achievements of outstanding athletes that have made history in the arenas of this world. The company develops products that embody this world in a fascinating way, and which promote a person's own achievements.

Openness: The current market and industry environment belongs to the fastest and most dynamic in the world. The requirements of this market can only be met by a company culture in which creative ideas and opinions are promoted, but in which old wisdoms are called into question over and over again. In such a corporate culture, respect and understanding for one another develop automatically, which enhances the competition for the best ideas and concepts, and thereby, the company's success.

Self-belief: Global companies have to meet new challenges on a daily basis, challenges that they can only master with qualified employees and their belief in their own capabilities. At PUMA, we are aware of this, and attach great importance to ensuring that every single employee understands and lives the corporate values and profits from the experiences and skills of his or her colleagues, in accordance with the company philosophy. Only the unconditional belief in their own abilities makes it possible for employees to move things, make difficult decisions, and realize visions that take themselves, and ultimately the company, further.

Entrepreneurship: New ideas are the key to success. The company has built its success on new ideas that necessitate the willingness to see beyond one's own nose, to say "yes" where others say "no," and to be inspired by the world outside of the sports industry, too. The brand has developed out of this creativity, and according to the management, this creativity will play an important role in future developments of the brand.

5. Virtual organization

The aim of becoming one of the most desirable sportlifestyle brands is supported by the constant improvement of the operational efficiency on the basis of the decentralized organizational structure. The company concentrates on continuously optimizing internal processes, whereby scale advantages arising from the company's size can be capitalized on by PUMA. The decentralized, virtual organizational structure makes it possible to allocate the available competencies at points within the company where they are most effective. In this way, PUMA achieves an even greater speed and efficiency along the value creation chain, and offers its customers an even better service. In the course of the strengthening of the decentralized corporate structure, an office has been located in London for the area of sports fashion and for the product area. As an international metropolis of culture, music, sports, and fashion, London is the ideal location to push the sportlifestyle concept further.

6. Environment and social matters

As a globally operating sports company, PUMA feels strongly committed to the protection of the environment and the adherence to social standards. This responsibility is expressed in the social, ethically motivated, and environmentally oriented dealings of PUMA with its partners. Through the continual optimization of its own activities in the area of environment and social matters, an efficient control system has been developed that helps the company to ensure high environmental and social standards in the entire value creation chain. The company has now assumed a leading role in the implementation of environmental and social management systems, as well as sustainable procedures. Thus, PUMA ensures that the objective of becoming the most desirable sportlifestyle brand is not only oriented to purely economic criteria. Analyses show that after implementing and/or optimizing their environmental and social standards, the suppliers were not only able to record significantly improved employee motivation, they were also able to achieve a higher value creation and competitiveness overall.

Phase 4: Company expansion

The growth phase of a company is usually accompanied by increased investments to open up new markets and, thus, sales potential. Objectives of a company in the expansion phase can, for example, be an increase in turnover, improvement in market share for its own products or possible acquisitions. In the majority of cases, this is also linked to an increase in the number of employees.

CASE   PUMA – Phase 4 of the company's development (2006-2010)

In Phase 4 of PUMA's long-term development plan, referred to as "Company Expansion," PUMA has the long-term mission of becoming the most desirable Sportlifestyle company and wants to reinforce its position as one of the leading multi-category Sportlifestyle brands. To achieve this goal, PUMA will adhere to a clear set of guiding principles: Desirability, Sustainability, Product Lifecycle Management, Corporate Values, Organizational Excellence and Value Creation. With these principles, among others, PUMA will drive Phase 4 and focus on three areas: Category Expansion, Regional Expansion and Non-PUMA Brand Expansion.

Category Expansion will encompass growth in existing business as well as entry into categories that are new to PUMA. In general, the company will take a multi-dimensional approach to category expansion, driving growth by making strong pushes across the full spectrum of Sportlifestyle, from performance to fashion. In addition to adding depth to PUMA via existing and new categories, the company will also add breadth by accelerating its Regional Expansion. Regional expansion is planned to occur in markets that are currently run by PUMA as well as through several selective joint ventures and takebacks of its licensed business in its core segments. Management has started its regional expansion with majority owned Joint Ventures together with its current license partners in Japan (apparel business), China/Hong Kong, Taiwan, Argentina and Canada as well as fully owned subsidiaries in India and Dubai for the Middle East region, all of which were operational as of 1st January 2006. Phase 4 will also be the first time that the company looks to expand selectively with brands other than PUMA. Towards the end of Phase 4, Non-PUMA brands could contribute up to 10 percent of overall business.

The goal of Phase 4 is to permanently establish PUMA as one of the top three brands in the sporting goods industry, and in the long-term, to make PUMA the most desirable Sportlifestyle company. Both brand and corporate communications support this strategic goal by strengthening the positioning of PUMA as a desirable Sportlifestyle brand and, thus, contributing to further increasing the brand and company value. PUMA has kicked-off Phase 4 in the World Cup year 2006, which will be marked by a significant increase of brand investments, in particular into marketing, sales (including own retail) as well as product development and design. These investments will be made with the aim of further strengthening the brand desirability within the scope of the World Cup as an outstanding sports event.

Outlook: The World Cup as a platform to increase brand desirability

The World Cup 2006 is the focus of the brand communication. It represents a great opportunity for the brand. The objective is not only to strengthen PUMA's position as one of the leading football brands, but to further underline the commitment to football. With a total of twelve teams PUMA is the dominant kit supplier at this year's event. In fact, well over half of the first round games will feature a PUMA team, which will give a substantial boost to our global visibility in football and reaffirm our commitment to the category. In addition, PUMA also works with numerous individual players and will convince through creative concepts as well as innovative technologies and designs. In order to do that successfully a closely harmonized internal and external communication must be guaranteed.

The 2006 African Cup of Nations, which took place this January in Egypt, served as a good test run for PUMA. The event, at which PUMA was supplier to eight out of the 16 teams competing in the tournament (Angola, Cameroon, Egypt, Ghana, Ivory Coast, Senegal, Togo and Tunisia) set the pace for 2006. In a dramatic all PUMA final host Egypt beat Ivory Coast after a penalty shootout. The strength, colourfulness and passion of this tournament made it the perfect stage to launch PUMA's new statement playing kit v1.06 that will also be worn by all PUMA teams in Germany later this year.

Over the following months further elements of the diverse brand activities – both sport and lifestyle-oriented will be introduced. The challenge will not only be to continuously forge new paths in the way the brand is communicated and, thus, differentiate the company from the competition, but also to establish further brand desirability through specific communication activities.

▶ Key Insights

- The development of brand desirability is defined by the interaction between certain factors. These include a long-term brand strategy, creativity, an innovative brand communication, design orientation, a selective distribution, and clear brand messages.
- The implementation of a concept that is harmonized to the creation of brand desirability has a defining effect on all phases of strategic company development.
- The creation of brand desirability ensures a permanent increase in the brand value, and serves, therefore, as the basis for the expansion of brand and company.
- In the areas of brand communication and design, creativity is the key for successful management of brand desirability. Only with a comprehensive creative deployment can the brand be connected with modern and up-to-date content that is in harmony with the zeitgeist.
- To define the brand desirability permanently, the brand must repeatedly be connected anew with contemporary norms and values that refer to the presence and uniqueness of the brand.
- The sustainable development of brand desirability can only be achieved by taking into consideration international perspectives. It must be based on a globally oriented brand strategy.

▶ Practical Guidelines

- Analyze the initial position of the company and its products with regard to the brand desirability. Integrate the findings into a long-term strategy for building up and expanding the brand.
- Ensure a modern and contemporary work environment in which creativity can develop. Use the potential of all employees to develop the brand desirability further.
- Detect new trends and try to integrate these quickly in the brand communication. Create an organizational structure that optimally supports a promotion of clear brand messages.
- Try to surprise again and again in brand communication through unusual and unconventional paths. Only through innovative topics and concepts are courses set that strengthen the image of a brand and, thus, the brand desirability in a sustained manner.

☐ In the creation of brand desirability, take into account international aspects such as cultural codes and regional influences that represent a particular lifestyle. Ensure that the brand has an unmistakable personality all over the world, one that is accepted and demanded by an international target group.

The Author

Dr. Ulf Santjer

Dr. Ulf Santjer has been Head of Corporate Communications at PUMA AG since 2002. From 1997 until 2001, he was Press Spokesman and Deputy Head of Marketing at PUMA Germany.

Literature Recommendations

D. A. Aaker, E. Joachimsthaler, "Brand Leadership. Die Strategie für Siegermarken," München 2001
M. Bruhn, "Unternehmens- und Marketingkommunikation. Handbuch für ein integriertes Kommunikationsmanagement," München 2005
C. L. Claywood, "Handbook of Strategic Public Relations & Integrated Communications," New York 1997
M. R. Czinkota, I. A. Ronkainen, "International Marketing," Mason 2004
Gladwell/Malcolm, "The Tipping Point: How little things can make a big difference," 2000
N. Mansaray, "Strategisches Marketingmanagement. In fünf Phasen zum Markterfolg," Wiesbaden 2001
H. Meffert, C. Burmann, M. Koers, "Markenmanagement. Grundlagen der identitätsorientierten Markenführung," 2nd ed., Wiesbaden 2002

Alexander Schwade – Akzo Nobel Deco GmbH

Umbrella Brand Strategy
Utilization of synergies in the management of more than one product group

▶ Executive Summary

- An integrated umbrella brand strategy brings several product groups together under one joint brand umbrella. In doing so, the resources of the company are bundled, thus increasing the efficiency of the funds used.
- With brand expansion, successive additional product groups are incorporated into the brand family, forming the basis for an extension of the competence of the umbrella brand. The introduction must be done gradually so that the end customer perceives it as credible and competent.
- In an umbrella brand concept, "1 + 1 = 2.5": every activity for an individual product contributes at the same time to the umbrella brand account, thus supporting all other members of the brand family, too.
- Cross-selling between the different product groups within the framework of an integrated and multi-dimensional marketing concept increases the efficiency of the individual (product) activities in favor of the umbrella brand, and vice versa.
- In a world of stimulus satiation, the umbrella brand strategy is an excellent option for reaching the customer with a clear, distinct, and sustained message across the entire range of products.
- If the individual products offer a transparent and credible price-performance ratio, the umbrella brand strategy, through its functional and emotional added value, makes it possible to achieve a premium price for all products of the brand family.
- On the basis of a well-founded analysis and strategy development, an elementary success factor is that the umbrella brand concept is implemented through a central brand management in a coordinated, timely, and consistent manner.
- By adhering to the umbrella brand positioning, a company can penetrate markets internationally, based on national/regional requirements, by flexibly expanding the brand in a timely fashion.
- Errors in the management of an umbrella brand not only affect the individual product and product group, but also the entire family.

▶ Theoretical Model of the Umbrella Brand Strategy

1. Definition and core principle

1.1 Detailed definition
When a company has several products and/or product groups in its portfolio, the question arises as to how these are presented on the market:

The individual brand strategy lends itself when an individual product has a clear and unmistakable performance promise to the consumer and, at the same time, has the potential to position and establish itself in a commercially successful manner on the market. The "Energy drink – Red Bull" or "duplo – the longest praline in the world," are successful examples of a single brand strategy.

With a family brand strategy, several product groups are positioned jointly on the market under one brand. The product groups can differ in nuances or in totally different fields of application. The decisive factor here is that they display a sufficiently large number of common features from the consumer's perspective so as to be perceived and accepted as a family. Family brands frequently develop out of single brands through the brand extension. Through line extension, the single brand becomes a family brand by being supplemented with additional products: Coca-Cola, Coca-Cola light, Coca-Cola Cherry.

The umbrella brand strategy comprises the approach that all products of a company are sold under one brand. In this approach, the umbrella brand is equivalent to the corporate brand. Examples are VOLVO, Nokia, and WOLF-Garten.

In practice, it can be noted that the crossover between a family brand and an umbrella brand is fluid. Brands such as Milka or Nivea have achieved such a size, and extend across so many product groups that they are often quoted in the trade as leading examples of a successful umbrella brand strategy, although in the conventional sense, they are family brands.

1.2 Core model

As the starting point for a marketing strategy, the consumers and their requirements stand on the one side, and the company that satisfies these requirements with a product, on the other side.

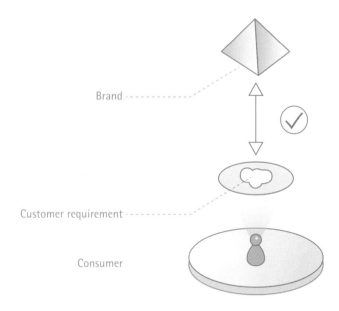

Fig. 1: Fit of brand and consumer requirements

Of fundamental importance is that the company knows precisely the requirements of its customers. The requirements can be openly known to the consumer, or also only present in a latent form. The more the company is aware of these wishes, the more precisely an offer can be developed that fulfills the requirements of the customer. Furthermore, when the offer is also perceived by the customer to be unique and relevant, in comparison to other suppliers, the company has a USP.

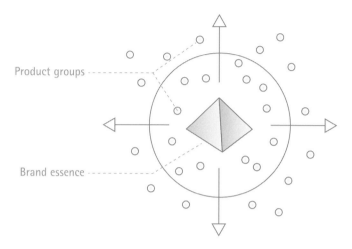

Fig. 2: Different distance of product groups to the brand essence

If the consumer has more than one singular need, the question arises as to which concept a company can use to satisfy these additional needs.

With an umbrella brand strategy, a company will offer different products under one common brand umbrella for the various requirements. The products can satisfy a chain of needs in a complementary manner or represent a completely self-contained problem solution. From the consumer's perspective, the company has a different competence for the various products. The product for which the company is regarded as being the most competent, forms the brand essence. For the other products, it is competent to differing degrees, depending on the perception of the consumer. Depending on the level of gradation, these products are at different distances from the brand essence.

With an umbrella brand strategy with different product groups, the following issues arise:

- With which products can the company grow in future under a joint brand umbrella?
- Are these products already part of the brand family, or do they have to be added to the brand for the first time (=> field of potential)?
- Can the company offer these products competitively on the market, and does the brand have the necessary credibility in the eyes of the consumers to make a corresponding offer (=> limitations of the brand competence)?

The brand essence analysis and the brand monitor are suitable instruments for answering these questions competently. (see 2.2.1 and 2.2.2).

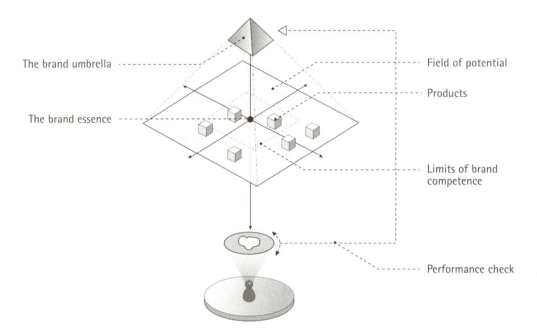

Fig. 3: Tracking and adaptation of umbrella brand and product portfolio

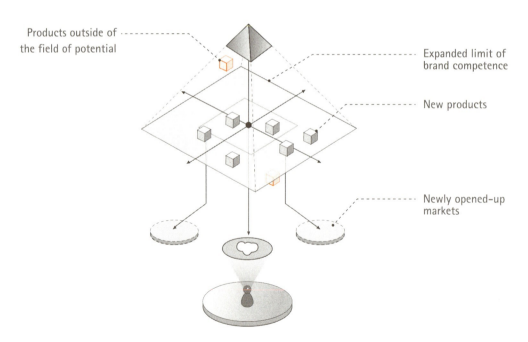

Fig. 4: Expansion of the brand competence to extend the product portfolio

Both instruments show where the brand still has potential for growth within the current borders of the brand. In addition, potential is also shown in products that, at the moment, do not yet fit the brand, but can be opened up for the brand through a successive procedure. This brand expansion is comparable with the construction of a house. First of all, the foundations have to be laid and then the overall work completed "stone by stone," In doing so, it is particularly important that the roof is not begun immediately, even if the potential of the corresponding product groups is very tempting. The brand monitor can also produce product concepts that are, on the one hand, very interesting from a commercial point of view, and for which the company has the corresponding know-how for their successful realization, but which, on the other hand, do not fit in with the umbrella brand. In this case, the development of a self-contained brand is recommended.

The principle of brand expansion can be done on the basis of a diversity of dimensions. The target market can be defined regionally, nationally, and internationally. Depending on different criteria, the target group can display one commonality: gender, age, hobby, consumer behavior, income, etc. The bigger the target market, the more commercially attractive it is for the company.

2. Factors of an umbrella brand strategy

2.1 Conceptual approach: the 4Ps of marketing

2.1.1 Product policy

With an umbrella brand strategy, products from different fields of application and experience are brought together under a joint brand umbrella. They complement one another and, thanks to their common brand essence, are perceived by the consumer as one large unit. With the positioning of the brand, the commonality is defined to which all members of the brand family are to be aligned.

The products must distinguish themselves through unique functional product features that offer the consumer a tangible and relevant additional benefit. If a premium umbrella brand is not constantly developed and updated, it is copied and is, thus, exchangeable both for the consumer and the trade. Product innovations are an elementary feature of a successful premium umbrella brand strategy. The introduction of innovative products not only updates the individual product group – it also has a positive effect on the entire brand family. However, care should be taken that these fit into the umbrella brand strategy. New products as a mere end in themselves are not sufficient. Rather, the consumer must recognize them as a genuine and worthwhile addition to the established brand family with regard to both the product benefit and the emotional added value.

CASE Using the example of WOLF-Garten, the main benefit of the umbrella brand strategy becomes clear: with its ranges of lawnmowers, scarifiers, grass seed, grass fertilizers, etc., WOLF-Garten covers a comprehensive variety of applications in the entire process of lawn maintenance. However, at the same time, the consumer also has the choice between different manufacturer and retail brands in each segment. However, no other brand offers the consumer the process of lawn maintenance as comprehensively as WOLF-Garten. The regular introduction of new products (e.g., automatic cable collection), or the improved technical equipment of existing products with new unique product features (Compact Plus electric mower), constantly update the brand as a whole. On this basis, WOLF-Garten has the USP of offering the most competent and most extensive range of products for lawn maintenance under one umbrella brand.

2.1.2 Price policy

The price positioning of an umbrella brand strategy is based on the positioning of both the individual product and the overall umbrella brand. The central aspect is that every product price must represent a credible price-performance ratio for the consumer. The value of a product is comprised of its functional and emotional values.

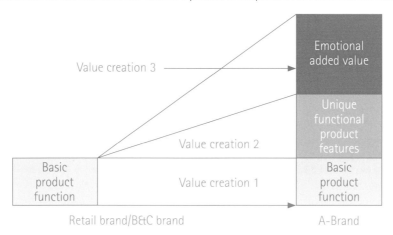

Fig. 5: Value creation through emotional added value

The functional value is based on the product equipment, on the "product features": products without special particular functional features are subject to particular price pressure from comparable competitor products as "me-too products" (value creation 1). If a product has innovative and unique product features, the consumer is prepared to honor this with an appropriate price premium (value creation 2). With a premium brand strategy, an emotional value is also generated in addition to functional values (value creation 3).

In an umbrella brand strategy with several product groups and products in different product equipment variants, the implementation of a multi-level price policy is possible. In the automotive industry, this becomes clear through different product types (makes of vehicles) that can be configured individually by the customer. As a result, the customer receives a car that individually corresponds to his or her personal requirement or desire for a functional and emotional use.

In the price policy, not only the right price positioning for the consumer needs to be taken into account, but also the successful sell-in to retail. With a strong umbrella brand, manufacturers are in a position to network their price and condition policies, so that their trade partners can be offered attractive financial incentives to list additional products or product groups from the umbrella brand family. Compared to a single brand, an additional and independent set of instruments offers itself to the umbrella brand. Price stability is a fundamental feature of a successful umbrella brand strategy. The consumer and the trade expect the brand product to keep its price stable at national and international level, as well as in the different sales channels within an appropriate price corridor. If the brand varies in price significantly between different channels, this can irritate the consumer. The willingness to pay the premium price falls, and the consumers naturally orientate themselves to the lower price in their price-performance perception. At international level, the trade reacts to different prices by setting the lowest price that it finds as the international standard price.

The internationalization and centralization on the part of the trade has led increasingly to the striving for an internationally harmonized price and conditions policy. With an existing umbrella brand range, it is recommended that the owner of a brand adopt the approach of defining the purchasing price for the trade through a weighted European average price. In individual cases, it can be more attractive for a manufacturer to withdraw completely from the market with individual national product groups, in order to maintain the international profitability of the product range family.

2.1.3 Communication policy

Within the scope of the marketing saying "do something good – and talk about it," communication fulfills the essential task of informing the user about the brand and the product, along with its product features. The basis for the communication policy is the determination of the brand essence, through which the brand image is defined, and with which the consumer should associate the product. Here, the communication must assume the actual situation as the starting point, in order to be able to plan the route to the target status. It is essential to decide which idea about the product and the brand the consumer is to have. A central task of communication is, therefore, to make a fundamental contribution to changing the brand perception of consumers.

Within the framework of communication, the emotional added value of the brand is created. The emotional added value is expressed in the consumers' trust in the brand and the product, as well as in an enhanced product experience. It is the task of communication to establish and maintain the trust in the umbrella brand and its performance. The emotional added value is the decisive difference between "me-too" products and the premium brand. If a brand concentrates exclusively on the functional product features, and does not maintain the emotional values, it does not capitalize on the brand potential, and will lose its premium position in the medium-term.

An umbrella brand strategy offers the unique opportunity to extend the emotional added value to the entire product family, and thus to ensure an emotional commitment of the consumer to the brand.

Within the framework of the umbrella brand strategy, communication has the pivotal task of linking new products and product groups to the brand. It is not sufficient to include new products in the product range. It must be conveyed to the consumer in a credible way that the new products represent a meaningful addition to the product range. The people responsible for communication should, therefore, be involved at an early stage of the product development, so that they can accompany the range extension in good time. Furthermore, communication has the task of stimulating the purchase of existing product groups, and particularly the introduction of new products and product groups. The breadth of the product range of an umbrella brand permits flexibility to bring different target groups to the brand via their different preference products. With a positive product experience, the consumer develops trust in the brand and makes additional purchases.

In a world of stimulus saturation, the sending of clear and harmonized signals is of central importance. The consumers are overloaded with purchase impulses, and are unable to record all of them because of their selective perceptions. In Germany alone, more than 50,000 brands are vying for the favor of the consumers. Against this backdrop, consistent brand signals are an important key to the success of the umbrella brand strategy. The brand signals that are defined in the Corporate Design Manual embrace not only the brand logo, but also define extensively the brand appearance, e.g., font type, color coding, packaging design, POS presence, pictorial language, etc. At the POS, every product cries out "Please buy me!" To ensure that consumers can recognize their brand products as early as possible, they have to perceive the consistent brand signals from a great distance away. The corporate designs of Milka and Coca-Cola are excellent examples of this. The harmonization of many communication elements significantly increases the chance that the brand message will actually reach the consumer.

With the umbrella brand strategy, the following applies in communication: "1 + 1 = 2.5." The communication for every individual product does not just promote the individual product, but also makes a positive contribution to the brand account. Consumers receive messages that they transfer directly or indirectly to other products within the brand family.

2.1.4 Distribution policy

With every product, the question arises as to which distribution channel is the best and most suitable. Here, the umbrella brand concept has a clear advantage. The portfolio of different product groups makes a tactical approach possible. The product group with the greatest potential is used as a door opener in the respective distribution channel, and is then followed by other product groups that are introduced on the market. Particularly on an international level, depending on the national competitive environment and different local/individual preferences of the consumer, an individual approach that is compatible with the brand can thus be chosen. With an umbrella brand concept, it is important not to lose sight of the strategic alignment, in order to ensure that, in the medium-to long-term, all family members are introduced into the market and, thus, the brand positioning is implemented.

With an umbrella brand strategy of consumer brands, there are different forms of placement at the POS. In a shop-to-shop system, all products can be presented together. This is where consumers experience their brand world in compressed form. Retail also pursues different strategies in product placement. Products of a brand family can be placed as a brand block or, in the most extreme form, as an individual product. A decisive factor is the search criteria that consumers use to find their products. Within the framework of category management, numerous different forms of goods placement are made in this respect.

It is decisive for the individual product that it already communicates its product benefits through its packaging design alone, and attracts the attention of the consumer for itself. Compared to a single brand product, the umbrella brand has the advantage that the consumer can receive the signals of the brand at many places in the retail outlet. Especially at the POS, the harmonized corporate design makes a fundamental contribution towards the consumers recognizing their brand product early on. As a guideline, consumers should already recognize their brand at a distance of at least ten yards.

The complementarity in the product family gives the umbrella brand another advantage over the single brand product. The umbrella brand can offer both the consumer and the trade topics from a single source. This is particularly important for secondary and campaign placements. Using the example of WOLF-Garten, this means that for example, scarifiers and fertilizers can be presented together. Selling a scarifier without grass fertilizer is like selling a car without petrol. Both are necessary for a technically correct application. The trade and the consumer have the advantage of receiving a complete solution from one source, that leads to application reliability and satisfaction amongst consumers, and, amongst the trade, leads to more sales with less handling effort.

Another essential aspect is efficient and effective logistics. The prompt and qualitatively faultless availability of the products for the trade and the consumer is a central competitive factor. For the umbrella brand, it has the advantage that it can offer, in particular the trade partner, a cost-effective solution per individual unit, through a larger and broader range of products. If in individual cases, disruptions to supply occur, the trade or the consumer can quickly be offered an alternative product, usually a higher-quality product, as a solution to the problem.

2.2 Practical approach: key factors of a successful umbrella brand strategy

2.2.1 The heart: the brand essence
With a range of products that consists of different product groups brought together under one brand umbrella, the question of positioning arises: What does the brand stand for? What is the performance promise of the brand? What do consumers think when they are woken up at midnight and asked what they think about their brand?

With an umbrella brand strategy, the aim on the one hand is to define the brand essence clearly, simply, and distinctly. On the other hand, however, the brand must also be strong and broad, in order to be able to carry the different product groups credibly. The brand essence is developed with the help of a so-called "brand essence analysis." For this, consumers are asked about their attitude towards the brand, e.g., in the form of group discussions.

- Which values do you associate with the brand?
- What does the brand stand for?
- If your brand were a memorial, what would it look like?
- etc.

In this group discussion, a picture emerges of what attitudes and associations the consumers have of/with the brand. Depending on the question and objective, this method can be scaled:

- Only loyal users of the brand.
- Not users, but persons who belong to the target groups.
- Users of competitors' products.
- Attitude of the target group towards competitors.
- etc.

With this method, brand management receives an excellent indication of where their own brands and those of their competitors stand. If this method is repeated regularly, i.e., every five to seven years, a time series about the development of the brand perception in the minds of the consumers emerges. In its core, this method answers the question of whether the marketing activities have achieved their objectives, and whether the desired positioning has actually been achieved in the minds of the consumers.

2.2.2 Growth through brand expansion
With an umbrella brand strategy, the temptation to position as much as possible, and as quickly as possible, under the umbrella brand on the market, is especially great. However, the establishment and maintenance of an umbrella brand is a long-term process that needs to be conducted carefully and with the necessary vision. The brand expansion starts with the brand monitor: With the brand monitor, the potential for the brand is developed through individual interviews in households:

- Which products still match the brand?
- What is the household penetration for particular products and product groups?
- What is the consumer and application behavior like?
- What is the attitude towards particular products and brands?
- etc.

The aim of the brand monitor is to provide the brand management with a reliable basis for decisions for the future introduction of completely new product groups.

With the brand monitor, different dimensions emerge in which the product groups lie nearer or further away from the brand essence. Here, the comparison with an onion can help. With an onion, the individual rings are also at increasing distances from the middle.

There are products here that match the brand directly and represent a worthwhile brand expansion in the next stage of brand growth (fields of potential). At the same time, however, there are products that do not, or do not yet, fit the brand. The decisive factor here is that the brand has the competence from the consumer's perspective to give a credible performance promise for this product. Example: if Nivea had launched the Nivea Beauté concept in the eighties, it would have flopped because the brand was not yet sufficiently sustainable. The long-term supplementation of the Nivea brand with new product groups, accompanied by the corresponding communication support, is an excellent example of a careful, but also a durably successful, brand maintenance.

An umbrella brand can promote international growth with different brand expansion concepts. Depending on the local situation, another product group can represent the next useful step of brand expansion. This depends, among other things, on the attitude of the consumers to the market, and on the competitive environment. If this process of different project stages is chosen, it is essential that care is taken, however, that this is only a tactically different approach. The overall objective, i.e., the implementation of the umbrella brand positioning through the introduction of all product groups, must still be the strategic orientation. If not all important product groups are introduced on the target market within a limited time frame, the brand runs the risk of losing credibility for the umbrella brand positioning.

2.2.3 Focusing

With the internationalization of the umbrella brand strategy, it is tempting to include "local beauties" under the brand umbrella. In practice, the national organizations are very creative at introducing or wanting to introduce national characteristics under the umbrella brand. Such creativity and dynamism should be used positively for the brand. It is positive to constantly remonitor and redocument the competitive environment, along with the trends in the trade and amongst the consumers. To make use of the synergies at international level, however, not every national wish can be acted upon. For a long-term, internationally successful umbrella brand strategy it is essential that all countries involved concentrate their strengths on the implementation of the umbrella brand strategy.

For international, centrally organized brand management, the skill lies in differentiating between the justified and the "nice to have" wishes. There are important national characteristics that must be taken into account even with an international approach. Here too, care should be taken that the product range and the brand appearance are competent from the consumer's perspective. The consumer is always national and local and not international. However, the international strategy is always dominant in the brand appearance!

2.2.4 Corporate design manual

A corporate design manual regulates the "dos" and "don'ts" when dealing with the brand. For a stringent and uniform brand management, it is essential to create a clear set of rules that precisely define the design of the brand at an international level. In doing so, it should be ensured that all objects that bear the brand logo, and which are passed on to third parties on behalf of the brand, are defined. For successful brand management, not only the definition, but also the control of the standardized implementation is important. A successful realization of an umbrella brand strategy includes a control mechanism that monitors its correct implementation. In this regard, international cooperation with internal marketing functions in different countries, as well as with external agencies, is like "looking after a bag of fleas." So that "artistic leeway" stays at an acceptance level, the design manual in combination with a functioning control mechanism is vital. The strict variation of quality assurance in the production process can serve as a comparison here. For all elements of the corporate design manual, the quality standards must be applied in the same way that they are on a day-to-day basis in the production process of every ISO-certified company.

2.2.5 Constant and moderate change

In the control of communication and production, a constant verification of the brand's topicality is necessary. In doing so, however, a company should not react to every "fashionable trend." A careful adaptation to the changing times and the changes in values within society is necessary, though. On the one hand, the skill consists of maintaining the tradition of the brand and the brand essence, while, at the same time, keeping the brand up-to-date and modern. Continuity in the core elements of the brand is of pivotal importance. A positive example for the reaction of a strong brand to the mega trends in a society is the product group Nivea Vital, that specifically addressed the aging population in the 90's. A negative example of missing out on a trend is the brand Coca-Cola that, up until to now, has not reacted sufficiently to trends such as wellness or relaxation. With Coca-Cola, this is expressed directly in a significant reduction of its market shares, as well as a reduction in the brand value of several billions.

2.2.6 Innovations

Innovations are a central factor for successful brand management. In doing so, innovations are usually initially related to the product range. Innovations can be completely new products or existing products that have been revised through a relaunch, and that are equipped with new product features. The decisive factor is that it creates a transparent and relevant benefit for the consumer. Example: the segment of rechargeable grass shears has had no relevant product innovation over a period of more than ten years.

In 2001, WOLF-Garten carried out a relaunch in which, in addition to a revised design, the product was given two new features. The rotary cutting head, in connection with an exchangeable cutting blade, gave the consumer a significant functional benefit. The result was that the market share in this segment grew more than threefold within three years. However, growth has not only taken place through displacement of the competition, but also through overall market growth. The latter is particularly important as, through innovation, even more people can be attracted to the product and gardening activities.

In addition to product innovations, however, there are also other forms of innovation that have a positive impact on international brand management, e.g., new forms of the marketing instruments.

An important advantage of the umbrella brand is that the introduction of an innovation under an umbrella brand has a considerably higher probability of success than for example, the introduction in the form of a single brand strategy. Consumers transfer their existing positive attitude towards the umbrella brand to the new product, and are significantly more willing to make a test purchase. An excellent example of this procedure is the expansion of the Milka range to include new tastes and forms of presentation.

Based on this mechanism, it is correspondingly easier to inspire retail to include the product in their program. A further positive effect is that relatively lower costs need to be budgeted for communication to reach consumers in the sense of the "marginal costs – marginal benefit perspective." In contrast to a single brand, the new product does not start off at "zero." Instead it can build on the balance in the brand account.

A further aspect of innovation is that it has a positive effect on the umbrella brand account. This is a fundamental element for keeping the brand up-to-date and modern. Established product groups, therefore, also profit under the umbrella brand from all the marketing activities of the successful introduction of the innovation.

2.2.7 Balance between functional and emotional benefit

The elementary benefit of a brand is that it can achieve added value as a result of emotions, although it might have the same product functionality as no-name products. Specifically, consumers are prepared to pay a higher price for their brand product. This increased price corresponds to the emotional benefit. Successful umbrella brand management is thus characterized by the fact that it gives the consumer not only a functional benefit, but also an emotional one. This emotional benefit can for example, lie in the area of image or purchase and application security. Nevertheless, it can be stated that, by concentrating purely on the emotional features of the product and neglecting at the same time its functional features, the umbrella brand runs the risk of losing its credibility. The functional product features with relevant USPs remain the backbone of the premium umbrella brand; the emotional factors build on them.

2.2.8 Umbrella brand account

The establishment and maintenance of an umbrella brand is a complex matter. Here, it is of elementary importance to ensure that every activity makes a contribution, positive or negative, to the brand account. With an umbrella brand strategy, this means managing a significantly more complex structure than for example, with a single brand strategy.

As an umbrella brand markets a large number of different products and product groups, there are a great many transactions on the brand account. With a positive development, a large number of deposits are made, with a correspondingly rapid development of the brand balance. At the same time, the risk, however, is also considerably greater. Every negative experience damages not only the individual product, but also the umbrella brand overall. The potential for damage with an umbrella brand is, thus, significantly greater than with a single brand.

2.2.9 Customer life cycle

An umbrella brand with several product groups and quality levels has the potential to make the consumers an attractive and relevant offer during their entire customer life, that corresponds exactly to their individual requirements and budget situation. If this is successful, consumers will build up a high level of appeal towards their brand and remain loyal to it during their customer life cycle.

Using the example of a garden owner, this can be explained at WOLF-Garten as follows: a young family that is building its first house is usually short of funds. As soon as they have completed the construction work, the interior is finished and then subsequently they devote themselves to the exterior of the house. Over the course of time, the debts are paid back and, at the same time, the freely available income of the household (usually) increases. When the parents are of retirement age, the children no longer live at home. The exterior is completely finished and is maintained with a love of detail and much effort.

For an umbrella brand in the gardening sector, it is therefore of pivotal importance to present consumers with a tailor made and relevant offering in every phase of their gardening life. This means specifically that it is more important at the beginning for the young family to invest in high-quality grass seed, and to select the price-entry in the brand segment for the lawnmower. At a later stage in their gardening life, they can then invest in a better quality and more powerful lawnmower.

The consumer expects fair advice, both from retail and from industry. Fair advice incorporates not only optimal problem solving, but also an offer that lies within the scope of their individual requirements and possibilities.

2.2.10 Central brand management

An umbrella brand strategy is not a market place for democratic decision processes. In the analysis and concept phase, it is important to survey the needs and requirements of the national and international markets, and to take them into account in an analysis and decision process accordingly. As soon as the brand positioning has been made by a central brand management, a clear differentiation must be made between strategic orientation and tactical implementation. Example: the brand WOLF-Garten represents perfect and individual gardening enjoyment. The positioning is unmistakable and may not be changed locally either. The flexibility on the interpretation of "perfect individual gardening enjoyment" can, however, differ locally. The English have a different attitude towards gardens than the Italians. National organizations need the freedom to adapt the strategic positioning to local requirements, e.g., in the form of different pictorial language or different focus articles.

2.2.11 Cross-selling

An umbrella brand concept offers the unique advantage that the marketing activities are not only aligned to the individual product, but, at the same time, are also used cross-functionally for other products of the brand family. With a vertical alignment, the marketing activities initially focus directly on the product concerned. From a horizontal perspective, the first cross-references to other products are made within the same medium, e.g., complementary promotions at POS (scarifiers and fertilizers). From the networking of horizontal and vertical possibilities into a multi-level, integrated marketing concept, unique communication options emerge for the umbrella brand. As a rule of thumb, it can be stated that it is seven times better to get a buyer of a brand to buy a new product from the same brand family than to get a new buyer to purchase the brand for the first time.

2.2.12 Use of the umbrella brand in relationships with the trade

The concentration process in European retail is a mega trend. Retail is reducing the number of its suppliers, but, at the same time, wants to present the consumer with as wide a variety of products as possible. Through the reduction in the number of trading partners, these are increasingly adopting a gatekeeper function for the industry.

The umbrella brand strategy is an instrument of the industry used to react to this concentration process. The trade still needs internationally operating industry partners that know the different requirements of local consumers in the countries, and that are capable, by means of an effective organization, of meeting these requirements with a market-relevant range of products. The strong international umbrella brand offers a solution to the requirements of internationally operating key accounts for a reduction in the complexity of their own working procedures, as well as the simultaneous need for fulfillment of the local individual wishes of consumers.

For the industry, the umbrella brand concept, therefore, has the advantage that negotiations with the trade are concentrated on concept discussions, and not on discussions about individual products. It is considerably easier to introduce a new product variant under an existing brand umbrella than to do so with a new product under a new brand name. The trade has three strategy approaches for profiting from a strong umbrella brand. With "image transfer," it makes use of the brand to transfer the brand's strength to itself. What would the image of a DIY center look like from the perspective of the consumer if it did not have leading brands such as for example, WOLF-Garten, Gardena or Bosch in its range of products?

With the strategy of "competency transfer," a trade partner carries as many products as possible from one brand. Thanks to the variety of products, the umbrella brand offers the trade partner a comprehensive possibility to transfer the manufacturer's competence to the trade partner. The shop-in-shop systems are an example of this. With a "frequency bringer" concept, the trade uses the strength of a brand to attract customers into the market. Example: presentation of Milka chocolate in 2nd level positioning and simultaneous advertising of the 100g bar of chocolate at EUR 0.59 in the sales flyers.

A further advantage for the trade partners under the umbrella brand concept of the manufacturers lies in the enhanced reliability of a successful product launch. The consumer applies brand trust to the product innovation. The subjective security when buying a product, combined with the desire to try it out, assures the trade of the expected product rotation in combination with the satisfaction of the customer.

▶ Process & Implementation

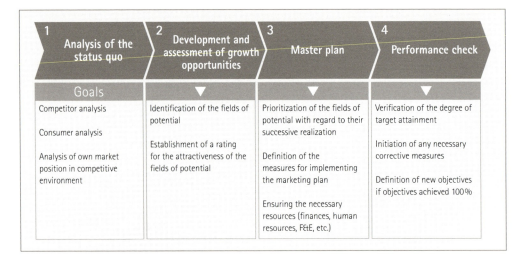

Fig. 6: Umbrella brand strategy process

Phase 1: Analysis of the status quo

The establishment of an umbrella brand concept starts with a successful stocktaking of the status quo. Here, all factors that have a fundamental influence on the strategic orientation of the brand are to be taken into account:

Own market position
- Current product mix, best-sellers/slow sellers, profitability, market shares.
- Price positioning.
- USP.
- History of the brand.
- Positioning of the products and brand.
- Distribution structure.
- Perception by the consumer and the trade.
- etc.

Competitive environment
- In an analogous manner to a company's own market position, the competition needs to be subjected to a comparable analysis.

Boundary conditions
- Law, technology, environmental protection, consumer protection, etc.
- Mega trends in society: changes in the purchasing and usage behavior of the consumer, change in the income structure.
- Changes in distribution structures: trade structure, growth of discounters, Internet, etc.
- etc.

Comprehensive approaches to different instruments lend themselves to the analysis: desk research, POS monitoring, evaluation of the communication mix, Gfk/Nielsen figures, sell-out figures of the trade, company-internal statistics, secondary studies. The "hunting and gathering," prepared in a structured SWOT analysis (strength/weakness/opportunities/threats), supplies a comprehensive picture of the status quo in the sense of a mosaic. This stocktaking is to be carried out for all actual and target markets on which the brand is to be extended or introduced for the first time.

In addition to the steps mentioned above, traditional market research offers particular methods that are of elementary importance for the establishment of an umbrella brand. As an example, reference is made here particularly to the brand essence analysis and the brand monitor (see 2.2.1 and 2.2.2)

Particularly against the backdrop of urgent day-to-day business and the desire for a quick solution, research is often not given sufficient time and attention. It should, however, be pointed out that the foundation is laid here for future strategic decisions. Furthermore, a well-founded analysis can help to avoid the wrong paths and, thus, make significant cost savings. Those who know their market, their competitors and their customers best will win in the long run.

Phase 2: Development and evaluation of growth opportunities

With an umbrella brand approach, international growth can be generated from different options:
- In existing product ranges and countries: increase in the market shares in existing countries by increasing the

clearance sale quantities: improvement of the distribution depth and breadth, change in the price positioning (increase/reduction), opening up new customers, increase in the usage intensity with existing customers, displacement of competitors, etc.
- Transfer of existing product ranges to new countries: international growth through the transfer of success layers from country A to country B.
- Line extension: Supplementation of existing product groups with new products, e.g., new bundled units, promotional variants, etc.
- Introduction of completely new product groups, innovations, "me-too" products to bridge the gaps in product ranges.

It is relatively easy to call for new products. However, it needs to be carefully checked whether the potential is already exhausted with the actual range of products and/or is sufficiently secured in its market position in terms of cash flow.

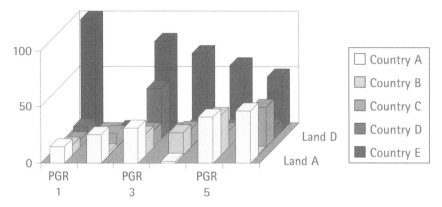

Fig. 7: Assessment of market potential for different product groups in various countries

In the selection of new products and product groups, a host of evaluation criteria need to be taken into account, e.g.:

- Do the products match the brand? From the consumer's perspective, does the manufacturer have the competence to give a credible product performance promise, etc.? Feasibility study: does the company have the necessary know-how? Time requirements? Complexity? etc. Profitability check: financial requirements for the development, production, and market introduction? When will the break-even point be reached?
- Potential for success?
- Competitive environment?
- Protection of the independence of the concept?
- Strategic importance for the brand?

Phase 3: Master plan

For the long-term development of an umbrella brand, the development of a master plan is necessary. Within the framework of the priority list creation, it initially has to be established what the umbrella brand represents in the short, medium, and long term. On the basis of the available options and their evaluation, a decision is then made on the order of implementation of the projects. The rules of the game are: in times of limited financial budgets, the projects that tell "the best story" to the company are the ones that are implemented. In doing so, a balance needs to be found between the financial importance (return on investment) and the strategic significance.

Simplified example: As a global leading skin care brand, Nivea was active in 50 large countries, in ten product categories, in 2001. With the claim of market leadership, the potential exists to be number one 500 times. At the time, Nivea had achieved market leadership in "only" 140 cases. Therefore, the question arises of with which means this number one position can be achieved in the remaining countries and product categories. As not all projects can be implemented at the same time, there is automatically a need to set priorities.

Once these priorities have been defined, a marketing concept is required for the implementation of individual projects, that defines the individual measures, and documents them in the framework of a milestone plan.

Phase 4: Performance check

The verification of the measures implemented, with regard to their degree of target attainment, is of central importance for the long-term development of an umbrella brand: have the quantitative and qualitative objectives been reached? If individual goals have not been reached, a decision needs to be taken regarding a corresponding readjustment of the measures.

Phases 1–4 should be regarded as a loop of recurring activities. An umbrella brand concept is a living process that has to react to change in the national and international environments in a moderate, yet constant way.

▶ Key Insights

- An umbrella brand concept is a strategy to optimally increase the efficiency and effectiveness of the resources used when several product groups are managed.
- The brand essence can be extended through brand expansions to thus enhance the potential of the brand.
- The central brand management manages the brand on the basis of a binding and standardized corporate design manual.
- All activities make a positive or negative contribution to the umbrella brand account.
- The balance between the functional and emotional benefit creates the added value of the brand.
- The umbrella brand concept transfers the brand image to new product groups. Through cross-selling, the trust of the consumers in the brand is transferred to new product groups and, in return, the product groups to date are given a positive boost.

▸ **Practical Guidelines**

- ☐ The detailed analysis of the status quo on the market is the starting point for the development of an umbrella brand strategy. The brand essence, as well as the potential for brand extension, is of particular importance here.
- ☐ The potential areas of growth need to be identified and weighted according to their attractiveness for the company and brand.
- ☐ Within the framework of a master plan, the target description and the corner parameters that are to be implemented for a successful attainment of the objective, are to be defined.
- ☐ A regular performance check is vital for the long-term development of the umbrella brand.

The Author

Alexander Schwade

After completing his studies in business administration (MBA) in 1989, in Germany and the U.S., Alexander Schwade began as a marketing trainee at Baiersdorf AG in Hamburg. In the subsequent nine years, he collected extensive experience in marketing in various functions at national and international level: international strategic product management, national product management in France, international key account management. In January 2000, Alexander Schwade moved to WOLF-Garten GmbH & Co. KG as category manager, where, from September of 2001, he took charge of international marketing in the roles of Corporate Marketing Director and Member of the Executive Board. An important focus of his work was the development of a new international umbrella brand concept. From June 2004, a new business division, Business Development, was set up. Since September 2005, Alexander Schwade has been active as Head of Marketing DIY at Akzo Nobel Deco GmbH.

Literature Recommendations

R. Köhler, W. Majer, H. Wiezorek, "Erfolgsfaktor Marke – Neue Strategien des Markenmanagements," München 2001
M. Gobé, "emotional branding," New York 2001
G. L. Urban, J. R. Hauser, "Design and Marketing of New Products," 1980
F.-R. Esch, "Strategie und Technik der Markenführung," München 2003

Guido Renggli, Philip Martin – Media Markt Switzerland

Regional Brand Expansion (Retail)
Strengthening and growth of a retail brand through international brand expansion

▶ Executive Summary

- In today's converging global community, strong retail brands need (multinational) competition in the various countries, markets, and cultures.
- The perspective of marketing (individualization for consumer orientation) and the perspective of management accounting (standardization for system precision) are permanent antagonists in this process.
- Decentralized, learning organizations have the opportunity of ensuring the adaptability of the organization that is behind a retail brand.
- The permanent learning process in a decentralized system ensures a continuous development of market share and, thus, the market leadership of the category killer.
- The following information is intended to familiarize the reader with the recipes for success of a special retail company in its international expansion. The main focus will be on presenting ideas, measures, and decisions in an understandable manner, based on the actions of Media Markt in Switzerland (abbreviated below as MM). The reader will then be able to derive the relevant success factors for his or her specific situation, and will have to adapt them individually.

▶ Theoretical Model of Regional Brand Expansion

1. Definition and core principle

The integration process that is taking place in Europe, and the associated development of a European attitude to life, forms the basis for the realignment of tried and tested company strategies. In parallel to this, retail has been confronted with a saturation of domestic markets, over-production in industry, and excess supply of sales areas.

In this situation, the solution for a market leader such as Media Markt must be "market expansion into international markets," in order to further strengthen its negotiating power with manufacturers, and to ensure the critical size of the company. These days, internationally active retail companies are the only attractive market partners for the industry's international marketing activities. This is particularly true in the sector of entertainment electronics and computers, where the borderless world of the WWW makes all national limitations redundant.

The background of increasing concentration, resulting in a rising ubiquity of business types and their associated retail brands, also gives international brand expansion an almost unavoidable aspect of brand strengthening.

CASE The retail company Media Markt found and finds itself faced with the challenge of aligning strategy in an international way, on the one hand, and having to pay particular attention to local interests, on the other hand. One of MM's principles for success is the supremacy of local interests in the company development process as a whole. One of the prime necessities for the alignment of decisions was always the aim of clear dominance of the relevant local competition, in order to achieve and ensure the "monopoly position in the psyche of the customer" (Domizlaff 1982) in a quick and sustainable manner.

This results in the standardization discussion problem with the question of which concrete, strategic design ensues from the step into foreign markets. The unification of methods, process, and systems, in order to exploit cost advantages, is one side of this design, but the success of MM is based, to the above-mentioned extent, on the effect of the strong brand, oriented to the specific, local market and competitive environment, in this case Germany, with the specific conditions of each separate location.

The countdown concept

Brand expansion already begins way before the concrete first steps in an expansion country. It is a permanent process of information concentration, the starting gun for that sounds with the general strategic decision by the company management to expand into foreign markets beyond the previous national borders.

The success on the home market and the company confidence this inspires bring the company to the starting line:

- "On your marks" is followed by the phase of
- "Get set!", up to
- "Go!", when the first opening creates a new reality.

This preliminary heat for entry into new markets requires three to five years of comprehensive analyses and case scenarios, in order to estimate the probability of success, and to prepare for success. We differentiate four phases of preparation leading up market entry. Each has different aspects for decision-making and/or implementation, but also overlaps with the next, both temporally and with regard to content.

Fig. 1: Countdown brand expansion

2. Factors in the brand expansion countdown

2.1 Market entry decision
The market entry decision follows after clarification of the relevant statutory framework conditions. With the introduction of the Euro, the financial regimentation around the currency topic in Europe has decreased. However, the slow-to-adjust legal conditions of every national state, in relation to the expansion of a retail branch, remain.

- Trade law with conditions for operational authorization for foreigners, for ranges of products, for company forms.
- Construction law, sometimes with regional differences, with conditions for the realization of own-brand operations that function well on the home market.
- Advertising law with limitations or conditions for the advertising of a retailer, price description regulations, etc.
- Company law and financial regulations for invoicing, financing and accounting.

Following the first approach to this analysis of statutory framework conditions, it quickly becomes clear whether the expansion can be carried out by the company's own "foreign" efforts, or whether the company-regulated inclusion of a "local" would substantially improve the trading conditions.

This cooperation (through to the purchase of a company), in whatever legal form, can also be particularly interesting from the point of view of competition aspects. Market shares, brand locations, real estate, and levels of recognition can quickly be purchased in this way, which can make a decisive difference to the initial position amongst national competition.

2.2 Market capture strategy
Tactical and operational planning begins with the market entry decision (Y/N). The individual steps to capture the market must be substantiated. Real estate as the point of sale, the product range as the sum of the demanded products, advertising to raise awareness, and personnel as the team of those people who make the range of products known to the customer in the real estate, and who process the sale (and the administration!). All this needs to be planned, searched for, and implemented and/or introduced.

This planning is oriented to the available market data (target group, buying power/needs, competition), in the temporal framework that is set with the first opening. The volume for the product, capital/finance and personnel planning results from the desired market shares.

This data orientation is not possible in the core field of retail marketing, i.e., the communication, in this form. In the first expansion step abroad, the marketing department, and particularly the person with responsibility for the brand (in the case of MM the company management), faces the particular task of carrying the trade personality into the new culture, or rather of transferring it!

Two cultures meet, the company's own culture and the foreign culture, whose compatibility must be anticipated. The selection and briefing of an agency are steps to determine the correct advisor in this matter, that can be decisive for the success of the brand expansion.

CASE The brand MM is based, among other things, on its clear dominance of the competition as perceived by the relevant consumer – i.e., generally the local competition. This must take place with the opening advertising (i.e., the first presentation of the new brand) in a sustainable manner, and with understandable words and images for the population (better: target group). The core competencies and, thus, the benefit to the customer, must be communicated. Then MM takes its place as the category killer from the opening onwards – first in the minds, and then in the market figures.

Fig. 2: Opening of MM Basel, 2003 at the main SBB railway station

2.3 Company organization

The necessary company organization is developed constantly in parallel to this countdown. National specialists have already been created in the international headquarters as a result of the market entry decision. The task now is to create and develop the national organization.

The recruitment of personnel is a consequence of the personnel requirements in the relevant countdown phase, and is accompanied by the provision and development of operational resources (especially administration of construction, finances, goods, and personnel).

2.4 First branch opening

With the first branch opening, the countdown has now reached the point of market entry. The timely construction and preparation of the real estate allow the industrial partners to stock the building. Once the creation, production, and placement of the above advertisements are complete, the staff, who have now been trained in the existing home market, are ready for their first customer contact on the opening day.

CASE Course of action: standardization vs. differentiation

Once the brand expansion is concrete and the national organization has been developed, the national managing director arrives on day X and takes over the management of the national organization from the international headquarters. This leader can already have been decided at the time of the first ideas in the market entry decision, and comes from internal management, or a person from the country or the branch is brought in. From this day onwards, the national interest is given a leader figure as a clear statement of its own national interests, concerns, and points of view. In this phase, a more or less confident and independent national organization is created according to the personality of the managing director.

"Centralized" or "decentralized" develop as a new dimension of the thinking, values, and actions within the organization. The marketing literature sees this ambivalence with standardization and differentiation as a central problem of action planning in international marketing (see Meffert/Bolz, "Internationales Marketing Management", page 28ff). Standardization and differentiation create a constant tension during this "countdown" in the international expansion of a retail company, whose market presence is based on power, strength, and dominance. They are the opposite poles in:

a) the consistent use of cost advantage through standardized performance components, with the result that the international expansion companies can no longer operate independently on a national level,

b) the differentiation through nationally specific adjustment and, thus, the specific alignment with the local market and competitive environment. Particularly this country-specific acclimatization has a specific effect on the motivation and management of the local organization and the staff (all business is local).

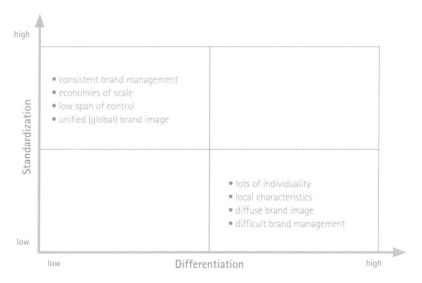

Fig. 3: Standardization/differentiation

For the successful expansion of a retail brand such as Media Markt, the management has the particular task of balancing the conflicting interests and combining them with one another. This tension was, however, not a new thing for MM, even in the first foreign expansion.

As already mentioned, MM's success is based on fast dominance of the relevant local market. Since opening the first market in Munich, this aim has been given the highest priority, and ranges of products, prices, and advertising have been aligned to the local market following the motto "structure follows strategy." Also, all the organizational prerequisites in the company organization have been made possible for this individualization of the MM system. Thus, the managing director of a market is personally involved in his market, and is mainly responsible for his own actions.

For the expansion into new countries, the additional aspects, as outlined above, have been added to the usual entry process that always takes place for the entry into new local markets. However, the discussion and necessity for an individual solution for the new market, or for taking over the tried and tested solution from previous learnings, has led to the practice that the

- customer-oriented factors, processes or measures in relation to marketing, demand maximum consumer orientation and, thus, local structure (differentiation), whereas
- customer-distant, backward factors, processes or measures, such as administration, the procurement of goods, accounting, etc. are more related to the implementation of centralized, standardized formulae (standardization).

▶ Process & Implementation

Background
With the opening of the first market, the start in the brand expansion process has been successfully carried out. A national organization has taken over the local management, and the classical marketing management process, with its typical characteristics, implementation, and control activities, begins. The marketing management remains characterized by the interplay between the central demand for standardization and the local demand for individualization.

Phase 1: Tracking
With the opening, the revolving marketing management process has rotated once, and the data and experiences of the first days and weeks after the opening initiate the control phase.

Centralized company units and the national organization are eager to see the daily data from the cashier and merchandise management, and the customer's direct feedback on the range from the opening event.

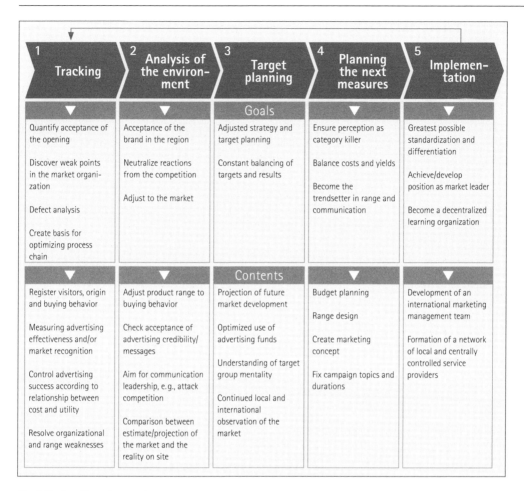

Fig. 4: Regional brand expansion process

Document frequency, turnover, contribution margin, and profit:

- Was the opening advertising seen?
- How many visitors came, and on which of the first days?
- How many visitors made a purchase (advertised articles, special placement articles, range articles)?
- Where did these visitors/customers come from and/or which advertisements did they see, and where? (Customer origin zip code is requested by the cashier system)

The market organization as a whole had to prove its functionality under extreme circumstances. This revealed weak points.

In addition to this analysis from all the company's own data, primary market research is also conducted, which usually takes the form of a representative recall in the target catchment area via market telephone interviews.

- Brand awareness
- Market visit
- Product purchase
- Impression
- Subsequent purchase plans

Are queried for the own brand and that of the main competitor

Fig. 5: Primary market research

This knowledge allows the exact determination of the route taken to market leadership. The data collected on site can be compared with the same data collected from other openings, in order to provide a detailed insight into the effect of the first measures, along with hints for further competitive action.

CASE   The following shows examples of how the MM position creates relevance and dominance, first in the minds of the consumers, and then on the market.

- Demonstrate price leadership with "the best price in town".
- Competitive attack against new competition opening in Zurich.
- Approach the consumers with persiflage on the cantons fighting amongst themselves (regional roots).
- Positioning as innovation leader.

Fig. 6 (various): Communication presence of Media Markt in Switzerland

This documents the ability and speed in which a "learning organization" such as MM can react. The balance between the standardized measures from the experiences to date from all openings, and the individualized and differentiated measures for local orientation, together demonstrate their contribution towards success in the internal competition.

The management of the MM organization, be it centralized or decentralized, ensures fast progress in this process and the tension between centralization and individualization:

- recognizing system coherence,
- promoting and demanding the pursuit of the best possible performance through business freedom,
- creating the culture of openness for new ideas in all levels of hierarchy,
- the mutual vision of a successful brand and
- the offer and the promotion of learning within the team ensures that the people (employees, suppliers, service providers, families, etc.) discover, that they are creating their own reality, and are part of this learning organization (compare this to Senge: "Die fünfte Disziplin").

Phase 2: Analysis of the environment

As a result of the first control phase, the feedback process works back to the original assumptions on the extended company environment and specific retail landscape:

- Were the economic conditions in the country/the region/the location estimated correctly?

- Which of the competitors reacted to the measures, and how? Where should increased competition be expected (particularly price attacks)?
- Are the socio-cultural conditions in relation to language, traditions, style, education, and media consumption being taken into account? Can the advertising be continued in this style/quantity and content?
- Based on the demand, must improvements be made to the range design or range of products?

The situation analysis and the expectations for the future are revised or confirmed in accordance with the new findings.

Phase 3: Target planning

The market conditions are known, the acceptance of the brand system by the consumer has been documented, and the attention effect and information have been established through advertising (in terms of style, volume, and frequency), along with the media acceptance. In this way, the performance capability of the brand system can be safety estimated in its effect against the competition. The strategic targets for the market and the brand performance are defined on this basis.

Phase 4: Planning the next measures

The next step is the further planning of measures for the year ahead. The financial framework planning and product innovation, or specific offers and agreements with industrial partners, are the ingredients for weekly consumer communication in the next year, in order to ensure frequency.

CASE Special target group communication is not generally an option in the case of MM, as the locally available media does not allow special selection. Daily papers, advertising papers, household distribution, posters, and radio communicate with the entire population of the catchment area, so that the MM advertising has to be geared towards the target group characteristics.

As the network of branches grows into a national presence (and to a justifiable level of loss due to non-selective advertising), new aspects of action planning come into play. For product areas such as computers, software, audio recordings, and white goods, more specialized, target-group specific media can be used. They give the national brand a new dimension when competing against retail competitors, who, in an ideal scenario, are not able to effectively utilize this media.

Phase 5: Implementation

In this step of planning national measures and/or their subsequent concrete implementation, the necessity of balancing the requirement for individual, decentralized use of the market's own advertising budget with the use of these funds to participate in collective "central" advertising, becomes apparent again. This necessity to make a decision is recognized and processed in the team of all those involved, in accordance with the principles of a learning organization.

A major challenge at this point in the life cycle of the organization is not to let this disagreement degenerate into a cultural war between centralized and decentralized.

In this management team (team of the local managing director), based on the first mutual management and decision task, a marketing management system is developed, that collectively works through the process. It is assisted by central specialist departments in the country, or by the international centers, agencies, other service providers, and the national managing director. This leader of the national organization is the guide in this process, that must achieve a balance between central concerns and local demand, in order to bring the brand onto the market in the strongest possible role.

CASE In the case of MM Switzerland, this route can be depicted as follows:

Media Markt began in Zurich with its first market in 1994. Within ten years, Media Markt became number 1 in Switzerland in 2004. Today MM has 14 markets in Switzerland and made a turnover of CHF 895 million in 2004. The number of employees was 996 (full-time).

In 2005, MM will continue its successful expansion by opening the fifteenth and sixteenth market. In October 2005, the new Media Markt in Muri, near Berne, will be opened. In November, the second Media Markt will follow in Geneva. This expansion will continue to help MM in its future business development to further strengthen its already strong market position.

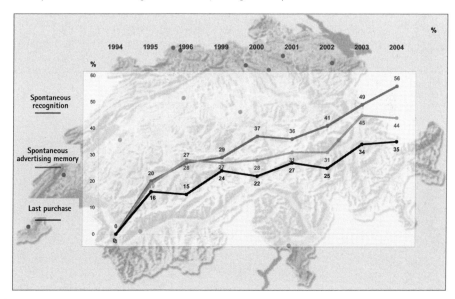

Fig. 7: Media Markt in Switzerland, Source: Media Markt (IMAS)

	1999 %	2000 %	2001 %	2002 %	2003 %	2004 %
Spontaneous recognition (all naming)	21	26	31	34	41	47
Spontaneous advertising memory (all naming)	20	24	25	26	36	39
MM preference for:						
Entertainment electronics	14	18	24	28	28	32
Electrical household appliances	8	10	12	12	15	17
Photography	7	8	11	12	17	21
Computers	13	16	20	21	22	25
DVD, CD, video cassettes	9	13	18	18	21	25
Telecommunication	10	14	13	14	16	18
Last purchase	18	21	26	24	25	31
Supported recognition	78	83	87	90	90	92
Supported advertising memory	42	44	55	55	68	68

Fig. 8: Media Markt – Summary, Source: Media Markt (IMAS)

▶ Key Insights

- The future of retail brands (in the sense of store brands) lies in the reduction to local specialties, or the expansion to internationally recognized brands with appropriate presence.
- Particularly in the product age of the all-powerful computer and software, international = attractive.
- On the way to this future, concept differentiation, to take account of local requirements, must take priority
- During the development and execution, company organization must make system advantages possible through standardization, without "suffocating" local requirements.
- The learning organization makes this fast and constant adaptation and adjustment possible.

▶ Practical Guidelines

- The core competencies of a brand should never be changed or differentiated too much during expansion into a new country. They are the real strength.
- You should not outsource the process of brand expansion. The brand and the associated culture make each company unique. Only the company's own resources can produce good brand expansion.
- Set yourself the target of achieving clear dominance of the relevant local competition in the new market, in order to achieve a "monopoly position in the minds of the consumers."
- All external and internal participants in the brand expansion process must understand and internalize the brand that is to be expanded, along with its core.

- A balance between the measures of standardization and differentiation is absolutely necessary. Customer-related functions, processes or measures must be differentiated. The non customer-related, backwards factors such as administration, goods procurement, accounting, etc. should be standardized, where possible.
- Integration measures are necessary in order to get to know the company culture and the foreign culture. Examples are exchange/introductory programs.
- Ensure a clear and continual strategy.
- Don't go with rushed decisions and/or actions that promise short-term communications success, if they might damage the long-term strategy.

The Authors

Guido Renggli

Guido Renggli studied economics, majoring in marketing, at Zurich University of Business. He took further courses in marketing and sales, at the University of St. Gallen, and in strategic business management, at IMD in Lausanne. He held the position of a Product Manager in the consumer goods sector. From 1985 until 1997 he was General Manager at Benckiser (Schweiz) AG in the FMCG sector. Since January 1st 1998, he has been the CEO of the Media Markt Group of Switzerland.

Philip Martin

From 1994 to 1997, after gaining his advertising qualifications, Philip Martin was employed as an advertising executive at a medium-sized advertising agency with a focus on B2B. From 1997 until 1999, he worked for Möbel Unger as Marketing Advisor. In 1999, he started work for Media Markt and Saturn Deutschland as Brand Management team leader. From 1997 until 2003, he was Senior Brand Manager for Switzerland and Hungary at Media Markt International, with an emphasis on international expansion. He has been an independent marketing advisor since 2003, responsible for national communication at Media Markt AG Switzerland.

Literature Recommendations
H. Meffert, J. Bolz, "Internationales Marketing-Management," Stuttgart 1994
Jr. Chandler, "Strategy and Structure," 1962
P. M. Senge, "Die fünfte Disziplin," Stuttgart 1999
H. Domizlaff, "Die Gewinnung des öffentlichen Vertrauens," 1992
O. Beisheim (ed.), "Distribution im Aufbruch," München 1999

Peter Caspar Hamel, Karoline Güller – Degussa AG

Corporate Brand Building

The development of a corporate brand for the employees and customers of an international company

▶ Executive Summary

- The importance of brands as a form of corporate capital will grow in the future. In times of increasing variety and similarity of products, brands take on a trust and orientation function for target groups and consumers, and simplify purchase decisions.
- Corporate brands bundle various products under a mutual company name. The corporate brand enables clear and lasting positioning with all target groups through its recognition effect, and creates acceptance for new products with business and end customers.
- The cornerstones of corporate brand building are:
  - the development of a corporate branding strategy,
  - content design of the brand identity and the brand values (corporate brand values),
  - corporate brand management (brand management and communication).

The entire process is divided into the as-is analysis, the development of a corporate branding strategy and its implementation and evaluation. Both the factors and the process steps of corporate brand building are explained in more detail below. The development and introduction of a new corporate brand for Degussa AG will be used as a case study to underpin the theoretical explanations.

▶ Theoretical Model of Corporate Brand Building

Summary
The factors of corporate brand building comprise corporate branding strategy, corporate brand values, and corporate brand management (Fig. 1). They are explained in the following.

```
              Corporate Brand
                Management


     Corporate Branding        Corporate Brand
         Strategy                  Values
```

Fig. 1: Factors of corporate brand building

1. Definition of corporate brand building

Corporate brand building describes the development of a corporate brand based on consistent value orientation, brand maintenance, and all activities and measures that increase the loyalty of all external and internal target groups towards the corporate brand.

2. Factors of corporate brand building

2.1 Corporate branding strategy

The first fundamental considerations should be devoted to the form in which the brand should be introduced by the company. The determination of brand strategy, which is also of central importance for brand communication, is a fundamental business decision. We differentiate between the following brand strategies:

- Individual brand and/or product brand strategy: each product made by the company is put on the market with its own brand, and positioned accordingly.
- Multi-brand strategy: the company manages several independent brands, from the same product segment, in parallel.
- Family brand strategy: a company manages several products under one brand name.
- Umbrella brand strategy and/or corporate branding strategy: the products and services, product and segment brands of a company are managed under an overall brand. In many cases, this brand name is also the name of the company.

The expansion of the reference group for a brand, from the actual group of users to all the company's target groups, is a typical characteristic of corporate branding strategy. The corporate brand thus reacts to various interests and needs simultaneously.

On the one hand, Degussa has a family brand concept in the company as a whole (Fig. 2). Many segment and product brands are managed within the company in a decentralized manner, but always with a clear reference to the corporate brand. The central management of the corporate brand is, however, the central focus of this analysis.

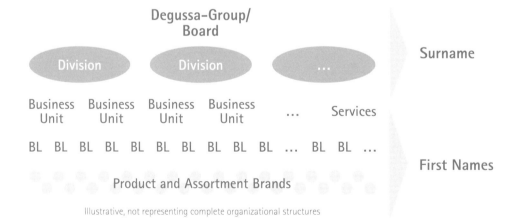

Fig. 2: Corporate brand Degussa "Surname"

The initial situation at Degussa was highly complex: the task was to unify five companies with long traditions, different products, and their own histories and corporate cultures, into a new group. This resulted in a challenge for company communication to, on the one hand, accompany the internal changes with information and, on the other hand, carry the new group strategy to external groups. Degussa found itself in this situation in February 2001. It was at this time that Degussa-Hüls and SKW Trostberg underwent a fusion as a last step in the creation of today's Degussa. Prior to the formation of the group, the predecessor company Goldschmidt had combined with SKW, and Hüls had combined with Rohm and Degussa. This last fusion gave the start signal for a new corporate strategy: the focus on specialist chemistry. "Degussa," the most traditional and well-known name, was selected for the new group. Customers, shareholders, employees and the public did not, however, associate the product portfolio of "specialist chemistry" with the name, but rather the activities of the predecessor company, the "old Degussa."

So the new corporate brand had to serve, on the one hand, as the carrier of the positive "old" image and, at the same time, represent the new alignment of the group. As the company item "fine and specialist chemistry" is complex and difficult to explain to non-chemists, the fundamental function principle of fine and specialist chemistry is instead described using the efficiency of Degussa products in their applications, that are universally well-known. The chemical cocoamidopropyl betaine, for example, is a term only recognized by experts. It is, however, simple to explain it to laypersons as the effective ingredient in almost all good shower gels. The active ingredient creatine in good skin creams ensures that skin looks younger for longer with regular use. This example, too, is easy for non-chemists to understand. The task, therefore, is to illustrate the contribution made by specialist chemistry to all stakeholders, in spite of the fact that Degussa products are not generally noticed as such by the end user.

At the beginning, it was important to explain the conversion process internally and externally, and to make the company aims clear to customers, shareholders, and employees, as well as the public. Degussa's new strategy was, therefore, to be bundled in a corporate brand. The company needed a new, unmistakable face and its own identity. The values and the positive image of the various business sectors, and of the predecessor companies, needed to be retained, but simultaneously combined into a uniform, mutual model. It was also necessary to communicate with various target groups and stakeholders: on the one hand, all those stakeholders who are affected by corporate decisions or who influence the behavior of the company themselves through their actions, on the other hand, the shareholders, i.e., the owners of the company, whose interests lie in a substantial increase in value.

2.2 Corporate brand values
The fundamental values of a corporate brand are decisive for its success. Companies act in the area between economic success and social responsibility. Companies today can only form relationships with their stakeholders through consistent orientation to socially recognized values and open and transparent communication of the principles behind their corporate actions. Values produce sympathies and appreciation of values, and create acceptance for the corporate activities. Values are simply orientation points that limit the availability of alternative actions and, thus, control human behavior. Orientation to these values raises company value in the long-term. It is for this reason that the principles of "value based management" are enjoying growing popularity in business practices.

At Degussa, the initial task was the formation of an efficient group, with a clear strategy and its own identity, from several chemical companies. As motivating as it may be for managers and employees to form a new company, irritations with regard to corporate identity also exist. The challenge was to create clarity and credibility with customers, shareholders, and opinion leaders when developing the corporate brand values. In a bottom-up process, the important, mutual characteristics were determined by carrying out opinion polls among customers, employees, and managers. The following characteristics of a corporate brand core took shape, as associated with the five predecessor companies (Fig. 3):

The capabilities
- Reliability and
- ability to innovate as well as
  the competencies
- excellence and
- intelligent linking throughout the company.

Fig. 3: The value pyramid of the corporate brand of Degussa AG

Uniqueness through intelligent linking is created when the capabilities of the ability to innovate and reliability are lived and linked with competence, in order to create first class market performance in all areas of the company. It is only the networking of the above capabilities and competences that creates the uniqueness of Degussa (Fig. 4). The characteristics of the corporate brand were condensed in the claim of "creating essentials," which stands next to the logo as an obligation. In a further step, these characteristics must be made "experiencable" among the internal and external target groups.

2.3 Corporate brand management
Besides corporate branding strategy, the management of the corporate brand is also an important part of corporate brand building. The basis for the management of the corporate brand is created through the fixing of the corporate branding strategy. Corporate brand management means the development, control, and execution of communication plans for the products of a company. It also consists in observing the course of results and taking corrective measures, if necessary. The management of the corporate brand begins at the first development step of the brand, i.e., at the moment when a brand name is to become a marketed product through marketing and communication activities. The management of the corporate brand accompanies the brand from this point on throughout its entire lifecycle.

Fig. 4: The corporate brand values of Degussa

The corporate identity and/or brand identity, with a clear alignment of its content, represents the basis for a successful brand, as described above. The communication of the brand content takes place via communication processes. Brand management encompasses all measures that are carried out by marketing, market communication, public relations, and internal communication, in order to structure and maintain the brand.

Corporate brand management at Degussa begins by fixing the corporate branding strategy and the first step of managing the corporate brand, i.e., the communication of the branded company name. The values and characteristics identified at Degussa are communicated to the internal and external target groups. The aim of all internal communication measures is to intensify the awareness amongst all employees of the meaning of the brand values and, thus, to change their "mindset" in the long-term towards the company values. Externally, the task is to build up and maintain the image and reputation of the Degussa brand. Thus, the corporate brand takes on the role of an internal management and development instrument. Its relevance and credibility play a decisive role (Fig. 5): communication makes a brand promise, which must be kept in the marketplace. A brand is relevant if it appeals to a central need of those it communicates with. Only if a brand promise is important for the recipient, will the brand have a chance of having any effect. Credibility means that the brand can keep its promises, and is clearly oriented towards its value categories. The company is only in a position to keep the brand promise if all employees live out the brand values consistently in their daily work and, thus, carry it outside the company.

Brand and communication management is aligned to the company values consistently in all phases and at all times. In their work, the employees and management of the company always orientate themselves to the company values, that take their structure from vision, missions, and guidelines.

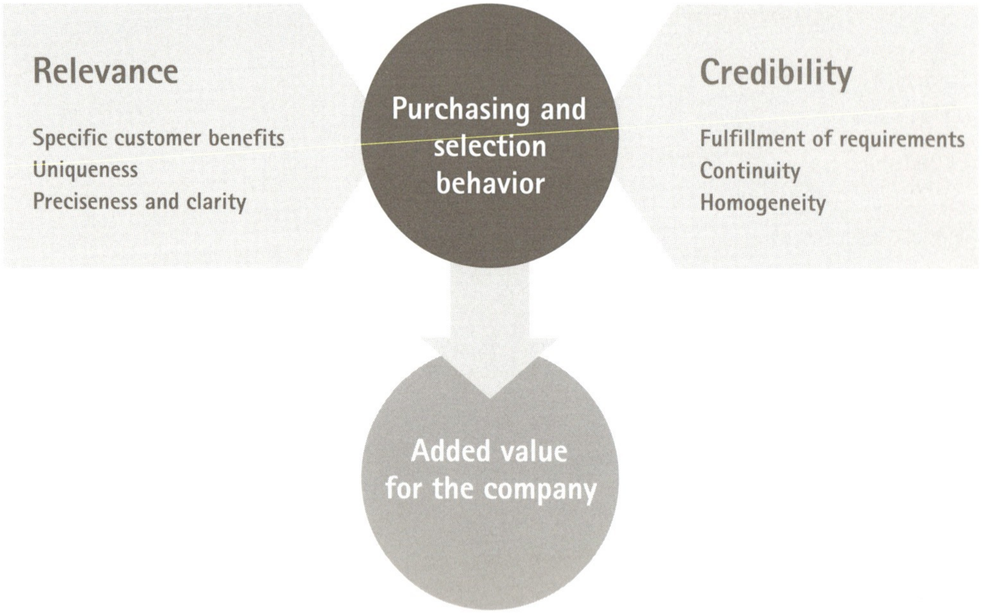

Relevance

Specific customer benefits
Uniqueness
Preciseness and clarity

Purchasing and selection behavior

Credibility

Fulfillment of requirements
Continuity
Homogeneity

Added value for the company

Fig. 5: Relevance and credibility of the corporate brand

▶ Process & Implementation

The process of corporate brand building comprises four steps, as described below. They are the as-is analysis, the development of a corporate branding strategy, the implementation of the corporate brand, and its evaluation.

Phase 1: Situation analysis of the corporate brand

Communication planning for the corporate brand begins with the analysis of the situation of the company, its market and the environment. Its structure is also based on an as-is analysis. It involves investigating the knowledge, opinions, attitudes, and behavior of all those who will be involved in the corporate brand.

The factors that are relevant to the strategic positioning of the corporate brand must also be taken into account. An internal analysis of the use of the brand also takes place in this phase. A further aspect of the first analysis is the external resonance analysis within the target groups of customers, journalists, opinion leaders, the financial community, and decision-makers in business and politics.

In order to be able to support the content and formulate the brand values, an analysis of the principles was carried out, which is important for the company from a historical point of view. In the stage of the development of Degussa's corporate brand values, the task was to clarify how customers and employees had rated Degussa in the

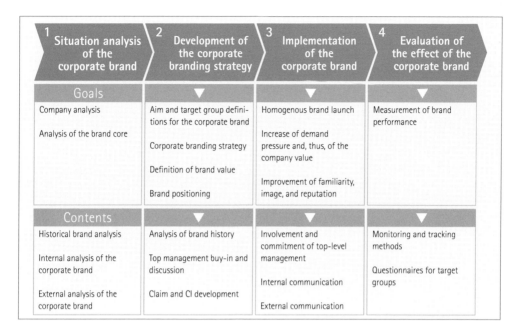

Fig. 6: Corporate brand building process

previous years, and what they associated with the predecessor companies. The results showed one outstanding overall statement: customers of the Degussa predecessor companies, who were asked in various waves over a long period of time, primarily selected the central characteristics and/or capabilities of great reliability and ability to innovate for the predecessor companies. The special core competence of Degussa, as seen by its customers, was and continues to be the excellence of its products and services. This external perception was used to formulate not only the current situation, but also the expectations for the new company. The existing special capabilities and competences of the company from a customer perspective must be developed further, through intelligent linking so that the exemplary performance of the whole company becomes the value-adding target (Fig. 4). This laid the cornerstone for the new corporate brand Degussa. It defines the core characteristics and promises of the company. A claim was developed based on these principles, which summarized the strengths and abilities of Degussa and, thus, the content of the corporate brand: "Creating Essentials." It includes a promise to customers, employees, shareholders, and society: constant creation of new, valuable, and essential products.

Phase 2: Development of the corporate branding strategy

In a second step, a concept of corporate branding strategy is developed. At this stage, the results of the analysis are concentrated into decisions and aims; measures and target groups are determined. Based on the analysis results, the values of the corporate brand are then formulated, a strategic concept of the corporate brand is developed, and the positioning of the brand is decided.

The most important target of every branding strategy is, of course, to increase the value of the company. With this aim as the basis, the group brand must achieve the presentation of the company to all the named target groups. The image is to be improved and familiarity increased. The company should, for example, appeal to qualified new professionals: respect and reputation should increase in the areas surrounding its business locations and among its customers; the public as a whole should recognize and acknowledge the contribution of the company, its products and services, its entire business operations, and the resulting meaning for society. The corporate branding strategy must, thus, become the carrier of a future-oriented, value-creating group strategy and represent its content clearly, holistically, and credibly.

This then leads to the question of the recipients: which target groups does the corporate brand have? For whom does the corporate brand play a role? The corporate brand Degussa orientates itself, broadly divided, towards four core target groups (Fig. 7).

Customers
The corporate brand acts as the "face" of the group for Degussa's external customers. They should associate clear and relevant expectations with the corporate brand, that are supported by the company and its employees during all business contacts. With the corporate brand, the company gives a promise from the entire group to its customers, and intensifies the promises of the many segments and product brands, that are managed by the operative units within the company. Thus, a complementary and interdependent, positive attraction is created for existing and potential customers.

Owners
The owners of the company – the shareholders – form the second central target group. The corporate brand Degussa is the first and most important argumentation level for the shareholders and financial community. To the financial community, the group brand represents a company that is developing its market position and, thus, generating company value. In relation to the creation of shareholder equity, the presentation of every listed company as an attractive and future-oriented investment is of great interest.

Society
The third public target group is the public and/or the social environment of the company. Degussa sees itself as a corporate citizen, i.e., as a member of society. As a global market leader in fine and specialist chemistry, the company and its activities are in the public focus more than other "corporate citizens." Thus, it is even more important to communicate clearly to society and the individual exactly who Degussa is and what Degussa does.

Employees
The Degussa employees form the fourth target core group. They are responsible for actually keeping the brand promise given to the three external target groups. A questionnaire regarding "Blue Spirit," the Degussa group guidelines, showed that most of the employees considered their real "home" to be in the relevant predecessor company for a long time after company fusion. Thus, the challenge was to create a new feeling of solidarity and, most importantly, to change the "mindset" of every single employee, if possible, for the sake of an overall increase in the efficiency of the group as a whole.

The corporate brand Degussa, thus, has various, clearly defined aims. It serves to present the company in society, has a decided orientation and control function internally, increases customer loyalty, and also serves as the "face" of the company to its shareholders. The message is always that each individual employee must contribute to the success of the company as a whole; each individual is responsible for keeping the brand promise. The brand contribution is to give the employees a vision and palpable targets. "Creating Essentials" stands for mutual understanding of values across all group departments. This understanding of values is described in more detail in "Blue Spirit," the internal group guidelines. Named after the cyanogen blue of the company logo, "Blue Spirit" illustrates the values and vision of the corporate brand for all employees.

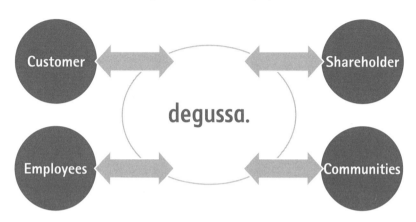

Fig. 7: Target groups of the corporate brand Degussa

Phase 3: Implementation of the corporate brand

The implementation of the corporate brand in the company marks the third phase. A brand develops its effect through people's emotional connections with it. Brand communications must achieve this for all target groups. The aim is to communicate a homogenous Degussa presentation within and outside of the company. Figure 8 illustrates the core target groups and the instruments to implement the corporate brand through internal and external communication. The aim is to strengthen the familiarity of the corporate brand. The external aim is to position the corporate brand within the target groups in the long term.

Brand promises must be kept in the market. A prerequisite for this is that the corporate brand is lived out within the company. Only then can it make a contribution towards the success of the company in the market, and increase its company value. For this purpose it is necessary to involve all employees in the strategy through suitable communication measures.

Communication at Degussa is carried out using a classic communication cascade, which begins with the so-called "brand manager." He informs the top management and leads the corporate branding team, with whose help middle management is informed about development, strategy, and content of the corporate brand and involved in the processes. Thus, the management at Degussa received standard presentations on CD-ROM, as well as accompanying information material that allowed the management to present the content of the corporate brand themselves at many events and meetings. So-called "brand ambassadors" are placed at the various locations as multipliers.

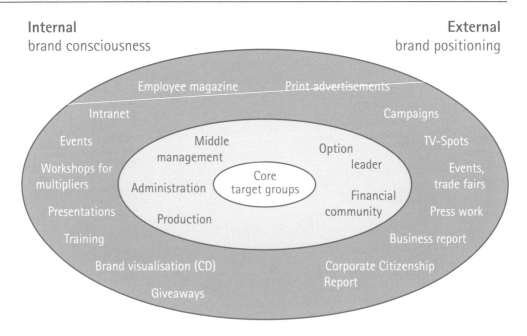

Fig. 8: Target group of the corporate brand Degussa

They inform the employees, through presentations that introduce product stories, and deliver the brand values indirectly via the contents of the corporate brand. They also enter into dialogue in discussions and conversations with the employees from middle management, administration, and production (Fig. 9).

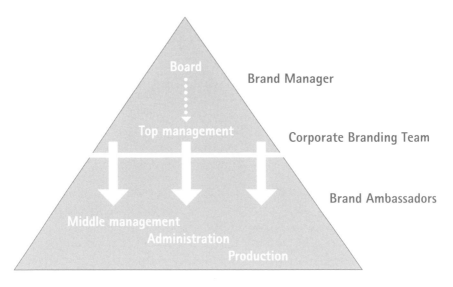

Fig. 9: Communication cascade

402 Manual of International Marketing

Internal communication of the corporate brand is carried out in two ways: the reference groups are approached directly via internal media and the knowledge is delivered indirectly by multipliers via the family brand (Fig. 10).

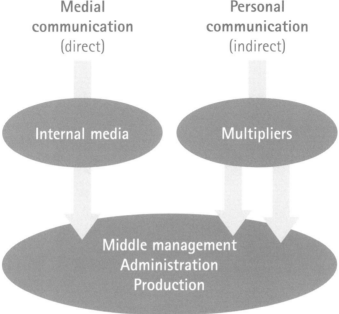

Fig. 10: Communication paths and internal target groups

Communication also accompanies the anchoring of the corporate brand in the company with numerous productions in the new employee magazine "Number 1": the corporate brand itself is reflected in the corporate design, from business reports to the employee magazine, trade fair presence, Intranet and Internet. Together with the group claim of "creating essentials," it forms the umbrella and the "face" of Degussa corporate culture. Continual change will continue to be a component of Degussa in the coming years. At present, further measures are being initiated for the optimization of the group. This relates, for example, to the solutions-to-customer concept that aims to make the company more customer-oriented and flexible. That is a particular challenge in the chemical industry due to the prevailing production conditions, and the optimization of the internal structure or measures concerning cost management. The corporate brand forms the framework for this concept. It provides orientation. Its contents clarify the "why" of the measures and translate the brand strategy.

External communication of the brand by various PR measures, image campaigns, press work, events, sponsoring, and lobbying, reaches all external target groups, as well as the public as a whole. Degussa produces chemical "ingredients" that give the end products, of which they are a component, their characteristics. Image campaigns were initiated in order to illustrate this to the end customer. While the text advertisements were aimed mainly at decision-makers in business and politics, image campaigns were aimed at the public as a whole. They break down the relevance of the Degussa products into concrete examples and make their point clear: whether you are at the Oktoberfest in Munich or at a nightclub – people everywhere benefit from Degussa.

Fig. 11: Nightclub motif in the image campaign "Creating Essentials"

These advertisements present the corporate brand to the public as a whole in several campaigns. The motifs clearly showed the benefits provided by Degussa to the individual through its products and services (Fig. 11 and 12). The advertisements are placed in the German business and financial press, in multi-regional daily newspapers, and in international business media in Europe, North and South America, as well as in Japan.

What function does the corporate brand have for customers? The product brand that carries a concrete performance promise is, of course, the most important factor. The Degussa corporate brand is intended to support the introduction of the business line, convey the primary values associated with the concrete performance promise and, thus, further strengthen customer loyalty and the formation of preferences. The intention is that the customer transfers his experience with a business line to segment and product brands via the corporate brand and decides to cooperate with another member of the Degussa family.

Phase 4: Evaluation of the effect of the corporate brand

Brand conversion and brand success are observed systematically and then measured. An evaluation is made whether the Degussa corporate brand is optimally suited to strengthening the direction of Degussa's strategic development and to raising its company value. The effectiveness of the corporate brand is measured with suitable monitoring and tracking methods – both with regard to brand perception and, also, the creation of added value. Image perception criteria are defined as a result of this and shareholder targets are finalized on the basis of clear

Fig. 12: "Rain forest" motif in the image campaign "Creating Essentials"

monitoring criteria. Employee targets that are directly connected to the brand are developed and communicated in cooperation with the "Blue Spirit," a kind of company constitution. The definitions of the measurement capacity for the branding process are effectiveness and the creation of company value (added value).

International expansion

As Degussa AG now achieves approximately three-quarters of its turnover outside of the German market, and approximately one-third of its employees work outside of Germany, an international roll-out of the company brand seemed to be essential. These image campaigns were, therefore, carried out on a global basis, not by indiscriminate distribution, but rather with a clear focus on the company's core markets. In this relation, it is important to recognize differences in language, culture, and society in advance, and to take these into account in the campaign concept and its motifs. Following this so-called culture check, it proved to be particularly problematic to use the above "nightclub" motif in the United States. Some details of the motif would have led to undesirable associations there, for example, the headline statement "never a night without special chemistry," which could be misunderstood in the U.S.A. as an instigation to abuse drugs.

An international check was carried out with the help of specialized service-providers before the campaign start, with the aim of ruling out this kind of friction in advance. Parallel to this, top management in the regions where the campaign was to run, were involved actively in the development of the campaign and the selection of the motifs. The results in this case speak for themselves: even though the original plan, for purely economic reasons, was to run the campaign only in Germany, North America, and some English-language business publications, the motifs and their statements were so popular with the management that the campaign also ran in the Japanese and Australian media with the corresponding requirements.

▶ Key Insights

- The corporate brand defines and formulates the core characteristics and promises of a company.
- A corporate brand creates a unique corporate and brand identity that is perceived by different target groups in the same way.
- The values upon which a corporate brand is based give rise to sympathies and appreciation in relation to the company, and create acceptance for its business activities.
- A corporate branding strategy enables the expansion of the group of brand recipients from the actual group of users to all the company's target groups.
- Internal communication measures intensify the awareness of all employees of the meaning of the values of the corporate brand and, thus, alter their "mindset" in the long term in relation to company values. Therefore, the corporate brand takes over the task of an internal management and development instrument.
- External communication measures aim to build up and maintain the image and reputation of the corporate brand with the relevant target groups.
- The corporate branding strategy is the carrier of a future-oriented and value generating group strategy, which represents its contents clearly, uniformly, and credibly.

▶ Practical Guidelines

- The credibility of the corporate brand is decisive. The group brand must keep its promises and be clearly oriented towards value categories.
- The corporate brand must address a central need in all recipients. Only then does the group brand become relevant. Only if a brand promise is of importance to the recipient does the corporate brand have a chance to have an effect.
- In their work, company employees and management must always orientate themselves towards the company values that take their structure from vision, missions, and guidelines.
- It must be ensured that all employees live out the group values consistently in their daily work and, thus, transfer them externally. Only then is the company in a position to keep the brand promise. The aim is to strengthen the awareness of the corporate brand. Externally, the corporate brand must be positioned with the target groups in the long term.
- Brand and communication management in the company must be oriented consistently and continually towards the company values of the corporate brand.
- The corporate brand must address the emotions of the various target groups. The group brand can only develop once people are emotionally attached to it.
- Communication work in the company must ensure a homogenous presentation of the corporate brand, inside and outside of the company. Only through the careful coordination and networking of content and activities does uniform, integrated, and effective group brand communication become possible.

The Authors

Peter Caspar Hamel

Peter Caspar Hamel has been Vice President Corporate Branding of Degussa AG, Düsseldorf, since 2002. He studied political science and economics, completed a traineeship in journalism and then became an economic correspondent with various specialist publications at Deutscher Fachverlag in Frankfurt am Main and at Handelsblatt in Düsseldorf. He then became Company Speaker for Gruner+Jahr AG in Hamburg, and Head of Group Communications at Heidelberger Druckmaschinen AG.

Karoline Güller

Karoline Güller is a freelance communications consultant. She studied at the Universities of Tübingen, Konstanz, and Lyon, France, and pursued various activities in the sectors of corporate communication and public relations. From 2002 until 2005, she was an assistant and doctoral candidate at the Faculty for Communication Sciences and Journalism at the University of Hohenheim (Stuttgart).

Literature Recommendations
M. Bruhn, "Handbuch Markenführung." Wiesbaden 2004
F.-R. Esch (ed.), "Moderne Markenführung. Grundlagen, innovative Ansätze, praktische Umsetzungen." 3rd edition, Wiesbaden 2001
M. Hubbard, "Markenführung von innen nach außen. Zur Rolle der Internen Kommunikation als Werttreiber für Marken." Wiesbaden 2004
C. Mast, S. Huck, K. Güller, "Kundenkommunikation. Ein Leitfaden." Stuttgart 2005
H. Meffert, C. Burmann, M. Koers (eds.), "Markenmanagement. Grundfragen der identitätsorientierten Markenführung." Wiesbaden 2002

Marketing Communications

→ www.marketingmanual.org/communications

Dr. Burkhard Henn – eBay Germany

Detection Marketing
Successful planning and implementation of marketing measures in the search for potential customers

▶ Executive Summary

- In almost all markets, customers have at their disposal significantly greater opportunities for obtaining information nowadays as opposed to ten years ago; at the same time, the quantity of information in the consumer environment has grown prodigiously, primarily due to the media.
- An evermore frequent response to the changing information environment is that the customer no longer waits for an appealing advertising message; rather, he articulates his needs himself.
- Companies wishing to sell products or services need to be in a place where their product range is being sought by the customer; this process of "detection" of products/services by potential customers should be actively managed by companies – they must provide guidance in those places in which the customer is searching for solutions to problems.
- Detection marketing achieves significance as an autonomous model through the interactive media, the importance of which has grown considerably in many markets as a tool in preparing decisions and as a distribution channel.

▶ Theoretical Model of Detection Marketing

1. Definition and core principle

Detection marketing takes into account the search strategies that potential customers employ to make the information overflow manageable. Search paths are identified so that marketing measures can be initiated in these areas. Irrelevant messages and coverage waste are minimized as a result.

Detection marketing: the integrated use of marketing instruments as orientation points along the search process of potential customers in order to lead them to a company's range of offerings.

2. Factors in detection marketing

2.1 Fiercer competition
International marketing conditions have fundamentally changed in the last decades. Competition has intensified due to a significant increase in products and services offered. Numerous international companies are fighting over market share in markets that were previously divided up between a few local and national providers. Trade barriers have fallen, infrastructure and logistical processes have improved, and companies have restructured in order to become competitive in international markets. Since the mid-nineties, moreover, the Internet has grown so significantly that, in the interim, a considerable volume is being sold via this channel in many markets. Examples include on-line banking, the tourist area, and many segments of mail order business.

2.2 Growth in media diversity

At the same time, the media landscape has become more complex and less manageable. In the traditional media, the range of television and radio broadcasters has grown; new special-interest magazines are constantly being launched. The Internet has meanwhile become an integral part of daily media use for many individuals. Mobile telephony and mobile data exchange via end devices such as smart phones have also created a multitude of opportunities. The new media are used increasingly for push communication. An example is the use of widely distributed banner campaigns on portal home pages to enhance awareness of products or services.

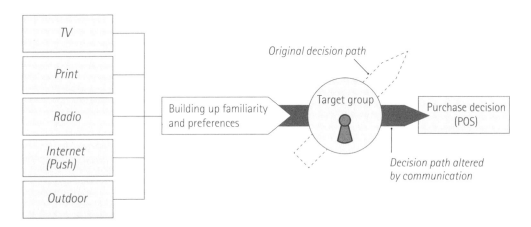

Fig. 1: Model of classic push communication

2.3 Information overflow

For some time now, consumer information overload has been a topic of discussion given the background of rapidly rising multiplicity of information and transaction offers. Companies often respond with ever more aggressive communication and with significantly higher marketing budgets. Via mass media, only those marketing messages for which high advertising pressure is created can still penetrate to achieve a significant share-of-voice. The consequences include high financial risks when launching new products and a jeopardized profit margin. Consumers, on the other hand, develop their own strategies in order to control the information overload. This results in disruptions of the push communication model (Fig. 2).

2.4 Individual search strategies

Many target groups have realized that they can become active in satisfying their own needs more efficiently by themselves. Individual search strategies constitute the response to a surfeit of information and non-specific advertising messages. Consumers track their own problem solutions – they take over the "detection" of offers of relevance to them on their own. Their strategies are determined by experience and preference with regard to media use and the involvement level in purchase decisions. For instance, the choice of a type of tea can occur at the point of sale, without prior establishment of preferences by means of communication measures or other influences and experience. Before purchasing a car, however, the same person will obtain detailed information on the Internet, configure a number of variants, and buy a new car in a dealership after additional consultation. This, however, assumes that companies offer appropriate information options, such as the suitable configuration tools in the Internet. Companies must be familiar with the search strategies of potential customers in order to

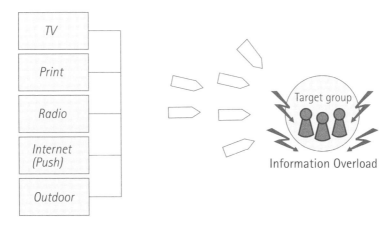

Fig. 2: Disruptions in push communication model

effectively place marketing messages and offers. They must investigate which paths customers choose in looking for information and transaction possibilities and place "orientation points" along these search paths.

2.5 Detection marketing strategy

Detection marketing has not become important as an autonomous model merely due to the growth in information overload in many areas. A decisive factor is that many target groups can now use instruments to filter information, that were not available only a few years ago. In particular, the research opportunities of the Internet, increasingly well-developed, should be mentioned here, both general search engines or special product search engines or price comparison offers. Such aids facilitate the conception and implementation of individual search strategies. These developments in turn compel companies to become intensely involved with the search strategies of their target groups and to devise their own detection marketing concepts. They must define at which points in the search process they can implement marketing measures (Fig. 3).

Figure 3 depicts an example of three search paths and the integrated placement of detection marketing measures. Potential customers utilize these media to obtain information or complete a purchase.

Search path 1:
Shows the path of a person who initially obtains an overview of the market by using an Internet search engine. Either in the editorial portion of the search engine, or as integrated advertising or contextual advertisements, the user finds a website with additional information on an appropriate product, as well as a dealer reference (provider's detection marketing measure). The transaction finally takes place at the physical retail outlet.

Search path 2:
In this case, a potential customer also initiates research via a search engine with a product-related query and finds a relevant link to a price comparison site. Here he compares prices among different on-line mail order dealerships and on-line market places that have placed their own range of products or a range at their disposal (detection marketing measures on the part of the mail order dealer and the market places). Finally, he selects a product from an on-line market place and purchases it via this platform.

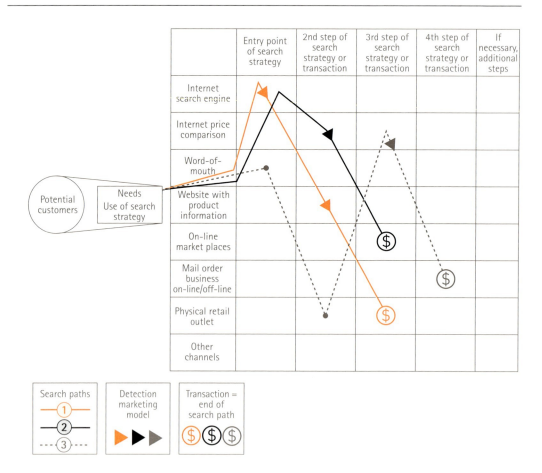

Fig. 3: Detection marketing model

Search path 3:
Shows the path of an individual who initially obtains information about a certain product by word-of-mouth. A physical retail outlet is found in order to obtain additional information on the product or to verify its properties and quality level. In the next step, a price comparison page is sought on the Internet and an order placed via the integrated product line of a mail order retailer (detection marketing measure of the retailer).

These examples demonstrate the importance of an analysis of the search strategies of potential customers. The fact that many search strategies have only been created in the last few years is often not taken into consideration sufficiently when deciding on activities in the marketing mix. Companies and sales partners must identify the most important routes in the detection matrix and implement measures at appropriate points. Frequently some detection marketing components are already being employed in marketing, but not inter-related as part of an integrated overall concept. Management of the distribution channels plays a key part from the company's perspective, since many measures need to be implemented by the sales partner. In analyzing the search paths, one should consider that individual channels can assume a communication or a distribution function. This is, for example, the case when obtaining information from a physical retail outlet and making the purchase with an on-line mail order retailer (and vice versa).

International aspects
The detection marketing model can be used in both national and international contexts. The complexity of the detection model will increase if heterogeneous search behavior is determined to prevail in markets. This is often the case in reality. Information behavior is extremely varied according to culture and stages of economic development. High levels of affluence, and thus generally higher market appeal, usual brings with it the information overload on the target groups as described above. In this connection, the targeted use of marketing measures as understood in detection marketing is essential.

▶ Process & Implementation

When developing and implementing detection marketing strategies in practice, a detailed advance analysis and checks of success after implementation are of decisive significance. The relevance of different search paths is determined during the analysis phase. The strategy establishes the selection of search paths that will be utilized for marketing purposes. When planning activities, the points in a search path at which marketing instruments will be employed are defined. The success check assesses and compares the efficiency of the various measures and the selected search paths. This allows individual marketing activities to be optimized on the one hand and the strategy to be reviewed on the other hand, i.e., the search paths chosen may be revised.

Phase 1: Analysis
The analysis phase serves to identify the various search strategies and transaction behavior in the target groups. Behavior patterns, that under certain circumstances can be complex and heterogeneous, must be captured. In the case of international marketing, moreover, it is indispensable to determine regional or national differences in behavior patterns of target groups.

1.1 Desk research
The first step in identifying search strategies is to review studies and available data on the search and transaction patterns of target groups in relation to one's own product or service range. Examples might include studies on changing search behavior on the Internet. Due to the high level of dynamism in this area, it is important that data is no more than one year old. Moreover, in this connection, competitive analyses can provide relevant indicators, such as the level of click prices that other providers pay to allocate certain concepts for search engine advertising. Studies and specialist literature in other areas of relevance to detection marketing are available, which can be used as the basis of decisions.

1.2 Qualitative analyses
In order to explore possible search strategies it can be useful to determine the spectrum of relevant behavior patterns by qualitative market research methods. Group discussions can provide indications as to which search strategies may be relevant to certain purchase decisions. One can then analyze which media should be used in

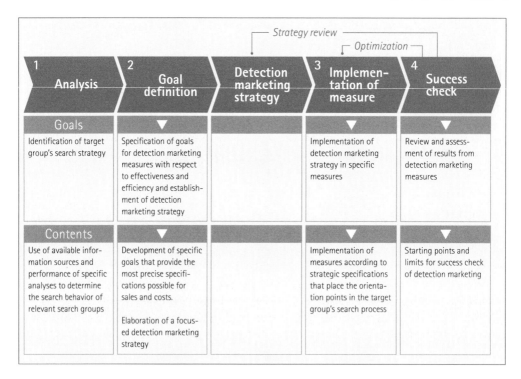

Fig. 4: Detection marketing process

which manner for obtaining information, and which should be used for eventual purchase transactions. Marketing managers often have a fixed idea of the way in which information and transactions are processed. Often, however, important aspects are neglected as a result; faulty strategic decisions can be the consequence. A thorough exploration of possible search strategies, including the target group, can prevent such failures.

1.3 Field tests

Based on the results of desk research and qualitative analysis, the scope of relevant search strategies can be outlined. Since detection marketing, however, is applied based on the information and transaction behavior of target groups, field research in realistic circumstances can be very revealing. Individual search paths must be clearly separated. Otherwise interdependencies may arise, such as when purchase decisions are prepared on-line but completed off-line and other non-isolated segments behave precisely in reverse. Refining the detection marketing concept is, therefore, a work process under constant development – strategies are developed and implemented, the effects analyzed and measures again refined, or the strategies revised.

1.4 Analysis of potential and competition

The analysis of potential is based on the knowledge gleaned from desk research, qualitative analyses, and field tests. The point is to estimate the maximum potential that can be achieved by applying detection marketing measures to a variety of search strategies. In addition to estimating market potential, analysis of competitive activities is also of key importance in order to realistically assess share of total potential that the company can address.

Phase 2: Goal definition and strategy development

The results of the potential and competitive analyses form the foundation for the definition of detection marketing goals. These goals define clear specifications for the sales and cost aspects. They determine the efficiency yardstick by which initiatives derived from the detection marketing strategy are measured. The strategy ensures that, commensurate with goals, the focus is on certain search paths. Based on the analytical data, the most efficient search strategies possible are delineated, from which sales goals can be generated that optimally use resources. This step is extremely important, since there is a danger that one might concentrate on paths not yet exploited by the competition, but too small in terms of volume to achieve overall goals. An example of a specific detection marketing strategy is the development of a personalization strategy for an on-line shop, that allows targeted placement of offers based on behavioral data.

Phase 3: Implementation of detection marketing measures

The implementation phase is concerned with the tangible implementation of strategy. "Orientation points" are applied that are geared to the target group's search strategies, in those channels that are to be utilized according to the detection marketing strategy. The possibilities of combining measures are manifold, so concentrating on the most significant search strategies is already essential in the strategic planning phase.

CASE Detection strategy for digital cameras

Target group search path identified:

- Research in search engines (entry point),
- Obtaining information on the manufacturer's website,
- Purchase in physical retail outlet.

The example shows a search strategy that has become increasingly important in the last few years in the digital camera product category. Implementation of appropriate detection marketing measures takes place at the three stages of the search process mentioned:

Research via search engines
Initially one must analyze which of the target group's search words are relevant in researching suitable product offers. If no knowledge is available in this respect, first ideas can be generated with the help of internal brainstorming sessions and group discussions with the target group. Assisted by software solutions that recognize and represent semantic relationships, additional concepts can be defined. If competitors are also active in this area, ideas for creating one's own semantic fields can be derived from their activities. The result is a list with search words and word combinations. Using search word databases the relative significance of the words arrived at can be determined. In order to place the appropriate "orientation points" in search engines – the entry point into the search process – there are two starting points for detection marketing measures:

Organic placement: the website that informs the target group about the product range should be easy to access when the relevant search word is entered. Criteria for ranking search results differ from one search engine to the next and change over time as the search algorithms are adjusted. By observing some simple ground rules, however, relatively good indexing of one's own information can be assured: contents must contain the search words defined and be programmed in such a way as to be legible by search engines. Links from other websites relevant to the topic may increase the profile of one's own Internet product range for the search words entered.

Paid placements: most of the large search engines offer advertising placements that are awarded according to the auction principle. Often this implies short advertising texts designed to include the relevant search word. The costs and quantity of access instances to one's Internet offers can be controlled using maximum bids and defined total budgets.

Obtaining information from the advertising website of the manufacturer
Information fields of relevance to the target group should have been determined during the analysis phase. Compact and easily legible presentations should characterize a company's Internet image. Detailed background information can be made available for printing in order to enhance legibility. A detailed dealer directory with research functions according to regions or postal codes should be made available so as to take into consideration the target group's search strategy (detection marketing measure).

Retail purchases
In the search process shown here, the retailer fulfills the key function in the completion of the purchase transaction. The potential customer's preselection should be confirmed by service and advisory skills at the point of sale. A comparatively superior distribution in the area can be a competitive advantage. At this stage, the manufacturer's sales function is required to assure the appropriate qualifications of dealers and distributors (detection marketing measure). Viewed individually, the measures used in the context of detection marketing are not new to many companies. Only a very few companies, however, exploit the synergy and efficiency gains that arise by systematically coordinating these measures for detection marketing.

Phase 4: Success check

The success check of the measures utilized in detection marketing is geared to the process chain of their application. Analysis and assessment of a certain measure is not systematically distinct from the success check in another context. The success check, however, has limits if media gaps occur in the information and transaction process, as described in the implementation example above. In this example, the costs of a visitor to the information site can be fairly precisely calculated and can be optimized by using paid search engine advertisements. It is, however, difficult to decode the relationship between information in the Internet and retail outlet transactions. In contrast, in the case of fully digitalized processes, efficiency can be better controlled and optimized.

Organizational implications

Successful implementation of a detection marketing strategy presents an organizational challenge for many companies. Existing organizational structures are often geared towards the communication disciplines and distribution channels. Frequently individual divisions develop their own interests. High levels of competence in the individual divisions are indispensable, of course; however, it is essential that the responsibility for the process spans all divisions and overrules any special interests. This will ensure successful implementation and continuous improvement of the detection marketing strategy.

▶ Key Insights

- Many target groups are confronted with a myriad of information and transaction offers that is becoming unmanageable.
- An increasing number of people use the Internet as a tool for their individual search strategies, thereby reducing the overload to manageable proportions.
- Detection marketing is the integrated use of marketing instruments as orientation points along the search process of potential customers with a view to leading them to one's own product range.
- Companies that correctly analyze their target groups' search strategies are in a position to considerably increase their marketing efficiency.
- A successful detection marketing strategy starts at the target groups' key search paths. In an international context, cultural and economic differences should be taken into account and, if necessary, strategies that span borders should be developed.
- Detection marketing measures are integrated into the relevant search paths and serve as orientation points for potential customers when researching problem solutions.
- Detection marketing's potential is not fully exploited by instituting individual measures. The key factor is integrated use of marketing instruments in the search process of the target groups and the optimization along this process chain.

▶ Practical Guidelines

- Detection marketing is a core business: companies must understand their target groups' search strategies and direct their activities accordingly.
- Definition of a detection strategy is a central management task – well-founded decisions can result in high efficiency increases.
- It is not enough simply to perform a one-off analysis of search processes: search behavior alters frequently and must be under continuous observation. The complexity increases with the heterogeneous nature of international markets that are ventured into.
- Flexibility and the courage to make radical decisions: changes in search behavior require new paths to be embarked upon. Established approaches and habits need to be questioned.
- A learning organization: employees must continuously expand their know-how in order to cope with the dynamic developments in search behavior.
- Measure and optimize: a detailed success check conducted on a continuous basis is a prerequisite for successful optimization. Measurement must be oriented to the detection marketing process.

> ☐ Successful implementation of the detection marketing concept in a company can require organizational changes: an overarching responsibility for process must trump responsibilities for individual communication disciplines and distribution channels.

The Author

Dr. Burkhard Henn

Dr. Burkhard Henn has been Head of Online Marketing at eBay Germany since 2003. Previously, the author worked in management positions in marketing of Internet advertising and international advertising agencies. After studying business at the University of Göttingen, he was engaged in the study of success checks on Internet advertising as part of his dissertation.

Literature Recommendations

J. Schneller, ACTA 2004. "Entwicklung des Internet als Transaktionsmedium und im E-Commerce." Institut für Demoskopie, Allensbach 2004

C. Anderson, "The Long Tail." In: Wired 12.10 October 2004
http://www.wired.com/wired/archive/12.10/tail.html

Dirk Miller – Siemens AG

Image Campaign
Relevance and credibility through a clear and consistent image of the company brand

▶ Executive Summary

"A clear and consistent image for a company brand is absolutely necessary. It provides all target groups with orientation and, in addition to relevance and credibility, creates significant added value for the company brand."

- Image campaigns for a company brand are often viewed as an "elite discipline" among experts. This is a myth. In principle, an image campaign for a company brand functions according to the same rules as any product campaign. The company brand merely adopts the "role of the product."
- For company brands, too, the aim is to demonstrate with an image campaign the relevant benefit for the appropriate target groups and to create preferences in the decision processes.
- In particular, international business activities and the necessity to differentiate the company in a sustainable manner from the relevant competitors in the respective markets, make establishing a consistent image for the company brand that creates preference with all target groups absolutely necessary.
- In complex company structures, individual product campaigns only have an effect on one section of the company brand. As a result, product campaigns are not capable of solving the communicative tasks for the image of the company brand, overall.
- An image campaign is therefore a suitable instrument for developing a consistent and emotional image for the company brand. It creates appeal and, thus, preference with the relevant target groups. An image campaign is able to generate a long-term and sustainable competitive advantage for a company.
- Ideally, individual product campaigns and the image campaign for the company brand complement each other in content and also show, wherever it makes sense, a harmonious overall picture in look and feel.
- A company brand usually appears worldwide, so care should be taken that this appearance is standardized and consistent across countries and markets. However, the communication status (in particular with the dimensions awareness and image) in different countries/markets can be very different. This reality must be taken into account in the planning and implementation of specific communication elements.

▶ Theoretical Model of the Image Campaign

1. Definition

Ever more frequently, the following boundary conditions are turning a clear and consistent company image into a decisive success factor:

- Shrinking differences in quality and performance of products and services, and competition that is intensifying on an international level.

- Continuing inundation of target groups with information, and a product and service offering that is becoming complex in its communication.
- More comprehensive product portfolios and shorter product life cycles, as well as shrinking differentiation possibilities for the instruments of price and quality compared to competitors.
- Regionally different and primarily product-related perception of the companies by various target groups.

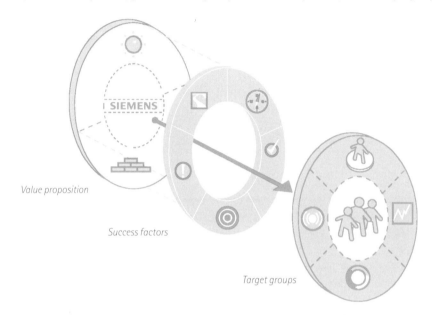

Fig. 1: Building on five success factors, the value proposition creates a clear brand image with the different target groups

Overall, this does not lead to a holistic perspective of the company brand and consequently to a lack of emotional and cognitive preference of the target group towards the company. This applies particularly to multinational companies.

The image of a company brand is generally the brand personality perceived in the relevant target groups. A "personality" with an attitude, with characteristics, with certain values, a "personality" that should also give a performance promise. This performance promise (value proposition) applies both to internal target groups, for example employees, as well as for all external target groups, such as customers and business partners. Special requirements of planning, creation, and implementation of an image campaign for a company brand result from this:

A The development of an image campaign for a company brand must always begin with the business strategy. This is an important prerequisite so that the image campaign supports the company objectives in a worthwhile manner.

B An image campaign must also reflect the defined brand values, the benefit promise of the company brand, and the identity of the company, in order to be authentic and credible.

C From an analysis of these elements, the communication objectives of an image campaign can be derived. Brand strengths and weaknesses become clear, brand drivers are identified.

D Relevant target groups for an image campaign are existing and potential customers and business partners, employees, as well as investors and analysts if the company is listed on the capital markets. Opinion leaders and multipliers can be another interesting target group. Not only do the various target groups need to be analyzed from a demographic point of view, they also need to be understood particularly in the aspects relevant for communication.

E It is important to define the relevant messages per target group. A message for all target groups is usually not sufficient; differentiation specific to target groups is a fundamental success factor of an image campaign.

F Taking into account the media usage behavior of the various target groups, the individual elements of an image campaign need to be defined and activities selected that can exactly address the respective target group in the best possible way.

G An image campaign, too, must be measurable by its results. For this, a metric system that is often the company's proprietary system needs to be set up. Key performance indicators (KPI) need to be defined, that document precisely the performance of an image campaign in the medium term and can be measured continually, both quantitatively and qualitatively.

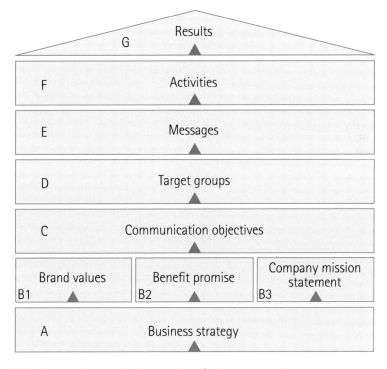

Fig. 2: Logics of planning, creation, and implementation of an image campaign

2. Factors

2.1 Value proposition

The basis, as regards content, for the successful planning, creation, and implementation of an image campaign, consists of the development of a consistent benefit and value promise (of a so-called value proposition) for a company. The development of a value proposition forms the basis for an attractive, relevant, credible, and differentiating positioning of a company and consists of the following three elements:

- **Benefit promise (benefit):**
  What unique benefit promise does the brand/company give?
- **Functional reason (reason to believe):**
  What are brand attributes that support the benefit promise?
- **Brand character:**
  What emotional attributes characterize the brand personality and reflect the tonality?

In addition to the development of a value proposition, the implementation of the value proposition within the company is also very important. The internal implementation of a value proposition forms the basis for the success of an image campaign. The value proposition must be lived on all levels and in all divisions of the company. Only then will the respective target groups of the company be able to really experience this performance promise.

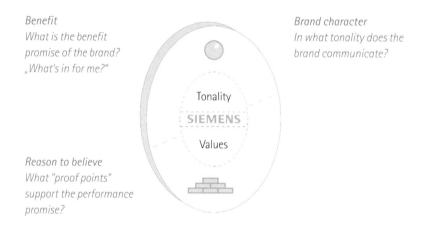

Fig. 3: Structure of the value proposition

2.2 Brand screen

A differentiation between the effectiveness of a product and image campaign can be made with the help of the brand screen concept. The brand screen describes the relationship between target groups and the respective company and depicts it in the dimensions of recognition, image, readiness to close/purchase, purchase, and loyalty. A product campaign has a predominant effect on the rear dimensions of purchase and loyalty of the brand screen and aims to increase the readiness to buy, or rather the readiness for a repeat purchase and/or the loyalty of the customers. An image campaign initially affects the front dimensions of recognition and image and increases the emotional preference of the target groups towards the company.

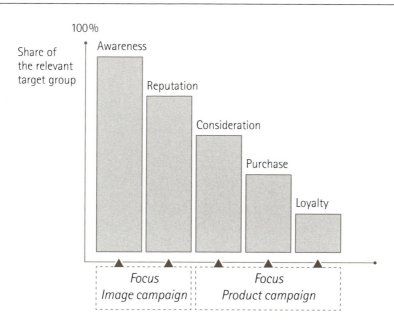

Fig. 4: Direct effect of image and product campaigns on the dimensions of the brand screen

To ensure the positive effect of an image campaign on the dimensions recognition and image of the brand screen, the company must fulfill the requirements that are briefly described below:

2.3 Success factors

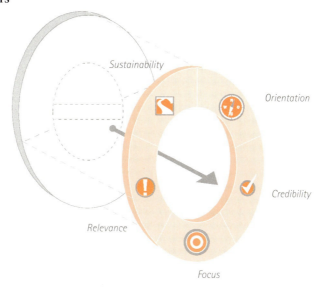

Fig. 5: The five success factors as the basis for the planning and implementation of the value proposition

2.3.1 Orientation
An image campaign must be able to be clearly assigned to a company brand. Arbitrariness and exchangeability are features that must be absolutely avoided. Only then does an image campaign actually give the necessary orientation. Siemens is represented in 190 countries around the world. Everywhere, the Siemens brand is used in practically an identical manner – this starts with the design of the business stationery and the factory signage, and must also be continued in image campaigns.

2.3.2 Credibility
An image campaign must be authentic and effectively reflect the company. Contradictions between actual performance and the performance promise must be absolutely avoided. For example, Siemens has defined a pictorial language that is valid across the company as a binding element of the corporate design. Here, they say, for example: "We talk with our customers. Not with ourselves. Our tonality is intelligent and cordial."

2.3.3 Relevance
An image campaign will only have an effect and generate preferences for the company's own corporate brand if it is relevant for the target groups that it addresses. Siemens checks the relevance of brand values in selected markets and customer segments on an annual basis and, more importantly, the relevance of these attributes in decision processes. These results are also the fundamental basis for the development of image campaigns.

2.3.4 Sustainability
In contrast to product campaigns, an image campaign for a company brand tends to be designed for the mid- and long-term. Sustainability and substance in the messages are therefore essential. In most cases, it is insufficient to follow communicative trends and/or to select company topics and messages as the basis for image campaigns that are relevant in the short term. A frequent change of the image campaigns, both in content and visually, more often than not has a negative effect. Werner von Siemens founded the company in 1847 and began the success story of Siemens with an innovation (pointer telegraph). Innovation is and will remain a core topic that has also been reflected in all image campaigns of the last years.

2.3.5 Focus
Image campaigns require a distinct focus. This creates clarity, gives the target groups a clear choice, and facilitates differentiation to competitors. In the majority of cases, wanting to please everyone and presenting a host of messages for every target group leads to a significant weakening of an image campaign. With a very broad portfolio, the factor "focus" is a special challenge. With its business areas, Siemens stands for gas turbines and light bulbs, for computer tomographs and hearing aids for toddlers, for complex production management systems and fire detectors, for complete mobile radio networks and cordless telephone terminals, for high-speed trains and car navigation systems, etc. Taking the success factors described above into consideration, an image campaign is an instrument for generating a competitive advantage in the long term.

▶ Process & Implementation

The image campaign is characterized by a clearly defined development process that is divided into preparation, planning, development, and implementation phases:

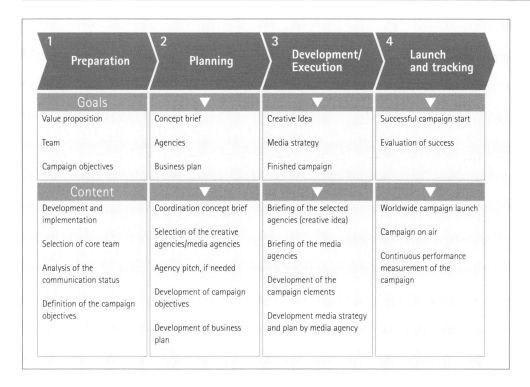

Fig. 6: Image campaign process

Phase 1: Preparation

In the preparation phase, the company must create the process-oriented platform for a successful implementation of the image campaign. For this, a core team for the development of the image campaign first has to be defined. The members of the core team should ideally represent the individual organizational units of a company, for example business areas and regions. Both with the core team and with all other departments relevant to the image campaign, a regular exchange and continual communication should take place during the development of the campaign.

Furthermore, the following three steps should be observed in the preparation phase:

- Development and implementation of the value proposition.
- Analysis of the communication status.
- Definition of the campaign objectives.

Development and implementation of the value proposition

The fact-based development process is important in the development of a differentiating and relevant value proposition. This is presented briefly below and comprises five stages:

- Data analysis/identification of positioning potential – in this first step, available data is analyzed and expert workshops carried out. Based on this, potential for a possible positioning of the brand is identified.
- Development of value proposition routes – at this level, first alternatives for a value proposition are developed.
- Internal validation (expert interviews) – the routes are validated internally in this step, particularly with regard to organizational aspects and whether they can be fulfilled. This step can be done in several iterative loops in order to reach a small selection of possible value proposition routes.
- External validation – the possible routes are now checked by market research (e.g., using moderated focus groups) for their market potential. In this phase, too, the benefit promise is honed and focused further.
- Fine tuning/recommendation – in this last phase, the internally and externally validated routes are now checked using higher-level strategic factors, and the final value proposition is formulated.

Analysis of the communication status

An image campaign represents an important part of the communication concept of a company. Accordingly, a detailed analysis of the communication status should be carried out in the preparation phase. Depending on the individual company, different factors can be incorporated in the analysis and various assessment standards created. The analysis of the communication status takes into account at least the following perspectives:

Business status
- What market share does our company have?
- How should we assess the market potential for our company?
- What communicative positioning does our company have?
- What communication values (e.g., awareness, image …) have been achieved so far?

Activities of the relevant competitors
- What communicative positioning do competitors use?
- What core messages are communicated?
- What communicative pressure do the competitors generate (media spending)?
- What creative central idea do competitors use?

Brand relevance
- What is the status of the brand?
- Which brand values are relevant?
- What are the brand drivers?
- Where are the current strengths? Where are the weaknesses?

Definition of the communication objectives

Before the start of the planning phase, the specific objectives of the image campaign should be derived on the basis of the challenges defined in the communication analysis. The objectives must be "smart" – "simple, measurable, attractive, reachable, and tangible": Only objectives that fulfill these criteria are suitable for substantiating the performance of an image campaign. These specific communication objectives can be, for example:

- Increase in the global brand value of the company.
- Enhancing the reputation at regional level.
- Implementation of the value proposition with the relevant target groups.

Phase 2: Planning

The recommended procedure in the planning phase of an image campaign consists of the following steps:

Decisions about the elements of the agency briefing
- Campaign objectives.
- Content of the campaign.
- Architecture of the campaign.
- Boundary conditions for the creation and execution.

Selection of potential creative agencies for an agency selection process (e.g., classical pitch)
- Selection of a creative agency.
- Selection of a media agency that accompanies the entire development process.
- Development of the campaign schedule.
- Creation of a business plan for the image campaign.

Phase 3: Creation phase

- Briefing of the creative agencies to develop a "creative idea."
- Briefing of the media agency to create a media strategy and definition of initial boundary conditions.
- Selection of a "creative idea" and the appropriate agency.
- Commissioning of the creative agency with the development of the image campaign.
- Commissioning of the media agency with the development of a concluding media plan.

Phase 4: Launch

- Zero measurement so that campaign controlling can start properly.
- Global launch with corresponding internal and external communication. Continual campaign controlling and success control.

> ### ▶ Key Insights
>
> ☐ An image campaign for a company brand works in principle along the same lines as any product campaign. The company brand merely assumes the "role of the product."
> ☐ The development of an image campaign for a company brand must always begin with the business strategy. That is an important prerequisite, so that this image campaign supports the company objectives in a worthwhile manner.

- An image campaign for a company brand is characterized by the following features: orientation, credibility, relevance, sustainability, and focus.
- A clear and consistent image for the company brand is absolutely necessary. It provides all target groups with orientation and, in addition to relevance and credibility, creates significant added value for the company brand.

The Author

Dirk Miller

Since October 2000, Dirk Miller has been Vice President of the department "Corporate Advertising" at Siemens AG. He and his team are responsible for topics such as strategic communication at Group level, Global Media Relations and global brand and image campaigns. Since December 2002, Dirk Miller has been a member of the German Advertising Council (DW) and also a Board Member of the Central Federation of the German Advertising Industry (ZAW).

For him, communication is always a "strategic task" and, thus, a fundamental part of the business process. Above all, communication is an investment and not a cost factor – what counts is always the return on investment (RoI).

Literature Recommendations

P. Argenti, Janis A. Forman," The Power of Corporate Communications," New York 2002
C. J. Fombrun, "Reputation, Realizing Value from the Corporate Image," Cambridge (Ma.) 1996
J. Marconi, "Image Marketing. Using public perceptions to attain business," Chicago 1996
D. Miller, "Marken- und Kundenwertmanagement in komplexen Konglomeraten – Das Beispiel Siemens," 2004
W. Bernd, O. Göttgens (eds.), "Integriertes Marken und Kundenwertmanagement. Strategien, Konzepte und Best Practices," pp. 499–514, Wiesbaden 2004
M. Schultz, M. J. Hatch, M. L. Holten, "The Expressive Organization, Linking Identity, Reputation, and the Corporate Brand," Oxford.
D. A. Aaker, "Brand Portfolio Strategy," New York 2004

Jens-Thomas Pietralla, Andreas X. Müller – Siemens Mobile

Marketing Communications Controlling
Using key performance indicators for integrated marketing communications controlling

▶ Executive Summary

- The highly competitive and challenging telecommunications equipment market calls for an especially diligent approach towards marketing communications (marcom): the industry is faced with reduced marketing budgets and staff while at the same time confronted with a situation where the acquisition of new orders becomes more and more difficult. By introducing key performance indicators (KPIs), Siemens installed a marcom controlling process to increase efficiency in its budget allocation within its communications unit. The following article introduces the methodology developed and illustrates its application in a case study.
- Strengthening the case for greater marcom efficiency on a general level, a recent study by McKinsey & Company revealed that more than half of the CEOs interviewed "were underwhelmed by the marketeers' analytical skills and business acumen." The study concludes that, "while there is no single formula for marketeers to establish credibility within their company, influential CMOs and successful marketeers put in place metrics and processes to track the impact of marketing initiatives."
- Out of the 4 Ps in marketing – product, placement, price, and promotion – controlling promotion is certainly the most challenging aspect of marketing communications controlling. Soft factors (emotion, trendiness, image, and style etc.) tend to evade numerical measurement. However, this article introduces an approach to improve marketing communication controlling also in areas where traditional controlling typically fails.
- Marcom controlling is more than just merely control. It is also about supporting the development of objectives and the strategies to reach them, monitoring deviations, providing analysis and recommendations to correct those deviations, and optimizing the results and the means to achieve them.
- Thus the focus of the model is based on controlling what to do (marcom objectives and the marcom budget, vehicles and schedule supporting them) – not on controlling how to do it (e.g., campaign testing).
- The following marcom controlling model is integrated into a regular marketing communication process (from analysis to strategy, concept, implementation, and finally to controlling). It introduces key performance indicators (KPIs) that are both concrete and measurable so that marketing communications objectives can be set along those marcom KPIs. The marcom KPIs being used are Awareness, Image, Consideration, Purchase, and Loyalty, as the model is based on the "marketing funnel" concept.
- A new qualitative and quantitative methodology is introduced to devise the optimal budget size, vehicle mix and communication timeline.
- In the specific example of one of our business units which is depicted in the case study we are differentiating between two types of budgets: the "pull budget" to increase the (unaided) brand awareness; the "push budget" to directly drive up purchases via point-of-sales measures. We are deducing the optimal size of the pull budget via regression analysis from the aspired unaided brand awareness, and the corresponding necessary advertising awareness respectively.

Theoretical Model of Integrated Marketing Communications Controlling

1. Core principle

Controlling marketing communications (marcom) is about controlling and measuring the financial impact on the business. Making marcom more accountable instructs the marketing decision-maker on how to spend advertising budgets more efficiently and more precisely, it translates into making greater impact for the same or less budget.

Making marketing more accountable means tying the measurement of its results to concrete business parameters. This can be done by applying a marketing funnel concept that explains and tracks how a potentially interested audience is turned into loyal customers. Tracking how this audience is attracted in greater numbers into this funnel is made possible by applying a key performance indicator (KPI) concept that delivers precise numbers at every stage of the funnel and shows the results of our marcom effort via a gap analysis between ex-ante and ex-post measurements.

The results of the KPI measurements can be used to derive the overall size of the necessary budget and the distribution of the budget on the various marcom vehicles and to track target achievement.

Thus the model offers a precise method to set marcom targets and to determine a sufficient budget for reaching those targets. These results can best be achieved in a deductive and quantitative approach instead of an intuition-based trial and error venture.

The typical annual marcom process (see Figure 1) starts with a review of the status quo, i.e. an analysis of the defined key performance indicators: How have they developed over time and vs. the targets set in the previous period? How have competitor marketing performance levels changed and how have customers reacted? Based on this analysis and the overall business objectives a comprehensive marcom strategy and subsequent marcom concepts and implementation plans are being developed. The final controlling step closes the circle by a successive measurement of the key performance indicators, by monitoring deviations and by providing analysis and recommendations to quickly correct those deviations. Governance is carried out by guiding and steering the process steps by guidelines and active interfering, if necessary.

The underlying assumption of our controlling model is the validity of a marketing funnel along the purchase decision-making process that guides prospective customers from first becoming acquainted with the brand and its offering, to inciting the customer to purchase, and to eventually even recommending the offering to others. It simply describes the steps in which you change an uninformed target group into loyal customers. All marcom activities are geared towards pulling a specific target group ever deeper into this funnel. While it is inevitable to lose some of these people along the way, the ultimate goal is to attract those customers with the highest lifetime value for the company, i.e., those that tend to make more purchasing decisions in favor of us and/or even recommend our products to others.

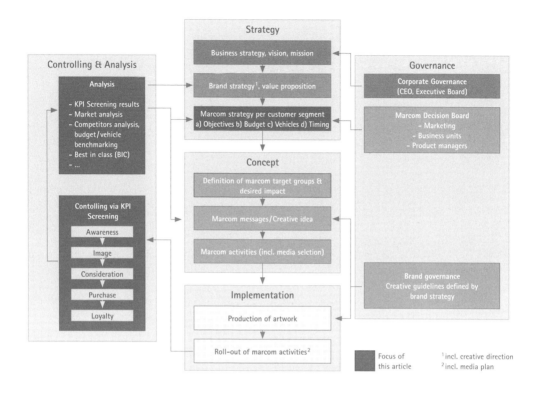

Fig. 1: integrated marketing communication process

2. Integrating marketing controlling in the marcom process

Successful marcom controlling requires sufficient up-to-date data points. Most fundamental is the KPIs analysis along the marcom funnel (see Figure 2) which we will introduce first.

2.1 Defining marcom key performance indicators

The purpose of the marcom KPI system is to analyze our own marcom achievements as well as any shortcomings while using the opportunity to learn from them. Learning from your own mistakes often proves to be the most difficult task, as one tends to become emotional and testy when it comes to own failures. Not surprisingly, in companies with thousands of employees, learning from organization's shortcomings is an ongoing challenge. The key to success lies in performance indicators that are as objective and as transparent as possible, and which fulfill the following criteria:

- specific,
- quantifiable and measurable,
- actively controllable.

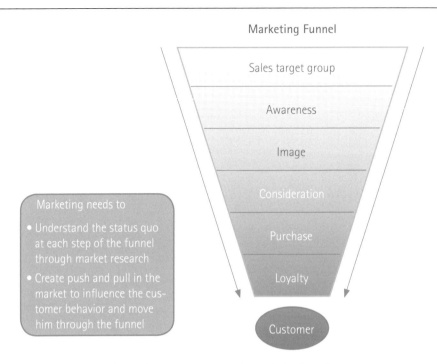

Fig. 2: Marketing is responsible for moving customers along the marketing funnel

The marketing funnel helps in that respect. It provides the basic key performance indicators that are measured as a percentage of the total sales target group (see Fig. 3) in a marcom KPI screening process.

2.1.1 Awareness
It is measured by the percentage of the target group that recalls the brand name, offering, or advertising efforts. It differentiates between aided and unaided awareness. The aided awareness offers the reference point (brand name, etc.) as a stimulus to the interviewed person and thus raises the recall level vs. the unaided measurement, where no stimulus is given.

2.1.2 Image
Prospective buyers have to trust the brand and believe in the qualities of the offer. You also want to know to what extent the target group associates your company with your aspired image values. Image is a multi-dimensional KPI, which can be consolidated to a one-dimensional value for numeric purposes.

2.1.3 Consideration
How many prospective customers consider your company in their relevant set or actively place your products on their shortlist? In B2B the equivalent is invited to submit a quote or tender.

2.1.4 Purchase
The ultimate proof is purchase. Did the customer decide to buy what you were offering? This is measured as the company's market share – ideally broken down by target segment.

2.1.5 Loyalty

The final question is whether or not the customers would purchase the offering again after all their experiences with the sales and after sales process. Those that stay excited about the product or service are your most valuable resource for expanding your share of the market (via recommendation) or your share of their purchasing power (via repurchase) – in other words the customer lifetime value. On the contrary, those that had negative experiences form the most dangerous threat to your image/reputation and your market share – especially if they were annoyed and actively denounced your product in their circles (e.g., web-logs or chat forums). Marcom also has a distinctive role in the customer loyalty process. Communication that either stops or is left entirely to the retailer once the product has been sold bears a substantial risk. A customer is still very perceptive of information about the product and an easy victim for negative news or messages. Targeted communication in the after-sales process will reassure the consumer that he made the right purchasing decision.

2.2 Using marcom key performance indicators

Usually the marcom KPI data are gathered via a representative number of interviews among the target group. The questionnaire for the interviews is structured along the funnel's parameters. For an in-depth analysis and validity check of the final data the parameters (Awareness, Image, Consideration, Purchase, and Loyalty) are each derived from a set of different sub-questions. The values of the different items are consolidated into one single KPI. This KPI is then compared with a minimum benchmark value which has to be reached in order to link a positive brand

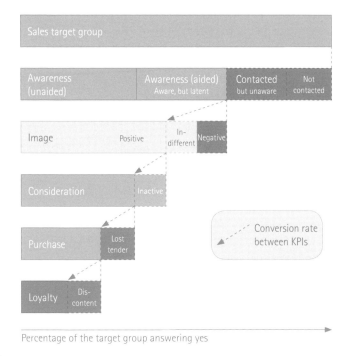

Fig. 3: Marcom KPI Screen

image with the respondent. For example, the average of the answers to the image sub-questions has to be at least a "4" on a scale from 1 to 5 in order to qualify as a "positive" image. Alternative to the "average" function you can also apply the "minimum" function, i.e. customers ranking the brand higher than x in more than y image values qualify as "having a positive image". The overall number of all such respondents in relation to the total number of respondents forms the percentage value we can attribute to the image bar in the funnel. The questionnaire can be presented in an interview or via an online tool accessible by password. Online questionnaires are usually cheaper than telephone interviews and computer-aided telephone interviews (CATI).

The percentage of customers answering favorably to the questions (in short: yes, I'm aware; yes, the brand has a good image; yes, I am considering buying it; yes, I've purchased it; yes, I'm loyal to this brand) generally decreases along the funnel, leaving a slice of negative or neutral attitudes.

To interpret these results the KPI values must be compared to the ones of main competitors. This provides an honest assessment of your competitive position and a starting point for defining future targets.

Secondly, the correlation coefficients between the KPIs will show the interconnections between the KPIs in a specific case and indicate how marginal increases and decreases in one KPI affect the performance of one or several others. In one business unit, for example, we found a direct and strong correlation between loyalty and image. Therefore, any investment with a positive impact on the brand image would directly influence the loyalty, driving re-purchase and recommendation. However, the same KPI analysis showed that purchase and unaided brand awareness had a comparatively weak correlation. Therefore investments with the mere objective of increasing unaided brand awareness turned out to be rather ineffective with regard to an increase in sales in this specific situation.

Thirdly, there should be an analysis of the conversion rates from one KPI to the other. Especially comparing these "loss rates" along the funnel steps with competitor data provides clear indications on where to focus and improve. If for example a substantial loss appears, from "awareness" to "image", it suggests that addressing the image shortcomings is more urgent than raising awareness levels (of a brand that is not being liked further). An example would be a global fast food chain within the health-conscious consumer segment: awareness is given, but the "healty" image needs to be developed first.

2.3 Complementing marcom key performance indicators with further data

In order to complement the marcom KPI screen, various additional analyses of the market requirements and competitors are necessary. While there should certainly be a tracing system of the main competitors' marcom KPIs in the above mentioned screening process, specific marcom strategy related benchmarks are also of interest. What are the major marcom activities and how much is spent on them? Which vehicle is used and how are their activities scheduled over time?

The purpose of all benchmarking is to continuously improve and emulate best practices. It is therefore mandatory to also look beyond your own business and search for the best in class companies in other industries and adopt their tools and processes.

3. Developing a marcom strategy with measurable success

Based on the analyses and results of the marcom KPI screening you can develop your targets and the strategies to reach them. Before you can formulate the marcom strategy included in the definition of the marcom KPI targets, you need to clarify the long-term business strategy and brand strategy, its two fundamental pillars. While the business strategy focuses on the tangible assets of a business, the brand strategy centers on the intangible assets of the brand.

The business strategy provides input and answers to questions regarding the 4 Ps in marketing: Product, Price, Placement, and Promotion (Marketing Communications).

The brand strategy defines the communicative positioning (e.g., how do we differentiate from our competitors?) and the brand identity system (e.g., what captures the soul of the brand?). From these aspects the value proposition and the message architecture are derived:

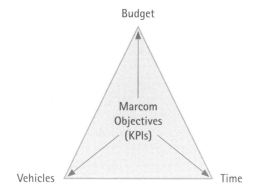

Fig. 4: Elements of the marcom strategy

The marcom strategy formulates communication objectives (expressed in marcom KPIs) and defines the means to achieve them: budget, timing, and marcom vehicles. While we define a marcom vehicle as a class of media, clustered according to its technical origin or distribution method (e.g., print, TV, Internet), we typify a marcom medium as an occurrence of such a marcom vehicle (e.g., New York Times, CNN).

To develop the marcom strategy, the following steps should be taken:

- Assess the status quo of your marcom KPIs (marcom objectives), your budget structure, vehicle usage, and timing of the marcom activities (marcom plan).
- Interpret the analysis of your competitor's KPIs.
- Analyze your customer target segments in terms of size and marcom vehicle preferences.
- Define new marcom objectives using the marcom KPIs to make those objectives concrete, measurable and controllable (e.g., increasing image by 15 percent in 12 months).
- Come to logical and mathematical (e.g., via regression analysis) conclusions on the necessary marcom means (budget, vehicles, time) to achieve your marcom objectives (defined as marcom KPI targets).

Steps 1–3 are part of the marcom process step "analysis." Step 4 obviously needs to be approved by senior management, with the quantitative analysis providing solid arguments for any "budget discussion."

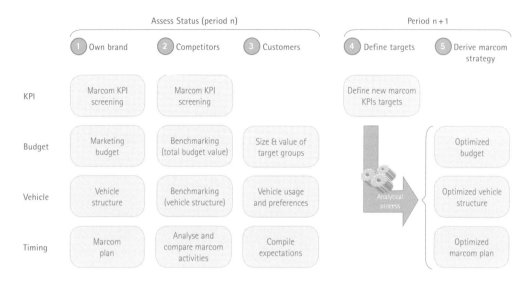

Fig. 5: How to move from marcom KPIs to budget and vehicle planning

Step 5 is at the center of an optimally fine-tuned marcom strategy. Attributing the right vehicles to the marcom KPIs is a challenging task. It needs to be done at an expert level considering the specific industry, country and situation, and taking into account the information from steps 1–3. Figure 6 shows a conceptual example of the relationship between communication vehicles and marcom KPIs.

An exemplary approach of attributing the right budget size for the defined marcom KPI-related task will be demonstrated in the following case study. It is important to note that a marcom strategy can lead to savings as well as to budget increases. If the interpretation of the marcom KPIs leads for example to the conclusion that the value for awareness is already at a sufficient level, ad spending in this sector could decrease.

The efficiency of advertising spending follows an s-curve. In the lower part of the "s" any change has minimal effects as the advertising is below the perception level. In the middle of the curve an increase has the greatest effect (efficiency zone). Spending above that level again yields decreasing marginal effects and is thus inefficient. Using the marcom KPI screen in this way helps to find an optimum level of advertising spending.

4. Controlling aspects to be considered in the marcom concept and implementation phase

4.1 Customer information and decision-making process

How is information retrieved and how are decisions by our customers made in the respective market? The question of information retrieval goes a long way to defining the right media and sequences of messages for our target group. Understanding this process also allows us to better interpret the results of our marcom KPI tracking. It can help us attribute the right media and the right amount of money for pushing the accurate indicator so

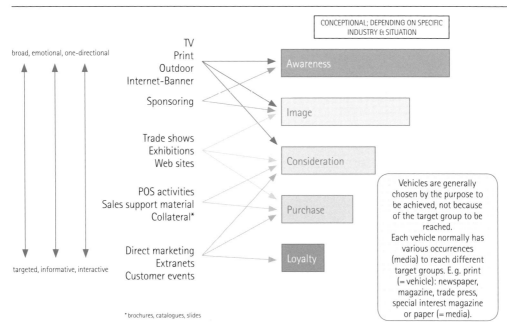

Fig. 6: Relationship between communication vehicles and marcom KPIs

that the desired results are achieved. In the process of finding the right budget size, we have already argued that reducing an advertising budget once having reached a certain market share level is an option. A logical explanation for this mathematical conclusion comes from our understanding of the information and decision-making process. It may show us, for example, that the business model of our customers demands at least two different suppliers for a certain infrastructure. In this situation, pushing further while having already achieved a high market share will hardly pay off the invest.

4.2 Target groups and desired impact

The sales target group should not be the only group addressed by communicative action. Instead all parties relevant to the purchasing process should be considered. In B2B we often face a decision-maker and a set of recommenders. However, reviewing the information process might produce the following results: the recommenders in turn rely heavily on consultants and analysts, which brings them into the focus of our communicative effort. A precise understanding of the purchaser's decision-making process and how to influence the parties involved is key to efficient marcom activities.

4.3 Implementing marcom activities

Creativity is hard to measure. Although we know that a good creative idea or Leitmotiv can have dramatic effects on the awareness and image factor there is still no generally proven method to produce good creative ideas and certainly none that translates money spent on the development of the idea into greater creativity of the idea. Even in cases where the creative idea and the corresponding artwork are known to have had an effect (e.g., the Marlboro man) it remains difficult to emulate this success by spending more money than before on creativity. With pre- and post-testing there is the possibility of learning about relative awareness and image improvements, but there is no theory that supports a "creativity for money" exchange rate mechanism.

With the marcom KPI controlling system and the marcom KPI target-driven budgeting approach we focus on what we should do (marcom objectives) – rather than on how to do it. The marcom activity plan adds timing to our budget and vehicle ideas. Usually the market and our marketing concept deliver a set of firm dates: the launch of a product, the most important trade show, the press conference, etc. Usually the business year has a calendar of its own – whether it contains Valentine's Day or CeBIT depends on the industry. The marcom activity plan is also the metronome for our marcom KPI screening efforts. The final controlling step closes the circle by a successive measurement of the marcom KPIs. The effects of the marcom strategy, the concept and its implementation can be directly controlled and deviations monitored. Those indicators lead directly into the next planning round and, together with additional analysis, will guide further recommendations on how to correct potential deviations.

CASE   Siemens

In the following case we depict an example of applying the marcom KPI-based controlling and strategy process; the introduction of a marcom KPI-based global budgeting process in one of our business units. We discern between "push" and "pull" aspects of a marketing budget based on the conclusions drawn from the marcom KPI model. In the following case we concentrate on the process steps "controlling" and "marcom strategy" of the marketing communication process depicted in Part 1.

1. Controlling and analysis

The highly competitive and challenging market for our B2C business unit called for an especially diligent approach to marcom spending. The local companies in the countries and the central effort and support from headquarters had to be synchronized and structured. A model for attributing advertising money

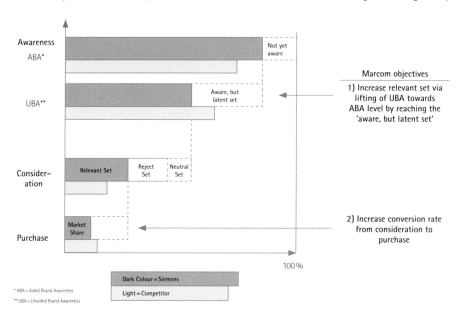

Fig. 7: KPI values of business unit analyzed at time of first measurement and derived marcom objectives

to certain regions and marcom vehicles was needed. In this situation a coherent line of thought was developed, about how marcom vehicles and the structure of an advertising budget influence certain marcom KPIs, that in turn influence sales. A first marcom KPI measurement had yielded the following results: firstly, aided awareness was sufficiently high, but the conversion rate to unaided awareness was not satisfactory in many countries. Secondly, the conversion rate from consideration to purchase was also not in line with expectations and market benchmarks.

2. Marcom strategy

Firstly, the marcom KPI consideration should be increased by lifting unaided brand awareness closer to the rather high aided brand awareness levels. For this an increase in above the line and PR measures was deemed necessary. Secondly, a substantial lift in point-of-sales measures was supposed to increase the conversion rate from consideration to purchase. Admittedly, the products themselves played the most important lever to address this issue.

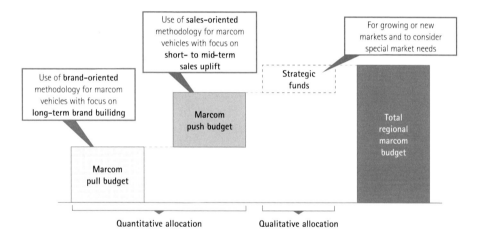

Fig. 8: Key driver of regional marcom budget is the quantitative allocation based on sales performance and regional brand requirements

2.1 Marcom Budgeting

The budgeting approach began with the assumption that regional brand requirements and sales performance should be the key drivers in the quantitative allocation of a regional marcom budget.

The basic distinction was made between:

- Pull budget, used for marcom vehicles with an assumed effect on long-term brand building, defined via a brand-oriented methodology. (Marcom KPI target: increase in unaided brand awareness).
- Push budget, used for marcom vehicles with an assumed effect on short- or mid-term sales, defined via a sales-oriented methodology. (Marcom KPI target: increase in purchase).

On top of that we added strategic funds allocated in special cases following qualitative criteria like market types (new, growing, etc.). The model integrated the results of the marcom KPI analysis and other research material in order to build a correlation between marcom spending, advertising awareness, brand awareness, and market share.

2.1.1 The pull budget

The pull budget is the part of the budget that produces a demand "pull" on the market. The objective is to indirectly increase the market share by making people more aware of the product and its benefits, and also by strengthening the brand, its identity, and values. Thus, the basic assumption behind the pull budget is that an increase in unaided brand awareness would also increase the consideration – ultimately resulting in more purchases.

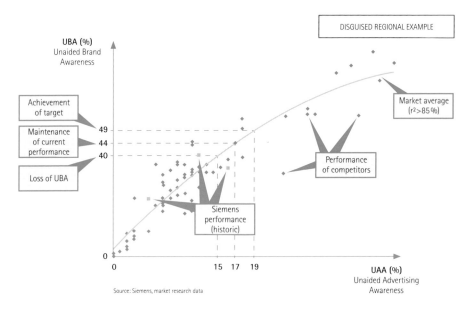

Fig. 9: Via regression analysis, the UBA target indicates necessary performance in unaided advertising awareness (UAA)

In order to efficiently allocate our global budget to the various regions we pursued the following process:

- Define unaided brand awareness (UBA) targets per region.
- Derive the needed unaided advertising awareness (UAA) levels to reach these UBA targets.
- Compute the required net spending to reach these levels – considering local costs per GRP.

With relevant data from previous periods, including our own and competitor data, a function to determine the correlation between unaided advertising awareness and unaided brand awareness was established.

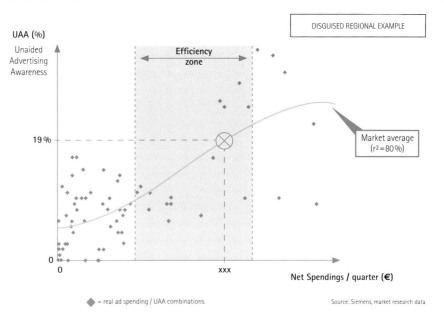

Fig. 10: A further regression analysis indicates necessary marcom pull investment to achieve aspired UAA performance

A further regression analysis then provided the budget needed to generate the required level of unaided advertising awareness. This methodology implicitly took into account the differing regional media price levels. It obviously needed a certain amount of data on previous advertising measures or competitor activities: the money that was spent on them and some post-advertising testing on their effect in building unaided advertising brand awareness (see data points in picture above).

With the theory that unaided brand awareness can best be moved via "Above-the-Line" (AtL) the media budget was attributed to AtL vehicles. Certainly AtL vehicles also have an effect on consideration and image.

2.1.2 The push budget

The push budget is supposed to be directly "pushing" or supporting the purchase decision, that is, to increase the marcom KPI "Purchase." In actual fact these activities directly influence specific point-of-sale KPIs like the "recommendation rate" (by shop assistants). For the sake of brevity we do not elaborate on these relationships in further detail. The push budget is mainly allocated to POS measures. The key question here is, what is the efficient amount of money to spend on such activities? We assumed that in order to reach the planned unit volume a certain amount of money per unit (varying from high, mid, low marcom priority category) is needed in the sales push effort to "move" the product to the customer. Based on the gross margins for the products, we categorized them in different marcom priority clusters to keep the budget efficient and spend it where it would reap the highest rewards. From another perspective the top products can more easily afford a premium on their attributable advertising costs. The total regional push budget is then calculated by multiplying the priority cluster

DISGUISED EXAMPLE

Formula

	Planned unit volume per marcom priority cluster		Multiplier in Euro per marcom priority cluster		Regional marcom push budget
		X		=	

Description
- Each product has a different priority with regard to supporting the business
- Each available and future product is therefore allocated to a specific marcom priority cluster "High", "Mid" and "Low"

- Depending on profitability targets and historic BtL-spending, a Euro-value is being assigned for each marcom priority cluster

- Planned sales volume by marcom priority cluster is being multiplied with assigned Euro-value
- Preliminary marcom push budgets of each marcom priority cluster are being added up, resulting in the total marcom push budget for each region

Low	3,000	€ 1	€ 3,000
Mid	2,000	€ 2	€ 4,000
High	1,000	€ 3	€ 3,000
Total	6,000 (in K units)		€10,000 (in € mio.)

Fig. 11: Planned product volume multiplied by specific Euro values per marcom priority creates regional marcom push budget

multipliers by the corresponding unit volumes planned. These funds are also updated according to the stage of the product lifecycle, generally decreasing towards the end of its life. In order to keep control of the likely difference between the forecast and the actual sales performance, the budget was subsequently aligned to the actual sales volume figures.

3. Conclusion

In our case the theory worked sufficiently well to help discern the relevant advertising budgets for the regions in an objective and fair process. This progress over previous methodologies was achieved at relatively minor additional costs, as the market research was needed anyway. The benefit was tremendous, as substantial improvements compared to the old process were made. In the past, budget allocation and support from headquarters were troubled by political infighting and erratic distribution of scarce resources. Now several theoretical aspects were combined in order to achieve practical advertising efficiency in the global budget allocation process. The marketing funnel at the core of our model helped us to define a set of objectively measurable marcom KPIs. Being aware of the old saying, "theory is if everything goes wrong, but we know exactly why – practice is, if everything works fine, but nobody knows why," we believe that the new approach successfully combines metric-oriented controlling with the expert judgment of experienced marketeers.

▶ Key Insights

- By placing metrics and processes to track the impact of marketing initiatives the credibility of marketing within senior management can be substantially increased.
- This progress can be achieved at relatively minor additional costs.
- The marcom funnel and the corresponding marcom KPI system, though simplistic, can serve as a pragmatic, efficient model to objectify the core issues to be solved via marketing communications.
- In order to achieve lasting improvements a regular marcom strategy/controlling/KPI screening process needs to be established.
- In our case study, we could prove via regression analysis the existence of an efficiency zone in advertising, a zone that creates sufficient increases in a certain KPI (awareness, in our example) by corresponding boosts in advertising. Below and above this zone, activities were less efficient because of the low marginal effect on the KPI. We translated this result into our global budget allocation process, leading to objective, balanced, and efficient regional advertising budgets.

▶ Practical Guidelines

- The marcom KPIs should not be measured in a one dimensional way (e.g., how would you rate the reputation of the following company?), because such generic questions yield generic answers lacking meaningful insights. To come up with substantial answers you need a thoughtfully assorted cluster of questions on any one KPI.
- It is advisable to employ a specialist agency for creating your own KPI screen.
- The screening questions should not center on actual marcom efforts and campaigns, but rather on long-term market issues. It is important to design the questionnaire in a way that leads to consistent and comparable results that can be used year after year. The development of the questions needs thought leadership and experience.
- Adapt the KPI screening flexibly to your sales target group. Certain B2B environments are so closely interwoven that awareness for the top players is almost at 100 percent and most customers have bought at least once from any one of the few available vendors. In such cases sticking to the basic methodology without adaptations leads to suboptimal results. As a rule of thumb: the more you go into B2B terrain, the more reasons to adapt you will find.

The Authors

Jens-Thomas Pietralla

Successfully combining key insights from different disciplines is a core belief of Jens-Thomas Pietralla. After receiving his Master of Science degree from the University of Ulm, he joined McKinsey & Company, the world's leading international management consultancy. Based in their offices in Munich and New York, he served companies in the high-tech and telecommunications sector as well as the consumer goods industry. Pietralla became a member of the firm's High Tech Leadership Group and Marketing Practice. Returning to Germany, he principally served Siemens in his role as a partner at McKinsey. In April 2002 Pietralla joined Siemens to become Executive Board Member of Mobile Devices as Senior Vice President for Strategy and Marketing. Two years later he became the Chief Marketing Officer of Siemens mobile and shortly after that joined the leadership team of the newly created Siemens Communications business group as CMO. In this role, he is responsible for all marketing activities of Siemens' largest business group with approximately € 17 billion revenues. Pietralla sees raising the Siemens brand profile and the efficient deployment of marketing resources as his primary task, thus paving the way for profitable growth.

Andreas X. Müller

After finishing his Master of Science at Stanford University and his post graduate studies at the Grande Ecole des Hautes Etudes Commerciales (HEC), Paris, Andreas X. Müller joined McKinsey & Company in Munich. Besides his work for leading clients in the high-tech and the telcom industries, he was part of the internal Marketing Practice. In 1999, Müller co-founded 12snap AG, the inventor and European market leader in mobile marketing. As board member he was responsible for the international expansion as well as important key accounts. In 2002, Müller led the company into profitability and is now member of the advisory board. In 2003, Müller joined the mobile phones division of Siemens AG. He is now responsible as Vice President Marketing Management for the marketing strategy and the marcom activities of Siemens Communications, the largest business unit of Siemens.

Literature Recommendations
McKinsey, "High-Tech Marketing and Sales: Aiming for Excellence," 2003
F. Cassidy, A. Freeling, D. Kiewell, "A credibility gap for marketers," The McKinsey Quarterly, No. 2, 2005
The CMO Council July 19th, "Assessing Marketing's Value and Impact" (whitepaper), 2005
http://www.cmocouncil.org
http://www.btobonline.com/article.cms?articleId=24546, Trends B2B marketing 2000-2005

Jörg Dohmen, Dr. Wolfgang Armbrecht – BMW Group

Marketing Innovations
Research & development for marketing

▶ Executive Summary

- Attracting new customers and securing the loyalty of today's target groups requires specific and distinctive communication channels.
- Key instruments for this purpose are marketing innovations.
- Marketing innovations reflect innovative product policy, consistently support the brand value's innovativeness, and set communication benchmarks in the industry. Innovation pilots can supplement or replace existing campaigns. If innovation measures are successful in the long-term, they even alter the organization with their related functions by replacing or complementing existing structures.
- Various results can be accomplished through marketing innovations – assessment of successful test channels, fulfillment of customer promise of innovativeness, expansion of innovative access to modern target groups, reinforcement of advertising acceptance, support of product innovations, extension of traditional marketing activities and functions within the organization.

This article is intended to provide the reader with a systematic approach to innovation management in marketing. Readers will recognize the need for marketing innovations, become familiar with its basic elements, and learn from examples how to create their own marketing approaches.

Background
Modern marketing communication is faced with numerous challenges. Markets that are stagnating or growing only feebly require differentiated, new solutions. On the one hand, unifying brand campaigns do not create awareness to the degree expected and are not associated with the advertised brand. On the other hand, products that are distinguished only by being slightly newer require additional differentiation. In addition to the supply side mentioned above, the demand side on the part of the consumer encourages a search for innovative approaches. Advertising targets are suffering from information overload. Messages no longer reach the target groups. Or target groups refuse above-the-line communications with media channels on the wane. Contrary to underprivileged families who prefer watching TV, well-off families spend less time in front of TV. This insight has been an alarm signal for years for exclusive brands, that react on this trend with shifting their TVC budget in favor of event, CRM, and web budgets. Interestingly consumers confirm this trend in trusting increasingly in new digital communications channels (e.g., AvantGo, Podcasting, RSS). Marketing innovations translate the Schumpeterian interpretation of innovation as the entrepreneurial mainspring that allows an enterprise to assert itself in the market in relation to the competition in the world of marketing. The magic triangle of brand, competition, and target group is affected by the dimension of technological progress. Marketing innovations that utilize new technology, in order to communicate current brand contents with appeal and intelligence, are based on this fundamental understanding. Innovative brands use marketing innovations in order to express their innovations leadership in marketing, as well as their innovations leadership in terms of the product. Marketing innovations then become part of the

unquestioned research and development aspect of marketing. They guarantee the strategic direction of marketing for future corporate success. "Marketing innovations are the key to modern target groups."

▶ Theoretical Model of Marketing Innovations

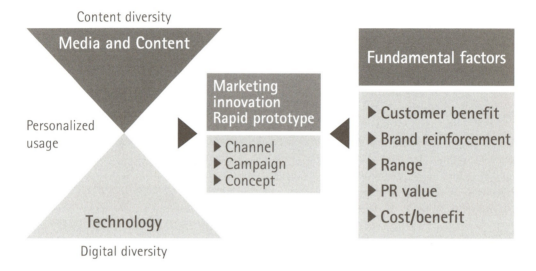

Fig. 1: Theoretical model: combinations of more new technologies and media and content should be personalized and converted as marketing innovations into a rapid prototype. Fundamental factors constitute the filter

1. Definition and core principal

Marketing innovations are new marketing activities with a unique character – campaigns, channels, or concepts focusing on additional customer benefit. They generate a USP (Unique Selling Proposition) that distinguishes a premium brand from the competition in a future-oriented and sustainable way. While in the narrow sense marketing innovations might be the successful "rapid prototypes" (pilots) of a specialist department with possible opportunities for broad implementation, in a wider sense they are the guiding principle of modern marketing communication for the entire marketing department. As a result, marketing innovation becomes strategy. On the one hand, the own brand is protected from the competition's marketing efforts. On the other hand, innovation-driven stimuli are used by media and technology to dynamically develop the brand from the inside. In addition to stimuli from technology, brand themes (content) also have considerable influence on marketing innovations. Three phases can be identified in working with marketing innovations: scanning, ideation, evaluation.

1.1 Scanning
The goal of increasing communication efficiency leads to a scanning order. This scanning task extends to two fundamental poles: content (communication content corresponds to the use categories of the groups demanding information) and technology. Both poles increase constantly over time in scope and specificity. They are based on the drivers of innovation, creativity, and technological progress.

1.2 Ideation

The ideation process builds on the innovation fields identified during scanning. The definition of an innovation field alone does not produce the desired brand reinforcement or the intended customer benefit. During the ideation process, the innovators concerned map existing brand contents in the newly discovered communication channel. A marketing innovation only attains the maturity of an innovation concept upon successful ideation. Channel, campaign, and target group then fit coherently.

1.3 Evaluation

The evaluation determines to which extent a rapid prototype grows from an innovation concept. The evaluation consists of reviewing the innovation concept with respect to fundamental factors. These basic factors measure the likelihood of success of a future marketing innovation.

2. The vision

It is anticipated that by 2010 there will scarcely be any television ad blocks. Time-shifted television, thanks to TiVo and digital personal video recorders (PVR), will force marketeers and advertisers to utilize new advertising formats. TiVo is a digital video recorder made by TiVo Inc, which allows time-shifted television viewing. The device is a TV box that stores digital photos and music, and which can display them via TV monitors. According to a survey by the Yankelovich Market Research Institute, approximately sixty percent of Americans indicated that they would consciously bypass advertising – among those who own a digital video recorder, this figure is even seventy percent. New channels and instruments are required. TiVo is an example for practically forced marketing innovation. However, it is not simply the changing technical environment brought about by digitalization, but also dynamic marketing conditions that argue for new approaches. Marketing innovation can be likened to research and development (R&D) for marketing. On the one hand, the use of R&D resources can be explained by the strategy of wanting to develop competitive advantages for the future. On the other hand, R&D investment in the future is appropriate for professional, planned marketing. Marketing channels can thereby be reserved at an early stage for one's own brand via first mover projects, and secured for the long term.

The vision is to achieve distinctive brand recognition and superior communication effectiveness. This effectiveness can be attained in two ways: by performance differentiation (both in terms of range, as well as quality of involvement) or by cost savings. Experimental iterative projects repeatedly lead, via clearly defined performance measurements, to new pilot projects (rapid prototypes).

3. The model

Content innovation (New School approaches) is the result of the creative design of formats using established technology. The catalyst in this case is the creativity in combining existing marketing formats with new appealing content. Marketing innovations, in contrast, are based on modern technology. They permit pioneering success based on technological progress. Approaches that simultaneously open up new usage categories are particularly innovative. Here, the example of PDA marketing shows that not just BMW brands and product contents are communicated, but that BMW events can also be linked to the user's personal calendar through organizer functions. The technology also puts the user in the position of being able to play with BMW contents (BMW 1 series Racer or Cross[3]) on the move, try out videos (BMW shorts, BMW driver training), configure his dream car (BMW 1 series Visualizer) and to transmit the data using Bluetooth/infrared. Entertainment and information value combine to

Fig. 2: Technology content Portfolio – combination of new communication methods with new technologies offer options for marketing innovation

offer a significantly more intense brand experience (involvement). The convergence of information and communication technology with consumer electronics provides diverse opportunities for marketing innovation and, thus, also for new marketing instruments.

The discussion as to what should be defined first (technology or target group) is clearly resolved in favor of the innovation driver – technology. This means that the scanning task is directed not at the target groups envisioned by market research, but at technological advances. Similarly to the theory known from strategic management of "structure follows strategy," here the formula is "target group follows technology." The prerequisite in this case is development that anticipates the customers' wishes. The instruments identified at that point offer a restricted communication channel, that combines the target groups from completely new (usually technical) perspectives. The

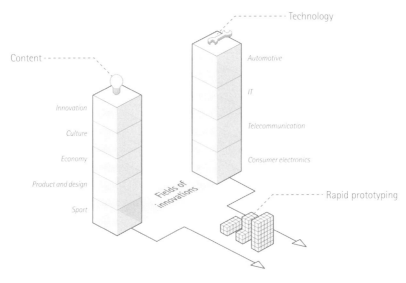

Fig. 3: Scanning of technologies and content is the basis for development of rapid prototypes for marketing innovation

original target groups described in so-called milieus merge as a result. In any case, a small spearhead is reached, that supplies a high multiplier effect by means of personal communication and press information. If the scanning task is limited to target groups in advance, then the true "enablers" are identified too late – in the innovation cycle after the peak of the trend – or not at all. The market would already have absorbed the innovation as routine. The marketing innovation would simply have come too late. Generic instruments are communicated by various competitors and claimed for themselves. The customer in turn will not directly allocate the "artificial marketing innovation" to any specific brand company. The marketing innovation will have gone up in smoke. First movers, in contrast, will not be affected by this disappearance. At the same time, a trial-and-error process results in numerous flops, although they are more manageable, since they are restricted to pilots. This is, in fact, the price paid by the pioneer.

4. The five fundamental factors in marketing innovation

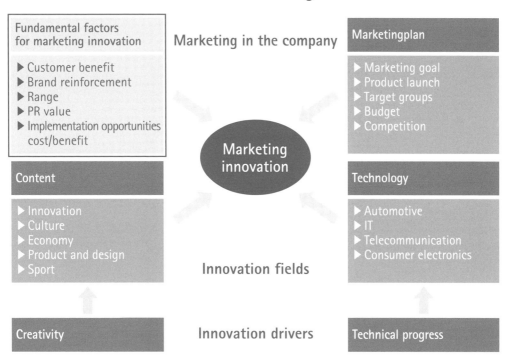

Fig. 4: The five fundamental factors in marketing innovation and further influential factors

The assessment of marketing innovation and its likelihood of success lead quickly to reflection on decisive fundamental factors. As already mentioned in the beginning, marketing innovation can provide the basis for strategic competitive advantages. There are, therefore, multidimensional requirements characterized by customers and products, marketing planning, and efficiency perspectives. The following five fundamental factors have emerged in practice:

4.1 Customer benefit

Innovation that merely serves the purpose of technical progress seldom achieves sustained success in the market. Consequently, the focus is on innovation with direct customer benefit. Trends should not simply be followed without reflection, but be used in a company-specific way, taking into consideration their relevance to customers. Customer benefit arising from a marketing innovation may be contained in an informational head-start, a service advantage or an entertainment value. For example, a digital product catalogue (BMW 1 series First Views) can generate an informational advance by PDA prior to the market launch of the product communicated. Music downloads via the BMW Player (a web radio with advertising window) allows, in addition to the primary benefit of "digital radio listening," the highly prized secondary benefit of "MP3 recording for private use." However, for the BMW brand, this also implies a tertiary use "offer of digital audio/video content" to the target group of web radio or MP3 player fans. Pre-installed MPEG4 videos on portable media players demonstrate the performance capabilities of the devices, as well as the dynamics of the new BMW 3 series limousine. Indirectly, this means an informational head-start for the users of Samsung product innovation YEPP YH-999. The entertainment electronics user elite can flaunt both the newest content of the BMW product film and ownership of the device. Experience with marketing innovation has shown us that activities are particularly successful if they have a strong relationship to the actual product and its use. Customers and interested parties favor interactive product catalogues and games accordingly.

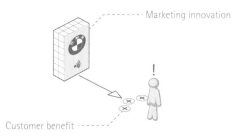

Fig. 5: Every marketing innovation must create a benefit

Fig. 6: The BMW 1 series player – web radio and pleasure principle win indicator

4.2 Range

The theory set forth initially, "target groups follow technology" applies with respect to range. Target groups define themselves according to a new dimension, as long as they have set their sights on digital lifestyle devices, such as smart phones, PDA's, MP3 players, LCD monitors. Innovative and technical brands clearly have a closer affinity with technological innovations. Socio-demographic descriptions of the target group take a back seat. PDA marketing, for instance, might be suitable for a brand that creates technical enthusiasm, such as the BMW. The BMW 1 series PDA portal is reserved for a user potential of almost four million PDA users. Surveys have revealed that an above-average number of CEO's and top managers are among this group. Marketing innovation thus reaches an ideal target group of technical enthusiasts, who are both modern and affluent. Coverage losses in the target buyer group are minimal, and the engagement with the advertising message considerably more intense than it would be if paging through a lifestyle magazine. The range should be accurately analyzed prior to launching a pilot via a new marketing channel; there are considerable efficiency risks inherent in these choices.

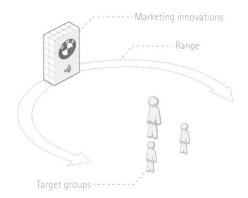

Fig. 7: The media range of marketing innovation is an additional key criterion

Figs. 8 and 9: BMW 1 series PDA Portal – Event Calendaring, interactive product catalogues, and games offer, via Palm OS organizers, a digital brand experience with diverse customer benefits and an attractive range. (Left) – BMW Activity Station – an infra-red-based download station for palm handhelds (Right)

4.3 Brand contribution

The performance differentiation in the marketing activities, as aimed for with marketing innovation measures, places high demands on the consistency with the original brand values. Ultimately, the marketing innovation not only becomes more authentic, but has a direct impact on the brand identity. Innovation management in marketing is essential for innovative brands, since strategic brand strengthening shapes brand profile in the long run. One example is the exhibit IT Lebensart, attended by 200,000 enthusiastic visitors in the brand showcases of Berlin and Munich. IT Lebensart offered digital brand experiences for the BMW 1 series on portable media players, notebooks, PDA's, and smart phones. The innovative technology of the BMW 1 series (Bluetooth technology, park distance control, iDrive) was credibly staged with the help of new media. At the same time, the "IT Lifestyle" instrument strengthened

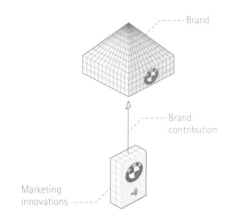

Fig. 10: An additional criterion is the contribution that the marketing innovation makes to brand strength

Fig. 11: IT Lebensart exhibit – part of the BMW 1 series market launch with digital BMW contents on innovative devices

the BMW brand value significantly, especially in its innovative facet. More traditional brands with conventional products can also enhance their perception as an innovative brand. This will also have a positive impact on the product portfolio.

4.4 PR value

The novelty character of marketing innovations often means that they are only reserved for small user target groups. These spearheads, however, tend to be particularly valuable communicators, since they have a strong multiplier effect on opinion-making, and are therefore likely to guide early adopters. Moreover, accompanying PR activities support the build-up of PR value, in order to communicate the innovation beyond the boundaries of the user target group and make it more accessible to the general public. Collaboration between the press department and technology partners proves to be particularly effective in this respect. It is precisely for representatives of the press that an engagement, demonstrating the utility of new channels, media, and devices can be of greatest interest. Marketing innovations should have the potential for a certain PR value in specialist magazines, lifestyle magazines, online, and the daily press. Publicity leverages the original advertising range by editorial integration into program elements of the media marketers. For example, the event innovation "BMW X3 Challenge" worked to extend its impact via the telecommunications partner Nokia. The challenge, consisting of three extreme sports, cross running, cross biking, and ice climbing, came up with a photo competition. Thirty-three participating teams took 1,200 photographs during the three contest days that were in turn transmitted by MMS (multimedia messaging) and received 140,000 votes on the Nokia photo portal. Not only the event in and around Berlin, but also the BMW X3 created a digital furor. The assumption is that the transmitted MMS reached the social network of the BMW X3 challenge candidates, who had been prequalified according to extensive criteria, and thus reached the heart of the target group.

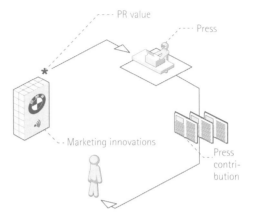

Fig. 12: The marketing innovation should be of interest to press and journalists in order to maximize its PR value

Fig. 13: BMW X3 Challenge – use of a photo portal in conjunction with the telecommunications partner Nokia, in order to communicate the event participants to the on-line community, through use of social networks via MMS and the web

Another example is the BMW activity station – the infra-red-based download station to PDA's –, that attracted the interest of the IT specialist press and marketing contests. The latter naturally experienced difficulties in allocation to the traditional competition categories, but this obviously did not lead to prize-winning results in the individual categories.

4.5 Implementation opportunities

The last fundamental factor combines several elements at once. If the two elements of degree of innovation and market maturity represent a technological trade-off, the two factors of implementation efficiency and effectiveness have a more economic focus. The degree of innovation influences the PR value, range, and customer benefit and, therefore, ensures the interdependency of these factors. The degree of market maturity alone minimizes customer benefit and range. A relevant example in this case is the BMW Activity Portal for the market launch of the BMW X3. In 2003, the PDA market in Germany had an attractive volume of approx. 2.8 million devices. Generally, however, only the calendar and address book functions were being used. The functions with advertising appeal, such as infrared downloads, video replay, and business card dispatch, still required considerable explanation. A high degree of innovation therefore encountered an insufficiently mature market; and the already available customer benefit could not be fully exploited. As a result, the user group was unfortunately restricted to the spearhead of an IT elite, that called up 5,000 direct downloads via the web and the BMW Activity Station in the space of half a year. The implementation opportunity of a variable that establishes the marketing innovation is the implementation efficiency. Innovative instruments initially have the disadvantage that development expenses are relatively high; they must be compensated by long-term advantages and savings engendered by their use.

Efficient development partnerships serve to minimize high levels of development expense. Development partners might include ITC and CE companies, suppliers from product development, and the agency network.

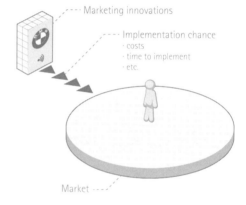

Fig. 14: The marketing innovation must be implementable at a reasonable cost and in the foreseeable future

The IT Lebensart exhibition is a prime example in which eleven innovation enterprises worked together according to a win-win philosophy. The element of implementation effectiveness determines the potential ability of a marketing innovation to attain its targets. Innovation goals may encompass all fundamental factors. The predominant goal in the case of media innovation, for instance, is a combination of range and brand contribution. Retro-reflecting, high-tech transparencies on the rear end of trucks ensure that attention is drawn to the presence of a vehicle exactly where BMW drivers and other interested parties are traveling in their own vehicles. In contrast, event innovations primarily focus on customer benefits and the brand reinforcement, since the interactive brand experience is in the forefront. The basic factor of range is engaged primarily in a quantitative way, since events are, as a rule, related to address generation measures.

Fig. 15: Retro-reflecting advertising – mobile ads for the new BMW 1 series on the rear end of trucks, using specially coated posters that intensely reflect headlight illumination. Three hundred truck drivers drive over nine million kilometers (five and a half million miles) in three months and are, thus, in the immediate vicinity of the target group of BMW drivers and interested parties

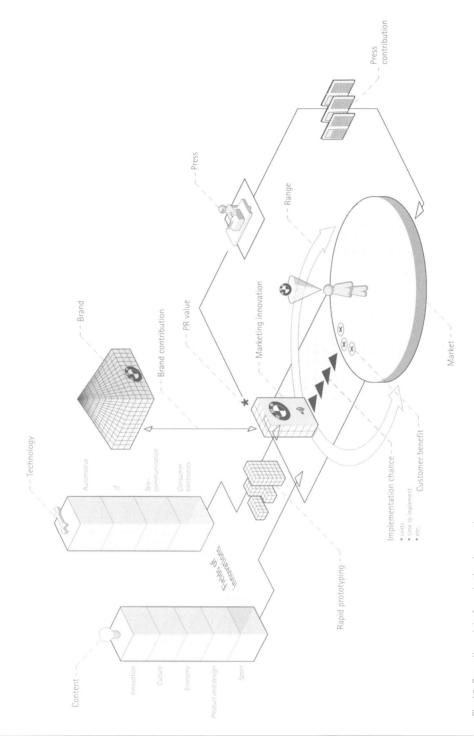

Fig. 16: Overall model of marketing innovation

Innovation Process for Marketing Intruments

"Efficient screening, tailor-made transfer to the brand, and a strong commitment towards implementing a pilot are already 80 percent of the entire process success of a rapid prototype."

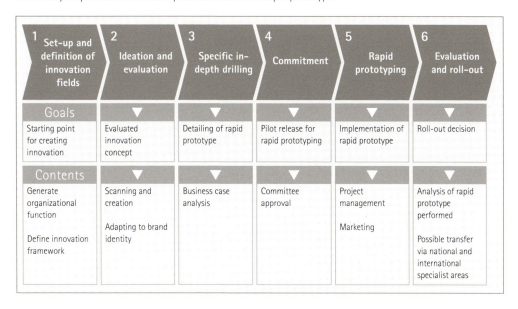

	1 Set-up and definition of innovation fields	2 Ideation and evaluation	3 Specific in-depth drilling	4 Commitment	5 Rapid prototyping	6 Evaluation and roll-out
Goals	Starting point for creating innovation	Evaluated innovation concept	Detailing of rapid prototype	Pilot release for rapid prototyping	Implementation of rapid prototype	Roll-out decision
Contents	Generate organizational function Define innovation framework	Scanning and creation Adapting to brand identity	Business case analysis	Committee approval	Project management Marketing	Analysis of rapid prototype performed Possible transfer via national and international specialist areas

Fig. 17: Marketing innovation process

Once the fundamental factors of marketing innovations have been presented, the innovation process must be visualized. Knowing that, in biology, the comparable process of mutation from genetic principles is similarly accidental, in innovation management a stable process should be defined that not only enables, but promotes spontaneous innovation. The entire process should ultimately be aimed at promoting the conceptual and cross-instrumental development of innovative avenues to clients and interested parties.

Phase 1: Setting up and defining innovation fields

At the set-up stage, the necessary prerequisites with respect to organizational design should be created, and innovation fields should be defined. The establishment of a separate functional division for marketing innovation has proven valuable at BMW, initially in the international arena, but now also in domestic practice. There are four arguments for creating an in-house function specifically tasked with innovation management:

- The advocate of ideas can function simultaneously as a clear contact point, and leaves the traditional areas of expertise to their daily routine.
- Responsibility for implementing ideas lies explicitly with innovation management.

- High motivation serves as a driver in research, pilots, and transfers to series.
- Clearly allocated budgets guarantee independence of action, thereby permitting appropriately fast responses.

The most recent example of the establishment of an innovation management function in the media industry is SevenOne Media, who anticipate their own systematic innovation impulses.

In terms of process, general innovation fields should initially be defined in concordance with the announced target groups. These fields could include content, media, product, IT, and POS innovations. As with all marketing work, the basis for innovation management should also be the marketing plan. Planning of innovation management itself, however, functions according to parameters that are extremely difficult to calculate. Innovation management requires that one be permanently up-to-speed. ITC and CE innovation windows, with a time-to-market of between two and six months, render ongoing planning for technology-based marketing innovation pointless, at least in relation to the operational level of activity planning on an annual basis. Certain innovation fields, however, can still be defined as part of the annual planning process. This is particularly true in the case of media and content innovation planning. Product innovations in the automotive industry have a lead time of up to 60 months. Clearly, in such cases, only innovations with very long-term advance lead times can be included in planning. The scanning process is undertaken within the innovation fields.

Phase 2: Ideation and evaluation

In the next phase, the innovation management team is occupied with the issue: which global innovation, not specific to the industry, can contribute to strengthening the brand, may explain a product innovation, and is likely to reach a particular target group?

During this step, the alignment of the idea with the fundamental factors of marketing innovation occurs. The fundamental factors of marketing innovation are simultaneously factors in the implementation decision, as well as measurement criteria for their likelihood of success. Fulfilling the range of criteria is essential, firstly, in the number of contacts actually reached and, secondly, in relation to the CRM measured value of qualified addresses generated.

The following approach has shown success in practice – the value of the scanning methods mentioned above increases until the marketing innovation workshops take place:

- External scanning via trend scout agency and agency network.
- In-house scanning via departments, market research, and international marketing expertise points close to development.
- Participation in trend circles, innovation forums, and trend labs.
- Marketing innovation workshops on a semi-annual basis.

The crowning finish for ideation and evaluation is the marketing innovation workshop organized on a semi-annual basis. This provides the agency network and those responsible for marketing internally with the opportunity to evaluate the measures deliberated upon.

In this respect, a considerable demand is placed on the assessment capabilities of the participants. The greater the level of specialist expertise gathered, the more results are obtained in active discussion.

Phase 3: Specific in-depth drilling

The goal of the in-depth drilling is a comprehensive analysis of the innovation concept. The specific in-depth drilling sets forth details of the concept from the ideation process and analyzes the business model, effects and efficiencies, of a rapid prototype. This also implies that the potential and impact of a later roll-out, based on the rapid prototype, can be calculated and enumerated. It is important to include expert knowledge from specialist departments in this phase, and to exploit their expertise. This means that ideas contributed, as well as implementation risks, are identified in workshops by the relevant marketing and sales colleagues. The motivation of colleagues to help systematically with ideas goes hand-in-hand with the acceptance of the marketing-innovation pilot discussed. The effectiveness and efficiency analysis is directly connected to the depth-drilling. As part of the effectiveness analysis, the innovation management team asks the question of whether the level of the objective strived for can even be reached. The goal level is increasingly shaped by addresses (CRM goal) in addition to contacts (advertising goal). This is particularly based on renunciation of marketing in favor of sales objectives, especially when markets are stagnant and the emphasis is on cost savings. The efficiency analysis, in contrast, examines the extent to which the envisioned goal can be reached with minimum resources. Here, too, costs can be a constraining factor. Efficiencies can be found precisely in collaboration with agencies; the latter are happy to accept contracts for the implementation of innovation pilots, since references can be utilized to generate business.

Phase 4: Commitment

The goal of this phase is the agreement of the organization on the execution of a rapid prototype. Innovation management requires quick decision-making and implementation, as trends and change have time-critical elements. Development departments therefore use the term "time competition." Committee decisions based on consensus may indeed bring a greater certainty of the commitment of the organization to the innovation, but under certain circumstances can hugely delay the decision-making process. This may jeopardize the pilot as a whole, if the competition has already seized on the idea and, therefore, no longer permits a first mover position. Decisions directly supported by top management accelerate the entire innovation process. From the organizational perspective, this means that innovation management should either be a staff function at the highest marketing level, or should possess privileges in terms of the idea contribution process for marketing campaigns.

Support of marketing innovation management with sufficient resources should also be assured, along with the commitment of the organization. Transparent allocation of budget funds for the subsequent year is a key element. This ensures that the marketing innovation function remains independent and prevents, to an extent, the widely prevalent "not-invented-here" syndrome. In working together with other specialist marketing areas, experience shows that the willingness to participate in additional marketing innovation projects alongside the scarce resources for traditional instruments is not particularly strong.

Once, however, solid findings are available from test pilots, the specialist areas concerned are quickly persuaded to assume the pilot as part of their established business.

Phase 5: Rapid prototyping

The goal of rapid prototyping is the implementation and marketing of the innovation concept. While the focus in Phases 1 to 4 has been primarily on creative and analytical processes, the phases that ensue require project management competencies. Rapid prototyping is successful if it can generate model findings in a clear and strictly limited area. In practice, measurable prototypes that provide transferable results within three to six months have proven themselves. Provided that the PR department and project partners are involved in the communication of the innovation project, a concerted build-up of PR value in the specialist press will result. An innovation culture that is firmly grounded in the company fosters acceptance of the implementation and marketing of pilots, as well as later roll-outs.

Phase 6: Evaluation and roll-out

The goal of this phase is to prepare an expansion of the marketing innovation in a series. Successful project results are to be presented to top (marketing) management staff, and subsequently communicated to the organization. The appropriate specialist departments accept the pilots; this may supplement or replace their functions. In order to increase acceptance of successful pilots, it is recommended that the departments concerned be addressed separately in order to break the ice with respect to the "not-invented-here" syndrome and the threat of job enlargement. Innovation "Jour Fixe" ("i-Jour Fixe" or fixed innovation days) provide regular information on new projects. General think-tank events make use of overarching themes, such as impulses received from the world's largest information technology fair, CeBIT, to describe trends that span all departments, and to stimulate interest in participating in rapid prototypes. The roll-out occurs on a national and more general level. If the pilot was restricted to one product in the regional test market, the expansion during the roll-out may include additional individual product groups, or possibly even successive roll-out of the entire brand.

The pilot implementation, and even more so, the series transition, support evidence of the sustainability of the innovation. The best example is the success of the world wide web, which took over traditional functions and revolutionized media planning, direct marketing, direct sales, and customer service.

International aspects

Marketing innovations are, of course, not limited to the geographical confines of the national market in terms of either origin or transferability. Rather, international implementation opportunities arise, provided comparable prerequisites pertain. The five fundamental factors must also be met in international scenarios. For example, a transfer of the PDA marketing portal would only be meaningful if the relevant market has access to the technically equipped devices and operating systems, and if an efficient range potential is available. Web-based and ITC-based innovations are particularly suitable in the case of internationalization, since the same technical standards often apply. The national marketing innovation array is communicated via international committees. Sales markets interested in marketing innovation can then work together with the pioneer countries and central innovators. Due to similar stages of industrialization, cooperation among the markets in Germany, the U.S., Japan, Great Britain, Italy, France, and Spain is particularly strong.

Summary

In summary, it is clear that marketing innovation can contribute decisively to integrated brand differentiation. Marketeers must decide for themselves which innovation fields are relevant with respect to the marketing plan, product, and target group. An effective aid is the adoption of the five fundamental factors of marketing innovation. Moreover, the described model process for innovation forms a practical orientation showing how the transition can be designed, from the definition of the target fields to the transfer to the specialist departments. Marketing innovations are a logical consequence and, at the same time, a promising response to the challenges that tackle modern marketing.

▶ Key Insights

- Marketing innovation is not an end to itself, but rather, secures the future of a brand through selective investment. It constitutes the Research and Development of marketing.
- Management of marketing innovation relies on a clear innovation strategy. This strategy must aim at the "fit" between brand identity, preliminary product development, and intended target groups.
- The innovation strategy defines clear innovation fields, that in turn spark opportunitiy cones.
- Numerous ideas regarding the innovation field flow into the innovation funnel. In-house evaluation is the first step in spreading the idea peer-to-peer.
- Effective innovation management requires the active support of top corporate management.
- Project management should remain with innovation management in order to minimize the "not-invented-here" syndrome within the organization.
- Inefficient marketing innovations should be discarded regardless of origin, if they have been filtered out based on the fundamental marketing innovation factors. Only efficient solutions will succeed.
- Innovation is favored in corporate cultures founded on a common spirit and with an openness towards innovation impulses that fosters competition within the company, but is ultimately consensus-oriented.
- Marketing innovations spread across national borders more easily, if similar conditions exist.

▶ Practical Guidelines

- Establish an innovation management function responsible for all initiatives in marketing development.
- Emotionally fascinating, interactive, personalized concepts, oriented to the digital lifestyle, are extremely promising, since such campaigns permit effective and ongoing CRM.
- Endow the whole company with a spirit for innovation from top to bottom. A common brand identity can function as the cohesive element.
- Integrate all marketing agencies into the innovation management process!
- Maintain close dialogue with the core users involved in the prototype, so as to obtain rapid feedback.

- Ensure that a clearly defined budget for marketing innovation exists. Without a clear budget, the marketing innovations are simply considered "nice-to-have," since the familiarity of experience with traditional instruments often prevents entering into new territory for reasons of security.
- Communicate successful marketing innovation to Group departments, country offices, and trade organizations to ensure greater brand impact.

The Authors

Jörg Dohmen

Jörg Dohmen, born in 1968, studied business at the University of Cologne and, in addition to obtaining his degree there, attained the CEMS Master of International Management through his studies at the Ecole des Hautes Etudes Commerciales (HEC) in Paris. He joined the automotive industry via a trainee program at Ford Werke AG. He held various sales and marketing positions there and finished his time at Ford as Zone Manager in Sales, after which he started as Marketing Manager at Land Rover Deutschland, placing an emphasis on alliances and dealership network changes at the time of the Freelander market launch. When business was transferred by the BMW Group to the Ford Motor Company, he changed to the BMW brand and, in his role as project leader, implemented the first on- and off-line campaigns in direct marketing. As Innovation Manager, he was responsible inter alia for the market launch of the BMW X3 for the BMW Group Deutschland.

Dr. Wolfgang Armbrecht

Dr. Wolfgang Armbrecht, born in 1957, studied business and journalism at the Freie Universität Berlin and received his doctorate in philosophy at the Institut für Publizistik- und Kommunikationswissenschaft (Institute of Journalism and Communication Sciences) at the University of Salzburg. After holding posts in human resources, as well as various management functions in PR and marketing within the BMW Group (including management of marketing communication for the Group in Munich and Tokyo), he is now responsible for leading BMW Marketing in the German market. Previously, he managed the central functional area of innovation management and predevelopment marketing. Wolfgang Armbrecht has taught at the Universities of Salzburg, St. Gallen, and Berlin as guest lecturer.

Literature Recommendations

T. Kelley, J. Littman, "The Art of Innovation: Lessons in Creativity from IDEO, America's Leading Design Firm," New York 2001

G. Corbae, J. B. Jensen, D. Schneider, "Marketing 2.0: Strategies for Closer Customer Relationships," Berlin 2001

A. M. Winkler, "Warp Speed Branding. The Impact of Technology on Marketing," New York 1999

C. Herstatt, J. G. Sander, "Produktentwicklung mit virtuellen Communities. Kundenwünsche erfahren und Innovationen realisieren," Wiesbaden 2004

P. F. Drucker, "The Essential Drucker: The Best of Sixty Years of Peter Drucker's Essential Writings on Management," New York 2003

A. Van de Ven, D. Polley, R. Garud, S. Venkataraman, "The Innovation Journey," New York 1999

P. Kotler, "Ten Deadly Marketing Sins: Signs and Solutions," 2004

P. Kotler, D. C. Jain, S. Maesincee, "Marketing Moves: A New Approach to Profits, Growth & Renewal," Harvard 2002

Markus Hinz – AutoScout24 and ScoutMedia24

Online Advertising

Maximizing the return on advertising (ROA) by applying the eight principles of online advertising

▶ Executive Summary

- Over the last few years, the requirements of marketing communication have changed drastically in the course of globalization, ever increasing competition and, above all, new technologies.
- Online advertising has now become a compulsory element of the communication mix of a competitive company.
- In the majority of cases, the objectives of online advertising can be described on an axis between "brand building" and "sales."
- The portfolio of online advertising disciplines for reaching these objectives is large and heterogeneous. Nevertheless, eight core disciplines can be identified.
- Only a few service providers cover the entire range of these disciplines with the products they offer. Salaried online advertising managers are therefore a worthwhile investment for any marketing department.
- Above all, the discipline "content integration" promises great communication potential. Up to now, little has been written about it although it helps to facilitate the broadest range of advertising effects.
- By using the online advertising model, this article describes the status quo of the eight basic online advertising disciplines, and by using "content integration" as an example, explains the process of implementing an online advertising activity.

▶ Theoretical Model of Online Advertising

1. Definition and core principle

By using various dimensions of online communication effectiveness as a basis, the online advertising model describes the eight basic disciplines or instruments of online advertising. From "attention" to "sales," online advertising instruments each have specific strengths and weaknesses with regard to their effect on target groups that can be reached via the Internet. As the objectives of online advertisers are primarily orientated towards branding or sales, the model concentrates on these two important directions. Within the scope of a definition of the disciplines, details that are relevant to implementation will also be taken into account, as well as national and international market trends and key figures, on a case-by-case basis.

Fig. 1: Factors of online advertising

2. Factors of online advertising

2.1 Display ads (classic online advertising)

Display ads or classical online advertising is most comparable with the well-known offline disciplines such as print, TV, or poster. Standardized means and/or formats of advertising are booked on the basis of a media or spread plan for a thousand contact price (TCP). The prices are oriented to the respective type of advertising and the quality of the target group (advertising medium). The advertising medium tends to have a stronger influence here. Today, the most well-known type of advertising "banner" can cost between 0.5 and 50 euros TCP, depending on the website. Yet, even within a website, there are often different price segments. The more specifically a target group can be selected, the higher the TCPs are – and the lower the losses, due to non-selective advertising among the target groups. Certain topic channels (categories), such as business and finances, car and travel, are often more expensive with multi-topic online portals than the other topic areas of the portal. Consequently, the industry defines the price, too. On monothematic websites such as AutoScout24, the target group can frequently be selected using so-called targeting criteria. The placement of an advertisement can be predefined on the market place of AutoScout24, e.g., depending on the brand sought, the model, or also the price. The campaign is particularly successful when different targeting criteria are combined. The advertising for a new Mercedes all-terrain vehicle can for example, only be shown to the purchasing planners of all-terrain vehicles of the brands BMW, VW, and Mercedes, who want to spend 35,000 EUR on the car. Advertising bookings without a target group selection like this are usually referred to as "run of site."

The agencies and/or advertising service providers for display ads on the Internet have now become almost identical with the established service providers for classical advertising. Most of the large advertising agencies also offer creation and media planning within their network. However, it is less the agency and rather more the technology of the ad server that defines the quality of the campaign controlling and/or reporting. Doubleclick and Falk, for example, offer independent established systems here in Germany. The major online marketers also have a decisive influence on the quality of the performance controlling, the standards of advertising media and the standardized net coverage measurement, too, in Germany.

These marketeers are organized in the online marketing circle (OVK). As a working group of the BVDW (Bundesverband Digitale Wirtschaft or the Federal Association of the Digital Industry), they primarily try to make the market for classical online advertising more transparent and, thus, promote it overall. With major online campaigns today, for instance, up to 100 different formats for the various advertising media (web sites) are created. In addition to "integrated ads," such as the standard banner, the super banner, the skyscraper or rectangles, the most frequent formats are also new window ads such as the pop-up or pop-under or interstitials and different types of "layer ads." Although more and more Internet browsers are offering pop-up blockers, the trend is still towards eye-catching advertising media such as layer ads that are superimposed across websites. With the growing number of people with broadband Internet access, the number of so-called rich media formats is also on the increase. The advertising media are no longer static or animated in a simple way – they also transport videos, audio files, and their own applications such as order forms, online games, or competitions. The most popular programming languages or technologies are HTML, Java, Flash, and Streaming Video.

In addition to online sponsoring and viral marketing, display ads are particularly good for brand building. With rich media formats, it is now also possible to advertise on the Net in a more emotional and striking manner. In the majority of cases, a classical online campaign is made even more successful by networking with offline activities such as TV spots or print adverts (cross-media campaigns). Through the current media and coverage study of the AGOF (Arbeitsgemeinschaft Online Forschung or Working Group on Online Research), the media and target group planning for display ads in Germany is now standardized in a similar way, and is accepted like the media planning for classical offline media. Consequently, the number of cross-media campaigns will definitely grow in the future, and classical online advertising will increasingly becoming a compulsory discipline in the communication mix of "brand building campaigns".

2.2 Paid search and search engine optimization

Those who talk about search engine marketing today nearly always mean keyword advertising (paid search) or the search machine optimization of one's own websites from a "programming and technical" perspective (also index optimization). Today, both are seen as the fastest growing disciplines in the online marketing mix as many people orientate themselves on the Internet with the aid of search engines or the major portals.

With paid searches, the respectively most attractive search terms are booked (or integrated), in line with the marketing objectives, with the search engine operators (e.g., Google) or special service providers (e.g., MIVA or Overture), either directly in the search results page (paid inclusion) or as a link in the thematic surroundings (sponsored link). When the consumer then looks for the term, it is ensured that the advertiser appears with the corresponding search word in one of the "top positions" (listing) on the results page or in the surrounding area. With most remuneration models, payment is only made when the search entry displayed is also then clicked on (pay per click). The starting price for one click is between 10 and 15 cents with most suppliers. However, the price increases rapidly in an analogous manner to an auction if other advertisers are also interested in the search term. The more sought after a search term is, the higher the payment for the click. To avoid this price war, keyword advertisers are optimizing their click budget by booking a host of other related search terms. Although the click probability is not as high as with the ideal search term, the price is then also lower. So through this effort just as many clicks can therefore be bought at a better price. However, the true price-performance ratio can only be measured when the conversion rate with regard to the individual marketing objectives is also measured after the click (e.g., calling up or leaving information behind, or online purchase). The success of a paid-search campaign is, therefore, not only dependent on the efficient purchasing of keywords, but also on the design of your own offer. This can range from the layout of a company information page to the usability of a shop.

As keyword advertising is so popular, competition for the limited inventory of successful search terms and/or top rankings is growing constantly. Some companies now have salaried search machine marketeers who frequently maintain 10,000 keywords and listings. In the optimization of paid search campaigns, the advertising text relating to the keyword, and the thematic context of the search, now also play an increasingly important role. Some service providers offer so-called "matching technologies" for this.

We no longer talk about search engine optimization merely in terms of our own pages, but also when service providers are commissioned with placing so-called "fake pages" on the Net. In the majority of cases, these pages are only found because, in the equal competition for an unpaid "top listing," the domain of these websites matches a certain search term. The content of this website often consists of core applications of the website of the advertiser and of manifold short-lived technical details that are only to be found on this page because they have a positive effect on the search algorithm of the leading search engine.

2.3 Classifieds (small advertisements)

Small ad market places belong to the most commercially successful and most frequented Internet websites. Jupiter Research forecasts a share of 16 percent of overall online advertising spending in Western Europe in 2005 for the classifieds business. For the U.S.A., the analysts have even predicted a doubling of the market by 2009.

Small ad advertising is the advertising of a specific product or a specific service. Similar to the ad markets of daily newspapers or advertising papers, the offer on the Internet is depicted with text information about the product and suppliers as well as picture and price. Through the integration in a database and the large memory space for the product information, the offers on the Internet can be presented in a more comprehensive manner, and can usually be found more quickly. Furthermore, the adverts on the Internet reach the corresponding target group without any losses due to non-selective advertising. In the majority of cases, the large market places such as Scout24 or eBay have the biggest respective available offer of commercial (B2C) and private (C2C) adverts on a national and regional basis. As with the daily newspapers, the most important category markets are cars, houses, contacts, travel, and jobs.

The prices and price logics for online small ads vary. Whereas with most suppliers you have to pay a "listing fee," which is related to how many offers are to be found for how long on the market place, auction platforms allow themselves to share in the success, too. A combination of success-based remuneration and "listing fee" is known from eBay. Often there is also the option of presenting your offer in an even more prominent way. With AutoScout24, dealers can also position their vehicles, for instance, on the home page of the vehicle exchange or in a top position on the search results page (see also 2.2).

Of course, in 99 percent of the cases, Internet small ads have the marketing objective of selling specific products or services. Every now and then, they also serve to make prospective customers aware of additional products and services on the website of the advertiser (click-through). For example, through extremely low-cost bait advertising.

As the users of Internet small ads market places are primarily acute purchasing planners for the corresponding products and services, advertisers are currently discovering these market places more and more as an environment for their classical online campaigns. For example, it is seldom the case that AutoScout24 is not represented in a media plan for a new or used car campaign of a car manufacturer. Extremely good key reporting figures and long-term commitments such as, for instance, "content integrations" (see 2.8) prove its success.

2.4 E-mail and newsletter marketing

E-mail marketing is the digital form of classical direct or dialogue marketing. The recipients receive the communication content not offline via the traditional postal route, but online via the Internet (web-based e-mail). Usually, e-mail marketing is used by advertisers in relation to a campaign or on a continuous basis, for instance, to maintain customer relationships. The regular sending of mostly standardized e-mails to a defined target group is also called newsletter marketing. Whereas advertisers usually acquire the e-mail addresses for the newsletters to customers and other dialogue groups of the respective company themselves, e-mail addresses for campaign e-mail marketing (e.g., acquisition of new customers) are often rented or bought from list brokers. The two most common marketing communication objectives for e-mail marketing are, therefore, customer care (dialogue, information, sales) and customer acquisition (acquisition, sales). In addition, through the dialogue, e-mail marketing is also a superb instrument for generating user insights (market research). The classical dialogue marketing agencies help in the implementation of e-mail marketing campaigns. From concept through creation, address management, and shipping, everything is mostly provided on a "one-stop shop" basis. However, for Internet companies or companies that regularly send out a relatively large number of newsletters, it is recommended establishing a part of the necessary know-how in-house. With the aid of content management systems, it is possible, for example, to have the newsletter created in the technology or marketing department. Specialized service providers such as e-circle or Falk take over the dispatching and the address management.

Today, e-mail marketing is one of the fastest and most cost-effective online advertising instruments with the greatest coverage. However, there are some criteria that should be observed without fail for successful e-mail communication. The most important criterion is undoubtedly that the recipient must have given his permission for the receipt of a mail beforehand (permission-based). E-mails without such permission are predominantly viewed as spam e-mails and are often already rejected by spam filters of the respective e-mail programs of the recipients. The "opt-in" or "double opt-in" procedure, for instance, should therefore be used with the registration for a newsletter subscription. With a newsletter that the recipient has already received, it should be possible at any time to cancel the newsletter again with one click (one-click unsubscribe). Another essential parameter of success is the design of the mail. In addition to general usability and dialogue perspectives, attention should be paid, above all, to a meaningful sender address and reference line, and to a personal form of address for the recipient. With the dispatching, care should be taken that the mail is sent from a fixed IP address where possible. Dynamic addresses are already viewed by many spam filters as a criterion for filtering. For this reason, the recipient address should not be written in the CC or BCC field. The time of sending (day and time) is another criterion for success, just like the test dispatch (variations, all links active?). E-mail and newsletter marketing should be continually optimized through the consistent analysis of possible measuring quantities such as e.g., opening rate, click rate, number of purchases or further recommendations, development of the subscriber numbers. According to a survey by the Web service provider Doubleclick (2005), the average response or click rate to an answer link is 8.6 percent globally. At the same, the opening rate of all "permission-based" advertising mails is 34.4 percent.

However, as a result of the spam problem and the distribution of computer viruses through e-mail, campaign e-mail marketing (acquisition e-mail marketing) does also have some limitations with regard to the target group. Only 32 percent of Internet users in Europe have any interest at all in receiving e-mails like these (Jupiter Research 2004). Southern Europeans, such as the Spanish (38%) and Italians (47%), are significantly more interested in "direct commercial communication" by e-mail than the Northern Europeans (D 30%, F 29%, U.K. 25%). However, according to Jupiter, the potential in "web-based e-mail users" is highest, in Germany (30.2 million users), England (19.3 million), and France (16.3 million). Users who give their permission for e-mail marketing communications are definitely not representative. Instead, like the target group for viral marketing, they have a greater affinity with technology and experience in dealing with the Internet. Many of these users are also so-called bargain hunters and competition pros.

2.5 Viral marketing

Generally, viral marketing refers to a distribution or communication strategy that puts its faith in the prompt epidemic and/or viral spread of services or communication content through multipliers in the Internet. Whereas the distribution strategy mostly follows expansionary objectives (e.g., free-of-charge spreading of new software, commission/snow ball systems for the acquisition of new customers), viral marketing is used in communication to make a brand better known or to update it.

With the spread of brand messages, the advertiser makes use of the rapid multiplication effects in social communication networks. Within a very short time, a viral marketing campaign can achieve huge coverage (reach). The advertising formats are mostly short videos (streaming video), images (e.g., jpg), games, eCards, text and presentation formats (e.g., Power Point) or links to websites. In the majority of cases, the advertising is spread through e-mails. However, chat rooms or community websites such as online exchange markets are also suitable as a breeding ground for viral communication.

In addition to the opportunity to establish a great coverage within a very short period of time, the strengths of viral marketing lie primarily in the high involvement of the target group and/or the impact of the advertising, and in the cost-efficiency of the activities. Furthermore, viral e-mail marketing is one of the best possibilities for avoiding spam filters. The weaknesses lie in particular in the measurability (e.g., coverage) and the control of the activities. Once the advertising has been published, you can no longer control who gets to see the message when, what, how much, and how often. The biggest problem here is without doubt the target group ("who"). According to Jupiter Research (2004), only four percent of the "onliners" in Europe are willing at all to forward advertising messages. In addition, the profile of these onliners is not representative of the web community. Approx. 65 percent are younger than 34, 56 percent are male, and 62 percent already have more than two years online experience.

The success factors for viral marketing are the distribution or first positioning of advertising (seeding the virus) and the creative idea of the implementation. With regard to the distribution, it is important to identify corresponding multipliers for the communication messages beforehand. With the idea, it has been shown that primarily humorous, current, and erotic content has the biggest chance of being distributed further.

2.6 Affiliate marketing

"Affiliate marketing" refers to the success-based rewarding of fixed advertising partners (website operators) within an advertiser's partner network of a desired size. The settlement model for advertising like this is often called CPX (cost per action). The advertiser (also merchant) defines himself what type of campaign or transaction necessitated by the advertising is paid, and how high the remuneration should be. "Affiliate marketing" is therefore a perfect instrument for sales and transaction-oriented online advertising. Originally, practically only Internet dealers such as Amazon.com ran their own affiliate or partner programs. It is only since 1999 that there have been service providers in Europe who provide advertisers or program operators with the technical infrastructure for external affiliate management. Affilinet, Tradedoubler, and Zanox are, for example, suppliers that have been running affiliate platforms like these in Germany and up to 20 other countries since 1999/2000. The service providers usually charge the advertisers around 30 percent of the monthly affiliate remuneration. For this, the program operator is provided with the individual technical infrastructure (e.g., management/admin tool) and is relieved of the entire monthly accounting with the individual affiliate partners.

Despite the possible outsourcing, at least one additional salaried employee should be employed for setting up and maintaining a partner program. On this subject, Jupiter Research published a survey of 174 affiliate advertisers in 2005. According to this, 74 percent have employed one or two affiliate managers. Only 10 percent of the companies have nobody from among their own employees who is responsible for the affiliate program.

With the incentivization of the affiliate partners, it has been shown that a remuneration system that is differentiated according to the length of the partnership and/or the overall sales is advantageous for retaining the best partners in this dynamic market in the long term.

2.7 Online sponsoring

Sponsoring on the Internet is still a relatively thinly spread and standardized discipline. Mostly, the term online sponsoring is equated with so-called content sponsoring. In a similar way to conventional sponsoring (e.g., sports, culture, social, or program sponsoring), the service of a sponsoring recipient (often the operator of an Internet website) is presented by a sponsor in content sponsoring, too. The service of the website is almost always exclusive content with high benefit for a specific target group that exactly matches the communication policy objectives of the sponsor. For example, every now and then, content that is normally available for a fee, is offered free of charge through the commitment of a sponsor for a limited period of time. In contrast to classical online advertising (see 2.1), the commitment of a sponsor to the advertising medium is more long-term. The service is paid in money, which is not, however, measured by classical media performance values (e.g., TCP or click) – it is defined beforehand as a fixed fee. However, in rare cases, the performance of the sponsoring recipient is also compensated with payment in kind or services.

The sponsoring normally only becomes visible through the depiction of a company emblem (logo) and the textual reference "sponsored by" or "powered by": the logo is then linked with the website of the sponsor just like a banner or a pop-up. Today, in addition to the logo, text, images, sound, and even moving picture content of a sponsor can be found on the page of an advertising medium. The boundaries to "content integration" and/or the "content placement" are fluid here (see 2.8).

Online sponsoring pursues predominantly branding objectives and is an excellent instrument for maintaining relationship management with defined target groups in a cost-effective and long-term manner (contact and dialogue option with the sponsor). For corporate communication, online sponsoring should actually be the first choice. Through the discreet, unremarkable appearance, you avoid the risk of increasing user reaction to online advertising (e.g., pop-ups). And by combining the brand with a direct added value for the user (attractive content), the sponsor profits through transfer effects in the perception. Furthermore, many of the sponsored topics (e.g., environment, culture, social) also have high additional potential for PR activities.

According to a Jupiter analysis, five to ten percent of the overall budget for pure event sponsoring should be reserved right from the beginning for additional online activities. The brand conditioning of an event is supported by the supplementary multi-dimensional medium Internet in a sustained and long-term way. For example, through e-mail messaging info concerning the event, video clips of the event, or forums about the event.

2.8 Content integration

By content integration, we understand the primarily long-term and comprehensive integration of online content of an advertiser in an Internet advertising medium. As a differentiation to online cooperations or strategic partnerships (also partnering), the integration always costs money and serves exclusively commercial purposes. In particular the inflationary used word "online cooperations" is often used in connection with "win-win partnerships" with regard to the supplementing or expanding of the value creation chains of two partners.

The difference to content placement lies in the dimension of the link. Whereas placement is often based on a short-term technical link, with integration, a longer term, deeper and technically more complex connection to the website of the advertiser exists. That is why content placement is assigned more to the discipline of display ads.

Content refers to any website content of an advertiser. From service and offer descriptions through market place databases, online calculators (e.g., financing), booking, and shop systems, to product configurators and specific search applications, any kind of online-based content is conceivable. The number of remuneration models is just as varied. Fixed fees, CPX (cost per action), and TCP models are the most popular accounting forms here. However, also hybrid systems (e.g., fixed fee + CPX) are by all means normal as remuneration of content integration. Mostly, the remuneration is oriented to the online advertising objective. The rule of thumb here is as follows: the more sales-oriented the objective is, the stronger the pay-per-performance (CPX) specification is. The more strongly that the objectives for content integration serve brand building, the more probable a fixed fee or a TCP model is.

Content integration supports practically all conceivable marketing communication objectives, but offers the greatest potential when it concerns the information of and interaction with very specific target groups. Or put another way: if the communication planning is based on the AIDA model, the use of "content integration" most probably supports the advertising impact parameters "interest" and "desire." However, action (e.g., online transactions) can also be a promising communication objective when the integration is designed accordingly from a content point of view. For "attention" there are undoubtedly more suitable online advertising disciplines, such as display ads. The fact of long-term integration on a well-known and popular Internet platform alone, can already be a communication objective with regard to a positive brand and/or image transfer.

In most cases, online agencies are involved in the implementation of content integration. For example, the so-called "car worlds" of the car manufacturers at AutoScout24 are created and supported almost exclusively by the same service providers that are also responsible for the manufacturers' own Internet presence (content). The media planning and purchasing is done primarily through the media agencies specialized in Internet advertising. As long-term content integration requires detailed descriptions of the product performance and performance measurements, there are often no standardized offerings and orders. Instead, there are individual contracts between advertising media and advertisers (respectively agencies).

In addition to the content itself, the most important criterion for the success of content integration is the placement of content on the respective website. This is done mostly according to target group criteria in related category fields and should be optimized continually using the defined performance key figures. Furthermore, the additional advertising of the integration contributes to the success, too. For example, through additional display ads, editorial reports, e-mail advertising (newsletter), or PR activities, the partnership should be made known and constantly supplied with related traffic in a targeted manner. The content should be up-to-date, wherever possible, and should give a service-oriented, factual, and informative impression rather than that of advertising. The user of the website should perceive the integrated content as a real benefit in terms of a service and/or editorial information added value.

▶ Process & Implementation

Overview

The process for content integration is largely exemplary for all other online advertising disciplines. Starting with the objective formulation for the advertising activity, the process change up to the control of performance and optimization of the activity is described using the most important criteria for success in each case.

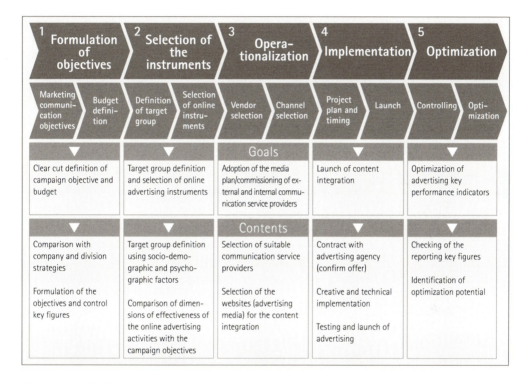

Fig. 2: Process of online advertising

Phase 1: Objective formulation

The online marketing communication objectives can be defined when they have been derived from the corporate strategy and the marketing strategy of the company. In nearly all cases, online advertising either has sales objectives, branding objectives, or market and competition oriented objectives:

- Brand building: create awareness, remove barriers, update brands, emotionalize, provide information about the performances of the brand, change the attitude towards the brand, etc.
- Sales: acquire new customers/users, more sales with existing customers, retain customers, etc.
- Market and competition: set market entry barriers, survey on market and consumer insights, etc.

The objectives for content integration are mostly long-term (long term > 6 months) and are often complex (see also 2.8).

CASE With the content integration "BMW Service World" at AutoScout24, BMW is aiming primarily to provide BMW drivers with information about the services of the service area, and the original parts and accessory products of BMW. However, at the same time, the content integration also facilitates direct contact (address, lead) through the ordering of information material or a newsletter subscription.

Fig. 3: Example for content integration. The content of the BMW Service World at AutoScout24 reflects the communication objectives

By searching for BMW service partners, the direct route to the supplier of the services is advertised and, furthermore, traffic for BMW original services is ensured on the BMW Internet site through the invitation "Visit our Internet site."

In principle, the following rule of thumb applies in online advertising for the objective formulation for content integration:

Product before brand communication: consumers are looking primarily for product and offer information on the Internet. The brand communication should therefore take place on the website of the advertiser and in a lower-ranking role within the framework of content integration on an advertising medium.

Parallel to the objectives, the budget framework for a content integration should, of course, be defined. As content integration covers so many potential communication objectives, the budget share of the online advertising budget can be up to 100 percent. With the calculation, you should take into consideration that fees for the service providers (planning, design, programming) and possible software costs (e.g., ASP solutions) occur, in addition to the media costs. It should be differentiated between one-off and running costs for the integration.

International aspects

Depending on the products advertised (portfolio), the market development, positioning, the brand status and the communication budget, the objectives of an advertiser can differ from country to country.

CASE However, the example of BMW shows that complex long-term measures such as a content integration can also be adapted in other countries.

Fig 4: BMW also advertises for services and original parts and accessories on the website of AutoScout24 in Italy

Phase 2: Selection of the instruments

Before the online advertising instruments are chosen, the communication objectives, and also the target groups for the activities, are defined. As there are no accepted market and media studies for the Internet in the majority of countries, the online activity planning is often still carried out on the basis of topic and interest areas of the target groups (e.g., car, business, lifestyle, etc.). However, more and more often, the target group is being described using socio-demographic or psychographic characteristics in the course of the standardization of coverage research. As addressing the suitable target group is a fundamental success factor for online advertising, it is recommended to make this as differentiated as possible. On the Internet, losses due to non-selective advertising can virtually be excluded if the communication is planned accordingly. The advertising medium AutoScout24 has therefore analyzed the value orientation of particular segments using the semiometry procedure to additionally verify the target group matching, for example.

CASE   The selection of the appropriate online advertising instruments is then done on the basis of advertising objective, target group, and budget. Part 2 of this article provides information on the respective effect dimensions, strengths and weaknesses, the market significance, and the remaining characteristics of the important instruments. The instrument content integration is primarily selected when long-term and cost-effective "top" target groups (e.g., car purchasing planners, BMW drivers, etc) are to be informed and an interaction is to be achieved with the target group on the basis of this information (e.g., transactions). It is still only a relatively small number of advertising media that offer the instrument of content integration in a standardized form in the course of the remaining media data.

Instruments					
Small Ads	E-Mail/Newsletter	Content Integration	Key Word Advert.	Classic Online Adv.	Sponsoring/Prom.
Car market	AS24 News	Premium partner	Top ad for	Banner/SuperBanner	Content-sponsoring
Motorcycle market	(1x week)	Car world	car dealers	Pop-up/-under/Layer	Competition
Commercial vehicles market	AS24 News Special	Service world		Interstitial/Sky-Scraper	Sponsoring
Parts/accessories	AS24 News/Targeting	Shop integration		LinkBox/TandemAd	Online-games
	List Brokerage			Rectangle-Formate	Voting-tools
					BrandDays
Dimensions of effectiveness					
Sales •• Brand-Building					
Sales, Transaction, Lead, Address, Contact, Dialog, Information, Response, Recall, Recognition, Attention					

Fig. 5: Online advertising offer portfolio from AutoScout24 (including content integration)

International aspects
Not every country offers the same possibilities for online advertising. The spread of the Internet, technical availability (broadband), and specific cultural peculiarities are important influencing factors on the shaping of the advertising disciplines in the individual countries. An example of cultural differences is described in point 2.4 "e-mail marketing."

Phase 3: Operationalization
Within the scope of the decision for an online advertising instrument, the selection of potential service providers is also performed. In the implementation of content integration, service providers usually support advertisers in the following topics:

- Strategy (e.g., selection online advertising instrument).
- Planning (e.g., selection advertising medium, address advertising medium).
- Implementation (e.g., contract negotiations, design, programming).
- Operation (e.g., performance reporting, updating, optimization).
- Dissolution (e.g., termination of contract, conclusion).

The usual service providers for content integration are marketing and/or management consultants, Internet advertising agencies, and media agencies with online unit, and/or online media specialist agencies, as well as online marketeers.

CASE   The BMW Service World at AutoScout24 is supported on the part of BMW by, for example, the online media agency PlanNet (selection advertising media) and the Internet agency BBDO Interone (design), and on the part of AutoScout24 by the marketeer Scout24 Media (integration).

The selection of a suitable advertising media is mostly done using these criteria:

- Range of the advertising medium (e.g., unique audience).
- Affinity with the target groups (e.g., user structure data, targeting and placement options).
- Image of the advertising medium (due to the possible brand and/or image transfer).
- Remuneration model and general price-performance ratio.
- Technical infrastructure (e.g., reporting tool, general site performance).

The aims of the advertisers and the advertising medium should be complementary in the long term and be oriented to the benefit of the target group with regard to their content and implementation. That is why the following online marketing rule of thumb applies, above all, in the selection of the advertising medium.

Consumer before technology orientation: the simplest design in the right environment works better than the most elaborate animations that are in the wrong place. The technical challenge of the advertising media should rather be the analysis of user insights to minimize losses through non-specific advertising. For instance, log file analyses of usage behavior and the resulting target group segmentation options, for instance, should therefore be part of the know-how of an advertising medium for content integration.

International aspects

Qualification and service spectrum of the online advertising service providers can also differ from country to country. In principle, it is recommended to contact classical advertising agencies. If in doubt, the agencies have cooperations or partners for specific online requirements, such as the design and programming of content integration. In the selection of the advertising media, it is undoubtedly an advantage to select "international" websites if the activity is to be carried out in different countries, too (see also AutoScout24/BMW case; Phase 1).

Phase 4: Implementation

The implementation phase extends from the service description to the launch of content integration. It thus incorporates the entire design and programming process, too. As most of the detailed decisions are made in this phase, and the coordination effort between advertisers, service providers and advertising media is at its greatest, a project plan that is accepted by all participants should be developed, at the latest, for the individual steps of the implementation. The master plan should include at least the following sub-projects:

- Service description (e.g., definition of the integrated content, placement etc.).
- Contract negotiation (e.g., remuneration model and conditions, duration, etc.).
- Design (e.g., corporate design, navigation logics, etc.).
- Programming (e.g., new applications, interfaces, level of linkage, etc.).

- Testing (e.g., links active?, usability, speed of page build-up, etc.).
- Launch (e.g. networking of the "going live date" with further activities such as PR)

The most important points in the service description and the contract and proposal design are mostly identical:

- Description of the placement on the advertising medium (incl. location, linkage).
- Definition of the content (type and scope).
- Definition of the branding logics (1. Co-Branding, 2. "Presented By" or 3. White-Label = Branding of the advertising medium). Exclusivity? (Competition exclusion for content integration or, additionally, other online advertising forms, as well).
- Pricing (remuneration model and conditions, see also 2.8).
- Additional services (e.g., classical online advertising for the launch or as an accompaniment).
- Reporting (which key figures of advertising performance are made available, when, and how).
- Legal issues (e.g., obligations, liability risks, data protection, warranty, trademark laws and copyright).
- Duration and/or terms of notice.

CASE Example for the branding logics "Presented By" AutoScout24 marketplace integrated at T-Online.

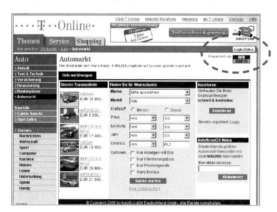

Fig. 6: Integrated in the "look and feel" of T-Online is the used car database of AutoScout24, from the vehicle search, right through to the results in the car category of T-Online. Only the reference "Presented by AutoScout24" indicates to the user the origin of the content

With regard to the definition of suitable content for content integration, the following rule of thumb in online advertising should be taken into account:

Practical value before experience value: where possible, the content should be oriented relevantly and directly to the core benefits of the advertised products and services, and primarily, should not be presented emotionally or indirectly (e.g., through competitions, games, advertising spots, etc.). For the implementation sub-projects design and programming, the following applies:

Information before entertainment: the medium Internet primarily offers interactive information and commerce environments, not classical one-way entertainment such as radio or TV. The design of the advertising forms should take this into account. Although broadband formats have been heralded as a mega trend for years, they very rarely match the media usage behavior of the Internet. This applies particularly for content integrations.

For the launch of long-term content integration, advertisers and advertising media should draw attention to the content partnership through additional activities.

CASE   Through the weekly AutoScout24 newsletter, BMW and AutoScout24, for example, have reported to more than 500,000 subscribers about the use of the BMW Service World, in addition to the standard placement of various display ads (link box, rectangle, etc), and have also started a classic online campaign based on the targeting criterion "Search for BMW."

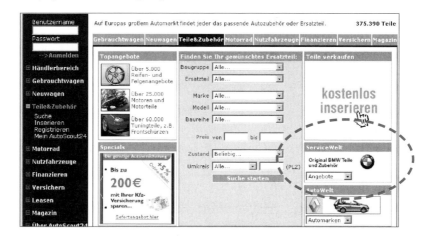

Fig. 7: Example of a standard placement of the BMW Service World at Autoscout24: "Original BMW parts and accessories" on the home page of the parts and accessory exchange of AutoScout24

International aspects

Particularly with regard to remuneration, there are international differences. With fewer standardized instruments, such as content integration, for example, the greatest differences can be seen. However, also the legal boundary conditions, such as liability, data protection, or warranty, must be checked in each country on an individual basis.

Phase 5: Optimization

The optimization of content integration is based on the definition, survey (reporting), and analysis of key figures for advertising performance. Depending on the marketing communication objective (e.g., brand building or sales promotion), measurable key figures should be determined in advance. The most common units of measurement for the performance control of content integration are for instance:

- Ad view (Ad impression): number of advertising contacts (content contacts).
- Brand awareness: increase of brand recognition or advertising recall (recall and recognition) in percent.
- Visits: number of visits on a defined area of content.

- Visits, pages and time per person: visits, called-up pages, and average visiting time per content user (unique).
- Ad clicks: number of clicks on defined links from the integrated content section.
- Lead: number of prospects (addresses) for products or services.
- Transaction: number of generated transactions (e.g., transactions or use of a service) in pieces and/or sales.

Most of these key figures can be surveyed in a standardized manner through the use of ad serving software (e.g. Falk or Doubleclick) by the marketer or the advertising medium. The performance control of branding objectives such as for example increase in awareness, appeal or also the change of attitudes, can only be achieved using "Before-After-Surveys". In the majority of cases, it is the advertiser who ensures the reporting of key sales figures (e.g. through the interface to the enterprise resource planning system. As content integration is a long-term online advertising activity, a survey of the key figures should be made in regular intervals so that optimization can take place within the framework of regular operation (e.g. updating of the editorial topics). For instance, AutoScout24 measures the key figures of the AutoScout24 subsidiaries from ADAC to T-Online (see below) on a daily basis. The decisive success criterion for AutoScout24 with content integrations on these portals is the directly measurable demand in the form of e-mails to car dealers who have placed ads.

CASE

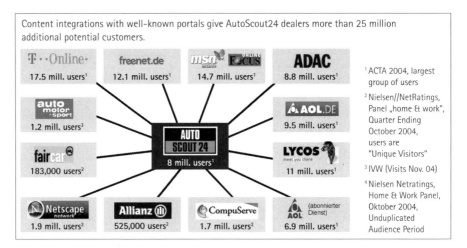

Fig. 8: The content partnerships of AutoScout24

International aspects

There are no international reporting standards for online advertising. In most cases, ad server technologies, units of measurement, and the methods of coverage measurement/research are already different. The Interactive Advertising Bureau Europe (www.iabeurope.ws) provides answers to questions regarding standards in individual European countries.

▶ Key Insights

- ☐ The Internet is the central technology for managing the market places of today and, therefore, compulsory in the marketing communication mix of a competitive company.
- ☐ Depending on the communication objective, the Internet offers eight fundamental online advertising disciplines.
- ☐ More than 90 percent of the objectives of online advertising can be described on an axis between "brand building" and "sales."
- ☐ The selection of online advertising instruments is done using the communication objectives and the respective dimensions of effectiveness on the defined target group.
- ☐ Content integration offers the biggest spectrum of advertising impact of all online advertising disciplines.
- ☐ As content integration is a very young discipline that has not been standardized very much to date, it still offers great development perspectives and opportunities for "first movers."
- ☐ The success of content integration depends above all on the clear definition of the objectives, the correct choice of partner, and the consistent optimization of key reporting figures

▶ Practical Guidelines

- ☐ Ensure that the online advertising activities are oriented to the value creation processes of the company.
- ☐ If you are continually investing in online advertising disciplines, such as affiliate management, paid search, or content integration, you should build up your own employees.
- ☐ With all the technical possibilities of online advertising, never lose sight of the target group: consumer before technology orientation.
- ☐ Information before entertainment: most people are looking for information on the Internet. Design the advertising in an informative way, too.
- ☐ Classical online advertising (display ads) must not necessarily be the first activity in the online activity mix. Check the strengths and weaknesses of all online advertising instruments against your objectives.
- ☐ On the Internet put your faith in established and well-known advertising media with a wide coverage within your media target group.
- ☐ Consistently observe the online advertising market. Above all, analyze how established Internet brands woo consumers on the Net.

The Author

Markus Hinz

Since February 2001, Markus Hinz, born in 1967, has been responsible, as one of the company's three managing directors, for the German activities of AutoScout24 and for Scout24 Media. His tasks include responsibility for marketing, key account and content management. After completing his communication studies, majoring in market and advertising psychology in Munich, he began his professional career in January 1993 at Media Markt und Saturn Verwaltungs GmbH in Munich, where his last position in 1997 was head of the product marketing team of the Media Markt headquarters. Before he moved to AutoScout24 in April 1999, he was head of marketing at Möbel Unger for just under two years.

Literature Recommendations

W. Fritz, "Internet-Marketing und Electronic Commerce," Wiesbaden 2004
M. Büttgen, F. Lücke (eds.), "Online Kooperationen," Wiesbaden 2003
M. Dannenberg, F.H. Wildschütz, "Erfolgreiche Online-Werbung," Göttingen 2004
Jupiter Research, "Paid Search in Europe, European Online Advertising Forecasts 2003 to 2009. Viral Marketing, Affiliate Marketing, Local Online Advertising, Pan European Online Advertising, Acquisition E-Mail Marketing," 2004
P. Kotler, D. Jain, S. Maesincee, "Marketing Moves," 2002

Michael Rüthnick, Robert Moffett – Masterfoods Inc.

Viral Marketing

Communication strategy at low cost that uses word of mouth as vehicle to reach a broad audience

▶ Executive Summary

"Even those deaf to the bragging cries of the marketplace will listen to a friend." *Paddi Lund*

Viral marketing offers an approach to "narrow-cast" communication that in an increasingly fragmented world is likely to become evermore important. It allows you to use your own current consumers as a means of transmitting your message by leveraging the latest technologies and understanding of human and group consumer habits. A powerful idea, correctly implemented can offer high-speed coverage, at potentially lower cost than classic, media routes. There are risks involved, however, and excellent preparation and planning is vital. To make it all happen:

- Start with a strong idea that is so newsworthy for your consumers, that not only will they try your product, but also reach for their address books to share your idea with other people.
- Build in elements that allow your idea to stick in the mind of your consumers.
- Create ways that make it as easy as possible for your consumers to share your idea or message with other people.
- Move to a "Tipping Point" by proactively seeding the "virus" to connect consumers and linking various target groups together.
- Track the progress of your message in real time to optimize its spread. Thorough up-front planning and contingency plans will help here.

A smart combination of all the above, plus lots of hard work and some luck, will maximize the chance of your idea or message becoming the next big viral epidemic.

▶ Theoretical Model of Viral Marketing

"Ignite consumer networks and then get out of the way and let them talk!" *Seth Godin*

1. Definition and core principle

One definition of viral marketing is "a communications strategy that aims to spread ideas to large numbers of potential customers using natural consumer communities and personal contacts as the key transmission medium." Viral marketing is a phenomenon of word of mouth exchanges through which ideas, products, messages and behaviors spread like biological viruses during epidemics. Marketing and biological viruses have three characteristics in common: firstly they are contagious, secondly the impact they can have is huge relative to their size, and thirdly the spread of the virus is not constant. There can be small isolated outbreaks and slow builds, but at some point a "tipping point" is reached, spread becomes exponential, and an epidemic starts. For a marketing virus, an epidemic occurs when your brand or product becomes the thing to have, to be seen with, to own and to talk about. It is the characteristic of a slow build-up that at some point "tips over" that distinguishes the viral method from other classic mass marketing approaches. Personal recommendation is a key part of the process and can be either explicit or implicit in nature (i.e., "I'm using it so I think it's good"). In either case, the most powerful executions of this form of word-of-mouth marketing spread not only because of the recommendations, but because there is some form or in-built low risk way a consumer can test, try, or experience the product or brand.

The drivers behind viral marketing

It is natural to want to find good advice and also to share what you think others will find useful with them. Over the course of human evolution, these behaviors have helped ensure our survival. Viral marketing "leverages this instinctive behavior to achieve a brand's objectives." When you find a consumer who is not only interested, but also passionate enough to promote the benefits of your product publicly to other personal contacts, it is likely that those contacts will also be interested in your product. Sharing in person, or increasingly, over the Net, your consumers find out about your product and the virus spreads.

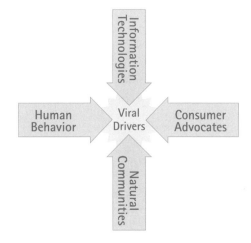

Fig. 1: The four drivers behind viral marketing

To make the most of viral marketing, we seek to understand and influence the spread of the idea by understanding under what circumstances it is infectious and which groups of people are most susceptible to catching and transmitting the idea. In this respect the marketeer does the same job as an epidemiologist. However, the latter is trying to minimize the spread while the former is doing all they can to enhance it.

For a marketeer to build this understanding, they will have to reach beyond the obvious communities to which we all belong, for example, our families, work place, neighborhood, churches, and clubs, etc. One reason for the increased interest in the viral approach has been the development of new virtual communities to which many of us belong. This may be via our Internet subscriptions, chat-rooms, e-mail, mobile phones, and SMS messages that make it easier for us to connect and share ideas with like-minded people at high speed and beyond traditional geographic boundaries. This ease of transmission and connection is why new technologies have been important in the development of viral marketing as a practical marketing tool.

Another factor in the development of viral marketing has been the increasing challenge faced by classic mass media marketing. At its best, viral marketing offers a valuable tool for high impact, low waste communication at a substantially lower cost than a classic mass media approach. New Yorker Magazine journalist, Malcolm Gladwell, brought much of this research to the mainstream in his article and subsequent book "The Tipping Point." Gladwell analyzed the different factors underlying various types of social epidemics and how these epidemics progressed from inception onwards. Since then the many renowned marketers including Seth Godin, Emanuel Rosen, and George Silverman have sought to help marketeers proactively leverage these techniques and stimulate marketing epidemics.

2. Factors in viral marketing

Since the birth of marketing, classic mass media channels (television, radio, and press) have been the marketeer's mainstay, and their use as a strategy in the progression to achieve maximum penetration in as short a time as possible is well known. Viral marketing differs in that the technique relies on a slow build approach. For example, rather than blasting your message to everyone, it is initially seeded within a select group of key influencers and lead users. As they are "infected" with the idea, and share it with others, momentum builds up until at a certain critical point, all being well, the idea explodes and the spread becomes exponential. This is the start of the epidemic. The moment of this explosion is known as the "tipping point."

The progression from seeding to explosion involves different types of consumers and influencers at various stages. These include "Innovators," "Early Adopters," and "Connectors." As well as a powerful core idea, there must also be a tightly focused target, enough virulence or "stickiness" to prevent it being lost in the maelstrom of other media and a contagion route that allows the virus to pass from one person or community to another – the "spreadability" factor.

2.1 Newsworthy idea

For viral marketing to work the consumer needs to be more than just interested, they must be "wild" about the idea. They also must be confident enough that others they know will find the idea interesting enough to risk sharing it with them. The idea must be unique, different, and noticeable: one that the consumer can identify with. The boring and banal just won't cut through. There will be many cases in which a product may not be interesting enough for a viral approach to work. It is also true that the challenges of deploying viral strategies are greater in product categories where products are relatively undifferentiated, everyday, or have negative associations. In these cases other techniques should be applied.

Fig. 2: The creation of the right situation for a viral activity requires different activities.

2.2 Focused target

You can unlock opportunities by digging deep into the consumer's psyche and finding out what matters to them about a product. Likewise, understanding how the process of idea transmission will play out is essential. This is at the heart of the viral approach. Typically there will be a small number of people who will have had a disproportionate impact on transmission. Gladwell termed this phenomenon the "Law of the Few." There are four main groups, whose role and influence vary as the process progresses:
- The "Innovators" or style leaders are crucial in introducing an idea. They are people who love to try out the new and are the first to be infected. They love the fact they are at the edge and may try wild and wacky ideas just for the hell of it. These are the people that make something cool.
- "Passionate Early Users." This group is key in the idea optimization, seeding and "crossover" stages while an idea moves from fashionable niche towards mainstream phenomenon. They take something that is "wacky" and "cool" and adapt it to make it more palatable to the masses. They are able to understand and articulate the different wants and needs of the masses.

- Key Influencers are critical in the spreading process as an idea amplifies and moves to the mainstream. Again these influencers can be split into highly credible and independent expert advocates or "Mavens," as well as sponsored "Salespeople" and "Spokespeople."
- "Connectors" are those people at the heart of various groups who are extremely well connected and regularly share what they know with others. They are key during the transmission stage.

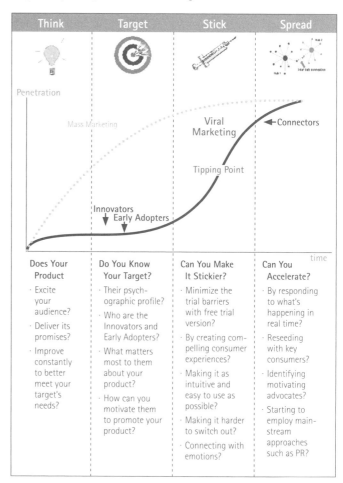

Fig. 3: Course of a viral marketing epidemic and the issues to be dealt with

CASE BlackBerry seeds the boardroom

Canadian company RIM developed and in 1999 launched the BlackBerry after some 10 years perfecting wireless e-mail. Rather than follow the usual route through the IT departments, RIM identified a small group of very senior executives working in investment banking, consultancies, and law firms, where fast information sharing is critical. They seeded their offer of a full experience of BlackBerry functionality via key conferences and trade shows. To remove another barrier, software was developed to allow this to happen without integration to the company servers. This activity allowed them to test the product, and recruit high influence advocates who were able to buzz together. This successful strategy meant BlackBerry did not need formal advertising for the first 18 months and today the BlackBerry has become a "must have" for the connected professional.

Given their importance to the process, a deep understanding of the values, demands, and motivations of these different groups is key to enabling the viral message to be refined and optimised as the idea rolls out. It is this understanding that allows the right choices to be made about what levers should be used for "seeding" and spreading your idea virus. Finding the highest quality targets – those with the greatest chance of getting infected and spreading an idea – is the way to maximize the efficiency of your seeding strategy.

2.3 Stickiness

For a message to become infectious, it must have "sticking power," otherwise it will get lost in the maelstrom of information, ideas, and commercials that consumers face every day. This "sticking power" depends on how many "stickiness factors" have been built into an idea. These can be divided into Physical Factors and Psychological Factors. Physical factors are inherent obstacles that have been designed into a concept that prevent easy switching to competitor products. The psychological factors are those that enhance the retention and activation of a message. This may be something that triggers a basic need or "hook" (personal safety, belonging, etc.), some kind of reward or bait (e.g., a means of benefiting from sharing a message) or may be natural reactions to layout and design. The Google example in the sidebar shows how both of these have been employed as part of their communications strategy. In general it is true to say that the simple, more focused, memorable, and relevant a message is, the stickier it will be.

CASE Google stickiness

Google used both physical and psychological means to spread their message. The layout, style, and feel is kept simple and clean. The company limits the number of words on the home page. This helps users – many of whom may lack confidence – to feel less threatened. The simplicity and user friendliness makes this search engine psychologically sticky. The various free tools give the physical stickiness. Once you've downloaded the free toolbar that integrates with Internet Explorer, it becomes easier to use Google – you no longer have to type in your Favourites link and stop using competitor search engines. The captive audience can then form a springboard to new services such as the auction site Froogle, Local search, mapping, and news services.

2.4 Spreadability

As in nature, once unleashed, the spread and impact of a virus or viral ideas is unpredictable and to a large extent uncontrollable. The best hope a marketeer has is great preparation, contingency planning, and monitoring. Intrinsic mechanisms can be built in to facilitate the sharing of the idea with others where possible (e.g., "one click to share with a friend"). What is necessary is a good idea of the contagion route – the sequence from person to person, and from group to group. It is in preparing for this phase of a campaign that identifying your key influencers becomes vital.

The first task is to get the word out there, and here it is your "Connectors" who are key. These people are natural networkers with large address books who love sharing ideas and keeping in touch with others. They have a disproportionately large number of regular contacts, who together form "hubs" of like-minded individuals. Often, given their love of collecting and sharing information with others, these people will be connected with several hubs – cross-infecting the different communities and spreading the idea. These "inter-hub connections" are critical in making the move from niche outbreak to epidemic. The significance of the connector in the process is not necessarily by giving the news credibility but by spreading the news. Building credibility is the job of the next key groups of influencers – the "Salespeople." The salesperson is someone with a clear vested interest in the product. While is could be an actual salaried salesperson, it could equally be a paid advocate, for example someone who has been offered a financial incentive for recruiting new users to a service. This strategy has been used by many of the newer phone and energy service providers, either way, they are masters of persuasion and influence, and that is their key role. Finally, before a consumer is ready to make a switch, especially to a high-cost item, they may require some more neutral advice. This is the job of the "Maverns." Typically they are people who love to be impartial experts, and freely share their knowledge and expertise with others. It is this impartiality and deep expertise that gives them such high credibility. It also means that a company must avoid overt influencing of this group as, in all likelihood, it will backfire. Here the strategy is to make it as easy as possible for them to deepen their expertise by providing them with objective data and information.

CASE   GMX – Germany's Hotmail

GMX provides free e-mail accounts for German consumers and by "copy cutting" Hotmail's famous viral approach. In so doing, it achieved both high awareness and recruitment levels.

- Interested users could register a no cost email account at GMX.de.
- Each mail carried a recruitment footer message "for a no charge email account visit GMX.de."
- Every mail receiver would see the message and the recruitment call.
- Many of them responded, setting up a GMX email account.
- And as they did, so more viral messages were spread!

Transitioning an idea to mass market
Carried out effectively, this slow build strategy can offer great rewards and build a solid reputation for the product as it marches towards the mainstream. Consumers who help a product to develop and evolve become personally invested with the product's success as it becomes the "must-have," "cool" product. The iPod is a good example of a brilliant idea that was initially brought to life and seeded with Apple Loyalists. Taking it mainstream, the functionality of the iPod was improved (use of PC platform and increased capacity) and the product experience was enhanced with related products. The design itself became the message, with the characteristic white earphones, that became the central idea in the mass market advertising approach. Staying true to the early adopters was essential and is reflected in their communication of an Apple computer as "from the creators of the iPod."

Viral marketing into the future
The concept of crafting ideas that "infect" consumers, using our understanding of contagion psychology and epidemiology, is here to stay. Furthermore, two factors are likely to drive viral marketing to become increasingly important. Firstly, the current seemingly unstoppable trend of consumer-base fragmentation, secondly an increase in our ability to understand the behaviors and motivations of our consumers and therefore precisely target micro-segments of the consumer base.

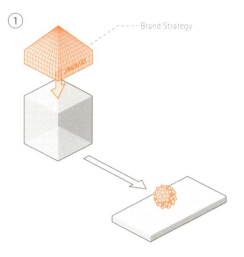

Fig. 1: Design of the virus
The design of a viral idea is always based on the brand strategy and the values that a brand is intended to represent. Only in this way can the subsequent virus create added value for the brand

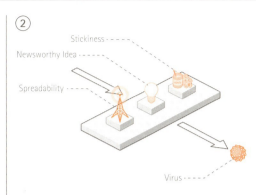

Fig. 2: Three success factors
To develop an effective virus out of the viral idea, three success factors need to be taken into account: newsworthiness (the narrative and news value of the idea), stickiness (the capacity to establish itself in the minds and in the behavior of the consumers), and spreadability (a design that permits dissemination with maximum speed – for instance a link in an e-mail that leads to the virus web page)

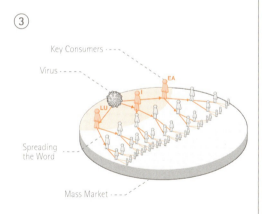

Fig. 3: The viral mechanism
The effect of a marketing virus is that it can be communicated to just a small number of key consumers at correspondingly low cost and then spreads exponentially like in a snowball system

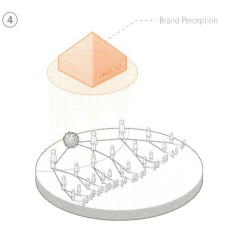

Fig. 4: Generating a collective brand perception
If the virus has been designed effectively in accordance with the brand strategy, it creates, through its dissemination, a collective brand image in the minds of the consumers – the objective of viral marketing has been achieved

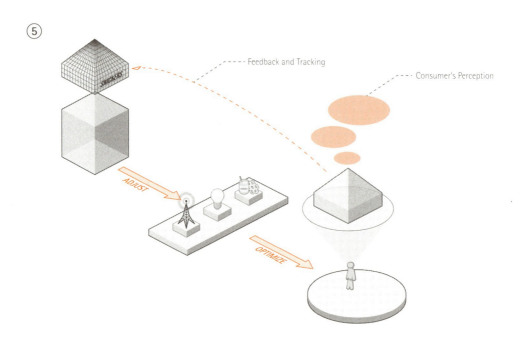

Fig. 5: Feedback, measurement, and optimization
Constant measurement, adaptation, and optimization of the viral activities is intended to prevent the course of the epidemic as well as the unwanted "side-effects" of the virus getting totally out of control

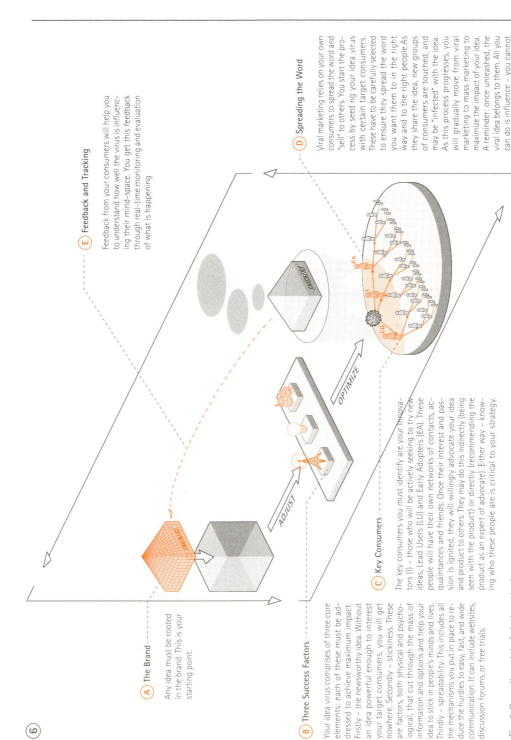

A) The Brand

Any idea must be rooted in the brand. This is your starting point.

B) Three Success Factors

Your idea virus comprises of three core elements; each of these must be addressed to achieve maximum impact. Firstly – the newsworthy idea. Without an idea powerful enough to interest your target consumers, you will get nowhere. Secondly – stickiness. These are factors, both physical and psychological, that cut through the mass of information and options and help your idea to stick in people's minds and lives. Thirdly – spreadability. This includes all the mechanisms you put in place to reduce the hurdles to easy, fast, and wide communication. It can include websites, discussion forums, or free trials.

C) Key Consumers

The key consumers you must identify are your Innovators (I) – those who will be actively seeking to try new ideas, Lead Users (LU) and Early Adopters (EA). These people will have their own networks of contacts, acquaintances and friends. Once their interest and passion is ignited, they will willingly advocate your idea and product to others. They may do this indirectly (being seen with the product) or directly (recommending the product as an expert of advocate). Either way – knowing who these people are is critical to your strategy.

D) Spreading the Word

Viral marketing relies on your own consumers to spread the word and "sell" to others. You start the process by seeding your idea virus with certain target consumers. These have to be carefully selected to ensure they spread the word you want them to in the right way and to the right people. As they share the idea, new groups of consumers are touched, and may be "infected" with the idea. As this process progresses, you will gradually move from viral marketing to mass marketing to maximize the impact of your idea. A reminder: once unleashed, the viral idea belongs to them. All you can do is influence – you cannot control what happens!

E) Feedback and Tracking

Feedback from your consumers will help you to understand how well the virus is influencing their mind-space. You get this feedback through real-time monitoring and evaluation of what is happening

Fig. 6: Overall model of viral marketing

Process & Execution

There are two basic approaches to viral marketing: riding the wave of a naturally occurring viral phenomenon where an idea finds the brand, or more commonly, where a viral marketing strategy is being purposefully developed to target core consumers. In this section we will be following the latter approach and outlining various steps you can take to help make sure your viral strategy stands the greatest chances of success.

A viral marketing campaign may be viewed as five distinct phases:

Phase 1: Getting that winning product with the built-in consumer "Wow"

The first job is to find a product or service with a strong identity that engages your consumers. It may be that they will admire it and identify with it as with high tech products such as the Blackberry or Apple's iPod. Over the past couple of years both of these have become life changing "must-haves" for consumers, with talk of "iPod widows" and Blackberry users who claim "I couldn't live my life without it."

1.1 Continuous improvement of your offer will help avoid "Vile Viral"

People can get really excited about a good idea, however they become more vocal about a bad concept, creating so called "vile viral" or the spread negative publicity about your product – obviously not something that you want. To avoid this happening make sure your product lives up to your consumer's expectations and delivers what it promises. Review this continuously as you move through the process.

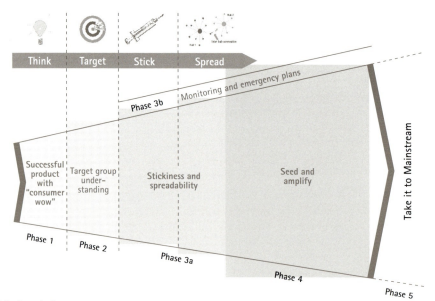

Fig. 7: Viral marketing process

1.2 Reinvent a low interest category, or don't even start
It may be that your product is just not special enough. And here we are talking about what your consumers really think rather than the view from the marketing department or boardroom. In this case, a different approach to viral marketing should be adopted or the use of viral marketing abandoned altogether. There are products in low interest, everyday categories that offer nothing differentiating or in the worst cases are perceived as inferior in some way. If this is your situation, the advice is not to attempt a viral strategy! On the other hand, even if you are in a low interest category, but can find something novel and interesting enough to spark interest, viral marketing may be a viable option for you. For example, French hotel chain Formule 1, offered such a unique stance on the budget hotel category that people would spend time telling their Formule 1 story to others at dinner parties.

It is also important to remember that no one likes to be taken for a ride or feel they have been manipulated, and even those companies with whiter than white credentials can come under fire for hypocrisy. In a world of unlimited information, if you pretend to be a small altruistic outfit, when in fact you are a big multinational accused of dubious ethical practices, you will be found out, and punished for the deception. Remember the old adage that trust is hard won, and easily lost. It is always pays to act with integrity.

1.3 Be open and responsive to all ideas
Finally, be open to ideas from all sources – remember that sometimes your idea can find you. The M&M's pinks story is a case in point. When an opportunity like this presents itself to you, it will be your ability to respond fast that will determine whether you are able to harness the potential of the idea or not.

CASE Pink M&M's – the case of the self-starting virus

M&M's candies in the U.S. decided to run a promotion together with the Susan Komen Breast Cancer Foundation to raise funds for breast cancer research. Special bags of pink and white M&M's were sold across the country. This much was planned. What had not been planned was an informal viral campaign, started by a consumer passionate about Breast Cancer research, who sent a simple, unbranded e-mail message to all her friends asking them to forward the message on to help ensure as much money as possible would be raised for the charity. This viral message increased awareness of the promotion, and by the end of December, the $650 000 donation target had been achieved. Breast cancer is such an important issue to many women, and the idea of raising money simply by enjoying some tasty chocolate (something else many women are passionate about) was enough for this virus to "self start."

Johnnie Walker's "Moorhuhnjagd" or "Grouse Shoot Game"

Despite being amongst the most well-known and popular examples of viral marketing in Germany, the "The Grouse Shoot Game" wasn't the result of a well thought out marketing campaign, it just happened totally by chance. Originally planned by Johnnie Walker brand as off-line promotion in delicatessens and specialist food outlets, the Grouse game flew onto the Internet in 1998, with no brand or agency involvement. Even today, no one knows who posted the game on the Internet. It was only when users started asking for updates, that the promotion agency found about the phenomenon. The Grouse was a huge benefit to the brand and achieved extraordinarily high awareness levels for Johnnie Walker across the country.

Phase 2: Get to know your targets and what matters to them

The successful diffusion of an idea, new product or message typically takes place in a set sequence. Firstly, the innovators or style leaders will try it – the main attraction for them being the originality and newness of the concept. It then travels through to early adopters, through to the early mainstream majority, followed by the late mainstream and finally the laggards – the group most resistant to change and anything new. It is worth mentioning that the profile of these groups will vary according to the situation and context. For example, someone may shun cable or satellite television as being unnecessary to him, while being an innovator in the latest forms of digital photography – driven by a hobby they are passionate about. You must be clear on who makes up these groups in your specific category.

Next, you must form a clear picture of what your target consumers value in your proposition. Whilst it is likely that there will be certain features and benefits that everyone in your target group considers important, as mentioned earlier, the motivations of these different groups will in all likelihood vary as the idea progresses. Herein lies an opportunity to engage and motivate different consumer groups by emphasizing different features and benefits as the idea diffuses through the market. For more on this, George Silverman in "The Secrets of Word of Mouth Marketing" describes a framework for identifying how best to help the different groups take a decision.

2.1 Find and seed with the important few for you

Clarifying whom you want to build an initial relationship with is crucial. If you have an existing business, you may have already identified your early adopters – they will be the first to buy and those who enquire about new product launches. Your consumer segmentation and customer database is your key source of information here.

Your mavens can be found at relevant conferences, exhibitions, and events. They will be active members of relevant Internet chat rooms and will be on the circulation lists of various specialist publications. Lastly, determine who would make suitable sales and spokespeople for your campaign. Your best strategy may be to target at a local level by seeking out key members of local organizations and clubs. Another option is to adopt a more mass-market approach and find a celebrity spokesperson or use other public relations activities.

2.2 Get clear on how your virus motivates the different target groups

Once you are clear on the different people you want to "infect" with your idea, it is important to determine the various psychological drivers that will have maximum effect. The most obvious of factors is a financial incentive for some kind of personal gain, however, other motivators that fit with your target's personal values, and/or enhance their personal credibility reputation and status may be worth much more to them than simply money.

Phase 3a: Trigger interest and make the message stick

As you move towards activation, consider the different ways that you can help increase the stickiness and spreadability of your idea. It is not necessary, and may not be possible, or desirable to incorporate all the stickiness factors mentioned earlier. Nevertheless, the more you are able to build in to your concept, the stickier your idea is likely to be. Likewise, the easier you make it for people to be exposed and pass on your idea, the more spreadable it will become. A free or low risk trial is a great way for potential consumers to experience your idea or product. "Free" is obviously much more powerful! Many software manufacturers use a "free trial period" to allow people to get used to the product and familiar with the benefits.

With different products you may need to be creative in how you can offer your consumers this product experience at a low risk to them. It is obviously not possible to give away free iPods to more than a select few key influencers, however, it is possible to create a space for them to try it out in a way that gives them as much excitement about the product as possible. For Apple, the Apple Store is one active expression of this concept.

One of the reasons why the Internet is such a great platform for viral marketing is that it is possible to build mechanisms into the total experience that makes implied and explicit recommendation much easier. Hotmail is a classic example, where at the end of each e-mail sent, the reader found the line "Get your free, private e-mail at Hotmail" together with a hyperlink enabling those who were interested to sign up immediately. Not only was the message clear, but in addition, because the mail was coming from someone the reader knew, typically during the launch phase, from a personal friend, it had much more credibility and impact than some anonymous flier, mail, or billboard advertising campaign.

Another route to explore, is how you can leverage social currency, finding expressions of your idea that allow people to sign up with the idea and share it. Examples could be free greetings cards, birthday reminders, newsletters, games, ring-tones, sponsored chat rooms, and message boards.

Phase 3b: Monitor progress and plan for contingencies

Once you have unleashed your idea, the control lies with consumers as to how they will interpret and engage with your message. It is up to them how, when and with whom they share your idea. This consumer ownership of your service or product message opens up some risks. The information flow is out of your control in terms of speed of information spread, degree of spread, as well as the geographies and consumers being touched by your message as it spreads. Several scenarios are possible.

Your desired target group may engage fully as planned. There may be some distortion of the original message, that may possibly even be positive in developing new perspectives that you have not yet considered. It may also be that your idea gets adopted by less desirable groups of consumers. Finally, it could be that nothing happens at all and the virus has no impact whatsoever. Anticipation of the various scenarios and planning your response is a good idea. It allows you to optimize, balance, and course-correct your strategy as necessary. For example, if a message gets to the wrong consumer group, this could be addressed by a specific PR campaign, targeted at this group. Establishing "observation posts" to monitor how and if your message is spreading and evolving is one good way to manage your campaign. Having as thorough a picture as possible of the situation, will allow you to reseed where necessary, adapting and correcting your engagement strategy. It will also let you know if your idea had failed and allow you to minimize any further waste of resource.

Once unleashed the campaign will move fast and various situations may play out at such speed that you may not have time to make the necessary corrections during the roll-out. Scenario planning is helpful here too as a means to anticipate and preempt recovery options without resorting to the temptation of manipulation or control of your message. Remember it belongs to them now and you must work with your consumers and allow them to lead the agenda.

Phase 4: Seed and amplify your idea

Having identified the vital few for each of your idea-diffusion groups, with an effective monitoring plan, you will be well placed to know who best to seed your ideas with and how. It is always a good idea to look beyond the most obvious targets and think as broadly as you can in your goal of building the most powerful relationship possible with them. Some examples could be leaders of a dog walking group for new pet care products, or an organization such as the U.K. Good Housekeeping Institute for products targeting home-makers and housewives.

As an idea grows, what your mavens are saying becomes increasingly important. They may be either public mavens such as Oprah endorsing selected authors through her bookclub in the United States or the U.K.'s Consumer Association magazine "Which?" that gives unbiased product test reports on various consumer goods. For example, with pet care products your maven may be the local vet. While another example of a local maven could be a sports trainer recommending a type of sports nutrition, or a gang leader who starts wearing a certain brand of clothing.

Accelerating towards your "Tipping point"
You can help your idea move from a cluster of hubs through to the "Tipping point" towards a full epidemic by following some guidelines and leveraging various other elements of your communication arsenal.

As a principle, make it as easy as possible for them to share the news, talk, discuss and thus create a buzz. Encourage your consumers to dialogue with you using the various communication vehicles you have put in place as it will maintain interest and increase their engagement. Through digital platforms such as internet, e-mail, or mobile telephony, digital friendly messages can spread more widely and much more rapidly than even virulent biological viruses that rely on physical proximity. PR and event marketing can also be a great way to encourage your current advocates to connect, share and buzz together. Do whatever you can to make sure other people know that these people are buzzing as if you don't, the group may get excited, but there will be no growth.

Some well-placed PR stories with recognized spokespeople can encourage those in the mainstream to think about testing the water. Events bring people together, and get visibility outside of the current consumer base. They are also great for providing a low risk trial of your idea experience. Continue to make the most of all your existing sharing tools, such as newsletters and chat rooms.

Phase 5: Moving from viral into mainstream

As you approach the bulk of your potential mainstream consumers you may chose to maximize your market potential through more traditional broadcast media rather than relying on buzz alone. However, what you say will need to adapt to your mainstream audience's concerns and values. This group is not interested in novelty for the sake of it, and needs good reasons to change their behavior and buy in to your idea. They will want to know why it is functionally better than what they have today. They will be concerned about reliability and customer service support. They will also want to be sure that socially, their peers will see their support as acceptable, and that they won't be seen as outlandish, bizarre, or on the fringes. The use of mainstream media is one way of legitimizing the idea and allaying any concerns.

Keeping your hard won consumers
Knowing that your innovators and early adopters will constantly be seeking the next big trend is what can give you an edge as a marketeer. Special editions, new models, and upgrades will keep your consumers engaged as will asking for their involvement in developing the next generation of your products such as Beta-testers for new software. It all involves a lot of hard work, great execution, and a fair amount of luck, but with the potential prize of your idea becoming the next Blackberry, the next iPod, or the next Hotmail, it is worth the effort.

International aspects

As a communication strategy tool, one of the major limiting factors a marketeer faces in applying viral marketing, internationally, is language. However, provided the product message delivers a "WOW" that is not culturally specific, there are no limits in spreading the virus beyond national boundaries. Global communication platforms such as the Internet facilitate the application of viral marketing internationally. Again, Google is a great example, with country specific websites and testing of new concepts in more advanced markets before rolling out to smaller and more cautious markets.

The starting point should always be local and with a specific consumer target. Although there are some really great ideas that travel, in most cases thinking about "global" or "European" consumers will reduce the tightness of your targeting and your understanding of the social networks, norms, and practices that you want to influence and break in to. Identifying and understanding your early adopters and mavens requires real consumer proximity and close understanding.

In many ways the planning and anticipation of communication scenarios are much more easily carried out at a local level, however, this is not always the case. Dependant on the type of media such as SMS or the Internet, for some global operators a "one size fits all" international approach, running a common strategy in parallel across different markets may be the smartest approach, as Jamba/Jamster have shown with their mobile phone ring-tones.

As an idea reaches tipping point internationally, with a move to mass communications, it naturally makes sense to employ an aligned international approach to ensure message consistency and reduce development costs wherever possible.

CASE SNICKERS "Wildkarts"

The SNICKERS brand wanted to strengthen its relationship with a group of difficult to reach younger and more active consumers in the Berlin region of Germany. The brand is all about energy and active lifestyles and has an edgier and adventurous personality than its competitors. The concept idea had to be something that would speak to this target group and had to capture the personality of the brand.

The winning idea

The brand team came up with the idea to create a once in a lifetime, unrepeatable experience with a very German feel, but at the same time a slightly irreverent spin. They would run a GoKarting race underneath the famous Reichstag building in Berlin, in the soon to be opened Metro station – destined to be one of the most visited stations in Berlin and possibly the whole of Germany. Once the Metro was running, it would not be possible to repeat the event.

The event itself

Seventy-five teams of three people (in mixed teams including VIPs, journalists and SNICKERS consumers) were competing against each other in one race, that was composed of a "real" go-kart race and a fun race at the Carrera race track. In addition, individual races for people who did not take part in the team competition were conducted. People could apply through the Internet, on-site by succeeding in one of the two "application tools" – "riding the bar" and underground battle, a computer game or through media partners. Furthermore, "double cart sessions" with professional drivers and a "grid-girl and grid-boy contest," to determine the starting order of the final race, was held. A SNICKERS chill-out lounge with live commentary, music, and LED screen were part of the framework program.

Knowing the consumer

A deep understanding of the brand's core target and their values was a prerequisite to ensuring the success of the event. SNICKERS consumers typically seek to experience their own limits and love to be on the edge, trying wild and sometimes wacky ideas. The location and GoKart racing itself met this need. We also knew that they like to have fun both as individuals and as teams. This led the brand team to choose to include both team and individual competitions, as well as various other fun elements as an integrated event experience. To seed the idea, the brand team posted information on the SNICKERS web homepage, as well as engaging opinion leaders, such as presenters from Music TV channels to publicize the event. With one of the channels, NBC Giga, consumers could vote for their preferred presenter to participate on the team, and for both NBC Giga and Viva channels, consumers could apply to join the VIP team.

Trigger interest and make message stick

It was the power of the idea that triggered most of the interest and research after the event showed that over 95 percent would recommend this event to friends because it was so entertaining, thrilling, new, and different. To enhance the stickiness of the message, various levers were used. Firstly, participation in the official race required teams of three people. This encouraged individuals to spread the word to other friends who might be interested in forming a team. Secondly, including celebrities and VIPs as participants that consumers could race with and against helped create further excitement and buzz. Thirdly, the opportunity to win free travel and accommodation to the event for those selected as the team provided a further incentive to pass on the word. To further stimulate word of mouth, more elements were added. Amongst others, these included – internet-based team applications: TV and internet support from NBC Giga in addition to participation at their games convention; E-card placement on Edgar providing links back to the SNICKERS home page, and a "send to friends or enemies" hyperlink to the event internet platform, and various guerrila activities across Berlin, including driver invasions, post-its, living banners, and a news flash initiative launched via SMS one day prior to the event.

Turn into viral: seed and amplify

The tipping point was reached just before the event, as the mass media started to pick up on the event, featuring it in daily newspapers and on local and national, TV and radio news programmes. In addition, various magazines and several national TV channels reported on the SNICKERS Wildkarts event beforehand. However, it was post-event when communications reached their peak, with nation-wide TV and radio coverage, a total of almost 20 hours of air time. While the goal had been to target consumers in the Berlin area, this broad, national media coverage did have an overwhelming benefit to the overall brand awareness for SNICKERS.

The 'viral' results

When asked how people initially found out about the event, word of mouth was the most frequently mentioned means. Over 95 percent saying they would recommend the event to friends because it was so thrilling, exciting, new and different. More than 60 percent recalled PR editorials and radio broadcasts, and over 40 percent said they had used the Internet to find out more about the event and visited the various links. The equivalent of over 20 hours of broadcast media air time was generated (including local and national TV and radio).

▶ Key Insights

- People's natural desire to share, discuss, and connect with each other gives a viral concept increased credibility and the power to cut through the clutter.
- An exciting and newsworthy idea has the power to infect conversations, mind space, and purchasing decisions.
- A small number of consumers have a disproportionate effect on the spread of an idea. Understanding these people and their motivations dictates your delivery strategy.
- Media costs of viral marketing are typically lower. However, investment upfront in consumer understanding and planning is critical.
- The creation of "global tribes" connected via the technology platforms offers potential new viral and business opportunities.
- Building in physical and psychological elements that can help your message to stick and hence impact on your consumer's behaviors.
- Viral messages belong to consumers, not marketeers. This unpredictability can be stressful!
- There are no geographic limits to viral marketing provided the product deliver against global consumer needs and a global consumer "Wow."

▶ Practical Guidelines

- Make sure you understand consumers – particularly those with the greatest influencing power. Understanding what motivates them will be key to your success.
- Get a product with a "Wow" factor. It has to matter to your consumer and be worth them risking sharing with others. If you don't have this, don't start.
- Sometimes a good idea can find you – look for subtle messages early on from consumer correspondence and leading edge consumers. React fast.

- ☐ If your product doesn't have intrinsic physical stickiness, look to enhance it by creating additional elements that help communicate the brand experience.
- ☐ Keep your eyes and ears open, and build in monitoring stations to track what is happening.
- ☐ If your message is not spreading as you would like, revise your seeding strategy and look for new ways to stimulate interest with your key opinion leaders.
- ☐ Focus your communications on addressing potential consumer concerns/potential barriers as you move your idea mainstream.
- ☐ For an international messaging campaign, approach deployment locally in order to effectively leverage consumer proximity benefits.

The Authors

Michael Rüthnick

Masterfoods European Brand Leader on SNICKERS & MILKY WAY brands. Following business study and MBA, 10 years working experience in various functions covering national and European brand development, national key account management and management consulting in marketing and sales. Since 2002, European Brand Leader with Masterfoods.

Robert Moffett

Robert Moffett is Masterfoods Marketing Capability Development Manager. With a BSc Food Technology (Reading University) and subsequent 17 years of experience with Nestle, British Sugar and Mars working in R&D, Product Development, Marketing, Organisational Effectiveness and Learning & Development. Since 2003 has lead Masterfoods' Marketing Capability Development team.

Literature Recommendations
M. Gladwell, "The Tipping Point: How Little Things can make a big difference," editor: Abacus 2002
S. Godin, "Unleashing the Idea Virus," London 2002
G. Silverman, "The Secrets of Word of Mouth Marketing," New York 2001
E. Rosen, "Anatomy of Buzz: How to create word of mouth marketing," Doubleday 2000

Customer Relations

→ www.marketingmanual.org/relations

Timo Schneckenburger – O$_2$ Germany

Community Marketing
Marketing efficiency through selective target group approach

▶ Executive Summary

At a time when markets are converging and society is becoming more heterogeneous, marketing activities with consumer-oriented approaches present ever greater challenges. Growing media pressure and increasingly demanding customers justify the question as to whether mass marketing can still be up-to-date and successful nowadays. In this context, community marketing can present an interesting alternative or addition to the traditional range of marketing instruments.

- Community marketing is characterized by the fact that a brand or product is initially publicized within a clearly delineated interest group, a community.
- The mass market is only approached in a second step via the community.
- In comparison with mass marketing, this multi-step communication concept significantly reduces coverage losses.
- Close cooperation with community members allows current market trends to be captured more rapidly, and the product and communication mix can be adapted to market changes at an early stage.

The following success factors should be taken into account for successful implementation of community marketing:

- Appropriateness of brand or product to the community.
- Identification of a profitable niche market.
- Selection of a community that fits with the company and has a high potential of influencing the mass market.
- Identification of community experts who are able to provide a credible entry point to the community.
- Development of a marketing mix tailored to the community, in cooperation with community experts.

▶ Theoretical Model of Community Marketing

1. Definition and core principle

The strategic core objective of community marketing is no different in principle from traditional mass marketing. Both concepts want to accomplish one thing: brand awareness and purchasing preference in as large a target group as possible. While mass marketing, however, targets the market as a whole and, therefore, carries with it high coverage losses, community marketing first takes a detour that ultimately leads to enhanced efficiency.

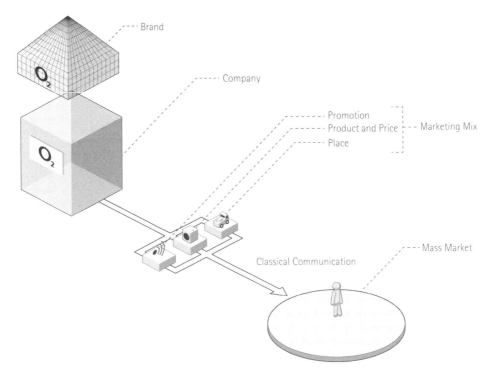

Fig. 1: Mass marketing model
In traditional mass marketing, the company communicates directly with the market as a whole

- Mass marketing addresses the entire market through media such as television and radio. The resulting coverage losses are high.

Community marketing aims to publicize a brand or product initially within a clearly delineated interest group, a so-called "community." The aim is to generate interest in a brand or product to such an extent that they identify with the product, its performance, and its profile. And because this persuasion effort occurs via a direct communication channel between the company and a manageable group of people (the community members), it is much more efficient than mass communication can ever be.

- Selected customer segments are approached via channels with affinity to target groups; these segments in turn will credibly convey certain messages to the mass market.

This approach creates a degree of loyalty and credibility amongst community members that can scarcely be achieved nowadays by means of traditional communication methods. If the positive attitude to the product is then carried over into the market, then this marketing approach can be deemed a success.

In the following, we provide an insight into the factors on which the success of this approach is based:

2. Factors in community marketing

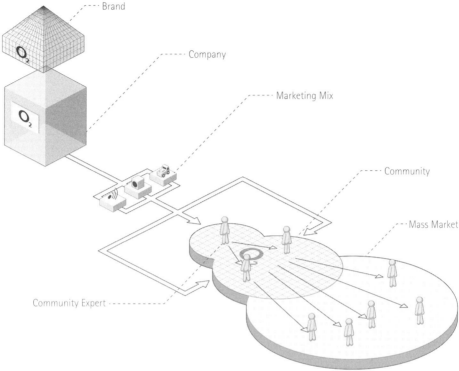

Fig. 2: Community marketing model
Community marketing concentrates on a small group of consumers – the community – and exploits its multiplier effects on the market

2.1 The brand
The success of community marketing rises and falls with the brand. The one key question a company must ask itself is: "Is my brand or my product even suitable for the community?" Generally, the following principle applies: the more a brand or product can be charged emotionally, the greater its community potential will be. Harley-Davidson, for example, with its hint of freedom and cool, is practically predestined for successful community formation. For a pound of branded German butter, it would be decidedly more difficult. However, it is not only a question of emotionality: brands with less awareness and a high "buzz effect" are also appropriate for community marketing as an innovative strategy for opening up new markets. The reason: most community members are so-called early adaptors. They are ahead of the times and prefer to buy products that have not yet made their way into the shopping basket of the masses. One successful example of this is Apple's iPod.

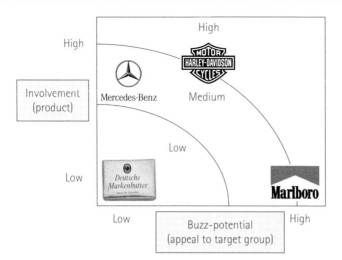

Fig. 3: Evaluation of a brand's community-potential

2.2 The market

Let's assume that the brand or product is suitable for a community. Then the second question of the conception phase arises: "In which market should I position myself?" For instance "Is my product lifestyle-oriented, or does it appeal more to high-performance sports freaks?" Only a clear and precisely-analyzed product or brand profile provides certainty here, a certainty that the right market segment and, thus, also a potentially successful community has been chosen. One thing should be obvious: the product must fit the community. Without acceptance in the group, success in the mass market will fail to follow. It is only when a community declares itself as an ambassador for the brand that the path to higher brand awareness is cleared.

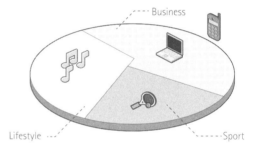

Fig. 4: Market with differing market segments

2.3 The community

"What is a community?" The answer to this question is simple: a community is a group of people that is formed in an uncoerced environment, usually leisure-related. This group speaks the same language, lives according to the same rules and values, and buys the same brands and products. And it has a certain common field of interest, such as sports, music, computer games – the possibilities are endless. However, it is important that the community must fit the brand or product.

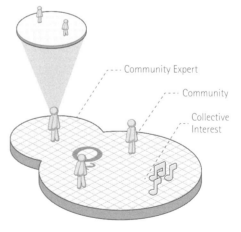

Fig. 5: Structure of a community

508 Manual of International Marketing

Moreover, there is a further, strategically decisive question that must be answered: should one count on an existing community, or should a new brand community be called into being, such as the community around the Harley-Davidson or the iPod?

Advantages and disadvantages of one's own brand community are summarized in Fig. 6. Advantages: high degree of probability that the brand and the community are really suited to each other, high chance of integration into the community, intensive possibilities for influencing the members. Disadvantages: the risk exists that no community will develop or that the members react differently than anticipated. Moreover, building a community is not done at the drop of a hat. It needs time. Products with short lifecycles, therefore, are more suited to existing communities.

	Pros	Cons
Own brand community	· Strong influence on community members · High degree of brand fit · Only presence in community	· Costly initiation and establishment of own community · Higher risk when establishing community (the wrong members)
Existing community	· Low risk · Quick implementation of community marketing · A new community need not be established · Access to existing community structures	· Often already occupied by other brands · Lower degree of brand fit · Less influence on community members · Community may reject brand

Fig. 6: Own brand community vs. existing community

2.4 Community experts

Community experts may include individuals, such as opinion leaders, but may also consist of institutions/agencies that represent certain interest groups. They have a common factor – they understand the "psychology" of the community very well – its language, its preferences, its etiquette, its approaches, and its communication dynamics. Community experts are both interpreters and ambassadors. In the conception phase of a community marketing strategy, they initially translate the code of the community to make it intelligible and useful to the brand company. Later, during the marketing process itself, they convey the brand or product profile into the community.

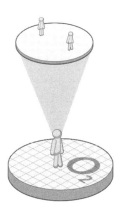

Fig. 7: Community experts

Opinion leaders play a dominant role here. As individuals within a community, they can assume a more powerful and directly effective position than institutions can, for example.

Characteristics of community experts are:

- they are well-known personalities within the community,
- they have a strong network,
- they identify and track down trends early.

2.5 Community marketing mix

Once promising communities and their "Insiders" have been found, the company and community experts need to develop a community marketing mix in joint creative workshops. As with mass marketing, here the mix also includes the traditional four P's: product, price, promotion, place. These must be geared to the existing and potential needs of the community, and integrated into the overarching brand communication concept. The following paragraphs indicate how this works in the field of community marketing.

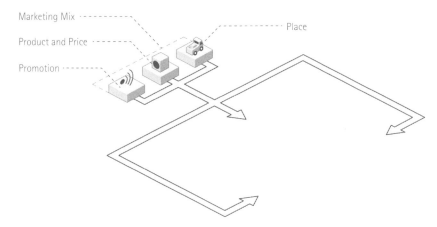

Fig. 8: Marketing mix

2.5.1 Product and price

Community marketing is successful only with products that are considered to be innovative and unique on the market. Me-too products should therefore be excluded from the start. "Cool" products with high-quality design and true brand personality, that primarily appeal to a younger target group, are promising. And it doesn't matter if they cost a little more. High price actually enhances the product's appeal for the so-called early adaptors. This is the – usually small – group of buyers that discovers a product long before it is accepted by the general public, and that enjoys a trendsetter reputation and, thus, a level of credibility that can later persuade the market as a whole of an innovative product's benefit. The iPod is a current example of how a product has managed the transition from a community niche to the mass market. After Steve Jobs brought out a silvery-white music box the size of a cigarette package, dyed-in-the-wool Apple fans rapidly bought up the first models. The iPod was born. The product, an MP3 player with integrated hard drive, was unique in the market, and its appearance struck a chord with design-oriented customers.

The high starting price did not pose a problem, either. On the contrary – uniqueness, appearance, and price helped the iPod to position itself as a high-end product, and the product was therefore of interest to a small, exclusive customer group demanding innovative function and design. This group had the credibility to perform a "proof of concept" for the iPod, which proved to be extremely helpful in the iPod's successful placement in the mass market.

2.5.2 Promotion

The traditional approach to promotion cannot begin to produce the clout of community marketing. Above-the-line campaigns are of negligible significance in practice, and should only be executed later when the brand is to be publicized in the mass market. Successful "discussion" with the community occurs below-the-line – with activities such as events, promotions, ambient media, or alliances. Creative and unconventional concepts are in the forefront – a simple sponsoring of big concerts has little impact on credibility within a community. Red Bull gears its community marketing promotion to a young, athletic, and off-beat target group. An important component consists of the extreme sports events, such as the Red Bull Flugtag (flying day), in which "daredevil men and women in their hand-made flying machines" give wings to their dreams of flying.

2.5.3 Place

Community-appropriate products are usually of an innovative and exclusive nature. Obviously, the distribution channels must fit this image and be accepted and utilized by the community. It is for this reason that distribution formats such as flagship or pop-up stores, that are opened for a very brief period of time in trendy city center locations – like nomads' tents – are becoming increasingly important. These are accepted as reputable sales channels in many communities. A short-term artificial scarcity of the product – e.g., induced by a choice of exclusive sales channels – can also stimulate interest in the relevant product, since it serves to enhance its cult character. Before Puma recreated itself as a lifestyle product, the shoes were sold in just about any athletic gear or shoe store. It was only when sales were restricted to the more exclusive Puma and Lifestyle shops that the brand shifted into the focus of the young and trendy dream target group, that from then on transformed the Puma shoe into a sort of cult object.

Core issues when using community marketing include:

- **Brand**
  Do the brand and product possess community potential? Is community marketing an approach that sits well with the company's strategy?

- **Market**
  In which markets does one wish to position the product/brand? Does the brand have sufficient potential?

- **Community**
  Is there an appropriate community? If yes, should one count on the existing community, or call one's own brand community into being? How great a potential to influence the mass market does the community exhibit?

- **Community experts**
  Are there community experts who are in a position to provide a credible entry point to a community?

- **Community marketing mix**
  Is the combination of product, sales channel, and promotion creative enough? Can the brand's community potential be strengthened by selective pricing? Which sales formats appeal most to the communities? Can a certain "cult character" be created through the marketing mix?

3. The three-step communication mechanism

The core philosophy of community marketing is a controlled interplay between the brand, the community, and the market. Due to the differing size (number of target individuals) of community and market, the nature of interaction must be adapted to the two groups. Personal communication that decreases in steps is appropriate.

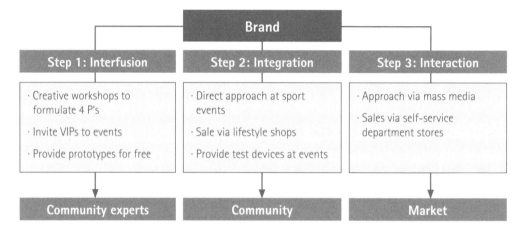

Fig. 9: Intensity of communication at touch points

Step 1: Interfusion: brand – community experts
Community experts and the company, draft, design, and implement the community marketing mix together. "Face-to-face interaction" and dialogue predominate. Since both parties work so closely together, a good term for this collaboration is "interfusion." During this phase, brand and community can still learn from each other – the brand learns to understand the "what" and "how" of the community. The community experts become familiar with the existing profile of the brand. The result of this close collaboration: a community marketing mix that is optimally tailored to the needs of the community and the brand, and a close bond between brand and community experts, who become credible representatives of the brand within the community.

Step 2: Integration: brand – community
When the brand communicates with the community, the phase is called "integration." The exchange between brand and user is less intensive than in the first step, but still marked by strong contacts from one person to the next. An example might be marketing via sales paths that are based on high levels of individual advice, such as in flagship stores. The goal of influencing the community and bringing the brand message to the mass market with its help can only be achieved through integration. But be careful – companies should ensure that they do not influence the internal dynamics of the community too much. A community must be independent. If it mutates into the extended arm of a company, it will be of little use.

Step 3: Interaction: brand – market

"Interaction" is the point at which the community, and not just the market as a whole, is being addressed. In this phase, the brand communicates with the market, no longer via personal contact, but through above-the-line mass media, such as print or television.

4. Community marketing in an international environment

Community marketing is an exceptionally appealing approach for companies operating internationally, provided that national characteristics are taken into account in conceptualizing the community marketing campaign. It is precisely during a time when markets are converging that it often happens that certain brands develop into a trend in different countries simultaneously and, thus, frequently become of interest to communities (e.g., Apple's iPod). The question naturally arises in this situation as to whether one can implement community marketing campaigns that span countries or regions in order to benefit from synergy.

Questions that need to be asked in an international community campaign include: are the brand and product values compatible or even identical in the target countries? Are the values in the target communities compatible or even identical?

It can certainly happen that brand or product values differ from one country to the other. If this is the case, then pure product campaigns must be adapted selectively in order to take into account regional characteristics. If, however, as in this case, a community is utilized that in turn has the same values, then synergies in marketing concepts can be exploited. Despite differing brand and product values, therefore, the possibility exists to convey a coherent message in the market, through the community's convergence of uniform values.

One must be aware, however, that regional differences may pertain from a communication perspective. If this is the case, adapting the campaign is unavoidable. Communities react with much greater sensitivity to the wrong approach or an incorrectly selected product than does the mass market. It is black and white – either demands are met or they are not. There is no middle ground.

Especially with international community marketing concepts, national marketing managers must work together closely, in order to understand the markets and their communities better and to recognize any differences. This is the only way in which one can be certain that a community marketing concept develops into a successful model in a number of different countries.

▶ Process & Implementation

"BELIEVE IT OR NOT: today at 7 pm, the Fantastic Four, free in the TUI Arena in Hanover! Bring your friends and rock along. O_2 can do!" Some O_2 customers have received this or a similar SMS in the recent past on their mobile phones. This is how the so-called flash mobs have been staged. These flash mobs are actually get-togethers of people with one and the same interest. The get-togethers take place spontaneously in public places. Meeting venues are communicated by Internet or mobile phone. The idea of positioning the O_2 brand as a skillful provider of mobile music services was conceived in close cooperation between members of music communities and O_2 employees.

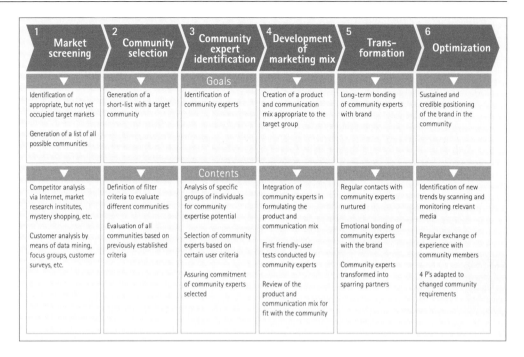

Fig. 10: Community marketing process

Phase 1: Market screening

Market research occurs at the outset of the community marketing concept. Existing customers or potential external target groups are analyzed in terms of their areas of interest, attitudes, and behavior patterns. This provides initial indicators for where communities might be created or may already exist. It is important to keep an eye on the fixed company strategy, so that only target groups that match the company's goals are the subject of focus.

Market research tools, such as focus groups, questionnaires, and telephone surveys, are also available to analyze behavior patterns. Secondary sources, such as trend magazines and special interest journals, e.g., for music or computer games, can be used. The outcome of the analysis is a long list of potential communities with promise.

CASE O_2 relied on focus groups for market analysis. People using mobile data services extensively in their leisure time, and who belonged to the "ambitious techie" or "young social" segments, were invited and interviewed. It soon became clear that both groups shared a fundamental interest in music and sports. Another important result: many of those interviewed were already active in structures similar to communities. They belonged to very specific music scenes, were aware of the latest product trends in MP3 players, or often exchanged sports news via MMS and SMS. The competitor analysis, however, revealed that two potential communities were already occupied by competitors.

Additional potential communities, which also belonged to O_2's actual core target group, were identified by focus groups in the music-related environment.

Phase 2: Community selection

The second step in the development of a community marketing concept is to generate a short-list or a single suitable community from the longer list of potential communities (Fig. 11). Initially, the appropriate criteria for community selection need to be defined in accordance with company goals and strategy. These criteria should be weighted according to their strategic importance.

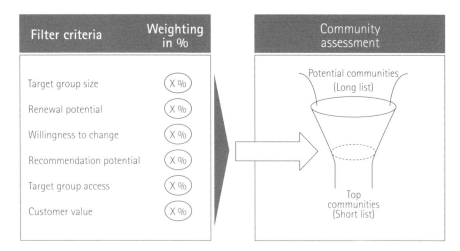

Fig. 11: Community selection

CASE O_2, used the following filter criteria:

- The target group size provides information on the number of community members.
- Renewal potential is documented by the fluctuation rate of community members.
- Willingness to change indicates the likelihood that customers will switch over from other mobile network providers.
- The recommendation potential, also called "word-of-mouth," is an indication of how strongly a community is networked internally. It is an important indicator for the speed of information dissemination and the possibility of bringing the brand into the community in a credible manner.
- O_2 defined target group access as the quantity and quality of potential cooperation partners (e.g., Universal in the music field) and community experts.
- Customer value, also known as ARPU (Average Revenue per User), is the indicator of the financial value that a customer represents for a mobile network company.

Phase 3: Community expert identification

Community experts are the key with which a company successfully unlocks the door to a community. The trick is to identify the true insiders in these interest groups. The first step in that direction is to approach potential experts via the hot communication channels, such as e-mail, SMS, newsletters, or the Internet.

CASE In order to identify these individuals within the selected community, O_2 first reviewed the entire customer base of the company for customers with a certain usage behavior (affinity with music, data and messaging). These customers were then selectively targeted via SMS, e-mail and the O_2 home page, and asked to keep a sort of journal or web log on their communication and information behavior. Based on these notes, 100 candidates were selected and invited to a one-day creative workshop. No financial incentive was offered to the workshop participants in order to ensure that the right people took part. In this way, O_2 could be sure that only "real freaks" participated in the workshops, those who were enthusiastic about the idea of a community, and who would have fun designing and implementing the relevant marketing concept.

Phase 4: Development of a marketing mix

Elaborating the marketing mix – working closely with the community experts (interfusion) – is the core of this step in the process, and its recipe for success. It is only through close cooperation with the true insiders and community experts that one can be sure of designing a targeted communication mix that is tailored to the needs and behavior patterns of the community, in order to position the brand credibly within the community. It is important that the community experts are convinced of the value of the brand and the underlying concept.

They should not feel that they are simply "selling" the brand. The same applies to the first contacts with the community as a whole. Here, too, the sales factor should not be in the forefront. The concept can only be successful if community members feel that they are benefiting from the brand.

CASE How did O_2 work when formulating the community marketing mix? At the beginning of the workshop, the O_2 "musicdownload" service was introduced. In subsequently formed small groups, community experts dealt with ideas and possibilities for further developing the product and communication mix. Teams with the most persuasive approaches met for additional workshops in which the community marketing mix was refined step by step. Workshop participants took part intensively in further product development. They defined functionality and content and helped O_2 to develop a holistic music concept that corresponded to the wishes of the target group. The first "friendly user tests" were conducted by friends of the workshop participants, by demonstrating the product and the associated concept to them in advance. Conceptual errors or defective functionality could be identified without any negative impact on the later launch. And the obvious enthusiasm of those engaged in development for the product resulted in a priceless word-of-mouth effect.

The marketing plan was also developed during the workshop. The focus was not on traditional above-the-line marketing, but rather on below-the-line measures designed to generate image and credibility within the target group. Music events lay at the core of the concept. This meant flash mobs organized by O_2 as described above. They were not marketed in advance. The place, time, and band were announced only on the day of the concert. Invitations were issued via SMS, e-mail, radio, and Viva TV clips. Admission to the concert was free. Alliances with partners, who financially support well-known bands in the community, were agreed, in addition to the music events. As a result, O_2 was able to authentically position itself on advertising surfaces appropriate to the target group (e.g., the concert tour bus for the band). A variety of music media channels known in the music scene reported on O_2's involvement. This is how, for example, editorials on flash mobs and ad campaigns were publicized in specially selected scene magazines, and album launches were supported by O_2 on television and radio.

Phase 5: Transformation

It is key to the success of community marketing that community experts are convinced of the product and the brand in the long-term. This is because frequently community marketing success only materializes in the medium to the long-term. The process described above – entering the community via community experts and entering the market only thereafter – can take several months, even years. Beyond this interval, the community experts should regularly be in close contact with the brand and the company. This makes them into sparring partners for the company.

CASE In order to guarantee this step, O_2 relied on regular contact with community experts, providing them with the most up-to-date handsets and offering them VIP cards for events sponsored by O_2. Opinion leaders were thereby emotionally bound to the O_2 brand, and developed into credible brand disciples within the community.

Phase 6: Optimization

People leave a community and others join. This so-called renewal potential can result in changes in the community's preferences and codes in short time intervals. The brand must keep step with these changes, since a missed scene code leads to the loss of credibility and negative effects on the target group. On-going scanning and monitoring of the community and the requisite adjustment of the 4 P's are, therefore, a must.

Market observation can occur in two ways – firstly, with the help of the community experts, and secondly, by analyzing trend and scene magazines. O_2 usually relies on magazine analysis due to time and cost constraints.

Another important tool in ensuring sustainability is a database with community member profiles. This facilitates personal and customized contacts, for example, via e-mail, via a free telephone hotline or even in chat rooms.

Community marketing – old wine in new bottles? Community marketing, opinion leader marketing, segment marketing, viral marketing this list could go on and on. New marketing approaches appear with regularity, designed to address target groups even more precisely. What are the differences in the approaches mentioned, though? A key difference is the nature of the target group. Communities are strongly networked internally, and the focus of their lives revolves around the same field of interest. In communities, the "we" concept is much more marked, as opposed to segments, that are distinguished by certain characteristics (e.g., socio-demographic features). The consequent close cohesion facilitates a much more intensive exchange of information between community members. A second difference is the step-wise approach. First community experts, then the community as a whole and, last but not least, the mass market are addressed. This means that selling does not take center stage at the beginning, but rather the generation of credibility. This process may be time-consuming, but it is sustainable.

Summary

It is not clear yet whether community marketing is simply another fad or whether it has the potential of developing into a mega trend. Nevertheless – the start has been very promising. The focusing on the requirements of a community, the personalized contacts with members, and the integration of community experts in the design of the product and communication concept, are becoming evermore important in authentic approaches to individual customer segments. It is precisely with community marketing that credibility can be engendered within a particular target group. In parallel with the "stingy is sexy" campaigns that are currently reduced to simple price messages, community marketing is increasingly applied in practice. It is precisely at this moment, when the appeal

	Segment marketing	Community marketing	Opinion leader marketing
Target group	· Cluster of individuals with similar or identical characteristics	· Groups that are strongly networked internally that view a common hobby/interest as their central focus	· Recognized trendsetters/ opinion leaders from different segments/ markets
Approach	· Direct approach to segment with a marketing mix tailored specifically	· Indirect approach to community via opinion leaders · Communication concept created together with opinion leaders	· Direct approach to opinion leaders · Communication concept created together with opinion leaders
Approach objective	· Primary: brand building and sales	· Primary: create credibility and acceptance in the community · High contact density · Secondary: brand building and sales in mass market	· Primary: credibility and sales among the opinion leaders and the mass market

Fig. 12: Differences between segment, community and opinion-leader marketing

is "cool," and "services" and "service landscape" are mentioned in the same breath, that community marketing, as a conscious counterpoint to mainstream communication, becomes a true differentiator and success factor in "new marketing."

▶ Key Insights

- Close networking amongst community members, an understanding of its code and etiquette, as well as a common interest, all facilitate optimum information flow within a community.
- Community marketing is a communication approach aimed at a very specific target group. Coverage losses are, thus, minimal.
- Early adaptors can be more selectively addressed in community marketing than in mass marketing.
- Early adaptors often have above-average purchasing power, and are prepared to spend a lot on certain products.
- The concept is also applicable in the international arena; it is important, however, to take national characteristics into account, since communities react more sensitively to the wrong approach than the wider market.
- Community marketing is particularly interesting when marketing innovative products that are not sufficiently mature for the mass market.

▶ Practical Guidelines

- Make sure that your brand or products are of interest to communities.
- Charge the brand/product emotionally.
- Select unusual, off-beat, and innovative communication concepts.
- Integrate community experts when developing the marketing mix.
- Don't give the community the feeling that you are using it for your own purposes.
- Don't make sales the main focus at the beginning – credibility is a must!
- In the case of international community marketing campaigns, local marketing staff and local community experts must be integrated into the entire project.

The Author

Timo Schneckenburger

Timo Schneckenburger, born in Munich, studied business at the Ludwig-Maximilian University in Munich from 1992 to 1998. After completing his studies, Timo worked for BMW AG as marketing and sales specialist, and participated in the internationally successful launch of the new MINI. In 2000, he moved to O_2, at the time still called Viag Interkom, as a consultant to the COO, with the brief of building up new sales channels. Currently, Timo Schneckenburger is Vice President of the marketing division of new customers.

Literature Recommendations

D. Banks, K. Daus, "Customer Community, Unleashing the power of your customer base," San Francisco 2002
F. Dudenhöffer, "Abschied vom Massenmarketing. Systemmarken und Beziehungen erobern Märkte," München 1998
A. Förster, P. Kreuz, "Marketing-Trends. Ideen und Konzepte für Ihren Markterfolg," Wiesbaden 2003
R. Rust, V. Zeithaml, K. Lemon, "Die Marke ist tot, es lebe der Kunde," in: Harvard Business Manager, No. 03/2005, pp. 38–51
A. Meyer, J.H. Davidson, "Offensives Marketing," Freiburg 2001
M. Sawhney, "Angriff aus der Blogosphäre," in: Harvard Business Manager, No. 02/2005, pp. 36–37

Rainer Bürkle – The Ritz-Carlton Hotel Company

Customer Service
Employee attitude as the focus of brand awareness

▶ Executive Summary

Service-oriented companies present themselves to the customer via two factors:

- the product or service, the "hardware,"
- the employees who sell the product or service to the customer, the "software."

These factors comprise the surface that the customer sees. In the best scenario, they represent the philosophy, strategy, and vision of a company. If they do not, however, and if they communicate other values and goals, a discrepancy arises within hardware, software, and corporate philosophy. This unavoidably leads to disappointment on the part of the customer, who will try to replace the service provider with one of its many competitors on the market at the next opportunity.

This article will explore more closely the "employee" factor. Employees are the most important interface between the customer and the company. The correct attitude and constant customer orientation is thus a key factor in attracting and retaining customers.

- From the point of view of the customer, the employees are the company.
- Employees must not simply learn corporate philosophy, they must live it.
- Daily communication of the company's core values and ongoing education can turn employees into ambassadors of the philosophy.
- Education and training cannot substitute for talent.
- A philosophy must be stable enough to resist short-term trends and flexible enough to integrate long-term changes.

▶ Theoretical Model of Customer Service

An orientation towards the customer should be a matter of course for every company. The will to offer the customer the optimal solution to his wishes is a cornerstone of entrepreneurial success. Customer orientation is, however, also a strategic statement. It is not simply the execution of a corporate philosophy, but the central starting point of the philosophy. Service to the customer, therefore, closes the circle between corporate philosophy and corporate reality. In an ideal situation the theoretical underpinning of the company is manifested in its service.

1. Customer service as a customer retention tool

The framework of customer service must be defined by a strong and clear company philosophy. The support of a well-founded value system allows the employee to interact competently and confidently, and thereby pleasantly and courteously. The employee's goal in each interaction with the customer should be to more than satisfy the services he wishes. It is only then that the customer becomes aware of the service not just cognitively, but also emotionally.

If a customer experiences a service as exceptionally good, he will subconsciously remember this moment with positive emotion. Emotions are an important part of our memory and complement Descartes' "cogito" with an essential component.

Satisfaction is central to a service-oriented company. This should not, however, be a goal marker, but the starting point of all efforts in order to fix the service brand in the customer's memory with a positive surprise effect.

CASE The Ritz-Carlton does not simply want to serve its guests – we want to win our guests over. Winning someone over means to be appealing, to draw attention in a pleasant way, to create a positive feeling, to see a winning smile during a conversation, or to feel a connection with someone. In order to find out what our customers truly expect, a system of numerous feedback loops exists that transmits precise information about our guests.

Guest Incident Action Form
This form is intended to document in standard fashion and to forward any special events or wishes on the part of the guest. Every employee is obliged to use these forms.

Guest Correspondence Comment Cards
Comment cards are laid out in all rooms. It should be noted, however, that most of our guests only communicate the most positive or negative experiences using the cards. Nevertheless, they are an important indication of the perception of our services.

Third party surveys
In order to explore certain target groups in more detail, surveys are conducted by independent institutes on a regular basis. Target groups are defined so as to design, rethink, and modify certain product areas, such as spa and wellness centers, club floor, guest areas, etc.

Telephone surveys
This involves phoning guests chosen at random, who have spent a night in one of our hotels (via GALLUP). Feedback is summarized in a monthly report with an emphasis on the standard level and the overall customer trends. We believe surveys should be conducted orally and not through questionnaires, since a conversation allows for more precise detail – this approach also corresponds to our principles of personal service.

2. Employees as representatives of the company

As already mentioned, service-oriented companies are largely represented by their employees. A customer requiring a service has many potential providers. It is possible that he can obtain the same products at different prices. The service, however, that he experiences during the process is unique, since he will be interacting with people.

Another 'P' must therefore be added to the well-known four marketing 'P's (Product, Placement, Promotion, and Price) – a 'P' for people who provide the contact between the company (the brand) and the guest (client/customer). It is clear that the employee is perceived as "the Company" by the customer and seen as its representative. The commitment and competence of individual employees thus makes the difference. We need to understand that strong core customer loyalty is impossible without positive human communication.

Quality has two aspects. One aspect consists of the products that satisfy the customer's needs to the extent possible. The other aspect is the quality of the perceived condition we term "freedom from flaws." Flaws can arise at many points and in many ways – poor material or poor workmanship or defective packaging – most frequently, however, they appear in the customer-employee relationship. This is not due to bad employees or inappropriate expectations on the part of the customer. These flaws occur if the communication on a product sparks expectations in a customer of which the employee is not aware and that he is not in a position to satisfy.

Flaws perceived by the customer are the evidence of unsuccessful communication of a corporate philosophy to the customer and employee. Quality management must, therefore, be equally concerned with communicating the corporate philosophy as with maintaining the hardware.

Another important point in quality management is to identify areas in which the employee can exceed expectations. In addition to the core competencies of a service company, there exists a multitude of potential interactions – both verbal and non-verbal – that tell the customer that he is the center of attention. In order to ensure that these opportunities do not disappear due to the daily routine, they must be actively elucidated and utilized as a field of action.

CASE Mr. Miller calls Hotel X and makes a reservation. During the call with the hotel employee, he emphasizes that he is only able to sleep on stones and that he would like these to be placed in his bed prior to his arrival. A few days later, Mr. Miller arrives at the hotel, the check-in is efficient and the receptionist who takes Mr. Miller is naturally friendly and demonstrates to Mr. Miller all the equipment in his room. Everything is according to expectations – even the stones in the bed. Up to this point, individual service has been provided. The guest wanted stones and he got them.

The next morning Mr. Miller drops by the reception. One of the employees recognizes Mr. Miller, addresses him by name and asks after his night's sleep on the stones. The employee wins over the guest.

This is the moment at which individual service is transformed into personal service. The employee shows true interest in the guest's well-being. This creates trust and transmits a feeling of belonging, of enthusiasm, or even passion.

There are many opportunities of this nature for employees, that occur throughout the day. It is management's task to stimulate creativity with regard to such moments in each employee. Creativity is a marketing tool that is still completely underestimated in service-oriented companies.

3. Only those talented become true experts

A talent is a natural ability that has not been attained by effort. Individuals with talent for a certain job experience deep satisfaction if they can live out their special abilities and improve them. This leads to an intuitively correct attitude on the part of the individual. A talent can be cultivated to such an extent that the resulting performance is almost perfect. Talents are constellations of the themes that make up the whole person.

A company that relies on intuitively correct attitudes from its employees must not make the mistake of using recruitment policies with a technical focus. If the customer's needs are understood, and the correct hardware installed, employees must be able first to understand the concept behind the company and its products, and second – and this is the key point – to live this concept themselves. Experiencing and living a concept is a highly complex process in which the factors of socialization, culture, and experience play an important role. These factors are extremely stable and develop and change only over lengthy time intervals, that cannot be substituted by in-house company training sessions. It is precisely for this reason that it is indispensable that the first selection criterion in recruiting new staff should be "talent."

Talents are often defined by certain themes that allow one individual to rise above others. A theme is a recurring pattern of thoughts, feelings, and behaviors that remains constant over time. It is essential and fundamental in the understanding of individuals. Themes allow us to describe a particular talent. In a certain way, they are the components of this talent. Observation of themes and overall talent allow us to explain and predict behavior. The following aspects are among those that are observed during the selection process for a specific "line" of employees: team work, work ethic, empathy, persuasive skills, interpersonal communication, precision, willingness to learn, etc.

(Talent + Fit) x Training = Performance + Competence

Talent is thus the basic condition to fulfill a requirement. In order to achieve excellence, however, two additional factors are necessary – "fit" and training. Fit describes the suitability of a talent to work in a certain environment. An employee who is talented with respect to service may, for instance, not agree with the dress code of the hotel or its team philosophy. These overall conditions, however, are the sole orientation point of the employee's daily routine, in addition to the philosophy. The intuitive combination of these two factors forms the foundation for spontaneously correct behavior in work processes, behavior that cannot be planned in advance. In addition the employee must be self-motivated. Refinement of talent occurs using meaningful and exacting training. A talent can only achieve excellence, if it possesses the right mix of behavior and themes, that are recognized and reinforced; this is never achieved without interpersonal relationships and investment. Training is equivalent to an investment with high yields – we recommend dividing this step into talent-oriented, technical, targeted, and principle-based basic value training and then strengthening the individual elements.

CASE Many companies concentrate too much on technical training. Demands on employees under the daily work routine should not, however, be dealt with only on a technical level, but require a comprehensive, interactive solution approach. At various levels in the hierarchy, therefore, The Ritz-Carlton concentrates on two basic values: philosophy and overall conditions. Together with a total training concept, therefore, these orientation points give each employee the liberty of making the right decision at the right time. Training contents and the relevant working standards required to master these two work orientation points alone are summarized in the Gold Standards. (The Ritz-Carlton Hotel Company L. L. C.) They include:

- The Credo,
- The Motto,
- The 3 Steps of Service,
- The 20 Basics,
- The Employee Promise.

All these are recorded on the "Credo Card" that every employee carries. The purpose is to ensure that everyone has access to and awareness of the philosophy, values, and goals of the company at all times. They can be communicated simply and precisely. When used as intended, a coherent philosophy becomes apparent in the employee's approach to work. In countries with a Ritz-Carlton, the Credo Card with its Gold Standards is extensively used and "lived" by the employees. This includes the management team in an exemplary role.

The Gold Standards are the foundation of the whole company. Their content is defined by The Ritz-Carlton pyramid model that is updated on an annual basis by the Steering Committee and employees. The vision establishes the approach for the next three to seven years.

Fig. 1: The Ritz-Carlton Credo

THREE STEPS OF SERVICE	THE EMPLOYEE PROMISE	
1 A warm and sincere greeting. Use the guest name, if and when possible. 2 Anticipation and compliance with guest needs. 3 Fond farewell. Give them a warm good-bye and use their names, if and when possible.	At The Ritz-Carlton, our Ladies and Gentlemen are the most important resource in our service commitment to our guests. By applying the principles of trust, honesty, respect, integrity and commitment, we nurture and maximize talent to the benefit of each individual and the company. The Ritz-Carlton fosters a work environment where diversity is valued, quality of life is enhanced, individual aspirations are fulfilled, and The Ritz-Carlton mystique is strengthened.	*"We Are Ladies and Gentlemen Serving Ladies and Gentlemen"*

Fig. 2: The Ritz-Carlton Gold Standards

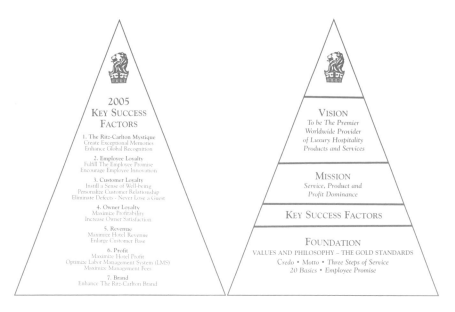

Fig. 3: Ritz-Carlton pyramid model

The following diagram shows the three Steps of Service to the customer and the behavior expected from employees, should the guest at some point be disgruntled for any reason. Here again it is clear that we have to rely on the trained talent of our employees - that they intuitively take the right course of action by combining our philosophy and the relevant situation spontaneously. A general principle is that every employee is authorized to placate a guest. This allows our employees to act efficiently

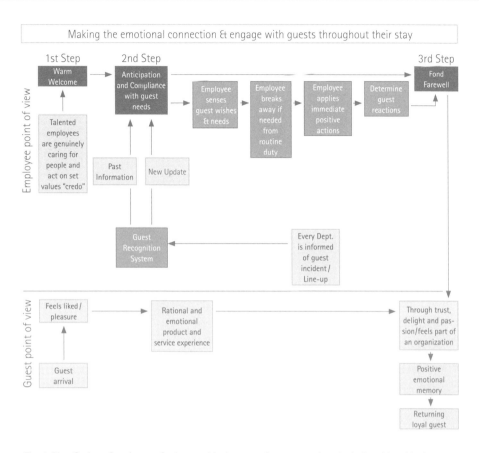

Fig. 4: Ritz-Carlton Continuum for Luxury Market: creating an emotional relationship with the guest during his stay

and confidently. In most cases this approach costs the company much less, and the probability that a guest will attempt to take advantage of the situation is low. The employee is thus authorized to interrupt his job of the moment in order to give his full attention to the dissatisfied guest. The event is then documented and disseminated throughout the hotel, so that all employees are informed of the event. The same information is kept in the guest file for future visits.

4. Summary: the talent-based company

The service rendered to the customer is one of the most important marketing instruments used to generate long-term brand loyalty on the part of customers. Many companies may already have recognized this, but a technically oriented perspective continues to dominate with respect to service performance. As a result, the company fails to utilize one of the key factors in market expansion – the employee – in communicating the company's philosophy.

The contact with the employee is the moment of truth that shows how reliably a company brings its entire product range to the customer, whether a discrepancy exists between the product and the service, whether the company even possesses coherence, or whether the brand claims, products, and services may in fact be under one roof, but are in fact worlds apart.

If, therefore, the company's philosophy is clearly defined and geared towards its product, the issue is to find the right people to represent the company. The most important part of this is talent selection, since without talent the best possible training will not lead to the right goals. Talent cannot be replaced, because it is on the one hand a natural gift and on the other hand determined by the long-term culture-dependent socialization process.

In order to ensure that this talent contributes to the company, training must be seen as an investment that allows talent to be expanded in all aspects. The goal of training must be that the employees are able to act intuitively in accordance with the situation, and to do so with strong self-confidence and inner freedom. The working environment should, therefore, not be excessively restrictive, but talent-oriented with the requisite freedom, productive guidelines, and clear goals.

Case: Selection and on-the-job training of employees in the Ritz Carlton. A standardized procedure to create and maintain a core of talent-oriented employees

▸ Process & Implementation

Phase 1: Selection

Guests pass on their high expectations of a luxury brand to the employees, who should provide consistent, excellent, and personal service at each guest contact. As a result, the preselection of suitable candidates should be undertaken with care and consistency throughout the departments. First, potential candidates are interviewed by phone by the department manager to receive a general impression. If the candidate appears suitable, the selection procedure is initiated; this consists of line staff, mentors, managers, and selected executive employees. The analysis of the candidate's profile is then transmitted to the department manager; he conducts a suitability test and initiates an interview. The Human Resources Director and the hotel manager are always involved in the selection procedure, and only if all participants agree, is the employment contract issued.

Phase 2: Orientation

Each new employee receives an initial orientation, lasting two days, prior to starting in a specific department. The structure of the orientation program is the same worldwide.

Beginning a new job implies getting to know a whole new work environment in which the employee is unfamiliar, both with the work routine and the colleagues. Typical worries are: "Will I meet the hotel's expectations? Who are

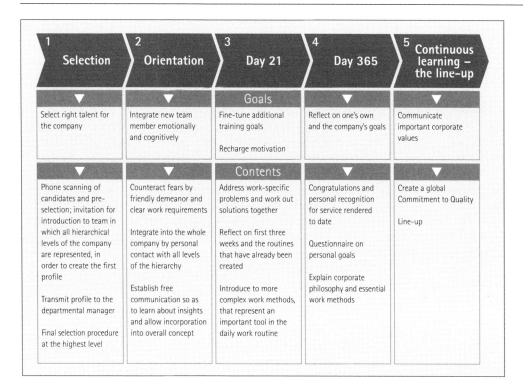

Fig. 5: Customer Service Process

my colleagues? Will I understand the philosophy and does everyone really live this philosophy?" Good management will have established the appropriate procedures to provide the new employee with the requisite information about the company and its philosophy. From the first day, he should receive a clear orientation and idea of where he is now working. Moreover, and this is the most important factor for everyone, he should be welcomed into the Ritz-Carlton family and given the feeling that he is the hotel's most important resource.

The first day begins with a warm welcome on the part of the management team. Each member introduces himself and wishes the new employee a good and successful start. After the introductory phase, employees perform an exercise called "Focus on You" in which they introduce themselves and get to know the other course participants better. The General Manager arrives and explains the company's history and the basic values of the hotel. This could, of course, also be done by the Training Manager, but the presence of the General Manager not only sets the appropriate expectations, but allows him to be identified with the hotel's basic values. This is a key element of the two-day orientation session.

In general, all meetings with management in the orientation phase should include as much interaction with the employees as possible, to pave the way for employees to always be ready to contribute new ideas and improvements. Orientation days should be especially memorable and we, therefore, always have a lunch break in our restaurants where the management team meets with the group and answers any questions. An important aspect, and therefore an important part of the training, is to experience the hotel as a guest.

The Human Resources Director explains the fundamental rules of the employee manual, distributed with an additional information file, that each employee is required to follow from the first day on. Any questions in this regard should be immediately clarified.

Phase 3: Day 21

It is common knowledge that after 21 days in a new job, morale drops for a variety of reasons. We want to know what the new employee has experienced in these 21 days and what he thinks and feels. We, therefore, organize the "Day 21 Meeting" in order to elicit feedback from employees. Have we met the employee's expectations? Have we fulfilled the promises given during orientation? Furthermore, we clarify future obligations.

Particular emphasis on Day 21 is laid on how to handle complaints. After the first three weeks, the employee will have experienced how important it is to handle guest complaints in a professional manner. Our employees must understand that complaints present new opportunities for them. We want them to decide individually what to do at the relevant moment in order to solve the problem.

The General Manager or Hotel Manager then joins in so as to explain why the "feeling of satisfaction" is so important and why it is the key factor in whether the guest returns or not. Then the employees provide general feedback on their experiences of the first 21 days. It is important to know whether someone was beside them at all times for support. Regardless of the discussion topic, responses to questions are thus first-hand. We also prepare a questionnaire for employees in which they are to assess the company's values on a scale of 1 to 5. This documentation is then provided to the management team, so that an action plan can be developed. The last activity of day 21 is a structured quiz concerning the hotel and occupancy ratios, relating to the points that all employees must be familiar with.

Phase 4: Day 365

Belonging to a company for a year is cause for celebration. Employees receive an anniversary pin and we expect feedback after 365 days with the company. We bring the Gold Standards – the company's basic values – to life.

First the Director of Human Resources congratulates every course participant and elucidates a series of topics, such as employee satisfaction, questionnaire results, appearance, line-ups, special recognition, and a repetition of the company's structure. A further important point is to stress the corporate philosophy. The employees are asked to fill out a questionnaire in which they describe why they have stayed with the company for a year, how the presence of the management team is felt in the hotel, whether the Gold Standards have been lived and which aspects we can improve upon in order to be among the very best. This questionnaire is evaluated by general management and presented in a separate feedback session.

Phase 5: Continuous learning – the line-up

The line-up offers a unique opportunity every day for today's Ritz-Carlton; everyone discusses the same topic at the beginning of the shift in every department throughout every hotel. Corporate standards are learned and repeated. Employees in Dubai talk about the same principles of the day as their colleagues in New York, the staff in Shanghai read the same employee story on Monday as those in Berlin. It is this consistency that allows us to strengthen the corporate culture in The Ritz-Carlton.

As the result of the daily line-up, not only is everyone clear about the corporate goals, but also about how we intend to achieve them. Every one of us helps achieve these goals and everyone is reminded of the individual role they play in their own hotel. The line-ups exist for our benefit. Regardless of how many hotels and companies we acquire, we are ONE organization with ONE vision and ONE mission.

In 1991, when the Ritz-Carlton was preparing for the Malcolm Baldridge National Quality Award, there was a multitude of information that had to be distributed to the hotels. The line-up seemed to be the best way to do this. Since then, the Daily Commitment to Quality has been implemented. It became a habit and, after the prize was won in 1993, the Commitment continued. To this date, it is the most significant daily means of communication. The Commitment of Quality is written by the Corporate Office and responds to the wishes and requirements of the ladies and gentlemen in The Ritz-Carlton. The majority of topics mentioned in the line-up are related to corporate goals. These are goals that help us to ensure that all employees work towards corporate goals in an effective and focused manner.

▸ Key Insights

- Establishing fundamental values, understood, lived by and believed in by all employees, is a prerequisite for any successful company.
- Employee selection must be based on their talents and appropriateness for the relevant job. The first training should take place based on the underlying company philosophy – advanced training can concentrate on technical aspects.
- Good communication and the repetition of basic values are assured by daily line-ups. Briefings include all employees concerned.
- Systems such as CLASS (The Ritz-Carlton Hotel Company) support the dissemination of customers' wishes.
- A continuous measurable feedback of customer satisfaction and resulting improvements motivate a team to work better.
- Rapid action on the part of skilled employees allows a guest to quickly forget bad experiences and prevents the guest from going to the competition at a later date.
- Train and inspire your employees in the art of winning over the guest for the company – it is not enough that guests like your hotel – they must love it.

▸ Practical Guidelines

- Basic values must be exemplified by the boss. Create direct contact with your employees, lead by example and describe your expectations clearly before you expect something.
- Don't put yourself in the position of having to hire the next best person who comes in the door, only so as to have two extra hands to help. Don't compromise – you may be dogged by the results and it is not fair on your colleagues, if something goes wrong as a result.
- Get to know the strengths and weaknesses of your team and pick the right job for each individual – fit them in! It is only if an employee shows sound competence (a combination of quick analysis, product knowledge, and problem solution systems) that a genuine atmosphere of confidence is created.
- Discipline among individuals and the team need not limit ideas and innovation. A certain healthy willingness to assume risk in the management team allows the trial and error process to flow.
- Suppliers must be chosen with care. They, too, must have the same quality standards and corporate philosophy as your company.
- Keep all those involved in the company informed. Owners must be aware of corporate goals and should be educated with respect to market situation and profit expectations. We need a holistic approach.
- Integrity and trustworthiness lead to confidence from the guests.
- Goals and participation should not be directed solely at financial benefits, but should also include employee and customer satisfaction. A satisfied and engaged employee results in satisfied guests and, ultimately, in positive financial results.

The Author

Rainer Bürkle

Rainer Bürkle started with The Ritz-Carlton Hotel Company in 1992 after studying at Cornell University, U.S. Previously, he had worked in Germany, Switzerland, and England for a variety of hotels and hotel chains, including Hilton and Savoy Hotels. During his time at The Ritz-Carlton, he has worked in a number of different hotels, and has held a number of different positions in the U.S., Germany, and Turkey. He has been General Manager of The Ritz-Carlton in Berlin since 2004. Moreover, he is Vice President and Area General Manager for hotels in Istanbul, Wolfsburg, and Moscow.

Literature Recommendations

D. Bowie, "Hospitality Marketing" Amsterdam, New York 2004
P. Mene, "Application Summary" The Ritz-Carlton Hotel Company, LLC – Malcolm Baldrige National Quality Award 1999 & 1992, 2000
C. Ober, "Hotel and Resorts Marketing Intelligence," Sydney 2000
A. Chastonay, "Cesar Ritz, Life and Work," 1997
T. Schumacher, "Wenn Du viel erreichen willst, tue wenig," Weinheim 2005

Harald W. Eisenächer, Sascia Hilverkus – Deutsche Lufthansa AG

Customer Retention System

Customer benefit, value appreciation, communication, and systems are all success factors of profitable customer retention

▶ Executive Summary

- Strategic investment in building an international customer retention program pays off if the program has clear goals and a business plan has been defined.
- In addition to loyalty and volume discounts, and the bonus points that a customer can earn when using a customer card, status logic is important. The actual customer differentiation occurs only on the basis of internationally identifiable status logic. This differentiation is based purely on the customer's quality rating. In addition to status and the related privileges, feelings of belonging and identity and a prestige effect vis-à-vis third parties are generated.
- A central role is played by the international partner portfolio in a customer retention program. From the customer's perspective, it considerably enhances the appeal of the program, and from the company's perspective, partners can greatly contribute to program profitability.
- This article shows those responsible for marketing a model as well as a process regarding customer retention and customer retention programs. Essential prerequisites and functional mechanisms of customer retention are enumerated for the reader, and the process of initiating customer retention and customer retention programs is illustrated.

▶ Theoretical Model of the Customer Retention System

Background

Companies introduce customer retention programs in order to attract, identify or get to know, develop, and retain customers much more efficiently than before in times of increasing competition. Brand loyalty is waning in many industries, while price criteria are becoming more important. In order to be able to attain a price premium in such markets, generating customer benefits that reach beyond the core product has become more important. Moreover, customization of individual services requires a more precise knowledge of the customer, which consequently leads to the stimulation of sales and, thus, to additional revenue.

1. Definition

Customer retention refers to the capability of identifying valuable customers and binding them to the company by means of customer benefits, in order to increase the company's revenues and profits.

2. Factors in customer retention

Successful customer retention programs are composed of the factors of basic services, supplementary services and value appreciation. A prerequisite for a customer retention system is a professional database system that not only supplies customer touch points with the correct information, but also provides a framework for individualized communication.

2.1 Basic services (basic values)

The basis of the customer retention program is formed by loyalty or volume discounts, as well as bonus points, that the customer can earn when using the customer card. An important issue is whether loyalty or volume discounts and bonus points are accumulated over a specified period of time or whether such discounts and points are valid indefinitely. Moreover, it must be determined whether there are different value ratings for loyalty or volume discounts, as well as for bonus points, and whether they can be used internationally. In order to receive these discounts and points, the customers are required to register for the program and, thus, provide their private addresses.

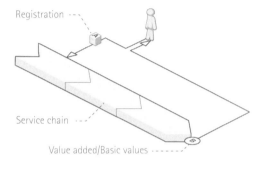

Fig. 1: After registering, the customer receives basic services (basic values) for the points he or she has earned from the normal service category, e.g., miles

2.2 Value appreciation

The company shows its value appreciation via the individualized products and services that the customer receives along the value creation chain, defined through status, preferential treatment, and personal service. In order to differentiate and personalize products and services for the customer, a certain status logic needs to be defined that is linked to certain privileges. A feeling of belonging and identity, as well as a prestige effect vis-à-vis third parties, is generated. This is the emotional moment in the customer retention program.

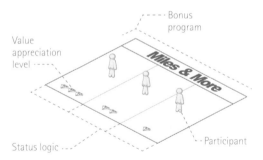

Fig. 2: Program participants are allocated to different value appreciation levels depending on their significance; these form a basis for selecting available added values

2.3 Supplementary services (added values)

Based on status logic, individualized added services (added values) are offered to the customer along the company's entire service chain, depending on the customer's quality rating. In order to be able to offer these individualized added services, the company must have access to the following information:

- Who are my valued customers and which countries do they live in?
- Which supplementary services provide the most utility value to my valued customers?
- How many customers can I service worldwide given the resources and infrastructure per status level?

In the event that knowledge concerning the customer is not yet available in the company, the information must be obtained by means of market research and customer surveys. In order to calculate customers' quality ratings, a customer-value based methodology (customer equity) can be used. The customer equity value is primarily determined by a customer lifecycle model. Important customers can be identified and approached at an early stage. This methodology is used for the focused development of supplementary services (added values) as part of the customer retention program. Based on customer knowledge, a precise analysis of the company's own worldwide value creation chain takes place.

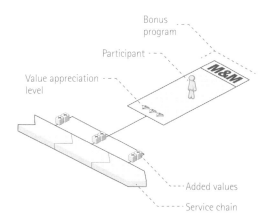

Fig. 3: Depending on value appreciation levels, the program participants receive supplementary services along the service chain – "added values"

2.4 Database system

It is only on the basis of reliable and up-to-date information that products and service processes can be tailored to the customer's needs more effectively, marketing activities can be conducted based on target groups, and sales channels can be utilized. The advantage of a customer retention program is that customers would like to stay informed about the status of their loyalty or volume discounts, as well as their bonus points, and, thus, have a self-interest in updating their data. This data flows into the database system, often called the Customer Retention Management System (CRM system). As a first step, the CRM system must be linked to all relevant, although not always compatible, IT systems. The data obtained in this fashion must be available for direct end user access for management analyses and reporting, as well as to provide information to existing internal and external systems. Reservation and sales data, status-relevant information, and advertising campaign information should all flow into the CRM system. This customer information is available at the customer touch points, so that the customer can be offered an individualized service. The CRM system also controls the global communication campaigns.

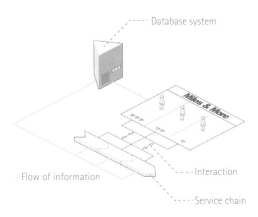

Fig. 4: A database system, in which data concerning customer interactions is stored and analyzed, forms the basis of focused customer retention

2.5 Customer touch points

All contact points that the customer has with a company are considered customer touch points. These contacts can be personal, but they can also take place via other media. Outstanding service experiences have a significant influence on customer satisfaction and, consequently, on customer retention. Particularly in the service sector, customer contact along the entire value creation chain is intense and, therefore, strongly affects customer retention. Manufacturing industries can expand their customer contact through after-sales care, for example. Complaint management is a critical customer touch point. Through appropriately proactive customer communication and compensation in case of disservice, customer retention can even be increased. If a complaint is poorly handled, however, a customer may cease to generate sales for the company, either temporarily or permanently.

2.6 Communication

The customer's attention can be drawn to the customer retention program at all available customer touch points. In addition, the communication channels Internet and traditional advertising can also make reference to the customer retention program. The integration of partners significantly increases the dissemination and communication opportunities of the program. If the customer is a member of the customer retention program, he can be invited to use a product with individual incentives via direct marketing (one-to-one marketing). The customer-value-based methodology (customer equity) can also be used in this case. Management of the customer's mailbox is enabled in such a fashion that the customer only receives offers or information that are of relevance to him or personalized for him. This management of marketing resources increases marketing efficiency by generating additional sales and/or lowering costs. Personalized communication consists, in part, in providing customers within a homogeneous segment with individual incentives or targets. Customers receive a target based on their prior consumer behavior in the form of additional consumption, and an incentive in the form of discounts or bonus points. One important aspect is the possibility of creating control groups in order to monitor the effects of communication measures.

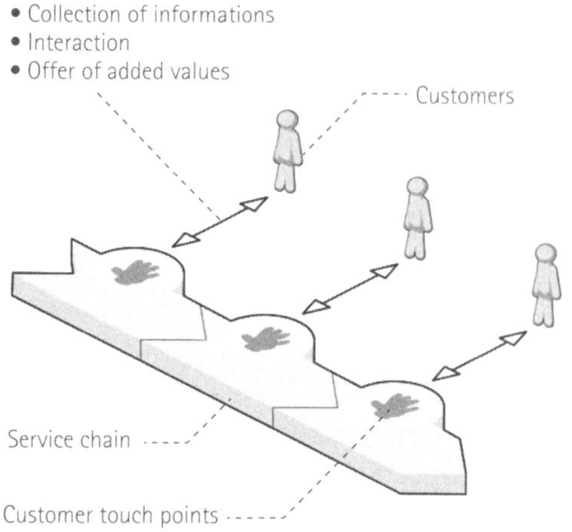

- Collection of informations
- Interaction
- Offer of added values

Customers

Service chain

Customer touch points

Fig. 5: Contact points with the customer can be defined at every point in the service chain at which information can be collected and added values offered

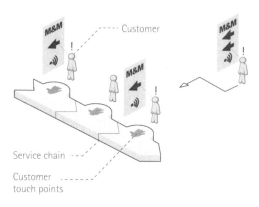

Service chain

Customer touch points

Fig. 6: Communication of the customer retention program occurs at the customer touch points and directly in the market

2.7 Partnership

The global partner portfolio plays a central role within a customer retention program. From the customer's perspective it considerably enhances the appeal of the program, and from the company's perspective partners can greatly contribute to program profitability. For program members, the more opportunities that exist for earning or redeeming bonus points or discounts, the more attractive it becomes to them. This is especially true abroad. Several influencing factors determine strategy when developing the partner portfolio: customer requirements and the relevance of the partners to the customers, the image or the brand power, and the economic size of the partners, as well as their "geographic fit." The advantage of the partners is in attracting and retaining new customers brought in by means of the program partnership. The larger the global network, the easier it is for the customer to shop within the network, and the higher are the switching costs.

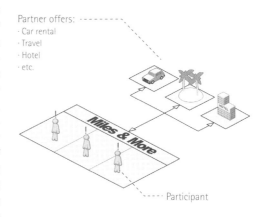

Fig. 7: Partnerships with other providers, that accept the program's bonus points, increase the appeal for the participants

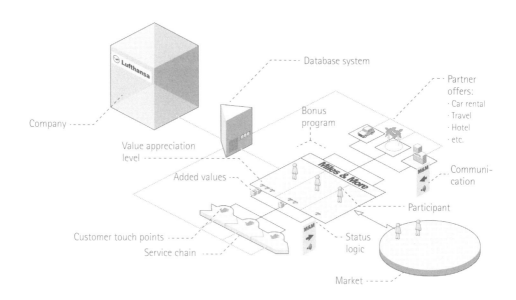

Fig. 8: Overall model of the customer retention system

CASE Miles & More

The Miles & More customer retention program was established in 1993 and has developed into an essential and profitable building block in the Lufthansa strategy. Miles & More is the largest customer retention program in Europe, with more than ten million members. The program includes c. 4.3 million members in Germany and c. 5.7 million members abroad. With 120 partners and the Star Alliance global network, Miles & More is a premium customer retention program with attractive earn and spend options.

Basic Values – Miles

Fig. 9: Miles & More members are credited with miles at the time of check-in

The Miles & More award miles represent the discount that Lufthansa or its partners award for the use of their respective services. As soon as a customer has become a Miles & More member, he can start to collect premium miles. These are credited to the customer's personal Miles & More account. Once he has reached a certain mile limit, the customer can exchange these award miles for the award of his choice. Customers can earn award miles with Lufthansa, its airline, hotel and car rental partners, and partners from the financial services, telecommunication and automotive industry. In total, the customer can earn miles at more than 22 million acceptance points. Members can redeem miles with almost all partners from whom they can collect award miles. Every award can be claimed against a certain mile value.

An award trip in Economy class from Hamburg to Lisbon and back requires 30,000 award miles; if booked within 14 days prior to departure, only 15,000 award miles need to be used. An award flight from Milan to New York via Frankfurt costs 60,000 award miles in Economy class (if booked at the last minute, 50,000 award miles), 90,000 in Business class, and 140,000 award miles in First Class. An around-the-world award flight in Economy class costs 180,000, in Business class 280,000 and First Class 400,000 award miles.

The award of miles is based on the number of miles actually flown, the service class booked (First, Business and Economy Class) and the booking class. Thus, there is a stronger incentive to purchase high-value tickets than there is for the more affordable tickets; this principle applies particularly in Economy Class.

Value Appreciation – Status logic

Fig. 10: The HON Circle card is the key to exclusive privileges

A key difference with regard to traditional bonus programs, such as Deutsche Telekom's Happy Digits or Payback, is the "status logic" based on so-called status miles. Customer differentiation is a function of status miles. This differentiation is oriented purely according to the quality rating of the customer, that again is based on the number of status miles earned in a year.

All the miles that are collected while flying Lufthansa or partners of Star Alliance are status miles. A customer who has flown more that 50,000 status miles in a year receives the status of Frequent Traveler; if he has traveled more than 150,000 status miles, he attains Senator status. While expanding customer differentiation at the beginning of December 2004, Lufthansa introduced the status of HON Circle member. A customer is given this exclusive top customer status if he has flown 600,000 HON Circle status miles within two calendar years on Lufthansa, Lufthansa Regional, Austrian Airlines Group, LOT Polish Airlines, Air Dolomiti, Air One, Croatia Airlines, Adria Airlines and SWISS. The HON Circle status is automatically extended if the participant again earns 600,000 HON Circle miles in the next two calendar years. Customer cards with credit card functions are an expression of the status that brings with it a feeling of belonging and identity, as well as the a prestige effect vis-à-vis third parties. Being named as the HON Circle member with its related privileges expresses extraordinary value appreciation.

Fig. 11: HON Circle communication – HON Circle member is addressed emotionally

Added Values – Easy travel

Fig. 12: Since December of 2004, the exclusive First Class terminal has been at the disposal of Lufthansa First Class guests and the HON Circle members.

Status logic allows Lufthansa to identify and differentiate their most valuable customers along the entire service chain, and to treat them according to their quality rating. A Senator, for example, can make a flight reservation using a dedicated telephone number; even if the chosen flight is fully booked, the Senator is able to make a reservation with the so-called booking guarantee for Senators. The resulting bill can be paid with the free Lufthansa Miles & More Visa card. At the airport, the Senator can check in at the exclusive First Class counter, even if he has booked only in Business or Economy Class. Excess baggage is not charged up to a certain limit. On the way to the departure gate, he can take time out in the exclusive Senator Lounge. And if a Senator wants to bring a companion on an award flight, he only needs to spend half the miles for the companion. The so-called Executive Bonus should be highlighted as well: Status customers are awarded an additional 25 percent award and status miles on all flights with Lufthansa or a Star Alliance partner. This helps to differentiate and provide targeted incentives to frequent flyers. .

Exclusive service for the HON Circle, an additional frequent flyer status above Senator status, begins on the ground in the newly constructed First Class Terminal in Frankfurt. Lufthansa is setting new international standards in the premium travel segment with this service. Concierge service, limousine transfer directly to the airplane, an exclusive atmosphere in a gourmet restaurant and personal service for guests, from arrival to departure, are part of the special service that Lufthansa uses to make their HON Circles and First Class guests even more comfortable when traveling. Lufthansa takes over the usual process of arriving at the airport, parking the car, check-in, security check, and customs for its customers in Frankfurt. HON Circle members and First Class Lufthansa passengers can use their time to departure effectively in the First Class Terminal in an area of c. 1,800 sq. meters. A "personal assistant" is available to the guest throughout his stay. He can decide how he wants to spend the time to departure – separate rooms, offices with telephones, notebook connection, and office supplies allow the guest the opportunity of working in absolute privacy. He can relax in specially equipped resting rooms. Modern and spaciously designed bathrooms with showers and bathtubs permit the passenger to freshen up before or after a long trip. The guests can make themselves comfortable on inviting sofas, armchairs and recliners, watch television or select reading material from a wide range of newspapers and magazines. In addition, there are opportunities for viewing individual films, listening to music and surfing the Internet with Wireless LAN. In the restaurant in the First Class Terminal, chefs prepare seasonal dishes in full view of the guests. A separate cigar lounge is available for smokers, providing snacks and drinks. First Class Terminal guests are chauffeured to the plane in good time before departure in a Mercedes Benz S-class or Porsche Cayenne. In Munich, a similar First Class service was established in 2005, and even in airports outside of Europe, HON Circle members will receive individualized service upon arrival.

Benefits for the HON Circle member include:

- Booking guarantee: HON Circle members have a more advantageous booking guarantee than Senators, under applicable tariff terms with Lufthansa, Austrian Airlines, and LOT Polish Airlines flights. They always benefit from a guaranteed reservation if they book their Business Class flights in booking classes C and D at least 24 hours in advance (for Economy Class flights in booking class Y, at least 72 hours in advance) of the departure.
- Waitlist priority: HON Circle members have the highest waiting list priority if a Lufthansa, Austrian Airlines or LOT Polish Airlines flight is fully booked.
- Improved award availability: the HON Circle member and up to three accompanying passengers are guaranteed an award reservation up to 14 days before departure, provided there are still seats available in the service class chosen (Business or Economy).
- Access to Lounges: in addition to the First Class Lounges in the Frankfurt airport and the lounge area in the First Class Terminal in Frankfurt, First Class passengers and HON Circle members can also use the Lufthansa Senator and Star Gold Lounges.
- Partner card: upon request, the spouse or partner of the HON Circle member will also be named as Senator.
- Executive bonus: the HON Circle member already has advantages when earning miles. For each flight on Lufthansa, Lufthansa Regional, Adria Airways, Air Canada, Croatia Airline, SWISS, Austrian Airlines Group, Air Dolomiti, Air One, LOT Polish Airlines, United Airlines, and US Airways, he receives an additional 50 percent of distance miles or 50 percent of the fixed mile value in Europe.
- Upgrade vouchers: HON Circle members receive six electronic upgrade vouchers when their status are named or extended.
- Credit card: all participants who have a bank account in Germany receive the Lufthansa HON Circle credit card, with no annual fee, that provides enhanced services. It combines the function of earning miles with those of a traditional credit card.
- Special hotline: an exclusive service hotline has been instituted for HON Circle members. Employees are available around the clock, every day, to answer travel queries.

Significant sales increases were noted after the launch of the HON Circle status. The supplementary service for the most valuable customers enhances customer satisfaction and, thereby, customer retention.

Database system

All data on Miles & More customers is administrated in a central CRM system that has interfaces with all related Lufthansa IT systems. The relevant customer touch point requires information on the customer's status in every process phase. Status customers have waitlist priority at the time of booking depending on their quality rating. Frequent Flyers are always permitted to check in at the Business counter, and Senators as well as HON Circle members can use the First Class counter. With the First Class Terminal, the check-in and boarding processes are shortened and made much more convenient for HON Circle members in Frankfurt. Additional lounge access is regulated via status as well. Advertising campaigns also flow into the CRM system, so that the customer's mailbox can be

Fig. 13: The Senator is automatically credited with miles when using Quick Check-in

managed. This is of key significance due, in particular, to the large number of partners. One essential point is the quality of the data in the database. Since Miles & More customers are interested in regular information on their mile balances, the address database is very up-to-date. In order to communicate more efficiently, e-mail addresses increasingly are used, provided permission has been granted by the customer. Use of personal customer data must be in accordance with EU guidelines on data protection, as well as data protection laws in the originator countries.

Customer touch points

An airline has the advantage that numerous customer touch points arise during a flight – from the reservation and check-in, through the time awaiting departure and the moment of boarding, to the flight itself. Intense customer contact occurs with colleagues on board and on the ground, so that the opportunity exists to enthuse customers for the program or to generate loyalty from existing customers by dint of extraordinary service.

Fig. 14: HON Circle members, Senators, and First Class guests have access to the Senator Lounge

On board, moreover, there is the in-flight magazine, duty-free sales and questionnaires, as well as in-flight entertainment on intercontinental flights, all of which offer opportunities to communicate with the customer.

Communication

The customer can obtain information on Miles & More from all customer touch points in Lufthansa's value creation chain. Communication with Miles & More members takes place on a periodic basis. Non-status customers receive the newsletter four times a year and a statement of account activity four times a year. The newsletter contains all the news about Miles & More. It is published in seven languages. Status customers in Germany receive the "Exclusive Magazine," which contains Miles & More information, as well as parts of the Lufthansa in-flight magazine. Status customers abroad receive the international Exclusive Magazine four times a year, which primarily contains information on Miles & More. This, too, is published in seven languages. Furthermore, all status customers are advised on their account balance six times a year. Upon request, customers can also subscribe to the monthly on-line newsletter. Twice a year, the Lufthansa WorldShop award catalogue is issued, and is sent to all status customers and all basic customers with over 30,000 award miles.

Fig. 15: Status customers in Germany receive the "Exclusive Magazine" on a monthly basis

All offers can also be obtained online. Currently, over 1.3 million flight, goods, travel, and experience awards are being issued around the world on an annual basis. Communication with the customer can be significantly more focused by means of status differentiation. This reduces costs on the one hand, and on the other, ensures that customers are addressed in an individualized manner. Experience shows that the more precisely the customer's needs are being addressed, the greater is his attention to the products offered. This is evermore important in an environment characterized by information overload. Traditional promotions of Frequent Flyer programs have a direct geographical relationship and, yet, also advertise offers that are the same across the board. Lufthansa nowadays only conducts promotions with uniform mileage incentives for new routes. In this case, the objective is to generate attention for, and gain market share in, the new route. The point, therefore, is not so much the generation of additional revenues, but the positioning of a new product (the new route) in the market. And Miles & More, in this case, becomes a component in the classical marketing mix of price, product, and distribution channel communication.

The next step in creating a promotion is individualization. Customers within a homogeneous segment receive individual incentives and individual targets. Based on their previous flying behavior, customers receive a target in the form of additional Lufthansa flights, and an incentive based on miles. The following example should clarify this individualization process: three customers – Maier, Schulze, and Schmidt – are contacted. Maier is a basic customer and flew Lufthansa four times a year in the past, within Europe, in Economy Class. Moreover, he used two competitor airlines at least twice. Customer Schulze is a Frequent Traveler and has flown Lufthansa ten times in the past year in Europe in Economy Class, and twice to Japan, also in economy. He flew at least four times with competing airlines in Europe, and at least once with a competitor in the U.S. And customer Schmidt is Senator with twenty Lufthansa flights in Business Class within Europe and ten intercontinental flights to South Africa and South America, also in Business Class. He did not use Lufthansa on at least four other European trips and two other intercontinental flights.

Customer Maier receives the following offer: fly three times with Lufthansa in the next four months to the European destination of your choice, in Economy, and you will receive an additional 5,000 award miles. Based on six known flights in an average "flight year" by customer Maier, the aim is to motivate him to take an additional flight with Lufthansa. The offer to customer Maier may, in certain cases, be supplemented with a "class factor"; he would receive twice the number of miles, if he made the flights in Business Class. Customer Schulze is contacted in the course of two promotions. In one promotion, similarly to customer Maier, an attempt is made to influence his internal European flight behavior, with a strong incentive to use Business Class – fly Lufthansa at least four times in the next three months, within Europe. For flights in Economy Class you will receive an additional 5,000 miles, for flights in Business, an additional 20,000 miles. This corresponds to one free flight based on miles within Europe. Since customer Schulze has not yet used Lufthansa on intercontinental routes to the U.S., he receives the following offer (with a time lag to the "Europe offer"): fly Lufthansa at least once to the U.S. in the next three months and you will receive an additional 6,000 miles, that will also count towards status miles. This offer contains the status miles component as a special incentive and is, thus, especially relevant for the customer. Customer Schmidt now gets similar offers; since, however, he is in jeopardy of losing his Senator status, these offers are linked directly with requalifying for Senator status. Status and award miles are issued and the incentive assures the customer that he can maintain his status. Example: customer Schmidt needs an additional 50,000 miles to requalify for Senator. Against this backdrop, he receives the following offer: fly Lufthansa eight times in Business Class in the next three months and you will automatically requalify for Senator. This offer can be supplemented with an award mile incentive, but experience shows that requalification is usually incentive enough.

The last step after the promotion has been conducted consists of the measurement of results. This already begins when defining the promotion during the "pre-campaign." The customer segment is divided into two groups: the target group and the control group. The target group receives the individualized offers to influence their behavior as described above. The control group, that constitutes c. 20 to 30 percent of the segment, does not receive offers. The control group customers thus behave "normally," that is, without being influenced. After the promotion has ended, revenues from the target group are compared to those from the control group. The difference is termed the promotion success. The success of a promotion is seen in two different time dimensions – the short-term success is the success that is directly achieved by the promotion. In the long term, it becomes apparent that the customers who regularly participate in promotions fly Lufthansa more often, on average. Within Lufthansa, the term "target customer promotion" has become common for this type of individualized promotion.

The range of possible uses for target customer promotions is large, though; in addition to the measures described for increasing revenue, target customer promotions aimed at targeted cost savings are also possible. Customers can be motivated to use cost-efficient Lufthansa services with selected incentives. Examples include the electronic ticket, Etix, and check-in machines at the airport. Customers who have in the past preferred to receive the physical paper ticket, receive an incentive in the form of miles if they switch to Etix, that is more cost-effective for Lufthansa; the miles can be credited to the Miles & More, or the credit card. The incentive lapses after a certain time; by then, however, the customer has become accustomed with the Etix and now uses nothing else. Or the customer may have been accustomed to checking in for his flights at the check-in counter. By using miles selectively as incentives, his behavior can be influenced to such an extent that he checks in by machine in the future. This saves time for him and is a more economical choice for Lufthansa, as well.

Partnerships

The Miles & More global network is a significant success factor from Lufthansa's perspective. Partners are selected based on customer needs, the relevance of the partner to the Miles & More customer, and the image and brand strength of the partner. The worldwide network in the fields of air travel, hotel, car rental, credit card, not to mention additional industries such as telecommunications, financial services, press and electronics and enable Miles & More customers to earn and spend miles everywhere in almost any life situation.

Visa and the Bayerische Landesbank are partners. In 1999 a Visa card was issued. For each Euro paid by the customer, one mile is credited to his Miles & More account. Moreover, award miles can be used indefinitely for all Lufthansa Miles & More credit card holders, regardless of whether they have been earned by flying, paying, or from any of the many Miles & More partners.

Fig. 16: The World Shop catalogue contains all the world Miles & More awards

The card's success is, above all, evidenced by its frequent use. The Lufthansa Miles & More credit card is used more than five times as often as other credit cards. After only five years on the market, therefore, every fifth Euro charged in Germany through Visa is via a Lufthansa Miles & More credit card.

In order to enhance the exclusivity of the HON Circle status, program partners are acquired who are in a position to complement the travel experience of the HON Circle members with additional services. Partners, for example, offer HON Circle members the highest status in their own customer retention programs for free:

- Avis: Membership in the President's Club & Express Preferred Card for spouses/partners.
- Sixt: Sixt Diamond Card & Sixt Diamond Card (for spouses/partners).
- Hilton: Honors Gold VIP membership.
- Hyatt: Platinum Gold Passport membership.
- Kempinski: Private Concierge membership & Suite Upgrade Voucher.
- Vodafone: Platinum Status Vodafone Stars in Germany.

Process & Implementation

Phase 1: Goals

In principle, customer retention can be obtained with companies, people, products, and markets. The company must be clear in this case as to what the customer should bond with. At the financial level, one should specify whether a customer retention program should be financed by marketing funds, should be self-financing by means of additional revenue generated, or should even be operated separately as a profit center. Three levels should be taken into consideration:

- The direct customer retention effect with a system-based incentive function of discounts and status.
- Revenue generated by the sale of customer retention services to the partners, above all in the form of discount and bonus points.
- Additional revenue earned by efficient and individualized direct marketing, the target customer management.

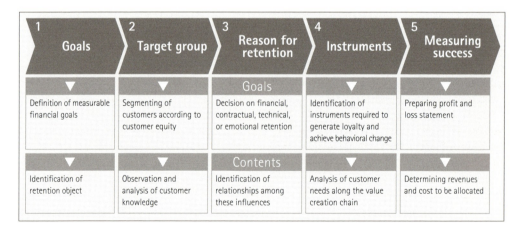

Fig. 17: Customer retention process

Phase 2: Target group

Prior to implementing a customer retention program, customers should be segmented into customer groups, since customer retention activities require considerable investment. A high level of familiarity with the customer is necessary for effective segmentation.

What consumer behavior do customers adopt? What sales do customers generate with the company? What share of total customer sales does the company have (Share of Wallet)? How valuable are the customers to the company based on a life-time value approach? Once the target group has been identified, consideration should be given to how these customers can be attracted to membership in the customer retention program by means of communication, as well as at the customer touch point. The appropriate customer touch points can be selected by means of an analysis of the value creation chain. An important and cost-effective instrument for generating new customers is to attract them by "member gets member" incentivs.

Phase 3: Reasons for retention

Prior to engaging in a customer retention program, the company must be clear about the reasons for retention. One reason may be contractual relationships. Monetary retention reasons exist if a customer receives a reward for loyal behavior and switching costs are therefore high. Technical reasons for retention pertain if a change to another provider is linked to compatibility problems, and barriers to change arise as a result. Customer satisfaction, personal relationships, and customer habits are among the emotional reasons for retention. The customer is, however, also retained due to value appreciation brought about by regular customer contacts.

Phase 4: Instruments

Instruments for retaining customers may be product developments in conjunction with customers and customer forums. Additional instruments could include free supplementary services, volume, and loyalty discounts or bonus programs, customer magazines, invitations to events, 24-hour service or express delivery, after sales care, or convenient locations. Customer clubs are designed for customer retention; they offer clusters of exclusive services, and are based on intense dialogue-oriented communication. A customer card frequently forms part of the customer club and entitles the holder to certain services and bonus services, and may be used as a payment method. Complaint management can also be used as a customer retention instrument. The target group, as segmented during Phase 2, should now be analyzed with respect to its needs, in order to discover the correct supplementary services for the customer retention program. Which offers should the company extend to the customer to fulfill their needs, on the one hand, but also to effect the behavior changes desired, on the other hand? Which instruments can be used to stimulate new needs? What up-selling and cross-selling potential exists among the customers? Are they receptive to offers from outside of the company? Infrastructure and database systems can also be included amongst these instruments. Only a high-quality customer retention system allows the answers to the above questions to be assessed based on customer data. If revenue is to be generated by sales of customer retention services to partners, the IT system must be scalable.

Phase 5: Measuring success

Regular success measurements against the goals defined in Phase 1 should be undertaken for profit and loss calculation purposes. All costs incurred in creating and integrating supplementary services in the value creation chain must be offset against revenue from partners, as well as additional revenue earned from efficient and individualized direct marketing. Communication efficiency in direct marketing is measured by constituting control groups.

▶ Key Insights

- Customer retention and customer retention programs should pursue clear goals.
- Customer retention programs have an effect on the company's entire value creation chain and shift company processes from a production-driven perspective to a customer-oriented perspective.
- Knowledge of customer behavior and needs, as well as clustering of customers according to segment, are among the key success factors in customer retention programs.
- Actual customer differentiation occurs based on status logic. This differentiation is based purely on the customer's quality rating. The status level may be differently defined internationally, since it depends on the opportunity of acquiring the relevant status abroad.
- In attracting high-quality partners, it is essential to know the customers' quality rating.
- The image and brand strength of partners, as well as the extent to which customer needs are taken into account, have a significant impact on the success of the customer retention program.
- The farther the global network of the partners extends, the easier it is for the customer to shop in the network, and the higher the switching costs are.
- A good customer retention program is profitable. It generates additional revenue in the core business, as well as via partners.

▶ Practical Guidelines

- Customer retention occurs at each customer touch point. Customer complaints are also customer touch points and, therefore, opportunities to (again) shape customer loyalty.
- Use of personal customer data must be in accordance with EU data protection guidelines, as well as the data protection laws in the originator countries.
- Professional database management is the prerequisite for a successful customer retention program.
- In assessing CRM systems, the company should concentrate on what the system should be able to do for the company and the customers, not on the "nice to haves." The system must be scalable for additional partners.
- Databases and communication tools should be scalable and able to be internationalized.
- Bonus points should be redeemed at marginal cost and not put off those paying full price.

The Authors

Harald W. Eisenächer

Harald W. Eisenacher has been Vice President of Marketing for Lufthansa AG since January of 2004. In his role, he has been responsible for the Lufthansa brand, communication, and customer retention. From 1999 to 2003, he was Vice President Marketing and Services at Lufthansa Cargo AG. Prior to that, he was Global Marketing Director at Hoechst AG.

Sascia Hilverkus

Sascia Hilverkus has been Head of Marketing Support at Lufthansa AG since November of 2004. Prior to that, she worked in Marketing at Lufthansa Cargo AG, from 2002 to 2004. Until 2002, she was Head of Product Management of Handelsblatt.com at the publishing group Handelsblatt GmbH.

Literature Recommendations

J. S. Thomas, W. Reinartz, V. Kumar, "Getting the Most out of all your Customers," 2004
D. K. Rigby, D. Ledingham, "CRM done Right," 2004
C. Homburg, H. Krohmer, "Marketingmanagement. Strategie – Instrumente – Umsetzung – Unternehmensführung," Wiesbaden 2003
H. W. Eisenächer, "Fallstudie Lufthansa: Profitable Kundenbeziehungen durch Kundenbindung," in: Handbuch für Kundenbindungsmanagement, Eds. M. Bruhn, C. Homburg, 5th edition, Wiesbaden 2005

Thorsten Schapmann – Imperial Tobacco Group

Interactive Marketing
How to generate and bind new customers through interactive communication

▶ Executive Summary

- The reality of an information overload via marketing messages in all media channels requires new and more effective ways to communicate with the consumer.
- The integration of all communication mechanisms into all consumer touch points with brands is important to achieve the most efficient interactive approach.
- Precise measurement of all different steps is essential for successful interactive marketing and campaign planning.
- Successful interactive marketing generates a vast amount of data, that has to be managed professionally in a database management as it forms the basis for further intelligent communication strategies.
- A global interactive brand communication requires substantial local know-how and can achieve wide synergy effects by using global platform solutions for local implementation.

▶ Theoretical Model of Interactive Marketing

Interactive Communication
Relationship with consumer generates learning

Interactive Production	Interactive Pricing	Interactive Distribution
(E.g., personalized products based on consumer feedback)	(E.g., individual pricing based on consumer interaction like "powershopping")	(E.g., individual distribution channels based on consumers' preference, like digital delivery, home delivery; optimizing POS investment based on regional consumer behaviour)

Fig. 1: The three areas of interactive communication

1. Definition and basic principle

Interactive Marketing describes the strategy to develop commercial relationships with the right consumers by allowing dialogue with brands. Based on the insights gained from the interactive communication, an interactive marketing strategy can influence all other areas such as production, pricing, and distribution (see Fig. 1). To achieve this approach, the integration of interactive elements in all relevant communication channels, using a response mechanism is required. The increase of communication effectiveness and efficiency can be achieved by developing and using the intelligence from the dialogue, managed by a consumer database and implemented into a CRM strategy. The aim is to acquire, convert, and retain the right consumer into the own brand and to build loyalty and advocacy for a longer-term profitable relationship.

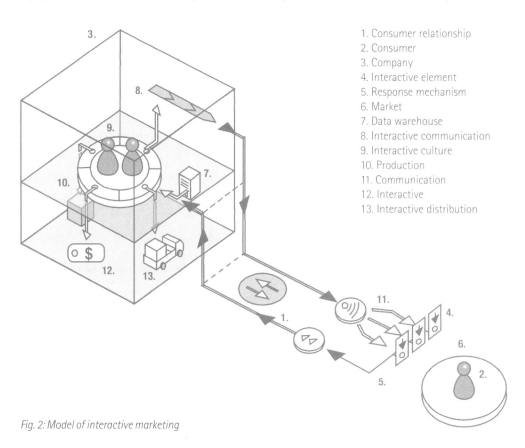

1. Consumer relationship
2. Consumer
3. Company
4. Interactive element
5. Response mechanism
6. Market
7. Data warehouse
8. Interactive communication
9. Interactive culture
10. Production
11. Communication
12. Interactive
13. Interactive distribution

Fig. 2: Model of interactive marketing

The goal of interactive marketing consists of establishing a stable relationship with the company's customers. It evolves from a steady interaction between customer and the company and its brands, that has to be enabled by interactive elements within the marketing communication mix. By providing these interactive elements, the company can react fast and precisely to the demands of the customers, who in return feel more valued and important to the company. By providing the foundation of an interactive communication, the company gains valuable information about the relevant target group that can be used to optimize all marketing activities.

2. Factors of Interactive Marketing

The following description of the model will focus on those factors that define the specifics of an interactive approach in comparison to a classical communication approach.

2.1 Interactive element (number 4)

The implementation of an interactive element differentiates the interactive communication from mass communication. This interaction provides feedback on the personal relationship between consumer and the brand. This, in turn, allows the brand to interact according to the previous dialogue content.

2.2 Response mechanism (number 5)

A response mechanism describes an invitational element that allows a direct response from consumer to the brand. This mechanism is an essential part of an interactive marketing strategy as it allows the brand/company to directly communicate with their consumers based on their feedback/responses on the first message sent.

2.3 Communication channels (number 11)

A successful implementation of an interactive strategy into a communication strategy can only be achieved by integrating the interactive element and the response mechanism in all relevant communication channels. The different communication channels achieve different communication objectives. Outdoor and print are more likely to generate quick awareness than direct mail and promotions, that are best used for example to provide product trials. Therefore the execution of the interactive element and the response mechanism should be considered carefully according to the needs of the different channels.

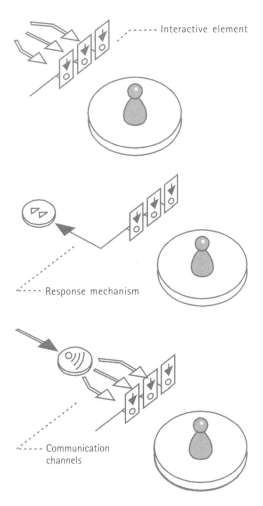

2.4 Data warehouse (number 7)

By allowing consumers to respond via the different communication channels, an enormous amount of data can very quickly be gathered: name and address (complete or partial), telephone number, e-mail address, preferred brand/product, promotion participation, historical data about former contacts with the brand or company etc. Professional management of a data warehouse is essential to combine all these data for a successful and effective interactive communication strategy. Using multivariate analysis methods, clusters of consumer groups can be created, which can be approached with different and relevant content.

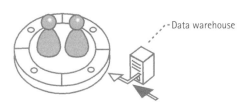

What is very important for a successful database, is the quality of the data source (internal or external sources should be considered and qualified) and the quality of the captured data in the system. Beside that, a clear strategy about the usage of this data is necessary to avoid a big investment into building a high-quality database but neglecting the possibility to use the data for communication due to budget limits.

Professional and intelligent database management allows a company to use the data for much more than interactive communication. The combination with market research data, POS data etc. can massively support further development of trade marketing strategies or even new brand/product development.

The development of an international consumer database is a very complex project, as there are numerous different kinds of address formats all over the world and a wide range of different legal requirements have to be considered when exchanging personal data worldwide and especially outside the European Union. In general the exchange of anonymous data is sufficient to analyze and understand international challenges in interactive marketing.

2.5 Interactive culture (number 9)

Especially the reliance on mass communication in the last decades in marketing makes it difficult to implement a culture that allows an interactive approach to achieve a bigger role in marketing. The ability to be contacted by consumers of fast moving consumer goods directly via different response mechanisms can sometimes be perceived more as a threat than a chance in brand management. Apart from watching research focus groups from behind one-way mirrored windows, many brand managers are not used to getting direct feedback.

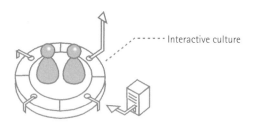

An interactive culture, though, enables companies to react more quickly to the different responses and requirements of their consumers and prospects. The learning from smaller test samples or coming out of different interactive campaigns can be implemented more quickly and more effectively into further development of communication and product ideas (number 10).

2.6 Communication strategy (number 8)

An interactive communication campaign must be implemented into the overall brand communication strategy. The integration into the brand communication, based on the brand proposition, is essential to achieve the maximum consumer effect from the entire brand experience.

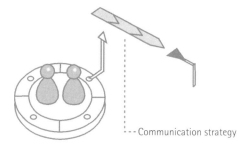

▶ Process & Implementation

Following the described process the marketing management will be able to develop interactive communication activities integrated into the brand strategy and based on communication objectives.

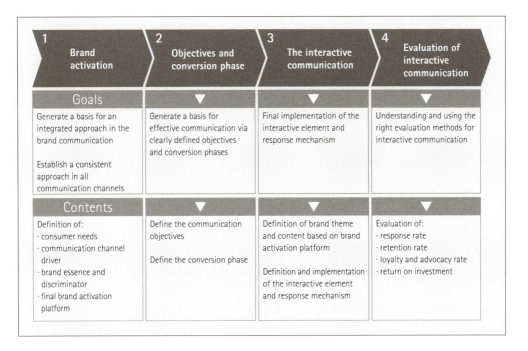

Fig. 3: Process of interactive marketing

Phase 1: Brand activation

1.1 Consumer needs
Essentially it is important to understand and uncover the genuine insights of a consumer. This will describe the needs a product or brand should satisfy for the consumer in using or buying it.

1.2 Communication channel driver
This step allows the marketing management to focus on the role of the environment in which the consumer will experience the brand communication. If your communication strategy is mainly focused in channels like gastronomic outlets or interactive communication (e.g., online), you need to define which role these channels play in the life of your target audience to create the most effective and relevant platform.

1.3 Brand essence and discriminator
Both parameters should have been defined already in the brand positioning. The essence of a brand distils the brand positioning to the question of how the brand will fulfill the requirements of the consumer. The discriminator defines why only this brand can satisfy the demand of the target group.

1.4 Brand activation platform
Based on the prior three steps the final platform is a compelling phrase that combines all information and creates a basis for consistent communication activities. All further communication activities will be measured against this platform and should meet the expectations that this phrase describes. The brand activation platform is a single compelling line that connects brand values with consumer needs. It stimulates ideas rooted in a common theme, and must be credible and realistic. The platform, copy line, and executions must be consumer relevant and appealing, differentiating, motivating, contemporary, and adaptable across a wide variety of communication channels.

Phase 2: Objectives and conversion phase

2.1 Definition of communication objectives
Communication activities should be based on goals such as:

- Generate awareness of the brand.
- Generate insight to bring the brand into the relevant mindset of the consumer.
- Generate trial of the brand.
- Generate loyal consumers, where your brand is the most often purchased brand.
- Generate advocacy for the brand.

Especially in generating and increasing trial and loyalty, interactive communication can play an important role in the total process, whereas the generation of awareness is limited if an interactive approach is the focus of a communication campaign. This objective can be achieved mainly via classical mass communication channels like out of home and print. However, an interactive element with a response mechanism should still be included to kick-start the dialogue with a consumer who shows interest in the brand.

2.2 Definition of consumer conversion phases
The objectives that have been defined above will determine specific activities based on the consumer conversion phases:

- acquisition,
- conversion,
- loyalty,
- advocacy.

Acquisition activities will support the brand awareness but will mainly generate a higher consideration of the brand via promotion mechanics etc. In the acquisition phase it is important to generate the first contact with the consumer and to achieve a significant start for further dialogue.

The conversion phase will support trial extension and should lead to converted consumers. In this phase an interactive communication is essential, based on the knowledge we have of the consumer and implementing intelligent mechanics that lead him to purchase the brand on a regular basis. This could be an interactive campaign based on proof of purchase, e.g., a code that is included in the pack that the consumer has to collect and to send in to get a prize.

The most challenging phase is to convert new "trialists" generated during the conversion phase, into loyal customers. This stage is important to generate a longer term profit out of the relationship with the consumer. In FMCG there are successful examples where a dialogue mechanism implemented after the trial activity could increase the retention of consumers in the brand. This can be achieved by different tools like e-mail, SMS, or mailing information including own content driven magazines that will keep the dialogue with the consumers alive.

At the end of the conversion process the brand will have generated loyal consumers who can be involved in an advocacy program. In this process the loyal consumer acquires new prospects for your brand, which is the most cost effective way to generate new consumers. Activities like a member-get-member mechanism or specific events for loyal consumers, with the option to invite friends, can generate an advocacy approach. In this phase it is very important to have the right consumers converted into loyalty consumers as this target group will be the multiplicators in their peer group. If they are not carefully generated, the brand could be damaged as it will have been taken over by a specific group of consumers that might not fit the brand image.

Phase 3: The interactive communication
3.1 Definition of brand themes and content
Each phase of the conversion process can be supported by an interactive element in brand communication to achieve the overall communication objectives. To generate the most effective interactive element, these elements should be derived from brand themes and content, that again are based on the brand activation platform that has been developed in the first phase. Brand themes like fashion, style, music etc. should be defined more precisely based on the brand activation platform.

To maximize the effect during an interactive communication campaign, a theme should be exploited in all channels for a limited period of time. The content of the different communication and promotion activities will be adapted according to the different communication channels. Every theme can be implemented in an integrated approach. The most important point at this stage is the development of the right interactive elements and response mechanism, implementing them in the different channels to achieve the most effective and efficient interactive communication approach.

3.2 Implementation of an interactive element with response mechanism
In the final stage of the process an interactive element has to be created that uses a response mechanism to secure the interactive dialogue between the brand and the consumer. The interaction allows the consumer to get in direct connection with another communication partner, that in some cases can be another consumer (indirect interaction), facilitated by the brand or with the brand itself (direct interaction). To create an effective interactive element the response mechanism plays a major role. There are different ways to allow a consumer to respond: via online, mobile, or classic direct mailing communication.

3.2.1 Online

In many markets the online penetration in the target group has achieved a critical mass so that this channel can be one of the most efficient response tools. It is important to analyze the usage of the online medium in your target group and market before offering this channel. The online medium provides a direct response channel to the consumer without a break in the communication channel. The brand can provide a response mechanism via e-mail contact, message board comments, chat forum, online questionnaires etc.

The technical infrastructure is an important criterion to provide an effective response channel. The technical platform and features of the website should be developed considering the penetration of broadband access and other technical requirements.

If the technical infrastructure is sufficient, the online channel has the advantage of being very cost efficient, very quick and flexible, and can provide a lot of information from both sides of the interactive partners. Brand management will face some challenges when using the online channel. Consumers will be able to publish their view on products, if a message board or chatroom is provided. An editing interface is worth considering to minimize the risk. On the other hand, the consumer expects the brand or company to respond to their remarks and questions in a reasonably short period of time.

The development of a basic and consistently branded online platform, that can be adapted into local markets to meet the different local consumer and user requirements, is a very cost effective solution for an international brand management.

The technical development of wireless access to the Internet, provided in different locations outside of home (see Fig. 4, wireless access points in Manhattan), the design of smaller, portable laptops or handsets that provide screens with an impressive resolution will further exploit the online communication in the near future.

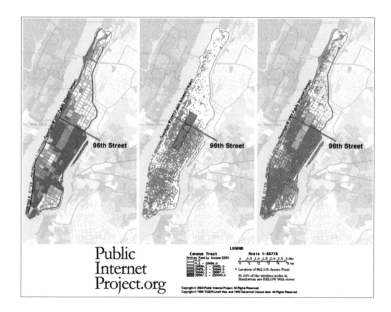

Fig. 4: Usage of online access outside office or home environment

3.2.2 Mobile

The penetration of mobile devices increased intensively in all major parts of the world in the last decade. In the very short history of mobile phones, the usage of text messaging, taking and sending pictures, and receiving ring tones and mobile logos has become a major part of the mobile communication business. Further technology like Infra Red and Blue Tooth as well as the UMTS network provide other interesting opportunities for exchanging information. A brand can create a multitude of response channels, from text messaging (SMS), multimedia messaging (MMS) to providing and receiving information via Blue Tooth technology (see Fig. 5).

Fig. 5: Bluecasting – Case: Coldplay

Where the "classical" mobile communication tools like SMS and phone calls are accepted for brand messages, the more innovative tools like Infra Red and Blue Tooth need to overcome resistance and technical barriers. The process of innovation in mobile devices shows a very promising future for this response channel. Combining mobile communication with entertainment facilities, high resolution screens on portable handsets and providing clear cost structures for the different services will get the consumer more and more used to relevant brand communications on their mobile devices. It is important to highlight that due to the very private characteristic of a mobile phone, the responsibilities of brand management when using this channel are extremely high. Legal requirements like a positive opt-in permission from consumers is the basis for a successful and responsible usage of the channel for commercial communication.

The cost effectiveness of the mobile channel can only be achieved by limiting the information that will be communicated. This is the biggest downside of this channel, as text and multimedia messaging can get very expensive if the content is not short and small enough.

3.2.3 Direct mail

The classical way of exchanging information and creating response is via mailings. Direct mail is still a very popular channel for interactive communication. In comparison to online and mobile this channel enables the sending of physical products as well as tangible, printed material that can have a bigger impact than just digital communication.

As direct mail can be a much more cost intensive way of communication, the quality of the addresses and the usage of the right data is very important. Direct mailing can only be a cost efficient interactive solution if the right target group is contacted with the right messages and products, and the consumer responses are analyzed for further increase of the quality in the mailing messages. Only a professional database management process for the generating, capturing, and analyzing of consumer data can build the bedrock for a successful direct mail campaign.

3.3 The implementation of interactive elements and response mechanisms in the different conversion phases

Ultimately a combination of all available response mechanism and interactive elements is necessary to increase the effectiveness of an interactive communication strategy. Derived from the above described process at this stage, the different communication channels, based on the different objectives, will define the right mix of the interactive elements and response mechanisms.

3.3.1 Acquisition strategy
- The generation of high quality consumer data is the main objective of a acquisition campaign.
- Responsive elements should provide quick access to a registration form and the communication should focus on the relevant benefits a consumer can expect when giving the data.
- The differentiation between quantity and quality is necessary, as classic channels like TV or Print campaigns which lead consumers to an online webpage with a free service or attractive prize, may provide high numbers of addresses but the quality may not be sufficient for further communication plans.
- Promotions in outlets, where the target group is present (gastronomic or retail channels), will be more expensive but can provide a higher quality of data if the promotion personnel are well-trained and the mechanism reduces any possibility to fake the information.

3.3.2 Conversion phase
- The interactive communication should be focused in channels that can provide product trials and generate feedback from the consumers who should be converted. Retail communication, classical direct mailing etc. are the relevant channels to focus on.
- An ongoing dialogue using online and mobile communication channels should be considered to support the conversion activities with relevant brand content.

3.3.3 Loyalty activities
- Communication channels that can provide direct communication with those consumers defined as loyal, like direct mailing, online web pages with specific entry areas, mobile channels with exclusive content etc. are essential.
- The combination of these channels with events and promotions for a closed consumer group will support the loyalty of the consumer.

3.3.4 Advocacy strategy
- Providing loyal consumers with further communication facilities for their peer group like special online content, customer magazines or special events is critical.
- Another relevant target group, acquired cost efficiently by the loyal consumers, will come into your brand franchise.

3.4 Legal requirements

The usage of interactive communication requires a detailed understanding of the law, basically the understanding and implementation of the EU directive for data protection. In many markets the consumer must give his permission to a company to use private data such as a mailing address and phone number for commercial communication. This permission must be signed or given via an "opt in" solution in an online environment. The consumer should always have the opportunity to opt out of his permission, completely or partly.

If a consumer does have doubts about the correct usage of his data, the company must be able to provide all personal data they collected and stored in the past. This data protection regulation is required to secure this communication channel for responsible and professional business. The vast amount of spam mailing and text messaging shows why the implementation of this legal requirement is necessary. It protects the brand and the company from damage through legal cases, adverse PR, or negative word of mouth effect.

Data protection rules define clear requirements for all parties and companies dealing with personal data. An external database agency storing consumer data, must also fulfill criteria to protect consumer privacy but the main responsibility is on the data user – i.e., the company or marketing department responsible for implementing the various activities. When dealing with interactive campaigns on an international level, the exchange of consumer data is very restrictive and requires particularly careful attention.

Phase 4: Evaluation of interactive communication

A big advantage of interactive communication is often described in the ability to evaluate every investment and step during a campaign. This can be a disadvantage when compared to classical communications, like out of home and print, where the evaluation of the return on investment is less realistic and rarely applied. Criteria for response, retention, loyalty and advocacy rates and their evaluation based on costs can lead to a controlling approach that is mainly focused on achieving a quick ROI. This approach can achieve very profitable communication but neglects a more long-term brand communication strategy via different, also non-interactive channels that cannot be measured in a short- or mid-term ROI.

The evaluation potential in interactive channels should be understood as a chance to learn in shorter time periods, test different ideas, and implement all these results to generate a permanent increase in effectiveness and efficiency in different solutions. This ability can be a driving factor to increase the budget allocation in this channel, as the measurement of success can be achieved much more easily than in other communication areas.

Nevertheless, a financial evaluation of an interactive approach can be valid and necessary. However, it should only be considered if the interactive tools and mechanisms are created and focused on changing the purchasing behavior of consumers and building a longer-term commercial relationship. A ROI calculation will then create a guideline for further investments into interactive communication solutions.

▸ Key Insights

- Interactive marketing is the strategy of creating an ongoing dialogue with consumers based on interactive communication by using interactive elements and generating responses.
- The implementation of all legal requirements for personal data protection is the basis for a professional interactive marketing strategy.
- Professional database management is the essential basis for successful interactive communication campaigns. Only one consumer database for all brand activities should be created to generate insights about consumer buying and switching behavior.
- Interactive communication must be implemented into an integrated brand communication strategy, based on consumer needs, brand essence, and communication channel drivers.
- The development of an interactive strategy must be managed with all relevant parties including brand management and trade marketing as well as classic, online, direct marketing, and media agencies.
- Testing all mechanisms and tools, and evaluating all activities is a key to achieving further budget allocation, increased knowledge and success.
- In global brand management a centrally produced interactive element/platform in online/mobile communication can generate cost savings and will secure a consistent brand communication approach. The sharing of best practices on an international level will further support local activities in interactive marketing.

▸ Practical Guidelines

- Interactive communication must be understood as a company-driven philosophy, supported by all management levels.
- A permanent dialogue with consumers requires a more mid/long-term communication approach that is reflected in all communication channels like out of home, print, TV, where an interactive element is included.
- Brand management should get easy access to consumer data and information about campaigns and should quickly understand the potential of interactive campaigns.
- The development and constant updating of the consumer database should be managed by an overhead function outside brand management and brand related budget. This secures a high quality of consumer data permanently available for interactive brand campaigns.
- The potential to test different approaches before investing in bigger campaigns should be considered at all stages of campaign planning.
- Consumer data can be generated via different sources. Internal data can be generated via promotion, online games etc; external sources can be lifestyle studies and other consumer data lists. Ideally the information about the consumed product or brand should be generated by an unbranded and anonymous source – internal or external.
- In a global approach to interactive marketing the know-how of the local communication structure is important as address quality and systematic, online penetration, and usage of mobile communication is essential to develop an ideal global platform and to achieve a cost effective local implementation.

The Author

Thorsten Schapmann

Thorsten Schapmann has been Senior Manager Retail Media/1to1 in the central Marketing department of the Imperial Tobacco Group, U.K. since February 2002. In his role he is responsible for the interactive communication concepts of the global brand portfolio, including brands like West and Davidoff-Cigarettes. Before that he was in charge of the development of the successful brand community www.west.de in Germany at Reemtsma Cigarettenfabriken as well as the international roll-out of interactive platforms in online and mobile communication.

Literature Recommendations

A. Tapp, "Principles of Direct and Database Management," New Jersey 1998
S. Godin, "Permission Marketing," München 2000
K. Backhaus, B. Erichson, W. Plinke, R. Weiber, "Multivariate Analysemethoden," Berlin 2003
EU-Datenschutzdirektive 95/46/EU, October 1995
www.trendwatching.com

Petra Meyer – Merck Consumer Healthcare, Gabriele Neuschaefer – morgenland

Innovation Management

Innovation Management reinvented: creating big ideas by an insight-fueled holistic innovation process

▶ Executive Summary

- Insightful innovation is driven by motive power and complexity – key words to success are "continuously" + "vivid" + "wholesome."
- Insightful-successful innovation means to innovate continuously based on continuously generated target insights.
- To deliver successful innovation breakthrough, big ideas are required to produce a flow of strategy-driven ideas to build on and fit to consumer insights – non-blue sky ideas.
- The "size" of the innovation is dependent on how well the new offer meets a consumer need or desire in all its aspects.
- True high-level insights need to be harvested continuously for refreshment and renewal in the company-consumer relationship.
- Big ideas are derived from the insight-platform base and translated into full-blown concepts targeting all the senses.
- Concepts are further developed and presented in a multi-sensory way to allow the consumer to fully understand, mentally integrate, and embrace the presented new product idea by relating it back to individual needs and desires.

▶ Theoretical Model of Innovation Management

1. Definition

Successful innovations, the real big ideas, are based on the insightful innovation process. This process includes three elements of idea implementation: insight generation; idea development; concept crafting. These three elements reconnect to each other; they form a holistic figure, following the principles of insight relation management and sensoric marketing. Insight relation management means that ideas and therefore innovations, consumer-relations, and strategic insights drive concept development. Sensoric marketing relates the generation of insights, the development of ideas and concepts as well as evaluation processes to multisensorial experiences. New product or service offers based on these principles add significant value to the brand and company. From a consumer's perspective they are perceived as an offer that they were always looking for. The insightful innovation process includes three phases:

1. Gold Mining: from insights to ideas.
2. Translation: idea-concept-recycling.
3. Correspondence: concept-insight-recycling.

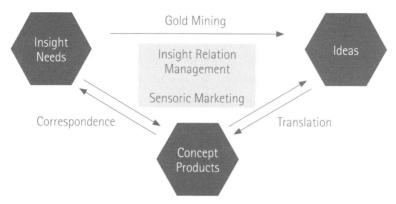

Fig. 1: The insight-innovation process

The approach is specifically useful to overcome inter- and intra-cultural barriers. Verbal expression depends on education and social development. Implementing a multisensoric language and including transport of information via images allows ideas/concepts to travel multiculturally. This thought applies to inter-cultural differences between countries and to intra-cultural differences between sub-populations like companies and consumers. Working on a global level, being international means leaving language-only communication behind and starting to use multi-sensoric language instead.

2. Principles of the insight-fueled innovation process

2.1 Insight relation management
- Identify the golden nugget insights, the needs that have not yet been met by a product or service offer and build the "nugget" product idea towards them.
- Think about insights in a differentiated way to develop insights with area-focused methodologies: discriminate between:

Insights to innovate: category and product insights.
Insights into consumer and brand relations: brand and competition insights.
Strategic innovation: insights about the future.

- Identify the target consumer and survey the competitive landscape: look into the consumers' life in its full reality and complexity concerning different experiences so as to come up with relevant insights that lead to meaningful ideas, for example Axe is "just" a shower gel – but in the socio-cultural context it stands for cleanliness = being an accepted person, and in a target specific context it stands for appetite appeal = sexiness.
- Generate insights continuously: the consumers' world is in constant change – it matches a system with an open door, where a stream of influencing variables can change the order of the overall system. A system that can be influenced by the introduction of one new product.
- Generate wide-ranging insights: insights that include full mindsets and complex experiences, from the first thought about a product to its discontinuation. Analyze the complete category context by exploring the full usage situation and its protagonists: the user in her/his environment, the product, and the brand.

- Analyze trends: find strategic insights by exploring a trend continuum: existing, approaching, visionary trends, trendsetters, and product manifestations.

2.2 Sensoric marketing

- Translate target insights into strategy-driven ideas by using multi-sensoric approaches:

  - idea development should integrate all the senses,
  - since by the end of the offer it will not just live on paper but will be integrated into the consumer's multidimensional world,
  - idea selection should focus on strategy: there is no good idea if there is no match to your marketing concept.

- Transfer concepts to consumers in an integrated way by using multisensoric approaches:

  - Consumers' minds are full of experiences, stored in form of images and sensoric impression clusters in a very organized way. To be understood, developed, and accepted the concept has to be integrated into this world of images,
  - An idea which is developed by using multisensoric approaches can be experienced,
  - To be fine tuned or developed, consumers have to have the chance to transfer their impressions from mind-language, i.e. images, to verbal language, meaning their first reaction towards a concept must be non-verbal, an image.
  - To be accepted by consumers a concept has to evoke images, that match existing images or add to them like a missing speech bubble in a cartoon.

▶ Process & Implementation

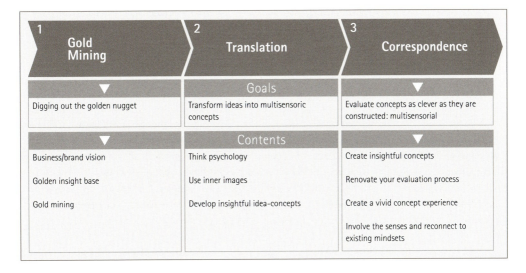

Fig. 2: Innovation management process

Phase 1: Gold mining

1.1 Starting point: a clear brand/business vision

Vision builds direction and the spirit to go and find that golden nugget. Like in the days of the gold rush, the prize is high – insightful innovation will build gold value for the company, but you have to wash a lot of rubble before you find a nugget – determination and drive is the key to success.

- Where do you see your business/brand in 10 years? What does it stand for in the consumer's mind? To help the mind capture the brand vision, describe the brand as a person: how is it going to live, how will friends see it, how does it make a difference in life? Apple, for example, enchants the consumer through design and style of the product combined with user-friendly technology. As a person Apple would be extrovert, stylish, trend setting, self-confident, and probably an inventor coming up with new ideas all the time. It has a few close friends to bounce ideas off and goes through life with open eyes.
- Build on the vision: imagine the potential value of your business/brand in 10 years to target your ambition. Do you want to be a billionaire – then you might need to dig for a few golden nuggets!
- Think about gold mining as a journey, set goalpost objectives you can achieve in a foreseeable time. Talk about them and celebrate when you have achieved them on the way to the long-term objective. Gold mining is going to be part of your thinking now and everyday.

1.2 Golden insight base

1.2.1 Consumer and product/brand insights

- Identify the target consumer and start getting to know him better than anyone else. Look into his life, his perspectives, attitudes, ever changing behavior, and developing needs and wishes. Understand his experiences with products/services in their entirety, i.e. Clearasil does not only fight a spot in a teenager's life, but also gives them confidence to go and face the world. Understand, what people like about products and what they would like to change: in the Clearasil case, they'd aspire to a miracle product removing a spot in two minutes. To get the full picture you need to step into consumers' shoes. Never stop looking. As with every other person, you can't know consumers a 100 percent. Develop and complete your understanding by adding every new bit and piece of information.
- There are a number of methods you can use to derive insights. Use wide-ranging approaches.
- Use your natural resources. At the start of an insight development process it is very valuable to talk to people like R&D inside the organization, and people working with you on the brand, for instance, agencies. They can tell you a lot about the whys and hows of products and can also share their perception of the brand. They are not only a great resource at the start of a project but are worth being integrated into an innovation process. In addition cross-cultural insight collection is a further source to build comprehensive insights.
- Forget classical research – think reality research. The classical tools to develop insights as a basis for innovations are surveys, questionnaires, and focus groups – a battery of research instruments to generate information from consumers and still about 80 percent of innovations based on their findings fail. This often causes a backwards step like generating tons of quantitative data creation to cope with the potential invalid human resource information. Consumers are the key to big ideas – they just don't talk in the language of insights, and they tend to not talk about their real selves at all. Who would expect a tiger in the zoo to behave naturally? Why does anyone expect the consumer in a test studio to express him/herself naturally? The key to reality is reality.

For example: to understand how a person uses toiletries, go where they are used. In a home, in bathrooms, in sport studios. Have a look at the bathrooms, let people show you how they use products, understand whether they share products with family members, talk to them about their product experience, understand how they feel about using the product, what the product makes them feel like, etc. Let them use the products in front of you – use them together with the consumer.

- You can also talk to people involved in product recommendation, for instance to the sales person in a perfumery and find out how they perceive your target consumer; or go on a shopping trip. Reality is rich and full of insightful experiences.
- Gain from variety. To find a clue is not about talking to people but talking to the right people. If research and recruitment is carried out with little effort, the output is uninspiring. It is a combination of different insights that generates an insight, that deserves to be called a nugget. And different insights come from different sources – the consumer triangle.

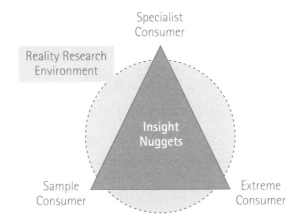

Fig. 3: The consumer triangle

Sample consumers are target consumers: user, non-user, and potential user. Extreme consumers are consumers with an extreme attitude and behavior concerning the focus area: for example extremely healthy or unhealthy. Specialist consumers are people with a special ability to drive innovation – like opinion leaders, cutting-edge creative people, experts in the focus area, for example professors or marketeers.

1.2.2 Strategic innovation insights

"The only stable factor in today's world is change."

Become a visionist: envision a picture of the future. How are people going to live, how will their attitudes, demands, values, and desires change? There are several options to generate a vision of the future: socio-economic trend data for people and cultures; general trend data, i.e., popcorn report; studies from the scientists. You can also interview people who are actively setting trends, for example for toiletry products you can work with perfume houses; in the medical area, you can talk to key opinion leaders who determine where research is going; or with creative consumers who are picking up trend waves and are able to articulate their views. Understand the gurus.

1.2.3 Category and product insights
Become a collector: survey the category and competitor landscape worldwide. What are the latest new offers and how was the consumers' acceptance. What is the latest big success in the market ? Find the parameter of success. Look at related categories. What is happening here? Watch out for transferable insights and findings. Consider general trends for applicability in your field. For example: ease of use is a key functionality criterion for electronics – how can you transfer this into a personal care market?

1.2.4 Sensoric insights
Innovations include a multisensoric experience – they are tangible on many levels. To evoke, create, express emotions, learn about the multisensoric aspects of an insight. Using all the senses makes more sense. Become a scholar: collect sounds, colors, shapes, tastes, scents, and fabrics expressing brand, product, insights – try to relate something to the latent need or desire.

1.3 Gold mining – derive "nugget" ideas
There are plenty of little ideas out there – but what you want is the big one, the non-blue sky idea. The golden nugget idea feels obvious, yet exciting and grips people's interest immediately. It describes a whole consumer experience in all aspects. Starting point: think big and exciting; be open to new methods; meet new people; and explore new cultural ground.

- Idea creation through events: build a team of creative people to springboard the most exciting insights that have been previously generated and come up with as many ideas as possible. You can use a variety of methods, namely creative workshops, brainstorming, ideation etc. to maximize the number of ideas and funnel them into high-quality ideas. Implementing a variety of different methods helps to view insights from different angles, ideally with all the senses, and combine them in a different way. Creative facilitators are there to stimulate the process as well as ensure focus on the task. Consider involving people, i.e. experts; creative consumers to challenge encrusted internal thinking. Generated ideas can be further clustered and developed to build even larger ideas.
- Daily ideas: allow yourself 20 minutes of creative time per day. Spend this time alone, with consumers, colleagues, or family. Use your insights to develop some quick ideas. Note them. Have an ideas box. Exchange ideas with other people. Give yourself targets for how many ideas you want to develop per week. Explore available creative methods; try out new methods. Have a large team of creative people, ideally cross-cultural, involved in the process. Work with people who challenge internal thinking. Review your ideas towards the vision and objectives.

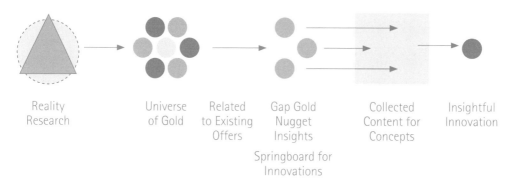

Fig. 4: Find winners – internalize the process

Phase 2: Translation

2.2 Starting point: think psychology! Gain from brain research and findings from social psychology

To survive in a world full of stimuli, people are driven to organize information. To keep this process as simple as possible, new and unique information is either devaluated or eliminated. As a result real innovations presented as verbal concepts have a low chance to find consumers' acceptance. Sensoric Marketing™ is a way to overcome this problem by creating multisensoric concepts – crafted concepts tested in a multisensoric approach.

2.2 Change your own approach: understand the sensoric marketing model and start to use inner images to create and establish real innovations

2.3 Develop insightful ideas – concepts

- You need to hit the sweet spot – not just generate tons of ideas – and select. Too many ideas is one reason why many innovations failed when they were launched into the real world.
- Big ideas match perfectly consumers' needs and desires: they are built on insights.
- Non-blue sky ideas are based on strategy.
- Watch both to develop great, insightful ideas.
- Strategy means: be a collector, look at competition, analyze markets and create data-material that clearly points to opportunities.
- Gather insights and form insight-platforms describing consumers' latent needs and desires in your opportunity fields.
- Use these insight-platforms to springboard sensoric ideas: ideas, that are springboarded from images and translated into images/sensoric materials to support the idea. It is a playful exercise that will produce impactful symbols and inspirational ideas reflecting collective knowledge and that, therefore, will capture consumers' imagination.
- Ideas which are made to play a role in consumers' lives and make the consumer happy; ideas forming your company's close relationship with the consumer's life.

Phase 3: Correspondence

3.1 Create insightful concepts

- To help consumers to fully understand concepts, the concepts need to be created and evaluated with a multisensoric approach involving images as well as tactile, acoustic, or olfactory experiences.
- With concept creation there are still words involved – but these words reflect the actual inner image that lies behind the concept. They are easy to associate with further images – they are understandable and rich in meaning.
- Watch out for the "typical" marketing vocabulary that will make the consumers alert and careful – the whole concept will be packed into the mindset of "selling," with no chance of being identified as "what I always wished for" and loved.

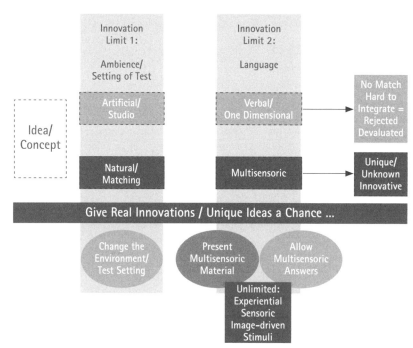

Fig. 5: Concept with multisensoric approach

3.2 Evaluate concepts in an insightful way

How it doesn't work

In the standard evaluation process consumers are confronted with verbal concepts where an innovative idea is pushed into the insight – benefit – reason to believe scheme – sometimes in addition executed through visuals. Consumers invited for money into an artificial ambience to look at a marketing artefact take a look at it – and react over-enthusiastically just to well-known material. Why? Because your customer's brain works like a closet in which you want to put your new and exciting idea/concept. If this idea/concept doesn't match the drawers, it is put aside – right in the middle of nowhere.

The harder it is for consumers to find the right drawer, the more you can anticipate rejection of an idea/concept. Hard for unique ideas, the real innovations, to survive!

How it works

The first way to have the target focus on the right drawers and make the information easy to take in, is to present the idea/concept in an appropriate environment. For example, a new soup concept should be presented in a kitchen and not in a test studio where the entrance sign "research" already triggers yes/no answers instead of real-life decisions. The next barrier to overcome is to present the idea/concept in a multisensoric way – why should an idea/concept target just one sense when people have so many? Supporting images, a dummy, a scent help the consumer to fully understand what the idea/concept is about. It is again about reality: make the stimulus as real as possible, present sensual experiences, evaluate prototypes.

The next barrier is the consumer: the recipient is confronted with new material – in the closet example it is clear that the idea/concept that is the easiest to store in the drawer, is the winner. Here the model gets a little more complicated if you look into personality traits: there is a minority of customers who belong to the group of challenge seekers. They handle the drawers differently – for them it is interesting to play around, try out, and even create new ones.

However, the average consumer wants it to be easy and over soon. To keep the consumer focused enough to let an innovative idea/concept have a chance to find a drawer it needs a feedback system. People think in images – let them answer via images – and let them explain their answer to you. Think whole again: let consumers get in touch with the idea by relating it to sensorial experiences. Vision is the most important sense by which human beings understand and explore their world, and to create a personal data processing center and relate collected information – everything is stored in the form of images. By answering through images and telling stories connected to these images consumers recognize what they "really" think. This process, that starts out non-verbally, works like a feedback system where consumers get to know their own thoughts. There is no chance for a yes or no – but for the all the facets in between. There is no chance for a loser to win either: by looking into the multifacetedness of his own answer the consumer will be able to explain in detail why there is "love" or "hate," which is very helpful for idea/concept recycling.

NOW: Go for success! Kick-start the insightful innovation process.

▶ Key Insights

- Many innovations fail because they are not based on real insights.
- Successful innovations are based on a holistic approach integrating psychological in-depth insights as well as a visionary market view.
- Ideas need to be generated and evaluated in a multisensorial language to create and select really big ideas.
- Truly unique ideas have a chance to succeed if they are presented on a multisensory level.
- The multisensoric approach overcomes cross-cultural problems.

▶ Practical Guidelines

- Open up for the richness of the real world.
- Start to understand your brand and products on a multisensory level.
- Collect insights with a reality-driven multisensory approach.
- Create ideas and concepts using the multisensoric language.
- Evaluate and fine-tune your concepts in a valid way: by using all the senses.
- Let "just verbalization" go – and seek the adventure of a multisensory world.
- Go for reality; understand a multistimuli world; give complexity a chance.

The Authors

Petra Meyer

Following a degree in business and languages, Petra started her marketing career at Unilever, where she mainly worked on personal care brands such as Axe and Rexona. She then joined Boots Healthcare International, the branded division of the Boots Co. in the U.K. taking up various roles in national and international marketing in the U.K., France, Germany and became Marketing Director for Europe. Since April 1st 2006, Petra Meyer is Vice President Strategic Marketing and Member of the Executive Commitee at Merck Consumer Healthcare.

Gabriele S. E. Neuschaefer

After studying psychology and economics she worked for several years as the head of a social marketing project at the University of Kiel, Germany. She then worked as a marketing consultant for diverse agencies collecting experiences in a broad variety of brands and products . She is now the CEO & President of morgenland Europe and morgenland U.S.A. Inc, taking care of multinational projects in the field of innovation and creativity, psychological marketing, qualitative research, and communication.

Literature Recommendations
G. Zaltman, "How Customers Think: Essential Insights into the Mind of the Markets," Boston: Harvard Business School Press, 2003
M. Gobe, "Emotional Branding: The New Paradigm for Connecting Brands to People," 2001
K. Robinson, "Out of Our Minds: Learning to Be Creative," 2001
D. Frey, "Cognitive Psychology"
E. Finkgraef et al (forthcoming), "The bullet point murder mystery"

Martin Kanis, Kathrin Henze – O₂ Germany

Integrated Customer Retention
Getting to know, keeping, and wooing back customers

▶ Executive Summary

- Over 75 percent of Germans today use a mobile phone. This represents 65 million users in Germany alone. Two billion mobile phone users are forecast for the year 2007 worldwide. This means that, pretty soon, every fourth person will be talking, sending SMS or downloading games or music on a mobile phone.
- For every minute a mobile phone is being used, we obtain customer data and thereby the chance to build our portfolio in a way that will interest the consumer. We have an opportunity to market our products in such a way that the customer will consume them with pleasure and, at the same time, assure our corporate profitability.
- Integrated Customer Retention covers all relevant corporate areas during the phases of the customer life cycle, i.e., from acquisition through the loyalty management phase to contract renewal. This is the only method by which continued enhancement of the customer experience along all customer contact points can be achieved.
- A corporate strategy with international orientation offers numerous opportunities in the mobile network industry. In terms of customer dialogue, however, country-specific peculiarities still play a key role.

▶ Theoretical Model of Integrated Customer Retention

1. Definition and core principle

Against the backdrop of ever shorter innovation cycles and an ever growing multitude of products, only those providers who actively use their customer knowledge to differentiate themselves from the competition will attract new customers. Once the customer has been acquired, there are numerous points of contact for interaction. The quality component is particularly important, because a positive customer experience has been proven to promote a company's growth. Proactive interaction with the customer, moreover, allows a customer's future potential to be forecast and offers opportunities for cross-selling and up-selling.

This potential can only be efficiently exploited if all the corporate areas involved in customer contact act in harmony. Information provided by the customer via a call to the call center, a visit to the on-line portal or at the point of sale (POS) must be consolidated and, even more importantly, made available at all customer contact points. Specifically, this implies that an incentive agreed between the customer and the call center agent on the phone must also be identifiable from the systems used by the POS. It is only continuous dialogue with the consumer throughout the entire customer relationship that makes it possible to obtain important information in order to develop the business relationship in the right direction at the right time. In the dynamic market environment of the mobile network industry, it will be the companies that are best able to capture the demands of the target group and to offer the customer a tailored problem solution who will win the battle for customers.

2. Integrated customer retention factors

But what distinguishes successful retention management, and what are the factors that lead to success? The central focus must be on the consumer. But customers vary from one company to the next. If a universally applicable recipe for success is not feasible in this context, there are nevertheless levers that have been proven to make retention management more successful. They can be summarized in four elements, which are defined by strategy and the organizational form of the company.

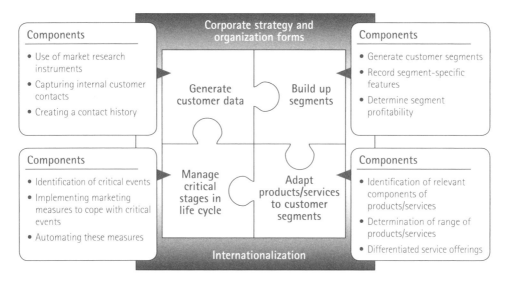

Fig. 1: Integrated retention management success factors

2.1 Customer data

The first step is to "simply" listen to the customer. The precise capture of data relevant to the customer relationship and its continuous update are the basis for all activities that take place as part of the dialogue with the consumer. There are many ways to do this. Customer interviews, customer cards that document a customer's purchasing behavior, or trend scouting are market research instruments that are frequently used. More informative, although often more difficult to implement, is an evaluation of the contacts that the customer is in touch with proactively. Queries and problems that are received at the POS or the call center are important information sources. In practice, the evaluation is made more difficult by the complexity of data that can usually only be captured as continuous text. The challenge is to select and systematically organize the information received in such a manner that it is possible to create and update a contact history at the level of the individual customer. The effort is worth it – for each piece of customer information offers the opportunity of responding more precisely to customer needs, thereby creating a positive customer experience and, finally, long-term customer retention.

2.2 Customer lifetime value

Mobile network providers are confronting, as are many other industries, the problem of catering to a very heterogeneous target group. Since one-product-for-all, however, seldom works, due to different expectations vis-à-vis the product, analysis and segmentation of the customer base play a decisive role. Which services does the consumer use and how much, which sales channels does he buy from, and via which channels does he complain if problems arise? It is important that all relevant information flows together. In selecting the target group, functional feasibility should be taken into account as well. A cluster should not be too small and possibly offer too little potential; on the other hand, it should not be too big and thus insufficiently homogeneous. The more distinctly a target group is defined, the better it is understood and the more effectively the service range can be adapted to its demands. But – and this is key to efficient retention management – this is not about what is best across the board for all customers. In order to assure profitability of the customer base, it is necessary to identify the value the individual customer represents for the company. In classifying the customers according to their Customer Lifetime Value (CLW), it is not just the final value that is significant. It is also important to identify what drives this value, that may differ depending on the industry and the company. Core factors include the sales for which individual customers are responsible, as well as the costs they give rise to during their use. It is only when these driving factors and their mutual interdependencies are understood that a realistic estimate of the actual and potential value of a customer can be known to a company.

2.3 Adapting the service portfolio

Companies invest large amounts on development and retention of their customer base. In order to guarantee efficient use of the marketing budget, constant deliberation is necessary: on the one hand, aimed at the fulfillment of customer expectations, on the other hand, as an ongoing review of the product portfolio for profitability. Based on the customer segments established, a targeted market approach, with intensity of varying levels, geared to the individual types, becomes possible. Usage behavior, profitability, and the customer's life cycle stage play a part here.

Value Added Services (VAS) have proven to be especially appropriate in differentiating products and services. VAS enables service groupings to be created as secondary services; this conveys a higher product value to specific target groups. It is key that an additional benefit is generated that is both individually recognized and valued by the customer. O_2, for example, offers special advantages as part of its VIP program, such as events or cell phone upgrades. Service classifications are used, if incentives are to be provided to the customer, generating loyalty to the company on his part. Treatment when calling the hotline, in which case customers are to be directly transferred to specialist teams and should on no account be made to wait, play an important part in this effort.

2.4 Identification and prevention of critical stages within the life cycle

What does a customer expect from a business relationship? Does he want to be approached actively by the company? What information does he want – and with what frequency? Customer Relationship Management (CRM) functions as the interface to the market and as coordinator among the various departments involved with customer contact. The content and intensity of the dialogue with the customer therefore becomes a CRM responsibility. The entire contract duration should be used to interact with the customer; this is how long-term links with the customer can be established. The dialogue may be initiated either by the company or by the customer himself, who may have proactively contacted the hotline or the POS. In both cases, the goal of the contact is a positive customer experience. This means that marketing campaigns that reach the customer must be tailored to his needs and hold his interest. A campaign must fit in terms of content, timing of approach, and the quality of the advertising medium. This means, too, though, that an irritated customer who turns to Customer Service must be helped courteously and competently. If the problem is resolved, in an ideal situation the irritation turns into a discovery: "They really care about me." Of decisive significance in this area is an efficiently organized complaint management system that is networked throughout the company and for which clear response time and service quality benchmarks have been defined.

The true challenge is to consistently bring together the "what" and "when" for the individual customer. The campaign management tool "Next Best Activity" (NBA) fulfills this task. Based on a scorecard system, NBA automatically determines which campaign is suited to which customer at what point in time. Each customer receives an individual mix of development and retention campaigns as a result of this system. NBA constitutes a learning system that combines all information sources with respect to a customer, and thereby aids in efficient use of the direct marketing budget.

2.5 General conditions

Markets, whether in the telecommunications or in other service provider industries, are in a constant state of flux. This is a dynamic that not only continuously presents new opportunities, but also at times results in time limitation on adopted strategies. If a company wishes to utilize market opportunities actively, it must constantly observe its competitors, test new strategies non-stop, and be faster than the competition. For a strategy employed by all does not offer differentiation and does not lead to success. In principle, a company has two possible strategies: price leadership and quality leadership. Both strategies, in their purest sense, harbor considerable disadvantages, in particular the risk of not being able to respond to changing customer requirements with sufficient speed. So there is still the middle road – a mixed strategy that selects the best from both worlds for the respective company. Examples include on-line based bonus programs, relatively inexpensive to handle, that offer the program participant an interesting premium portfolio; or selected call center services, that are offered free of charge to certain customer segments.

The goal of the organizational form is the efficient implantation of corporate goals. If the strategic orientation alters due to changing market conditions, the direct connection between the corporate goals and the organizational structure ceases to exist. The constant is the customer, whose demands are at the core of all activities, regardless of any strategy discussion that may be taking place. In order to ensure that consumers experience the company's customer orientation, it must be firmly grounded in the entire company structure as one of its corporate values. The company must create the foundation for closeness and interaction with the customer to become part of the corporate culture and this orientation is rewarded by appropriate incentive systems. Information and processes must be established and institutionalized in an integrated fashion across departmental boundaries, in order to assure a vision that spans all departments. A prerequisite for this scenario is continuous employee training and education, since this is the only way in which customer needs can be accurately elicited. If the consumer is constantly used as an information provider, then customer preferences can be taken into account in all stages of product development and sales processes. Mass offerings turn into services for particular segments or even for individual customers.

2.6 Internationalization

"The global appetite for mobile phones has exceeded the most optimistic expectations," summarizes Ben Wood, analyst of the market research company Gartner. According to forecast, 779 million mobile phones will be sold worldwide by the end of 2005. Over 85 percent of sales achieved in Europe by calling via these devices are concentrated in the ten top players of the European mobile network market. Vodafone, Orange, and T-mobile – the three largest European providers – are all represented internationally, too. A total of 24.6 million customers in Germany, England, and Ireland telephone using O_2 alone.

A corporate strategy with international orientation offers advantages both in exploiting additional market opportunities as well as in efficient utilization of existing capacity, for example in product development. In the mobile network market the considerable differences among countries with respect to buyer behavior and governmental and legislative influences act as a restricting factor. The result of these country-specific differences has been to subordinate the role that customer service and retention play. And exactly what does the customer want in terms of internationalization? Studies show – he wants to be able to be reached everywhere. Seventy percent of Germans take their mobile phone with them on holiday; every third takes a camera phone. Network availability is expected, in other words, mobile access in the most remote regions of the world is no longer a way for a network provider to distinguish itself, but simply a hygiene factor.

▶ Process & Implementation

The path to successful customer retention management is a process of continuous discovery of the customer and his demands. It involves the entire company, because only close interaction between all process steps and the departments concerned allows for consistent improvement of customer experience. O$_2$ defines three phases in the life cycle of its customers: acquisition, a loyalty management phase during the course of the contract, and the contract renewal period.

Rapid successes are a precondition for change when the topic is "process improvement" in a company. The goal is to test the chances of success for as many ideas as possible by virtue of pilot tests, so that decisions can promptly be made concerning company-wide implementation. O$_2$ uses a test lab for this purpose, that rapidly and flexibly investigates how new products and services resonate with customers by means of outbound calls. A prerequisite for valid results that can survive a test in practice is the use of teams spanning all functions. They assess an idea and propel it forward in an integrated fashion through all phases and ensure that any innovation is illuminated and approved from different perspectives.

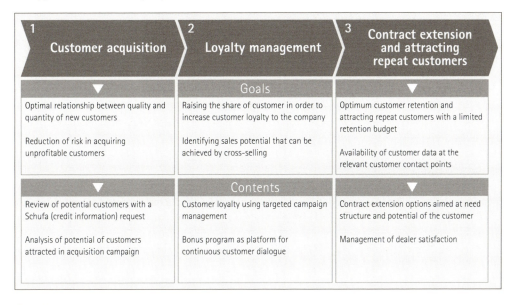

Fig. 2: Process overview – integrated customer retention

Phase 1: Customer acquisition

Not just attracting many customers, but the right ones

Growth by attracting new customers – this is indispensable. But in the world of mobile networks, every additional customer initially means an investment on the part of the network provider. These acquisition costs, that in the German market primarily entail subsidizing new end devices, are compensated for by the profitable customer from sales generated and the resulting revenues for the company. If, however, the customer does not pay his bills or consumes less than anticipated, the company bears the costs. What opportunities exist to lessen the risk of unprofitable new customers? In practice, two approaches are pursued, both of which are based on the generation and targeted assessment of potential customer data. O_2 checks the creditworthiness of the potential customer with a credit check in order to avoid the danger of taking on high-risk customers. This approach, however, means that potentially profitable customers may be refused. A second option for assessing the potential of new customers is to review the development of customers that have been attracted by special acquisition campaigns. For, in the case of acquisition, not just the number of new customers and their associated campaign costs, but also any subsequent costs incurred, must be included in the calculation. Such costs may arise if unprofitable customers are approached and acquired. Continuous reporting for at least six months after acquisition provides clarity with respect to the potential and profile of these customers.

Coordination between all corporate areas involved is particularly useful when attracting new clients. While sales staff are primarily interested in the numbers of new customers acquired, existing customer and risk management staff are more concerned with the quality of these new customers. The optimum point is somewhere in the middle, and it is in the interest of the company as a whole to find this optimum mid-point, in other words, as many customers as possible with the least possible risk.

Phase 2: Loyalty management

Efficient customer retention during the life cycle

Loyal customers are of key value to any company. Due to the high initial investment, payback periods are relatively long. Higher customer retention, therefore, directly impacts profits. And this applies as long as retention costs, or the costs incurred when a customer renews his contract, are lower than new acquisition costs.

The more the mobile network industry discovers other services to offer, besides pure voice telephony, and the more it enters into other areas, such as the photography or music industry, the more interesting the question of "Share of Customer" becomes. This indicator – the market share of a company with a single customer – provides information about the customer's loyalty to the company. The indicator, however, also permits conclusions to be drawn concerning the level of sales potential that can arise via cross-selling with the existing customer base. Analyses show that customer loyalty is directly rated to sales. Customers who generate a high level of sales have up to a 30 percent lower chance of straying than those who seldom use their phones. A prerequisite for increased sales, however, is that the customer needs to know the service portfolio. O_2, therefore, defines the first three months as a discovery phase in which the customer is introduced to the cell phone functions, rates, and services. In order to provide the consumer with information on the company or on product innovations at a later date on a regular basis, enclosures are sent out with the monthly bill, or the customer magazine "can do" is utilized. It seems that it is precisely this regularity that is important. Experience shows that customer retention measures that start shortly before the contract expires do not work. O_2 uses NBA in this case, in order to approach the customer automatically at the right time with the right campaign. The customer life cycle offers numerous opportunities for increasing customer satisfaction and loyalty – always assuming that appropriate moments can be identified and used to offer services of a type and quality that suits the customer's individual needs.

In November, 2003, O_2 introduced its bonus program. What goals motivated this decision? A distinction should be drawn between open and closed customer retention programs. Numerous partner companies work together in open programs, such as Payback, Webmiles, or Happy Digits, systems that earn points for future redemption. Such programs are particularly suitable for attracting new customers, providing the companies participating have a high degree of recognition. O_2 prefers a closed system, with the goal of managing and developing existing customers via an incentive system. The bonus program provides a foundation for an individual dialogue with the consumer. When the awarding of bonus points is used as a communication tool during the entire life cycle, new or increased utilization of selected products are fostered. The advantages of a closed program can be seen particularly during critical time intervals of the customer relationship. Customers are, for example, advised of their bonus point levels and the resulting premiums they can earn during the phase in which they are deciding whether to renew or terminate their contract with O_2. At the same time, awarding bonus points to specific target groups is an option as part of service differentiation. Those customers who are most likely to switch are offered greater opportunities to collect points by participating in campaigns; barriers to changing service providers are thereby erected. It is important to integrate the bonus program to the extent possible in existing communications and, finally, also in the NBA. On the one hand, it is more economical; on the other hand, it shows the customer that the program is an integrated component of the company's product range. The bonus program thus provides a significant contribution to getting to know the customer and fostering his commitment to O_2.

But critics exist. The launch of a bonus program is expensive. Is it worthwhile nevertheless? A strong focus on objectives that have been set is a prerequisite for a program that is successful from a budget perspective. The decision on how much money to invest in customers with bonus points depends on how greatly program participation causes sales to increase or churning to decrease. The key criterion for assessing the success of a bonus program is, therefore, not the number of participants, but their quality and development potential.

Phase 3: Contract renewal and attracting repeat customers
Keeping the customer from drifting away and wooing him back

At which point does the customer decide to terminate his contract and switch to the competition? And how – in other words, with which product offers and which approach – can a company still keep him? Sixty percent of individuals terminating their contracts seek contact with their provider in advance, possibly with a complaint. These "critical events" must not just be resolved competently, but should be used proactively to help retain the customer. The latter must believe that the company can and will help him. A very different, albeit equally critical, situation can arise if a customer repeatedly fails to pay his bill. In order to ensure that a non-payer is not handed over to a collection agency, processes and communications involved in the dunning procedure are of singular importance. The experience of employees, who are constantly in contact with the customer during the dunning period, permits differentiated forms of dunning to be applied.

In order to convince a customer to remain with the provider for contract renewal, an offer that is interesting from his point of view must be made. At this point, both those service elements that are relevant to the customer and the customer's profitability should be known. According to the premise that as many customers as possible of the highest possible quality are to be retained, with a limited retention budget it is useful to create a decision matrix. This offers a chance to tailor special promotions for profitable customers and customers at risk of switching services, and to address them by means of a variety of media. The approach can be made proactively with a mailing or reactively with a fulfillment.

If a company in the mobile network business wants to effectively counter the loss of customers, the dealer must be included as an additional cog in the communication and budget allocation wheels. It is not only the customer, but also the distribution partner, who must be satisfied. In the case of O_2, the dealer controls 60 percent of all customer contacts that occur during the contract renewal stage. In order to keep customers with a high risk of churning and to reattract customers who have already terminated their contracts, it is useful to grant employees ex-gratia payments within certain limits. To check the efficiency of these incentive awards, prompt tracking in conjunction with a system that includes the goal of customer retention in dealer and call center agent commissions is necessary. Information that may affect the payment should be accessible via all channels to assure uniform advice. If a customer is promised an add-on by the call center, then the dealer must have access to this information via his system. A precondition is a link to CRM systems: this ensures that customer information reaches the customer contact points quickly and transparently. Even if the individual systems differ depending on the type of distribution channel, a guarantee must exist that the corporate strategy, with respect to attracting new customers and retaining customers, is identifiable in all such channels.

New technologies, high investment levels, and increasing competitive pressures – no-frills providers are dispensing almost completely with service, but are setting new price lows. But other models exist. The segment of price and cost-conscious customers opened up October 2004 for O_2 due to the cooperation with Tchibo. One thing is clear: many things change and change can be very swift. Opportunities arise and promptly vanish. The challenge is to stay true to one's own brand and thus recognizable, and yet still to open new doors to our customers. Our success will depend on how well we succeed in orienting ourselves to our customers' wishes and anticipating the needs of potential customers. As services become more easily replaceable and, at the same time, ever more complex, the deciding factor will be who listens best to the customer.

▶ Key Insights

- Marketing guides the extent and intensity of integration between the customer and the company. Customer potential can only be exploited if the life cycle of the customer is used efficiently for interaction.
- Capturing and updating relevant customer data is a prerequisite for identifying and predicting the usage behavior of the customer.
- Customer profitability is assured by a differentiated service offering that relates to the customer's expectations and the value that he brings to the company through his usage behavior.
- The customer will select the provider who offers him the best problem resolution. Providers can only distinguish themselves by thoroughly tailoring their service offerings.

- The content and intensity of the customer dialogue is controlled by marketing, which functions as the interface to the market and as a coordinator among the corporate areas that are engaged in customer contact.
- A common vision of customer orientation can only succeed if it is supported by top management, grounded in the corporate culture, and integrated in all areas of the company's organization.
- A supra-national corporate strategy orientation offers growth potential in international or global competition. In order to initiate and fully utilize individual customer contacts, knowledge of national characteristics is, however, a deciding success factor.

▶ Practical Guidelines

- Act quickly when you test. Review as many ideas as possible in pilot test in order to subsequently be able to decide quickly whether a roll-out throughout the company is advisable.
- Manage customer acquisition: as many customers as necessary with as little risk as possible.
- Continuously collect information from customer contact points and make it available to all relevant areas.
- Use loyalty programs that can serve as a platform for realizing cross-selling potential and increasing customer loyalty.
- In deciding on the form and content of a contract renewal offer, use all available information about a customer, e.g., needs, sales generated, profitability, risk of changing provider or media affinity.
- Equip and train your sales staff so that they can offer varying advice to customers depending on their different value to the company and nevertheless leave each customer with the feeling that they have received friendly and professional treatment.
- Clarify your role as international player to the customer by ensuring that he is aware of the associated benefits, e.g., by means of global mobile accessibility.

The Authors

Martin Kanis

Since May of 2004 Martin Kanis (38) has been responsible for the CRM division of O₂ Germany GmbH & Co OHG in the role of Vice President. Customer relationship management focuses on customer retention, customer development and communication. The central focus in this respect is the orientation of the programs to the customer's value – every customer relationship is valuable, but it is the company's and not the customer's role to make it profitable. Martin Kanis has more than ten years of experience in the telecommunications industry and has been working for O₂ since 1997.

Kathrin Henze

Kathrin Henze is responsible for strategic development of customer retention programs as Head of CRM Retention at O_2. Together with her team she controls life cycle, contract renewal, and repeat customer management, including O_2's bonus program. Kathrin Henze has had experience in the banking and software sectors, in addition to the telecommunications industry. She has been with O_2 since 2001.

Literature Recommendations

A. Meyer, J. Davidson, "Offensives Marketing," Planegg 2001
A. Coenenberg, R. Salfeld, "Wertorientierte Unternehmensführung," Stuttgart 2003
M. Marn, E. Roegner, C. Zawada, "The Price Advantage," New Jersey 2004
www.inside-handy.de

visit → www.marketingmanual.org

latest editions – latest knowledge – latest Executive Science!

THE WALL STREET JOURNAL.
EUROPE

The Wall Street Journal Europe is an integral part of the world's leading business news franchise which also includes The Wall Street Journal, The Wall Street Journal Asia and The Wall Street Journal Online at WSJ.com, the largest paid subscription news site on the Web. Together, these publications have a paid circulation of 2.7 million readers, providing business leaders around the world with unsurpassed coverage of global business news edited from a local perspective, and hold 31 Pulitzer Prizes for outstanding journalism.

Published by Dow Jones & Company, The Wall Street Journal Europe draws on more than 1,800 news staff, the largest network of business and financial news staff in the world, including more than 350 in Europe, the Middle East and Africa, working from 43 bureaus and serving 34 cities across the region. In 2005, the newspaper won seven "Business Journalist of the Year" awards presented by the World Leadership Forum, more than any other publication, and was named "Best Global Business Media" by international research institute Media Tenor last year.

The Wall Street Journal Europe is delighted to work with the Executive Science Project and Scholz & Friends on the Manual of International Marketing, bringing to marketeers a comprehensive and authoritative guide to the world of marketing.